The Writer's Express

The Writer's Express:

A Paragraph and Essay Text with Readings

Kathleen T. McWhorter
Niagara County Community College

HOUGHTON MIFFLIN COMPANY   BOSTON   TORONTO

Dallas   Geneva, Illinois   Palo Alto   Princeton, New Jersey

Sponsoring Editor: Mary Jo Southern
Senior Basic Book Editor: Martha Bustin
Project Editor: Robin Bushnell Hogan
Senior Production/Design Coordinator: Karen Meyer Rappaport
Senior Manufacturing Coordinator: Priscilla Bailey
Marketing Manager: George Kane

Cover illustration: Cover design by Perennial Design.

Art Credits: Art Credits begin on page 546.

Acknowledgments for reprinted material appear on page 546.

ISBN: 0-395-59895-8

123456789-DH-96 95 94 93 92

Contents

Rhetorical Contents

(Note: Many selections appear under more than one heading. An asterisk (*) denotes a textbook excerpt.)

Thematic Contents

(Note: Many selections appear under more than one heading. An asterisk (*) denotes a textbook excerpt.)

Social Issues

Science and Humanity

Sports and Sports-Related Issues

Preface

To succeed in college, in the workplace, and in today's information-laden society, students must be able to **express their ideas clearly and correctly in written form**. *The Writer's Express* teaches developmental students the fundamentals of paragraph and essay writing through structured, sequential instruction and practice. The text approaches writing as a process, providing encouragement, support, and practical applications throughout. Students begin by writing simple paragraphs and gradually progress to rhetorical modes and essay writing. The text stresses writing as the effective expression of ideas; correct grammar and mechanics are presented as tools for achieving effective expression, rather than as ends in themselves.

Although writing skills are vitally important, they are not sufficient to handle the demands of college coursework. Students must also be able to **read, think critically, and interpret and react to what they have read**. Twenty-five years of experience teaching developmental students has convinced me that these essential skills—writing, reading, and critical thinking—are most effectively taught when integrated. Many students need help to "see" the connections among these skills; they need instruction that emphasizes connections, overlap, and cross-applications. They also need to build a repertoire of thinking strategies useful for writing, as well as reading. *The Writer's Express* links writing with reading and critical thinking by using high-interest, up-to-date readings as springboards to writing and critical thinking. Numerous writing and collaborative activities throughout the text foster critical thinking and analysis.

Organization of the Text

The text is organized into five parts, opening with a chapter that establishes the importance of effective writing and places it within the context of the college experience. To encourage writing as early in the course as possible, the chapter includes six assessment exercises. It concludes with a "How to Use This Book" section that explains the organization of Chapters 3–15 and describes the features within each chapter.

Part I focuses on paragraph writing strategies. It covers the writing process (Chapter 2), paragraph structure and topic sentences (Chapter 3), developing a paragraph with details (Chapter 4), and the revision process (Chapter 5). Chapter 5 introduces a Revision Checklist feature that is further developed in each of the remaining chapters of the book.

Part II presents methods of developing paragraphs, including narration and process; description; example, classification, and definition; comparison and contrast; and cause and effect. Each chapter describes the rhetorical mode and provides practical advice for organizing, developing, and writing in that mode. As in other sections, writing assignments build sequentially. Students generate ideas about a topic, prepare a first draft, and revise using the Revision Checklist.

Part III discusses essay writing techniques. Chapters 11–12 cover planning (including selecting and narrowing a topic and generating ideas), drafting, and revising the essay. Chapters 13–15 cover expository and persuasive essays and essay exams. Topics include analyzing audience, selecting and organizing convincing evidence, and choosing a tone.

Part IV contains fifteen additional readings, including questions for discussion and writing assignments. These readings give additional examples of good writing and further represent the rhetorical modes. The themes of these selections parallel those in the chapters and thus give instructors greater flexibility in assigning readings.

Part V, "Reviewing the Basics," is a brief handbook with exercises. It reviews principles of grammar, sentence structure, mechanics, and spelling. A set of error correction exercises is included.

Special Features

The following features distinguish *The Writer's Express* from other developmental writing texts and make its approach unique:

• *Readings* Beginning with Chapter 3, each chapter includes an engaging reading around which prewriting, critical thinking, and writing assignments are structured. Readings touch on topics within the students' realm of experience, such as sports, art, community policing, the environment, and family relationships. Each reading offers students a model for the writing skills taught in the particular chapter, as well as a source of ideas and a base for discussion and collaborative learning activities.

• *"Getting Ready to Write" Strategies*   After the first two introductory chapters, each chapter contains three activities that prepare students to write about the reading. First, students are taught strategies for reviewing its literal content, including underlining, annotating, outlining, and idea mapping. Next, students learn a critical thinking strategy that enables them to analyze and evaluate the reading. Skills include making inferences, understanding connotative language, and distinguishing fact from opinion. Finally, students are given questions for reaction and discussion, which may form the base of class discussion or be used as collaborative learning activities. These introductory activities provide students with opportunities to use prior knowledge and build confidence.

• *Writing Assignments*   Three types of writing assignments follow each chapter reading. Writing About the Reading involves students with ideas expressed in the reading. Writing About Your Ideas allows students to write about personal experiences related to the topic of the reading. Journal Writing Suggestions encourage students to react to topics related to the reading. This variety of writing assignments encourages practice with a range of writing tasks.

• *Revision Checklists*   A Revision Checklist appears at the end of each chapter, starting with Chapter 5. This feature provides a review of writing strategies learned in the chapter as well as cumulative review of strategies learned in previous chapters.

• *Writing Success Tips*   Each chapter includes a boxed insert that offers practical advice on topics related to writing. The Success Tips are intended to address student concerns, suggest new strategies, and help students overcome common writing problems. Topics include word processing, journal writing, peer review, and researching a topic.

• *Skill Refreshers*   Each chapter offers a review of a topic related to sentence structure, grammar, or punctuation. The Skill Refresher begins with a brief section of instruction, followed by a ten-item self-assessment quiz. Students are directed to record their score on the Skill Refresher Score Chart located at the back of the book. Students who score below 80 percent on the self-assessment quiz are directed to pages in Part Five, "Reviewing the Basics," that present a more detailed explanation of the topic.

• *Assessment Exercises*   Chapter 1 contains six assignments that will enable the student and instructor to assess the student's experience, attitude, and approach toward writing. These assignments encourage writing early in the course and emphasize its importance as a vehicle of communication between instructor and student.

• *Visual Learning Aids* Many developmental students are visual learners; that is, they process information visually rather than verbally or auditorily. The text uses idea maps—visual representations of a paragraph's content and organization—to appeal to visual learners. Tables, charts, lists, and photographs used throughout the text also accommodate a visual learning style.

• *Student Writing Samples* Each chapter contains one or more pieces of student writing used as an example or model of a particular writing strategy. The samples are motivational and enable students to establish realistic expectations for their own writing.

Auxillary Materials

Two teaching aids accompany the text:

Software: Expressways. Available in IBM and MacIntosh versions, *Expressways* provides a tutorial review of the key writing strategies presented in the text. The software is interactive: the student completes a range of writing activities and exercises that maintain interest and motivation. Each unit models the pedagogical structure of the text, providing skill instruction, demonstration, practice, and a brief on-screen reading. The program guides the student through the writing process and culminates with a writing assignment that may be printed and evaluated by the instructor or by peer reviewers.

Instructor's Resource Manual. This manual provides an overview of the text, explains pedagogical features, discusses the role of critical thinking in the writing class, and offers practical suggestions for teaching writing. It also contains suggestions for using the readings and has notes on each chapter, including additional class activities. Overhead Transparency Masters and a complete answer key to the text are also included.

Acknowledgments

I appreciate the excellent ideas, suggestions, and advice of my colleagues who served as reviewers:

Nancy G. Allen
Angelo State University, TX

Pamela Besser
Jefferson Community College, KY

Nancy Cox
Arkansas Tech University

Ian Cruickshank
St. Louis Community College, MO

Susan F. DeBoard
University of Central Arkansas

Michael W. Donaghe
Eastern New Mexico University

Craig Frischkorn
Jamestown Community College, NY

Mary Gilbert
Tompkins Cortland Community College, NY

Lyman Grant
Austin Community College, TX

Sandra Hanson
La Guardia Community College, NY

Margaret E. Harbers
Nashville State Technical Institute, TN

Judith Harway
Milwaukee Institute of Art and Design, WI

Julie Hawthorne
Sacramento City College, CA

Susan D. Huard
Manchester Community College, CT

Steven Katz
State Technical Institute at Memphis, TN

Mark Ledbetter
Wesleyan College, GA

Cecilia Macheski
La Guardia Community College, NY

Patricia Malinowski
Finger Lakes Community College, NY

Suellen Meyer
St. Louis Community College at Meramec, MO

Blair Morrisey
Muskegon Community College, OR

Gerald G. Niebauer
Duluth Community College Center, MN

Bonnie Orr
Wenatchee Valley College, WA

Karen J. Patty-Graham
Southern Illinois University at Edwardsville

Frances Peck
University of Ottowa

Ruth E. Ray
Wayne State University, MI

Ann M. Salak
Cleveland State University, OH

Steve Serota
San Jacinto College-South, TX

Meritt W. Stark, Jr.
Henderson State University, AR

Ward Tonsfeldt
Central Oregon Community College

Russel Ward
Aims Community College, CO

Roberta Wright
Lee College, TX

Gary Zacharias
Palomar College, CA

The entire editorial staff with whom I have worked deserves praise and credit for their assistance throughout the writing of this text. In particular, I wish to thank Mary Jo Southern for her warm and generous support throughout the project, Sue Warne for her vision in overseeing the development of the book, Martha Bustin for her creative talent and energy, and Robin Hogan for her meticulous attention to the production process. I also wish to thank Beverly Ponzi for her most valuable assistance in typing and manuscript management. Finally, I thank my students who continue to make teaching a challenging and rewarding profession.

Kathleen T. McWhorter

The Writer's Express

1 An Introduction to Writing

In this chapter you will

1. learn some basic features of effective writing.
2. assess your writing skills.

During the first week of classes Leon, a new freshman, was talking to his friend, Maria, a second-year student. Leon had just learned that he had to write two three-page papers for introductory sociology and that they would count for 30 percent of his grade. "I've never been good at writing, and every time I try I panic—I don't know what to say or how to begin," said Leon. "I'm worried about that course already." Maria smiled. "Leon, it'll be all right. Don't worry—you'll get lots of help in your writing course. I felt the same way last year, but my writing instructor, the textbook, and the other students were great. I don't panic about papers any more—I know what to do."

Like Leon and Maria, this course will give you the practical help that you need with writing. This course is designed to make you feel more comfortable and confident about writing. And let's face it, you will need to be. Both in college and on the job, you will need to write and to do so with confidence.

WHY IS WRITING IMPORTANT?

Regardless of your curriculum or major, writing will be an important part of your college courses. Although not all introductory courses require writing, advanced courses in your chosen discipline will demand a great deal of writing.

Here are a few examples of the kinds of writing you will do in your courses:

- essay exams and short answer questions
- research papers and reports
- reaction papers and critiques
- précis (summaries)
- logs and journals

As you probably know, writing is also a key to success in the workplace. Regardless of the career path you follow, you'll probably find that your job application and the job itself require writing. Professionals in businesses and industries rely on memos, letters, reports, directions, and logs to communicate with each other and to keep accurate records. And just as those students who write well get the best grades in college courses, those professionals who can write and communicate effectively usually get the best jobs. Writing well can add a whole new dimension to your life and your potential for success.

Because writing is so fundamental both in college and on the job, it is important to write clearly and correctly. You will find good writing skills will help you get better grades and a better job. In addition, knowing how to write well and being comfortable expressing yourself in writing have benefits in your private, daily life.

The assessment exercises in this first chapter are designed to help both you and your instructor assess your writing skills. Based on what you write for these exercises, you both can identify those areas that require more attention and those skills that have already been mastered.

Assessment Exercise 1–1   Write a brief paragraph describing the kinds of writing you have done over the past year for school, a job, or in everyday life.

IMPROVING YOUR WRITING SKILLS

■   Your writing instructor can be your best and most helpful resource for developing your writing skills. Make an effort to discuss his or her written comments on your papers and to set realistic goals for improvement together. Your writing classmates can also be a source of support and assistance. Get together informally to discuss assignments, share problems, and read and react to each other's papers.

And finally, this text will help improve your writing skills. You will learn how to get started, how to generate ideas, and how to organize them in paragraph and essay form. You will discover how to strengthen your writing by revising it thoughtfully and how to polish it through careful proofreading. The final unit of this text contains a complete review of basics such as sentence structure, grammar, and punctuation.

This book also gives you a chance to see how other writers express and organize ideas. Reading samples of both student and professional writing will give you ideas about how to organize and express your own thoughts in writing. If you have difficulty coming up with ideas to write about, use the readings as a springboard for developing your own thoughts on the subject.

Assessment Exercise 1–2   Write a paragraph about your reading habits. Do you ever read for pleasure? If so, what do you like to read? How well do you understand and remember what you read? If not, explain why you don't read frequently.

WHAT IS GOOD WRITING?

■ To answer the question "What is good writing?," you might say, "correct grammar, spelling, and punctuation—no errors." Actually, writing is much more than just avoiding errors. Listed below are a few new ways to think about it.

Good Writing Is Thinking

Good writing is a thinking process. As you read this book, you'll see that writers do a great deal of work before they pick up a pen and put words on paper. They decide what they want to say, plan how to say it, and organize their ideas. Once their ideas are on paper, they evaluate them carefully to work out the best way to express them.

Good Writing Involves Change

Finding the best way to express your ideas involves experimentation and change. This process is called *revision*. It involves rethinking ideas and making changes in what you have said as well as improving the way you have expressed it.

Writing Expresses Ideas Clearly

The primary focus of this text is to help you express ideas clearly. Good writers communicate with their readers in a direct and understandable way, making clear main points and supporting them with details. They provide facts, reasons, or examples to show that their main points are correct and believable. And they use a variety of techniques to arrange ideas logically.

Good Writing Is Directed Toward an Audience

Suppose you were going to interview for a part-time job. You would probably dress differently for the interview than you would to meet a friend for lunch. How you dress is partly determined by whom you are going to see and by what is expected of you there. In a similar way, writers vary their writing to suit the people for whom they are writing—their audience. What is appropriate for one audience may be inappropriate for another. For example, you would not write to a close friend about a car accident in the same way as you would to your professor. Because your friend knows more about you, she would be interested in all of the details. Conversely, you and your professor don't know each other well, thus she would want to know less about the details and your feelings and more about how the accident will affect your course work. Study the following excerpts. What differences do you notice?

> *Letter to a friend:*
> Jeff was driving the car. As we got to the light at Cedar Road it turned red. Jeff was changing the radio station because Sue hates country music, and I guess he didn't notice. I yelled, "Stop!", but he went through the intersection, and a van hit the back of the car. I was terrified, and I felt sick. Fortunately, we were all O.K. Jeff felt really terrible, especially because by the time we got to school, I had missed my biology exam.

> *Letter to a professor:*
> I missed the exam today because I was involved in a car accident. Although I was not injured, I didn't arrive on campus in time for class. Please allow me to make up the exam. I will stop by your office tomorrow during your office hours to talk.

The letter to a friend is casual and personal, while the letter to the professor is business-like and direct. The writer included details and feelings about the car accident for his friend, but talked only about the exam to his professor.

Writers make many decisions based on the audience they have in mind. Here is a partial list of questions they ask themselves before and while they write:

- How much detail is appropriate?
- What kinds of details should I include?

- How many and what types of examples should I use?
- What kind of vocabulary makes sense?
- What tone should my writing have? How should I sound to my readers?
- How formal should my writing be?

In later chapters you will learn more about writing to suit your audience. Also, as you work with the chapter readings, you will have an opportunity to study how other writers address specific audiences.

Good Writing Achieves a Purpose

When you call a friend on the phone, you have a reason for calling even if it is just to stay in touch or keep up your friendship. When you ask a question in class, you have a purpose for asking. When you describe to a friend an incident that happened to you, you are relating the story to make a point or to share an experience. These examples demonstrate that you communicate orally to achieve specific purposes. Similarly, in written communication, you write for a specific reason or purpose. At times you may write for personal reasons—to record an assignment, to take notes in class, or to help you learn or remember information for an exam. Many other times, your purpose for writing is to communicate information, ideas, or feelings to a specific audience.

Good writing, then, must achieve your intended purpose. If you write a paragraph to explain how to change a flat tire, your reader should be able to change a flat tire after reading the paragraph. Likewise, if your purpose is to describe the sun rising over a misty mountain top, your reader should be able to visualize the scene.

More about writing to achieve your purpose appears in later chapters. Working with the chapter readings will help you see how other writers accomplish their purpose.

Assessment Exercise 1–3

Think of a favorite TV program or a family event you have attended recently.

1. Write a paragraph describing the TV episode or the event to a friend who usually watches the program with you or who knows you well.
2. Write a paragraph describing the same episode or event to your English instructor.

Assessment Exercise 1–4	Write a letter to your instructor explaining what you would like this course to do for you.

WAYS TO THINK ABOUT WRITING

■ If you start off with the right attitude, the right equipment, and a basic understanding of the processes involved in writing, you can become a good writer. Here are a few tips for getting off to the right start in your writing course.

1. *Approach writing as a skill.* Just like driving, typing, or basketball, writing is a skill that can be learned. As with other skills it requires practice and hard work.

2. *Think of writing as a process.* Writing involves a series of steps you work through in order to produce an effective piece of writing. It is a process of developing and explaining ideas. You certainly do not have to know everything you're going to say before you start.

3. *Consider writing as a way of telling people what you think.* Writing is a channel of communication between you and your reader and can create a new dimension to your relationships with others. You can share ideas with others through writing just as you do through speech.

4. *Plan on spending time.* It takes time, usually more than you think, to complete a writing task. Write when you've got a reasonable block of time (45 minutes or more). It is usually best to work for a while, then take a break—even a day—and then work for another stretch of time.

5. *Write at peak periods of concentration.* Because writing is so demanding, write when you're mentally sharp. If you are tired, upset, or restless, refresh yourself before you attempt to write.

6. *Apply new techniques.* Writing improves through a conscious effort to apply the new approaches and techniques you will learn in this book, from your instructor and classmates, and by reading other writers.

7. *Plan on making changes.* The most important steps in the writing process are rethinking and revising. Professional writers change what they write several times before they are satisfied with what they have produced.

8. *Jot down notes if interrupted.* If interrupted or stopped before being able to finish a writing task, jot down a few notes about what

you were thinking or going to say or do next. These notes will enable you to get back on track when you begin again.

9. *Write notes to yourself.* Sometimes your mind works faster than you can write. When this happens, make marginal notes to yourself.

10. *If you get stuck (cannot think or write), take a break.* Walk around, get a snack, watch a TV show, or make a phone call. Discuss your ideas with a friend. In addition to clearing your mind, you may discover new ideas or clarify those you already have. To get started again, reread what you've already written. If you are still stuck, try backtracking to a prewriting technique, such as freewriting, brainstorming, branching, and questioning. You'll learn about these techniques in Chapter 2.

11. *If you handwrite your drafts, use full 8½-by-11-inch sheets of paper.* You need as much space as possible to see how ideas connect. Write on only one side of the paper. Consider using a word processor if your handwriting is very poor. (See Writing Success Tip 6, p. 104.)

Assessment Exercise 1–5

Suppose you have just been asked to write a one-page paper on street crime for your criminology course. Describe, step-by-step, how you would go about doing this assignment. (What is the first thing you would do? What would you do after that, and so forth?)

Assessment Exercise 1–6

Write a paragraph on one of the following topics, or a topic of your own choosing.

1. Drug abuse among teenagers in your community
2. A childhood game or fantasy you still play
3. Your favorite neighborhood restaurant
4. A money problem you faced recently
5. The next purchase you would like to make
6. What you do to relax when you feel tense

HOW TO USE THIS BOOK

■ To get maximum benefit from this book, it is helpful to know how this book is structured and how to use it. There are five parts, consisting of 15 chapters. Part One provides an overview of the writing process and focuses on basic paragraph writing techniques. Part Two presents methods for developing paragraphs. You'll learn how to write topic sentences and support them using relevant and sufficient details. Part Three discusses essay writing techniques and strategies for writing various types of essays. Part Four contains 15 additional readings, which can serve as writing examples or topics for writing. Part Five reviews basic concerns about sentence structure, grammar, and punctuation. You can refer to this last section any time you have a question about these topics.

Each chapter is organized the same way. Beginning with Chapter 3, each contains the ten parts described below.

Writing Strategies

This section presents and explains a key aspect of the writing process. Here you will learn to use specific techniques in order to improve your writing. In Chapter 3, for example, you will learn how to write effective topic sentences. The next chapter demonstrates how to develop details to support that topic sentence. In the writing strategies section you will work on exercises and complete short writing assignments. Because this section is the most important part of each chapter, use it to learn and try out each new writing strategy. Study the sample paragraphs to discover how they illustrate each technique.

Thinking Before Reading

This section of each chapter introduces you to the reading that follows. It will ask you to skim quickly through the article before you read it. This skimming method is called *previewing*. As you preview, try to discover what the reading is about and how it is organized. Then, you will create a mental outline of the key ideas it covers. After you have previewed the article, you'll find several questions designed to activate your thinking—or put your mind in gear. Use these questions to discover what you already know about the subject of the reading. Once you have started thinking about the subject, reading about it will be easier and more enjoyable.

Reading

The reading gives you an opportunity to see how other writers work with the writing techniques presented in the chapter. For example, in the chapter that shows you how to write a descriptive paragraph, the reading will demonstrate descriptive writing. In the chapter that shows you how to write a persuasive essay, you will then read a persuasive essay written by a skilled writer.

As you work with each reading, study the writer's techniques. Look at *how* he or she organized and developed ideas. Pay particular attention to the feature(s) of the writing discussed in the *Writing Strategies* section of the chapter, and then study how the writer applies this strategy.

Getting Ready to Write

This section of the chapter provides three steps to help you get ready to write about what you have read. The first demonstrates a method for reviewing and organizing the author's ideas. You will learn techniques for outlining, underlining, and idea mapping. All of these techniques apply to textbook assignments for other courses as well.

The second step in the *Getting Ready to Write* section offers a strategy for thinking critically about the reading. Here you will learn how to react to, interpret, and evaluate what you read. Each of these strategies works with other readings in the text, and with other things you read and hear, too. A critical thinker analyzes everything, including news reports, commercials, editorials, textbooks, magazine articles, and even conversations.

The third step in this section offers questions for discussion and reaction. Your instructor may choose to discuss these in class or ask you to write a response. You can use these questions when you talk informally with classmates about the reading. They will provoke your thinking and allow you to see how others react to and interpret the reading.

Writing About the Reading

This section contains one or more writing assignments about the ideas expressed in the reading. Use these assignments to develop your skill in applying the writing strategies and critical thinking skills you learn in each chapter.

Writing About Your Ideas

This section contains several writing assignments that give you the opportunity to express your own ideas on topics related to the reading. Use these assignments to practice developing and organizing your own ideas while you apply strategies you learn in each chapter. Journal Writing Suggestions are also included in this section.

Revision Checklist

A Revision Checklist at the end of chapters 4 through 15 will help you with every writing exercise in that chapter. Use it to check that you are applying strategies you learned in previous chapters as well as the new ones in the current chapter.

Writing Success Tip

Each chapter includes a boxed insert that offers practical advice on topics related to writing. These tips will suggest new strategies or give advice about how best to overcome common writing problems.

Skill Refresher

Each chapter offers a review of a topic related to sentence structure, grammar, mechanics, or punctuation. The review begins with a brief refresher, followed by a 10-item check-test. For example, one Skill Refresher reviews run-on sentences; another discusses how to use commas. Study the refresher carefully before you complete the checktest. Check your answers using the Answer Key on page 537. Then record your score on the Skill Refresher Score Chart page. If you score below 80 percent on the check-test, you need a more thorough review of the topic. Each Skill Refresher directs you to pages in Part Five that present a more detailed explanation of the topic. Work through that section several times until you are comfortable with the material. Be sure to ask your instructor or classmates if there is something you don't understand.

Summary

A brief summary that reviews key points ends each chapter. Read the summary several different times. Read it the first time before you read the chapter; this will give you an overview of the chapter and tell you what to expect. Read it a second time when you've finished the chapter; this will help you draw together all of the material in the chapter. If you feel confused while you are working with the chapter, or if you are working with it over a period of several days, read both the summary and the headings listed in the Table of Contents to get your bearings.

WRITING

SUCCESS

TIP 1

Keeping a Writing Journal—Part One

A writing journal is a fun, exciting, and meaningful way to improve your writing, keep track of your thoughts and ideas, and develop a source of ideas to write about. Writing in your journal can also add a new dimension to the way you think about events in your daily life.

How It Works

1. Buy an 8½-by-11-inch spiral bound notebook and use it exclusively for journal writing.

2. Take 10–15 minutes a day to write in your journal. You can do this during "dead time"—waiting for a bus or for class to begin, for example. Some students prefer to write at the end of each day.

3. Record your ideas, feelings, and impressions of the day. Don't just record events; analyze what they mean to you.

4. To get started, ask yourself some thought-provoking questions. A few examples follow.

- What was the best/worst/most unusual thing that happened today? Describe how you feel about it.
- What was a particularly pleasurable experience? Think beyond events. Maybe it was smelling a chocolate cake baking or feeling your dog's wet nose nudging you to wake up.
- What new ideas did you encounter today? Perhaps you started thinking about world hunger or the value of religion. Describe your thoughts.
- What interesting conversations did you have? Jot down some of your dialogue.
- What new people did you meet? Think about what type of relationship might develop between you.
- What are you worrying about? Describe the problem and write about possible solutions.
- What are your interests? Sometimes you may want to choose a topic and write about it. The topic may be an event, person, or subject that interests you. You might write about a movie you have seen or about a dream vacation you would like to take.

A Sample Journal Entry

Today Dad and I took his boat out and went fishing in the river. It's been three years since I've gone fishing with him. I guess the last time was before I moved out of the house. We had a chance to talk like we used to when I saw more of him. He told me some stuff about my sisters and problems they were having with Mom. He seemed depressed about it and was glad to talk about it. I probably should spend more time with him but . . .

Why It Works

An obvious benefit of keeping a journal is that it gives you practice writing, and the more you write the better you become. However, the journal has many other benefits as well:

1. Journal writing shows you how to write for yourself. Class assignments and papers are written for someone else to read. You will begin to see writing as a means of personal expression. Writing can release pent-up feelings and make you feel better about your problems.

2. Journal writing gives you experience in using writing to think about ideas, react to problems, and discover solutions. You'll learn to use writing to discover and sort out ideas, adding a new dimension to the way you think.

3. Your journal will be a valuable source of ideas. When you are asked to write a paragraph or essay on a topic of your choice, refer to your journal.

4. Many students find that they enjoy journal writing and continue it long after they complete their writing course. A journal provides a valuable record of a person's ideas and experiences. Rereading a journal written several years ago is like looking at old photographs—it brings back memories and preserves the past.

I
. . . .

Paragraph Writing Strategies

2

The Writing Process: An Overview

CHAPTER
OBJECTIVES

In this chapter you will learn to

1. understand writing as a process.
2. follow the steps in the process.

In the third week of the semester, Mo had a writing assignment for his sociology class. This was the assignment:

> Visit the local zoo and spend at least one hour in the monkey house. Write a paragraph briefly describing what you saw and how it relates to our introductory unit on group behavior.

This assignment did not make much sense to Mo, but one Sunday afternoon he and a friend went to the monkey house. He actually had fun watching the monkeys' antics. Later that day he began the assignment since it was due Tuesday. He pulled out several sheets of paper, said to himself, "Well, here goes nothing," and started to write the following paragraph.

> I visited the monkey house over the weekend and saw many interesting things.

At that point Mo was in trouble; he didn't know what to say next. He stared at the blank paper awhile. Realizing that he *had* to write something, he started to describe what three monkeys did while he was there. When he finished writing, Mo put the assignment in his notebook and handed it in on Tuesday. The next week, when the professor returned the paragraphs, Mo was angry and disappointed when he saw his grade of C−. The instructor's note said, "This should really be a

D, but I know you tried." Mo thought—"You bet I tried, and this is what I get!"

THE FIVE STEPS

■ Where did Mo go wrong? Actually, he made several mistakes, but they all stem from a larger problem. He was viewing writing as a single-step activity. But writing is a *process*. It is a series of steps in which you *decide* what to say, *plan* how you'll organize your ideas, *write, revise,* and *proofread*. Mo neither thought nor planned before he began writing; consequently, he had trouble knowing what to say. Then, in desperation, he resorted to simply reporting events, without placing his observations into a unifying framework. When he finished writing, he put the assignment away. He hadn't reread his paragraph to see how he could improve it, nor had he proofread for errors.

In this chapter you will begin to approach writing as a process and avoid Mo's mistakes. Don't be concerned if this process is not entirely clear by the end of this chapter. The rest of the book will show you more about the process. You'll understand more and more as you work through each chapter and examine each step in the process more closely. The five steps you will learn are:

1. Generating Ideas
2. Organizing Your Ideas
3. Writing a First Draft
4. Revising and Rewriting
5. Proofreading

If you use each of these steps, you will find that writing will be much easier for you than it was for Mo. You will not find yourself frustrated, staring at a blank sheet of paper. Instead, you will feel as if you are putting your ideas into words and making headway toward producing a good paragraph.

Generating Ideas

The first step before writing is to generate ideas about your topic. Although Mo spent time in the monkey house, he did not spend time thinking about what he saw or how it related to what he had learned in his course. He did not develop any ideas to write about. There are four techniques you can use to do this: (1) freewriting, (2) brainstorming,

WRITING

SUCCESS

TIP 2

Keeping a Journal—Part Two

·   ·   ·   ·   ·   ·   ·   ·   ·   ·   ·   ·   ·   ·   ·   ·   ·

In Success Tip 1 (pages 11–12) you learned to use a journal to record experiences and explore ideas. You can also use your journal to keep a record of your learning and to evaluate how well you are doing.

How a Learning Journal Works

1. You can create a separate section in your journal or you can integrate learning journal entries with your other, more personal entries.

2. At least once a week, more often if possible, write an entry that describes what you are learning about writing.

3. Focus on your reactions to the writing strategies you are learning. Write about what worked and what did not. Describe what you did to get a technique to work. Record your questions and problems, frustrations and successes. Include things you know you will have to keep working on.

4. Keep a list of errors you make often. (Also see Chapter 5, pages 88–89 for suggestions on error logs.) Update and revise it as your writing improves.

5. Record suggestions your instructor has made for improving your writing.

Here is a sample journal entry one student wrote after learning the four methods for generating ideas discussed in this chapter.

(3) branching, and (4) questioning. Each of these techniques can help you overcome the common problem of feeling as if you have nothing to say. They can unlock ideas you already have and help you discover new ones. Each of these four techniques provides a different way to generate ideas. Feel free to choose from among them, although you will probably need to use only one of them for any writing assignment.

Freewriting

Freewriting involves writing nonstop for a limited period of time, usually three to five minutes. Write whatever comes into your mind, regardless of whether it is about the topic or not. If nothing comes to

Sample Entry

I never knew there were so many ways to get ideas for papers. I tried them all on a paper for my career planning seminar. I didn't like questioning because I felt like I was asking questions when I already knew the answer. Freewriting and brainstorming worked O.K. For me, branching worked super for this paper. I like drawing and seeing things and branching hardly seemed like I was writing. But I don't think branching will always be best. Some topics don't divide up that easily. For topics that I know very little about, I think questioning would help me the most.

Why It Works

1. Writing about learning to write adds a new dimension to your learning. It focuses your attention on the *process* instead of the *product* (the piece of writing you produce).
2. Writing these entries forces you to think about and evaluate what does and does not work.
3. Your journal is a useful personal reference. If you get discouraged, look back and see the kinds of concerns you had last week or last month—you will see how much progress you have made.
4. When you get stuck on an assignment, rereading your journal may help you realize what's wrong or give you an idea about what to do next.

mind, you can just write "I'm not thinking of anything." As you write, don't be concerned with grammar, punctuation, or spelling, or with writing in complete sentences. Words and phrases are fine. Focus on recording your thoughts as they come to you. The most important thing is to keep writing without stopping. Write fast; don't think about whether what you are writing is worthwhile or makes sense. After you finish, reread what you have written. Underline everything that you might be able to use in your paper.

Mo discussed his sociology assignment with his writing instructor, who explained how to use freewriting to generate ideas. He suggested that Mo redo the monkey house assignment to see how freewriting works.

Sample Freewriting

> The monkeys are behind bars like prisoners. They leap and jump and play but seem to know they can't get out. They eat with their hands—they look like impolite humans. There's an <u>old monkey who been there forever and he's crabby and nasty to the others</u>. People like to go there during feeding time. Monkeys eat bananas. It smells in the monkey house. The monkeys seemed to enjoy being watched by us. <u>They seemed to be showing off for us</u>. The monkey house is located next to the reptile house. I hate going there. <u>Some monkeys threw things at us and at other monkeys and they looked angry. One monkey stole another's food but the monkey whose food was stolen didn't fight back</u>. Most people go the zoo during the summer. Sometimes I wonder if the zoo is really humane. <u>Monkeys were grooming each other by picking each other's hair</u>. Monkeys in the zoo don't act like they would in the wild though either. I felt sorry for some of them they looked so confused. <u>Sometimes they seemed to compete with each other</u> to see who could do the most antics.

Freewriting is a creative way to begin translating ideas and feelings into words without being concerned about their value or worrying about correctness. You'll be pleasantly surprised, as Mo was, by the number of usable ideas this technique uncovers. Of course, some of your ideas will be too broad, others might be too personal, others may stray from the topic. In the sample, the underlining show which ideas about group behavior Mo considered usable when he reviewed his freewriting. He did not underline ideas about the monkeys' eating habits, smell, or the location of their house because they did not relate to the topic of group behavior.

Exercise 2–1   Using a clock or timer, freewrite for five minutes each on three of the following topics. Be sure to write without stopping. After you finish each freewriting, reread and underline any ideas that might be usable in writing a paragraph on that topic.

1. your mother's or father's eating habits
2. your favorite rainy day activity
3. how rap music affects drivers
4. giving neckties as presents
5. what children should eat for breakfast

___

Brainstorming

Brainstorming is a way of developing ideas by making a list of everything you can think of about the topic. You might list feelings, ideas, facts, examples, or problems. There is no need to write in sentences; instead, list words and phrases. Don't try to organize your ideas, just list them as you think of them. Give yourself a time limit. You'll find ideas come faster that way. You can brainstorm alone or with friends. With your friends you'll discover a lot more ideas, because their ideas will help trigger more of your own. When you've finished, reread your list and mark usable ideas. Here is an example of a group brainstorming session on the topic of sports fans.

Sample Brainstorming

sit in bleachers	baseball card collections
stadiums and ball parks	beer
have tailgate parties	betting
do the "wave"	cost of tickets
excitement and shouting	parking
disappointment	traffic jams in and out
restrooms, long lines	dress funny
food costs	chanting
bored	cold and snow
fanatical	hotseats
radio sports talk show	

The topic of sports fans is too broad for a paragraph, but there are several groups of usable paragraph-sized ideas here: the behavior and attitude of fans at games, the costs and inconveniences of being a fan, tailgate parties, and radio sports talk shows.

Exercise 2–2   For two of the following topics brainstorm for about five minutes each. When you finish, review your list and mark ideas you could use in writing a paragraph.

1. How do you feel about female anchors on television news programs?
2. Should chemical weed killers be outlawed?
3. Are car telephones dangerous?
4. How did you spend your last birthday?
5. What do you do while waiting for a bus or subway?

Branching

Branching is a visual way of generating ideas. To begin, write your topic in the middle of a full sheet of paper. Draw a circle around it. Next, think of related ideas and write them near your center circle. Connect each to the central circle with a line. Call these ideas the primary branches. Your topic is like a tree trunk, and your ideas are like primary limbs that branch out from it. Here is an example of a branching diagram that one student did on the topic of shopping at convenience stores.

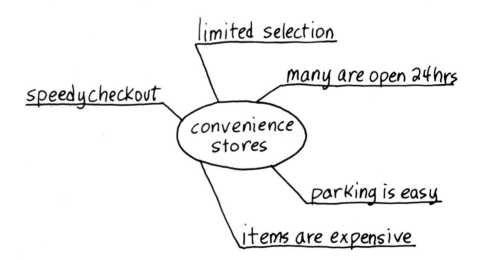

You can collect other related ideas to main branches with smaller, or secondary branches. In the example below, the student looked at his first branching diagram and decided to focus on one of the narrower topics (the limited selection at convenience stores) he had put on a primary branch.

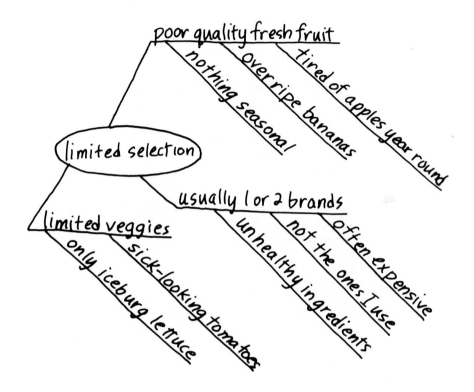

The student used "limited selection" as the trunk, then created three primary branches: poor fruit, limited veggies, and limited brand selection. He drew secondary branches onto each of these primary ones and could have kept going. If you use this technique, you can branch from your branches until you run off the paper. But there's no need to develop branches for every one of your main branches. It is fine to choose one branch that interests you or that you're familiar with and to ignore all the other possibilities.

When you have finished branching, use a different color pen to mark those branches that seem usable for your paragraph.

Exercise 2–3   Draw branching diagrams for two of the following topics.

1. salaries for football players
2. homeless people's rights to free shelters

3. tourists (sightseers) who litter
4. outdoor wedding receptions
5. waiting in hospital emergency rooms

Questioning

Another way to generate ideas about a given topic is to ask questions. The questions *What? Why? Where? When? How?* and *Who?* are effective to begin exploring any topic. As with freewriting and brainstorming, write any question that comes to mind. Don't worry if it seems silly, and don't stop to evaluate whether it is really related to the topic. If you can think of answers, include them as well, but don't limit yourself to questions for which you know the answers. When you have finished, reread and underline questions or answers that you might be able to use in writing a paragraph. Here are the questions one student wrote on the topic of dreams.

Sample Questions

Why do we dream?

Do dreams have meaning in our everyday life?

How do you interpret a dream?

Why are they so frightening when they hardly make sense?

When at night do we dream?

Do some people not dream at all?

Can we control our dreams?

How long do dreams last?

What do our bodies do while we are dreaming?

Why do people sleepwalk? Do they remember it?

Do I remember all of my dreams?

Are dreams predictions?

Are dreams warnings?

What are the most common dreams?

How are dreams studied?

Do men and women have different dreams?

Do children have different dreams?

What scary dreams can I remember?

Exercise 2–4   Use questioning to generate ideas on two of the following topics.

1. Giving candy for Valentine's Day
2. Your favorite room in your home

3. Should there be benefits for part-time jobs?
4. Keeping wild animals as pets
5. Should smoking be allowed in public places?

When to Use Which Technique

Now that you have tried freewriting, brainstorming, branching, and questioning, you are probably wondering when to use each technique. In general, there are no rules to follow. The best advice is to use the technique that you are most comfortable with. You may have already discovered that you like one better than another. Perhaps one or more techniques didn't work very well for you. Don't try to decide yet; instead, try to use each more than twice to determine which really works for you. You may find that for certain topics one technique works better than the others. For example, suppose you decided to write a paragraph about your mother's sense of humor. While it might be difficult to think of questions, freewriting might help you remember important, humorous events in your life together. In a different situation, however, questioning might be the most effective technique. Suppose you are studying religious institutions in your sociology class. Your instructor has assigned a paper that requires you to explain your personal religious beliefs. Asking questions about your beliefs is likely to produce useful ideas to include in your paper.

Sorting Usable Ideas

Freewriting, brainstorming, branching, and questioning each produce a wide range of usable ideas. Many of the discussions in later chapters of this book will help you decide what kinds of ideas are valuable for writing. However, once you've identified usable ideas, you shouldn't feel as if you need to write about them all. You can sort through them to decide which ones you can put together to produce your paragraph. Sometimes you may find that you would like to develop just one idea in your paragraph and narrow down your topic, as the student who did the branching diagram on the limited selection at convenience stores. Here is another example. Suppose you freewrote on the broad topic of noise in your neighborhood. One of your ideas was "noise pollutes ability to think." This topic would be a more manageable one for a single paragraph because it is more specific. You could then do a second freewriting focused on noise and thinking. You'll find that the more specific your topic is, the easier it will be to generate ideas and write about it. You will read more about narrowing topics in Chapter 3.

Exercise 2–5   Select one of the topics listed below or one of your own choosing. Try all four techniques—freewriting, brainstorming, branching, and questioning—on the same topic. When you have finished all four samples, reread each one and mark usable ideas. Then, write short answers to the questions that follow.

Topics
1. Are vacations necessary?
2. Who are those people who bring babies to rock concerts?
3. Should supermarkets have candy in checkout lanes?
4. How can we eat well without spending a lot of money?
5. Can health foods taste good?

Questions
1. Which technique produced the most usable ideas?

_____

2. Which technique were you most comfortable using?

_____

3. Which technique were you least comfortable using? Why?

_____

_____

ORGANIZING YOUR IDEAS

■ Once you have used freewriting, brainstorming, branching, or questioning to generate ideas about your topic, the next step is to decide how to organize these ideas. Ideas in a paragraph should progress logically from one to another. Group or arrange your ideas in a way that makes them clear and understandable.

Suppose you used brainstorming to generate ideas on the topic of giving a party. You've identified the following ideas for possible use in your paragraph.

```
food and decorations        people park in neigh-
are expensive               bors' spots

shopping is hard—           neighbors get annoyed
don't know how much         about noise
food to buy
                            friends meet each
lots of fun                 other
```

```
get to talk to              more fun than I ever
friends                     thought
friends from differ-        people come and go—no
ent places might not        fixed time
get along                   people bring extra
not always able to          food
reach those you want        get invited to other
to invite                   people's parties
clean up is work            there are different
a good excuse to            kinds of parties—
clean apartment             small and large
```

If you reread your list, you'll observe that most of the items are either disadvantages or advantages of giving a party. The following ideas do not fit very easily into this organization, so you can eliminate them.

```
there are different kinds of parties—small and
large not always able to reach those you want
to invite people come and go—no fixed time
```

Next, rewrite your list, grouping the ideas into advantages and disadvantages. Then reread your list and cross off ideas that you don't like, or ideas that are too similar to another idea. For example, "lots of fun" is too similar to "more fun than I ever thought," so cross it out. Number the ideas in each group to indicate the order in which you will write about them (see below). There are a number of different ways to arrange ideas. These include most to least important, first to last as they occur in time, and general to more specific. Chapters 4 and 6 through 10 discuss this topic further.

```
Advantages:
4. get to talk to friends
3. people bring extra food
6. get invited to other parties
1. more fun than I ever thought
5. friends meet each other
2. a good excuse to clean apartment
Disadvantages:
4. neighbors get annoyed about noise
1. food and decorating are expensive
```

2. shopping is hard--don't know how much food
   to buy
5. friends from different places might not get
   along
3. people park in neighbors' parking places
6. clean up is work

These ideas are numbered first to last as they occur in time. Not all ideas will sort out as neatly as these, but trying to organize your ideas will help you develop a topic sentence for your paragraph. Sometimes new ideas will grow out of your efforts to rework and rearrange others.

Exercise 2–6   Select one of the topics you developed in Exercises 2–1, 2–2, 2–3, 2–4, or 2–5. Organize and rearrange the usable ideas into a logical order.

WRITING A FIRST DRAFT

■   Suppose you are taking a weekend trip and have begun to pack your suitcase. You have in mind what you'll be doing and whom you'll see. To pack, you start by looking through your entire closet. Then you narrow your choices to several workable outfits. You arrange outfits, mix and match them, figure out how much will fit in the suitcase, and finally decide what to take.

Writing a draft is similar to packing for a trip. You have to try out different ideas, see how they work together, express them different ways, and, after several drafts, settle upon what your paragraph will say. You may have to "try out" several different arrangements. Drafting is a way of trying out ideas to see if and how they work. You might experiment with expressing your ideas one way, then try them out again a different way. In your first draft you might use examples to explain your idea; if that does not work, you might switch to using reasons.

A first draft expresses your ideas in sentence form. Work from your organized list of ideas, focusing on expressing and developing each one more fully. Don't be concerned with grammar, spelling, or punctuation; instead, concentrate on what you are saying, not on whether you are writing it correctly. Here are a few tips to follow in writing first drafts.

1. After you have thought carefully about the ideas in your list, try to write one sentence that expresses the main point. Think of this as a working topic sentence.

2. Write down more fully developed ideas from your list in the order in which you organized them.

3. If you are unsure of whether to include an idea from your list, include it. You can always delete it later. Add new ideas as you think of them.

4. Do not get caught up in finding the best wording for an idea. Just write it as you think of it. You will have time to fix it later as you revise.

5. Think of a first draft as a chance to experiment with different ideas and organizations. While you are working, if you think of a better way to organize or express your ideas, make changes or start over.

6. Concentrate on developing and explaining your working topic sentence.

7. As your draft develops, feel free to change your focus or even your topic. For example, you might find you have more to say about attending a party than about giving one. When this happens you might want to develop new ideas using freewriting, brainstorming, branching, or questioning.

8. Plan on changing things around later. What you write as your last sentence might turn out to be a good beginning.

9. If your draft is not working out, don't hesitate to throw it out and start over. Most writers have many "false starts" before they produce a draft with which they are satisfied.

10. If you think you need more ideas, go back to the generating ideas step. It is always all right to go back and forth among the steps in the writing process.

11. When you finish your first draft you should feel as if you have the *beginnings* of a paragraph you will be happy with.

Here is a sample early draft of the paragraph on giving a party.

```
     Giving a party is more fun than I ever
thought. You get to talk to your friends and
your friends get to meet each other. My best
friend met his wife at a party I gave a few
years ago. People invite you to their parties
if you give parties. Ever since I've been
giving parties, I've received more invitations
than I can accept. People also bring food to
your party. There are a few disadvantages of
having a party. Buying food is expensive.
Preparing it is a lot of work. Cleaning up
```

```
afterwards takes time. Also, people don't know
where to park, and they park in neighbors'
spots.
```

Exercise 2–7   For the topic you chose in Exercise 2–5, write the first draft of a paragraph.

REVISING AND REWRITING

■   Let's think again about the process of packing a suitcase. At first you may think you have included everything you need. Then, a while later, you think of other things you'll need. Because your suitcase is full, you have to rethink everything. You might eliminate some items, add others, and switch around or combine outfits.

A similar thing often happens with first drafts. When you finish a first draft you are more or less satisfied with it. Then, when you reread it later, you see you have more work to do. Revision is a process that involves evaluating and changing a draft to make it more effective.

Before you are satisfied with what you write, you may need to write two, three, or even four drafts. Revising often involves much more than changing a word or rearranging a few sentences. Revising requires that you *rethink* your ideas. It might mean changing, adding, deleting, and rearranging them. Revision is not concerned with correcting spelling, punctuation errors, or making sentences grammatical. Make these changes later when you are satisfied with your ideas. Here is a later draft of the paragraph shown on page 27. In this draft the author organized his ideas to follow the process of giving a party and to make all points support the topic sentence.

```
       From beginning to end, the positive
aspects of giving a party outweigh the
negative. It is true that preparations can be
time-consuming and expensive. Cleaning may take
many hours, and buying food can be hard, espe-
cially if the party is large and you are not
sure exactly how much to buy. If you buy
decorations too, you can end up spending a lot
of money. However, people often bring food and
drink as presents, and that cuts down on the
expense. Once guests start to arrive, neighbors
```

can get annoyed about the noise and parking problems. If you are careful, you can make sure things don't get out of control, and then you can enjoy seeing and talking to your friends. Occasionally friends you know from different places might not get along well. More often, friends enjoy meeting each other, and they become friends themselves. My best friend met his wife at one of my parties. After everyone leaves, there is usually some mess. But while cleaning up, you can think about the good time everyone had and also about other invitations you will receive. All in all, party-giving is worthwhile.

Use the following suggestions to revise effectively.

1. Try to let your first draft sit awhile before you begin revising it. If possible wait until the next day, but even a few hours away from the draft will be helpful.

2. Reread the sentence that expresses your main point. It must be clear, direct, and complete. Experiment with ways to improve it.

3. Reread each of your other sentences. Does each relate directly to your main point? If not, cross it out or rewrite it to clarify its connection to the main point. If all of your sentences relate to a main point that is different from the one you've written, rewrite the sentence.

4. Make sure your paragraph has a beginning and an end.

5. Reread again to see whether your sentences connect to one another. If necessary, add words or sentences that connect your ideas.

6. Delete or combine sentences that say the same thing.

7. Replace words that are vague or unclear with more descriptive words.

8. If you get stuck at any of these stages and cannot see what changes are needed, ask a friend to read your paragraph and mark ideas that are unclear or need more explanation.

9. After you have made one set of revisions, wait a few hours and then repeat all of these steps.

10. When you have finished revising you should feel satisfied both with what you have said and with the way you have said it.

Exercise 2–8   Revise the first draft you wrote for the previous exercise, following steps 1–10 above.

PROOFREADING

■ Proofreading is checking for errors. It is a final polishing of your work, in which you are concerned with correctness. Don't be concerned with proofreading until all your rethinking of ideas and revision are done. Check for each of these types of errors:

- run-on sentences
- fragments
- spelling
- punctuation
- grammar
- capitalization

The Skill Refreshers at the ends of the remaining chapters and Part Five of this text provide a good review of these topics.

Use the following tips to be sure you don't miss any errors.

1. Review your paragraph once for each type of error. First, read it for run-on sentences and fragments. Then read it four more times, each time paying attention only to grammar, spelling, punctuation, and so forth.

2. To spot spelling errors, read your paragraph from last sentence to first sentence and from last word to first word. The flow of ideas will not matter, so you can focus on spotting errors.

3. Read each sentence aloud, slowly and deliberately. This will help you catch missing words, endings you have left off of verbs, or missing plurals.

4. Check for errors again as you rewrite or type your paragraph into final form. Don't do this when you are tired; you might introduce new mistakes.

Exercise 2–9   Proofread and prepare the final copy for the paragraph you have developed throughout this chapter.

SUMMARY

■ The five steps in the writing process are:

1. **Generating Ideas.** Use freewriting, brainstorming, branching, and/or questioning to develop ideas about your topic.

2. **Organizing Your Ideas.** Look for relationships among ideas and discover how to present ideas logically.

3. **Writing a First Draft.** Express your ideas in sentence form. Focus on ideas, not grammar or correctness.

4. **Revising and Rewriting.** Rethink your ideas and evaluate how effectively you have expressed them. Rewrite your draft—adding, changing, deleting, and reorganizing your ideas.

5. **Proofreading.** Check your paper for errors in sentence structure, grammar, spelling, and punctuation.

3   Writing Topic Sentences

**CHAPTER
OBJECTIVES**

In this chapter you will learn to

1. understand the structure of a paragraph.
2. write effective topic sentences.

WHAT IS A PARAGRAPH?

■   Writing, in many ways, mirrors speech. The way we organize and present ideas in writing is similar to the way we present them orally. When we speak, we speak in groups of sentences. Seldom does our conversation consist of single statements or a series of unrelated statements. For example, you probably would *not* simply say to a friend, "I think you are making a mistake if you decide to marry Sam." Rather, you would support your general remark by offering reasons or by giving an example of someone else who made the same mistake. Similarly, in writing we group ideas together into paragraphs. A paragraph is a group of related sentences that develops one main thought about a single topic.

Chapter 2 showed you that writing a paragraph is a complex process that involves thinking, writing, and rethinking. But the structure of most paragraphs is not complex. There are usually two basic elements: (1) a topic sentence and (2) supporting details.

The topic sentence states your main point. The sentences that explain this main point are called supporting details. These details may be facts, reasons, or examples that provide further information about the topic sentence. If you were to write a paragraph based on the example above, *I think you are making a mistake if you decide to marry Sam* would be the topic sentence, and all of your reasons and examples would be supporting details.

A paragraph begins with the first sentence indented five letter spaces from the left margin. This indentation separates paragraphs from one another and signals the reader that a new idea is about to begin.

Read the following paragraph, noticing how the details explain the topic sentence, which is underlined.

> Acupuncture is an ancient and still widely used treatment in Oriental medicine that is alleged to relieve pain and other maladies. The method is based on the idea that body energy flows along lines called channels or meridians. There are fourteen main channels, and a person's health supposedly depends on the balance of energy flowing in them. Stimulating channels by inserting very fine needles into the skin and twirling them is said to restore a balanced flow of energy. The important spots to stimulate are called *Ho-Ku points*. Modern practitioners of acupuncture also use electrical stimulation through needles at the same points. The needles produce an aching and tingling sensation called *Teh-ch'i* at the site of stimulation, but relieve pain at distant, seemingly unrelated parts of the body.
>
> Douglas A. Bernstein, et al. *Psychology*

In this paragraph, the topic sentence identifies the topic—acupuncture—and states its primary use—to relieve pain. The remaining sentences provide further information about how acupuncture works.

You can visualize a paragraph as follows:

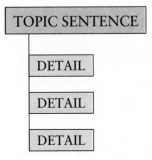

WRITING

SUCCESS

TIP 3

Organizing a Place and Time to Write

.   .   .   .

You'll find that you may be able to write more easily if you write in the same place and at the same time each day. Use the following tips to organize a place and time to write.

Organizing a Place to Write

1. If you live at home or in an apartment, try to find a quiet area that you can reserve for writing. If possible, avoid areas used for other purposes, such as the dining room or kitchen table, because you'll have to move or clean up your materials frequently. If you live in a dorm, your desk is an ideal place to write, unless the dorm is too noisy. If it is, find a quiet place elsewhere on campus.

2. You'll need a table or desk; don't try to write on an arm of a comfortable chair. Choose a space where you can spread out your papers.

3. Eliminate distractions from your writing area. Photos or stacks of bills to pay will take your mind off your writing.

4. Have adequate lighting and a straight, comfortable chair.

5. Collect and organize supplies: plenty of paper, pens, pencils, erasers, tape, stapler, white-out, and so forth.

You might visualize the paragraph on acupuncture as follows:

> Acupuncture is an Oriental treatment to relieve pain.
>
> It is based on the idea of energy flow lines.
>
> A person's health depends on energy flow through 14 channels.
>
> Needles are used to stimulate flow of energy.
>
> Points of stimulation are called Ho-Ku.
>
> Electrical stimulation can be used.
>
> etc.

6. Organize separate folders to keep completed and returned papers, quizzes, class handouts, and so on.

7. Keep a dictionary nearby, as well as any other reference materials recommended by your instructor—a thesaurus, for instance. (See Writing Success Tip 8 for advice on what type of dictionary to buy.)

8. Use your writing place for reading, studying, and writing for your other courses, as well.

Organizing Time to Write

1. Reserve a block of time each day for reading this book and working on writing exercises and assignments. Also reserve time for writing in your journal. (See Writing Success Tips 1 and 2 on pages 11–12 and 16–17.)

2. For now, reserve an hour a day for writing. This may seem like a lot of time, but most instructors expect you to spend a minimum of two hours outside of class for every hour you spend in class.

3. Try to work at the same time each day. You'll establish a routine that will be easy to follow.

4. Choose a time during the day when you are at the peak of your concentration. Don't try to write at times when you are likely to be interrupted.

5. Begin assignments well ahead of their due date so that you have time to plan, organize, write, revise, and proofread. It's best to leave a day or more between finishing your first draft and beginning to revise.

As you saw in Chapter 2, topic sentences are general statements, and details are smaller, more specific pieces of information. To help you understand the concept of general versus specific, here are a few examples. The first three use one-word topics and details; the last two use topic sentences and detail sentences.

General: fruit
Specific: apples, oranges, bananas

General: emotions
Specific: love, fear, anger

General: music
Specific: rhythm, beat, tempo

General: My sister-in-law is selfish and self-centered.
Specific: She talks about herself constantly.
            She shows no interest in the opinions of others.
            She focuses attention on herself by dressing boldly.

General: Newspapers include a wide variety of information.
Specific: Newspapers contain advertisements for products and
            services.
            Newspapers report world and local news events.

Notice that in each of these examples, the specific explains or describes the general by giving examples, reasons, or further information. In the same way, supporting details in your paragraph must explain or describe your topic sentence.

Exercise 3–1   Complete the following sets by supplying the missing information. Write complete sentences for items 3–8.

1. General: world problems
   Specific: hunger, _____ , _____

2. General: ways to pay for college
   Specific: _____ , _____ , _____

3. General: There are several reasons to buy a new car rather
              than a used car.
   Specific: 1. Used cars may have mechanical problems.

              2. _____

              3. _____

4. General: Advertisements are often misleading.
   Specific: 1. Products often appear larger than they really
                 are.

              2. _____

              3. _____

5. General: Television provides several types of entertainment.
   Specific: 1. _____

               2. _____

               3. _____

6. General: Many careers require specialized training.
   Specific: 1. Nurses must learn anatomy and physiology.

               2. _____

               3. _____

7. General: _____
   Specific: 1. Some television commercials use humor to sell
                  their product.
               2. Other commercials use celebrities to convince
                  the audience to buy the product.
               3. Some commercials use an "everyone's buying
                  it, so why don't you?" appeal.

8. General: _____
   Specific: 1. Newspapers provide news of local and regional
                  interest.
               2. Newspapers offer news of state-wide policies
                  and regulations as they affect the local com-
                  munity.
               3. Newspapers contain advertising by local busi-
                  nesses.

WRITING EFFECTIVE TOPIC SENTENCES

■ Purpose of a Topic Sentence

An effective topic sentence does two things. First, it makes clear what
the paragraph is about—the topic. Second, it expresses a view or makes
a point about the topic. In the following examples, the topic is circled
and the point about the topic is underlined.

1. The first week of college is a frustrating experience.
2. Fanny's serves the best hamburgers in town.
3. State-operated lotteries are growing in popularity in America.
4. Time management is a vital skill for college students.

Exercise 3–2   For the following topic sentences, circle the topic and underline the view the writer takes toward the topic.

1. Sunday morning is a time for reading and relaxing.
2. My part-time job at a department store is providing me with valuable sales experience.
3. Publicly funded FM radio stations need your financial support.
4. *Time,* a weekly newsmagazine, presents thorough coverage of world events.
5. Danny Everett, my favorite morning radio personality, gets my day off to a bright and humorous start.

Exercise 3–3   Complete the following topic sentences by supplying a view about each topic.

1. Liquor advertisements _____ .

2. Most fast-food restaurants _____ .

3. Monday morning is _____ .

4. Violence on television _____ .

5. College professors _____ .

Choosing a Manageable Topic

To write a good paragraph, you need a manageable topic, one that is the right size. Your topic must be general enough to allow you to bring together interesting details that will engage your reader. But it must be specific or narrow enough so that you can cover it adequately in a few sentences. If your topic is too general, you'll end up with a few unrelated details that do not add up to a specific point. If your topic is too narrow, you will not have enough to say.

Suppose you have decided to write a paragraph about sports. You write the following topic sentence:

```
Sports is a favorite national pastime.
```

The topic of sports as a national pastime is too broad to cover in one paragraph. Think of all the different aspects you could write about. Which sports would you consider? Would you write about both playing sports and watching them? Would you write about professional, college, and high school sports? Would you write about the reasons people enjoy sports? Because you cannot include all the aspects in one paragraph, you could revise the topic sentence to be more specific:

```
Watching professional football on Sunday
afternoons is a form of relaxation for me.
```

Here you have limited your topic to a specific sport (football), a specific time (Sunday afternoon), and a specific fan (you).

Here are a few other examples of sentences that are too general. Each has been revised to be more specific.

Too General: My parents have influenced my life.
Revised: My parents helped me make the decision to attend college.

Too General: Sex education is worthwhile.
Revised: Sex education courses offered in high school allow students to discuss sex openly.

If your topic is *too* specific (narrow), you will run out of details to use in the paragraph. Or, you may include details that do not directly explain the topic. Suppose you decide to write a paragraph about using a computer for word processing:

```
Using the word processor for my paper allowed
me to correct spelling errors without retyping.
```

What would your paragraph say? Beyond saying that the computer corrects your mistakes, you may have little else to say. This sentence is too specific. It might work as a detail, but not as a main idea. To correct this problem, ask "What else does the word processor allow me to do?" You might say it allows you to change the order of paragraphs, correct punctuation, and replace words. Your revised topic sentence could be:

```
The word processor has several features that
save time and make revision easy.
```

Here are a few other examples of topic sentences that are too narrow, along with revisions for each one.

Too Narrow: Only 36 percent of Americans voted in the 1990 election.
Revised: Many Americans do not exercise their right to vote.

Too Narrow:	The television commercial that shows talking cereal boxes is annoying.
Revised:	Television commercials that use gimmicks are annoying.
Too Narrow:	My psychology exam contained 150 multiple choice questions.
Revised:	My psychology exam was difficult and long.
Too Narrow:	A yearly subscription to *With the Grain* costs $20.
Revised:	*With the Grain* is a magazine devoted to environmental issues.

Suppose you used brainstorming or branching to generate ideas. If you find you can develop the topic in many different directions, or if you have trouble choosing details from a wide range of choices, your topic is probably too general. You will know your topic sentence is too specific if you cannot think of anything to explain or support it.

Exercise 3–4   Evaluate the following ineffective topic sentences. Label each "G" for too general or "S" for too specific.

> _____ 1. Learning foreign languages is difficult.
> _____ 2. Dinner for two at my favorite Italian restaurant costs $15.
> _____ 3. Attending graduate school is worth the time and money.
> _____ 4. Many rules of etiquette have changed over the past 25 years.
> _____ 5. Passive cigarette smoke makes me nauseous.

Tips for Writing Effective Topic Sentences

Use the following suggestions to write clear topic sentences.

1. **Make sure your topic sentence is a complete thought.** Be sure your topic sentence is not a fragment or run-on sentence. (Refer to section C in Part Five for a review of sentence errors.)

2. **Place your topic sentence first in the paragraph.** Topic sentences often appear other places in paragraphs. But until you become a more experienced writer, it will be easier for you to put yours at the beginning.

3. **Avoid announcing your topic.** Sentences that sound like announcements are usually unnecessary. Avoid such sentences as: "*This paragraph will discuss* how to change a flat tire," or "*I will explain why* I object to legalized abortion." Instead, directly state your main point: "Changing a flat tire involves many steps," or "I object to abortion on religious grounds."

Not all expert or professional writers follow all of these suggestions. Sometimes, a writer may even write a paragraph without a topic sentence. And some writers use one-sentence paragraphs. You will find these paragraphs in news and magazine articles and other sources. Although professional writers can use these variations effectively, you probably should not experiment with them too early. It's best, while you are polishing your writing skills, to follow more standard guidelines.

Exercise 3–5   Evaluate each of the following topic sentences and mark them as follows:

E = effective   G = topic too general
A = announcement   N = not complete thought
S = topic too specific

_____   1. This paper will discuss the life and politics of Alexander Hamilton.
_____   2. Japanese culture is fascinating to study because its family traditions are so different from ours.
_____   3. A large box of my favorite breakfast cereal costs 2.39 dollars.
_____   4. The discovery of penicillin was a great step in the advancement of modern medicine.
_____   5. I will talk about the reasons for the removal of the Berlin Wall.
_____   6. Poor habits may lead to weight gain.
_____   7. Oranges and lemons are a good source of Vitamin C.
_____   8. The White House has many famous rooms with an exciting history.
_____   9. There are three factors to consider when buying a CD player.
_____ 10. Iraq has a long and interesting history.

Exercise 3–6   Analyze the following topic sentences. If a sentence is too general, too specific, or if it makes a direct announcement or is not a complete thought, revise it to make it more effective.

1. World hunger is a crime.

Revised: _____

_____

2. Freud, a founder of a school of psychotherapy in which patients talk about their problems and past lives.

Revised: _____

_____

3. I will point out the many ways energy can be conserved in the home.

Revised: _____

_____

4. Congress is very important in this country.

Revised: _____

_____

5. Pollution is a serious problem.

Revised: _____

_____

_____

Exercise 3–7   Write a topic sentence for four of the following topics, using the tips given above. Then select one of your topic sentences and use it to develop a paragraph.

  1. Should suicide ever be encouraged?
  2. Who deserves football or college scholarships?
  3. Do children learn better with computers?
  4. Why are baseball games fun to watch?
  5. Should we use comics or cartoons to teach children to read?
  6. Is space exploration a waste of money?

7. Does the news coverage of presidential campaigns unfairly influence voters?

THINKING BEFORE READING

■ Following are two strategies designed to get you thinking before you begin reading. Just as you must think about writing before you actually put words down on paper, thinking about another author's writing before you read will help you get the most from your reading. For example, the next section of this chapter contains an article written by Seattle newspaper columnist, Fred Moody. As you read it, watch how he constructs paragraphs and how the writing moves from general to specific thoughts in each paragraph.

Previewing

Previewing is a way of learning what a reading is about before you actually read it. By reading selected portions of a reading, you can discover a great deal about its content and its organization. Previewing is like looking at a map before driving in an unfamiliar city. When you preview an article, you become familiar with its layout so that you can understand it more easily as you read. Previewing is not time-consuming. You can preview a brief selection in a minute or two by following these basic steps.

1. **Read and think about the title.** What does it tell you about the subject? Does it offer any clues about how the author feels about the subject or how he or she will approach it?

2. **Check the author.** Is the author's name familiar? If so, what do you know about him or her?

3. **Read the first paragraph.** Here the author introduces the subject. Look for a statement of the main point of the entire reading.

4. **Read all dark print headings.** Headings divide up the reading into pieces and announce the topic of each section.

5. **Read the first sentence under each heading.** This sentence often states the main point of the section.

6. **Read the first sentence of each paragraph.** You will discover many of the main ideas of the article. If the reading consists of very short paragraphs, read every third or fourth first sentence.

7. **Read the last paragraph.** Often this paragraph summarizes or concludes the reading.

The more you practice previewing, the more effectively you will find it works. Use it for all of your college textbooks.

Making Connections

Reading is always easier if you are interested in the subject and feel it has something to do with you. Before you begin to read, take a minute to discover what you already know about the subject, what connection it may have to your life, or how you can associate the ideas with your experience.

For example, the reading in this chapter discusses the negative effects of divorce on the couple as well as on the children. You might ask yourself the following questions about the topic:

1. Think about a couple you know who are divorced. What effects has their divorce had on the couple? How has their divorce changed them?
2. What effects of divorce have you noticed among children?
3. Think of a married couple you know well. What problems would you expect them to have if they decided to divorce?

READING

DIVORCE: SOMETIMES A BAD NOTION

Fred Moody

Divorce, along with high-school graduation, marriage, and death, is now an established American rite of passsage. Everyone, either directly or indirectly, is touched by it. A first marriage undertaken today stands (avert your eyes, squeamish reader) a 66 percent chance of ending in divorce. For the first time in history, an American marrying now is more likely to lose a spouse through divorce than through death.

Divorce most often is portrayed as liberating. The ease with which we divorce is regarded as a proof of the individual freedoms Americans enjoy. It is one more means we have of achieving self-fulfillment—the *raison d'être*[1] of the baby-boom generation. When no-fault divorce was ushered in 20 years ago, it was hailed as a quick and easy solution to relationships gone sour. Now, a generation later, legions of divorced parents and their children are emerging to paint a far different picture: one of financial travail, psychological devastation, and endless emotional turmoil. Study after study documents so much discontent surrounding divorce that it now appears to be an even greater source of disillusionment than marriage is.

Divorce is particularly disillusioning for women and children. No-fault reforms have robbed women of alimony, and no-fault's lax child-support enforcement has allowed men to default on their obligations to the point where many divorced women and children are reduced to poverty. Instead of reducing inequality between the sexes, no-fault divorce has widened the gap in status between men and women, and is the leading cause of the well-documented feminization of poverty in America.

3

There's no question that the fundamental right to divorce should be available to anyone; the ability to divorce a monster or an addict, or to get out of a marriage that is an incurable mistake, is a humane and civilized right. But the notion that every unhappy marriage is a bad one, or that individuals are morally as well as legally entitled to place their own pursuit of happiness above the well-being of their offspring, is *ruinous*.[2] Opting for divorce before having exhausted every effort at preserving a relationship is self-destructive. . . .

4

The emotional fallout of divorce is easy to see. Legions of divorced people, their attorneys, their therapists, their children, and their children's therapists have learned that divorce is shattering.

5

"Quite often, divorce is much more devastating than people who go into the process anticipate," says Seattle pyschiatrist Dr. Herbert Wimberger. "They are surprised by how painful it is, by how long the pain lasts. Divorce very often is a serious loss, bringing on a severe grief reaction." Adds Seattle psychotherapist Diane Zerbe, "Everybody knows somebody five years later who is still emotionally invested in their failed marriage, still angry at their ex-spouse, and their bitterness is a major part of their life. They haven't been able somehow to come to terms with what happened and go on to find a more satisfying relationship."

6

1. reason for being
2. causing ruin; destructive

The evidence also seems to suggest that second marriages are no happier, with even less likelihood of working than first marriages (for some reason, third ones have better odds). 7

No-fault has also become a source of no-limit frustration and bitterness for wronged spouses, by shifting the power overwhelmingly from the spouse who wants to stay married to the spouse who wants a divorce. It offers an amoral solution to a problem many people regard as moral. It also has backfired psychologically. The idea that a procedure providing no outlet for anger would somehow do away with anger has proven an illusion. "I keep telling my lawyer," says one furious woman currently going through a divorce, "that my husband is sleeping with other women, that he won't even talk to me, that he neglects our children, and the lawyer keeps answering, 'Irrelevant! Irrelevant!' It isn't fair!" 8

In many divorces, the rage that formerly came out during the debate over grounds for divorce now is redirected into interminable custody disputes and negotiations over child support. In one recent case, the husband, being divorced by his wife, was determined to get sole custody of their children, even though he had had little to do with them during his marriage. He made extravagant accusations against his wife—of abandonment, child abuse, and incest—all of which were dutifully investigated and dismissed by the court. 9

As all this suggests, no-fault also failed to deliver on its promise of convenience and lower cost. "People are spending more time and money on divorce than ever before," says Seattle family-law attorney Nancy Hawkins. 10

Worst of all has been the disastrous impact of no-fault divorce on women and children. In Washington state, for example, property is divided equally between divorcing spouses, regardless of who is primarily responsible for the failure of the marriage. Before 1973, the wounded party—usually the wife—was awarded a greater share of a couple's property as a form of compensation for pain and suffering. No-fault's attempts to make divorce law gender-neutral, and therefore more fair, have created a raw deal for women. It has led to the virtual elimination of alimony payments to wronged or financially disadvantaged wives, and to drastic reductions in the amount and duration of maintenance payments to wives who gave up career goals for their families. 11

Judges have further disadvantaged such women by refusing to regard a husband's future earnings as community property, even in cases where a wife could demonstrate that her support and the sacri- 12 fice of her own career contributed to her husband's success and earning power.

Consequently, divorced women who win custody of their children now suffer, on the average, a 33 percent decline in their standard of living, while their ex-husbands enjoy a corresponding rise in theirs. This is largely due to the dismal complexities of court-ordered child support. In Washington, research shows that court orders for child support are almost always too low to cover the actual costs of raising children. Further, only 50 percent of divorced dads in Washington pay the full amount of their child-support judgment; 25 percent pay part of what they're ordered, and the remaining 25 percent simply ignore the order and pay nothing at all.   13

The effect on children is enormous. According to University of Washington sociologist Diane Lye, more than 70 percent of America's black children and 50 percent of its white children will live in single-parent homes by the time they are 16 years old. "There are 18 million poor children in our country now," she says, "and over half of them are living in single-parent homes caused by divorce." . . .   14

Clearly, far more sweeping reforms are called for. At the very least, courts need enough time and money to study divorce decrees and determine whether they adequately provide for women and children. As things stand now, they simply rubber-stamp agreements reached between people who are in no shape to keep their children's best interests in mind.   15

There should also be lawyers representing children in divorce hearings, as they do in child-abuse hearings. A child's lawyer should be able to argue on behalf of the child's best interests—that the divorce be denied, that parents undergo further counseling, that children be compensated for the emotional and material damage divorce will bring down on them.   16

Rampant divorce is dangerous not only to children—it also harms, often permanently, the husbands and wives who suffer through it. It lowers the moral tone of the entire nation, as society seconds the motion that we are entitled to look first of all after ourselves. Since the mid-1960s, divorce has had almost unremittingly good press, and the better divorce's public image, the greater priority many people give to self-fulfillment over obligations to others. Those who shape and mold opinion in this country—writers, reporters, moviemakers, and advertisers, to name a few—need to de-romanticize divorce.   17

Young people need to be made aware of the dire consequences of   18 marriages carelessly undertaken: Marriage and divorce education is as critical to our society's health as sex education. Divorce's romanti-cized[3] image as a harmless quick fix is a lie. That fantasy has led legions of naive and discontented people into even greater unhappiness than they had suffered in their marriages.

Since the advent of no-fault, one of the fundamental truths about divorce has been discounted: that love or marriage may be fleeting, but divorce is forever. Those contemplating divorce should understand that it often affords not a new beginning, but only a new form of anguish. "You never get divorced for real," says one woman, who left her husband six years ago. "You never get rid of that person." Another woman concurs: "I thought divorce would be like jumping through a hoop," she says. "But it's not a hoop—it's a tunnel."   19

Utne Reader, Nov./Dec. 1990

GETTING READY TO WRITE

■   Throughout college, you will be required to write about materials you have read. For example, you may be asked to analyze a short story in an English class, summarize a news article for sociology, or react to a research report in biology. To write about something you have read, you must first have a complete understanding of the material, both its content and its organization. Writing is helpful in increasing your comprehension and your ability to remember what you have read.

In the "Getting Ready to Write" section of each chapter you will learn strategies that will help you to identify what is important and to organize ideas and get ready to write about them. In this chapter, you will learn two strategies: immediate review and underlining.

Step 1: Immediate Review and Underlining Topic Sentences
When you have read any piece of material once, do not expect to have complete mastery of it. You probably can remember many of the key points and some of the supporting details, but there will be ideas you cannot recall. Also, your level of understanding may be literal—that is, you can recall facts and details, but you're not ready to interpret and react to the ideas expressed.

---

3. Not based on fact; imaginary

A quick review of the reading is often useful in making its content stick in your memory. The review will also bring to your attention portions or ideas that need to be reread or thought about more carefully. Questions may come to mind.

An easy way to review the selection is to follow the same steps you followed in previewing before reading (see p. 43). Review the reading "Divorce: Sometimes a Bad Notion" now by following the previewing steps. The best time to review is *immediately* after you've finished reading, while the content is still fresh in your mind.

Another valuable form of review is to underline either the topic sentence of each paragraph or the most important words in that sentence. This activity forces you to decide what each paragraph is about and, at the same time, helps you to remember it. You can also reread your underlining to refresh your memory for a class discussion and to locate specific sections quickly without rereading.

Exercise 3–8   Underline each topic sentence of the paragraphs in the reading, "Divorce: Sometimes a Bad Notion." *Helpful Hint:* If you have difficulty identifying the topic sentence, ask yourself, "What one key, general idea do all of the sentences in the paragraph discuss or explain?"

Step 2: Thinking Critically: Discovering the Author's Purpose

A writer always has in mind a purpose for writing. A writer may write to defend an action or policy (abortion, gun control, or mercy killing). Or a writer may write to present information on an issue. Other times, a writer intends to entertain or amuse, express emotions, or describe an event or person. As a reader, it is your job to recognize the author's purpose and to judge whether he or she accomplishes it effectively.

To discover the author's purpose, use the following suggestions:

1. Answer the questions: What is the writer trying to tell me? What does he or she want me to do or think?

2. Pay close attention to the title of the piece and the source of the material because these may offer clues. Suppose an article is titled "Twenty-six Reasons to Vote in National Elections." The title suggests the author's purpose is to urge citizens to vote. If an essay on the lumber industry appeared in *Eco-Ideas*, a magazine devoted to environmental preservation and improvement, you might predict that the author's purpose is to call for restrictions or limitations on the industry.

3. Look for clues or statements about purpose in the beginning and concluding paragraphs of the material. Suppose an essay concluded with a statement such as, "The above evidence clearly suggests that gun control laws have little effect in reducing crime." This reveals that the author's purpose is to oppose gun control laws.

Step 3: Reacting To and Discussing Ideas

After you read someone else's ideas, it is helpful to talk about them. As you discuss those ideas, you may get a clearer picture of what the writer was trying to say. You might also discover new ways of looking at the subject, realize new problems, or clarify your own thinking. By talking about ideas, you will also find yourself generating language— that is, expressing your ideas and feelings in words. This activity will be particularly helpful when you begin to write about what you have read.

The questions in this section are intended to initiate discussion and provoke thought about the reading.

1. Summarize Moody's attitude toward divorce.

2. Do you agree or disagree with the statement in paragraph four, "But the notion that every unhappy marriage is a bad one, or that individuals are morally as well as legally entitled to place their own pursuit of happiness above the well-being of their offspring, is ruinous"?

3. Must all divorces involve anger, frustration, and bitterness?

4. Discuss the idea that children should have their own attorney in a divorce dispute.

5. Do you agree that divorce has been "romanticized" as a quick fix for couples with problems?

WRITING ABOUT THE READING

■ *Assignment 1*

Write a paragraph to explain how you think Moody wanted his audience to react to this article. Start your paragraph with a topic sentence that begins, "Moody wanted the people who read 'Divorce: Sometimes a Bad Notion' to . . ." Complete your paragraph by including details that explain your topic sentence or give examples to support it.

WRITING ABOUT YOUR IDEAS

■ *Assignment 1*

Write a paragraph explaining whether you feel divorce is sometimes a bad notion. Include details that explain why you feel as you do.

Assignment 2

Write a paragraph describing the positive or negative effects of divorce that you have observed. Support your topic sentence with examples.

Assignment 3

Moody states that the effects of divorce are most disastrous on women and children. Write a paragraph explaining why you agree or disagree with this statement.

Journal Writing Suggestions

1. Write a journal entry explaining what you think are the major causes for the high divorce rate in our country.

2. Divorce is a stressful situation. Write a journal entry describing a stressful situation that you have experienced.

Sentence Fragments

A sentence fragment is a group of words that (1) lacks a subject, (2) lacks a verb, or (3) is a subordinate (dependent) clause unattached to a complete sentence, and therefore it fails to express a complete thought.

NOTE: A **subject** is the noun or pronoun that performs the action of the sentence. A **verb** is a word that conveys the action or state of being of the subject. A **subordinate clause** is a group of words beginning with a subordinating conjunction like *although, because, if, since, unless, wherever, while* or with a relative pronoun like *which, that, what, who, whoever.*

In the examples below, the fragments are underlined.

> My friend Anita called me last night. Calls me every night. [The second group of words lacks a subject.]

> Anita, a friend I have known all my life, and excellent at math. She asked if I had finished doing my taxes. [The first group of words lacks a verb.]

> I planned to fill out the tax forms that evening. Because the deadline was approaching. [The second group of words is a subordinate clause unattached to a complete sentence.]

How to Spot Fragments

A fragment begins with a capital letter and ends with a period, like a complete sentence, but it is not a complete sentence. To identify fragments in your writing, ask the following questions of each group of words.

1. **Is there a verb?** To find the verb, look for a word that conveys what is happening, what has happened, or what will happen. Do not confuse a verb with verbals (*-ing, -ed,* or infinitive *"to"* forms of verbs that are used as nouns or modifiers). A true verb changes form to communicate a time change. A verbal does not.

FRAGMENT: A nervous, pressured feeling and a headache.
CORRECT: A nervous, pressured feeling and a headache struck me.

FRAGMENT: The express train leaving the station at four.
CORRECT: The express train will leave the station at four.

FRAGMENT: To get a taxi and hurry downtown.
CORRECT: I need to get a taxi and hurry downtown.

2. Is there a subject? To find the subject, ask "who?" or "what?" is performing the action of the sentence.

FRAGMENT: Asked Mr. Gomez how he grew rhubarb. [Who asked Mr. Gomez?]
CORRECT: Gail asked Mr. Gomez how he grew rhubarb.

3. If the group of words (clause) starts with a subordinating conjunction or relative pronoun, is this subordinate clause attached to a complete sentence? A subordinate clause cannot stand alone. It needs to be combined with a related sentence.

FRAGMENT: Although we wanted to go to the softball game.
CORRECT: Although we wanted to go to the softball game, we could not find the right park.

FRAGMENT: If we had asked directions or bought a map.
CORRECT: We might have found the park if we had asked directions or bought a map.

How to Correct Fragments

1. Revise by combining the fragment with an appropriate existing complete sentence.

FRAGMENT: My sister loved her job at the jewelry store. Until she got a new boss.
REVISED: Until she got a new boss, my sister loved her job at the jewelry store.

2. Remove the word or phrase that makes the statement incomplete.

FRAGMENT: While I was waiting for class to begin.
REVISED: I was waiting for class to begin.

3. Add the missing subject or verb.

FRAGMENT: Waiting for my paycheck to be delivered.
REVISED: I was waiting for my paycheck to be delivered.

SKILL   REFRESHER

· ·

Rate Your Ability to Spot and Correct Fragments

Place a checkmark in front of each item that contains a fragment, then correct each fragment so it is a complete sentence.

1. Leaving the room, she turned and smiled.
2. Until the exam was over, the professor paced in the front of the room.
3. I remembered her birthday. Because we're good friends.
4. I realized I forgot my book. After I left the classroom.
5. Jason asked a question about centrifugal force. Before the professor moved on to the next topic.
6. Until the phone rang and the answering machine answered.
7. Hoping I would do well on the test.
8. Scheduling a conference with her art history professor to discuss the topic for her final paper.
9. I got a "B" on the quiz. Because I reread my notes.
10. Marcus was interested in the course. Focused on the rise of communism.

Score _____

Check your answers using the Answer Key on page 537. If you scored below 80 percent, you need additional review and practice recognizing and correcting fragments. Refer to section C.1 of Reviewing the Basics in Part 5.

SUMMARY

■   1. A topic sentence states the main point of your paragraph. Be sure that your topic sentence

- identifies the topic you are writing about.
- expresses a view or makes a point about the topic.

2. To write an effective paragraph, choose a manageable topic. Your topic must be

- specific enough so that you can cover it adequately in a single paragraph.
- general enough to allow you to bring together interesting details that explain it.

4   Developing and Arranging Details

CHAPTER
OBJECTIVES

In this chapter you will learn to

1. use details to develop your topic sentence.
2. select relevant and sufficient details.
3. arrange details in a paragraph.
4. use specific words.
5. use transitional words.

Imagine that you have decided to request a raise from the manager at your part-time job. You walk into her office and say, "Based on my performance over the past year, I feel I deserve a raise." Of course, your manager's response would be, "Why?" She would expect you to explain exactly what you have done to deserve a raise. When you state your main point in the topic sentence of a paragraph, your reader, too, will ask "Why?" You must provide supporting details so that he or she will accept your main point.

USING RELEVANT AND SUFFICIENT DETAILS

■ The details you choose to support your topic sentence must be both relevant and sufficient. *Relevant* means that each detail must directly explain and support your topic sentence. For example, if you were to write a paragraph explaining why you deserve the raise, it would not be relevant to mention that you plan to use the money to go to Florida next spring. A vacation has nothing to do with, or is not relevant to, your job performance.

Sufficient detail means enough information to make your topic sentence understandable and convincing. In your paragraph requesting a raise, it would probably not be sufficient to say that you are always on time. You would need to provide more information, highlighting the fact that you always volunteer to work holidays, describing improvements you've suggested, or giving examples of customer satisfaction.

Selecting Relevant Details

Relevant details help to clarify and strengthen your ideas, whereas irrelevant details make your ideas unclear and confusing. Here is the first draft of a paragraph written by a student named Edward to explain why he decided to attend college. Can you locate the detail that is not relevant?

> I decided to attend college to further my education and achieve my goals in life. I am attempting to build a future for myself. When I get married and have kids, I want to be able to offer them the same opportunities my parents gave me. I want to have a comfortable style of living and a good job. As for my wife, I don't want her to work because I believe a married woman should not work. I believe college is the way to begin a successful life.

Sentence five does not belong in the paragraph because the fact that Edward does not want his wife to work is not a reason for attending college.

Now suppose you were writing a paragraph on nuclear weapons. As a topic sentence you write:

> Nuclear weapons should be eliminated because they pose safety and health threats.

Which of the following details are relevant to the topic sentence?

1. Nuclear weapons threaten the safety of those who live near storage areas.
2. Nuclear weapons are expensive to produce and maintain.
3. Nuclear energy provides an important alternative to oil.
4. Nuclear weapons are housed underground to protect them from sabotage.
5. Long-term health problems may result from the exposure to radiation.

Detail two is not relevant because it does not concern health or safety. Detail three is not relevant because it does not discuss nuclear weapons. And detail four is not relevant because it does not give a reason for their elimination.

Use the following simple test to be sure each detail you write belongs in a paragraph you have written.

1. Reread your topic sentence with other sentences in your paragraph. For example,

Read topic sentence + last sentence
Read topic sentence + second to last sentence
Read topic sentence + third to last sentence

2. For each pair of sentences ask yourself, "Do these two ideas fit together?" If your answer is "No," then you have found a detail that is not relevant to your topic. Delete it from your paragraph.

Now revise the following paragraph by crossing out the details that are not relevant.

The legal drinking age should be raised to age twenty-five. Those who drink should be old enough to determine whether or not it is safe to drive after drinking. Bartenders and others who serve drinks should also have to be twenty-five. In general, teenagers and young adults are not responsible enough to limit how much they drink. The party atmosphere enjoyed by so many young people encourages crazy acts, so we should limit who can drink. Younger people think drinking is a game, but it is a dangerous game that affects the lives of others.

Did you delete the third sentence? It does not belong in the paragraph because the age of those who bartend or serve drinks is not relevant to the topic. Part of the sentence about partying should also be eliminated or explained because the connection between partying and drinking is not clear.

Exercise 4–1   For each of the topic sentences listed, place a check mark by those statements that provide relevant details.

1. Magazines are published about hundreds of different subjects.
   _____ a. Fashion magazines are popular among women in their twenties.
   _____ b. Advertising in specialty magazines is very reader specific.
   _____ c. There is a magazine for almost every sport.

WRITING
SUCCESS
TIP 4

College Services for Writing

• • • • • • • • • • • • • • • • • • • •

Many colleges offer services to assist students with their writing skills. Most of these services are free and available upon request. Common services are described below; check to see which are available on your campus.

Tutorial Services

Many colleges offer tutoring in a variety of disciplines, including writing. Tutoring is usually provided by other students who are paid by the college. A fellow student can often explain a technique in a manner that is easy to understand. Most tutors have already taken a writing course, so they can understand your concerns. Tutoring may be offered by the English Department, the college learning lab, student services, or the academic skills center.

Computer-Assisted Instruction

Some colleges have labs or libraries that house individual instructional programs to be used on a computer. These programs often review

2. Although the words sound similar, astronomy and astrology are very different fields of study.

_____ a. Astrology is an unscientific method of making predictions about events in people's lives, based on where stars are in the sky.

_____ b. Many popular magazines include astrological predictions.

_____ c. Astronomy is the scientific study of the stars, planets, and space.

3. Water can exist in three forms, which vary with temperature.

_____ a. At a high temperature, water becomes steam; it is a gas.

_____ b. Drinking water often contains mineral traces.

_____ c. At cold temperatures ice is water in its solid state.

4. Outlining is one of the easiest ways to organize facts.

_____ a. Formal outlines use Roman numerals, as well as Arabic letters and numerals to show different levels of importance.

principles of grammar, spelling, or punctuation and give you practice applying them. Even if you have never used a computer before, these programs are easy to use and have very clear, straightforward directions.

College Learning Lab

Most colleges have a Learning Center or Lab that offers instruction in reading, writing, and mathematics. The Lab may have instructors available to assist you or may sponsor workshops that review specific writing skills. Many labs have an extensive library of videotapes, workbooks, audio tapes, and manuals on a variety of topics. Visit the Lab and find out what services are available.

Your Instructor's Office Hours

One of the most valuable sources of assistance on campus is your instructor. Most instructors reserve several hours a week during which they are available to meet with you in their offices. Don't hesitate to visit your instructor during these office hours. If, for example, you are having difficulty organizing the details for a writing assignment, go and see your instructor. Take copies of all your work up to that point—freewriting, drafts, and so forth.

_____ b. Outlining emphasizes the relationship among facts.
_____ c. Outlines make it easier to focus on important points.

Exercise 4–2   Write a paragraph beginning with one of the topic sentences listed below. Complete the paragraph by including at least three *relevant* details. When you've finished, use the test described on page 57 to make certain each detail is relevant.

1. Hunting wild animals should (or should not) be allowed.
2. My hometown (or city) has changed in the past five years.
3. Religion is (is not) important in my life.
4. White parents should (should not) be allowed to adopt black children.
5. Medical doctors are (are not) sensitive to their patients' feelings.

Including Sufficient Detail

After reading your paragraph, your reader should know *why* you believe your topic sentence is true. You must give him or her a sufficient amount of specific information to understand your main idea.

Let's look at a paragraph another student wrote on the topic of billboard advertising.

> There is a national movement to oppose billboard advertising. Many people don't like billboards and are taking action to change what products are advertised and what companies use them. Community activists are destroying billboard advertisements at an increasing rate. As a result of their actions, numerous changes have been made.

Notice that this paragraph is very general. It does not explain who dislikes billboards or why they dislike them. It does not tell what products are advertised or name the companies that use them. No detail is given about how the billboards are destroyed and the resulting changes are not described. Here is a revised version. Notice the addition of numerous details.

> There is a growing national movement among residents of inner-city neighborhoods to oppose billboard advertising. Residents oppose billboards that glamorize cigarettes and alcohol and target people of color as consumers. Community activists have organized and are taking action. They carry paint, rollers, shovels, and brooms to an offending billboard. Within a few minutes the billboard is painted over, removing the damaging advertisement. Results have been dramatic. Many tobacco and liquor companies have reduced their inner-city billboard advertising. In place of these ads, some billboard companies have placed public service announcements and ads to improve community health.

If you have trouble thinking of enough details to include in a paragraph, try brainstorming or one of the other prewriting techniques described in Chapter 2. Write your topic sentence at the top of a sheet of paper. Then list anything that comes to mind about that topic. Include examples, events, incidents, facts, and reasons. You will be surprised at how many useful details you think of.

Once you have finished, read over your list and cross out details that are not relevant. (If you still don't have enough, your topic may be too specific. See pages 39–40.) The next section helps you decide in what order you will write about the details in your list.

Exercise 4–3   Reread the paragraph you wrote for Exercise 4–2 to see if it includes sufficient detail. If necessary, revise your paragraph to include more relevant details. Use a prewriting technique, if necessary, to generate additional ideas.

METHODS OF ARRANGING DETAILS

■ Bill had an assignment to write a paragraph about travel. He wrote the paragraph and then revised it. As you read each version, pay particular attention to the order in which he arranged the details.

Version 1

> This summer I had the opportunity to travel extensively. Over Labor Day weekend I back-packed with a group of friends in the Alleghany mountains. When spring semester was over I visited my seven cousins in Florida. My friends and I went to New York City over the Fourth of July to see fireworks and explore the city. During June I worked as a wildlife preservation volunteer in an Ohio State Park. On July 15 I celebrated my twenty-fifth birthday by visiting my parents in Syracuse.

Version 2

> This summer I had the opportunity to travel extensively in the States. When the spring semester ended, I went to my cousins' home in Florida to relax. When I returned, I worked as a wildlife preservation volunteer in an Ohio State Park for the month of June. Then my

```
friends and I went to New York City to see
fireworks and look around the city over the
Fourth of July weekend. On July 15th, I cele-
brated my twenty-fifth birthday by visiting my
parents in Syracuse. Finally, over Labor Day
weekend my friends and I backpacked in the
Alleghany mountains, trying not to think about
the upcoming school year.
```

Did you find Bill's revision easier to read? In the first version, Bill recorded the details as he thought of them. There is no arrangement or connection among them. In the second paragraph he arranged the details in the order in which they happened. Bill chose this arrangement because it fit his details logically. Time sequence is one of four common methods for arranging details:

1. time sequence
2. spatial arrangement
3. advantages/disadvantages
4. least/most arrangement

We will discuss each of these methods below. In Part Two of this book, additional methods of arranging ideas are discussed.

Time Sequence

When you write about an event or a series of events that took place over a long period, it is often easiest to describe them in the order in which they happened. For example, if you were to write about a particularly bad day in which everything went wrong, you might begin with waking up in the morning and end with going to bed that night. If you were describing a busy or exciting weekend, you might begin with what you did on Friday night and end with the last activity on Sunday. (You will learn more about this method of arrangement in Chapter 7, "Narration and Process.")

Spatial Arrangement

Suppose you have an assignment to describe the room in which you are sitting. You want your reader, who has never been in the room, to visualize it. You need to describe, in an orderly way, where items are positioned in the room. You could describe the room from left to right, from ceiling to floor, or from door to window. In other situations your choices might include front to back, inside to outside, near to far, east to west, left to right, and so on. This method of presentation is called *spatial arrangement*. Notice how the details are arranged from front to back in the following paragraph.

> Keith's antique car was gloriously decorated for the Fourth of July parade. Red, white, and blue streamers hung in front from the headlights and bumper. The hood was covered with small American flags. The windshield had gold stars pasted on it, arranged to form an outline of our state. On the sides, the doors displayed red plastic tape stripes on them. The convertible top was down, and Mary sat on the trunk dressed up like the Statue of Liberty. In the rear, a neon sign blinked: "God Bless America." His car's decor was not only a show-stopper but the highlight of the parade.

The topic you are writing about will often determine the arrangement you choose. In writing about a town you might choose to begin with the center of town and then move to each surrounding area. In describing a building you might go from top to bottom.

Exercise 4–4   Indicate which spatial arrangement you would use to describe the following topics. Then write a paragraph on one of the topics.

1. a local market
2. your best friend
3. a bus you have ridden in
4. your hometown
5. your campus snackbar or bookstore

Advantages and Disadvantages

Another way to organize ideas is to divide them into advantages and disadvantages. Suppose you are writing a paragraph about shopping at convenience stores. You could explain your shopping experience by discussing advantages and disadvantages. Here's a sample paragraph using this method of arranging of details.

> There are both advantages and disadvantages of shopping at a local convenience store. Convenience stores offer many benefits. First, the stores are nearby, are easy to reach by car, and have ample parking space. Also, locating items is easy because you don't have to search through many long aisles. Finally, speedy checkout enables you to get in and home in no time. On the other hand, convenience stores have two

primary disadvantages: price and selection. Nearly all products cost more at a convenience store than at a large supermarket. The product selection is very limited. Often you only have one or two brands from which to choose. Not all sizes or varieties of a product are available, either. Finally, some items are not stocked at all, particularly certain fresh meats, vegetables, and fruits. All in all, convenience stores are time-savers, yet they come with a stiff price tag.

This writer presented the advantages first, but you can also begin with disadvantages. The order you choose depends, in part, on your purpose in writing. Readers tend to remember the last point most clearly. The disadvantages of convenience stores tend to stick in your mind, and the paragraph does discuss disadvantages in its second half.

Exercise 4–5   Write a paragraph supporting one of the following topic sentences with advantages and disadvantages.

1. buying a new rather than a used car
2. owning a pet
3. working while attending college
4. living in an apartment
5. studying with a friend

The Least/Most Arrangement

Another method of arranging details is to present them in order from least to most or most to least, according to some quality or characteristic. For example, you might arrange details from least-to-most expensive, least-to-most serious, or least-to-most important.

By arranging the details from least-to-most frustrating in the following paragraph, the writer describes the events of a day that went wrong.

Have you ever had a day when everything seems to go wrong? Yesterday ranks as a disaster for me! Everything I tried to accomplish seemed to take twice as long as it should. For example, I had to wait in line for my coffee, then wait again for another cup when I spilled the first one. When driving to work, I got caught at all nine traffic lights. Even worse, if there was a mistake to be made, I made it. I made careless mistakes on my math test, and, at work I fed the register tape in backwards and made errors counting back change. The day's worst episode happened when I was driving home. While waiting at still another red light, a car hit me from behind and damaged my taillights and bumper.

Notice that the writer wrote more about the minor annoyances first and progressed to more serious mishaps.

You can also arrange details from most to least. This structure allows you to present your strongest point first. Many writers use this method to construct a case or an argument. For example, if you were writing a business letter requesting a refund for damaged mail order merchandise, you would want to begin with the most serious damage and put the minor complaints at the end, as follows:

> I am returning this merchandise because it is damaged. The white sneakers have dark streaks of dirt across both toes. One of the shoes also has a red mark in the heel. The laces are frayed and look already worn. I trust you will refund my money promptly.

Exercise 4–6   Write a paragraph supporting one of the following topics. Organize your details using the most-to-least or least-to-most arrangement.

1. reasons why you like or dislike your part-time job
2. five special items in your closet
3. three favorite restaurants
4. things to remember when training a puppy
5. why you like city (or small town) living

USING SPECIFIC WORDS

■   When you are writing a paragraph, use specific words that give your reader as much information as possible. You can think of words the way an artist thinks of colors on her palette. Vague words are brown and muddy; specific words are brightly colored and lively. Try to paint pictures for your reader with specific, vivid words. Here are a few examples of vague words along with more specific words for the same idea.

Vague: fun
Specific: thrilling

Vague: dark
Specific: hidden in gray-green shadows

Vague: good
Specific: appetizing

Vague: tree
Specific: red maple

Use the following suggestions to develop your details.

1. **Use specific verbs.** Choose verbs (action words) that help your reader picture the action.

Vague: The woman left the restaurant.
Specific: The woman stormed out of the restaurant.

2. **Give exact names.** Include the names of people, places, brands, etc.

Vague: A man was eating outside.
Specific: Anthony Hargeaves lounged on the deck of his yacht *Penelope,* spooning Franco-American spaghetti out of a can.

3. **Use adjectives before nouns to convey details.**

Vague: Mary had a dog on a leash.
Specific: A short, tangle-coated dog strained at the end of the leash in Mary's hand.

4. **Use words that appeal to the senses.** Use words that describe touch, taste, smell, hearing, and sight.

Vague: The garden was lovely.
Specific: The brilliant red, pink, and yellow roses filled the air with their heady fragrance.

To summarize, use words that help your readers create mental pictures.

Vague: Al was handsome.
Specific: Al had a slim frame, curly brown hair, deep brown almond-shaped eyes, and perfectly ordered, glittering white teeth.

Exercise 4–7   Reread the paragraph you wrote and revised in Exercises 4–2 and 4–3. As you read, underline any vague or general words. Then replace the underlined words with more specific ones.

USING TRANSITIONAL WORDS

■ Transitional words allow readers to move easily from one detail to another. They show how details relate to one another. You might think of them as "guide and signal" words that guide the reader through the paragraph and signal what is to follow. As you read the following paragraph, notice the transitions (underlined) this writer used.

I have so many things to do when I get home today. First, I have to take my dog, Othello, for a walk. Next, I should do my homework for my sociology class and study that last mind-boggling chapter of business. After that I should do some laundry, since no one has any underwear left. Then, my brother is coming over to fix the tailpipe on my car. Afterwards, we will probably order a pizza for a speedy dinner.

Here are some commonly used transitional words and phrases for each method of arranging details discussed on pages 62–64:

Arrangement	*Transition*
Time Sequence	first, next, during, eventually, finally, later, meanwhile, soon, then, suddenly, currently, after, afterward, before, now, until
Spatial	above, below, behind, in front of, beside, next to, inside, outside, to the west (north, etc.) of, beneath, nearby, on the other side of
Advantages/ Disadvantages	one, another, first, second, on the one hand, on the other hand, however
Least/Most	most important, above all, especially, particularly important, even more

To understand how these transitions work, review the sample paragraphs for each of these arrangements (pp. 61–62, 63, 64). Underline each transitional word or phrase.

Exercise 4–8   Review the paragraphs you wrote for Exercises 4–5 and 4–6. Underline any transitions you used. Revise each paragraph by adding transitions to clarify your details.

THINKING BEFORE READING

■   The following article, "The Greening of the Golden Arches," by Bill Gifford, appeared in an issue of *Rolling Stone* Magazine. Gifford describes how the McDonald's fast-food chain has become environmentally aware. In this reading you can observe how Gifford develops topic sentences using relevant and sufficient details. You can also study how he organizes his details. Overall, Gifford organizes the essay using a time sequence arrangement. He begins with a scientist at McDonald's working to discover ways the company could reduce its wastes. Then the author moves to describing the resulting changes.

1. Preview the reading using the steps listed on p. 43.
2. Discover what you already know about "green" or environmental concerns by answering the following questions.
   a. Is disposal of garbage an issue in your city or town? What efforts have been made to reduce waste?
   b. Do you think fast-food chains such as McDonald's contribute to the waste problem?

READING

THE GREENING OF THE GOLDEN ARCHES

Bill Gifford

It looked like a plastics executive's dream come true. There stood Jackie Prince, a scientist with the Environmental Defense Fund [EDF]—the enemy—at a McDonald's stove, flipping Big Macs. To industry thinking, it was just where she and her kind belonged, forever. 1

But in the end, it was bad news for plastics. Prince and two other EDF staffers worked in a McDonald's for a day last summer as part of a joint EDF-McDonald's task force searching for ways the fast-food chain—the sacred ark of the throw-away society—could reduce its 2 million-pound-per-day Niagara of waste. 2

The first answer came in November, when McDonald's announced it would deep-six its signature polystyrene clamshell sandwich boxes. Then in April, McDonald's released the task force's sweeping 138-page report, which went well beyond clamshells. Among forty-odd other changes, the chain said it would recycle all its corrugated cardboard, use less paper in its napkins and test a refillable coffee mug. . . . 3

The strange marriage between EDF and McDonald's dates to 1989, when the company's general counsel, Shelby Yastrow, was scheduled to appear opposite EDF's executive director, Fred Krupp, on a cable-TV show. Yastrow called Dan Sprehe, a legislative analyst with the company, and told him to check out Krupp's group. "It's hard to believe," Sprehe says, "but nobody around here knew much about them two years ago." 4

Founded by Long Island scientists in 1967 to fight local DDT[1] spraying, EDF's motto in the old days was Sue the Bastards! But since Krupp assumed leadership in 1984, EDF has promoted a kind of environmentalism that tries to satisfy economic needs as well as ecological concerns. Spend more than a half-hour with Krupp, a slightly nerdy but persuasive thirty-six-year-old, and he'll launch into a spiel about Solving the Big Problems—global warming, rain-forest depletion, protecting Antarctica—by harnessing market forces and removing the incentives to plunder and pollute. . . .

The task force began work in August, focusing first on the fate of the clamshell. Its seven members spent long meetings debating various new wrappers and boxes submitted by suppliers. They even considered an edible wrapper, which McDonald's operations director Keith Magnuson described as "a little chewy," before settling on a layered tissue-and-plastic wrapper with insulating air bubbles.

But in late October, word reached EDF that a proclamshell faction within McDonald's was attempting an end run around the task force. The company was about to renew its commitment to polystyrene. Krupp called Rensi and put the project on the line. The task force has come up with an alternative, he said. If the announcement were made, EDF would publicly blast it. The next Monday, Krupp flew to Oak Brook and made his pitch to senior management. Two days later, McDonald's said goodbye to its beige, sky blue and pearly white boxes.

But the move to paper "wasn't much of a switch," says Jan Beyea, senior scientist with the National Audubon Society. "It sent the wrong message, that by switching to paper you're doing the environment a favor. Paper is made with tremendous chemical and industrial processes." The new wrapper, concedes Richard Denison, an EDF member of the task force, "is by no stretch of the imagination a recyclable material." And besides, McDonald's didn't fully kick the polystyrene habit: Breakfast entrees are still encased in bad old plastic.

The real reason McDonald's switched can be found in the company's 1990 annual report, which states: "Although some scientific studies indicate that foam packaging is environmentally sound, customers just didn't feel good about it." Or as Yastrow put it: "That

---

1. a powerful insecticide

clamshell package was the symbol that everyone glommed onto. We knew if we got rid of that thing, it would be like pulling forty thorns out of our paw."

But if the market force of consumer reaction provoked the dubious clamshell move, it also motivated more positive gains. The final plan, released in April, contains three dozen or so initiatives, of which customers will notice only a handful. Ketchup packets will get larger so customers will use fewer. Carryout bags will be made of recycled, unbleached paper. Napkins will be shrunk by a fifth (but refolded to appear the same size).   10

Most of the changes will take place behind the counter. In part, that's by design: McDonald's wouldn't dare inconvenience its customers in the slightest way. But it's also because more than eighty percent of trash at a McDonald's comes from behind the counter, as the task force learned from a waste audit of franchises in Denver and Sycamore, Illinois. Bulk shipping containers and corrugated cardboard alone account for a third of the typical franchise's garbage output. So the task force decided to recycle all the corrugated—eliminating, in one stroke, nearly 350 tons per day of landfill-destined trash. Then, to create demand for recycled corrugated, McDonald's ordered its suppliers—the companies that sell everything from meat to coffee cups to McDonald's—to use boxes with a minimum of thirty-five-percent-recycled content.   11

McDonald's resisted the whole concept of reusables—plates and service—though EDF pushed hard for months. The chain rejected proposals for refillable cold cups and serving burgers on plates because customers tend to leave with their drinks and because hot-off-the-grill sandwiches go into the same wrapper for both take-out and eat-in customers. McDonald's did agree to test reusable shipping pallets and a refillable coffee mug.   12

EDF also nudged McDonald's into testing far-out waste-disposal techniques such as composting. Ten McDonald's are sending coffee grounds, eggshells and food-coated paper to a Maine composting plant, where organic waste decays naturally into dirt that's sold to farmers and landscapers. Such tests are just a tiny step toward dealing with food waste, which constitutes a third of the typical store's trash. Every day, the average McDonald's tosses out 81 pounds of unsold Big Macs, mushed fries and other perishable items, which adds up to a whopping 694,000 pounds of wasted food nationwide.   13

The task force ignored at least one other environmental disaster propagated by the McDonald's system: cows. Their grazing habits cause erosion, their dung seeps into ground water and greenhouse   14 gases pour from their nether regions. "The best thing McDonald's could do," says a scientist with a rival environmental group, "would be to get out of the business of marketing meat."

Many environmentalists seem to have difficulty condoning the existence of McDonald's. Few would be caught dead eating there. Greenpeace executive director Peter Bahouth says that if he were president of the company, he'd "shut the doors." But Krupp, who occasionally eats at McDonald's with his two children, doesn't see it as black or white, McDonald's or Mother Earth. EDF's brand of environmentalism takes what it can get and counts even small steps as progress. . . . 15

EDF took no money from McDonald's. In the competitive world of environmental groups, however, results equal donors, and EDF's direct mail now boasts of slaying the clamshell. But donors are also customers, not only for McDonald's but for Safeway, Anheuser-Busch, Procter & Gamble and hundreds of other firms now feeling the pressure of green consumerism. Krupp loves to talk about harnessing market forces, but it's more than that. As the greening of McDonald's shows, Krupp and the movement he represents have become a market force. 16

Rolling Stone, August 22nd, 1991

GETTING READY TO WRITE

Step 1: Recognizing Types of Supporting Details

Before you can write about an author's ideas, you must understand how that author supports and explains his or her main points. Gifford uses a variety of details to support his main ideas. Specifically, Gifford uses facts, events, dialogue, examples, and comparisons. He also uses lively verbs, exact names, and descriptive words and phrases that appeal to the senses and allow you to visualize events.

Exercise 4–9   Analyze Gifford's use of supporting detail by indicating in which paragraph(s) Gifford uses:

1. specific verbs _____
2. exact names _____
3. adjectives to add detail _____
4. words that appeal to the senses _____

Step 2: Thinking Critically: Making Inferences

An inference is a conclusion about something unknown based on available facts and information. Suppose you are driving on an expressway, and looking in your rear view mirror you notice a police car coming up behind you with its red lights flashing. You glance at your speedometer: it reads 65 mph. What do you think is going to happen next? By predicting that you are going to be pulled over for speeding, you have made an inference.

Writers sometimes leave ideas and relationships unstated but expect their readers to make the necessary inferences. You can think of making inferences as a process of reading between the lines. Here are a few tips for making inferences:

1. **Notice details.** Details often provide clues about what is to happen or what the author is suggesting. For example, in paragraph one the detail "To industry thinking, it [at a McDonald's store] was just where she [Jackie Prince] and her kind belonged," reveals the plastics industry's attitude toward environmental concerns.

2. **Notice descriptive language.** These words often suggest the writer's attitude toward the subject. For instance, the phrase "slaying the clamshell" suggests the author and EDF regard the plastic cartons as an adversary or enemy.

3. **Add up the facts.** Consider what all of the facts taken together mean. Ask yourself, "What do all of these facts point toward or suggest?" All the small changes that McDonald's has made, for instance, will eliminate considerable waste.

Exercise 4–10   Answer the following questions about the reading. You will need to make inferences in order to answer them.

1. Why was the EDF's relationship with McDonald's bad news for the plastics industry?

2. How have the EDF's methods of operation changed since it was founded in 1967?

3. Explain the statement in paragraph 14, "The best thing McDonald's could do would be to get out of the business of marketing meat."

4. Why were most of the changes made behind McDonald's counter?

5. Explain the statement in paragraph 16, "results equal donors."

Step 3: Reacting to and Discussing Ideas

Use the following questions to generate ideas about the readings.

1. Explain the meaning of the title of the article.
2. Why is the relationship between EDF and McDonald's described as a "strange marriage"?
3. Do you think other corporations are becoming more concerned with eliminating unnecessary waste? Why or why not?
4. To what extent did McDonald's accept EDF's recommendations?

WRITING ABOUT THE READING

■ *Assignment 1*

Write a paragraph explaining whether you think other fast-food chains should be required to make changes similar to those that McDonald's has made.

WRITING ABOUT YOUR IDEAS

■ *Assignment 2*

Think of a specific fast-food restaurant, other than McDonald's. Describe changes the restaurant could make to reduce waste.

Assignment 3

Write a paragraph explaining possible uses for the food that McDonald's wastes each day.

Journal Writing Suggestions

1. Write an entry describing what you do to recycle or make less trash.
2. Write an entry describing a situation in which you've experienced conflicting feelings. Use relevant and sufficient details to describe your ideas.

Run-on Sentences

A run-on sentence (also known as a fused sentence) consists of two complete thoughts placed within the same sentence, without any punctuation to separate them. Each thought could stand alone as a separate sentence.

> RUN-ON: **Political science is a difficult course I am thinking of dropping it and taking it next semester.**

> RUN-ON: **My younger sister will visit us this weekend I probably will not have much time to study.**

How to Spot Run-ons

You can often spot run-ons by reading them aloud. Listen for a break or change in your voice midway through the sentence. Read the two above examples to see if you can hear the break.

How to Correct Run-ons

Simply adding a comma to correct a run-on sentence does *not* work. Doing so leads to an error known as a comma splice. There are four basic ways to correct a run-on sentence.

1. Create two separate sentences. End the first thought with a period and begin the next with a capital letter.

My younger sister will visit us this weekend. I probably will not have much time to study.

2. Connect the two thoughts using a semicolon.

My younger sister will visit us this weekend; I probably will not have much time to study.

3. Join the two thoughts by using a comma and coordinating conjunction (*and, or, but, for, nor, so, yet*).

My younger sister will visit us this weekend, so I probably will not have much time to study.

• •

4. Subordinate one thought to the other. To do this, make one thought into a subordinate clause (a dependent clause) by adding a subordinating conjunction (words like *although, because, since, unless*) or a relative pronoun (words like *which, that, what, who, whoever*). Then connect the subordinate clause to an independent clause (a group of words with a subject and a verb that expresses a complete thought and that can stand alone as a complete sentence).

Since my younger sister will visit us this weekend, I probably will not have much time to study.

Rate Your Ability to Spot and Correct Run-Ons

Read the following sentences and place a checkmark in front of each run-on sentence. Some sentences are correct. Then correct each run-on using one of the methods described above.

1. The Civil War ended in 1865 the period of Reconstruction followed.

2. Although light and sound both emit waves they do so in very different ways.

3. The Constitution forms the basis for our federal system of government and divides the government into the executive, legislative, and judiciary branches.

4. Archaeologists study the physical remains of cultures anthropologists study the cultures themselves.

5. The body's nervous system carries electrical and chemical messages these messages tell parts of the body how to react and what to do.

6. Neil Armstrong was the first human to walk on the moon this event occurred in 1969.

7. Robert Frost is a well-known American poet his most famous poem is "The Road Not Taken."

8. Algebra and geometry are areas of study of mathematics calculus and trigonometry are other branches.

9. There are two parts of the British parliamentary system, the House of Lords and the House of Commons; the American Congress also has two parts, the Senate and the House of Representatives.

10. It is easy to become distracted by other thoughts and responsibilities while studying it helps to make a list of these distractors.

Score _____

Check your answers using the Answer Key on page 537. If you scored below 80 percent, you need additional review and practice recognizing and correcting run-on sentences. Refer to section C.2 of Reviewing the Basics in Part 5.

SUMMARY

■   1. Use details to support and explain your topic sentence. The details you include must be

- relevant. Each detail must directly explain and support your topic sentence.
- sufficient. You must provide enough detail to make your topic sentence clear and understandable.

2. Arrange your details in a logical order. Four common methods of arrangement are

- time sequence—events are presented in the order in which they happen.
- spatial arrangement—objects or places are described by their location in relation to one another.
- advantages/disadvantages—ideas are grouped into positive and negative features.
- least/most arrangement—ideas are arranged from most-to-least or least-to-most according to a particular quality or characteristic.

3. Present your details using specific words—words that help your reader create mental pictures.

4. Use transitional words to relate your details to one another.

5　Strategies for Revising

· · · ·

In this chapter you will learn to

1. revise your ideas.
2. correct your errors.

Suppose you are planning a special picnic for the weekend. Since it's July and it has been hot all month, you decide on cold fried chicken, cold salads, watermelon, and brownies. The day of the picnic, a sudden weather change drops the temperature to 50 degrees, and you realize that your warm weather menu won't work. You have to rethink and revise your menu, adding warm foods, deleting the watermelon, and so forth.

A similar situation occurs in writing. Planning and organizing are very useful and important steps, but they do not produce a workable finished product right away. In your first draft, you try out ways of fitting ideas together. But when you look at it again, you may find that the fit is not perfect. Therefore, you need to rethink and rewrite to express your ideas more clearly and vividly.

This chapter suggests strategies to help you with this kind of revising and editing. Revising involves looking at every idea and sentence again and often making major changes in your writing. Editing is a part of the revision process that involves adding or deleting words and sentences, as well as correcting your grammar, spelling, and punctuation. It may be helpful to review the steps in the writing process (Chapter 2) to see how revision fits within the process.

EXAMINING YOUR IDEAS

■ The most important part of revision is evaluating your ideas. Think of revision as an opportunity to reassess and change your ideas to make your paragraph as effective as possible. Once you've finished your first draft, try not to revise right away. Revising during and immediately after finishing the first draft can diminish the results of your revision process. If you can afford the time, wait until the next day. While you're working on something unrelated, new ideas about your topic may emerge. The next day, with the benefits of time and distance from your writing, you'll have a fresh outlook and will see your draft differently than when you just finished it.

One way to begin examining your first draft is to consider the topics we have discussed in the last few chapters. Some of these issues reappear here. Although this may seem like a lot to think about, revising does not require learning new material. Instead, you need to apply the principles you have already learned, using the questions that follow to guide you.

Is Your Paragraph Suited to Your Purpose and Audience?

As we mentioned in Chapter 1, good writing achieves your purpose and is directed toward a specific audience. When you are ready to revise, read your paragraph through once or twice to get an overall impression of it. Then, decide whether the paragraph accomplishes what you want it to. If it doesn't, try to identify what went wrong. (The remaining questions in this section will be helpful.) Sometimes, however, it is difficult to identify the reasons why a paragraph doesn't achieve its purpose. When this happens, ask a friend or classmate to read your paragraph and to summarize what the paragraph does accomplish. Often, this information will give you clues about what's wrong with the paragraph. (See Writing Success Tip 5 on p. 80 of this chapter for more suggestions on using classmates or friends in the revision process.)

To evaluate whether your paragraph is suited to your audience, read the paragraph from the viewpoint of your audience. Try to anticipate what ideas might be unclear, what additional information might be needed, and whether the overall reaction will be positive or negative.

Exercise 5–1   After prewriting, write a first draft on one of the following topics. Then evaluate whether your paragraph is suited to your purpose and audience. Revise your paragraph if it is not well-suited.

1. the ideal part-time job
2. a famous person you would like to meet
3. healthy eating habits
4. an irrational fear
5. your first experience using a computer

Have You Provided Relevant and Sufficient Detail?

When you begin to revise, check whether all the ideas in your paragraph are really related to one another and whether you have provided enough detail.

As we saw in Chapter 4, unrelated ideas will distract your reader and dilute the force of your message. Simply rereading a paragraph may not show you whether your ideas are related. When this happens, draw an idea map as shown below. An idea map is a visual display of information. In the same way a road map allows you to see cities and towns in relation to one another, an idea map enables you to see how ideas relate to one another.

To draw an idea map, write an abbreviated topic sentence at the top of your paper. Then, working through your paragraph sentence by sentence, list underneath the topic sentence only the details that directly explain it. If one of your details does not support the topic sentence, write that detail beside the list. If you are not sure where to place a detail, write it in a separate column, to the right of the list. List examples or facts that explain more about a detail directly under it.

Idea Map

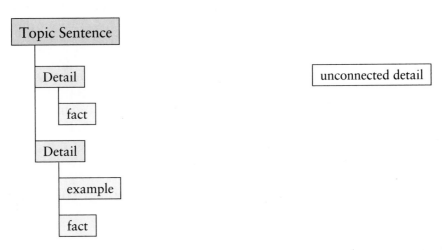

WRITING
SUCCESS
TIP 5

Peer Review

Many students have found that their peers (classmates) can offer valuable suggestions for revision. Peer review is an excellent way to find out what is good and what needs to be improved in your draft. Often your classmates will see things you don't because you are too close to or too personally involved with the topic. Here are some tips on using peer review.

How to Find a Reviewer

A good source of reviewers is other students in your writing class. They are familiar with what you are learning and are working on the same skills themselves. Friends who have already taken a writing course also make good reviewers. Get the opinion of more than one reviewer, if possible.

What to Ask Your Reviewer

1. Give your reviewer a copy of your draft that is easy to read. It's best if you provide a copy that your reviewer can write on. Ask him or her to underline and mark any parts of your draft that are unclear or confusing.

Here is the first draft of a paragraph written by a student named Joe. His idea map follows.

Draft 1

```
    A nutrition and health company that I am
currently involved with is Herbalife. Cur-
rently, Herbalife is one of the top companies
in the world for rate of growth and also for
leading the industry in research and develop-
ment of nutritional products. You may begin
your own distributorship as I did with as lit-
tle as fifty dollars. The potential of your in-
```

2. Ask your reviewer who he or she thinks your intended audience is and what your purpose for writing is. Does the answer match what you think? If not, think about how you can get your own message across more clearly.

3. Give the reviewer a copy of the revision questions in this chapter or those found in later chapters. Ask the reviewer to focus on these questions.

4. Don't accept everything your reviewers say. Weigh their comments carefully.

5. If you are uncertain about advice you've been given, talk with your instructor.

How to Be a Good Reviewer

If you're asked to be a reviewer, use these suggestions:

1. Read the draft through completely at least once before making any judgments.

2. Offer some positive comments first. Tell the writer what is good about the paper.

3. Avoid general comments. Don't just say that the topic sentence is unclear. Instead, explain how it could be improved or what it lacks.

4. Offer specific revision suggestions. For instance, if you feel a paragraph needs more explanation, tell the writer what type of information to include.

come depends on the effort you put forth. Herbalife stands alone because they deal with overall health and are backed by a team of doctors and scientists who are the leaders in weight loss research and maintenance on a daily basis. Herbalife will continue to be a leader because their products are of high quality, and they care about the health of the entire world. My involvement with Herbalife is just beginning, and I look forward to a profitable future.

Sample Idea Map

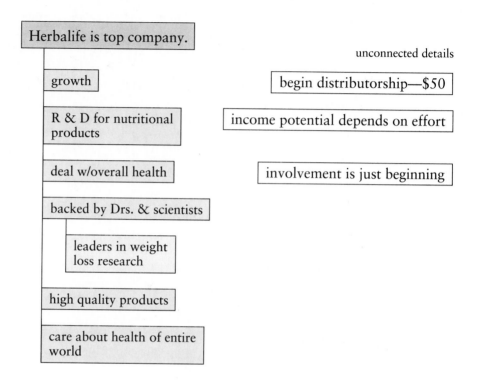

Joe's map shows him how he structured his paragraph. It allows him to see whether his ideas connect and whether he has enough detail to support his main ideas. By studying this map, he can spot details that do not fit and ideas that need further development or explanation. Joe found three details (see right side of map) that did not directly support his original topic sentence. He realized that these details related to a slightly different topic that focused on why he felt Herbalife was a good company with which to begin his own business. Joe rewrote his topic sentence to include this idea and added more explanation in his revision.

Draft 2

Because Herbalife is one of the top companies in the world for nutrition and health, it is a good way for me to start my own business. It is a company that is not only growing rapidly but also is becoming a leader in research and development of nutritional products. Herbalife products are easy to sell because they are backed by medical doctors and scientists. The products are appealing because they are of high quality and the company demonstrates its concern for worldwide health through its advertising. You can start your own distributorship for only fifty dollars. There are no other hidden costs, and you are not required to maintain a large inventory. I'm expecting Herbalife to be the start of a business that will help me pay for college.

This second draft focuses more directly on the topic and includes relevant and sufficient detail. Further decisions might focus on improving sentence structure, strenghtening the connection among details, and adding transitions.

Exercise 5–2   Read the following student paragraph and draw an idea map for it. Use your map to identify details that are not relevant to the topic. Delete these details from the paragraph.

Labor unions are valuable to employees of large companies. They represent workers' rights that would not seem as important to employers if workers were not organized and represented by leaders. Being a union leader is a difficult but important job. Unions are also important because they make sure that all employees are treated equally and fairly. Before unions were created, each employee had to make his own deal with his employer, and some workers ended up doing the same job as others for less pay. Employers listen to unions because they can organize strikes and contact federal agencies about violations. Sometimes strikes don't work and people are out of work for long periods of time. A lot of times this is on the news. Labor unions also make sure that work sites are safe and that there are no health hazards.

Exercise 5–3   Draw an idea map for the paragraph you wrote in Exercise 5–1. Revise the paragraph by adding or deleting details.

Is Your Paragraph Logically Organized?

Another major issue to consider as you revise is whether you have arranged your ideas in a way your readers can follow. As we saw in Chapter 4, even if you have plenty of detail, the wrong organization can throw your readers off track. In addition, you need to make sure you use transitional words to help readers follow your thoughts.

Idea maps are also useful for checking your organization. By listing the ideas in the order in which they appear in your paragraph, you will be able to see if they are arranged logically. Study the following first draft paragraph along with its idea map.

Draft 1

> The women's movement has produced important changes in women's lifestyles. Women started the movement with rallies and marches. The Nineteenth Amendment to the Constitution gave women the vote. A lot of men were not happy about that. Women never used to be able to vote, and they were not supposed to drink or swear or wear pants. That was ridiculous. Women now have more rights and freedoms. But women still don't get paid as much as men. Many women have jobs plus families that they take care of. Women do a lot more than men. Women now have a choice about what they want to do for a career but are not rewarded as much as men.

Idea Map

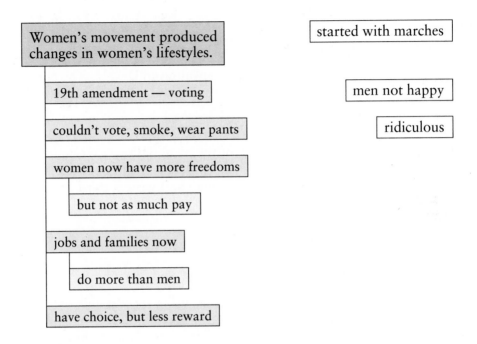

The map shows that the details are not arranged in any specific order. Since most of them relate to changes in women's rights, these details could be arranged from past to present. The writer arranged the details in chronological order in her second draft.

Draft 2

> The women's movement has produced important
> changes in women's lifestyles. Before 1900,
> women never used to be able to vote and were
> not supposed to drink, swear, hold certain
> jobs, smoke, or wear pants. They were
> oppressed. The Nineteenth Amendment to the
> Constitution, passed in 1920, allowed women to
> vote. Other rights have come gradually over the
> years. Drinking, swearing, smoking, and wearing

pants are no longer prohibited. Now women have a wide variety of job possibilities. Women have more freedom now, but they still do not earn as much as men. Today women have more choices, but they are still short on rewards.

Notice the added transitions in Draft 2. The phrase "Before 1900" was added to emphasize that the writer will review the early status of women.

Exercise 5–4   Study the idea map of the paragraph you wrote in Exercise 5–1. Evaluate your arrangement of details. If they are not arranged logically, number them on your map and write a third draft of your paragraph.

Is Your Language Specific and Vivid?

In Chapter 4 we discussed using specific and vivid words and phrases to provide accurate and interesting detail. As you revise a paragraph look for drab, nondescriptive words and phrases. Replace them with lively words that enable your reader to create a mental picture of your topic.

Here is a paragraph a student wrote on the topic of aerobic dancing. Notice how she changed and replaced words to make her details more specific and vivid.

Aerobic dancing is ~~great~~ *energizing and enjoyable* exercise. It makes you ~~use a lot of~~ *stretch and exert* muscles *from nearly all muscle groups*. It also gives your cardiovascular system a good workout because ~~it gets~~ *starts* your heart pumping and ~~increases~~ your rate of breathing. You maintain the pace for ~~awhile~~ *twenty or thirty minutes*, which is also beneficial. Aerobic dancing builds endurance and stamina that makes you ~~feel as if you are in good~~ *come alive and scream, "I'm in shape!"* ~~physical condition~~ body. In aerobics the risk of injury is slight since there is no intense strain on any one part of the body.

Exercise 5–5   Evaluate your use of specific and vivid language in the paragraph you wrote for Exercise 5–1. Revise the paragraph.

REVISION CHECKLIST

Here is a list of questions that will help you analyze and evaluate your ideas. Use them to decide whether you have organized and expressed your ideas clearly and concisely. Chapters 6 through 15 will have a revision checklist very much like this one.

1. Who is your audience? How interested are they in your subject, and how much do they know about it? Is your paragraph shaped to fit your audience?
2. What is your purpose? Will your paragraph accomplish your purpose?
3. Is your main point clearly expressed in a topic sentence?
4. Is each detail relevant? Does each explain or support the topic sentence directly?
5. Have you supported your topic sentence with sufficient detail to make it understandable and believable?
6. Do you use specific words to explain each detail?
7. Do you connect your ideas with transitional words?

Giving Yourself a Break

If you have tried idea mapping and you still can't see what to do with your paragraph, try taking a break. When you come back, you'll have a fresher outlook. Try reading your paper aloud, or ask someone else to read it. Ask him or her to identify your main point and to explain how you supported it. Compare these statements with your purpose for writing. If a revision still seems impossible, don't be afraid to start over. Sometimes a paragraph is not worth revising. Begin with a new topic (if possible) or try a different approach to the same topic. Generate ideas and write a new paragraph.

EDITING FOR ERRORS

■ Errors in grammar, spelling, and punctuation can make your writing less effective. Many readers are less likely to believe what a writer says if he or she makes careless errors. Making corrections, then, is an important *final* step to writing a good paragraph. As we saw in Chapter 2, you should not focus on corrections until you are sure your thinking is sound. Look for errors only after you are satisfied with the content and organization of your paragraph. Of course, if you do notice an error while you are revising your ideas, be sure to correct it.

What Errors to Look For

Chapters 3–15 contain Skill Refreshers that will help keep your errors to a minimum. Part Five provides a thorough review of basic grammar and punctuation. Here is a list of common errors to watch for; turn to the correct page numbers for help or review.

sentence fragments (page 52)

run-on sentences (page 74)

subject-verb agreement (page 98)

pronoun-antecedent agreement (page 120)

pronoun reference (page 139)

dangling modifiers (page 166)

misplaced modifiers (page 186)

coordinate sentences (page 206)

subordinate clauses (page 232)

parallelism (page 263)

comma usage (page 289)

colon and semicolon usage (page 315)

capital letter usage (page 341)

Keeping an Error Log

Many student writers consistently make certain types of errors and not others. You can identify and learn to avoid your problems by keeping a record of your mistakes. Use the form shown in the sample error log shown on page 90. Each time your instructor returns a paper, count how many errors you made of each type, and enter that number in the log. Soon you will see a pattern. You can then review your final drafts specifically to locate your common errors.

If you make frequent spelling errors, keep a separate list of the words you misspell. Study and practice writing them correctly.

Exercise 5–6   Check the paragraph you wrote for Exercise 5–1 for errors and correct any you find. Enter them in an Error Log.

Exercise 5–7   Evaluate each of the following student paragraphs using the guidelines suggested in this chapter. Write a list of specific suggestions the writer could use to improve his or her paragraph.

Paragraph 1

Today more people are interested in the control of pollution than ever before. On earth day approximately 200 million people in 140 countries celebrated by participating in ecological events. More and more people are buying environmentally safe products and more businesses are trying to produce safer products. Together we can all save the earth.

Paragraph 2

Waiting; I love waiting it makes life seem long. I can't understand why people are in such a hurry all the time. Be in a hurry, and you will be wrong. Wait a while and things will come your way. I was in a hurry once crossing the street and got run over. This is when I was 24 years old, I lived, but you can bet anything I'm going to wait from now on.

Paragraph 3

Two friends, Mark and Bob, I grew up with have been friends since childhood. They have been called twins before. The both like rock music, football, and classic cars. They do everything together everyday and never get angry with each other. Except on one thing. Bob doesn't get along with his family. While Mark respects and gets along with his very good. But the other is helping his friend out and that's what friends are for.

Sample Error Log

Types of Error	Assignment		
	1	2	3
Sentences			
run-on	one	two	one
fragments	one	0	0
Grammar	subject-verb agreement verb tense pronoun reference	— verb tense abbreviation	subject-verb agreement verb tense pronoun reference
Punctuation	comma	comma quotation	comma semi-colon
Misspelled Words	favorite relies knowledge	chemicals majority especially leisure	necessary hoping definitely

THINKING BEFORE READING

■ This reading demonstrates how a professional writer, E. B. White, revised his work. The reading contains three drafts of the same paragraph. The paragraph describes Neil Armstrong and Edwin Aldrin, Jr., as they make the first human contact with the moon. The first moon-walk was televised, and E. B. White watched Armstrong and Aldrin plant the U.S. flag on the moon's surface. He describes his thoughts in the reading titled "Moon-walk."

1. Preview this reading by reading the final draft (3) *completely.* Be sure to read it again, more thoroughly, after you have studied the first two drafts.

2. Connect the topic of the moon to your own experience by completing the following:
   a. What meanings does the moon have for you? Brainstorm a list of ideas.
   b. If outerspace travel became commonplace, would you consider traveling to the moon?
   c. What do you think it would be like to step out of a spaceship onto the moon?

MOON-WALK

E. B. White

(DRAFT 1)

white

comment

Planning a trip to the moon differs in no essential
respect from planning a trip to the beach. You have to decide
what to take along, what to leave behind. Should the thermos jug
go? The child's rubber horse? The dill pickles? These are sometimes fateful decisions on which the success or failure of the
whole outing turns. Something gets goes along that spoils everything because it is always in the way. Something gets left
behind that is desperately needed for comfort or for safety. The
men who drew up the moon list for the astronauts, planned long
                               to suck up moondust and save
and hard and well. (Should the vacuum cleaner go?) Among the
                                          the world?)
items they sent along, of course, was the little jointed flagpole
and the flag that could be stiffened to the breeze that didn't
blow. (It is traditional among explorers to plant the flag.) Yet
the two men who stepped out on the surface of the moon were in a
class by themselves: they were of the new race of men, those
who hadseen the earth whole. When, following instructions, they
colored the moon red, white, and blue, they were stepping out of
character---or so it seemed to us who watched, trembling with awe
and admiration and pride. This was the last scene in the long
book of nationalism, and they followed the book. But the moon
still holds the key to madness, which is universal,; still controls
the tides, that lap on every shore everywhere, and xxx blesses
lovers that kiss in every land, under no particular banner. What
a pity we couldn't have played the scene as it should been played,
planting, perhaps, a simple white handkerchief, symbol of the
                  like the moon   all and recognizes no
common cold, that belongs to mankind imperially and knows no

borders

(DRAFT 2)

white

comment

Planning a trip to the moon differs in no
essential respect from planning a trip to the beach. You have to
decide what to take along, what to leave behind. Should the thermos
jug go? The child's rubber horse? The dill pickles? These are
sometimes fateful decisions on which the success or failure of the
whole outing turns. Something goes along that spoils everything
because it is always in the way; something gets left behind that
is desperately needed for comfort or for safety. The men who drew
up the moon list for the astronauts planned long and hard and well.
(Should the vacuum cleaner go, to suck up moondust?) Among the *inevitable*
items they sent along, of course, was the little jointed flagpole
and the flag that could be stiffened to the breeze that did not
blow. (It is traditional among explorers to plant the flag.) Yet
the two men who stepped out on the surface of the moon were in a
class by themselves and should have been equipped accordingly:
they were of the new breed of men, those who had seen the earth
whole. When, following instructions, they colored the moon red,
white, and blue, they were fumbling with the past---or so it seemed
to us, who watched, trembling with awe and admiration and pride.
This moon plant was the last *chapter* scene in the long book of nationalism,
one that could well have been omitted. The moon still holds the
key to madness, which is universal, still controls the tides
that lap on shores everywhere, still guards lovers that kiss in
every land under no banner but the sky. What a pity we
couldn't have forsworn our little Iwo Jima scene and planted instead
a banner acceptable to all---a simple white handkerchief, perhaps,
symbol of the common cold, which, like the moon, affects us all.

(DRAFT 3)

that

it tu~rn out;

The moon is a great place for men, a~nd when
did they rocking little
Armstrong and Aldrin danced from sheer exuberance, it was
                              a poor place for
a sight to see. But the moon is ~no place for banners~ flags.
a flag   ~for the breeze~ doesn't blow   a flag is out
~They~ cannot float on the breeze, and ~they don't~ belong there
of place on the moon anyway.
anyway. Like every great river, every great sea, the moon

                    none
belongs to ~no one~ and belongs to all. What a pity we

couldn't have forsworn our little Iwo Jima flag-lanting

scene and planted instead a universal banner acceptable

to all---a limp white handkerchief, perhaps, symbol of the

common cold, which, like the moon, affects us all.

Of course, it is traditional that explorers plant the flag,

and it was inevitable that our astronauts should follow thw
                        as we watched
custom. But the act was the last chapter in the long book

of nationalism, one that could well have been omitted---or

~so it seemed to us.~ The moon still holds the key to madness,

still controls the tides that lap on shores everywhere, still

guards the lovers that kiss in every land under no banner but th

the sky. What a pity ~was an idiot~ that, in our triumph, we
                                                            instead
couldn't have forsworn the little Iwo Jima scene   and planted
                                      simply
a banner acceptable to all---a ~simple~ white handkerchief,

perhaps, symbo_l of the common cold,whcih, like the moon, affects
us all.

GETTING READY TO WRITE

■   *Step 1: Drawing Idea Maps*

Earlier in this chapter you learned to draw idea maps to check the consistency and organization of your own writing. Idea maps can also help you analyze someone else's writing. They can help you understand how the writer's ideas relate to one another and discover how the piece is organized. You will also find that by expressing the writer's ideas briefly in your own words, you'll remember the material better.

Exercise 5–8   Construct an idea map of each of White's three drafts of "Moonwalk." (The maps will make it easier to see the revision process White went through.)

Step 2: Thinking Critically: Understanding Symbols

A symbol is an object that stands for something else. Usually, a symbol stands for something abstract, often an idea or belief. For example, a dove is a symbol of peace, a cross is a symbol of Christianity, a wedding band is a symbol of marriage vows, an eagle is a symbol of the United States. Here are a few other common symbols. Decide what each represents:

a.   swastika
b.   skull and crossbones
c.   Uncle Sam
d.   shamrock

E. B. White in "Moon-walk" discusses several symbols. First, he describes the act of planting a flag—a symbol of ownership or conquest. Then, he discusses the U.S. flag, a symbol of patriotism and nationalism. White suggests that Armstrong and Aldrin should have been equipped with a universal symbol, instead of the U.S. flag. White concludes the paragraph by suggesting that the men should have planted a limp, white handkerchief, the symbol of the common cold. However, the white handkerchief may have other symbolic meanings as well. The color white symbolizes something pure and unspoiled. A white flag is used during battle to symbolize truce or surrender. A white handkerchief is often used as a substitute. Hence, the white handkerchief may suggest other meanings, as well.

Here are a few questions to think about:

1. Was White creating a new symbol when he said the white handkerchief could stand for the common cold?

2. Is the common cold itself a symbol? Could it be a symbol of shared human misery or the universality of man?

3. Does White mention any other symbol in the paragraph?

Step 3: Reacting To and Discussing Ideas

Get ready to write about the reading by discussing the following questions:

1. How did Armstrong and Aldrin feel when they touched down on the moon?

2. Do you think Armstrong and Aldrin should have planted an international flag instead of the U.S. flag?

3. What did you discover about the revision process by studying White's drafts?

WRITING ABOUT THE READING

■ *Assignment 1*

Write a paragraph describing E. B. White's revision process. Describe the types of changes he made to produce his final draft.

Assignment 2

Write a paragraph explaining what other symbol or symbols (other than flags) might have been appropriate to place on the moon during man's first moon-walk.

WRITING ABOUT YOUR IDEAS

■ *Assignment 1*

Write a paragraph describing what you think it would be like to land and walk on the moon or to travel in outerspace.

Assignment 2

Landing on the moon was an important "first" for Armstrong and Aldrin, for the United States, and for the world. Write a paragraph describing a "first" experience that you are proud to have accomplished.

Journal Writing Suggestions

1. Write a journal entry describing how you feel about space exploration. (Is it worth the cost? What are the benefits? What are the risks?)

2. Landing on the moon was an important event in the lives of Armstrong and Aldrin. Write a journal entry describing an important event in your life.

·   ·   ·   ·   ·   ·   ·   ·   ·   ·   ·   ·   ·   ·   ·   ·   ·   ·   ·

Subject-Verb Agreement

A verb must agree with its subject in number. A subject that refers to one person, place, or thing is called a *singular subject*. A subject that refers to more than one thing is called a plural subject.

Guidelines

1. A singular subject must be used with a singular verb.

   The <u>dog</u> <u>wants</u> to go jogging with me.

2. A plural subject must be used with a plural verb.

   The <u>dogs</u> <u>want</u> to go jogging with me.

Mistakes to Watch For

Subject-verb agreement errors often occur in the following situations:

1. With compound subjects (two or more subjects).

INCORRECT: <u>Yolanda</u> and <u>Lion</u> <u>wants</u> to lead the way.

CORRECT: <u>Yolanda</u> and <u>Lion</u> <u>want</u> to lead the way.

2. When the verb comes before the subject.

INCORRECT: There <u>is</u> four gas <u>stations</u> on Main Street.

CORRECT: There <u>are</u> four gas <u>stations</u> on Main Street.

3. When a word or phrase comes between the subject and verb.

INCORRECT: The <u>woman</u> standing in the waves with the other swimmers <u>win</u> a prize for her endurance.

CORRECT: The <u>woman</u> standing in the waves with the other swimmers <u>wins</u> a prize for her endurance.

4. With indefinite pronouns (pronouns like *someone* or *everybody* that do not refer to a specific person). Some indefinite pronouns (*everyone, each, neither, such as*) take a singular verb; others (*both* or *many*) always take a plural verb. Some indefinite pronouns may take either a singular or a plural verb (*all, any, none*). Treat the pronoun as singular if it refers to something that cannot be counted. Treat the pronoun as plural if it refers to more than one of something that can be counted.

SKILL   REFRESHER

• •

INCORRECT: Everybody wish to become a millionaire.

CORRECT: Everybody wishes to become a millionaire.

Rate Your Ability to Use Subject-Verb Agreement

Circle the word or phrase that correctly completes each sentence.

1. Someone (want, wants) to make a left turn.
2. Chalkboards (is, are) not always black.
3. The sheriff, together with three deputies (agree, agrees) to establish a road block.
4. Trisha and I (swim, swims) together every morning.
5. Neither Bo nor Jeff (know, knows) the answer.
6. Here (is, are) your lottery tickets.
7. Pizza and chicken wings (is, are) my favorite take-out foods.
8. (Candy, Candies) harms teeth because of its high sugar content.
9. (Sabrina, Sabrina and Mary) is going to the fireworks display tonight.
10. On my front lawn (was, were) two discarded pop cans.

Score _____

Check your answers using the Answer Key on page 537. If you scored below 80 percent, you need additional review and practice recognizing and correcting subject-verb agreement. Refer to Section C.7 of Reviewing the Basics in Part 5.

SUMMARY

■   1. Revising involves examining your ideas and rewriting to improve them. To revise effectively ask the following questions:

- Is your paragraph suited to your audience and purpose?
- Have you provided relevant and sufficient detail?
- Is your paragraph logically organized?
- Is your language vivid and specific?

2. Editing involves correcting errors in grammar, spelling, and punctuation. Use an error log to keep track of your error pattern.

II

Methods of Developing Paragraphs

6 Narration and Process

In this chapter you will learn to

1. organize events in a narrative sequence.
2. explain processes and procedures.

Imagine that you are describing to a friend a recent disagreement you had with a sales clerk when attempting to return a defective CD player. Probably, you would repeat the conversation in the order in which it occurred: "I said. . . , then he said . . ." and so on. Now suppose you were explaining to a family member how to program your VCR. The easiest way to explain this is to describe each step in the order it is to be done. "First you . . . , and then you. . ."

In each of these instances, you organize ideas in the order in which they occur in time—that is, in chronological order. Organizing ideas using time order is a common and effective writing technique. Describing events that have already occurred using time sequence is called *narration*. Such writing is often referred to as a *narrative*. Describing how something is done using time sequence is called *process*. There are many everyday and academic situations in which you will find narration or process to be a clear and useful way to organize your ideas. Here are a few examples.

Narration

Everyday Examples
- telling a friend how you spent the weekend
- describing a frightening event

Academic Examples
- summarizing the plot of a short story.
- describing a series of historical events

Process

Everyday Examples
- giving directions to a shopping mall.
- explaining how to file a health insurance claim

Academic Examples
- explaining how to do an experiment or research project
- explaining how to solve a math problem

WRITING NARRATIVES

■ Writing a narrative is similar to telling a story. Story-telling exists as one of the oldest, most appealing and enjoyable ways of communicating ideas. Throughout history, ideas have been communicated and recorded through stories, myths, fables, and legends. We all know stories of Robin Hood, Pinocchio, and Cinderella. Stories remain popular today: movies, television shows, soap operas, and even many jokes involve a series of events organized and presented in story form.

A narrative is different from a simple recounting of events, however. A narrative makes a point through the story. By recounting what happens, you communicate an idea about the topic. The following narrative paragraph explains a Native American legend.

> Face Rock, a striking arrangement of rocks off the coast of Oregon near Bandon, gets its name from a Native American legend. A princess, the daughter of Chief Siskiyou, was warned by her father not to wade too far into the dangerous coastal waters. She disobeyed and walked far into the pounding surf. Her dog and two kittens followed her. The Princess was unaware that an evil spirit, Seatka, lurked in the waves. Seatka willed the Princess to look at him so he could place her within his power. She refused, and instead, stared directly at the moon, set high in the sky. To this day, the Princess and her faithful animals stand in the water, stonily determined not to succumb to evil. Seatka is there too, still awaiting her glance.

This narrative makes the point that it is dangerous for children to disobey their parents. Now here is a narrative paragraph written by a student.

> Our trip to Fantasy Amusement Park was not a fantasy. It was a nightmare. When we arrived, the parking lot was full and we had to park in the alternate parking areas and wait twenty minutes for a bus to take us to the park. When we entered the park, we realized it was children's day—everyone under age eight gets in at half price. There were kids everywhere. It felt like one big kindergarten class during recess. First, we wanted to ride the high speed roller coaster, so we had

Should You Use a Word Processor?

• • • • • • • • • • • • • • • • • • •

Word processing uses a computer program to enable you to type papers onto a computer disk and print them using a printer connected to the computer. Word processing programs let you revise and correct errors without retyping your entire paper. Some basic information about word processors follows that will help you decide whether to use one.

Advantages

1. Word processors produce neat, easy-to-read copy. Most instructors prefer to read printed rather than handwritten copy, but they do not always require it.

2. Word processors make revision and correcting errors much easier. If you want to add, change, or delete a sentence, for example, you don't have to rewrite the entire paragraph or page. You simply make the change on the computer screen and then reprint your paper.

3. Word processing makes it easy to experiment with different arrangements of ideas without tiresome recopying. Word processors have a copy function that allows you to make a copy of your writing. Once you've copied it, revise the copy and compare it to your original.

4. Your paper is stored on disk, so you always have a copy of papers you've submitted without having to use a photocopier.

to wait in line for 30 minutes. Then we waited in line for the water slide. Finally my girlfriend said, "I can't take this anymore. Let's get out of here." Amusement parks are not amusing when it costs ten dollars apiece for the privilege of standing in line.

This student makes a clear point about amusement parks: they aren't fun when overcrowded with small children.

Selecting a Topic and Generating Ideas

It is usually best to limit your paragraph to a single event or experience. Otherwise, you will have too much information to cover, and you won't be able to include sufficient detail. Don't try, for example, to

5. By saving time not having to recopy your work, you'll have more time to spend on revising the paper itself.

6. When you recopy a final draft, you can introduce new errors, such as leaving out a comma or misspelling a word. This problem does not happen with word processing.

Disadvantages

1. You have to write where and when a computer is available, unless you own one.

2. You need some basic typing skills. You need not type fast, but you do need to be familiar with the keyboard. (Many colleges offer key-boarding workshops or credit courses that teach the basics.)

Availability

Many colleges have computer labs or writing labs with computers and computer software available for your use. Usually, an assistant is present who can help you become familiar with their use. Other colleges offer periodic workshops on how to use a specific word processing program.

Advice

Give it a try! The hours you'll save over the course of your years in college will be substantial. The initial extra time it will take to learn word processing will be saved many times over. Besides, most businesses and offices use computers: your familiarity with them will be an asset when it comes time to apply for jobs.

describe an entire weekend or several childhood experiences in a single paragraph. Instead, choose one exciting weekend activity or one particularly memorable childhood experience.

To generate ideas, write a list of events that occurred. Don't worry, at this point, about expressing each in sentence form or listing them in the order in which they occurred. Record in the margin any feelings you have about the events. Although you may not include them in the paragraph, they will be helpful in writing your topic sentence.

Exercise 6-1   Think of an experience that illustrates one of the following situations. Write a list of events that occurred.

1. a big mistake
2. leaving a loved one for the first time
3. a last minute change of plans
4. having to "sleep on" a problem in order to solve it
5. a seemingly endless but worthwhile wait

Writing a Topic Sentence

Your topic sentence should accomplish two things. First, it should identify your topic—the experience you are writing about. Second, it should indicate your view or attitude toward that experience. For example, suppose you are writing a paragraph about your first college registration. Your view might be that it was confusing and frustrating or that it required you to make decisions for which you felt unprepared. Here are a few possible topic sentences.

1. Registration was a frustrating experience because course selection was limited.
2. Registration was an endless stream of paperwork to complete and procedures to follow.
3. Registration was simpler than I expected because the system is now computerized.

Sometimes you may discover your view toward the experience as you are writing about it. For example, a student wrote the following first draft about her first college registration.

I was overwhelmed by the number of human bodies crammed into one room and didn't realize that I would be there for almost four hours! I was terribly late for work, and my boss was pretty annoyed. I didn't think I would have to fill out so many forms and wished they had planned for more available seating. The crowded room was so noisy and warm that I had trouble thinking. I almost cursed when I learned that the courses I wanted were closed and I didn't know where to go to ask for advice about what to do next.

As she was writing she realized that she wished she had known more about the process before she began. Then she wrote the following topic sentence:

```
My first registration at college might not
have been so frustrating if someone had ex-
plained the process to me ahead of time.
```

Exercise 6-2   For the experience you chose in Exercise 6-1, write a topic sentence that expresses your attitude toward the experience.

Sequencing and Developing Your Ideas

The events in a narrative paragraph should usually be arranged in chronological order—the order in which they happened. Sometimes you may want to rearrange events in chronological order to emphasize a point. If you do, make sure the sequence of events is clear enough for the reader to follow.

You can visualize a narrative paragraph as follows:

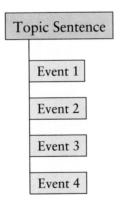

To place the events in the correct sequence, review and number your list of events.

A clear, well-written narrative should provide sufficient detail to allow your reader to understand fully the situation you are writing about. Try to answer for your reader most of the following questions about the experience.

When did it happen?

Where did it happen?

Who was involved?

What events occurred?

Why did they happen?

How did they happen?

Be sure to include only essential and relevant details. Other details distract readers from the events you are describing.

Because a narrative should maintain the reader's interest and build suspense, it is sometimes effective to place your topic sentence at the end of the paragraph, as in the following student example. (Notice that even though the events are not all listed in chronological order, the writer makes it easy for the reader to follow the story.)

> After a lot of discussion, my friends and I finally agreed to meet that night for dinner at the Night Owl near campus. Earlier that day, Lisa, a rather argumentative friend, told me that she was getting tired of our group of friends. She felt they were dull and that she might not come out with us. When I arrived at the Night Owl, Lisa wasn't there, and everyone asked me where she was. I didn't want to hurt their feelings, so I finally announced that she was sick. After dinner we decided to visit the Ten Drummers. As we walked in, I noticed Lisa having a great time with some people we didn't know. Obviously, she was not sick. Everyone looked at me, and I was embarrassed about having lied to my friends.

Exercise 6–3   For the experience you selected for Exercises 6–1 and 6–2, write a first draft paragraph. Be sure to present the events in the order in which they occurred.

Useful Transitions

Transitions are especially useful in narratives to lead your reader from one event to another. Notice how transitions like "that night," "earlier," and "when" help you follow the sequence in the student paragraph above. Here are some frequently used transitions:

TABLE 6-1	**Frequently Used Transitions**			
	first	then	in the beginning	next
	second	later	after	during
	third	at last	following	after that
	finally			

Exercise 6–4 Revise the paragraph you wrote for Exercise 6–3. Add transitions to make your ideas clearer.

WRITING PROCESS DESCRIPTIONS

■ A process paragraph describes how something is done or how something works. A "how to" paragraph, for example, may explain how to change a flat tire, aid a choking victim, or locate a reference source in the library. A "how it works" paragraph may explain the operation of a pump, how the human body regulates temperature, or how children develop speech. Here is an example of both types of paragraph. The first explains how to eat an ice cream cone. The second describes how hibernation works.

"How To" Paragraph

In trying to make wise and correct decisions about the ice-cream cone in your hand, you should always keep the objectives in mind. The main objective, of course, is to get the cone under control. Secondarily, one will want to eat the cone calmly and with pleasure. Real pleasure lies not simply in eating the cone but in eating it right. Let us assume that you have darted to your open space and made your necessary emergency repairs. The cone is still dangerous—still, so to speak, "live." But you can now proceed with it in an orderly fashion. First, revolve the cone through the full three hundred and sixty degrees, snapping at the loose gobs of ice cream; turn the cone by moving the thumb away from you and the forefinger toward you, so the cone moves counterclockwise. Then, with the cone still "wound," which will require the wrist to be bent at the full right angle toward you, apply pressure with the mouth and tongue to accomplish overall realignment, straightening and settling the whole mess. Then, unwinding the cone back through the full three hundred and sixty degrees, remove any trickles of ice cream. From here on, some supplementary repairs may be necessary, but the cone is now defused.

                       L. Rust Hills, *How to Do Things Right: Revelations of a Fussy Man*

"How It Works" Paragraph

Hibernation is a biological process that occurs most frequently in small animals. The process enables animals to adjust to a diminishing food supply. When the outdoor temperature drops, the animal's internal thermostat senses the change. Then bodily changes begin to occur. First, the animal's heartbeat slows, and oxygen intake is reduced by slowed breathing. Metabolism is then reduced. Food requirements become minimal. Finally, the animal falls into a sleep-like state during which it relies on stored body fat to support life functions.

Selecting a Topic and Generating Ideas

Write about a procedure or process that you are familiar with, preferably something you have done often or have a complete understanding of. Both "how to" and "how it works" process paragraphs involve steps that occur *only* in a specified order. Begin developing your paragraph by listing these steps in the order in which they must occur. It is helpful to visualize the process. For "how to" paragraphs imagine yourself actually performing the task. Draw diagrams of complicated "how it works" objects and use them as a guide in listing the steps.

Exercise 6–5   Think of a process or procedure you are familiar with, or select one from the following list, and make a list of the steps it involves.

1. how to read a map
2. how to waste time
3. how to learn to like _____
4. how the NFL football draft works
5. how to win at _____

Writing Your Topic Sentence

For a process paragraph, your topic sentence should (1) identify the process or procedure and (2) explain why familiarity with it is useful or important. In other words, your topic sentence should explain to your reader *why* he or she should learn about the process. It should state a goal, offer a reason, or indicate what can be accomplished by using the process. Here are a few examples of topic sentences that contain both of these important elements.

> Reading maps, a vital skill for vacations by car, is a simple process.
>
> Because leisure reading encourages a positive attitude toward reading, every parent should know how to select worthwhile children's books.
>
> To locate books in the library, you must know how to use the computerized card catalog.

Exercise 6–6   Revise the following topic sentences to include a reason why the topic is important or relevant.

1. Making pizza at home involves five steps.
2. Taking notes in a lecture class requires good listening and writing skills.
3. Through a smell-identification process, bloodhounds can locate criminals.
4. My dentist showed me how to use dental floss.
5. Here's how to change a flat tire.

Exercise 6–7   Write a topic sentence for the process you selected in Exercise 6–5.

Sequencing and Developing Your Ideas

Use the following tips to develop an effective process paragraph.

1. The only order in which the steps in a process can be presented is the order in which they happen.

2. Be sure to include only essential, necessary steps. Avoid comments, opinions, or unnecessary information because it may confuse your reader.

3. Assume, unless you know otherwise, that your reader is unfamiliar with your topic. Be sure to define unfamiliar terms and identify clearly any technical or specialized tools, procedures, or objects.

4. Use a consistent point of view. Use either the first person "I" or the second person "you" throughout. Don't switch between them.

5. Place your topic sentence first. This position provides your reader with a purpose for reading.

6. Use transitional words (like those in Table 6-1, page 109) to help your reader follow the process.

Exercise 6–8   Write a first draft paragraph for the process you chose in Exercise 6–5.

Exercise 6–9   Revise the paragraph you wrote for Exercise 6–8. Add transitions to make your ideas clearer.

THINKING BEFORE READING

■ The following reading is taken from the autobiography of Gordon Parks, *Voices in the Mirror*. Parks is a famous photographer, well-known for his work in *Life* magazine. In this narrative Parks relates an experience early in his career as a photographer, and the racial discrimination and bigotry he faced in Washington, D.C.

1. Preview the reading using the steps described in Chapter 3, page 43.
2. Connect the reading to your own experience by answering the following questions:
   a. Can photographs capture and communicate feelings?
   b. Can photographs communicate ideas?
   c. Do discrimination and racism still exist today? In what forms?

READING

■

THE CHARWOMAN

Gordon Parks

I have one formidable, overwhelming and justifiable hatred, and that is for racists. Thorn-wielding is their occupation and I can attest to their proficiency. Throughout my childhood they kept their eyes glued to my tenderest parts, striking me, impaling me, leaving me bloodied and confused—without my knowing what had provoked their hostility. I came at last to think of them as beasts with cold hearts; of lost souls impassioned with hatred, slithering about in misery, their feelings severed of all humaneness and spreading over the universe like prickly cloth. Rancor[1] seems to have been their master, and any good that befalls the targets of their grudges sets them to brooding. And though the wind sings with change they remain deaf to it; change to them is the unbearable music of imaginary monsters, which they resist. Their actions and attitudes easily identify them. Their smiles have a curl. Their voices, no matter how gentle, are bedded in loathing. At times I can only look at them in a curious silence, wondering about their feelings, and the climates that bred them. I recall having a sort of innocence about the source of their bigotry,[2] but naïveté was no antidote for the bleeding. Washington, D.C., in 1942, bulged with racism.

I arrived there in January of that year with scant knowledge of the place, knowing only that beneath the gleaming monuments and gravestones lay men who had distinguished themselves. What I had learned along the way had little to do with this sprawling city where Washington and Lincoln had been empowered. Sensing this, Roy Stryker, the photographic mentor at FSA [Farm Security Administration], sent me out to get acquainted with the rituals of the nation's capital. I went in a hurry and with enthusiasm. The big blue sky was without clouds and everything seemed so pure, clean and unruffled. It appeared that the entire universe was pleasured in peace.

My contentment was short-lived. Within the hour the day began opening up like a bad dream; even here in this radiant, high-hearted place racism was busy with its dirty work. Eating houses shooed me to the back door; theaters refused me a seat, and the scissoring voices of white clerks at Julius Garfinckel's prestigious department store riled me with curtness. Some clothing I had hoped to buy there went unbought. They just didn't have my size—no matter what I wanted.

In a very short time Washington was showing me its real character. It was a hate-drenched city, honoring my ignorance and smugly creating bad memories for me. During that afternoon my entire childhood rushed back to greet me, to remind me that the racism it poured on me had not called it quits.

Not only was I humiliated, I was also deeply hurt and angered to a boiling point. It suddenly seemed that all of America was finding grim pleasure in expressing its intolerance to me personally. Washington had turned ugly, and my angry past came back to speak with me

1. bitter hate
2. narrow-minded intolerance

as I walked along, assuring me that, even here in the nation's capital, the walls of bigotry and discrimination stood high and formidable. In all innocence, I had gone to a restaurant to eat, to a store to buy clothing and a movie theater for enjoyment. And Washington was telling me, in no uncertain terms, that I shouldn't have done it. Now I was hurrying back to Roy Stryker's office like an angry wind.

When I reached there he looked at me for a few moments without speaking. He didn't have to. The gloom shadowing my face told him everything. "Well," he finally asked, "tell me—how did it go?"   6

I answered him with a question. "What's to be done about this horrible place? I've never been so humiliated in my life. Mississippi couldn't be much worse."   7

"It's bad—very bad. That's why I was hesitant about taking you on here. The laboratory technicians here are all from the Deep South. You're not going to have an easy time. Their attitude about photographers is not the best. To them they are a glorified lot who roam the world while they slave away in the back rooms doing the dirty work. And slaving for a black photographer isn't going to improve that attitude. You're on your own here, and you'll have to prove yourself to them—with superior work." He rubbed his chin, thinking. "As for that city out there, well—it's been here for a long time, full of bigotry and hatred for black people. You brought a camera to town with you. If you use it intelligently, you might help turn things around. It's a powerful instrument in the right hands." He paused, thinking things through for me. "Obviously you ran into some bigots out there this afternoon. Well, it's not enough to photograph one of them and label his photograph *bigot*. Bigots have a way of looking like everyone else. You have to get at the source of their bigotry. And that's not easy. That's what you'll have to work at, and that's why I took you on. Read. Read a lot. Talk to other black people who have spent their lives here. They might help to give you some direction. Go through these picture files. They have a lot to say about what's happening here and other places throughout this country. They are an education in themselves. The photographers who produced those files learned through understanding what our country's problems are. Now they are out there trying to do something about those problems. That's what you must do eventually."   8

Eventually. All well and good—but I was still burning with a need to hit back at the agony of the afternoon. I sat for an hour mulling over his advice and the humiliation I had suffered. It had grown   9 late; the office had emptied and Stryker had left for the day. Only a black charwoman remained but she was mopping the floor in an adjoining office. "Talk to other black people who have spent their lives here," he had said. She was black, and I eased into conversation with her. Hardly an hour had gone by when we finished, but she had taken me through a lifetime of drudgery and despair in that hour. She was turning back to her mopping when I asked, "Would you allow me to photograph you?"

"I don't mind." 10

There was a huge American flag hanging from a standard near 11 the wall. I asked her to stand before it, then placed the mop in one hand and the broom in the other. "Now think of what you just told me and look straight into this camera." Eagerly I began clicking the shutter. It was done and I went home to supper. Washington could now have a conversation with her portrait.

Gordon Parks, *Voices in the Mirror*

GETTING READY TO WRITE

■ *Step 1: Using Idea Mapping*

Before you write a narrative or describe a process you must have a clear understanding of the sequence of events. A sequence map—a visual representation of key events or steps in the order in which they occur—can help you keep events straight. A sequence map looks like this:

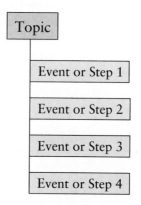

For complicated narratives or processes, you can include key details about each step, as shown below.

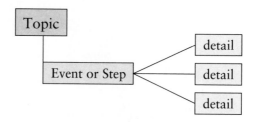

You'll find sequence maps useful in reading as well. For example, plots of novels and short stories frequently switch back and forth in time, and a sequence map can help you follow events.

Exercise 6–10   Complete the following sequence map for the reading by filling in the blank boxes.

PARKS' DAY IN WASHINGTON
Parks recall past experience with racism
Stryker sends Parks out to learn about city
Parks storms into Stryker's office
Parks goes home to supper

Step 2: Thinking Critically: Point of View

Narratives are always told from a point of view—that is, from a particular perspective. Think of point of view as the eyes through which the story is seen. The point of view of the reading "The Charwoman" is that of the photographer. His impressions, reactions, and feelings are conveyed.

A writer's point of view is important to recognize and evaluate as you read and write about narratives (or any other type of writing that express attitudes and feelings). Point of view often allows you to look beyond events to see how they are perceived by the people involved. The same event, from a different person's perspective, can create quite different results.

Exercise 6–11 "The Charwoman" could be told from several points of view other than that of the photographer. For example, the story could be told from the viewpoint of Roy Stryker, the author's mentor, from the charwoman's viewpoint, or even from the viewpoint of the clerk at Garfinckel's department store. Each story would, necessarily, include a different series of events and feelings. Write a paragraph telling the story from Roy Stryker's viewpoint.

Step 3: Reacting to and Discussing Ideas

Get ready to write about the reading by discussing the following questions.

1. Do you think Roy Stryker knew what Parks would experience that afternoon when he sent Parks out to get acquainted with the city?
2. Describe Parks' feelings as he rushed back to Stryker's office.
3. How can a camera be a "powerful tool in the right hands"?
4. Describe your reaction to the photograph of the charwoman.
5. How does the photograph of the charwoman attack bigotry and racism?
6. Stryker told Parks he must eventually do something about our country's problems. Do you think the charwoman photograph "did something"?

WRITING ABOUT THE READING

■ *Writing Assignment 1*

The narrative is told from Parks' point of view because he relates how he met, spoke with, posed, and photographed the charwoman. Write a narrative paragraph relating these same events from the point of view of the charwoman. Feel free to add details and try to include those that reveal how you think the charwoman felt toward Parks.

WRITING ABOUT YOUR IDEAS

■ *Writing Assignment 2*

Stryker told Parks that he must prove himself through superior work. Write a narrative paragraph describing a situation in which you had to prove yourself.

Writing Assignment 3

Parks followed a process in posing the charwoman in order to accomplish his goal. Think of a goal you have accomplished and write a process paragraph describing how you accomplished it.

Journal Writing Suggestions

Write a journal entry about photography. When and why do people take photographs? What do they do with them after they have taken them?

Parks experienced anger and frustration as a result of his treatment. Write a journal entry describing a situation in which you felt angry or frustrated.

REVISION CHECKLIST

1. Is your paragraph appropriate for your audience? Does it give them the background information they need? Will it interest them?
2. Will your paragraph accomplish your purpose?
3. Is your main point clearly expressed in a topic sentence?
4. Is each detail relevant? In other words, does each directly explain or support the topic sentence?
5. Have you supported your topic sentence with sufficient detail to make it understandable and believable?
6. Do you use specific words to explain each detail?

   For Narrative and Process Writing:
7. Have you made a point about your narrative? Have you told the reader why it is important to be familiar with the process you describe?
8. Are the events arranged in the order in which they occurred? If not, will your reader be able to follow the sequence?
9. Have you used transitional words to help the reader follow events?
10. Have you told the story from a consistent point of view?

Pronoun–Antecedent Agreement

A pronoun substitutes for a noun (*he, she, it*) and must agree in person, number, and gender with its antecedent (the word it replaces).

Rules to Follow

1. If the noun is singular, the pronoun replacing it must also be singular.

Robert wanted to lend me his classnotes.

2. Likewise, if the noun is plural, then the pronoun substitute must be plural.

Mark wrote lyrics for songs; many were depressing and sad.

3. Some indefinite pronouns are singular; others are plural. Use a singular pronoun to replace a singular noun and a plural pronoun to replace a plural noun.

One of the team members could not find his keys.

Both of the instructors said they planned to vacation in Maine.

4. Some indefinite pronouns are either singular or plural, depending on how they are used. If the pronoun refers to something that cannot be counted, use a singular pronoun to refer to it. If the pronoun refers to something that can be counted, use a plural pronoun to refer to it.

Too much ice on airplane wings is dangerous, so it is removed before takeoff.

Many students think they will register for an economics course.

5. Use a plural pronoun to refer to two or more nouns linked by *and*.

Sam and Mark lost their keys.

. . . .

6. If a pronoun substitutes for two or more nouns joined by *or* or *nor*, the pronoun agrees with the noun it is nearer to.

Either Mrs. Marcus or her sons will drive their car.

Rate Your Ability to Use Pronoun–Antecedent Agreement

Circle the word or phrase that correctly completes each sentence.

1. Ellen and I are going to pool (their, our) money and buy a couch.
2. Gene or Bo brought (his, their) drumsticks for the practice session.
3. Each student received (his or her, their) transcripts by mail.
4. Either the sweater or the turtleneck will be returned to the store (it, they) came from because I don't need both.
5. Everyone opened (his or her, their) book to page 50.
6. When the play was over, the audience rose from (its, their) seats to give a standing ovation.
7. When a speaker makes a joke (he or she, they) is trying to maintain audience interest.
8. No one handed in (his or her, their) exam before the time was up.
9. At some point in (their, his or her) lives, men and women will stop to evaluate their goals and accomplishments.
10. Every foreigner must master Portuguese if (they, he or she) expects to succeed in Brazil.

Score _____

Check your answers using the Answer Key on page 537. If you scored below 80 percent, you need additional review and practice recognizing and correcting pronoun–antecedent agreement. Refer to section C.8 of Reviewing the Basics in Part 5.

SUMMARY

■   1. Narration is a method of describing events using time sequence. To write effective narratives

- limit your paragraph to a single event or experience.
- identify your topic and express your view or attitude in the topic sentence.
- arrange your details in chronological order.
- use transitions to lead your reader from one event to the next.

2. A process paragraph describes how something is done or how something works. To write effective process paragraphs

- write about a topic that is familiar.
- be sure your topic sentence identifies the process or procedure you are writing about.
- be sure your topic sentence explains why your topic is useful or important.
- arrange your details in the order in which they should occur.
- use transitions to connect your details.

7 Description

. . . .

In this chapter you will learn to

1. establish a dominant impression in your descriptive paragraphs.

2. choose details that will support your dominant impression.

3. choose details that vividly describe your topic.

4. organize details to convey your topic clearly.

Imagine that you are searching through a brochure for a cottage to rent for a week during the summer. You find two cottages listed that meet your basic requirements and price range. The ad for each is shown below. Which would you be more interested in viewing? Which cottage would you be more interested in renting?

> *Ad A* Two bedroom cottage on Lake Simon. Kitchen, living room, full bath. Deck and fireplace. $375/week.

> *Ad B* Cozy, secluded, shorefront cottage on Lake Simon. Two comfortable bedrooms, modern kitchen and bath. Living room with lake view. Woodburning fireplace and redwood deck. $375/week.

Each cottage has the same basic features and the same price and location, but you are probably drawn to cottage B. Why? Ad B offers descriptive details to help you visualize the apartment. You begin to imagine what it looks like and to "get a feel for it." Ad A, on the other hand, contains only factual information, and when you have finished reading, no real impression emerges.

Descriptive writing, then, creates an impression. It helps the reader visualize the topic. Now suppose summer is over and you just spent a week at cottage B. You might write the following paragraph describing it.

The rented cottage was rustic and completely charming. The bedrooms had colorful bed quilts, porthole windows, and antique pictures on the walls. On entering the living room, one's immediate desire was to fling oneself onto a huge puffy blue sofa. Tunes from an old-fashioned radio combined with the woodburning fireplace created a relaxing atmosphere. From the redwood deck there was a marvelous view of the lake and of a playful family of goslings.

Notice that this paragraph begins with a topic sentence that identifies its topic (the cottage) and indicates how the writer feels about it. This feeling or attitude toward the topic is called the *dominant impression*. The remainder of the paragraph offers details that help the reader visualize the cottage. In effect, each detail explains the dominant impression. Each sentence contains colorful and descriptive words and phrases. In this chapter you will learn to write descriptive paragraphs that convey a dominant impression and contain descriptive details, and to express them effectively.

ESTABLISHING A DOMINANT IMPRESSION

■ The dominant impression of a descriptive paragraph is the overall sense you want to convey about your topic. It is expressed in your topic sentence, usually at the beginning of the paragraph. Suppose your topic is the audience at a recent concert. If you felt the audience was appreciative, you might write the following topic sentence.

> The audience at the recent Billy Joel concert was appreciative and responsive to both the old and new songs he performed.

However, two different dominant impressions of the audience are created by the following topic sentences.

> The antics and immature behavior of the audience at the Billy Joel concert ruined the concert for me.

> Because the audience at the recent Billy Joel concert was bored and listless, I did not enjoy myself.

The dominant impression often reflects your first reaction to a topic. Let's say you are writing about your bedroom. Think of a word or two that sums up how you feel about it. Is it comfortable? messy? organized?

WRITING
SUCCESS
TIP 7

Spelling Tips

Correct spelling is important to a well-written paragraph. Use the advice below to help you avoid misspellings.

1. Don't worry about spelling as you write your first draft; checking a word in a dictionary at this point will interrupt your flow of ideas. If you don't know how a word is spelled, spell it the way it sounds. Circle or underline the word so you remember to check it later.

2. Keep a list of words you commonly misspell. This list can be part of your error log (see Chapter 5) or of your writing journal (see Writing Success Tip 2). Every time you catch an error or find a misspelled word on a returned paper, add it to your list.

3. Study your list. Ask a friend to "quiz" you on the list. Eliminate words from the list after you have passed several "quizzes" on them.

4. Develop a spelling awareness. Your spelling will improve just by being aware that spelling is important. When you encounter a new word, notice how it is spelled and practice writing it.

5. Pronounce words you are having difficulty spelling. Pronounce each syllable distinctly.

6. Review basic spelling rules. Your college library or learning lab may have manuals, workbooks, or computer programs that review basic rules and provide guided practice.

7. Be sure to have a dictionary readily available when you write. (See Writing Success Tip 8.)

8. Read your final draft through once. Look at each word carefully, and check only for spelling errors. Check the spelling of any words of which you are uncertain.

your own territory? a place to escape? Any one of these could be developed into a paragraph. For example, your topic sentence might be:

> My bedroom is a comfortable escape, a place where I am surrounded by things that are of personal value.

The details that follow would then describe objects on which you place personal value. If you have difficulty deciding or thinking of a dominant impression for a topic, brainstorm a list of words to sum up your observations and reactions. For example, for the topic of your college health office you might write things such as "smells like doctor's office," or "antiseptic and clean." The topic of a double-dip ice cream cone could produce details like "icy and delicious" or "messy" or "calories galore." If brainstorming does not help, hold off on writing a topic sentence until you've made a list of details about your topic.

Exercise 7–1   For three of the following topics, write three topic sentences, expressing a different dominant impression in each.

1. thunderstorm

   a. _____

   b. _____

   c. _____

2. professional athletes

   a. _____

   b. _____

   c. _____

3. favorite food or beverage

   a. _____

   b. _____

   c. _____

4. recent film you have seen

   a. _____

   b. _____

   c. _____

5. your wristwatch

a. _____

b. _____

c. _____

Exercise 7–2   Write a topic sentence for a paragraph that will describe *one* of the following. Be sure to include a dominant impression.

1. your most boring or most exciting family event
2. a favorite piece of clothing
3. a television personality you like or dislike
4. someone who is self-centered
5. someone who is always late

DEVELOPING AND SELECTING DESCRIPTIVE DETAILS

■ All the details in a descriptive paragraph must be relevant to and help create your dominant impression. Begin by brainstorming a list of all the details you can think of that describe your topic or support your dominant impression. Try to visualize the person, place, or experience and write down what you "see." Your details should enable your reader to paint his or her own mental picture of the topic. Here's a list of details a student wrote on movie theaters.

```
fold-up seats          greasy smell of popcorn
big screen             kids running up the aisle
previews               squishy seats you sink into
people whispering      ushers with flashlights
trash on floor         "Excuse Me"
ticket stubs           "Sshh"
sticky floors          lines at the box office
dim lights             always crowded-sit next
popcorn-salty          to others
```

If you have not formed a dominant impression, review your list looking for a pattern to your details. What feeling or impression do many of them suggest? In the above list, many of the details convey the feeling of annoyance or dislike. After you have decided upon an impression, eliminate those details that do not relate to that impression. For example, the details about the screen, ticket stubs, and lighting should be eliminated because they do not support the impression of annoyance.

Now read the following student paragraph on the topic of movie theaters. Notice how the student developed ideas from the above list. The paragraph still contains some details that do not directly support the dominant impression. Watch for them as you read.

```
    Movie theaters are crowded, annoying
places. I don't enjoy sitting next to
strangers, especially rude or noisy ones. And,
I don't appreciate practically arm wrestling
with them for the privilege of using the arm
rest. Ushers are usually people I know. People
talk during the film and others say, "Sshh."
Waiting in line at the concession stand irri-
tates me because the prices are always outra-
geous and service is poor. The air smells like
popcorn, and usually you want to buy some, al-
though it's always too salty and you get
thirsty. I wish theaters would show more pre-
views. I am convinced that they make their pop-
corn overly salty on purpose. I think they
should serve pizza, since it is such a popular
food. It's annoying when people eat this salty
stuff and make such loud crunching noises. Peo-
ple trash the floors and spill so much soda
that my feet stick to the floor.
```

Details about ushers, serving pizza, and previews of coming attractions should be deleted since they are not reasons for the writer's annoyance.

Exercise 7–3   For the following topic sentences circle the letter of the detail(s) that are not relevant to the dominant impression stated.

1. Airplane flights allow an opportunity to fantasize.
   a. I imagine I'm flying by myself like a bird.
   b. I watch the people around me.
   c. I think of what all the people we are flying over are doing.
   d. I study the clouds.
2. You don't need a lot of equipment to enjoy fishing.
   a. The only necessary items are a rod and reel.
   b. There are many different types of rods.

    c. A net is helpful if you're fishing from a boat.

    d. Take a picnic lunch if you're fishing from a boat.

3. Gambling is addictive and can lead to financial disaster.

    a. Some people are unable to stop because they want to win just one more time.

    b. Money is exchanged for gambling chips at casinos.

    c. Las Vegas is a place where many people go to gamble.

    d. I know a gambler who often bets his entire paycheck on one horse race.

4. The common cold virus is unpleasant and often untreatable.

    a. Common colds produce non-stop runny noses.

    b. Viruses give us measles, mumps, and polio.

    c. The common cold virus cannot be treated with antibiotics.

    d. The virus cannot attack animals, only humans.

5. Officials at sporting events must be knowledgeable, skillful, and have strong personalities.

    a. Officials must be able to withstand crowd reactions to unpopular calls.

    b. Officials must know the technicalities of the game.

    c. Officials must exert authority and win respect of the players.

    d. The pay officials receive is not commensurate with their responsibilities.

Exercise 7–4   Select one of the topic sentences you wrote in Exercise 7–1 or 7–2. Develop a descriptive paragraph for this sentence.

USING DESCRIPTIVE LANGUAGE

■ Descriptive language is exact, colorful, and appealing. It enables the reader to envision the observations and impressions of the writer. Here are two sentences about a day at the beach. The first presents lifeless, factual information; the second describes what the writer sees and feels.

1. I went to the beach today to lie on the sand and read a book.

2. As I lay reading on my sand-sprinkled blanket at the beach today, I felt the sun's warming rays and heard the constant crash of waves as the seagulls cried above me.

You might think of descriptive language as a way the reader sees the world through the eyes of the writer. A section of Chapter 4, pp. 65–66 discusses the use of descriptive language. Review that section before continuing with this chapter.

One of the best ways to help your reader see, as you'll remember from Chapter 4, is to use words that draw on your readers' five senses—sight, hearing, smell, touch, and taste. The student whose paragraph appeared on page 128 used details like the touch of sticky floors, the smell of popcorn, and the sound of the audience's whispers to make you see why she dislikes movie theaters.

Make sure you use specific words wherever possible. The student didn't simply say that theaters are dirty. She said the floors are sticky with spilled soda. You yourself have probably been in theaters where your feet stuck to the floor, so this detail immediately gives you a mental picture.

Use vivid verbs, adjectives, and adverbs to help your readers see what you are describing. When you can, use exact names of people, places, and objects ("a red Toyota," not "a car").

Exercise 7–5   For each of the following items, write a sentence that provides a vivid description. The first one is done for you.
1. an old coat
   Mr. Busby wore a tattered, faded, stained-around-the-neck, deep burgundy leather coat.
2. a fast-food meal

   _____

3. a bride (or groom)

   _____

4. a sidewalk

   _____

5. the dog behind a "Guard Dog on Premises" sign

   _____

Exercise 7–6   Revise the paragraph you wrote in Exercise 7–4, adding descriptive words and phrases.

Exercise 7–7   Write a paragraph describing what you think is happening in the photograph shown below. Be sure your paragraph conveys a dominant impression. Use descriptive language to make your details vivid.

ORGANIZING DETAILS AND USING TRANSITIONS

■   The arrangement of details in a descriptive paragraph is determined by your topic and by the dominant impression you want to convey. You want to emphasize the most important details, making sure your readers can follow your description.

One of the most common arrangements is a spatial organization (which we discussed in Chapter 4, p. 62). If you were describing your college campus, for example, you might start at one end and work toward the other. You might describe a stage set from left to right or a building from bottom to top.

Transitions help your reader follow a spatial arrangement. Some common transitional words for such an organization include: *above, below, behind, in front of, beside, next to, inside, outside, to the west (north,* etc.), *beneath, nearby,* and *on the other side.*

If you were describing a person, you might work from head to toe. But you might prefer to follow another common organization: from least to most important. If the dominant impression you want to convey about the person's appearance is messiness, you might start with some characteristics that are only slightly messy (an untied shoe, perhaps) and work toward the most messy (a blue-jean jacket ripped to shreds, stained with paint, and covered with campaign buttons).

Again, transitions will help your reader see where you are going. Common transitions for a least-to-most-important organization include: *most important, above all, especially, particularly important,* and *even more.*

Exercise 7–8   Evaluate the arrangement of details in the paragraph you wrote for one of the previous exercises in this chapter. Does it support your dominant impression? Revise it and add transitions, if needed.

THINKING BEFORE READING

■   The following reading, "Obachan," is a good example of a descriptive essay that uses vivid, sensory detail to capture the reader's interest. The author describes her Japanese family heritage as revealed through the life of her grandmother.

1. Preview the reading using the steps provided in Chapter 3, p. 43.
2. Connect the reading to your own experience by completing the following.
   a. Brainstorm a list of details that describe your grandmother, grandfather, or other close relative. Next, review your list. What feelings does the list reveal?
   b. Do older members of your family hold different ideas and values than younger members? Think of several situations that demonstrate these differences.

READING

■

OBACHAN[1]

Gail Y. Miyasaki

H er hands are now rough and gnarled from working in the canefields. But they are still quick and lively as she sews the "fu-
ton" cover. And she would sit like that for hours Japanese-style with
legs under her, on the floor steadily sewing.

She came to Hawaii as a "picture bride." In one of her rare self-
reflecting moments, she told me in her broken English-Japanese that
her mother had told her that the streets of Honolulu in Hawaii were
paved with gold coins, and so encouraged her to go to Hawaii to
marry a strange man she had never seen. Shaking her head slowly in
amazement, she smiled as she recalled her shocked reaction on seeing
"Ojitchan's" (grandfather's) ill-kept room with only lauhala mats as
bedding. She grew silent after that, and her eyes had a faraway look.

She took her place, along with the other picture brides from Japan, beside her husband on the plantation's canefields along the Ha-
makua coast on the island of Hawaii. The Hawaiian sun had tanned
her deep brown. But the sun had been cruel too. It helped age her.
Deep wrinkles lined her face and made her skin look tough, dry, and
leathery. Her bright eyes peered out from narrow slits, as if she were
constantly squinting into the sun. Her brown arms, though, were
strong and firm, like those of a much younger woman, and so different from the soft, white, and plump-dangling arms of so many old
teachers I had had. And those arms of hers were always moving—
scrubbing clothes on a wooden washboard with neat even strokes,
cutting vegetables with the big knife I was never supposed to touch,
or pulling the minute weeds of her garden.

I remember her best in her working days, coming home from the
canefields at "pauhana" time. She wore a pair of faded blue jeans
and an equally faded navy-blue and white checked work shirt. A Japanese towel was wrapped carefully around her head, and a large
straw "papale" or hat covered that. Her sickle and other tools, and
her "bento-bako" or lunch-box, were carried in a khaki bag she had
made on her back.

1. Grandmother.

I would be sitting, waiting for her, on the back steps of her plan-   5
tation-owned home, with my elbows on my knees. Upon seeing me,
she would smile and say, "Tadaima" (I come home). And I would
smile and say in return, "Okaeri" (Welcome home). Somehow I always felt as if she waited for that. Then I would watch her in silent
fascination as she scraped the thick red dirt off her heavy black rubber boots. Once, when no one was around, I had put those boots on,
and deliberately flopped around in a mud puddle, just so I could
scrape off the mud on the back steps too.

Having retired from the plantation, she now wore only dresses.   6
She called them "makule-men doresu," Hawaiian for old person's
dress. They were always gray or navy-blue with buttons down the
front and a belt at the waistline. Her hair, which once must have
been long and black like mine, was now streaked with grey and cut
short and permanent-waved.

The only time she wore a kimono was for the "Bon"[2] dance. She   7
looked so much older in a kimono and almost foreign. It seemed as
if she were going somewhere, all dressed up. I often felt very far
away from her when we all walked together to the Bon dance, even
if I too was wearing a kimono. She seemed almost a stranger to me,
with her bent figure and her short pigeon-toed steps. She appeared so
distantly Japanese. All of a sudden, I would notice her age; there
seemed something so old in being Japanese.

She once surprised me by sending a beautiful "yūkata" or sum-   8
mer kimono for me to wear to represent the Japanese in our school's
annual May Day festival. My mother had taken pictures of me that
day to send to her. I have often wondered, whenever I look at that kimono, whether she had ever worn it when she was a young girl. I
have wondered too what she was thinking when she looked at those
pictures of me.

My mother was the oldest daughter and the second child of the   9
six children Obāchan bore, two boys and four girls. One of her
daughters, given the name of Mary by one of her school teachers,
had been disowned by her for marrying a "haole" or Caucasian.
Mary was different from the others, my mother once told me, much
more rebellious and independent. She had refused to attend Honokaa
and Hilo High Schools on the Big Island of Hawaii, but chose instead to go to Honolulu to attend McKinley High School. She

2. The Lantern Festival, the Buddhist's All Soul's Day.

smoked cigarettes and drove a car, shocking her sisters with such un-heard of behavior. And then, after graduation, instead of returning home, Mary took a job in Honolulu. Then she met a haole sailor. Mary wrote home, telling of her love for this man. She was met with harsh admonishings from her mother.

"You go with haole, you no come home!" was her mother's ulti-   10
matum.

Then Mary wrote back, saying that the sailor had gone home to   11
America, and would send her money to join him, and get married. Mary said she was going to go.

"Soon he leave you alone. He no care," she told her independent   12
daughter. Her other daughters, hearing her say this, turned against her, accusing her of narrow-minded, prejudiced thinking. She could not understand the words that her children had learned in the Ameri-can schools; all she knew was what she felt. She must have been so terribly alone then.

So Mary left, leaving a silent, unwavering old woman behind.   13
Who could tell if her old heart was broken? It certainly was enough of a shock that Honolulu did not have gold-paved streets. Then, as now, the emotionless face bore no sign of the grief she must have felt.

But the haole man did not leave Mary. They got married and had   14
three children. Mary often sends pictures of them to her. Watching her study the picture of Mary's daughter, her other daughters know she sees the likeness to Mary. The years and the pictures have soft-ened the emotionless face. She was wrong about this man. She was wrong. But how can she tell herself so, when in her heart, she only feels what is right?

"I was one of the first to condemn her for her treatment of   15
Mary," my mother told me, "I was one of the first to question how she could be so prejudiced and narrow-minded." My mother looked at me sadly and turned away.

"But now, being a mother myself, and being a Japanese mother   16
above all, I *know* how she must have felt. I just don't know how to say I'm sorry for those things I said to her."

Whenever I see an old Oriental woman bent with age and walk-   17
ing with short steps, whenever I hear a child being talked to in bro-ken English-Japanese, I think of her. She is my grand-mother. I call her "Obāchan."

Asian Women's Journal, 1971

GETTING READY TO WRITE

■ *Step 1: Marking Revealing Actions, Descriptions, and Statements*

Writers often reveal how they feel and what they think through description rather than through direct statements. For example, Miyasaki never directly states her feelings for Obāchan, but the details demonstrate that she loved and respected her.

As you read descriptive writing, it is helpful to underline words, phrases, or bits of conversation that are particularly revealing about the writer's attitudes toward the subject. For example, in paragraph 7 the following words reveal Miyasaki's attitude toward her grandmother dressed in a kimono. "She seemed almost a stranger to me. . . . She appeared so distantly Japanese. . . . there seemed something so old in being Japanese."

Actions, too, may reveal an author's feelings. In paragraph 5, the author describes wearing her grandmother's boots. This action suggests Miyasaki admired Obāchan and wanted to be like her.

Exercise 7–9   Review the reading, underlining other particularly revealing actions, descriptions, and statements.

Step 2: Thinking Critically: Understanding Connotative Language

Many words have two levels of meanings—denotative and connotative. A word's denotative meaning is its precise dictionary meaning. For example, the denotative meaning of the word *mother* is "female parent." A word's connotative meaning is all the feelings and attitudes that come along with that word. These are sometimes called emotional colorings or shades of meaning. The common connotation of "mother" is a warm, caring person. Connotative meanings vary, of course, among individuals.

Think of the word *rock*. The dictionary defines it as "a large mass of stone." But doesn't *rock* also suggest hardness, inability to penetrate, and permanence? Now think of the words *bony* and *skinny*. Their connotations are somewhat negative. The word *slender,* although similar in denotative meaning, has a more positive connotative meaning.

Here are several groups of words. Decide how each word differs from the others in the group.

1. fake, synthetic, artificial (they all mean not real, but how are they different?)
2. difficult, challenging, tough
3. inspect, examine, study
4. expose, reveal, show, display

Now look at some words from the reading and consider their connotative meanings.

paved with gold coins (para. 2)

haole (para. 9, 10)

independent daughter (para. 12)

silent, unwavering old woman (para. 13)

Connotative meanings, then, can provide additional clues about the writer's meaning.

Step 3: Reacting To and Discussing Ideas

Get ready to write about the reading by discussing the following questions.

1. What was Obāchan's reaction when she first met her husband?
2. Describe the life that Obāchan led in her early years in Hawaii.
3. Why did Obāchan object to the marriage of Mary to a Caucasian?
4. How would you describe Mary?
5. Why does the author's mother regret accusing Obāchan of prejudice and narrow-mindedness?

WRITING ABOUT THE READING

■ *Assignment 1*

Write a paragraph describing Obāchan's feelings and reactions when Mary married the Caucasian. You may use details from the reading to support your dominant impression.

WRITING ABOUT YOUR IDEAS

■ *Assignment 2*

Write a paragraph describing your grandmother or grandfather, or other close family relative. Reveal your attitude toward him or her through your choice of detail and connotative language.

Assignment 3

Write a paragraph describing a belief, custom, or attitude within your family that has changed from one generation to another.

Journal Writing Suggestions

1. Write a journal entry describing a changing attitude within your family.
2. Write a journal entry describing the most difficult aspects of descriptive writing.

REVISION CHECKLIST

1. Is your paragraph appropriate for your audience? Does it give them the background information they need? Will it interest them?
2. Will your paragraph accomplish your purpose?
3. Is your main point clearly expressed in a topic sentence?
4. Is each detail relevant? Does each explain or support the topic sentence directly?
5. Have you supported your topic sentence with sufficient details to make it understandable and believable?

For Descriptive Writing

6. Have you created a dominant impression in your paragraph? Do your details support that impression?
7. Have you used vivid and specific language to convey your details?
8. Is your organization appropriate to your topic and the dominant impression you want to create? Have you used transitional words to help your reader follow your description?

Pronoun Reference

A pronoun refers to a specific noun and is used to replace that noun. It must be always clear to which noun a pronoun refers.

Rules to Follow

1. A pronoun must refer to a specific word or words. Avoid vague or unclear references.

INCORRECT: <u>They</u> said on the evening news that the President would visit France.
CORRECT: <u>The evening news commentator</u> reported that the President would visit France.

2. If more than one noun is present, it must be clear to which noun the pronoun refers.

INCORRECT: Jackie told Amber that <u>she</u> passed the exam.
CORRECT: Jackie told Amber, "<u>You</u> passed the exam."

3. Use the relative pronouns *who, whom, which,* and *that* with the appropriate antecedent.

INCORRECT: Sam, <u>whom</u> is the captain of the team, accepted the award.
CORRECT: Sam, <u>who</u> is the captain of the team, accepted the award.

Rate Your Ability to Use Pronouns Correctly

Evaluate each of the following sentences. If there is an error in pronoun reference, revise the sentence so that each pronoun is used correctly.

1. Marissa told Kristin that her car wouldn't start.
2. Brian found a book in the trunk his mother owned.
3. Naomi put the cake on the table, and Roberta moved it to the counter after she noticed it was still hot.
4. The professor asked the student about a book he wanted to borrow.
5. Our waiter, which was named Burt, described the restaurant's specials.

6. Aaron's sister was injured in a car accident, but it would heal.
7. In the professor's lecture, he described the process of photosynthesis.
8. Another car hit mine, which was swerving crazily.
9. In hockey games, they frequently injure each other in fights.
10. The hunting lodge had lots of deer and moose antlers hanging on its walls, and Ryan said he had killed some of them.

Score _____

Check your answers using the Answer Key on page 537. If you scored below 80 percent, you need additional review and practice recognizing the correct usage of pronouns. Refer to section C.9 of the Reviewing the Basics in Part 5.

SUMMARY

■ Descriptive paragraphs create an impression and enable your reader to visualize your topic. To write effective descriptive paragraphs

- establish a dominant impression—an attitude or feeling about your topic. Express this impression in your topic sentence.
- select relevant and sufficient details to support your dominant impression.
- use descriptive language—exact and colorful words that appeal to the senses.
- organize your details logically.
- use transitions to link your details.

8 Example, Classification, and Definition

CHAPTER OBJECTIVES

In this chapter you will learn to

1. use examples to develop your ideas.
2. explain a topic by dividing it into parts.
3. explain a topic by using definition.

Suppose you have become friends with an international student in one of your classes. During class your professor mentions bumper stickers; after class your friend asks you what bumper stickers are. There are several ways you could explain. First, you could give examples: "You know, signs like 'I Brake For Animals,' 'Vote No On Question 3,' and 'Ugly, But Paid For,' that people put on the back of cars." Or, you could explain bumper stickers by describing the different types: some state the values of the driver or urge action; some are intended simply to be humorous. Or, you could define the term: "Bumper stickers are adhesive signs placed on the back of cars. They express a message the car owner wants to convey to other drivers." Finally, you might use a combination of these techniques. For instance, you might define bumper stickers and then give several examples.

As the previous situation illustrates, example, classification, and definition are three useful ways to explain a topic. Examples are particular instances or situations that explain an idea. Classification divides the topic into groups or parts. Definition explains a word's meaning. In this chapter you will learn to use all three of these approaches to develop effective paragraphs.

USING EXAMPLES TO EXPLAIN

■   Examples are specific details that explain a general idea or statement. You already use them to describe daily situations to your friends. Textbooks and instructors also use them to make abstract, general statements more real and understandable. Here are a few sample general statements along with specific examples:

Everyday

General Statement	*Examples*
I had an exhausting day.	1. had two exams 2. worked four hours 3. swam 20 laps at the pool. 4. did three loads of laundry
General Statement	*Examples*
The food in the hotel is expensive.	1. french fries cost $2.50 2. pizza slice costs $2.00 3. yogurt costs $2.05

Academic

General Statement	*Examples*
Aggressive behavior displays violent emotions directed at other people or things.	1. smashing a malfunctioning soda machine 2. shouting and honking at a slow driver 3. calling his girlfriend an idiot
General Statement	*Examples*
Snowshoe rabbits are well-adapted to their environment.	1. thick fur provides warmth in sub-zero temperatures 2. white in winter, brown in summer to blend in with background, fool predators 3. powerful hind legs for crossing broad areas quickly

In each of these samples, the examples make the general statement clear, understandable, and believable by giving concrete details.

Writing Your Topic Sentence

To write a paragraph in which you use examples to explain a general statement, you follow the same process described in Chapters 6 and 7. Use freewriting, brainstorming, branching, or questioning to generate ideas. Then use the ideas to compose a first draft of a topic sentence. Be sure it states your topic and your view toward it. (See Chapter 3, pages 37–38, if necessary, for a review of developing a viewpoint.) You will probably want to revise this topic sentence once you've written the paragraph, but for now, use it as the basis for gathering examples.

Selecting Appropriate and Sufficient Examples

Next, use brainstorming to create a list of as many examples as you can think of. Suppose your topic is dog training. Your tentative topic sentence is, "You must be firm and consistent when training dogs; otherwise, they will not respond to your commands." You might write the following list of examples:

My sister's dog jumps on people; sometimes she disciplines him and sometimes she doesn't.

Every time I want my dog to heel, I give the same command and use a firm tone of voice.

If my dog does not obey the command to sit, I always repeat it again more firmly, while pushing on his back.

The dog trainer at obedience class showed us his dogs. He used a set of hand signals to give commands.

Now review your list and select between two and four examples to support your topic sentence. Use the following guidelines.

1. **Each example should illustrate the idea stated in your topic sentence.**

2. **Each example should be as specific and vivid as possible, accurately describing an incident or situation.** Suppose your topic sentence is, "Celebrities are not reliable sources of information about a product because they are getting paid to praise it." For your first example you write: "Many sports stars are paid to appear in TV commercials." "Sports stars" is too general. To be convincing, your example has to name specific athletes and products or sponsors: "Michael Jordan is paid to tell us how good Nike Air Jordan sneakers are; Chris Evert promotes athletic shoes."

Dictionaries and Other Reference Works for Writers

Every writer needs help at one time or another in spelling a word, recalling a grammar rule, or thinking of the best word for a particular context. A dictionary, grammar handbook, and thesaurus are valuable reference tools for writers. Becoming familiar with these books and comfortable in using them can improve your writing tremendously. Consulting them can also be enjoyable, allowing you access to the fascinating world of words and the study of language.

A Dictionary

Every writer needs at least one good dictionary to check for spelling and word meanings. Buy a full-sized or collegiate dictionary; smaller condensed dictionaries do not contain enough words or meanings to meet your reading and writing needs. Several good ones exist, such as:

The American Heritage Dictionary
Webster's Collegiate Dictionary
Random House Dictionary

If you can't afford a new hard-bound dictionary, look for used copies at garage sales or used book stores. Some are available in paperback editions.

Dictionaries contain a wide variety of useful information. In addition to listing a word's meanings, dictionaries indicate its origin and pronunciation and may include variant spellings and synonyms.

3. **Choose a sufficient number of examples to make your point understandable.** The number you need depends on the complexity of the topic and your reader's familiarity with it. One example is seldom sufficient. The more difficult and unfamiliar the topic, the more examples you will need. For instance, if you are writing about poor service at a restaurant, two examples may be sufficient. Your paragraph could describe your long wait and your rude waiter and make its point quite powerfully. However, if you are providing examples of ways to control test anxiety, you probably would need more than two examples. In this case, you might discuss the need to improve study habits, set realistic goals, practice relaxation techniques, and work on self-esteem.

A Grammar Handbook

A grammar handbook provides complete and extensive review of all aspects of grammar and mechanics (capitalization, punctuation, and so forth). For example, you can use a handbook to check whether you have used a verb tense correctly or to review the correct way to include a quotation in a sentence. Consult your handbook if you have a specific question or an unusual writing or format problem that you don't know how to handle, or if you want to check on grammar rules and exceptions to those rules. Most libraries shelve several handbooks for your reference, and many recommend:

The Riverside Handbook
The Little, Brown Handbook
The Bedford Handbook for Writers

Be sure to obtain a recent edition that contains up-to-date information on how to document sources using parenthetical references.

A Thesaurus

A thesaurus lists synonyms, that is, words that have similar meanings to each other. *Scrutinize*, for example, is a synonym for *examine*. A thesaurus is not a dictionary because it does not contain definitions. In general, people use a thesaurus when seeking a precise or interesting alternative to a word being written. Because the meanings of words have many subtle nuances, you will want to double check in a dictionary the words you select in a thesaurus. Otherwise, you might select a word that doesn't make sense in your sentence or use a new word incorrectly. The most widely used thesaurus is *Roget's Thesaurus*, which is available in paperback.

4. **Draw the connection for your reader between your example and your main point, as is done in the following student paragraph.**

My dad always remains calm, even in emergency situations. One night my husband cut his hand badly on a knife, and blood was everywhere. I felt so frightened that I couldn't look at the wound, and I didn't know if I should call 911. Instead, I called my dad who lives next door. He came right over. He looked at the cut, applied direct pressure to stop the bleeding, washed and bandaged it, and then decided we should go to the emergency room. He was calm and knew what to do even though I could tell that he was worried, too.

5. **Check that your examples truly do illustrate your main point.** Sometimes you may find that your examples do not clarify your main point or that each example you think of seems to illustrate something slightly different. If your topic is too broad, narrow your topic, using the suggestions in Chapter 3, pages 38–40.

Exercise 8–1   Select one of the topics listed below, write a topic sentence, and list at least five possible examples.

1. slang language
2. daily hassles or aggravations
3. the needs of infants or young children
4. over-commercialization of holidays
5. irresponsible behavior at public events

Arranging Your Examples

Arrange your examples in a logical order so your paragraph will flow well, have impact, and make sense to your reader. The least-to-most arrangement (see p. 64) is often the clearest and easiest to use. For instance, you might arrange examples from least-to-most complicated, presenting your reader with the easiest to understand example first. Or, if you are giving examples of a friend's surprising behavior, you might begin by saying, "I was surprised when . . . Even more surprised when she . . . The biggest surprise was . . ." Now study the following paragraph, noticing the arrangement of ideas:

> My ex-girlfriend annoys me with her habit of procrastinating. It angered me when she left dirty dishes in the sink overnight. I was even more irritated when she would not decide what to do on the weekend until Saturday morning. However, the most infuriating example of procrastination had to be when I asked her to marry me and she waited a week to tell me "no."

In this paragraph, the writer organized his examples from least-to-most annoying.

Exercise 8–2   Using the topic sentence and examples you wrote for Exercise 8–1, develop a paragraph. Select the best examples and arrange them in least-to-most order.

USING CLASSIFICATION TO EXPLAIN

■ Classification is a method of explaining or describing by dividing the topic into categories. For instance, an easy way to explain reptiles is to divide (or classify) them into categories: crocodiles, alligators, snakes, turtles, tortoises, and lizards. Or you can explain the defensive line of a football team by classifying players as nose tackle, cornerbacks, safeties, linebackers, and defensive ends. If you wanted to explain the personnel who make up an orchestra, how could you classify the various musicians? You could divide them into subgroups by age (under 30, over 30), by sex, by level of proficiency, or by type of instrument played. You can visualize classification as follows:

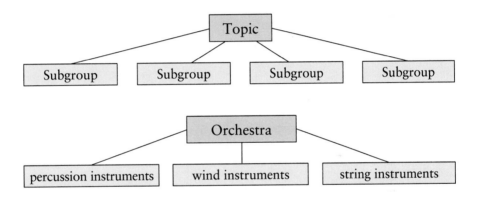

Classification is a particularly useful way to organize complex information. It is used in many situations—in daily life and in academic environments. Restaurant menu items are classified as appetizers, main courses, and desserts. Airline TV monitors classify flights by arrivals and departures. Grocery stores classify and arrange items by product type: paper products, canned foods, frozen foods, dairy, produce, and so on. Biologists classify plants by genus and species. Psychologists classify people by behavior types (normal, neurotic, psychotic), and mathematicians classify equations by complexity (binomials, trinomials). In each of these situations, the classification makes information more understandable and usable.

Deciding How to Classify

To divide a topic into groups or categories, first decide on what basis you will make the division. Suppose you must classify the restaurants in your town or city into groups. You could classify them by price, by location, or by food type. Each group represents a different way of classifying. Brainstorm to select a method of classification, then list all of the different ways you can think of to divide your topic. Here is a sample list a student wrote for classifying her friends.

age

length of friendship

type of relationship

sex

personality

occupation

marital status

closeness

shared interests

Exercise 8–3   For each of the following topics, brainstorm to discover different ways you might divide them.

1. Topic: apartments
   Ways to divide:

   _____

2. Topic: vacations
   Ways to divide:

   _____

3. Topic: boring evenings
   Ways to divide:

   _____

   _____

4. Topic: criminals
   Ways to divide:

   _____

5. Topic: travel
   Ways to divide:

   _____

   _____

Once you have brainstormed to discover possible ways of classifying, select the one that best represents or describes the topic and best fulfills your purpose for writing. Assume your topic is college professors. You could classify them according to personality, teaching style, style of dress, or age. Teaching style would be a good choice because it focuses on their job responsibility and would be very descriptive. Age, however, would not be particularly useful, unless your purpose is to show an aging trend among professors, for example.

Once you decide how you will classify, the next step is to divide your topic into subgroups. If you've decided to classify college professors according to teaching style, there are a few different subgroups to identify:

1. formal (highly structured)   3. student-oriented
   informal (casual)   subject matter-oriented
2. lecture style   4. practical
   discussion style   theoretical
   workshop style

You can create lists like these by brainstorming. If you are writing a single paragraph, select just one of these subgroups to write about. In an essay, you could write about each subgroup in a different paragraph.

Exercise 8–4   For each of the following topics, brainstorm to discover ways of classifying. Choose one way, underline it, and list the subgroups into which you could divide the topic.

1. Topic: Movies
   Ways of classifying:

   _____

   Subgroups:

   _____

   _____

2. Topic: Languages
   Ways of classifying:

   _____

   Subgroups:

   _____

   _____

3. Topic: Overnight Accommodations (Hotels/Motels)
   Ways of classifying:

   _____

   Subgroups:

   _____

   _____

4. Topic: Environmental Pollutants
   Ways of classifying:

   _____

   Subgroups:

   _____

   _____

5. Topic: Computers
Ways of classifying:

_____

Subgroups:

_____

_____

Developing Your Topic Sentence

Once you have chosen a way to classify and have identified the subgroups, you are ready to write a topic sentence. Your topic sentence should not only identify your topic, but it should also indicate the way in which you will classify items within your topic. The topic sentence also may mention the number of subgroups you will use. Here are a few examples:

1. An automobile exhaust system has four main sections.
2. Clocks come in many sizes, from watches and alarm clocks to grandfather clocks and huge outdoor digital displays.
3. Three common types of advertising media are radio, television, and newspaper.
4. By working at Denny's, I've discovered that there are three main types of customers.

Explaining Each Subgroup

The details of your paragraph should explain and provide further information about each subgroup. Depending on your topic and/or your audience, it may be necessary to define each subgroup. For instance, suppose you are answering an essay exam question that asks you to discuss how psychologists classify behavior. Because the subgroups they use are normal, neurotic, and psychotic, you would thoroughly explain each of the terms. It is often helpful to include examples as well as definitions. Examples of normal, neurotic, and psychotic behavior would demonstrate your grasp of these categories and improve your answer.

If possible, provide an equal amount of detail for each subgroup. If you define or offer an example for one subgroup, you should do the same for each of the others, as is done in the following paragraph.

Parents discipline their children in different ways. Some use physical punishment, but this can hurt the child. Others yell constantly, yet this approach does not work well because the children get used to it, and it can destroy their feelings of self-esteem. Other parents make their children feel guilty if they do something bad. This works, but then the child can suffer from guilt for his or her entire life. Some parents talk to their children and explain how to act, and when the child misbehaves, the parents explain why the action is wrong. This seems to work pretty well because the children grow up to understand right from wrong.

Arranging Your Details

In discussing your groups or categories, arrange your details in a logical sequence. A most-to-least organization can be effective because you begin with the largest or most important group or category and proceed to lesser ones. If you mention the group names in your topic sentence, be sure to list them in the order in which you will discuss them, as the following first draft exemplifies.

Unquestionably the three best football players of all time are Johnny Unitas, Jim Brown, and Joe Montana. Unitas starred as a quarterback who could pass and run the ball stunningly. Jim Brown, a running back, set a record for running the most yards. Joe Montana skillfully led winning defenses and went to the Superbowl many times.

This paragraph does divide the topic effectively. However, the writer needs to develop the paragraph further by providing additional details.

Exercise 8–5   For one of the topics in Exercise 8–4, write a paragraph classifying it into the subgroups you identified.

Testing the Effectiveness of Your Classification

In order to test the effectiveness of your groups or categories, try to think of exceptions (items or situations that don't fit into any one of your established categories). In the example mentioned earlier—orchestras—you could consider possible exceptions. Hammered dulcimers, for example, are both string *and* percussive instruments; electronic synthesizers are neither string, percussion, nor wind instruments. If you discover many exceptions, you might need to redefine your groups or expand your number of groups so that you can accommodate the exceptions. You can also revise your topic sentence to indicate that you will discuss only several large or common categories. You can restrict your topic by adding a limiting word like "most" or "common." Here are two examples:

1. Most childhood temper tantrums stem from one of the following . . .
2. Several common varieties of wine are . . .

USING DEFINITION TO EXPLAIN

■ All of us have had to explain the meaning of a term or concept at one time or another. Perhaps you've had to define your new favorite hobby or sport for a friend. Or, you may have explained new slang terms to older adults or grandparents. Maybe you defined the functions or features of a word processor to a friend who was learning to use one. In some cases, people may ask you to explain vague terms. If you said, "The movie was so *great*, I've seen it three times," your listener might ask what you mean by "great." Relative terms (those that imply a comparison with something else) also require definition. For example, you might say a coat is expensive and a car is expensive. But your listener would not assume that the coat and the car had the same dollar value. Instead, he or she would want to know what "expensive" means for each item. Finally, any discipline (history, English, biology) contains specialized vocabulary terms associated with that subject area. When you take short answer and essay exams for your college courses, you will sometimes be asked to define the terms that have been discussed in class or used in assigned readings.

Writing Your Topic Sentence

The topic sentence of a definition paragraph should identify the term you are defining. It should also place the term in a general group or class and offer a distinguishing characteristic. Here is an example:

A *mythomaniac* is a person who has an abnormal tendency to exaggerate.

The term being defined is "mythomaniac." The general group or class is "person" and the distinguishing feature is "abnormal tendency to exaggerate."

Here are two other examples:

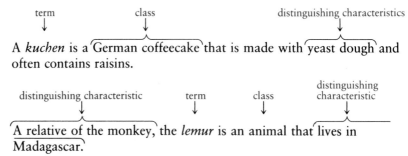

A *kuchen* is a German coffeecake that is made with yeast dough and often contains raisins.

A relative of the monkey, the *lemur* is an animal that lives in Madagascar.

The class places the term in a general group or category. In this example, it tells the reader that a lemur is an animal—*not* a person, plant, or object. The distinguishing characteristic tells how the term is different and unique from others in the same class. The lemur is distinguishable from other animals because it is monkey-like and lives in Madagascar. You can distinguish a kuchen from other coffeecakes by the fact that it contains yeast and raisins.

In writing about any term, especially an unfamiliar one, it is helpful to do some research. If possible, talk to others about their understanding of the term. Check the meaning of the term in a dictionary or glossary. Don't copy what you find. Instead, express its meaning in your own words.

Exercise 8–6   Write a topic sentence that includes a class and distinguishing characteristic for each of the following terms.

1. brat
2. holiday spirit
3. sex appeal
4. loneliness
5. autumn

Developing Your Paragraph

Usually your topic sentence will not be sufficient to give your reader a complete understanding of the term you are defining. For instance, suppose you are defining the term *discrimination,* and you write the following topic sentence:

        Discrimination is the unfair treatment of
    people because they belong to a particular
    group.

This sentence is not enough to explain the term completely to your reader. Study the several ways that follow to explain discrimination further.

1. **Give examples.** Examples can make a definition more vivid and interesting to your reader.

> Discrimination is the unfair treatment of people because they belong to a particular group. When my parents didn't talk to a new family in the neighborhood because they were of a different religion, it was discrimination. When my cousin Joan interviewed for a job and it went to a man, even though she had more experience, it was discrimination.

2. **Classify the term.** Breaking down your subject into sub-categories helps to organize your definition. For example, you might explain discrimination by classifying some of the types: racial, gender, and age.

> Discrimination is the unfair treatment of people because they belong to a particular group. One kind of discrimination is racial, as when someone is treated differently because of their ethnic background. When a person is treated differently because of his or her sex, it is gender discrimination. A third kind of discrimination is age discrimination. That occurs when people are treated differently because of how old or young they are.

3. **Explain what the term is not.** To bring the meaning of a term into focus for your reader, it is sometimes helpful to give counter examples, or to discuss ways that the term means something different from what one might expect.

> Discrimination is the unfair treatment of people because they belong to a particular group. Discrimination is not rare in America, even though America is committed to equal opportunity for all. Most people experience discrimination in some form at some time in their lives. People are discriminated against because of their race, color, age, religion, handicap,

sex, appearance, national origin, family background, or other factors that have nothing to
do with their qualifications or abilities.

4. **Trace the term's meaning over time.** If the term has changed or
expanded in meaning over time, its development may be a useful means
of explanation.

Discrimination is the unfair treatment of
people because they belong to a particular
group. In the past, discrimination meant the
ability to tell the difference between things.
People were said to have discriminating taste
in food or fashion. The ability to discriminate
was considered a positive trait. More recently,
discrimination has come to have a negative
meaning. The term now refers to prejudice
against certain people. At first, it was used
to mean only racial discrimination. Then there
was sexual discrimination against women and homosexuals. Now we have age discrimination, too.
Some businesses and organizations discriminate
against teenagers and senior citizens because
of their age.

Your details should follow a logical arrangement. Review the
previous sections of this chapter for suggestions on ways to arrange
examples or to classify. If you include both, it is usually best to give
examples first, since they are often more practical and familiar to the
reader.

Depending on the term you are defining, you may also want to
describe it or explain its function. If you are defining a centrifugal
pump, you might describe what it looks like and then explain how it
works. (Refer to Chapter 6 on Process and Chapter 7 on Description
for suggestions on developing these types of paragraphs.)

Exercise 8–7   Select one of the topic sentences you wrote for Exercise 8–6. Develop
a paragraph defining that topic.

Exercise 8–8   Revise the paragraph you wrote for Exercise 8–7. In particular, consider your organization, use of examples, and the clarity of your explanation.

HELPFUL TRANSITIONS

■   When you are writing a paragraph that uses example, classification, or definition to explain your topic, strong transitional words and phrases will help your reader follow your presentation of ideas. The table below offers useful transitions for each method of organization.

TABLE 8.1	Useful Transitions for Each Method of Organization	
Method of Organization	**Transitions**	
Example	for example, for instance	
	to illustrate, an example is . . .	
Classification	one, another, first, second, third, last, finally	
Definition	also, in addition, too, first, second, third . . .	

THINKING BEFORE READING

■   The reading "The Uses of Advertising" is an excerpt from an introductory business marketing textbook. In this skillful example of classification, the authors explain how advertising works by dividing the topic into types or subgroups, based on the different purposes that ads serve.

1. Preview the reading using the steps listed in Chapter 3, p. 43.
2. Discover what you already know about advertising by completing the following.
   a. Think of three recent television commercials you have seen. Analyze each, deciding what the advertiser wanted to accomplish and what appeals were used.
   b. Why do businesses advertise? Brainstorm a list of reasons.
   c. Write a list of the different types of appeals you've observed.

READING

■
THE USES OF ADVERTISING

William M. Pride and O. C. Ferrell

A dvertising can serve a variety of purposes. Individuals and
organizations use it to promote products and organizations, to
stimulate demand, to offset competitors' advertising, to make sales-
persons more effective, to increase the uses of a product, to remind
and reinforce customers, and to reduce sales fluctuations. [1]

PROMOTING PRODUCTS AND ORGANIZATIONS

Advertising is used to promote goods, services, ideas, images, issues, [2]
people, and indeed anything that the advertiser wants to publicize or
foster. Depending on what is being promoted, advertising can be classified as institutional or product advertising. **Institutional advertising**
promotes organizational images, ideas, or political issues. For example, some of Seagram's advertising promotes the idea that drinking
and driving do not mix, in order to create and develop a socially responsible image.

   Product advertising promotes goods and services. Business, gov- [3]
ernment, and private nonbusiness organizations turn to it to promote
the uses, features, images, and benefits of their products. When Johnson & Johnson introduced Acuvue disposable contact lenses, it used
advertising to tout the benefits of disposable lenses. Some magazine
advertisements for Acuvue lenses included a toll-free telephone number to call or postpaid card to send in to obtain more information
about the uses and benefits of the new product.

STIMULATING PRIMARY AND SELECTIVE DEMAND

When a specific firm is the first to introduce an innovation, it tries to [4]
stimulate *primary demand*—demand for a product category rather
than a specific brand of the product—through pioneer advertising. **Pioneer advertising** informs people about a product: what it is, what it
does, how it can be used, and where it can be purchased. Because pioneer advertising is used in the introductory stage of the product life
cycle when there are no competitive brands, it neither emphasizes the

Figure 1 *Stimulating primary demand.* The National Dairy Board stimulates primary demand for dairy products through the promotion of their nutritional value.

Source: Courtesy of America's Dairy Farmers. National Dairy Board.

brand name nor compares brands. The first company to introduce the compact disc player, for instance, initially tried to stimulate primary demand by emphasizing the benefits of compact disc players in general rather than the benefits of its brand. Product advertising is also used sometimes to stimulate primary demand for an established product. Occasionally, an industry trade group, rather than a single firm, sponsors advertisements to stimulate primary demand. For example, to stimulate demand for dairy products, the National Dairy Board sponsors advertisements that promote their nutritional value (see Figure 1).

To build *selective demand,* or demand for a specific brand, an advertiser turns to competitive advertising. **Competitive advertising** points out a brand's uses, features, and advantages that benefit consumers but may not be available in competing brands. For example, Volvo heavily promotes the safety and crash-worthiness of Volvo automobiles in its advertising.

An increasingly popular form of competitive advertising is **comparative advertising,** in which two or more specified brands are compared on the basis of one or more product attributes. This type of advertising is prevalent among manufacturers of hamburgers, soft drinks, toothpastes, aspirin, tires, automobiles, and a multitude of other products. However, under the Trademark Law Revision Act of

5

6

1988, marketers using comparative advertising must not misrepresent the qualities or characteristics of the comparison product. For example, a commercial for Sorrell Ridge fruit preserves told viewers that the firm's preserves are made only from fruit and fruit juice, whereas competitor J. M. Smucker Co.'s preserves consist mostly of corn syrup and refined sugar but little fruit. Although Smucker did not file suit over the advertisements, its management worried that consumers might regard Smucker's preserves as less healthy, even though Smucker, too, has an all-fruit line of preserves—a fact the comparison made by Sorrell Ridge failed to mention.[1] Thus marketers must avoid misrepresenting either their own products or those of their competitors in advertising. . . .

OFFSETTING COMPETITORS' ADVERTISING

When marketers advertise to offset or lessen the effects of a competitor's promotional program, they are using **defensive advertising.** Although defensive advertising does not necessarily increase a company's sales or market share, it may prevent a loss in sales or market share. For example, when McDonald's test-marketed pizza in Evansville, Indiana, and Owensboro, Kentucky, Pizza Hut countered with defensive advertising to protect its market share and sales. The pizza maker advertised on both television and in newspapers in the two test cities, emphasizing that its product is made from scratch while McDonald's uses frozen dough.[2] Defensive advertising is used most often by firms in extremely competitive consumer product markets, such as the fast-food industry. . . .

REMINDING AND REINFORCING CUSTOMERS

Marketers sometimes employ **reminder advertising** to let consumers know that an established brand is still around and that it has certain uses, characteristics, and benefits. Procter & Gamble, for example, reminds consumers that its Crest toothpaste is still the best one for preventing cavities. **Reinforcement advertising,** on the other hand, tries to assure current users that they have made the right choice and tells

---

1. Jeffrey A. Trachtenberg, "Advertising: New Trademark Law to Increase Perils of Comparative Advertising," *Wall Street Journal,* June 1, 1989, p. B6.
2. Scott Hume, "Pizza Hut Is Frosted; New Ad Takes Slap at McDonald's Test Product," *Advertising Age,* Sept. 18, 1989, p. 4.

them how to get the most satisfaction from the product. The aim of both reminder and reinforcement advertising is to prevent a loss in sales or market share. AT&T's advertising tells customers that its services are "the right choice." . . .

A firm's use of advertising depends on the firm's objectives, resources, and environmental forces. The degree to which advertising accomplishes the marketer's goals depends in large part on the advertising campaign.

9

Marketing, Seventh edition.

GETTING READY TO WRITE

■ *Step 1: Using Idea Mapping to Review and Organize Ideas*

Your knowledge of example, classification, and definition provides you with a useful way to organize the information that you read. By summarizing a reading's main points in chart form (see below), you will find the material easier to remember and review. Classification, definition, and examples form three headings, as shown below.

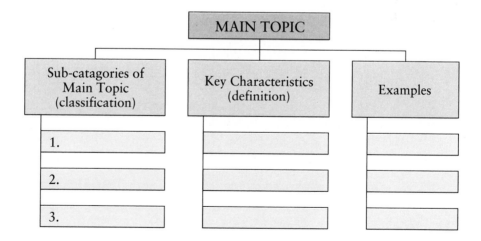

Now, complete the following idea map for *The Uses of Advertising.*

ADVERTISING		
Types of Advertising	Characteristics	Examples
1. institutional		
2. product		
3. pioneer		
4. competitive		
5. comparative		
6. defensive		
7. reminder		
8. reinforcement		

Step 2: Thinking Critically: Applying and Transferring Information

The purpose of the reading is to explain the various types of advertising. On your idea map you've recorded and learned each type and its characteristics. However, this information, like much textbook information, is of little practical value to you unless you can use and apply it to new situations. For example, knowing what defensive advertising is in the abstract or knowing that Pizza Hut once used it to defend its product against McDonald's has little practical value. What *is* important, however, is to be able to recognize defensive advertising when you see it.

A critical thinker, then, is concerned with how ideas and information can be applied or transferred to real situations. Application and transfer are often what college instructors expect, as well. They want you to be able to use what you are learning. Many assignments and test questions require this level of thinking.

Develop the habit of applying new information that you hear in lectures and read in textbooks. Ask yourself such questions as: *How can I use this? To what situations does this information apply? Where have I observed this? What are some examples of this?* When you think of an application, make a note. You'll find, too, that this type of thinking will help you remember the information. Applications connect new ideas to what you already know or have experienced, and thereby, increase your retention.

Exercise 8–9   Apply the information in *The Uses of Advertising* by thinking of or locating an example of at least five types of advertising.

Step 3: Reacting To and Discussing Ideas

Get ready to write about the reading by using the following questions to generate ideas.

1. What type(s) of advertising do you feel are most commonly used?
2. Do you think all types of advertising are equally effective?
3. Is advertising deceptive? misleading?
4. Do you listen to television and radio commercials, or do you ignore them or block them out?
5. If only a few people listen to commercials or read ads, how can they be effective?
6. Is advertising necessary? Valuable? If so, how?

WRITING ABOUT THE READING

■ *Assignment 1*

Select one type of advertising; write a paragraph explaining it by giving examples.

Assignment 2

Select a second type of advertising; write a paragraph that defines it.

WRITING ABOUT YOUR IDEAS

■ *Assignment 1*

Write a paragraph in which you classify the various responses you have to television commercials.

Assignment 2

Write a paragraph in which you explain your reactions to the use of celebrities and athletes in advertising. Use examples to support your viewpoint.

Journal Writing Suggestions

1. Write an entry describing your reaction to a recent ad or commercial. Evaluate its effectiveness.

2. Write an entry discussing your experiences with writing example, classification, and definition paragraphs. Which is easiest? Which is most difficult? Why?

REVISION CHECKLIST

1. Is your paragraph appropriate for your audience? Does it give them the background information they need? Will it interest them?
2. Will your paragraph accomplish your purpose?
3. Is your main point clearly expressed in a topic sentence?
4. Is each detail relevant? Does each explain or support the topic sentence directly?
5. Have you supported your topic sentence with sufficient detail to make it understandable and believable?
6. Did you use specific words to explain each detail?

For EXAMPLE Paragraphs
7. Does the topic sentence express a viewpoint toward the topic?
8. Does each example clearly illustrate the topic sentence?
9. Is each example understandable by itself?
10. Are there sufficient examples to explain the topic sentence to the intended audience?
11. Are the examples arranged in a logical order?
12. Are ideas connected with transitional words and phrases?

For CLASSIFICATION Paragraphs
7. Does the topic sentence identify the topic and method of classification?
8. Is each subgroup adequately explained?
9. Is equal detail provided for each subgroup?
10. Are the subgroups presented in a logical order?
11. Are ideas connected with transitional words and phrases?

For DEFINITION Paragraphs
7. Does the topic sentence identify the term to be defined?
8. Does the topic sentence identify the class to which the term belongs and include a distinguishing characteristic?
9. Does the paragraph include sufficient detail (examples, classification, negation, tracing its origin, or description)?
10. Are details arranged to make the term easily understandable (simple to complex)?
11. Are specific words and phrases used?
12. Are ideas connected with transitional words and phrases?

Dangling Modifiers

A modifier is a word or group of words that describes, qualifies, or limits the meaning of another word. When a modifier appears at the beginning of the sentence, it must be followed immediately by the word it describes. Dangling modifiers are *not* followed by the word they describe. Dangling modifiers either modify nothing in the sentence or do not clearly refer to the correct word or word group in the sentence.

DANGLING: After getting off the bus, the driver pulled away.

REVISED: After I got off the bus, the driver pulled away.

How to Correct Dangling Modifiers

There are two ways to correct dangling modifiers:

1. Add a word or words so that the modifier describes the word or words it is intended to describe. Place the new word(s) just after the modifier.

DANGLING: While sitting under the maple tree, ants started to attack.

REVISED: While sitting under the maple tree, I was attacked by ants.

2. Change the modifier to a subordinate clause. (You may need to change the verb in the modifier.)

DANGLING: After giving the dog a flea bath, the dog hid under the bed.

REVISED: After I gave the dog a flea bath, she hid under the bed.

Rate Your Ability to Spot and Correct Dangling Modifiers

Correct any dangling modifiers used in the following sentences. If the sentence is correct, mark C in front of the sentence.

1. While standing on the ladder with tar paper, Harvey patched the roof.
2. Being nervous, the test seemed more difficult than it was.
3. Waiting to drop a class at the Records Office, the line seemed to go on forever.
4. After many years, Joan had received her degree in engineering.
5. Moving the couch, the elevator was, of course, out of order.
6. Watching the evening news, the power went out.

7. After deciding to mow the lawn, it began to rain.
8. Being very tired, the long wait was unbearable.
9. Skiing downhill, the wind picked up.
10. At the age of eighteen, the phone company hired me.

Score _____

Check your answers using the Answer Key on p. 537. If you scored below 80 percent, you need additional review and practice recognizing and correcting dangling modifiers. Refer to Section D.1 of Reviewing the Basics in Part 5.

SUMMARY

■   1. Examples are particular instances or situations that explain an idea. To develop a paragraph using examples be sure that
  • your examples are relevant and sufficient.
  • each example is as specific as possible.
  • it is clear how each example illustrates your main point.
  • your examples are arranged in a logical order.
  • you use transitions to connect your ideas.

2. Classification is a way of explaining by dividing the topic into groups or parts. To explain a topic using classification,
  • decide how you will divide the topic into groups.
  • develop a topic sentence that identifies your topic as well as your method of classification.
  • explain each subgroup by giving adequate detail.
  • arrange your details in a logical order.
  • use transitions to connect your ideas.

3. Definition is a method of explaining a word's meaning. When writing definition paragraphs, be sure
  • your topic sentence identifies the term you are defining.
  • your topic sentence places the term in a general group and offers a distinguishing characteristic.
  • the paragraph is developed using examples, classifying the term, explaining what it is not, or tracing its meaning over time.
  • you use transitions to connect your ideas.

9 Comparison and Contrast

· · · ·

In this chapter you will learn to

1. Analyze similarities and differences.
2. Develop paragraphs using comparison and contrast.

Shopping for a used car? Imagine that you eventually narrow your choice to two cars—a Nissan and a Chevrolet. Each meets your basic requirements in terms of cost, mileage, and mechanical soundness. Which do you buy? How do you decide? Or, suppose you are thinking of changing your major from accounting, but you can't decide whether to switch to marketing or business administration. Again, how do you decide? In each situation, your decision-making process involves looking at similarities and differences among your options. When you consider similarities, you are comparing. When you consider differences, you are contrasting.

In your college course work, instructors will ask you to compare and contrast a variety of different ideas, events, or things. For example, your biology instructor may want you to compare two early biologists— Mendel and Darwin; your psychology instructor may ask you to analyze the differences between two (or more) theories of motivation. In some instances you will be asked to discuss only similarities or only differences, but in many instances you will need to write about both. This chapter addresses these kinds of issues. You will learn how to analyze similarities and differences and to use different methods of organization to record the results of your analysis.

Comparing and contrasting ideas can get complicated. It requires excellent planning and organization. Consequently, a major portion of this chapter is devoted to strategies for organizing your material and planning your paragraph.

IDENTIFYING SIMILARITIES AND DIFFERENCES

■ If you have two items to compare or contrast, the first step is to figure out how they are similar and how they are different. There is an effective two-step approach for this task: (1) brainstorm to write a two-column list of characteristics, and then (2) match up the items and identify points of comparison.

Brainstorming to Produce a Two-Column List

Let's say you want to write about two friends—Rhonda and Maria. Here is how to identify their similarities and differences.

1. Brainstorm and list the characteristics of each person.

Rhonda	*Maria*
shy, quiet	age, 27
age, 22	single parent, two children
reserved, private person	outgoing
friends since childhood	loves to be center of attention
married	loves sports and competition
hates parties	plays softball and tennis often
fun to shop with	
tells me everything about her life	
fun to shop with	
tells me everything about her life	

2. When you have finished your list, match up items that deal with the same feature or characteristic—similar age, personality type, marital status—as shown below.

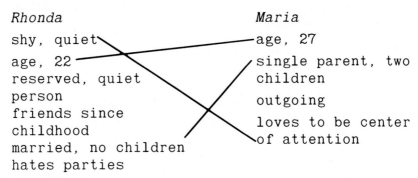

WRITING
SUCCESS
TIP 9

Building Your Concentration

• • • • • • • • • • • • • • • • •

Writing, like studying, listening, and reading, requires peak concentration. If you find that you are easily distracted, that your mind wanders while you are working, or that you are having trouble sticking with an assignment, try the following suggestions.

Eliminate Distractions

1. **Identify distractions.** As you are working, make a list of what bothers you. When you have finished working, study your list and work on finding solutions.

2. **Write down bothersome details.** When you think of an errand you need to do or a call you need to make, jot it down on a separate pad on your desk. In all probability, you'll stop thinking about it.

3. **Be "tough" with yourself.** Don't allow yourself to think about problems, friends, or other concerns. If you find you are, stand up, walk around, and clear your mind. Then return to work.

4. **Enlist the cooperation of family or roommates.** Discuss with them when and where you plan to study and write and what distracts you.

5. **Organize a place and time to write.** See Writing Success Tip 3 for hints on how to do this.

3. When you have listed an item in a certain category for one person but not for the other, try to think of a corresponding detail that will balance the lists. For instance, you listed "friends since childhood" for Rhonda, so you could indicate how long you have known Maria.

Exercise 9–1   Make a two-column list of similarities and differences for three of the following topics.

1. breakfast and dinner
2. two courses you are taking
3. two tasks (one difficult—one easy)
4. two forms of communication
5. two decisions you made recently
6. two businesses
7. two types of insurance

Build Your Motivation and Interest

No one has trouble concentrating on tasks they want to do or are interested in. Create your own motivation and interest as follows:

1. **Choose a topic that genuinely interests you.** Although it might seem faster and safer to use a topic suggested by your instructor, or the first one that pops into your head, take the time to discover a topic that you feel like writing about.

2. **Give yourself deadlines.** It is tempting to procrastinate or to work on another course assignment instead of writing. When you have a paper due, make a written list of deadlines for yourself. For example, plan that you will complete a first draft by Tuesday, complete revision by Thursday, and do a careful proofreading on Friday.

3. **Use psychological rewards.** Reward yourself with an enjoyable task like making a phone call or reading a book, after you complete a writing task.

Identifying Points of Comparison

The next step is to add a third column to your list and reorganize the list so that the items you have matched up appear next to each other. In the new, third column write the quality or characteristic that describes or categorizes each set of items in your two lists. As you do this, you may find it easier to group several items together. For example, you might group some details about Rhonda and Maria together under the category of personality. Study the following list, noticing the points of comparison that have been added in the left-hand column.

Points of Comparison	Rhonda	Maria
personality	shy, quiet reserved, private person	outgoing, loves to be center of attention
marital status	married, no children	single parent, two children
length of friendship	friends since childhood	met at work last year
shared activities	go shopping and jogging together	play softball together, go to parties

Exercise 9–2   For the three topics you chose in Exercise 9–1, match up the items and identify points of comparison.

This two-step process can work in reverse order as well. You can decide points of comparison first and then brainstorm characteristics for each point. For example, suppose you are comparing and contrasting two restaurants. Points of comparison might be location, price, speed of service, menu variety, and quality of food. Or, if you are comparing or contrasting two professors, Professors Rodriquez and Meyer, you might decide to compare them on the following points.

Point of Comparison	Professor Meyer	Professor Rodriquez
amount of homework		
type of exams		
class organization		
how easy to talk to		
grading system		
how they teach		

Then you could fill in columns two and three with appropriate details, as shown below.

Point of Comparison	Professor Meyer	Professor Rodriquez
amount of homework	assignment due for every class	hardly any
type of exams	essay	multiple choice and essay
class organization	well-organized	free and easy
how easy to talk to	always around	difficult to find
grading system	50% class participation 50% essay exams	100% exams
how they teach	lecture	class discussion, questions

Once you have completed your 3-column list, the last step is to study your list and decide whether to write about similarities or differences, or both. It is usually easier when writing a single paragraph to concentrate on one or the other. You might need to add specific examples to support your assertions.

Exercise 9–3   List at least five points of comparison for each of the following topics. Then choose one topic and make a three-column list on a separate sheet of paper.

1. Two films you have seen recently.
Points of Comparison:

a. _____

b. _____

c. _____

d. _____

e. _____

2. Hard rock and soft rock music.
Points of Comparison:

a. _____

b. _____

c. _____

d. _____

e. _____

3. Baseball and football players.
Points of Comparison:

a. _____

b. _____

c. _____

d. _____

e. _____

DEVELOPING YOUR TOPIC SENTENCE

■ Your topic sentence should identify the two subjects that you will compare or contrast. Select subjects that are neither too similar nor too different. If they are, you will have either too little or too much to say. Your topic sentence should also state whether you will focus on similarities, differences, or both. It may also indicate what points you will compare or contrast. Suppose you compare two former U.S. presidents—Reagan and Ford. Obviously, you could not cover every aspect of their presidencies in a single paragraph. Instead, you could limit your comparison to their personalities, administrative style, or popularity.

Here are a few sample topic sentences that meet the above requirements.

1. Former presidents Reagan and Ford have vastly different personalities.

2. Both Ford and Reagan used a hands-off administrative style in which they allowed their staffs to make important decisions.

3. Reagan was much more popular with the press while in office than was Ford.

Be sure to avoid topic sentences that announce what you plan to do. Here's an example: "I'll compare network news and local news and show why I prefer local news."

Exercise 9–4   Select three of the topics you worked with in either Exercise 9–1 or 9–2. Write a topic sentence for a paragraph that develops each topic you have selected.

ORGANIZING YOUR PARAGRAPH

■ Once you have identified similarities and differences and written a tentative topic sentence, you are ready to organize your paragraph. There are two ways you can organize a comparison or contrast paragraph: (1) subject-by-subject or (2) point-by-point.

Subject-by-Subject Organization

Subjects are the two specific entities you are comparing. In the subject-by-subject method, first you write about one of your subjects, and then you switch to write about the second subject. Ideally, you cover the same points of comparison for both and in the same order. Let's return to the comparison between Professors Meyer and Rodriquez. In the first half of the paragraph you discuss Professor Meyer—his class organization, exams, and grading system; in the second half you discuss Professor Rodriquez—her class organization, exams, and grading system. You can visualize this arrangement as shown below.

Subject 1	*Professor Meyer*
point A	class organization
point B	exams
point C	grading system
Subject 2	*Professor Rodriquez*
point A	class organization
point B	exams
point C	grading system

Focus on the same kinds of details to develop each subject. Discuss the same points of comparison in the same order for each one. If you are discussing only similarities or only differences, then organize your points within each topic using a most-to-least or least-to-most arrangement. If you are discussing both similarities and differences, then you might discuss points of similarity first and then points of difference, or vice versa.

Here is a sample paragraph using subject-by-subject organization.

Two very good teachers, Professor Meyer and Professor Rodriquez, present very different teaching styles. Professor Meyer is very organized. He conducts each class the same way. He reviews the assignment, lectures about the new chapter, and explains the next assignment. He gives essay exams, and they are always based on important lecture topics. Because the topics are predictable, you know you are not wasting your time when you study. Professor Meyer's grading depends half on class participation and half on the essay exams. Professor Rodriquez, on the other hand, has a free and easy-going style. Each class is different and seems to reflect whatever she thinks will help us understand what she's teaching. Her classes are fun because you never know what to expect. Professor Rodriquez gives both multiple choice and

essay exams. These are difficult to study for
because they are unpredictable. Our final grade
is based entirely on the exams, so each exam
requires a lot of studying beforehand. Although
each professor teaches very differently, I am
figuring out how to learn from each particular
style.

Exercise 9–5   Write a comparison and contrast paragraph using the subject-by-subject method of organization. Use one of the topics you worked with in Exercise 9–1 or 9–2.

Point-by-Point Organization

In the point-by-point method of organization, you discuss both of your subjects together for each point of comparison. For the paragraph on Professors Meyer and Rodriquez, you would talk about how each organizes his or her class, then move to your next point of comparison—exams—describing each, and then describe the grading system each uses.

You can visualize this organization as follows:

Point A: class organization	Subject 1: Professor Meyer
	Subject 2: Professor Rodriquez
Point B: exams	Subject 1: Professor Meyer
	Subject 2: Professor Rodriquez
Point C: grading system	Subject 1: Professor Meyer
	Subject 2: Professor Rodriquez

When using this organization, keep your paragraph parallel by consistently discussing the same subject first for each point. (That is, always discuss Professor Meyer first and Professor Rodriquez second for each point.)

If your paragraph focuses on only similarities or only differences, then arrange your points in a least-to-most or most-to-least pattern. If you're discussing both similarities and differences, discuss similarities first and the differences second, or vice versa.

Here is a sample paragraph using point-by-point organization.

Professor Meyer and Professor Rodriquez demonstrate very different teaching styles in how
they operate their classes, how they give exams, and how they grade us. Professor Meyer's

classes are highly organized; we work through the lesson every day in the same order. Professor Rodriquez uses an opposite approach. She creates a lesson to fit the material, which enables us to learn the most. Their exams differ too. Professor Meyer gives standard, predictable essay exams that are based on his lectures. Professor Rodriquez gives both multiple choice and essay exams, so we never know what to expect. In addition, each professor grades differently. Professor Meyer counts class participation as half of our grade, so if you talk in class and do reasonably well on the exams, you will probably pass the course. Professor Rodriquez, on the other hand, counts the exams 100 percent, so you *have* to do well on them to pass the course. Each professor uses unique, enjoyable teaching styles, but I feel more relaxed with Professor Rodriquez.

Exercise 9–6   Write a comparison and contrast paragraph using the point-by-point method of organization. Use the same topic you chose for Exercise 9–5.

Developing Your Points of Comparison

As you discuss each point, don't feel as if you must have a comparison or contrast in every sentence. Your paragraph should not just list similarities and/or differences. For every point, provide explanation, descriptive details, and examples.

Try to maintain a balance in your treatment of each subject and each point of comparison. Give equal attention to each point and each subject. If you give an example for one subject, try to do so for the other subjects as well.

USEFUL TRANSITIONS

■   Transitions are particularly important in comparison and contrast paragraphs. Because you are discussing two subjects and covering similar points for each, your readers can easily become confused. Table 9-1 lists commonly used transitional words and phrases.

TABLE 9-1	**Transitions for Comparison-Contrast Paragraphs**
To show similarities	likewise, similarly, in the same way, too, also
To show differences	however, on the contrary, unlike, on the other hand

Each method of organization uses different transitions in different places. If you use a subject-by-subject organization, you'll need the strongest transition in the middle of the paragraph, when you switch from one subject to another. You will also need a transition each time you move from one point to another within the same subject. In the following paragraph, notice the underlined transition sentence.

Two dogs of the same breed may look similar, but they can have completely different personalities. My two golden retrievers, Meg and Dude, are good examples. Meg is shy and is afraid of her own shadow. When guests arrive, she quivers and whines and runs to hide in the basement. Dude, on the other hand, is completely the opposite. He is forward and pushy. He eagerly greets guests and lets them know whether he likes them. Dude is alert and protective. He occupies a good part of each day watching cars pass the house, growling at any that drive by too slowly. Despite their differences, Meg and Dude are both lovable companions.

This paragraph uses a subject-by-subject organization. A strong transition emphasizes the change from Meg to Dude.

If you use point-by-point organization, use transitions as you move from one subject to the other. Your reader needs to know quickly whether the two subjects are similar or different on each point. Here is an example:

Although colds and hay fever are both annoying, their symptoms and causes differ. Hay fever causes my eyes to itch and water. I sneeze excessively, bothering those around me. Colds, on the other hand, make me feel stuffy, with a runny nose and a cough. For me, hay fever arrives in the summer, but colds linger on through late fall, winter, and early spring. Their causes differ, too. Pollens produce hay fever. I am most sensitive to pollen from wild flowers and corn tassels. Unlike hay fever, viruses, which are passed from person to person by air or body contact, cause colds.

Notice that each time the writer switched from hay fever to colds, a transition was used.

Exercise 9–7   Reread the paragraphs you wrote for Exercises 9–4 and 9–5. Add transitions to make your organization clearer.

THINKING BEFORE READING

■ This reading was taken from an article that originally appeared in the periodical, *American Demographics*. The article includes statistics that indicate a discrepancy between Americans' concern for the environment and the action they are willing to take to improve it. This reading is a good example of comparison and contrast organization. As you read, notice how the writer organizes his ideas.

1. Preview the reading using the steps described on page 43.
2. Activate your thinking by answering the following.
   a. What environmental problems exist in your state, city, or community?
   b. What actions are taken in your community to protect the environment?
   c. What actions have you taken to preserve or improve the environment?

READING

■

THE ENVIRONMENT:
WHAT WE SAY VERSUS WHAT WE DO

Joe Schwartz and Thomas Miller

Saving the environment is a high priority for most American citizens. But as consumers, most of us are not willing to act on our beliefs. Over three-quarters (78 percent) of adults say that our nation must "make a major effort to improve the quality of our environment," according to a recent study commissioned by S. C. Johnson and Son and conducted by the Roper Organization. But at the same time, most say that individuals can do little, if anything, to help improve the environment.

Public concern about the environment is growing faster than concerns about any other issue monitored by Roper—at least before the Persian Gulf crisis and the softening of the economy. Businesses are tuning into this trend by producing "green" products, services, and advertising campaigns. But banking on environmental awareness can backfire, because the majority of Americans are already convinced that businesses are not environmentally responsible. . . .

2

Americans tend to blame businesses for the environmental problems they see at global, national, and local levels. More than eight in 10 Americans say that industrial pollution is the main reason for our environmental problems, and nearly three-quarters of the public say that the products businesses use in manufacturing also harm the environment. Six in 10 Americans blame businesses for not developing environmentally sound consumer products, and an equal share believes that some technological advancements made by businesses eventually produce unanticipated environmental problems.

3

Americans tend to blame businesses for the environmental problems they see at global, national, and local levels. More than eight in 10 Americans say that industrial pollution is the main reason for our environmental problems, and nearly three-quarters of the public say that the products businesses use in manufacturing also harm the environment. Six in 10 Americans blame businesses for not developing environmentally sound consumer products, and an equal share believes that some technological advancements made by businesses eventually produce unanticipated environmental problems.

4

5

Consumer behavior usually affects the environment at two points. First, consumers can either buy or reject environmentally unsound products. After the purchase, they affect the environment by either recycling products or sending them to the dump.

6

At the moment, recycling appears to be the most rapidly growing pro-environmental behavior. Between March 1989 and February 1990, the share of Americans who say they regularly recycle bottles and cans rose from 41 percent to 46 percent, and the share who regularly recycle newspapers rose from 20 percent to 26 percent. Those who sort their trash on a regular basis rose from 14 percent to 24 percent of all adults.

7

Altruism[1] isn't the only force behind the recycling boom. Many states and municipalities have passed "bottle bills" and other mandatory recycling laws. People may be complying with the new rules and may even be doing more than is required. But in many cases, legislation stimulated their behavioral changes.

8

1. concern for the welfare of others

More than half of all adults (52 percent) never recycle newspa- 9
pers. Only 16 percent say they avoid products that come from environmentally irresponsible companies, and just seven percent regularly
avoid restaurants that use foam containers. Only eight percent of
Americans say they regularly cut down on their driving to protect the
environment. More than three-quarters (76 percent) say they just mo-
tor on as usual, even though most acknowledge that emissions from
private automobiles are a leading cause of air pollution. . . .

The first stage—deep public concern about environmental prob- 10
lems—has certainly been reached. So far, voters have been largely un-
willing to take the next step and approve sweeping changes. But the
important attitudinal shifts of the 1980s should gradually change environmental behavior in the 1990s.

Vast majorities of Americans are worried about our environmen- 11
tal future. So far, only a minority have adopted more environmentally responsible lifestyles. But attitudinal changes generally precede
behavioral ones. The stage is finally set for the "greening of
America."

American Demographics, February, 1991.

GETTING READY TO WRITE

■ *Step 1: Using the Three-Column List for Review*
The three-column list that you constructed to organize your ideas before
writing also may be used as an effective study and review technique.
As you read other writers' comparison and contrast pieces, organize
your notes on their ideas into three-column format. A three-column list
for the reading, "The Environment: What We Say Versus What We
Do" would be organized as follows:

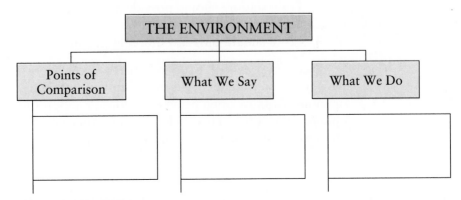

Exercise 9–8   Complete the above three-column list by supplying details contained in the reading.

Step 2: Thinking Critically: Distinguishing Fact from Opinion

Facts are statements that can be tested as either true or false. Opinions are statements that express attitudes, feelings, judgments, and beliefs. Opinions are neither true nor false. Here are a few examples of each:

> *Facts*
> 1. It is raining outside.
> 2. My math instructor canceled class yesterday to enter an advanced math contest.
> 3. Fifty-two percent of Americans never recycle newspapers.
> 4. Twenty-four percent of all American adults sort their trash.

> *Opinions*
> 1. It looks like it might rain later.
> 2. My math instructor is overqualified, but he is undermotivated.
> 3. Train stations should provide bins so commuters can more easily recycle their newspapers.
> 4. Cities should pass laws forcing people to sort their trash.

Facts, if provided by a reliable source, are generally accepted. However, you have the right to question and disagree with an author's opinions. Authors often provide reasons or supporting evidence for the opinions they offer. This evidence helps you evaluate and decide which ideas to question and which ideas to accept.

To evaluate opinions, ask questions such as:

- What evidence does the author give to support these opinions?
- Have you heard or read differing opinions on the same topic?
- How does the author's opinion fit with what you already know about the subject?

Exercise 9–9   1. List five opinion statements for which the author gives supporting evidence in the reading on pages 179–181. After each, indicate what supporting evidence is provided.

Opinion   *Supporting Evidence*

1. _____   _____

    _____   _____

2. _____   _____

    _____   _____

3. _____   _____

    _____   _____

4. _____   _____

    _____   _____

5. _____   _____

    _____   _____

2. Review the reading to locate opinion statements for which supporting evidence is not provided. List them below.

Unsupported Opinions

_____

_____

_____

_____

_____

_____

Step 3: Reacting to and Discussing Ideas

Use the following questions to generate ideas about the reading.

1. What method of organization did the author use?

2. Why do you think there is a discrepancy between belief and action about environmental problems?

3. What can or should be done to encourage Americans to *act* responsibly toward the environment?

4. For what other issues do you think a discrepancy between belief and action exists?

5. Describe what you consider an environmentally responsible lifestyle includes.

WRITING ABOUT THE READING

■ *Assignment 1*

Drawing from the information contained in the reading, write a paragraph that compares an environmentally responsible lifestyle with an environmentally irresponsible one. Develop your paragraph using subject-by-subject organization.

Assignment 2

Rewrite the paragraph you wrote in Assignment 1. Use a point-by-point organization.

WRITING ABOUT YOUR IDEAS

■ *Assignment 3*

Write a paragraph discussing the discrepancy you have observed between someone's belief and his or her subsequent actions regarding one of the following topics.

a. telling lies
b. nutritional or eating habits
c. job responsibility
d. punctuality
e. loyalty to friends or family

Assignment 4

Write a paragraph contrasting what is said versus what occurs on your campus or in your community regarding one of the following issues.

  a. date rape
  b. racial discrimination
  c. gay rights
  d. cheating

Journal Writing Suggestions

  1. Write a journal entry about a situation in which your actions were or were not consistent with your beliefs.
  2. Write a journal entry describing your success and/or difficulty in writing or organizing comparison and contrast paragraphs.

REVISION CHECKLIST

  1. Is your paragraph appropriate for your audience? Does it give them the background information they need? Will it interest them?
  2. Will your paragraph accomplish your purpose?
  3. Is your main point clearly expressed in a topic sentence?
  4. Is each detail relevant? Does each explain or support the topic sentence directly?
  5. Have you supported your topic sentence with sufficient detail to make it understandable and believable?
  6. Do you use specific words to explain each detail?

For COMPARISON AND CONTRAST Writing
  7. Does your topic sentence identify the two subjects that you compare or contrast?
  8. Does your topic sentence indicate whether you will focus on similarities or differences, or both?
  9. Is your paragraph organized using a subject-by-subject or point-by-point arrangement?
  10. For each point of comparison, have you provided sufficient explanation, descriptive details, or examples?
  11. Have you used transitions to indicate changes from subject to subject or point to point?

Misplaced Modifiers

Misplaced modifiers are words or phrases that do not modify or explain the words the way the writer intends them to explain.

> MISPLACED: Crispy and spicy, the waitress served the chicken wings to our table. [Was the waitress crispy and spicy or were the wings?]
> CORRECT: The waitress served the crispy, spicy chicken wings to our table.
> MISPLACED: I saw a dress in a magazine that cost $1200. [Did the magazine or the dress cost $1200?]
> CORRECT: In a magazine, I saw a dress that cost $1200.
> MISPLACED: Already late for class, the red light delayed'Joe even longer. [Was the light or Joe delayed?]
> CORRECT: The red light delayed Joe, already late for class, even longer.

How to Avoid Misplaced Modifiers

To avoid misplaced modifiers, be sure to place the modifier immediately before or after the word or words it modifies.

Rate Your Ability to Spot and Correct Misplaced Modifiers

Identify and correct the sentences containing misplaced modifiers.

1. Studiously, the test was previewed by Marietta before she began answering the questions.

2. The book was checked out by a student that Mark had returned late.

3. Keshim proudly turned in his research paper that had taken two months to complete.

4. Shocked, the article about the large donations political candidates receive from interest groups caused Lily to reconsider how she viewed candidates and their campaign promises.

5. The student loan check was cashed by Bryant that was desperately needed.

6. Angry with the delay, the referee finally arrived and the crowd booed.

7. Called aboriginals, the native people of Australia have a culture rich with hunting skills and legends.

8. Young, unhappy and love-lorn, the poetry of Emily Dickinson reveals a particular kind of misery and pain.

9. A national problem, the governors of all the states met to discuss homelessness.

10. Concerned about the risk of being exposed to the virus, many AIDS patients are refused treatment by health care workers.

Score _____

Check your answers using the Answer Key on page 537. If you scored below 80 percent, you need additional review and practice in recognizing and correcting misplaced modifiers. Refer to Section D.1. of Reviewing the Basics in Part 5.

SUMMARY

■   1. Comparison and contrast paragraphs explain similarities and/or differences between two or more subjects.

2. To develop ideas
   • use a two-column list to identify similarities and differences.
   • add a third column to your list to describe or categorize items in your list.

3. Your topic sentence should
   • identify the two subjects that you will compare or contrast.
   • indicate whether you will focus on similarities or differences, or both.

4. Organize your paragraph using either
   • subject-by-subject organization, or
   • point-by-point organization.

5. For each point of comparison, be sure to provide sufficient explanation, details, or examples.

6. Use transitions to indicate changes from subject to subject or point to point.

10   Cause and Effect

In this chapter you will learn to

1. Understand cause and effect relationships.
2. Plan and organize cause and effect paragraphs.

Each day we face situations that require cause and effect thinking. Some are daily events; others mark important life decisions. Why won't my car start? Why didn't I get my student loan check? What will happen if I skip class today? How will my family react if I decide to get married? We seek to make sense of and control our lives by understanding why things happen (causes) and what will happen as a result (effects).

Cause and effect is a common method of organizing and discussing ideas. Cause and effect thinking is used in many courses of study. In psychology, for example, you might study:

why children are self-centered	(causes)
what causes phobias (fears)	(causes)
the effects of depression	(effects)
how people react to stress	(effects)

You will also find yourself writing in the cause and effect mode or pattern in both personal and academic situations, as illustrated below.

Personal Examples	**Academic Examples**
a letter to a bank explaining why a loan payment is late	essay exams that begin with "Explain why" or "Discuss the causes of . . ."

a car accident report to an insurance company explaining how an accident occurred

a letter to your parents explaining why you need money

assignments that ask you to agree or disagree with a statement and explain your reasons

exercises that ask you to predict outcomes of a recent political event

DISTINGUISHING BETWEEN CAUSE AND EFFECT

■ To write about causes and effects, you must understand their relationship. The first step is to distinguish the causes from the effects. Let's consider an everyday situation: You turn the ignition key, but your car won't start because it's out of gas. This is a simple case in which one cause produces one effect. You can visualize this situation as follows:

Cause   **Effect**

out of gas ─────────────→ car won't start

Here are a few other examples of one cause producing one effect:

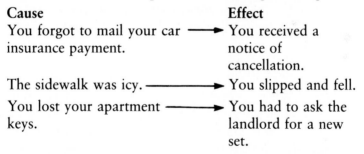

Cause	Effect
You forgot to mail your car insurance payment.	You received a notice of cancellation.
The sidewalk was icy.	You slipped and fell.
You lost your apartment keys.	You had to ask the landlord for a new set.

Most situations, however, are much more complicated than those shown above, and even a simple cause and effect sequence may contain hidden complexities. Perhaps your car was out of gas because you forgot to buy gas last night, and you forgot because you were making other preparations for the upcoming visit of a good friend. Suppose you missed your math class because the car would not start, and an exam was scheduled that day. Missing the exam gave you a low average and, as a result, you failed the course. You can see, then, that cause and effect often work like a chain reaction, each affecting the next.

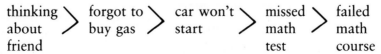

thinking about friend > forgot to buy gas > car won't start > missed math test > failed math course

Using a Computer to Organize and Write Papers

Word processing has numerous advantages for writers (see Success Tip 6). Among them are some features that are particularly helpful in planning, organizing, and drafting essays. Here are some ideas of how to use a computer for each step in the writing process.

1. Generating Ideas

Three methods of generating ideas—brainstorming, freewriting, and questioning—work well on the computer. (Branching is best done with pen and paper). Try dimming your screen so you don't see what you're typing, and don't become concerned with correctness or typing errors. After you have finished, usable ideas can be easily moved to a new list or unusable ideas easily deleted.

2. Organizing Your Ideas

Word processing allows you to change and rearrange ideas easily. The copy function allows you to try two or three arrangements of ideas at once. Because two or three different versions won't fit on the screen at one time, you may find it easier to print paper copies and use them for comparison.

3. Writing a First Draft

When you type your first draft on the computer, it is reassuring to know that you won't have to rewrite it to make changes and revisions. If you find you cannot compose on the computer, handwrite your first draft and then type it in. As you're typing, you'll find yourself making changes and getting ideas for further revision.

Other times, there are many causes that contribute to a single effect or many effects that result from a single cause. For example, there may be several reasons why you decided to major in accounting:

Causes	Effect
1. liked business in high school	
2. attractive salary	accounting major
3. uncle is an accountant	
4. good with mathematics	

4. Revising

The add, delete, move, and copy commands allow you to make numerous changes easily. If you decide to take out several sentences or an entire paragraph, move them to the end of the essay (separated from the essay by a few blank lines) instead of deleting them entirely. You may find in further revisions that you want to use some or all of the ideas.

You may find that you get more ideas for revision if you print and read a hard copy of your essay. Without a printed copy, you can only see a screen-full at a time and it may be difficult, at first, for you to evaluate your flow of ideas.

5. Proofreading

Final error correction is easily done on the computer. If you find it difficult to spot errors on the screen, work from a paper copy instead.

Finally, be sure to save your document frequently—every five or ten minutes, so you don't lose your work. When you have finished, save your finished product, even if you don't plan to make further changes. You'll want a record of what you've submitted.

There may be several effects of a decision to reduce your hours at your part-time job.

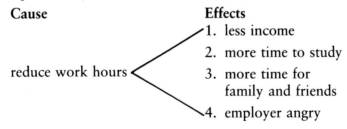

Multiple causes and multiple effects, then, are common. To distinguish among them, ask questions. To find causes ask, "Why did this happen?" To identify effects ask, "What happened because of this?"

When analyzing a cause and effect situation that you plan to write about, ask yourself the following questions:

1. What are the causes? What are the effects? (To help answer the questions, draw a diagram of the situation.)
2. Which should be emphasized—cause or effect?
3. Are there single or multiple causes and single or multiple effects?
4. Is a chain reaction involved?

Exercise 10–1   Indicate whether each of the following statements could be a topic sentence for a paragraph about causes or a paragraph about effects.

1. There are several reasons I decided to move to a different apartment. _____

2. The location of my new apartment has made transportation much less of a problem for me. _____

3. The price of luxury items is determined by public demand for them. _____

4. There are numerous reasons for the popularity of cable television. _____

5. Because advertising can be misleading and deceptive, both state and federal laws were passed to regulate it. _____

Exercise 10–2   Choose two of the following topics and write lists of possible causes and effects. Label each either "C" for cause or "E" for effect.

1. the popularity of _____ television program
2. children who misbehave
3. the popularity of horror films
4. alcoholism among teenagers
5. employee theft

DEVELOPING THE TOPIC SENTENCE

■   To write effective topic sentences for cause and effect paragraphs, follow these suggestions:

1. **Clarify the cause and effect relationship.** Before you write, carefully identify what are causes and what are effects. If you are uncertain, divide a sheet of paper into two columns. Label one column "causes" and the other "effects." Brainstorm about your topic, placing your ideas in the appropriate column.

2. **Decide whether to emphasize causes or effects.** In a single paragraph, it is best to focus on either causes or effects—not both. For example, suppose you are writing about students who drop out of college. You need to decide whether to discuss why they drop out (causes) or what happens to students who drop out (effects). Your topic sentence should define the relationship and indicate whether you are discussing causes or effects.

3. **Determine if the events are related or independent.** Analyze the causes or effects to discover if they occurred as part of a chain reaction or whether they are not related to one another. Your topic sentence should suggest the type of relationship you are writing about.

If you are writing about a chain of events, your topic sentence should reflect this. For example, "A series of events led up to my sister's decision to drop out of college." If the causes or effects are independent, then your sentence might indicate this. For example, "Students drop out of college for a number of different reasons."

Now read the following paragraph a student wrote on the topic of advertising for children. Notice that the topic sentence makes it clear that she is focusing on reasons and that they are independent of one another.

> Advertising intended for children should be limited to facts for three reasons. First, because parents teach children to obey and respect adults, children tend to accept as truth whatever an adult on a commercial tells them. Second, children do not have the ability to sort out accurate claims from misleading ones. They do not have enough experience or sophistication to question the claims advertisers make. Finally, because children are not emotionally mature, they tend to overreact to emotional appeals. Therefore, it is unfair to appeal to and to manipulate them in the same way in which advertisers treat adults.

Exercise 10–3   Review the lists you wrote for Exercise 10–2. Write a topic sentence for a paragraph that will explain either causes *or* effects of each situation.

ORGANIZING SUPPORTING DETAILS

■ Providing supporting details for cause and effect paragraphs requires careful thought and planning. You must provide relevant and sufficient support and organize your details effectively.

Providing Relevant and Sufficient Support

Each specific cause or effect you describe must be relevant to the situation introduced in your topic sentence. Suppose you are writing a paragraph explaining the reasons you decided to attend college. Each sentence must explain why you are attending college. You could not include ideas, for example, about how college is different from what you expected.

If, while writing, you discover many ideas about how college is different from what you expected, then you need to revise your topic sentence in order to refocus your paragraph on this new topic.

Each cause or reason requires explanation, particularly if it is *not* completely clear or obvious. For example, it is not sufficient to write, "One reason I decided to attend college was to advance my position in life." This sentence needs further explanation. For example, you could discuss the types of advancement (financial, job security, job satisfaction) you hope to attain.

Jot down a list of the causes or reasons you plan to include. This process may help you think of additional ones and will give you a chance to consider how to explain or support each cause or reason. You might decide to eliminate one or to combine several. Here is a list of reasons one student wrote for deciding to attend college.

```
get a better job

meet new friends

get higher salary

get more respect from family

get interesting job I enjoy
```

By listing his reasons, this student realized that the first reason—to get a better job—was too general and was covered more specifically later in the list, so he eliminated it. He also realized that "get higher salary" and "get interesting job" could be combined. Then he wrote the following paragraph.

```
     There are three main reasons I decided to
attend Ambrose Community College. First, and
most important to me, I want to get a high pay-
ing, interesting job that I will enjoy. Right
now, the only jobs I can get pay minimum wage,
and as a result, I'm working in fast-food
places or stores. This kind of job doesn't make
me proud of myself, and I get bored with rou-
tine tasks. Second, my parents have always
wanted me to have a better job than they do,
and I know my father will not respect me until
I do. A college degree will make them proud of
me. A third reason for attending school is to
```

```
meet new friends. It is hard to meet people,
and everyone in my neighborhood seems stuck in
a rut. I want to meet other people who are in-
terested in improving themselves like I am.
```

Organizing Your Details

There are several ways to arrange the details in a cause and effect paragraph. The method you choose depends on your purpose in writing, as well as the topic about which you are writing. Suppose you are writing a paragraph about the effects of a hurricane on a coastal town. Several different arrangements of details are possible:

1. **Chronological.** A chronological organization consists of arranging your details in the order in which they happened. The order in which the hurricane damage occurred becomes the order for your description in the paragraph. This arrangement is similar to the arrangement you have learned to use for narration and process (Chapter 6). A chronological arrangement works for situations and events that occurred in a specific order.

2. **Order-of-importance.** In an order-of-importance organization, the details are arranged from least-to-most important or from most-to-least important. In describing the effects of the hurricane, you could discuss the most severe damage first and then describe damage of lesser importance. Or, you could build up to the most important for dramatic effect.

3. **Spatial.** Spatial arrangement of details uses physical or geographical position as a means of organization. In describing the hurricane damage, you could start by describing damage to the beach and work toward the center of town.

4. **Categorical.** This form of arrangement divides the topic into parts or categories. To describe hurricane damage using this arrangement, you could describe what the storm did to businesses, roads, city services, and homes.

As you can see from the example of hurricane damage, there are many ways to organize cause and effect details. Each has a different emphasis and achieves a different purpose. The organization you choose, then, depends on the point you want to make.

Once you have chosen which method of organization to use, return to your preliminary list of causes or reasons. Study your list again, make changes, eliminate, or combine items. Then rearrange or number your list to indicate the order in which you will include them in your paragraph.

Exercise 10–4   Write a paragraph developing one of the topic sentences you wrote in Exercise 10–3. Be sure to include relevant and sufficient detail. Organize your paragraph using one of the methods described above.

Exercise 10–5   Choose one of the following topic sentences and develop a paragraph using it. Organize your paragraph using one of the methods described above.

1. Caffeine has several negative effects on the body.
2. Professional athletes deserve (or do not deserve) the high salaries they are paid.
3. There are several reasons why parents should reserve time each day to spend with their children.
4. Video games are popular among teenagers for several reasons.

HELPFUL TRANSITIONS

■ To blend your details smoothly, use the transitions listed below:

TABLE 10-1   **Useful Transitions**

For causes	**For effects**
because, due to, one cause is . . . , another is . . . , since, for, first, second	consequently, as a result, thus, resulted in, one result is . . . , another is . . . , therefore

The student paragraph on p. 194–195 is a good example of how transitions are used. Notice how the transitions function as markers and help you to locate each separate reason.

Exercise 10–6   In the blank provided, supply a transitional word or phrase that strengthens the connection between the two ideas.

1. No known cure exists for the common cold _____ it is a virus.

2. Computers provide an easy way to store and process information quickly. _____ computers have permeated every aspect of society.

3. Animal skins are warm and very durable; _____ almost every culture has made use of them for clothing or shelter.

4. _____ some people refused to accept his views and beliefs, Martin Luther King, Jr. was brutally murdered.

Exercise 10–7   Reread the paragraphs you wrote in Exercises 10–4 and 10–5. Add transitional words and phrases, if needed, to connect your details.

THINKING BEFORE READING

■   The following reading is a good example of cause and effect organization. It is taken from a book titled: *Deadly Consequences: How Violence Is Destroying Our Teenage Population and a Plan to Begin Solving the Problem*, written by a medical doctor.

1. Preview the reading using the steps listed on p. 43.
2. Activate your thinking by completing the following.
   a. Write a list of words that describe your attitude toward police.
   b. Describe the attitude toward police in your community.
   c. Are crime and drug sales problems in your city or community? What is being done to control them?
   d. Do you think the 911 emergency phone system is effective in controlling or reducing crime? Why or why not?

READING

■

COMMUNITY POLICING

Deborah Prothrow-Stith, M.D. with Michaele Weissman

Reducing adolescent violence in poor neighborhoods requires   1
the effort of all the institutions that shape people's lives—especially the police. The police are inextricably involved in the violence
that bedevils poor communities. Many poor people blame the police
for instigating violence and for failing to curtail violence in their communities. They think that if the police really cared they would restore
order and end the mayhem on city streets. African-Americans in particular resent the way their sons and other males are demeaned by
the police. They interpret the search-on-sight policies of many urban
police forces as proof that the police despise and assail black man-
hood. For their part, many white police officers look at non-white
communities and all they see is trouble and disarray. They do not recognize the strength, the health, the diversity, and the resilience in minority families, in minority churches, and in other minority institutions. Many police officers have trouble even seeing that poor people
of color are victimized by violence and by crime more than any other
of our citizens. Instead, the police focus on the hostile attitude with
which their presence is often greeted and they feel betrayed by the
very citizens they say they are risking their lives to protect.

Neither side in this round robin of dislike and misunderstanding   2
has much sympathy for the other, and neither side approaches the
other in a manner likely to reduce violence. Instead, there is a stalemate.[1] Those in desperate need of police services and those who are
paid to provide desperately needed police services often do not understand, like, or communicate with one another. In general, this is the
case even when the police officers in question are members of minority groups.

So long as police officers spend their shifts in patrol cars, I think   3
this stalemate will continue. Inside a car police officers are basically
anonymous, unaccountable, and far removed from the life of the
street. Much of the ill will between police and local people stems
from the absence of contact between them. When police officers walk

---

1. deadlock, situation in which further action is impossible

a beat the relationship is changed for the better. Anyone can approach a cop on the beat. People get to know one another. Officers become part of the community they serve. The sense of menace disappears from the relationship.

A new brand of policing that advocates the return of foot patrol interests me very much—not only as a tactic for improving police-community relations, but also as a method of combatting crime. Community policing, as it is called, is the public health of police work. Like public health, community policing emphasizes prevention. Numerous police departments are already experimenting with this far-reaching new method of police work. The most prominent convert is New York City's Police Commissioner Lee Brown, who served as the chief of police in Houston from 1982 to early 1990.   4

Community policing is based on a handful of hard-hitting realizations about the failure of modern police techniques to curb crime, violence, or social decay. Each of these insights is supported by computer-generated data. Among them: 5

—As many as half of all police calls come from as few as 3 percent of locations, or "hotspots."

—A vast increase in the number of arrests has over-crowded courts and prisons, but done nothing to reduce crime.

—Deploying officers in patrol cars to respond to radio calls is a poor way to fight crime and an ineffective way to make the streets safe.

—The 911 system is an albatross.[2] Responding quickly to crimes that have already occurred does nothing to make the streets safe.

—The current police emphasis on responding to major crime such as murder, rape, and robbery, while ignoring minor crime such as vandalism, purse snatchings, and public drinking hastens the decline of deteriorating neighborhoods, while failing to lead to an increase in public safety.

Supporters of community policing say the first crucial step toward improving big city policing is restoring foot patrols. The second even more radical step on the community policing agenda is to reorganize the way police work is done. Instead of reacting to every criminal act as if it were a unique occurrence, supporters say officers need to approach the problem more holistically.[3] What are the larger   6

2. constant burden
3. emphasizing the whole and relationship of its parts

problems connecting apparently unrelated events? Instead of intermit-
tently arresting the low-level drug dealers who congregate on a darkened basketball court in the park, community policing boosters suggest police should approach this "hotspot" analytically. If night after
night dealers gather on a darkened playground, instead of arresting
them only to see them released a few hours later, why not change the
circumstances that create the problem? One community policing solution might be to flood the park with high density light, creating a desirable environment for basketball, softball, and rugby, but an undesirable one for dealing drugs.

The community policing approach does not measure success by   7
the number of arrests made. In fact, a successful solution can mean a
reduction in the number of arrests. When the now brightly lit park is
used for recreation instead of drug dealing, the number of violent incidents and arrests there will decline. In their book, *Beyond 911*,
Mark Moore, Malcolm Sparrow, and David Kennedy report that this
is just what happened in the Link Valley section of Houston in 1988
when a coalition[4] of community activists and a local police sergeant
joined forces to drive the cocaine dealers out of the neighborhood.
Link Valley is near the freeway. Most of the users who purchased
drugs there were white suburbanites who took a quick detour off the
highway on their way home from work. Believing that this kind of
user would do anything to avoid exposure, the coalition heavily pub-
licized the fact that they would be setting up roadblocks and arresting drug buyers in Link Valley, and that's just what they did. After several months of planning, police sealed off most access routes
into the neighborhood. Residents received stickers so they could enter and depart unbothered. Everyone else who entered the neighborhood was questioned politely by police. Few drug purchasers showed
up to buy drugs that day, or ever again. There were few arrests.

The coalition, of course, considered this a success, not a failure.   8
The anti-buyer initiative, however, was only one piece of an overall
strategy. Other steps included tracking down the landlords of the
abandoned buildings where drug dealers did their business and legally compelling them to raze[5] or secure their structures. The police
and community also organized a highly successful garbage cleanup.
In one day, ten semitrailer-sized dumpsters full of filth were hauled
out of the neighborhood. This is hardly the way the police fight
drugs on *Miami Vice*, but it worked! Before, police had made hun-

4. group with a specific purpose
5. tear down, demolish

dreds of arrests in Link Valley. Still, the community was dying a drug-induced death. After the campaign, the community was revived. Residents felt safe again. Calls for police service in this neighborhood decreased by 44 percent. Nor did the dealers simply move next door. Calls for service in surrounding communities also declined significantly.

What worked in Link Valley would not necessarily work in East Harlem. Each police problem requires different solutions. One of the strengths of the community policing model is that it sets free the intelligence of the police. Officers no longer simply react to events. They look for root causes. Within a specific community the mission of the police becomes one of stopping crime by preventing crime. When police and community people work together to solve problems, the result can heal old wounds. Officers who work side by side with local residents get to know young black males as someone's son, someone's nephew. The ill will between anonymous cop and anonymous kid can be defused. Young males, too, can get a chance to know police officers as people who are present in the community to help. In this new police context, I hope some of the terrible bitterness that has poisoned relations between police and inner city communities can begin to recede.

From *How Violence is Destroying Our Teenage Population and a Plan to Begin Solving the Problem.*

GETTING READY TO WRITE

■ *Step 1: Reviewing and Organizing Ideas*

This reading discusses both causes and effects. Prothrow-Stith explains causes of current problems between the police and the community. She also gives reasons why the present system is ineffective in preventing crime and explains the positive effects that community policing produces.

As you have discovered in previous chapters, an idea map is a useful way to record, organize, and review ideas. Since cause and effect relationships are often complex, this kind of diagramming can clarify relationships, simplify them, and reduce them to a basic form. The ideas in this reading can be organized as shown below.

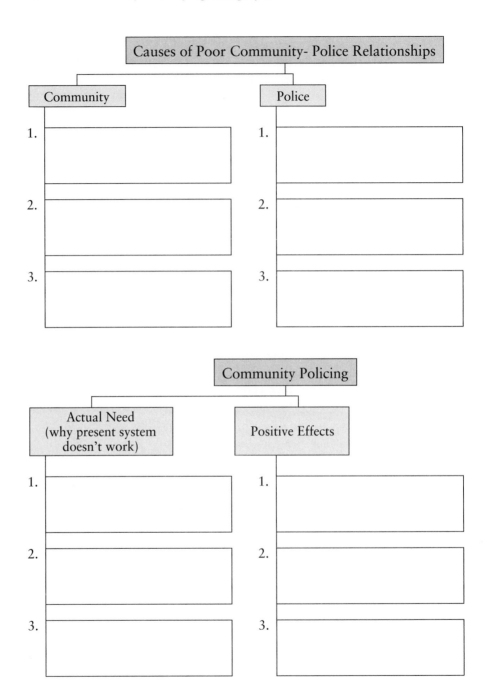

Exercise 10–8   Complete the above idea map by supplying details from the reading.

Step 2: Thinking Critically: Evaluating
Cause and Effect Relationships

Critical thinkers do not accept everything they read as true. Instead they evaluate the author's claim and make a decision about whether or not to accept or agree with the ideas presented. In this article the author attempts to establish that community policing is a solution to current police/community problems and that it controls crime effectively. Are you willing to accept this assertion?

To do this, you will need to analyze the cause and effect relationships and the evidence the author offers to support them. Cause and effect relationships will establish one thing that is the cause of another thing. The author, for example, asserts that one of the causes of poor police/community relationships is the police search-on-sight policy. Your task as a critical thinker is to question or evaluate this assertion. You might ask:

> What evidence does the author offer in support of this? Is it relevant and sufficient?
>
> Is the connection logical? Plausible?
>
> Can you think of situations which support this assertion?
>
> Can you think of situations in which this connection does not hold true?
>
> Are there other causes the author has not thought of?

There are no right or wrong answers to these questions. Your answers will be based on judgment and personal experience. You may even disagree with classmates on whether evidence is sufficient or whether to accept an author's assertion.

Prothrow-Stith provides no evidence in support of the search-on-sight policy as a cause of poor community-police relationships. However, the connection does seem logical. For those connections for which evidence is provided, you'll need to decide whether the evidence is relevant and sufficient. For example, is the Link Valley example (paragraph seven) adequate proof that community policing is effective in reducing crime?

Exercise 10–9   For each cause and effect you listed in your idea map for Exercise 10–8, review the reading to determine if the cause and effect relationship is supported with evidence.

Step 3: Reacting to and Discussing Ideas

Get ready to write about the reading by using the following questions to generate ideas about the reading.

1. Do you think police foot patrols are effective in building better police/community relationships?

2. In what other ways could police/community relations be improved?

3. Do you agree that police should be problem-solvers rather than those who respond to crimes as they occur? Why or why not?

4. Does cleaning up a neighborhood prevent drug sales, or do you think the sales just occur elsewhere?

5. The author asserts that when police officers and kids get to know one another, bitterness will recede. Do you agree?

WRITING ABOUT THE READING

■ *Assignment 1*

Write a paragraph explaining why community policing would (or would not) be effective in reducing crime. If you use reasons given in the article, be sure to express them in your own words.

Assignment 2

Write a paragraph explaining (giving reasons for) whether or not you feel the author provided sufficient evidence for you to agree that community policing is effective in reducing crime.

WRITING ABOUT YOUR IDEAS

■ *Assignment 1*

Write a paragraph explaining why you respect (or do not respect) police.

Assignment 2

Write a paragraph explaining why crime or drug dealing is (or is not) prevalent in your neighborhood or community.

Assignment 3

Write a paragraph explaining the effects police foot patrols would have (or have had) in your community.

Journal Writing Suggestions

1. Write an entry describing your attitude toward police. Describe a particular incident you experienced, observed, or read about that illustrates your feelings.

2. Write an entry describing your success and/or problems in planning and organizing cause and effect paragraphs.

REVISION CHECKLIST

1. Is your paragraph appropriate for your audience? Does it give them the background information they need? Will it interest them?

2. Will your paragraph accomplish your purpose?

3. Is your main point clearly expressed in a topic sentence?

4. Is each detail relevant? Does each explain or support the topic sentence directly?

5. Have you supported your topic sentence with sufficient detail to make it understandable and believable?

6. Do you use specific words to explain each detail?

For CAUSE and EFFECT Writing

7. Does your topic sentence indicate whether you will emphasize causes or effects?

8. Does your topic sentence indicate whether the events are related or independent?

9. Are your details arranged using one of the following arrangements: chronological, order-of-importance, spatial, or categorical?

10. Have you used transitions to blend your details smoothly?

Coordinate Sentences

Two or more equally important ideas can be combined into one sentence. This type of sentence is called a *coordinate sentence.*

How to Combine Ideas of Equal Importance

There are three ways to combine ideas of equal importance. (Each idea must be an independent clause, which is a group of related words that contains a subject and a predicate and that can grammatically stand alone as a sentence.)

1. Join the two independent clauses using a comma and a coordinating conjunction (*and, so, for, but, yet, or, nor*).

EXAMPLE: 1. Russell recommended that we try the Mexican restaurant down the street.
2. The restaurant turned out to be excellent.

COMBINED: Russell recommended that we try the Mexican restaurant down the street, and it turned out to be excellent.

2. Join the two clauses using a semicolon.

EXAMPLE: 1. The candidates for mayor made negative comments about each other.
2. Many people disapproved of the candidates' tactics.

COMBINED: The candidates for mayor made negative comments about each other; many people disapproved of their tactics.

3. Join the clauses using a semicolon and a conjunctive adverb (words such as *however, therefore, thus*) followed by a comma.

EXAMPLE: 1. Professor Sullivan did not discuss the chapter on polar winds.
2. The exam included several questions on polar winds.

COMBINED: Professor Sullivan did not discuss the chapter on polar winds; however, the exam included several questions on the topic.

Rate Your Ability to Write Coordinate Sentences

Combine each of the following pairs of sentences to form coordinate sentences.

1. A field study observes subjects in their natural settings. Only a small number of subjects can be studied at one time.

• • • • • • • • • • • • • • • • • •

2. The Grand Canyon is an incredible sight. It was formed less than ten million years ago.

3. Many anthropologists believe that Native Americans migrated to North and South America from Asia. Alaska and Siberia used to be connected twenty-five thousand years ago.

4. Neon, argon, and helium are called inert gases. They are never found in stable chemical compounds.

5. The professor returned the tests. He did not comment on them.

6. Ponce de Leon was successful because he was the first European to "discover" Florida. He did not succeed in finding the fountain of youth he was searching for.

7. The lecture focused on the cardio-pulmonary system. The students needed to draw diagrams in their notes.

8. Rudy had never read *Hamlet*. Rufus had never read *Hamlet*.

9. Presidents Lincoln and Kennedy did not survive assassination attempts. President Ford escaped two assassination attempts.

10. Marguerite might write her paper about *Moll Flanders*. She might write her paper about its author, Daniel Defoe.

Score _____

Check your answers using the Answer Key on page 537. If you scored below 80 percent, you need additional review and practice in working with coordinate sentences. Refer to Section D.3 of Reviewing the Basics in Part 5.

SUMMARY

■   1. Cause and effect paragraphs are concerned with why events occur and what happens as a result.

2. To write an effective topic sentence
   • clarify the cause and effect relationship
   • decide whether to emphasize causes or effects
   • determine if the events are related or independent

3. Four useful ways to organize your details are
   • chronological
   • order-of-importance
   • spatial
   • categorical

4. Use transitions to blend your details.

III

. . . .

Strategies for Writing Essays

11 Planning Your Essay

· · · ·

In this chapter you will learn

1. to choose and narrow your topic.

2. to generate ideas about your topic.

3. to organize your ideas.

If you can write paragraphs, you can write an essay. An essay is simply a group of paragraphs about a common subject and main point.

Essay writing does not require high levels of creativity or special talent. If you can write single paragraphs, you will be able to group them together to form an essay. Essays need not be long or complicated; an essay can have as few as three or four paragraphs. Your subject does not necessarily have to be complex, either. You could write an essay about everyday, familiar topics such as a recent film, soap operas, or your family or friends. Writing an essay does require time, planning, and organization. The purpose of this chapter is to help you plan and organize essays.

WHAT IS AN ESSAY?

■ An *essay* is a group of paragraphs about one subject. Essays give the writer the opportunity to expand ideas. Essays also allow the writer to relate and develop ideas in order to support a larger point. Like a paragraph, it contains one key idea about the subject, called the *thesis statement*. It is like the paragraph's topic sentence, but it is usually about a broader subject. The paragraphs in an essay, like supporting details in a paragraph, explain some aspect of the thesis. Essays use transitional words and sentences to connect ideas among paragraphs.

210

The chart below shows that the parts of essays are very much like those of paragraphs.

Paragraph	Description	Essay
topic	the one thing the writing is about	subject
topic sentence	states the one key point of the writing	thesis statement
supporting details	explain the key point(s)	supporting paragraphs or body
transitional words	make connections among ideas	transitional words or sentences
last sentence	connects all ideas back to key point	conclusion

Paragraphs differ from essays primarily in the size or complexity of ideas discussed. A topic sentence is more specific than a thesis statement. A thesis statement contains a "bigger" idea.

HOW ESSAYS ARE ORGANIZED

■ In conversation, we often lead up to or introduce an idea before we state it. Suppose you wanted to convince some friends to go on a fall weekend camping trip. Before asking them, you would probably lead up to or introduce the idea of camping. You might mention the fun you had the last time you camped. "Remember the great time we had camping at Letchworth Park? Well, let's do it again." Then after you stated your main point, you would follow it with details—when, where, how—or reasons—it wouldn't cost much, the leaves will be turning, the weather is still warm, and so forth. You might conclude by saying, "So, when are we leaving?" or "So, what about it?"

An essay follows a similar organization: it introduces an idea, states it, explains it, and draws a conclusion. As you can see, this order follows the same order as the list of parts shown above. Most essays begin with an *introductory paragraph* that states the *subject* of the essay. It also states the key point the essay will make in a *thesis statement. Supporting paragraphs* contain ideas that explain the when, where, and how of the key point. Usually an essay has two or more of these paragraphs. The paragraphs are linked by transitional words and

WRITING
SUCCESS
TIP 11

An Overview of Library Resources and Services

Your college library is one of the most helpful and useful places on campus. It offers a wide variety of services and has numerous resources that can make your life easier as a student. Although libraries differ in what they offer, a brief review of key resources and services most college libraries offer follows.

1. A Reference Librarian

Most libraries have one or more librarians available at all times to help you locate what you need. They can suggest how to get started on a research project or direct you to the best source of information for your particular needs. Don't hesitate to ask for assistance. A quick question asked of a reference librarian might save you hours of frustrating or unsuccessful searching.

2. Periodical Collection

Your library subscribes to numerous periodicals—both popular magazines such as *Sports Illustrated* or *Glamour* and professional and scholarly journals such as *The Journal of Personality and Social Psychology*. The popular magazines are a source of "fun" reading as well as an excellent source of topics to write about.

sentences. The concluding paragraph ties all of the ideas in the essay together in relation to the thesis statement. Once you know the parts to include, it is easy to arrange your ideas this way. The following sample essay shows where each of these essential elements appears.

Science Versus Religion

subject

introductory paragraph {
Disagreement exists among evolutionists and creationists about the origin of human beings. Evolutionists believe that all life forms, including humans, developed from more primitive life forms. Creationists believe humans were created by God. As it stands now, creationist theory has two primary advantages that give it the edge in many people's minds over evolutionary theory.
} *thesis statement*

3. Interlibrary Loan

Most libraries have an arrangement with other public and college libraries to borrow each other's books. If your library doesn't own a book you need, the library can obtain it for you from another library. You can pick up and return the book to your own library. Some libraries may charge a fee for this service, so check with your librarian. It usually takes a week or more to obtain a book through interlibrary loan.

4. Audiovisual Services

Many libraries have extensive collections of videotapes, films, records, and audiotapes available for your use.

5. Quiet Study Areas

Many libraries have floors or sections reserved for quiet study and research. Take advantage of facilities designed to meet your needs.

supporting paragraph {

Creationist theory has been around for centuries and has become part of our culture. Religious influences begin at the time of birth and are strong in many families. Churches, friends, even television reinforce the religious view. Evolutionary theory, on the other hand, has only been around for two or three hundred years.

supporting paragraph {

Another advantage the creationist theory holds is that it is fixed and unchanging, while evolutionary theory, like much in science, is uncertain and changeable. Creationism is based on faith. The Bible, which many people believe is the inspired word of God, is considered indisputable, constant, and unchanging. There remains no room for interpretation, no issues to decide, no decisions to make. Evolution, however, is based on scientific inquiry, which is always open to change and interpretation. Many people find it easier to go with the "facts."

conclusion {

Which side will win this dispute? It may never be decided. However, since creationism is based on faith, which does not require proof, it will probably continue to hold its advantage.

In this essay, the writer introduces the theories of creationism and evolution by defining each. Then, in her thesis statement, she states that creationism holds the advantage. Paragraphs two and three explain these two advantages. The concluding paragraph indicates that the dispute remains unresolved and restates the writer's opinion.

Exercise 11–1   Read the following essay and answer each of the questions below.

When A Home Is Not A Home

The good news is that mobile homes offer affordable housing for people who want to own their own house but cannot afford the substantial down payment a free-standing house requires. The bad news is that America discriminates against mobile homes and their owners. Despite its advantages, numerous barriers stand in the way of mobile home ownership.

Did you know that if you purchase a piece of property and purchase a mobile home, your local government may not let you place your home on your property? Local zoning laws severely restrict placement of mobile homes. Why this arises leads to the issue of discrimination. People associate mobile homes with unruly children, beer cans on the lawn, and rusted-out, abandoned cars. The fact that many solid citizens live in mobile homes and more would if laws didn't prohibit them does not enter the picture.

A second type of discrimination is financial. Home buyers need every break they can get. But loans for mobile homes are treated differently than for permanent homes. The loan rates are usually two or three points higher, and government agency financing is still difficult to obtain as well. Unfortunately, all these disadvantages are tied to the image of mobile home owners. They are unfairly thought of as unreliable people who are poor financial risks.

What does America have against mobile homes? The answer is rooted in discriminatory attitudes toward mobile home owners.

1. What is the subject of the essay? _____

2. Which sentences introduce the subject? _____
3. Underline the thesis statement.

4. List the supporting ideas the writer uses. _____

    _____

5. How does the writer conclude the essay? _____

CHOOSING AN APPROPRIATE TOPIC

■ When your instructor assigns a topic or provides a choice of topics, in a sense, he or she has done part of your paper for you. You may not like the topic(s), but at least you know where to start. If your instructor assigns a paper on a topic of your choice, your first reaction may be "I don't know what to write about!"

Although you may be tempted to grab any topic and get on with writing, remember that the most important ingredient in clear writing is clear thinking. Invest your time in thinking about what you want to write about. Then consider your topic and review the writing activities you learned in Chapter 2. The two most important guidelines for choosing a topic are simple:

1. **Write about something familiar.** Select a topic you know a fair amount about. Otherwise, you will have to research your topic in the library. Your experience will provide the content of your essay.

2. **Choose a topic that interests you.** You will feel more like writing and will find that you have more to say.

Where to Look for Topics

If you are an active thinker who notices, becomes involved with, and reacts to the world around you, you'll never run out of topics to write about. For example:

1. **Think of activities you have done over the past week.** Suppose you saw a horror film, went to a shopping mall, to work, to church, and played softball. Each of these could become a topic of an essay: What I like about horror films; the mall as a social arena; the trouble with my boss; why more people don't attend church.

2. **Look around you or out the window.** What do you see? Perhaps it is the television, a dog lying at your feet, or children playing tag. Possible topics are: the influence of television on what we buy, pets as companions, or play as a form of learning. ·

3. **Think of what time of year it is.** Think about what you do on holidays, or what this season's sports or upcoming events might mean to you.

4. **Consult your writing journal.** It is an excellent source of topics.

5. **Think of a topic you have read about, heard or seen on radio or TV news, or discussed with a friend.**

As you think of topics, write them down. Keep the list, and refer to it when your next paper is assigned.

Exercise 11–2   Using the above suggestions, make a list of five possible topics you could use to write a one- or two-page essay.

GENERATING IDEAS ABOUT YOUR TOPIC

■   Once you have chosen a working topic, the next step is to generate ideas about it. This step will demonstrate that you have chosen a usable topic. It will also provide you with a list of ideas you can use in planning and developing your essay. Review the four methods for generating ideas on pages 17–22 of Chapter 2.

1. **Freewriting:** Write non-stop for a specified time, recording all ideas that come to mind.
2. **Brainstorming:** Write a list of all ideas that come to mind about a given topic.
3. **Questioning:** Write a list of questions about a given topic.
4. **Branching:** Draw a diagram showing possible subtopics into which your topic could be divided. Choose the one that seems best for your topic, and try it out. If that method doesn't work, try one of the others.

When a student named Teresa was assigned a two-page paper on a topic of her choice, she thought of activities she had been involved in recently. She decided to write about health and fitness centers. To generate ideas, Teresa used brainstorming, and wrote the following list of ideas:

Fitness Centers

free assessment
develop a program
classes
use equipment
instructors and trainers
nutritional advice
weigh-ins
aerobic
meet friends

lockers
go after work
workouts with weights
hard to go sometimes

In the remaining sections of this chapter you will see how Teresa used this list to plan and organize her essay.

Exercise 11–3   Select one of the topics you listed in Exercise 11–2. Use freewriting, brainstorming, questioning, or branching to generate ideas about the topic.

NARROWING YOUR TOPIC

■   Students often try to work with a topic that is either too broad or too narrow. If your topic is too narrow, you will find you don't have enough to write about. If it is too broad, you will have too much to say, which will create several related problems:

1. you will tend to write in generalities;
2. you will not be able to explore each idea in detail;
3. you will probably wander from topic to topic;
4. you will become unfocused.

It is difficult to know if your topic is too broad, but here are a few warning signals:

- you feel overwhelmed when you try to think about the topic
- you don't know where to start
- you feel as if you are going in circles with ideas
- you don't know where to stop

You can use the ideas you generated during brainstorming, freewriting, questioning, or branching to help narrow your topic. One or more of those ideas may be a more manageable topic. For example, Teresa's brainstorming produced several narrower topics:

facilities
types of equipment
services offered

Often more than one round of narrowing is necessary. You may need to reduce a topic several times by dividing it into smaller and smaller subtopics. You can do this by using one of the prewriting techniques again, or you can use a simple diagram to help you. The following diagrams show how Teresa narrowed the topic of fitness center services. First she wrote the topic on the left side of the paper, than listed examples for it on the right.

Then she put several of the examples on the left to narrow them further. For example:

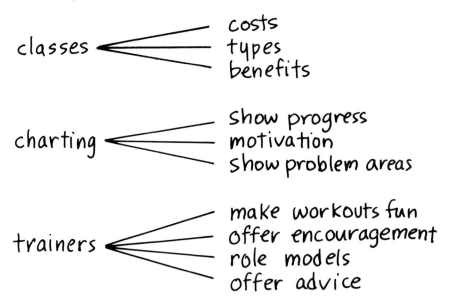

In this way, she wound up with quite a few manageable topics to choose from. Finally, she decided to write about the cost of classes since she had checked out the cost of many in her neighborhood.

In the example above, Teresa narrowed each topic to a narrower topic. You do not always have to narrow each topic. Sometimes you might eliminate some topics and narrow further only those that remain, as this student did for the topic of television viewing:

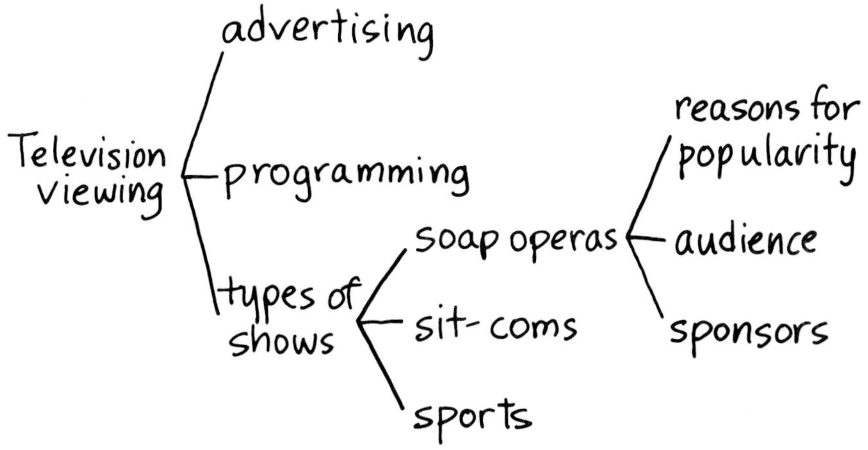

advertising

Television
viewing — programming

reasons for
popularity

soap operas — audience

types of
shows — sit-coms   sponsors

sports

Notice that this student did not make lists next to advertising or programming in the first round, or next to sit-coms and sports in the second round. She made choices at each of these stages and decided to pursue only one path. She decided to write about soap opera sponsors, because she felt she knew more about why people watch soap operas than she did about their audience or the reasons that soap operas are popular.

A question many students ask is: "How do I know when to stop narrowing?" For an essay, you will need at least two or three main points to support your thesis. And each of these points will need to be explained. Let's suppose you have narrowed the topic of television viewing to the topic of soap opera sponsors. To narrow the topic further, you would list each reason, as shown below.

Soap Opera
Sponsors
make ads appeal to women
advertise products women buy
advertise household products

Now, could you write an entire essay with at least two or three main supporting points and adequate detail? If not, you'll know you have narrowed too far.

Exercise 11–4   Complete the narrowing process for one of the items in the last list for each topic.

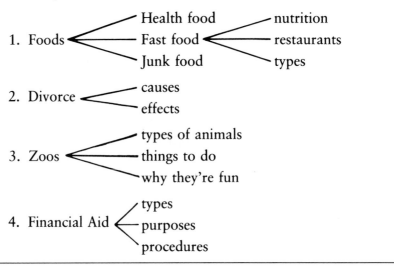

1. Foods — Health food — nutrition
             Fast food — restaurants
             Junk food — types

2. Divorce — causes
             effects

3. Zoos — types of animals
          things to do
          why they're fun

4. Financial Aid — types
                   purposes
                   procedures

Exercise 11–5   Narrow three of the following topics using the diagramming procedure illustrated above. Continue narrowing each until you find a topic about which you could write a four- to five-paragraph essay. Circle your final topic choice for each.

1. advertisements
2. radio
3. junk mail
4. colleges
5. news reporting
6. wild life preservation
7. telephone solicitation

DEVELOPING YOUR IDEAS

■ Once you have a workable topic, you still have some thinking to do before you begin to write your first draft. You must organize your ideas and plan how you will develop your essay. This involves developing a thesis statement and deciding how to support it. The process parallels that of developing a topic sentence and supporting details for a single paragraph, which we discussed in Chapters 3 and 4. The two steps work best if they are done together.

As you decide how to support your thesis statement, you may

decide to revise the statement itself. Or, you might realize that the thesis statement is too broad and decide to narrow it.

Developing Your Thesis Statement

Your thesis statement explains what your essay is about and also gives your reader clues about its organization. The thesis statement should not only identify your topic, but also express the main point. It should be as specific as possible. In order to write a clear and effective thesis statement, you usually have to organize your ideas about the topic first.

If you have done the narrowing diagrams described above, then you already have a topic. Now you need to decide what point to make about it. To develop your point, you may find one more round of narrowing useful. For example, look at Teresa's diagram on page 218. After seeing her list next to the topic "classes," she decided her topic would be the cost of classes. She drew another bracket and list:

Cost of classes —— worth the cost
                    equipment expensive
                    instructors need
                    living wage

She decided that she was most interested in the first statement: The classes are worth the cost. But she knew that people who didn't belong to fitness clubs might need convincing. So she asked herself the question "*Why* are they worth the cost?" Then she listed her answers again.

trainers help
you develop a routine
see others working out
have support of others
becomes a habit
have fun with others
aerobics
jogging teams
exercise classes
social — meet people

By studying this list Teresa saw that there are three main groups of reasons why health clubs are worthwhile: they offer 1) a variety of physical activities, 2) advice and support and, 3) social benefits. Then, she expanded her thesis to include these three reasons:

> ```
> Health and fitness clubs are worthwhile
> because they offer a variety of physical activ-
> ities, training and support, and social ben-
> efits.
> ```

This statement suggests to the reader how the essay will develop by indicating the three major topics Teresa will discuss. It also provides information about the essay's organization. The thesis statement indicates that first she will discuss physical activities, then training and support, and finally, social benefits.

Suppose you have chosen the popularity of soap operas as a topic, and you write the following thesis statement:

> ```
> Soap operas are popular for a variety of
> reasons.
> ```

You could improve this statement by being more specific. You could brainstorm a list of reasons, as for the fitness center example above. You could also write topic sentences for the paragraphs in the body of the essay and then revise your thesis statement. For example, you might write the following topic sentences:

> ```
> Soap operas entertain viewers by allowing
> them to become involved in the characters'
> lives.
>       Soap operas allow viewers to escape their
> own problems.
>       Soap operas help viewers place their own
> problems in perspective.
> ```

Your revised thesis statement might be:

> ```
> Soap operas provide entertainment, escape,
> and a healthy perspective on life.
> ```

If you are having trouble making your thesis statement specific, you may not have planned your ideas well enough. You may need to generate and organize more ideas about the topic. Use a different method than you used initially. That is, if you have already used brainstorming, use freewriting or questioning instead.

If generating more ideas does not help, you may need to choose a different topic. If your topic is assigned, then discover more ideas about the topic by talking to someone about it or by reading about your topic in the library.

Exercise 11–6   Revise each of the following thesis statements to make them more specific.

1. Jogging has a lot of benefits.
2. Counseling can help people with personal problems.
3. Getting involved in campus activities has really helped me.
4. Budgeting your time is important if you are working and going to school.
5. Commuting to college presents problems.

Exercise 11–7   For one of the topics you used in Exercise 11–5 develop a thesis statement.

Arranging Your Ideas

The ideas that support your thesis statement should follow a logical order. The paragraph development methods you learned in Chapters 6 through 10 are useful in organizing essays. Depending on your topic and purpose, use one or more of the following methods of organization:

- narration
- process
- description
- definition
- example
- classification
- comparison and contrast
- cause and effect

Sometimes, your topic lends itself well to a particular method of organization. For example, if your essay is about how to improve your skills in playing racquetball, a process method of organization works well. You could discuss the techniques in the order in which they should be used. Or, if your topic compares two musical groups, then a comparison and contrast organization would be appropriate. Other times it is difficult to know what method of organization to choose. When this happens, focus on your audience. Choose an organization that arranges your ideas clearly so your reader can follow them. For example, if you are describing a place, use spatial arrangement. If you are explaining a complicated idea or theory, cover the basics first and work up to more complicated ideas. Often a combination of methods is effective. You might use both process and cause and effect, for instance, in explaining how to use a computer data base system.

Exercise 11–8   For each of the following topics, identify at least one method of organization that would be appropriate. For some items more than one method may be appropriate.

1. professional versus college football
2. the advantages of public television
3. graphic media reporting of violent crimes
4. how to prevent home burglary
5. changes in the motion picture rating system
6. what makes a motion picture a box-office hit

Using Outlining and Idea Mapping

The best way to prepare a solid, effective essay is to plan its development using an informal outline or idea map. An informal outline is a list of ideas you will present in the order in which you will present them. It should be set up like this:

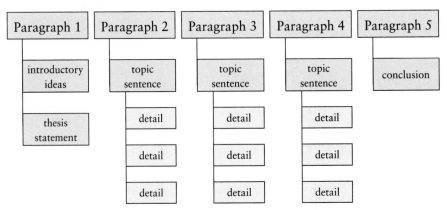

An idea map is a visual representation of the arrangement of ideas. In Chapters 6 through 10 you learned to map each method of paragraph development. You can expand these maps and use them to organize essays, as well. Here is a sample map for Teresa's essay.

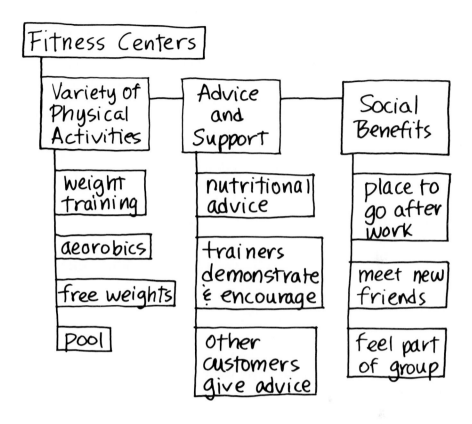

Whether you use outlining or mapping is a matter of personal preference. Experiment with each to learn which one works best for you.

Exercise 11–9   Prepare a map or outline of an essay on the topic you chose in Exercise 11–7.

THINKING BEFORE READING

■   This reading first appeared as an editorial in the *Wall Street Journal*. It is a good example of how an essay is organized. As you read, notice how the author states and develops her thesis statement. Journalists often add headings and write very short paragraphs, especially if their essays appear in newspapers or popular magazines. For most of your essays, it is not necessary to use headings and your paragraphs should be fully developed.

1. Preview the reading using the steps described in Chapter 3, page 43.
2. Activate your thinking by answering the following:
   a. What types of jobs have you had? What did you learn from them?
   b. What types of jobs do teenagers usually hold?
   c. How do teenagers you know respond to their part- or full-time jobs?
   d. What is a dead-end job?

READING

THE DEAD-END KIDS

Michele Manges

If just showing up accounts for 90 percent of success in life, as Woody Allen claims, then today's teenagers ought to make great recruits for tomorrow's permanent work force.   1

Well over half of them are already showing up in the part-time work force doing after-school and summer jobs. In times past, this kind of youthful zeal was universally applauded; the kids, we thought, were getting invaluable preliminary training for the world of work. But now a lot of people are *worried* about the surge in youth employment. Why?   2

Because a lot of today's eight million working teens—55 percent of all 16- to 19-year-olds—aren't learning anything much more useful than just showing up.   3

TASTE OF ADULTHOOD

Not that long ago many youngsters could get part-time or summer jobs that taught them the rudiments of a trade they could pursue later. If this wasn't the case, they at least got a taste of the adult world, working closely with adults and being supervised by them. Also, in whatever they did they usually had to apply in a practical way at least some of the skills they'd learned in school, thus reinforcing them.   4

Today, however, a growing majority of working youngsters hustle at monotonous, dead-end jobs that prepare them for nothing.   5

They certainly make up one of the largest groups of underemployed people in the country.

Many work in adolescent ghettos overseen by "supervisors" barely older than they are, and they don't need to apply much of anything they've learned in school, not even the simplest math; technology has turned them into near-automatons. Checkout scanners and sophisticated cash registers tot up bills and figure the change for them. At fast-food joints, automatic cooking timers remove the last possibility that a teen might pick up a smidgen of culinary skill. 6

Laurence Steinberg, a Temple University professor and co-author of a book on teenage employment, estimates that at least three out of every four working teenagers are in jobs that don't give them any meaningful training. "Why we think that wrapping burgers all day prepares kids for the future is beyond me," he says. 7

In a study of 550 teens, Prof. Steinberg and his colleagues found that those working long hours at unchallenging jobs tended to grow cynical[1] about work in general. They did only their own defined tasks and weren't inclined to help out others, their sense of self-respect declined, and they began to feel that companies don't care about their employees. In effect, they were burning out before they even joined the permanent work force. 8

A lot of teenaged workers are just bone-tired, too. Shelley Wurst, a cook at an Ohio franchise steakhouse, got so worn out she stopped working on school nights. "I kept sleeping through my first-period class," she says. "If it wasn't for the crew I'm working with, I wouldn't want to work there at all." 9

This sort of thing is all too common. "Some kids are working past 2 A.M. and have trouble waking up for morning classes," says Larry Morrison, principal of Sylvania (Ohio) Northview High School. Educators like him are beginning to wonder whether teenage work today is not only irrelevant to future careers but even damaging to them; the schoolwork of students who pour so much time and energy into dead-end jobs often suffers—thus dimming their eventual prospects in a permanent job market that now stresses education. 10

As for the teens themselves, a great number would much rather be working elsewhere, in more challenging or relevant jobs. Some, like Tanya Paris, have sacrificed to do so. 11

A senior at Saratoga (Calif.) High School, she works six hours a week with a scientist at the National Aeronautics and Space Administration, studying marine algae, for no pay and no school credit. The 12

1. questioning the value of

future biologist hopes that her NASA work will help her decide which area of biology to pursue.

But most others either are lured by the money they can make or   13
can't find what they're looking for. Jay Jackson, a senior at North-view High, says he'd take a pay cut from his $3.40-an-hour job as a stock boy if he could find something allied to psychology, his prospective career field. He hasn't been able to. Schoolmate Bridget Ellenwood, a junior, yearned for a job that had something to do with dentistry but had to settle for slicing up chickens at a local Chick-fil-A franchise—a job, she says, "where you don't learn much at all."

AND MORE TO COME

Expect more teen jobs where you don't learn much at all. The sweep-   14
ing change in the economy from making things to service, together with the growth of computerized service-industry technology that leaves almost nothing to individual skill and initiative, is expected to accelerate.

So the mindless and irrelevant part-time jobs open to teens in the   15
near future will probably increase, while the better jobs continue to decline. On top of that, a growing labor shortage, which would drive up pay, figures to draw more kids into those jobs—against their interests. "Teen-agers would be much better off doing a clerical-type job or studying," says Prof. John Bishop of Cornell University's Industrial and Labor Relations Center.

Efforts have been under way to cut back the number of hours   16
teens can work, but the worsening labor shortage is undercutting them. Many educators are instead urging the states to start or expand more high-school cooperative education programs. These plans tie school and outside work to future career goals and provide more structure and adult supervision than ordinary outside work.

Employers also prefer students with this kind of experience. A re-   17
cent study by the Cooperative Work Experience Education Association found that 136 of 141 businesses in Arkansas would hire a young applicant who had been in such a program over one who had worked independently. "The goal is not to get kids to stop working," says Prof. Bishop of Cornell. "It's to get them to learn more."

Wall Street Journal, February 2, 1990

GETTING READY TO WRITE

■

In organizing and developing her ideas for this essay, Manges may have written an informal outline. To understand her ideas and their relationship to one another, it may help to reconstruct that outline.

Exercise 11–10   Reconstruct Mange's outline of this essay. Be sure to include each key point and all of its supporting details. Use the informal outline shown on p. 224, as a guide.

Step 2: Thinking Critically: Examining Assumptions

Assumptions are ideas a writer believes to be true but does not try to prove. A writer may take it for granted that the reader will agree with those ideas because they share a common set of values or background. Assumptions can be opinions or beliefs. Assumptions often deal with what is good or bad, right or wrong, valuable, worthwhile, or important. The author may state them, or they may be implied by other things he or she says. As a reader, it is your job to examine these assumptions and decide whether they are really true. Then you can evaluate whether arguments or ideas based on these assumptions make sense.

An example of an assumption appears in paragraph 15 of the reading: "Teen-agers would be better off doing a clerical-type job or studying." The author does not give evidence that this statement is correct. Do you accept this assumption that all teenagers, regardless of their academic abilities and interests, would be better off with clerical jobs or studying? Is it possible that for some students a "meaningless" job provides a welcome break from studying and gives them a chance to interact with other people, and students would *not* be better off studying?

An assumption on which the entire article is based is that meaningful work is valuable, while meaningless (routine, unchallenging) work has no value. Do you agree with this assumption? Is it possible that meaningless jobs are valuable in encouraging teenagers to stay in school or go to college so they can eventually get more interesting and meaningful jobs? The author does not prove this assumption. The author does describe negative effects of meaningless work in paragraph 8, but the assumption itself is not proven.

Other assumptions contained in the reading are listed below. Reread the paragraph in which each appears and decide which ones you agree with. If there are any you do not agree with, try to think of reasons why you disagree.

1. A taste of the adult world is helpful to teenagers (paragraph 4).
2. It is not valuable for teenagers to be supervised by those only slightly older than themselves (paragraph 6).
3. Sleeping through classes is undesirable (paragraphs 9 and 10).
4. Challenging, relevant jobs are important to teenagers (paragraph 11).
5. It is desirable to cut back the number of hours teens can work (paragraph 16).

Exercise 11–11   Select one of the assumptions listed above and write a paragraph explaining why you agree or disagree with it.

___

Step 3: Reacting to and Discussing Ideas

Get ready to write about the reading by discussing the following questions.

1. What might teenagers learn from dead-end jobs?
2. The author suggests cooperative education programs as an alternative to dead-end jobs. Would this type of job interest you?
3. Why are there so many "meaningless" jobs?
4. What could a teenager do to make a meaningless job more meaningful?
5. What makes a job "meaningful"?
6. Should teenagers' work hours be restricted? If so, by whom?

WRITING ABOUT THE READING

■ *Assignment 1*

Write an essay explaining whether you agree with the author that meaningful work is valuable while meaningless work is not.

Assignment 2

Write an essay describing the ideal, meaningful job.

WRITING ABOUT YOUR IDEAS

■ *Assignment 1*

Write an essay describing a job you have held and explain your reactions to it.

Assignment 2

Write an essay in which you identify your major or course of study and explain how it will lead to a meaningful job.

Journal Writing Suggestions

1. Write an entry about your observations of teenagers in the work force.

2. Write an entry describing your experiences with essay writing. How is it similar to and how does it differ from writing paragraphs?

PLANNING CHECKLIST

1. Have you chosen a topic that is familiar to you and interests you?
2. Have you generated ideas about your topic, perhaps by using freewriting, brainstorming, questioning, or branching?
3. Have you narrowed your topic so that it is limited enough to cover in a few paragraphs but not so narrow that you will run out of things to say?
4. Have you expressed your main point in a clearly worded thesis statement?
5. Have you arranged your ideas in a logical way that will be easy for your readers to follow?

Subordinate Clauses

Subordination is a way of showing that one idea is more important than another. When an idea is related to another idea, but less important, the less important idea can be expressed as a subordinate clause. Subordinate clauses contain a subject and a verb but do not express a complete thought and cannot stand alone as grammatically complete sentences. They are always used in combination with a complete sentence or independent clause.

One Way to Combine Ideas of Unequal Importance

When a less important idea is combined with one of greater importance, it is helpful to show how the ideas relate to one another. Use words such as *after*, *although*, *before*, *while*, *when*, and *because* to begin the subordinate clause and show its relationship to the more important idea. In the examples below, the subordinating conjunctions are underlined.

> After I finished the exam, I went to the coffee shop. [The word *after* indicates that the two ideas are related by time sequence.]

> Because I missed the bus, I was late for my math class. [The word *because* indicates that missing the bus was the reason for being late to class.]

> I won't be able to make my tuition payment unless my student loan comes in soon. [The word *unless* indicates that the tuition payment depends on the student loan.]

The two clauses can appear in either order. When the subordinate clause appears first, a comma follows it. (Refer to the first and second examples above.) When the independent clause comes first, a comma is usually not needed. (See the third example above.)

Rate Your Ability to Use Subordinate Clauses

Combine each of the following pairs of sentences to form a sentence in which one idea is more important than the other. Add or delete words as necessary.

1. Mushrooms are a type of fungus. Some types are safe to eat.
2. Grape juice is fermented. Grape juice becomes wine.

· ·

3. It is important for children to be immunized. Children who are not immunized are vulnerable to many dangerous diseases.

4. A poem should be read carefully. Next, it should be analyzed.

5. The Vikings were probably the first Europeans to set foot in North America. Columbus "discovered" America much later.

6. I was giving a speech in my communications class. At the same time, Carl Sagan was giving a speech on campus.

7. I started my assignment for French class. I was relieved that it was a very easy assignment.

8. Infants may seem unaware and oblivious to their surroundings. They are able to recognize their mother's voice and smell from birth.

9. Neo-Freudians disagreed with Freud's focus on biological instincts and sexual drive. They formed new theories.

10. The hypothalamus is a tiny part of the brain. It has many very important functions, including the regulation of hormones, body temperature, and hunger.

Score _____

Check your answers using the Answer Key on page 537. If you scored below 80 percent, you need additional review and practice in working with subordinate clauses. Refer to Section D.4 of *Reviewing the Basics* in Part 5.

SUMMARY

■   1. An essay is a group of paragraphs about one subject. It consists of a thesis statement and details that support it.

2. Essays are organized as follows:
   • introductory paragraph (includes thesis statement)
   • supporting paragraphs
   • conclusion

3. To choose a topic, select one that is familiar and interesting.

4. Be sure that your topic is neither too broad nor too narrow.

5. To write an effective thesis statement, organize ideas about your topic first. Do this by
   • using the methods of paragraph development you learned in Chapters 6 through 10.
   • using outlining or idea mapping

12 ···· Drafting and Revising Your Essay

CHAPTER OBJECTIVES

In this chapter you will learn to

1. develop the body of the essay.
2. write introductory paragraphs.
3. write concluding paragraphs.
4. select an appropriate title.
5. revise your essay.

Suppose you are renovating a building, and your job is to create a modern office complex within an existing structure. You begin by brainstorming about possibilities and finally decide on a basic layout. Next, you make sketches of various interior arrangements. However, you find you have to make many sketches to include all necessary components. You plan, change, and rearrange to get an arrangement that works.

Drafting an essay is like sketching. Once you have chosen a topic and developed some ideas about it (steps we discussed in Chapter 11), you are ready to draft your essay. Think of drafting as an initial laying out of ideas in sentence and paragraph form. Drafting involves arranging the pieces of your essay—its introduction, body, and conclusion—and seeing how they work together. Just as the components of an office space must work together to produce a functional building, so must the pieces of an essay fit together to create a clear and understandable essay. Your introduction must lead into the body. The body must contain relevant and sufficient support for the thesis you presented in the introduction. Your conclusion must tie the essay together and bring it to an end.

WRITING THE INTRODUCTORY PARAGRAPH

■ An introductory paragraph has three main purposes:

1. To present the thesis statement and suggest the organization of your essay;

2. To set the tone of your essay and suggest the audience for whom it is intended;

3. To interest your reader and/or provide necessary background information.

Although your introductory paragraph appears first in your essay, it does *not* need to be written first. In fact, it is sometimes difficult to introduce ideas you haven't fully developed yet. It may work better to write the introduction after you have developed ideas, written a thesis statement, and drafted your essay.

Writing Your Thesis Statement

As we saw in Chapter 11, in planning your essay you have already developed a working thesis statement. The remainder of the introductory paragraph is built around it. Remember the following guidelines for writing a thesis statement (also see Chapter 11, pages 221–223):

1. The thesis statement must be a complete sentence.

2. It should state, as clearly as possible, the main point of your essay.

3. It should be as specific as possible.

4. It should give your reader a clear picture of what is to follow. If it mentions key points, they should be in the order in which you will discuss them. In other words, your thesis statement should parallel the order of your supporting paragraphs. If your thesis statement reads: "Public school budget cuts will have negative effects on academic achievement, student motivation, and drop-out rate," then discuss effects on academic achievement first, motivational effects second, and drop-out rate last.

Establishing the Tone

Your introductory paragraph should establish the tone of your essay. *Tone* is the way you say something and reflects your attitude toward your subject and your reader. The volume and character of your speaking voice—or tone of voice—can express a wide range of attitudes:

WRITING
SUCCESS
TIP 12

Locating Reference Sources in the Library

•   •   •   •   •   •   •   •   •   •   •   •   •   •   •   •   •   •

Libraries have a wealth of information. The key to researching a topic is to know how to find what you need rapidly and efficiently. The following tips will help you locate materials in a library.

1. *Identify Correct Subject Headings*

The first step in researching a topic is to discover under what subject headings to look in order to locate information on your topic. A useful source is *The Library of Congress Subject Headings*. It lists possible headings for particular topics.

2. *Consult the Card Catalog*

Many libraries now have a computerized card catalog that enables you to determine if your library owns a particular book or to locate books on a given topic. You'll find it easy and convenient to use. Directions for using the system often appear right on the computer screen.

anger, disgust, respect, approval, and so forth. Because your reader cannot "hear" your spoken voice, you must convey attitudes through your writing, not only by what you say but also by *how* you say it.

Your tone relates directly to your purpose in writing. For example, if your purpose in writing is to explain your objections to pornography, then your tone should reflect your feelings about pornography. In the statement, "Pornography is a cheap disgusting attempt to victimize women," you can "hear" the writer's anger and strong disapproval. The words "cheap," "disgusting," and "victimize" convey the writer's feelings. If your purpose in writing is to express concern about a recent case of discrimination on campus, then your tone should convey your disapproval: "The recent racial discrimination case on campus presents shocking and disconcerting evidence that discrimination still exists."

Tone relates directly to your audience as well. Your tone of voice would differ when speaking to a close friend and when speaking to a stranger, for example. Similarly, in writing your tone should reflect your relationship with your reader. In writing an article for the campus

3. Consult Bibliographies and Indexes

These publications list by subject the articles published in journals and magazines over the previous year. There are hundreds of indexes, usually at least one for each academic discipline. Here are a few examples: *Social Sciences Index*, *Psychological Abstracts*, and the *Business Periodicals Index*.

4. Consider Using Computerized Indexes and Searches

Many libraries have access to computerized data base systems that combine information from many indexes. These systems allow you to search for sources on a topic quickly and easily. Some libraries may charge a fee for this service.

newspaper on a recent change of grade policy, your audience consists of other students, most of whom you do not know. Your tone should be direct, straightforward, and somewhat formal: "I support the addition of pluses and minuses to our letter grade system because it will give me a more accurate assessment of my performance in my courses." Now, suppose you are writing about this grade change to a friend at another college: "You can believe I was glad to see the new policy on pluses and minuses! Now I'll really be able to see how close I came to a higher or lower grade."

Tone can be established in several different ways. One way is through word choice. Notice how one word changes the tone of the following statement.

1. The parade was an <u>obvious</u> display of patriotism.
2. The parade was an <u>appalling</u> display of patriotism.
3. The parade was a <u>heart-warming</u> display of patriotism.

Action words (verbs) too, can reveal tone, as in the following examples.

1. Recent world events <u>comforted</u> the group.
2. Recent world events <u>shocked</u> the group.
3. Recent world events <u>surprised</u> the group.

There are other ways to vary your tone. Your choice of personal pronouns will influence how you speak to your reader. First and second person pronouns ("I" and "you") create a more direct tone than third person pronouns ("they"). Using contractions makes your writing sound less formal. Notice the difference personal pronouns and contractions make in these two sentences:

1. You know, it's been a long time since I've really felt excited about school, but now I am.
2. College is an unexpected but exciting experience.

You'll also notice that the more rambling sentence structure of the first sentence makes it sound more relaxed than the second sentence.

Exercise 12–1   For each of the following topics, write a sentence in a tone that clearly shows your attitude toward the topic.

     1. abortion   4. political campaigning
     2. TV sitcoms   5. your writing class
     3. romance or mystery novels

Exercise 12–2   For each of the sentences you wrote in Exercise 12–1, identify the audience for which your tone is intended. Then rewrite the sentences for a different audience.

Exercise 12–3   For each of the following statements, describe the tone and the potential audience.

1. We farmers should stop playing second fiddle to the government and take active steps to get higher prices for our crops and better financial help in event of crop failure.

Tone: _____

Audience: _____

2. How many muggings is it going to take to make you realize that you cannot go about your daily business without taking precautions?

Tone: _____

Audience: _____

3. When Elvis Presley died in 1977, America lost its King. I treasure the picture he autographed for me after a performance. It was the happiest day of my life.

Tone: _____

Audience: _____

4. Homelessness conveys human tragedy. Society should take action to help those poor souls recover their livelihood and self-respect.

Tone: _____

Audience: _____

Exercise 12–4   Choose one of the statements above. Think of a different audience for it and rewrite it, changing the tone to suit the new audience.

Capturing Your Reader's Interest

A final function of the introductory paragraph is to capture the reader's interest, urging him or her to continue reading. Many writers use a "hook" as their first sentence to pull the reader in immediately. The thesis statement usually follows this hook. Here are a few different hooks to try. Choose the one that suits your audience as well as your purpose in writing.

1. **Ask a question.** Engage your reader by asking a provocative or controversial question related to your subject.

> What would you do if you were sound asleep and woke to find a burglar in your bedroom?

2. **State a startling fact or statistics.** Your reader will be curious to know more about it.

> Did you know that the federal government recently spent $687,000 on a research project to study the influence of valium on monkeys?

3. **Begin with a story or anecdote.** The story must illustrate or relate to your thesis.

> Mark Brown, a 14-year-old convicted auto thief, has spent the last two months riding in a police cruiser. Already his attitudes have changed. He's back in school and a member of a community crime patrol group. His punishment is part of an experimental youth reform program.

4. **Use a quotation.** An amusing or startling quote or one by a well-known person will focus your reader's attention.

> Oscar Wilde once said, "Always forgive your enemies—nothing annoys them so much."

5. **State a misunderstood fact, myth, or misconception.** Explaining why it is incorrect can lead to a statement of your thesis.

> It's hard to lose weight and even harder to keep it off. Right? Wrong! Until I started combining exercise with sensible eating I would have agreed.

Certain hooks may be appropriate for certain audiences, but ineffective for others. For example, an amusing story or anecdote about an overstressed college friend may be an effective way to introduce an essay about the effects of stress on college students to an audience of college students or professors. But your parents or hometown friends might not understand the anecdote or find it funny.

Your introductory paragraph does not require a hook. You can begin directly with your thesis statement, as follows.

```
     My dream vacation that I spent two years
saving up for was a complete disaster!
```

This straightforward beginning captures the reader's interest instantly. Immediately, you want to know what went wrong.

After stating your thesis, you'll often need one or more transitional sentences that lead into the next paragraph. These sentences should sustain the interest that you've created using a hook or by dramatically stating your thesis. These sentences may offer more information, clarify, explain, or limit your treatment of the thesis, as shown below:

```
     My dream vacation that I spent two years
saving up for was a complete disaster! It all
began when my cousins invited me to go to New
York City with them, but I couldn't afford it.
I felt so jealous and disappointed that I
scrimped on lunches and worked overtime for two
years, and finally I was ready to leave.
```

These sentences fill the reader in on background information and heighten the suspense. You learn where the writer was going, what motivated him to go, and how he saved the money to go. It also brings you up to the point of departure. You expect, then, that the next paragraph will pick up at that time.

Exercise 12–5   Read each of these opening sentences from introductory paragraphs and identify the hook.

   1. My name is Lisa, and I am a videoholic.

   hook: _____

   2. Why do some men refer to women as "chicks" or "foxes"?

   hook: _____

   3. It was a perfect evening. I was watching Monday Night football and my wife was reading one of her trashy novels. Suddenly, she looks up and asks "Hon, who's your fantasy woman?"

   hook: _____

   4. Mark Twain once said, "Man is the only animal who blushes, or has need to."

   hook: _____

   5. By the time an average child is 18-years-old, he or she will have seen over 350,000 television commercials.

   hook: _____

Exercise 12–6   Return to Exercise 12–1. Select one of the topics and generate ideas using brainstorming, freewriting, questioning, or branching. Develop a preliminary thesis statement. Now write an introductory paragraph using one of the hooks described above.

WRITING THE BODY

■   The body of your essay provides information to support your thesis statement. Base your first draft on the outlining or idea mapping (see Chapter 11, pages 224–225) you've done to identify the ideas you want to include and the order in which you will present them. Don't hesitate to change these, however, as you begin writing.

   When you write your first draft, concentrate on expressing your ideas in sentence and paragraph form. Don't worry about spelling, punctuation, or grammar. You can pick up and correct any errors later when you revise and proofread. Instead, focus on:

   1. developing each paragraph effectively
   2. arranging your paragraphs in a logical sequence
   3. connecting your paragraphs

Read the following student essay. The next three sections will refer to this essay and explain how it is developed.

Lengthening the School Year

If I were given eight weeks of vacation each year, I know exactly what I would do. I would visit family, catch up on household chores, and do everything I haven't had time to do over the past year. Kids do get eight weeks of vacation each year, but they haven't any idea of how to use it. Lots of talk has surfaced lately about lengthening the school year **thesis statement** and I, for one, favor it. [In fact, extending the school year from 180 to 220 days will make children value their time, make their summer meaningful, and improve their academic skills.]

This summer I watched my children closely. They would stay up late watching television and then sleep late the next morning. When I asked my son why he did this he said, "There's nothing to do in the morning, so I kill the morning by sleeping." His answer rang in my head: He's killing time. No one should kill time—life is too valuable. Attending school in the summer will give him and other children something to do with their time. They will come to value free time instead of looking for ways to kill it.

Another reason for lengthening the school year is that the eight-week vacation is no longer needed. A hundred years ago, children were needed during the summer to work on the family farm. Summers included hard work, but they were meaningful. Children made a contribution to the family income and felt needed. Now, most children don't live on farms and aren't needed to work. In fact, in many families both parents work outside the home. Children, then, are left to invent their own meaning for the summer days. Furthermore, they end up spending their time on the streets, seeing and hearing too much of what's wrong with the world. The extended school year will make summers meaningful once again.

<u>Perhaps the most important reason for lengthening the year is to improve our children's academic skills.</u> Compared to many other countries, our children are falling behind, especially in science and math. And we hear about increasing illiteracy and declining SAT scores, as well. Education is like many other things—the more time you spend at it, the better you become. Increased time in school will give children more time for instruction and practice. Hopefully, this will help them catch up and develop the skills they need to function in this world.

Those who are opposed to lengthening the school year say it will cost too much. But what could we possibly buy that would be worth more than the education of our children?

Developing Each Paragraph

Each paragraph in the body of your essay should be built around an idea and topic sentence that support your thesis statement. Each topic sentence should be supported by relevant and sufficient detail, as we saw in Chapter 4. Most supporting paragraphs are organized using one or more of the methods of development (narration, description, and so on) you learned in Part 2. Notice the underlined topic sentences in the body of the sample student essay above. Each addresses a key aspect of the thesis statement. The remaining sentences in each paragraph support the topic sentence and use a clear method of development. Paragraph two uses example, Paragraph three uses comparison and contrast, and Paragraph four uses cause and effect.

Arranging and Connecting Your Paragraph

The paragraphs in the body should progress logically from one idea to another. Follow the organization you developed when you planned the essay, testing as you go. See whether your paragraphs in fact support your thesis and whether they follow logically one to the next. Don't be afraid to abandon your plans if they don't work out. You may even want to do a new idea map or outline.

Writers often combine methods of development. You may use one method for one paragraph and a different one for the next, for example. The overall method of development for the essay may differ from that of individual paragraphs, as well. For instance, in writing a cause and effect essay, you might develop a paragraph using time order; another might be developed using example. In the sample essay above, the overall method of development is least-to-most important. Each paragraph, however, used a different method of development.

Write a first draft essay for the topic you chose in Exercise 12–6.

The body paragraphs of your essay should flow smoothly. You should connect your ideas in clear and obvious ways. There are several ways to do this:

1. **Use transitional words and phrases.** The transitional words and phrases you learned for connecting thoughts and sentences in Chapters 6 through 10 are also useful for connecting paragraphs. Table 12–1 lists useful transitions for each method of organization.

TABLE 12-1	**Useful Transitions**
Method of Development	**Transitions**
Most-Least	most important, above all, especially, particularly important
Advantages/Disadvantages	one, another, first, second, etc.
Spatial	above, below, behind, beside, next to, inside, outside, to the west (north, etc.), beneath, near, nearby, next to
Time Sequence	first, next, now, before, during, after, eventually, finally, at last, later, meanwhile, soon, then, suddenly, currently, after, afterward, after a while, as soon as, until

Process/Narration	first, second, then, later, in the beginning, when, after, following, next, during, again, after that, at last, finally
Description	see Spatial and Most-Least above
Example	for example, for instance, to illustrate
Classification	one, another, second, third
Definition	means, can be defined as, refers to, is
Comparison	likewise, similarly, in the same way, too, also
Contrast	however, on the contrary, unlike, on the other hand, although, even though, but, in contrast, yet
Cause and Effect	because, consequently, since, as a result, for this reason, therefore, thus

2. **Write a transitional sentence.** This sentence is usually the first sentence in the paragraph. It might come before the topic sentence or it might *be* the topic sentence. Its purpose is to link the paragraph in which it appears with the paragraph before it. In the sample essay on pages 242–243, the first sentences of paragraphs two, three, and four, function as transitional sentences.

3. **Repeat key words.** Repeating key words from either the thesis statement or from the preceding paragraph helps your reader see connections among ideas. In the sample essay on pages 242–243, notice the repetition of key words and phrases such as "lengthening the school year," "vacation," "summers," and "free time."

Exercise 12–8 Review the first draft essay you wrote for Exercise 12–7. Add transitions as needed. Check to see if you've repeated key words and add them if needed.

Determining the Length of Your Essay

The length of an essay depends on your audience, purpose, and topic. An essay may be as short as three or four paragraphs or as long as 10 to 15 pages. Your essay should be as long as necessary to cover your topic adequately. Estimate the length of your essay by counting the number of main points you have developed to support your thesis. Usually each main point is developed in a separate paragraph. If your essay seems too long, your topic may be too broad. When this happens, replan your essay, focusing on one aspect of your topic. If your essay is too brief, your topic may be too narrow or you may need to generate more ideas in support of your topic.

WRITING THE CONCLUSION

■   The final paragraph of your essay has two jobs. It should reemphasize your thesis statement and draw the essay to a close. It should not be a direct announcement such as "This essay has been about . . ." or "This paper has shown that . . . ." It's usually best to revise your essay at least once *before* working on the conclusion. During your first or second revision, you often make numerous changes in both content and organization which may, in turn, change your conclusion.

Here are a few effective ways to write a conclusion.

1. **Restate your thesis.** If your essay is written to prove a point or convince your reader of the need for action, it may be effective to end with a sentence that restates your point or calls for action. But if you choose this way to conclude, be sure not to merely repeat your first paragraph. Be sure to include all of the thoughts you developed in the body of your essay.

The sample essay on pages 242–243 might have ended with the following restatement:

> Extending the school year will have im-
> portant advantages. Children will learn to han-
> dle their time in meaningful ways and become
> better educated.

2. **Suggest a new direction for further thought.** Raise a related issue that you did not address in your essay, or ask a series of questions. The sample essay on pages 242–243 uses this strategy.

3. **Summarize key points.** Especially for longer essays, briefly review your key supporting ideas.

4. **Look ahead.** Project into the future. Consider future outcomes or effects.

If you have trouble writing your conclusion, it's probably a tip-off that you need to work further on your thesis or organization. In the next section, we discuss how to reexamine your work to strengthen your message.

Exercise 12–9   Write a conclusion for the essay you wrote in Exercise 12–7.

REVISING

■   Once you have written your first draft, the next step is to revise. Chapter 5 "Strategies for Revising," p. 77, discusses the revision process in detail. Although the chapter focuses on paragraph revision, the same steps apply to essay revision.

Examining Your Ideas

As is true for paragraph revision, the most important part of essay revision is examining and evaluating your ideas. Revision is an opportunity to rethink and rearrange your ideas to produce a more effective essay.

When examining ideas, you should have two primary purposes:

1. to evaluate the overall effectiveness of the essay
2. to evaluate the effectiveness of each individual paragraph

Your first purpose concerns the introduction and support of your thesis statement. Your second purpose examines whether each paragraph is well-written and develops and explains a topic sentence. Use the questions listed in the Revision Checklist on p. 262 to guide your evaluation.

Using Idea Maps

In Chapter 5, p. 77, you learned to draw idea maps to evaluate paragraphs. The same strategy works well for essays, too. The idea map will enable you to evaluate the overall flow of ideas as well as the effectiveness of individual paragraphs. To draw an essay idea map, work through each paragraph, recording your ideas in abbreviated form as shown below. Then write the key words of your conclusion. If you find details that do not support the topic sentence, write that detail beside the list.

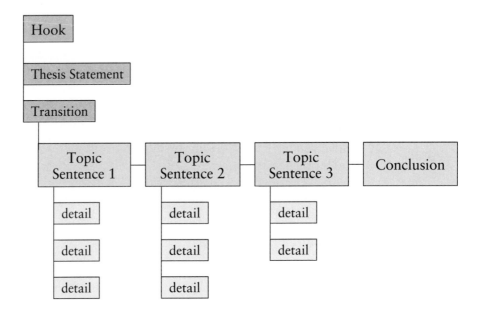

A sample idea map for the essay on pages 242–243 is shown below.

Sample Map

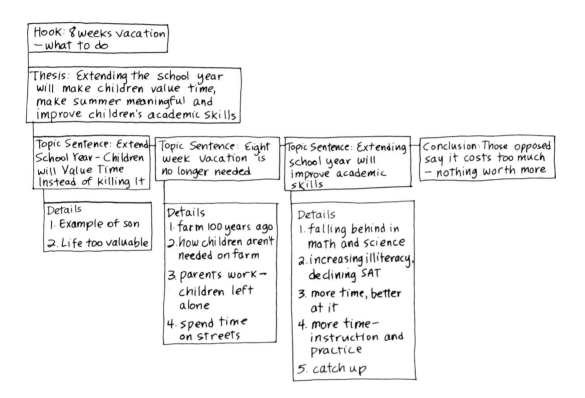

Hook: 8 weeks vacation
— what to do

Thesis: Extending the school year will make children value time, make summer meaningful and improve children's academic skills

Topic Sentence: Extend School Year – Children will Value Time Instead of killing It

Topic Sentence: Eight week vacation is no longer needed

Topic Sentence: Extending school year will improve academic skills

Conclusion: Those opposed say it costs too much — nothing worth more

Details
1. Example of son
2. Life too valuable

Details
1. farm 100 years ago
2. how children aren't needed on farm
3. parents work – children left alone
4. spend time on streets

Details
1. falling behind in math and science
2. increasing illiteracy, declining SAT
3. more time, better at it
4. more time – instruction and practice
5. catch up

When you've completed your idea map, conduct several tests:

1. **Read your thesis statement along with your first topic sentence.** Does the topic sentence clearly support your thesis? If not, revise to make relationship clearer. Repeat this step for each topic sentence.

2. **Read your topic sentences, one after the other, without corresponding details.** Is there a logical connection between them? Are they arranged in the most effective way? If not, revise to make the connection clearer or to improve your organization.

3. **Examine each individual paragraph.** Are there enough relevant, specific details to support the topic sentence?

4. Read your introduction and then look at your topic sentences. Does the essay deliver what the introduction promises?

5. Read your thesis statement and then your conclusion. Are they compatible and consistent? Does the conclusion agree with and support the thesis statement?

To learn more about the revision process, read the following first draft essay and the idea map. Use the five tests listed above to evaluate the essay. Then study carefully the writer's revisions.

First Draft Essay

When I took my son to his first day at pre-kindergarten, I wondered if I was making a huge mistake. Then, as I turned to leave him and saw his big, beautiful, brown eyes fill with tears, I knew for sure I had made a bad decision. That was a year ago. Now I am convinced that sending Jason to pre-kindergarten is one of the best decisions I've ever made. Pre-kindergarten helps children grow and change in many ways.

Before Jason started his school experience, he was very shy. He wouldn't talk to anyone unless he knew them well. He wouldn't even talk to my cousin's kids when they came over. After attending pre-kindergarten a while, he started to lose his shyness. He learned to meet new kids and get along with them.

In addition, Jason learned his ABC's, numbers, and to write his name, which was the greatest thing in the world to him. He also learned many different songs, stories, games, and other fun things.

Now, Jason even eats a wide variety of foods because other kids do. He plays different games too. Now Jason is a completely different person which makes me proud.

Idea Map

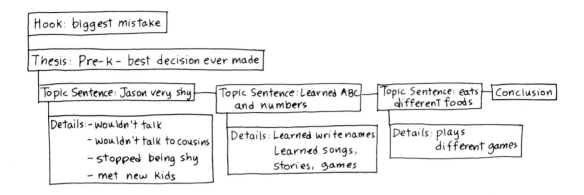

The map reveals several weaknesses in the essay. Paragraph two needs more detail or an example of how Jason stopped being shy. Paragraph three lacks a topic sentence. The writer lists three types of things that Jason learned in pre-k, but it does not have a sentence that says this. The writer decided that paragraph four is too specific—it's only about foods. The writer decided to broaden this paragraph by including Jason's experiments with new things and using food as one example.

First Revision

Growing Up at Pre-K

> As I walked my son, Jason, to his first
> day at pre-kindergarten, I wondered if I was
> making a huge mistake. Then, as I turned to
> leave him and saw his big, beautiful, brown
> eyes fill with tears, I was certain I'd made a
> bad decision. That was a year ago. Now I am

convinced that sending Jason to pre-kindergarten is one of the best decisions I have ever
made. Pre-kindergarten helps children grow and
change in many ways.

Before Jason started pre-k, he was very
shy. He wouldn't talk to anyone unless he knew
them well. In fact, he wouldn't even talk to my
cousin's kids when they came over. After a
while at pre-k, he started to lose his shyness.
He learned to meet new kids and get along with
them. Now, when new kids moved in next door, he
is anxious to play with them.

Pre-k also helped Jason learn things in
preparation for kindergarten. He learned his
ABC's and numbers; he learned to write his
name, which was the greatest thing in the world
to him. He also learned many different songs,
stories, and games. Now he'll know how they do
things in story and music hour and during
recess.

Jason has learned to try new things. Before
he wouldn't try anything new. For example, before pre-k he never tried new foods. Now Jason
eagerly tastes new foods. I think he wants to
try new things because he sees other kids trying them. He also attempts different ways of
talking. I can tell when he tries talking like
one of the other kids, or one of the aides.

Now Jason is a completely different person,
and I am proud of him.

In subsequent revisions, the writer added more examples, more
detailed explanations, and added vivid and descriptive language. She
also included several anecdotes that illustrated her main points.

Exercise 12–10   Draw an idea map for the essay you wrote in Exercises 12–6
through 12–9. Use it to revise your essay.

SELECTING A TITLE

■ The title of your essay should identify the topic and interest your reader. It may also suggest the focus you present in your essay. To select a title, reread your final draft, paying particular attention to your thesis statement and your overall method of development. Here are a few examples of effective titles.

> "Surprise in the Vegetable Bin" introduces an essay on vegetables and their effects on cholesterol and cancer.

> "Denim Goes High Fashion" introduces an essay describing uses of denim for clothing other than jeans.

> To write accurate and interesting titles, try the following tips:

> 1. Write a question that your essay answers.
> Question: Why Change the Minimum Wage?
> 2. Use key words that appear in your thesis statement.
> Thesis Statement: The new international trade ruling threatens the safety of the dolphin, one of our most intelligent mammals.
> Title: New Threat to Dolphins

Exercise 12–11   Select a title for the essay you wrote in Exercises 12–6 through 12–10.

PROOFREADING

■ Proofreading, an important final step in writing an effective essay, is checking for errors in grammar, punctuation, spelling, and mechanics such as capitalization. Also, look for typographical errors if you typed your paper. Errors left uncorrected detract from your essay. They indicate to your reader that you are careless or unconcerned with correctness. This impression detracts from your believability; consequently, your reader is less likely to accept the ideas you have presented. (Chapter 2, p. 30, lists useful tips for proofreading, and the error log discussed in Chapter 5, p. 88 is a valuable aid, as well.)

If you have difficulty catching all of your errors, ask a friend or classmate to proofread your paper. Be sure to understand why he or she made each correction.

THINKING BEFORE READING

■   This reading appeared in the *New York Times Magazine*. The author, Barbara Ascher, relates the experience of her brother's death from AIDS. The reading illustrates a well-developed essay.

1. Preview the reading "A Brother's Death" using the steps listed on p. 43.

2. Activate your thinking by completing each of the following activities.

a. List all of the different attitudes or feelings (both positive and negative) that you've heard expressed about AIDS and or AIDS victims.

b. People respond to grief in different ways. Some become quiet and withdrawn, and others become angry. Some immerse themselves in their work. List some ways you have observed that people handle grief.

READING

■

A BROTHER'S DEATH

Barbara Lazear Ascher

It could have been a parade of Civil War soldiers, wounded and near defeat, marching toward another battle. They stared ahead with eyes from which all joy had been banished.   1

They had marched in too many funeral processions, they had watched as disease dismissed courage and defiantly claimed their friends. This day, three months ago, they marched in a New Orleans jazz funeral for my brother, Bobby, dead of AIDS at 31.   2

I rode with my sister, mother and father, and my brother's companion, George, in a mule-drawn wagon, ahead of the parade of friends, and behind the musicians, old black men who knew the route and the music by heart.   3

The street was closed for the occasion. The citizens were shuttered inside cool interiors away from the fireball that is New Orleans' August sun. The day was ours, the streets were ours. The sun beat down on us alone. We, in the cart, sat as still as stones.   4

George cradled a carved wooden box that looked like an ornate bird house—the house of ashes that had been my brother's bones.   5

Still as stone we rode through the streets of New Orleans as jazz rose up around us and the old men played "The Old Rugged Cross" to lead us to the church. If we moved, if we cried, we might never stop moving, never stop crying. It was better to be still.   6

My brother was a wild thing. The confines of our New England home could not contain him. He kept flying into windows. Released, he flew south to warmth, to a landscape large enough to absorb his exuberance. To sympathetic souls who held him when exuberance failed.   7

A friend who volunteers at the Gay Men's Health Crisis tells me, "You would be surprised how many families first learn that their son or brother is gay at the same time they learn he has AIDS. They get a phone call that says, 'I've got two things to tell you.'" My family was more fortunate. We knew that my brother was gay, and his openness had enabled my parents to share the happiness he and George were finding together, to know and accept that in a careless world, love is precious whatever the pairing. But there is no accepting that one's child is doomed.   8

We are not alone in our anger, grief and disbelief. The horizon is filling up with parents burying young sons. Fewer and fewer of us are allowed the smug certainty that AIDS has nothing to do with our lives. Soon, each of us will have a child, brother, friend, friend of a friend, a distant relative who is doomed.   9

Until recently, the statistics have insulated many of us. We've read that the risk group comprises homosexuals, bisexuals and intravenous drug users. If we didn't fit in the categories, we said, "Well, I'm safe," and turned the page. To number fatalities is to depersonalize them. The body count in Vietnam. The deaths from drunk driving. Numbers don't touch our hearts.   10

My parents, well known in their community, broke through those barriers of denial by making it clear, in their son's prominent obituary, that the cause of Bobby's death was AIDS. Not "pneumonia" or "heart attack" or "respiratory failure," or other causes of death we now see in obituary columns when we read about single men dying in their prime.   11

The letters of sympathy began to come in immediately.   12

"Thank you for being honest about Bobby's illness. My best friend's son has AIDS."   13

"When my cousin died of AIDS, it was a family secret. That robbed us of the opportunity to mourn and be supported in our grief."   14

"My best friend in college, captain of the football team, a   15
Rhodes scholar, just died of AIDS."

It became clear from the letters that AIDS was coming home.   16
AIDS had come to Donna Reed America, to Father Knows Best
America. AIDS was killing kids who once wore Mickey Mouse Club
caps and wrote mash notes to Annette Funicello.

When we first learned of Bobby's illness it seemed incomprehensi-   17
ble that this could be happening to our baby brother. My sister and I
began a journey into paralysis. There were days when it seemed we
had to concentrate on putting one foot in front of the other if we
were to walk at all. If we traveled more than a couple of blocks, we
were exhausted for the rest of the day.

We were hungry, we weren't hungry. We made chocolate chip   18
cookies and chocolate brownies and didn't eat them. We opened and
closed the refrigerator door, looking for something that might cush-
ion the pain, fill the chasm that was opening from within.

Now I realize that this was the beginning of grief which starts in   19
the stomach, yawning like the gaping mouth in Munch's painting,
"The Scream." But what did we know of grief? We were young, our
beloveds had not yet died. I began to understand that grieving is like
walking. The urge is there, but you need a guiding hand, you need
someone to teach you how.

I went to speak with a wise and trusted minister at my church   20
who warned that there were bad times ahead. The death of a sibling,
he said, grievous in itself, is also a startling reminder of our own mortality. I suppose it's not dissimilar to the time in youth when we first
learned of our origins and began to understand, if they made me,
then they can make another. After that we became the nervous senti-
nels of our territory. When a sibling dies, the absolute certainty of
death replaces the cherished illusion that maybe we'll be the exceptions. When a sibling dies, death tugs at our own shirt tails. There's
no unclasping its persistent grip. "You too," it says. "Yes, even
you."

When you are new to grief, you learn that there's no second-   21
guessing it. It will have its way with you. Don't be fooled by the statistics you read: Widows have one bad year; orphans three. Grief
doesn't read schedules.

One morning, three weeks after Bobby died, I arose feeling happy   22
and energetic. Well, now, I thought, I guess we've taken care of that.
Wrong. The next morning I was awakened by a wail I thought was
coming from the storm outside until I realized it was coming from
me.

Grief will fool you with its disguises. Some days you insist that   23
you're fine, you're just angry at a friend who said the wrong thing.
One day I wept into the lettuce and peaches at our local market
when an acquaintance approached to scold me for my stand in an
old battle. Of course, we both assumed that she was responsible for
my tears.

You learn that you can cry and stop and laugh and even follow a   24
taxi driver's commands to "Have a nice day," and then cry again.
You learn that there is no such thing as crying forever. Three months
ago I was certain that I would never be happy again. I was wrong.

Grief is like the wind. When it's blowing hard, you adjust your   25
sails and run before it. If it blows too hard, you stay in the harbor,
close the hatches and don't take calls. When it's gentle, you go sail-
ing, have a picnic, take a swim.

You go wherever it takes you. There are no bulwarks to with-   26
stand it. Should you erect one, it will eventually tire of the game and
blow the walls in.

We cannot know another's grief, as deeply personal as love and   27
pain. I cannot measure my own against the sorrow of my brother's
friends who must wonder every day which among them will be next.
Who must have wondered, as they marched through the streets of
New Orleans, which of their families would sit one day in the mule-
drawn cart. I shy away from the magnitude of my brother's own
grief when, upon being diagnosed, he heard the final click of a door
as it closed on possibility.

A friend of mine said of her son when he died at 30, "He was   28
just beginning to look out at the world and make maps." So was my
brother. And then there was no place to go.

New York Times Magazine, November 19, 1989

GETTING READY TO WRITE

■ *Step 1: Annotation*

In this reading the writer reveals her personal feelings and experiences
surrounding her brother's death from AIDS. She discloses very personal
thoughts and shares details of her grieving process. She intends that
you become emotionally involved with her.

To prepare to write about an essay, it is helpful to mark key
passages and jot down your own ideas, reactions, and feelings in the
margin. This process is known as *annotating*. Annotation helps you

keep track of your ideas and reactions and helps you to separate your own feelings from those of the author.

Here's a partial list of the types of annotations you might make.

questions

key terms or definitions

statements that reveal the author's feelings

summary statements

inconsistencies

figures of speech

ideas that you disagree with

assumptions (ideas the writer assumes to be true but doesn't prove)

vivid examples

sections you want to reread or think about

A sample annotation for the first few paragraphs of the reading is shown below. Your annotation need not look exactly like this. Each reader's reactions and impressions may differ.

Sample Annotation

their lives have changed

It could have been a parade of Civil War soldiers, wounded and near defeat, marching toward another battle. They stared ahead with eyes from which all joy had been banished.   1

They had marched in too many funeral processions, they had watched as disease dismissed courage and defiantly claimed their friends. This day, three months ago, they marched in a New Orleans jazz funeral for my brother, Bobby, dead of AIDS at 31.   2

is this usually done?

I rode with my sister, mother and father, and my brother's companion, George, in a mule-drawn wagon, ahead of the parade of friends, and behind the musicians, old black men who knew the route and the music by heart.   3

not involved

not a pleasant day to "own"

The street was closed for the occasion. The citizens were shuttered inside cool interiors away from the fireball that is New Orleans' August sun. The day was ours, the streets were ours. The sun beat down on us alone. We, in the cart, sat as still as stones.   4

George cradled a carved wooden box that looked like an ornate   5
isolation

Exercise 12–12   Reread "A Brother's Death" and record your reactions using annotations.

Step 2: Thinking Critically: Figurative Language

Figurative language refers to words or expressions that make sense on a creative or imaginative level, but do not make sense literally. Here are a few everyday figurative expressions.

The exam was a piece of cake.

George eats like a horse.

She's as skinny as a scarecrow.

The meaning of each of these is clear, but you can see that they are not factually or literally true.

Figurative language is a creative way of expressing ideas. It appeals to your imagination, senses, or emotions. It usually involves a comparison between two unlike things that share at least one common characteristic. The expression "George eats like a horse" takes two dissimilar things (George and a horse) and says they are similar in one way (how they eat). The expression creates a mental image and suggests more than it says about George's eating habits. When you visualize a person eating like a horse, what do you see?

The article "A Brother's Death" contains numerous figurative expressions. For example, in riding in the mule-drawn wagon, the author says "Still as stones we rode through the streets" (paragraph 6). Ascher compares the riders to stone that is hard and cold, that lacks life or feeling. This expression suggests that the author felt cold and hard because she was numbed by the death. Her immobility made her feel lifeless. Later Ascher says, "If we moved, if we cried, we might never stop" (paragraph 6). That is, if she allowed herself to become lifelike, her feelings might overwhelm her.

Figurative expressions that compare two unlike things are called similes when they use the words "like" or "as," and metaphors when they do not use any comparison words. For example, if Ascher had written, "we were stone in the wagon," that would be a metaphor.

Another figurative expression in the article, called personification, appears in this sentence: "Grief doesn't read schedules." (paragraph 21) It is a comparison that gives human qualities to an inanimate (not alive) object or idea. Grief is given the human ability to read (or not read) schedules. This expression emphasizes the power of grief and helps the reader understand that it cannot be controlled.

Exercise 12–13   Review "A Brother's Death" and circle each use of figurative language.

Step 3: Reacting to and Discussing Ideas

1. What is the author's attitude toward Bobby's homosexuality?

2. How does the author describe the homosexual community in New Orleans?

3. Do you think the death of a sibling would be a startling reminder of one's own mortality? Why? How is it different from the death of a close friend who is close in age?

4. What types of "maps" (paragraph 28) was Bobby just beginning to make?

5. What kind of hook does Ascher use to open the essay? Evaluate its effectiveness.

WRITING ABOUT THE READING

■ *Assignment 1*

Build a four- to five-paragraph essay using the following thesis statement or your revision of it.

> Barbara Ascher, in the article "A Brother's Death," uses figurative language to help the reader understand her brother and her reaction to his death.

In each of your supporting paragraphs, give one example of a figurative expression used in the article. Explain what it means and what it tells you about Bobby, or about his sister's reaction to his death. Be sure to reread the sentences surrounding the expression in the article before you write about what it means. Below is a list of some of the figurative expressions used in the article, "A Brother's Death."

Paragraph	Expression
7	"He kept flying into windows."
7	"he flew south"
17	"My sister and I began a journey into paralysis."
19	"grieving is like walking"
20	"death tugs at our own shirt tails"
21	"It (grief) will have its way with you."
23	"Grief will fool you with its disguises."
25	"Grief is like the wind."
27	"he (Bobby) heard the final click of a door as it closed on possibility."

Assignment 2

Write a three- to four-paragraph essay that answers this question: Do you think the article is primarily about AIDS or about death and grief? (This question asks you to identify the author's purpose in writing. Refer to Chapter 3, p. 44 for further information.) Support your answer with specific examples from the reading.

WRITING ABOUT YOUR IDEAS

■ *Writing Assignment 1*

Write a three- to four-paragraph essay about the subject of grief. Narrow the subject before planning your essay.

Writing Assignment 2

Write a three- to four-paragraph essay about AIDS. Narrow the subject before planning your essay.

Writing Assignment 3

The author states that "fewer and fewer of us are allowed the smug certainty that AIDS has nothing to do with our lives" (paragraph 9) and that "Until recently, the statistics have insulated many of us" (paragraph 10). What other problems or social issues do you feel many of us are ignoring? Select one issue or problem and write a three- to four-paragraph essay explaining why it is a growing problem or issue and/or why or how we are ignoring it.

Journal Writing Suggestions

1. Write an entry describing your feelings about AIDS or homosexuality.
2. Write an entry describing your success in establishing a tone in your writing.

REVISION CHECKLIST

1. Is your essay appropriate for your audience? Does it give them the background information they need? Will it interest them?
2. Will your essay accomplish your purpose?
3. Have you narrowed your topic so that you can cover your subject thoroughly in your essay?
4. Is your main point clearly expressed in a thesis statement in the introductory paragraph? Does your introductory paragraph capture the reader's interest and lead into the body of the essay?
5. Does each paragraph of your essay have a topic sentence that supports your main point?
6. Is each paragraph's topic sentence supported by relevant and sufficient detail?
7. Are your paragraphs arranged in a logical sequence and connected by transitions?
8. Is the tone of your essay appropriate for your purpose and audience?
9. Does your conclusion reemphasize your thesis statement and draw the essay to a close?
10. Does your title identify the topic and interest the reader?
11. Have you proofread your paper and corrected any errors in grammar, mechanics, and spelling?

PROOFREADING CHECKLIST

1. Does each sentence end with appropriate punctuation (period, question mark, or exclamation point)?
2. Is all punctuation within each sentence correct (commas, colons, semicolons, apostrophes, dashes, and quotation marks)?
3. Is each word spelled correctly?
4. Have you used capital letters where needed?
5. Are numbers and abbreviations used correctly?
6. Are any words omitted?
7. If your paper is typed, have you corrected all typographical errors?
8. If your paper is handwritten, is your handwriting always legible?
9. Are your pages in the correct order and numbered?

Parallelism

Parallelism means that words, phrases, or clauses in a series should have similar grammatical form. Keeping corresponding parts of a sentence parallel in structure and length will make your writing clearer and easier to read.

What Should Be Parallel?

1. Words in series. When two or more nouns, verbs, or adjectives appear together in a sentence, they should be parallel in grammatical form. Verbs should be written in the same tense.

INCORRECT: All night long the music from the next apartment was banging, thumping, and pounded so loudly I couldn't sleep.

CORRECT: All night long, the music from the next apartment banged, thumped, and pounded so loudly that I couldn't sleep.

2. Phrases.

INCORRECT: My sister likes wearing crazy hats, dressing in funky clothes, and to go to classic movies.

CORRECT: My sister likes wearing crazy hats, dressing in funky clothes, and going to classic movies.

3. Clauses.

INCORRECT: While Yolanda studied math and worked on psychology, her husband was watching the baby.

CORRECT: While Yolanda studied math and worked on psychology, her husband watched the baby.

Rate Your Ability to Use Parallel Structure

Identify the sentences that lack parallelism and correct them.

   1. Melinda's professor drew an organizational chart of the human nervous system on the board, passing out a handout of it, and lectured about the way the nervous system is divided into subcategories.
   2. Down's Syndrome is caused by the presence of an extra chromosome, a microscopic deviation from the norm that has important consequences.

SKILL   REFRESHER 10

. . . .

3. Ski jumping, speed skating, and hang glide are sports that require consideration and manipulation of velocity and wind resistance.

4. Professor Bargo's poetry class read famous poets, analyzed their poetry, and researches their lives.

5. The clam, oysters, and the mussel are examples of mollusks.

6. There are many alternative sources of energy available including solar, wind, and atomic energies.

7. The United Nations was formed in 1945 to renounce war, uphold personal freedoms, and bringing about worldwide peace and well-being.

8. In the 1980s, Sandra Day O'Connor was appointed the first female Supreme Court Justice, Geraldine Ferraro became the first female presidential candidate, and the Equal Rights Amendment is defeated.

9. The Eighteenth Amendment to the Constitution implemented Prohibition, but the twenty-first amendment, ratified fourteen years later, repeals it.

10. Black holes, pulsars, and quasars are studied by astronomers and physicists.

Score _____

Check your answers using the Answer Key on page 537. If you scored below 80 percent, you need additional review and practice in using parallel structure. Refer to Section D.5 of Reviewing the Basics in Part 5.

SUMMARY

■   1. Your introductory paragraph should
   • present your thesis statement and suggest the organization of your essay.
   • set the tone of your essay and suggest its audience.
   • interest your reader and provide background information.

2. Your thesis statement should clearly and specifically state the main point of your essay.

3. Tone reflects your purpose and is related to your audience. Tone is established through word choice, use of personal pronouns, and use of contractions.

4. Several types of hooks can be used to capture your reader's interest: questions, a startling fact, story, quotation, or misunderstood fact.

5. The body of your essay provides information to support your thesis statement. Focus on
    - developing each paragraph effectively.
    - arranging your paragraphs in a logical sequence.
    - connecting your paragraphs using transitional words and sentences or by repeating key words.

6. Your conclusion should reemphasize your thesis statement and draw your essay to a close. You might
    - restate your thesis.
    - suggest a new direction for further thought.
    - summarize key points.
    - look ahead.

7. Revision involves examining and evaluating ideas. Evaluate
    - the overall effectiveness of your essay.
    - the effectiveness of each individual paragraph.

8. The title of your essay should identify your topic and interest your reader.

9. Proofreading is an important final step and involves checking for errors in grammar, punctuation, spelling, and mechanics.

13 Writing Expository Essays

In this chapter you will learn to

1. plan expository essays.

2. analyze your audience and purpose.

3. organize and develop expository essays.

WHAT IS AN EXPOSITORY ESSAY?

■ An expository essay presents information on a specific topic; its purpose is to explain. For example, you might want to explain your qualifications for a job, describe how to operate a microscope, or trace your family tree. For all of these topics, you want to focus clearly on facts and objective detail. Expository writing usually does not include opinions, judgments, or arguments. Expository essays follow the basic organization you learned in Chapters 11 and 12. They contain an introductory paragraph with a thesis statement, supporting paragraphs, and a concluding paragraph. You generate ideas and organize them as you do for other types of essays.

Much of the writing you do in college and at work will be expository. In college, essay exams, class assignments, and term papers all demand expository writing skills. The reports, memos, and summaries at work should present information clearly and effectively.

Depending on your topic, you may need to obtain additional information about your topic through reading or research. Although you may have general information about your topic, you may need to locate specifics—facts, statistics, or examples to support your main points. Here is a brief expository essay that a student wrote for an assignment for her interpersonal communication class. Her essay is based on her own observations and on an article by Desmond Morris.

How to Spot a Liar

If you suspected a friend were lying to you, what would you do to confirm your suspicions? Most of us would listen more carefully to what the person says, and try to "catch" him or her saying a slip or something contradictory. Most liars are experienced—they've been practicing for a long time. They are very careful about what they say; therefore, they seldom make a slip. To spot a liar stop paying attention to *what* is said. Instead, pay attention to the person's voice, face, and body.

How a person speaks reveals more than what he or she says. While choice of words is easy to control, the voice often betrays one's emotions. Because areas of the brain involved with emotion control the voice, the voice tends to reveal emotion. When a person lies, the voice tends to be higher pitched and the rate of speech tends to slow down.

Even more revealing than voice is a person's face. The face is the primary place we display emotions. We use different facial expressions to convey fear, anger, happiness, or guilt. Facial expressions are harder to fake than words because you can rehearse or practice what you will say, but you cannot practice how you will feel. Liars tend to make exaggerated expressions—a smile that is drawn out too long or a frown that is too severe. Eyes are especially revealing. Liars' eyes lack the genuine, warm twinkle when they smile, and they make less eye contact with the other person.

The body is the most revealing of all. While many liars try to control their voice and face, many do not know that their body has its own language. Posture and gestures reveal a person's feelings. Liars tend to make less enthusiastic gestures. At times, the gesture may not fit with what is being said. Liars tend to hold themselves at a greater distance from other people. They also have a less relaxed body position. You may notice, too, nervous behaviors such as twisting a ring or toying with a button.

Spotting a liar is never easy, but you will have the most success if you watch rather than listen. As we all know, actions are more important than words. (Desmond Morris. "Nonverbal Leakage: How You Can Tell if Someone is Lying." *Manwatching*. New York: Abrams, 1977.)

Notice that this essay is factual. The author does not include opinions about or personal experience with liars. The introductory paragraph interests the reader by posing a hypothetical question. The next sentence tells us that what we frequently assume is wrong and

WRITING
SUCCESS
TIP 13

Taking Notes When Researching a Topic

When researching a topic, be sure to take accurate and detailed notes. Use the following tips to record information.

1. **Use note cards.** Purchase $3'' \times 5''$ index cards. Write on only one side of the card. Record only closely related facts or ideas on a single card. Use a separate card for each source, even if the information is on the same topic. This method will allow you to rearrange your cards in the order in which you will use them as you write your paper.

2. **Record the source of the information on each card.** Include title, author, and exact page(s).

3. **Record the specific topic of the note at the top of the card.** Suppose you are researching the topic of pollution of residential water wells. If you are writing a note about chemical spraying of farm crops as a source of pollution, write "Source: Crop Spraying" at the top of the card.

4. **Search for useful information that explains, supports, or develops your thesis statement.**

explains why. The last sentence states the author's thesis. The next three paragraphs explain how voice, face, and body can be used to spot liars. The concluding paragraph restates the thesis in more general terms and ends with a widely accepted expression.

PLANNING YOUR ESSAY

■   Since the purpose of an expository essay is always to provide information that your audience can understand and use, be certain that all of your information is clear and correct. This involves selecting an appropriate level of detail, choosing a logical method of development, obtaining complete and correct information, and deciding on an appropriate tone.

Selecting an Appropriate Level of Detail

A student wrote the following paragraph as part of an expository essay for a class assignment. His audience was his classmates.

5. **Be selective.** You will not be able to record every detail each source contains. Record information that is directly related to your purpose in writing. Search for information that is useful and appropriate for your audience.

6. **Summarize, paraphrase (restate in your own words), or write a direct quotation.** For example, depending on the type of information and its usefulness, you might summarize background information, paraphrase facts, and quote the opinion of an authority on your topic.

7. **Use separate cards to write notes to yourself.** Record questions, personal reactions, or additional information needed.

8. **Use 3″ × 5″ cards to record complete bibliographic information of each source.** Use a separate card for each source. Write the information in correct documentation form. This method will save you time as you prepare your bibliography.

When the small long-iron clubhead is behind the ball, it's hard to stop tension from creeping into your arms. When this happens, your takeaway becomes fast and jerky. Your backswing becomes shorter and you lose your rhythm. Even worse, this tension causes your right hand to uncock too early. One result is that the clubhead reaches its peak speed before it hits the ball. Another result is the clubhead goes outside the line of play and cuts across the ball steeply from outside to in. A slice or pull results.

Did you find the paragraph clear and easy to understand? Unless you know a lot about golf, you probably found it difficult, confusing, and not understandable. This writer made a very serious error: he failed to analyze his audience. He assumed they know as much about golf as he does. Readers who do not play golf would need more background information to understand his essay. Terms would also have to be defined.

Analyzing your audience is always the first step for any expository essay. It will help you assess how much and what type of detail to include. Here are some key questions to begin your analysis:

- Is my reader familiar with the topic?
- How much background or history does my reader need to understand the information?
- Do I need to define any unfamiliar terms?
- Do I need to explain any unfamiliar people, places, events, parts or processes?

Suppose you are writing an expository essay on how to locate an apartment to rent. As you plan your essay, you need to decide how much information to present. This decision involves analyzing both your audience and your purpose.

First, consider how much your audience already knows about the topic. If you think your readers know a lot about renting apartments, review briefly what they already know and then move to a more detailed explanation of new information. On the other hand, if your topic is probably brand new to your readers, then capture their interest without intimidating them. Try to relate the topic to the readers' own experience. Show them how renting an apartment resembles something they already know. For example, you might compare renting an apartment to other types of shopping with certain desired features and an established price range. If you are uncertain about your audience's background, it is safer to include information they may already know rather than to assume that they know it. Readers can skim or skip over information they know, but they cannot fill in gaps in their understanding without your help.

The author of the sample essay on liars on p. 267 did not assume any knowledge by the reader about nonverbal communication. Each idea was explained completely.

Once you have made these decisions about your audience, you will want to specify your purpose. Is your purpose to give your readers an overview of the process? Or, do you want to give your readers specific, practical information so that they can begin shopping for a car right away? You would need much more detail for the second purpose than you would for the first. The author's purpose in writing the sample essay on liars on p. 267 was very practical. She intended to tell you exactly what to look for in identifying when someone is lying.

Exercise 13–1   For two of the following topics, define your audience and purpose and generate a list of ideas to include in an expository essay.

1. the lack of privacy in our society
2. the value of sports

3. the functions of billboards
4. attitudes toward senior citizens
5. how to make new friends

Choosing a Logical Method of Development

Analyzing your audience and purpose will also help you choose which method or methods of development to use. Expository essays use the same methods of development that you learned in Chapters 6 through 10—narration, process, description, definition, example, classification, comparison and contrast, and cause and effect. You can select the best one to suit your audience and purpose. The sample essay on liars was based on the process method of development. However, the supporting paragraphs were arranged from least-to-most important. Now, suppose you are writing an expository essay on stages of child language development. If your audience is unfamiliar with the topic, practical, realistic examples of a child's speech at each stage may be the most effective method for helping your readers understand the topic. If your audience is more knowledgeable about the topic, examples or definitions may be unnecessary. A more direct, straightforward process explanation would be appropriate.

Your method of development depends on purpose. Here are a few examples.

If your purpose is to	*Use*
explain how something works or perform a specific task	Process (See Chapter 6)
give practical understanding using specific situations	Example (See Chapter 8)
explain a topic by showing the parts into which it can be divided or the group to which it belongs	Classification (See Chapter 8)
explain what something is	Definition (See Chapter 8)
emphasize similarities or differences between two topics or explain something by comparing it to something already familiar	Comparison and Contrast (See Chapter 9)
explain why something happened	Cause and Effect (See Chapter 10)

Suppose you are majoring in accounting, and you must write an expository essay about why you chose accounting as a career. You could explain your choice in several different ways. If your purpose is to show others that you made the right choice, you would probably trace the history of your decision. If your purpose is to encourage other students to choose accounting, you would probably describe the job of an accountant, giving vivid details about its opportunities and rewards. If your purpose is to get a job with an accounting firm, you might give examples of problems accountants solve and challenges they face. If you choose the first approach, narrative or cause and effect would be the best methods for developing your essay. Description would be best for the second approach, and example would be best for the third. The chart below demonstrates how audience and purpose work together in your choice of method.

Audience	*Purpose*	*Method(s) of Development*
family, friends, interested others	show that you made the right choice	narrative, cause and effect
students	encourage them to major in accounting	description
potential employers	demonstrate your understanding of the job and its challenges	example

Although your essay should have logical overall development, you can use more than one method of development within the essay. Assume you are writing an essay on family responsibility. You might choose definition for your first paragraph and define how you will use the term—"responsibility." The next three paragraphs could classify family responsibility by types, such as financial responsibility, physical care responsibility, emotional support responsibility, and so forth. In your last three paragraphs, a well-developed example of each type could work. Although you chose several different methods of development, the essay followed a logical overall development. You progressed from general to specific, beginning with the broad concept of family responsibility and ending with examples of specific types. The essay might also progress from less to more personal, concluding with examples from your own family life.

Exercise 13–2   For each of the following thesis statements, suggest at least one possible method of development. If it is appropriate, suggest several methods. Then select one thesis statement and draft an outline that demonstrates your method(s) of development.

1. Thesis Statement: The story of Saddam Hussein's rise to power reveals an exciting, yet terrifying, lesson in history.

Method of Development: _____

2. Thesis Statement: Soap operas allow viewers to escape into a fantasy world in which they can share the characters' problems and joys.

Method of Development: _____

3. Thesis Statement: A listener reveals his or her attitude toward a speaker through nonverbal signals.

Method of Development: _____

4. Thesis Statement: Children inherit much from their parents, including good or bad financial habits.

Method of Development: _____

5. Thesis Statement: Many schools are revising their history courses to include contributions of Afro-Americans, Native Americans, Asians, and Hispanics.

Method of Development: _____

Obtaining Complete and Correct Information

Many times, you will already know enough about your topic to explain it clearly and completely, especially if it is something with which you have direct experience. At other times, however, you will need more information. Here's a quick review of useful sources.

The College Library

Your college library is usually the best source of additional information. It is also one of the easiest and fastest sources to use. Information is readily available, and you can use it at your convenience. In addition, a librarian can help you locate what you need quickly. See Writing Success Tip 12 for suggestions on locating library information sources.

Consulting an Expert

Depending on your topic, it may be helpful to consult someone who is an expert in the field you are writing about. Suppose you are writing about types and features of homeowner's insurance. If your brother-in-law is an insurance agent, he may be able to provide all the information you need or direct you to appropriate sources. Prepare a list of questions to ask your expert. As you talk to or interview him or her, be sure to take detailed notes.

News Media

If you are writing about a current topic, magazines, newspapers, radio and television news, documentary programs, and videos contain a wealth of information. If you want to write a paper on wildlife preservation, for example, you could keep an eye out for public television news specials and check the educational videos at your local rental store.

Documenting Sources

When you take information from other sources, you must indicate that you have done so. You must acknowledge, or give credit to, other authors when you use their information, ideas, interpretations, explanations, or theories. Even if you are not quoting them directly, you must let your reader know where you obtained your information, as the student did in the essay on lie detection on page 267.

There are two commonly used documentation formats: the MLA (Modern Language Association) style and the APA (American Psychological Association) style. Usually, your instructors will indicate which documentation style they prefer or require. Both styles involve placing brief source notes in your paper. They give the author and page in parentheses within the essay following the acknowledged material. A complete source reference is listed in a bibliography at the end of the essay. The complete source reference for a book includes the author(s) full name, title of book, edition, place of publication, publisher, and date.

Here is an example of a citation within an essay, followed by its complete source reference using MLA style.

CITATION: Young children are capable of regenerating some missing body parts. There are several documented cases of regrown fingers, complete with nails and finger prints. (Wallace 362)

COMPLETE   Wallace, Robert A. *Biology: The World of Life.* 5th ed.
REFERENCE: Glenview, IL: Scott Foresman, 1990.

Each documentation style has specific formats for books, periodicals, newspapers, and other reference sources. To obtain further information on the MLA and APA styles, consult the most recent editions of:

The MLA Handbook for Writers of Research Papers
Publication Manual of the American Psychological Association

Exercise 13–3   Select one of the topics you chose for Exercise 13–1. Evaluate the level of detail you need and review the ideas you generated. Decide if you need additional information, and if so, use one or more of the sources described above.

Deciding on an Appropriate Tone

Since the purpose of an expository essay is to present information, your tone should reflect your seriousness about the topic. A humorous, sarcastic, flip, or very informal tone will detract from your essay and suggest that what you say should not be taken seriously.

As a general rule, your tone should reflect your relationship to your audience. The less familiar you are with your audience, the more formal your tone should be.

A few examples of sentences in which the tone is inappropriate for most academic and career expository writing follow.

INAPPROPRIATE: Making jump shots is a mean task, but I'm gonna keep tossing 'em till I'm the best there is.
REVISED: Learning to make jump shots is difficult, but I'm going to practice until I'm the best on the team.

INAPPROPRIATE: I just couldn't believe that my best friend was a druggie.
REVISED: I was shocked to learn that my best friend uses drugs.

INAPPROPRIATE: The math exam was a real bust, and I'm sure I bombed it.
REVISED: The math exam was difficult, and I think I failed it.

The following suggestions help keep your tone appropriate.

1. Avoid slang expressions.
2. Use few if any contractions (don't, we'll).
3. Use first person pronouns (I, me) sparingly.
4. Your writing should sound more formal than casual conversation or than a letter to a close friend.
5. To achieve a more formal tone, avoid informal or everyday words. For example:

use "met" instead of "ran into"
use "children" instead of "kids"
use "annoying" instead of "bugging"

Exercise 13–4   Revise each of the following statements giving each a more formal tone.

1. I used be a goof-off when I was in high school, but now I am trying to get with education.
2. Sam is the kind of guy every woman would like to sink her claws into.
3. Because Marco is one of those easy-going types, people think they can walk all over him.
4. Ronald Reagan was a big hit as president and his staff made sure we knew it.
5. Emily Dickinson is a fabulous poet; some of her poems really hit me.

DRAFTING YOUR ESSAY

■   Because expository writing is often highly factual and detailed, readers, especially those who are not familiar with your topic, can easily become lost or confused. There are several things you can do to help your readers stay on track and grasp your ideas more easily.

Begin with an Informative Introduction

Factual essays can be just as lively and interesting as personal ones. You can use the same kinds of "hooks" to engage your readers' interest in the essay's introduction. (See pages 239–241 in Chapter 12.) You might

- relate the topic to the reader's personal experience;
- emphasize the value or importance of the information you are presenting;
- present a little known or surprising fact;
- relate your topic to a current event or concern (for example, connecting an essay on homeless people to a recent fund-raising event held for them in your community).

Your introduction should also present your thesis statement. For expository essays, your thesis statement should announce your topic clearly and directly as well as your approach to it. (See pages 239–241 in Chapter 12.) If possible, try to suggest, in advance, the organization your essay will follow. This technique is known as *foreshadowing*. Here are a few examples of thesis statements that foreshadow the organization of the essay.

1. There are five types of schizophrenia: residual, disorganized, catatonic, paranoid, and undifferentiated. (This thesis statement indicates the order in which the five types will be discussed.)
2. The id, the ego, and the superego are key aspects of Freud's theory of personality.
3. Psychologists who have made significant contributions to the field include Wundt, Watson, and Skinner.

Maintain a Balance Between Technical and Non-technical Information

If your essay contains a great deal of highly factual or technical explanation, it is helpful to break it up with examples, illustrations, or practical advice. For example, in the following excerpt from an essay on human communication, notice that the writer makes comparisons and offers examples.

> Human communication does not occur in a vacuum. It always takes place in a series of interacting contexts, which influence the communication that occurs. The context for communication is similar to the environment or setting in which a party occurs. Where it's held, who attends, and what is occurring affect whether you will have a good time.
>
> The first context is the temporal context. The time of day during which the communication occurs influences its effectiveness. For example, some of us are "day people"; others are "night people." When a day and a night person talk at midnight, the day person is not fully alert or receptive to conversation . . .

Use Clear Transitions

In earlier chapters, you learned to use transitional words and phrases to link ideas. Transitions are particularly important in expository essays. They keep your readers on track by showing how previous ideas connect with those that follow. Transitions also reveal your train of thought. A summary chart of transitional words is reprinted below for convenient reference.

Method of Development	*Transitional Words*
Most-Least	most important, above all, especially, particularly important
Advantages/Disadvantages	one, another, first, second, etc.
Spatial	above, below, behind, beside, next to, inside, outside, to the west (north, etc.), beneath, near, nearby, next to
Time Sequence	first, next, now, before, during, after, eventually, finally, at last, later, meanwhile, soon, then, suddenly, currently, after, afterward, after a while, as soon as, until
Process/Narration	first, second, then, later, in the beginning, when, after, following, next, during, again, after that, at last, finally
Description	see Spatial and Most-Least above
Example	for example, for instance, to illustrate
Classification	one, another, second, third
Definition	means, can be defined as, refers to, is
Comparison	likewise, similarly, in the same way, too, also
Contrast	however, on the contrary, unlike, on the other hand, although, even though, but, in contrast, yet
Cause and Effect	because, consequently, since, as a result, for this reason, therefore, thus

Repeat Key Words

Repeating key words also enables your reader to stay on track. Key words often appear in your thesis statement and by repeating some of them, you can remind reader of your thesis and encourage them to connect each new idea to it.

You need not repeat the exact same word or phrase as long as the meaning stays the same. You could substitute "keep your audience on target" for "enables your readers to stay on track," for example. The following excerpt from an essay on clothing illustrates the use of key word repetition.

The Real Functions of Clothing

Just as a product's packaging tells us a lot about the product, so does a person's clothing reveal a lot about the person. Clothing reflects the way we choose to present ourselves and reveals how we feel about ourselves.

Clothing reveals our emotions. We tend to dress according to how we feel. If we feel relaxed and comfortable, we tend to dress in comfortable, relaxed clothing. For instance, some people wear sweatshirts and pants for a relaxed evening at home. If we feel happy and carefree, our clothing often reflects it. Think of how fans dress at a football game, for example. Their dress reflects casual comfort and their team-supporting hats, T-shirts, etc. reveal their emotional support for the team.

Clothing also reveals our expectations and perceptions . . .

Make Your Conclusion Strong

The conclusion of an expository essay should remind your reader of your thesis statement. Do not simply restate it. Summarize your main points and what your essay says about your thesis. Finally, your conclusion should draw the essay to a close. Ask questions that still need to be answered or make a final statement about the topic.

Exercise 13–5   For the topic you selected in Exercise 13–1, write a first draft essay. Then revise the essay, using the revision checklist at the end of the chapter. Pay particular attention to your introduction, transitions, repetition of key words, technical/non-technical balance, and your conclusion.

THINKING BEFORE READING

■ This reading, "Understanding Society and Culture Through Eating," illustrates an expository essay. The authors' main purpose explains the importance of eating in every society. You can observe how Farb and Armelagos present key concepts and support them by using concrete examples from a variety of cultures.

1. Preview the reading using the steps outlined in Chapter 3, p. 43.
2. Discover what you already know about eating by completing the following:
   a. Think about special events and holidays that are important in your family. Do they include food?
   b. For what other reasons than nutrition do people eat?
   c. Do ethnic groups seem to have their own special foods? Why?
   d. Make a list of various events and places (other than restaurants) where food is served. (Examples: baseball games, movie theaters)

READING

■
UNDERSTANDING SOCIETY AND CULTURE THROUGH EATING

Peter Farb and George Armelagos

All animals feed but humans alone eat. A dog wolfs down every meal in the same way, but humans behave in a variety of ways while eating. In North American and European societies, for example, business negotiations are conducted over cocktails and lunch; seductions may begin with champagne and oysters; wedding and birthday parties center around an elaborately decorated cake; and gifts of food are part of the exchange at Christmas time. In simpler societies, eating is associated with initiation and burial rites, the roles of the sexes, economic transactions, hospitality, and dealings with the supernatural—virtually the entire spectrum of human activity. . . . 1

In all societies, both simple and complex, eating is the primary way of initiating and maintaining human relationships. In fact, the English word "companion" is derived from French and Latin words that mean "one who eats bread with another." The Bantu of south- 2 ern Africa regard exchanging food as the formation of what amounts to a temporary covenant[1] between individuals—"a clanship of porridge," as they call it. For most Chinese, social transactions are almost inseparable from eating transactions. The giving and sharing of food is the prototypic[2] relationship in Chinese society, as if the word were literally made flesh. Only a Chinese living alone and in abject poverty would sit down to a solitary meal. It is usual to eat with one's family or kin; when these are unavailable, people eat in teashops or at work rather than by themselves. No important business transaction and no marriage arrangement is ever concluded without the sharing of food. The quality of the meal and its setting convey a more subtle social message than anything that is consciously verbalized; attitudes that would be impolite if stated directly are communicated through the food channel.

Food and drink have such intense emotional significance that they are often linked with events that have nothing to do with nutrition. The perpetrators of the Boston Tea Party were angry not over tea but over taxation; the breadline and apple-sellers of the Great Depression became symbols of what was wrong with the economy. Guests at a dinner party usually leave a little food on the plate to let their hosts know they have been fed to repletion. A child who misbehaves is sent to bed without dinner, while obedience is rewarded with candy or ice cream. The simple fact of sitting down to eat together may convey important statements about a society. The civil-rights movement in the southern United States during the 1950s began as a dispute about the right of blacks not simply to eat at lunch counters but to sit down there with whites; blacks insisted on that right because in North American society people customarily sit down to eat only as equals.

Eating is intimately connected with sex roles, since the responsibility for each phase of obtaining and preparing a particular kind of food is almost always allotted according to sex. Members of one sex, generally the males, may be served first, and particular foods may be regarded as appropriate to each sex. Husbands and wives in some parts of Melanesia and Polynesia are not supposed to see each other eat; in Arabia, Japan, and parts of eastern Europe, women do not eat until the men in the family have finished their meals. In some societies, on the other hand, eating with the family is so traditional that workers are given long midday breaks so that they can go home for lunch. After World War II, hungry Greeks preferred to carry home

1. agreement
2. model

the hot soup given them by the Red Cross and eat it there with their families rather than in the warm Red Cross canteens. At marriage celebrations in northern Europe during the Middle Ages, it was considered an important moment when the couple ate together—which is apparently the origin of the custom that prevails today in North America and in parts of Europe of watching the new bride and groom share the first slice of wedding cake.

Each society's culture is transmitted to children through eating with the family, a setting in which individual personalities develop, kinship obligations emerge, and the customs of the group are reinforced. Children learn at mealtimes to express a formal reverence for food through the custom of saying grace, as in what Christians know as the Lord's Prayer ("Give us this day out daily bread"), and they become acquainted with the regulations governing what their society considers edible. For many African children, this amounts to learning that a meal is not a meal unless it includes porridge. Europeans are brought up to feel much the same way about bread, and many North Americans genuinely believe that dinner is not really dinner without meat.

Finally, what is eaten establishes one's social, religious, and ethnic memberships. The coarse black bread that is the standard fare of a European peasant is a function of social rank, and so is the meal of roast dog that was served to the Aztec noble. Who can mistake the status of a German who drinks Trockenberenauslese, a wine made from grapes so rare that finding enough to produce a single bottle is a day's work even for a skilled picker? The surest way of discovering a family's ethnic origins is to look into its kitchen. Long after dress, manners, and speech have become indistinguishable from those of the majority, the old food habits continue as the last vestiges[3] of the previous culture. Taboos against certain foods mark one as an adherent of a particular religion: Moslems and Jews reject pork, Hindus beef, and some Protestant denominations alcohol. Food customs as a badge of rank are particularly evident in India, where rules for each caste define both whom a person is permitted to marry and also with whom that person is permitted to eat; the interweaving of these prohibitions tends to keep young people in the same caste as their parents.

With so much cultural importance attached to eating, it is no wonder that food to a large extent is what holds a society together.

3. visible trace

For example, the rice that is fundamental to the existence of the Malays of Southeast Asia is believed to possess an essential life force; so the ceremonials that mark every stage of life—from birth through coming of age, marriage, and death—involves a symbolic meal of rice. For a Malay, rice is synonymous with food, and its presence is what distinguishes a meal. The Malays' first food of the day, at what North Americans and Europeans think of as the breakfast meal, usually consists of a sort of cake and coffee. Malays regard this as a snack rather than as a meal, simply because no rice is eaten. People in modern societies as well have notions about what is appropriate food for each meal. A typical North American breakfast consists of fruit, cereal, and a milk product—but strawberry shortcake, which includes all three, is considered inappropriate. . . .

For all that we denigrate[4] the magical beliefs connected with food in simpler societies, it should be remembered that some of us throw salt over a shoulder to ward off bad luck, or eat fish in the belief that it is a superior brain food, or oysters with the hope of increasing sexual potency. All the major religions continue to attach symbolic meanings to food and drink (even though the Roman Catholic prohibition against eating meat on Friday has been lifted): the bread and wine of the Christian communion service, the taboo observed by Jews against mixing meat and dairy products at the same meal, and the reverence for the sacred cow in Hindu India. In the political sphere, injustice is dramatized by fasting, as practiced by Gandhi and Martin Luther King, Jr., among many others. And we continue [. . .] to observe the rites of passage—birth, coming of age, marriage, and death—with food and drink.

4. belittle, treat as unimportant

from *Consuming Passions: The Anthropology of Eating*

GETTING READY TO WRITE

■ *Step 1: Summarizing*

Before you write about ideas you have just read, it is important to be sure you understand them completely. Summarizing is a good way to test your understanding. If you can condense the authors' ideas and express them in your own words, you can be certain that your comprehension is complete. Also, when you summarize you are making yourself a written record of the reading's key ideas that you can use later for a quick review.

Use the following steps to summarize:

1. First reread the material you want to summarize. Underline topic sentences (see Chapter 3, p. 37) and annotate (see Chapter 12, p. 257). Review your underlining and annotating.

2. Write a sentence that expresses the author's main thesis.

3. Write sentences that explain the author's most important supporting ideas. (Refer to your underlining.) Be sure to express ideas in your own words. Don't copy phrases or sentences. If you can't express an idea in your own words, you probably don't understand it.

4. Include definitions of key terms, important concepts, procedures, or principles.

5. Do not include examples, descriptive details, or quotations.

6. Reread your summary to determine whether it contains sufficient information. Use this test: Would your summary be understandable to someone who had not read the article? If not, revise your summary to include additional information.

Exercise 13–6   Write a summary of "Understanding Culture and Society Through Eating."

Step 2: Thinking Critically: Analyzing Source and Authority

As you learned earlier in this chapter, because the purpose of expository essays is to present information, it is imperative that the information be complete, reliable, and correct. You can present correct information by consulting sources and through careful research. However, how do you know that material you *read* is reliable, complete, and correct? How do you know that an author is knowledgeable about the topic or has consulted expert sources or conducted careful research? All critical readers must address these concerns. To find out whether information you are reading is reliable, you must consider the source of the material and the authority of the author.

Analyzing the Source

Source refers to where the material was originally published. It might be a book, newspaper, professional journal, or magazine. The source provides clues about the reliability of the material. Some publications have reputations for presenting carefully researched information. Others are known for providing personal opinion, less carefully researched material, personal interest stories, or even "newsy gossip." For example, the source of the reading in this chapter is a book titled *Consuming Passions: The Anthropology of Eating*. This is a scholarly book, one that usually indicates time-consuming research was involved and verifiable sources were sought, and it examines the role of eating in society and culture. Because of its sources, you can be reasonably confident that the information is reliable. If you were reading about eating habits in an encyclopedia or in a journal titled *The Journal of Anthropology*, you could be equally confident about the reliability of the information. However, reading about eating habits in a general interest magazine that you bought in the supermarket gives you less confidence about reliability due to the lack of sources and adequate research.

Sources for material that is not original to the book or publication you are reading are often included in footnotes or in acknowledgment sections such as the one at the back of this book. If you are uncertain about whether a source is reliable, check with your college's reference librarian.

To evaluate a source, ask the following questions:

1. What is the reputation of this source?
2. For what type of information is it best known?
3. Who is the intended audience?
4. What type of documentation does it provide? (Does it list sources of information?)

The Authority of the Author

The authority of the author(s) will also affect your judgment about a work's reliability. If the author is an expert or scholar in the field about which he or she is writing, then you can be reasonably confident that you are reading correct, current information. The authors of the reading in the chapter are professionals in their field, so you can assume the information they present is reliable. In general, if the writer has no advanced degree or experience in the field, then you cannot be as confident. If a writer lacks credentials, it does not automatically mean the information is unreliable; however, it signals that you should check for documentation and take into account the source of the material.

In books, the author's credentials are usually included on the jacket, on the title page, or in the preface. Articles and essays often include a footnote or introductory note about the author. Many periodicals such as newsmagazines and newspapers, however, will not include any information about their authors. In these instances you are forced to trust the publisher's judgment.

Step 3: Reacting to and Discussing Ideas

Get ready to write about the reading by using the following questions to generate ideas.

1. What impact have fast-food restaurants had upon American eating habits?
2. Discuss the effects of the microwave oven and frozen microwaveable food.
3. Discuss the meaning of the statement, "You are what you eat."
4. Are the eating habits of your family changing? If so, how?

WRITING ABOUT THE READING

■ *Assignment 1*

Write an expository essay explaining how the reading in this chapter is organized and what types of supporting information the author provides.

WRITING ABOUT YOUR IDEAS

■ *Assignment 2*

Write an expository essay explaining the function and importance of eating in your life and that of your family. Explain what your eating habits demonstrate about your social habits and your religious or ethnic background.

Assignment 3

Write an expository essay explaining how eating habits are changing in our country.

Assignment 4

Write an essay explaining how food preparation responsibilities are divided among males, females, and children in your family.

Journal Writing Suggestions

1. Write an entry describing your attitudes toward food and/or its social importance.

2. Write an entry describing how writing expository essays differ from other types of writing you have done this semester.

REVISION CHECKLIST

1. Is your essay appropriate for your audience? Does it give them the background information they need? Will it interest them?
2. Will your essay accomplish your purpose?
3. Have you narrowed your topic so that you can cover your subject thoroughly in your essay?
4. Is your main point clearly expressed in a thesis statement in the introductory paragraph? Does your introductory paragraph capture the reader's interest and lead into the body of the essay?
5. Does each paragraph of your essay have a topic sentence that supports your essay's main point?
6. Is each paragraph's topic sentence supported by relevant and sufficient detail?
7. Are your paragraphs arranged in a logical sequence and connected by transitions?
8. Is the tone of your essay appropriate for your purpose and audience?
9. Does your conclusion reemphasize your thesis statement and draw the essay to a close?
10. Does your title identify the topic and interest the reader?

FOR EXPOSITORY ESSAYS

11. Have you obtained complete and correct information?
12. Have you documented all information sources?
13. Does your tone reflect your seriousness about your topic?
14. Does your essay maintain a balance between technical and non-technical information?

PROOFREADING CHECKLIST

1. Does each sentence end with appropriate punctuation (period, question mark, or exclamation point)?
2. Is all punctuation within each sentence correct (commas, colons, semicolons, apostrophes, dashes, and quotation marks)?
3. Is each word spelled correctly?
4. Have you used capital letters where needed?
5. Are numbers and abbreviations used correctly?
6. Are any words omitted?
7. If your paper is typed, have you corrected all typographical errors?
8. If your paper is handwritten, is your handwriting always legible?
9. Are your pages in the correct order and numbered?

When to Use Commas

Commas separate parts of a sentence from one another. Commas most often separate

1. Items in a list or series.
   I need to buy jeans, socks, T-shirts, and a new tie.

2. Introductory phrases.
   After a cup of coffee, I was awake enough to read the paper.

3. Information that interrupts the sentence.
   My biology professor, Dr. Rodriquez, has been teaching for fifteen years.

4. Direct quotations.
   Barbara Walters always says, "We're in touch, so you'll be in touch."

5. Two independent clauses joined by a comma and a conjunction.
   The cat climbed on my lap, and I remembered that I hadn't fed her today.

6. A dependent clause from an independent clause when the dependent clause comes first in the sentence.
   Because I enjoy watching animals, I visit the zoo often.

Commas are also used in dates, addresses, numbers, and openings and closings of letters.

December 13, 1993

Yours truly,

Rate Your Ability to Use Commas Correctly

Punctuate each of the following sentences using commas.

1. Although I was late my sister was still waiting for me at the restaurant.
2. Tom invited Marie Ted Leah and Pete.
3. Following the movie we had a late lunch.
4. I bumped into a beautiful woman Lisa's mother on my way into the grocery store.

SKILL   REFRESHER

· · · · · · · · · · · · · · · · · · ·

5. The phone rang but I was outside.
6. My niece began to yell "I'm Tarzan king of the jungle."
7. Bill a friend from school sent me a postcard from Florida.
8. When I entered the room everyone was watching television.
9. I heard her call "Wait for me."
10. Although I have visited Vancouver I have never been to Vancouver Island.

Score _____

Check your answers using the Answer Key on page 537. If you scored below 80 percent, you need additional review and practice recognizing when to use commas. Refer to Section E.1 and E.2 of Reviewing the Basics in Part 5.

SUMMARY

■   1. An expository essay presents information on a specific topic. Its purpose is to explain.

2. To select an appropriate level of detail, analyze your audience. Assess their familiarity with your topic.

3. Consider your audience and purpose in choosing an overall logical method of development. Individual paragraphs within an essay can have their own method of development.

4. Be sure to obtain complete and correct information about your topic. Consult the college library, experts, and news media.

5. Be sure to document sources correctly using a standard documentation format.

6. Select a tone that reflects your seriousness about the topic.

7. Be sure to maintain a balance between technical and non-technical information.

8. Use clear transitions and repetition of key words to connect ideas.

14 Writing Persuasive Essays

. . . .

In this chapter you will learn to

1. plan a persuasive essay.

2. select convincing details.

3. present a convincing argument.

If you turn on the television or radio, or open a magazine or newspaper, you will encounter almost immediately one of the most common forms of persuasion—advertising. Commercials and ads are attempts to persuade you to buy a particular product or service. Here are a few examples.

1. "You've tried just about everything for your hay fever . . . now try your doctor. Your doctor has an advanced prescription medicine called Seldane that can relieve your allergy symptoms without drowsiness."

2. "Question: How can I get luscious taste with low fat? Answer: Simplese. The all-natural ingredient that replaces fat and keeps the taste you want."

Persuasion is an attempt to convince others to agree with an idea or to take a specific action. In advertising, the specific action is purchasing a product or service.

You probably use persuasion in your daily life more than you realize. You may try to persuade your spouse or friend to see the movie of your choice, convince your child to try a new food, or persuade your employer to give you Saturday nights off.

Most of the persuasion that is important in academic and career situations will require you to write. Here are a few examples:

Academic

1. a sociology paper defending or rejecting a new theory

2. writing a position paper for environmental science on pollution controls for industry

3. an essay on your college goals for a scholarship application

Career

1. memo defending a budget request

2. letter to support an employee's promotion

3. a proposal to secure a contract with a prospective client

WHAT IS A PERSUASIVE ESSAY?

■ A persuasive essay presents reasons and arguments for accepting a belief or position or for taking a specific action. For instance, a persuasive essay might try to convince readers that our current welfare system is injust, that parking regulations are unfair, or that a plus and minus grading system for colleges is desirable. Or, a persuasive essay might urge readers to take a specific action, such as voting against a political candidate, contacting their congressional representative to support the creation of a new park, or preventing their children from viewing violent television programs.

A persuasive essay has the same basic parts as other essays: introduction, thesis statement, supporting information, and conclusion. It requires that you follow the same steps in the writing process: pre-writing, planning, drafting, and revising. You are, therefore, already well-equipped to learn how to write a persuasive essay. However, the most important feature of a persuasive essay may be new to you: the presentation of convincing reasons and explanations. In this chapter you will learn how to plan a persuasive strategy, select convincing evidence, and present it effectively.

Here is a sample persuasive essay.

Buckle Up

As a paramedic, I am the first to arrive at the scene of many grim and tragic accidents. One horrid accident last month involved four women in one car. The front seat passenger died instantly, another died during a mercy flight to the nearest hospital, one lost both legs, and one walked away from the accident without serious injury. Only one woman was wearing a seat belt. Guess which one? Though many people protest and offer excuses, seat belts do save lives.

Many people avoid wearing seat belts and say they'd rather be thrown free from an accident. Yet, they seldom realize that the rate at which they will be thrown is the same rate at which the car is moving. Others fear being trapped inside by their seat belt in case of fire. However, if not ejected, those without a belt are likely to be stunned or knocked unconscious on impact and will not be alert enough to escape uninjured.

Seat belts save lives by protecting a passenger from impact. During a crash, a body slams against the windshield or steering wheel with tremendous force if unbelted. The seat belt secures the passenger in place and protects vital organs from injury.

Recent statistics demonstrate that a passenger is five times more likely to survive a crash if a seat belt is worn. Life is a gamble, but those are good odds. Buckle up!

Notice that the author introduces the topic using an interesting example from his personal experience. The thesis statement is stated at the end of the first paragraph. The second and third paragraphs offer evidence that support the writer's thesis. The last paragraph concludes the essay by offering a convincing statistic and reminding the reader of the thesis: "Buckle up."

FIRST STEPS IN PLANNING A PERSUASIVE ESSAY

■   The first step in planning a persuasive essay is to identify your subject. What issue or problem are you going to write about and what position you will take or solution you will offer? Suppose you have an assignment to write about the issue of mandatory testing for drug use. You need to decide whether you support mandatory testing or oppose it. As for other essays, begin by using freewriting, brainstorming, questioning, or branching to generate ideas. Your goal is to identify reasons, explanations, examples, and situations that will convince readers to accept your position.

If you choose your own topic, be sure to choose an issue about which you have definite feelings. It is difficult to write convincingly about a position in which you don't believe. On the other hand, if you feel you are so emotionally involved with an issue that it upsets you to think about it, consider selecting a different issue. You may find it difficult to separate your emotions from the facts and present a reasoned appeal.

Writing for College Courses

Throughout this book we've focused on writing paragraphs and essays within the context of a writing class. Throughout college you'll be required to write for a variety of academic disciplines. You might write a reaction paper in political science or a lab report in biology, for example. The skills you've learned for writing paragraphs and essays provide a solid foundation for successful writing. You'll need to adapt your writing to fit the requirements of each assignment as well as the nature of the discipline. Here are a few tips to help you get started writing for other courses.

1. Think of yourself as part of a group or community of writers. Members of a group tend to do things the same way. In biology, for example, lab reports are written to follow a specific format.

2. Be sure to use the same five-step process—generating ideas, organizing, drafting, revising, and proofreading—that you've used throughout this book. It's tempting to skip over some of these steps when you're not writing for an English class. The steps are essential to good writing in any discipline.

Analyzing Your Audience

Analyzing your audience is a crucial second step in planning a convincing essay. You must decide whether your audience is in agreement, neutral, or disagreement with your position. In addition, decide how familiar your readers are with the issue and how reasoned or well-thought out their position is.

Audiences who agree with your position are the easiest to write for, since they already accept most of what you will say. *In-agreement audiences* will also be likely to feel positively about you because you think the way they do about the issue. For this audience, your essay can be structured very much like an expository essay. State your position and explain why you think it is correct.

Neutral audiences have not made up their minds or have not given much thought to the issue. They have questions or misunderstandings, and they may have heard arguments supporting the opposing viewpoint. An essay written for a neutral audience should be direct and straightforward, like those written for an in-agreement audience. However, a

3. Pay close attention to an assignment as it is given. Write down everything your instructor says about the assignment. He or she may give examples of topics, suggest how to begin, or offer hints on how to organize the assignment.

4. Be sure to define your audience and purpose before you begin.

5. Select a tone that is appropriate for the discipline. A sentimental or angry tone, for example, would be inappropriate in social science courses, even though you may be writing about issues about which you feel strongly.

6. Use language appropriate to the discipline. Each subject area has its own set of specialized terminology that helps to make communication clear and exact. Use this language whenever possible.

7. If you are unsure of the assignment, ask your instructor what is expected. Suppose, for instance, your economics instructor asks you to write an analysis of a recent change in interest rates. If you are uncertain of how to organize an analysis or how to write it, talk with classmates and your instructor.

fuller explanation of the issue is necessary to answer questions, clear up misunderstandings, and respond to opposing arguments. State your position and offer reasons in support of it.

Disagreeing audiences are the most difficult to address. Some have thought about the issue and then have chosen a position that opposes yours. Others who disagree may not have examined the issue at all and are making superficial judgments or are relying on misinformation. Both types think their position is correct, so they will not be eager to change. They may also distrust you, since you think differently than they do. For such an audience, your biggest challenge is to build trust and confidence. Before writing, carefully analyze your audience and try to answer these questions:

1. Why does your audience disagree with your position?

2. Is their position based on real facts and sound evidence, or on personal opinion? If it is based on evidence, what type? Supply strong evidence to support your position.

3. What type of argument or reasons are likely to appeal to your audience? For example, will they be persuaded by facts and statistics, or by statements made by authorities? Would personal anecdotes and examples work well?

Once you have a grasp of their thinking, in your introduction you might include sentences that openly recognize their opposing viewpoint. Here is an example:

> Advertising, like other expenditures, should be taxed. What better way to generate income and, at the same time, reduce the flood of advertising that bombards us daily on radio and television. Major corporations and radio and television stations will, of course, oppose such tax legislation, arguing that taxing advertising will reduce the amount of advertising, which in turn will reduce public service programming that is aired.

For a disagreeing audience, include more preliminary discussion of the issue than you would for other audiences. For example, you might establish your authority on the issue, relate an amusing or convincing anecdote to engage your audience, or present surprising statistics or a shocking example to startle your audience. You might also offer reasons for your thesis statement before you directly state it.

RESEARCHING YOUR TOPIC

■ A persuasive essay must provide specific and convincing evidence that supports the thesis statement. Often it is necessary to go beyond your own knowledge and experience to locate such evidence. You may need to investigate your topic by researching your topic in the library. For example, if you were writing an essay urging the creation of an environmentally protected wetland area, find out what types of wildlife live there, which are endangered, and how successful other wetlands have been in protecting wildlife.

At other times you may need to interview people who are experts on your topic or those directly involved with it. Suppose you are writing a persuasive essay urging other students to volunteer their time at a local shelter for homeless men and women. The director of the shelter or one of its employees could offer useful statistics, share personal experiences, and provide realistic details that would make your essay vivid and convincing.

Here are a few tips for researching your topic.
When consulting written sources—

1. use current, up-to-date sources.
2. sample a variety of sources to get different viewpoints on your topic.
3. move from general to more specific sources.
4. take careful notes as you read and use quotation marks for all material you copy directly.
5. keep track of all sources used to include in your bibliography.

When interviewing—

1. prepare a list of questions ahead of time.
2. consult individuals who are experts or who have direct experience with your topic.
3. if possible, talk with more than one person. For instance, the director of the homeless shelter may provide a different viewpoint than one of its employees or one of its clients.
4. be sure your "experts" understand your purpose for interviewing them. Ask permission to use their names and to quote them in your paper.
5. take detailed notes during the interview. Fill in ideas you didn't have time to write immediately after the interview.

STRUCTURING YOUR ESSAY

■ After you have chosen your position, generated ideas, and analyzed your audience, you need to devise an approach that will both support your position and appeal to your audience. There are three major decisions to make:

- What will you include in your thesis statement and where will you place it?
- What evidence will you include?
- In what order will you present your evidence?

There are no rules to follow in making these decisions. You must consider your topic, your purpose, and your audience in making them. The next sections discuss each of these decisions in more detail.

Exercise 14–1   For three of the following issues, take a position and generate ideas to support it.

1. increasing the national speed limit to 65 mph
2. The rights of insurance companies to deny medical coverage

3. banning smoking in public places
4. outlawing sports hunting of wild animals
5. mandatory counseling for drunken drivers

Exercise 14–2   For one of the issues you chose in Exercise 14–1, identify an audience that you would like to convince of your position. Think of a specific person or group. Then analyze your audience and summarize your findings.

Position: _____

Audience: _____

Analysis: _____

_____

_____

_____

Developing Your Thesis Statement

Your thesis statement should identify the issue, state your position toward it, and, if possible, foreshadow your supporting points. The following thesis statement makes it clear that the writer will argue against the use of animals for medical research.

> The use of animals in medical research should be outlawed because it is cruel, unnecessary, and disrespectful of animals' place in the chain of life.

Notice that this thesis identifies the issue, makes it clear that the writer opposes animal research, and suggests the three major reasons in her argument: (1) it is cruel (2) it is unnecessary, and (3) it is disrespectful. It is not always necessary to include the major points of your argument in your thesis statement, but it does help the reader know what to expect.

This thesis statement also makes clear what action the author thinks is appropriate: medical research should be outlawed. Here are a few more thesis statements. Notice that they use the verbs must, would, should, and ought.

> If we expect industries to dispose of their wastes properly, then we should provide tax breaks to cover the extra expense.

It would be a mistake to assume racial discrimination has been eliminated or even lessened significantly over the past twenty years.

The proportion of women and minority tenured faculty on our campus should be increased.

Place your thesis statement where it will be most effective. There are three common choices:

1. In the beginning;
2. After you respond to objections to the position, but before you provide reasons for accepting it;
3. At the end, after you state reasons for accepting the position.

You can visualize these three organizations as follows:

1. Thesis statement in the beginning

Paragraph 1 ⎱ Introduction
⎰ Thesis Statement

2 ⎫
3 ⎬ Supporting Evidence
4 ⎭

5 Conclusion

2. After responding to objections
Paragraph 1   Introduction
2   Response to Objections

3 ⎫ Thesis Statement
4 ⎬
5 ⎭ Supporting Evidence

6   Conclusion

3. Thesis statement at the end
Paragraph 1   Introduction

2 ⎫
3 ⎬ Supporting Evidence
4 ⎭

5   Concluding Paragraph with Thesis Statement

In general, placing the thesis in the beginning is best for in-agreement or neutral audiences. For disagreeing audiences, a later placement gives you the opportunity to meet the audience's objections before you present your thesis.

Exercise 14–3   Write a thesis statement for a persuasive essay on three of the following topics.

1. recycling garbage
2. lengthening the public school year
3. television sitcoms
4. volunteer work
5. athletics and the use of steroids

Exercise 14–4   Write a thesis statement for the issue you selected in Exercise 14–2.

Selecting Convincing Evidence

When you write a persuasive essay, your goal is to provide readers with evidence that they cannot easily refute (disagree with or prove wrong). It is important to evaluate each piece of evidence you include. Ask yourself questions such as: What does this prove? Are there other ways it could be interpreted? How might a disagreeing reader disagree with this information? The evidence you choose to include will depend on your topic and your analysis of the audience.

The most commonly used types of evidence are

1. facts and statistics
2. quotes from authorities
3. examples
4. personal experience

Facts and Statistics

Facts are statements that can be verified as correct. (To review the distinction between fact and opinion, see Chapter 9, page 182.) As in writing any other type of paragraph or essay, the facts you choose must directly support the position you express in your thesis statement. Here is an excerpt from a persuasive essay using facts as evidence that the American diet is not health conscious.

> Americans are not as conscious of health and nutrition as everyone thinks. The average American diet is 37 percent fat. This is well above the 30 percent that is recommended and far from the 20 percent that medical researchers suggest to reduce heart disease and control cancer. Surprisingly, American women are eating less fruit and vegetables than they did in the 1970s, . . .

Facts expressed as numbers are called statistics. It is usually more effective to present more than one statistic. Suppose you are writing to persuade taxpayers that state lotteries have become profitable businesses. You might state that more than 60 percent of the adult population now buys lottery tickets regularly. This statistic would have little meaning by itself. However, if you were to state that 60 percent of adults now purchase lottery tickets, whereas five years ago only 30 percent of adults purchased them, then the first statistic becomes more meaningful.

In selecting statistics to support your position, be sure to:

1. **Obtain statistics from reliable sources such as almanacs, encyclopedias, articles in reputable journals and magazines, or other trustworthy reference material from your library.**

2. **Use up-to-date information, preferably from the last year or two.** Dated statistics may be incorrect or misleading.

3. **Make sure you define terms and units of measurement.** For example, if you say that 60 percent of adults regularly play the lottery, you should define what "regularly" means. Does it mean daily, weekly, monthly?

4. **Verify that the statistics you obtain from more than one source are comparable.** For example, if you compare the crime rate in New York City to that of Los Angeles, be sure that each crime rate was computed the same way and that each included the same types of crimes from similar report sources.

Quotations from Authorities

You can also support your position by using statements of opinion or conclusions drawn by experts or authorities. Experts or authorities are those who have studied extensively, conducted research, or written widely about your subject. For example, if you are writing an essay calling for stricter pre-school monitoring requirements to avoid child abuse, the opinion of a psychiatrist who works extensively with abused children would provide convincing support.

Examples

Examples are specific situations that illustrate a point. Refer to Chapter 8, pp. 143–146, for a review of how to use them as supporting details. In a persuasive essay, your examples must represent your position. They should illustrate as many aspects of your position as possible. Suppose your position is that a particular movie should have been X-rated because it contains excessive violence. The examples you choose to support the position should be clear, vivid examples of violent scenes.

The examples you choose should, if possible, relate to your audience's experience. Familiar examples will be more appealing, convincing, and easily understandable than those they have not experienced. Suppose you are writing a persuasive essay advocating a prochoice position on abortion. Your audience is career women, 30–40 years old. It would be most effective to use examples involving women of the same age and occupational status.

Personal Experience

If you are knowledgeable about a subject, use your personal experiences effectively as convincing evidence. For example, if you were writing an essay supporting the position that physical separation from parents encourages a teenager or young adult to mature, you could discuss your own experiences when you left home and had to face new responsibilities.

ORGANIZING YOUR EVIDENCE

■ The evidence you include to support your position should follow a logical sequence. Choose one of the methods of organization you learned in Chapters 4, or 6 through 10. For example, you could state your most important evidence first, using a most-to-least arrangement. Or, you could build toward your most important evidence, using a least-to-most arrangement. Many writers feel the least-to-most arrangement has more effect on readers who tend to remember best the last thing they read. Other arrangements are possible, as well. You might use a cause and effect arrangement, for example, if your essay explains positive effects a particular action would have. Or, imagine you were trying to show that a particular law is unenforceable. You might use time sequence, providing case studies of unsuccessful attempts to enforce it.

Exercise 14–5   For each of the following thesis statements, indicate what type or types of supporting evidence would be convincing. Then give an example of that evidence, "making up" an example or statistic, if necessary.

1. Winter carnivals, such as Mardi Gras, are beneficial; they provide a welcome escape from the doldrums of the gloomy, late winter season.

Type(s) of Evidence: _____

    2. A change in the minimum wage is necessary to upgrade the American standard of living.

Type(s) of Evidence: _____

    3. People spend large amounts of money purchasing novelty items and toys for their pets; they should stop wasting their money.

Type(s) of Evidence: _____

    4. The vicious cycle of unemployed workers who suffer loss of self-esteem which, in turn, makes them less employable can be changed through training programs.

Type(s) of Evidence: _____

    5. Public health is not improving because there has been a significant lack of progress in the cleanup of hazardous waste.

Type(s) of Evidence: _____

Exercise 14–6   Generate evidence to support the thesis statement you chose in Exercise 14–3. Evaluate your evidence and research your topic further, if needed. Write the first draft of an essay.

THE INTRODUCTION AND CONCLUSION

■   The introduction of a persuasive essay should interest the reader in the issue and suggest why it is important. It may include your thesis statement, a definition of a key term, or other explanatory information.

    If you delay stating your thesis until the end of your essay, make sure your conclusion contains a clear, direct statement. If you state your thesis earlier, then your conclusion should summarize key points and make a final call for action. You may request that your reader take specific action, such as writing a letter to a congressional leader or joining a local environmental concern group.

Exercise 14–7   For the essay you drafted in Exercise 14–6, add to or revise your introduction and conclusion to be more clear, effective, or powerful. Then revise your essay using the checklist at the end of this chapter.

THINKING BEFORE READING

■ The reading "Crack and the Box" is a good example of a persuasive essay. Pete Hamill takes the position that the increase in drug use in America relates to excessive television viewing. As you read it, observe the types of supporting evidence Hamill provides.

1. Preview the reading using the steps listed in Chapter 3, p. 43.
2. Activate your thinking by answering the following questions.
   a. Why do you think people take drugs?
   b. Why do people watch television?
   c. In what ways are taking drugs and watching television similar?

READING

■
CRACK AND THE BOX

Pete Hamill

One sad rainy morning last winter, I talked to a woman who was addicted to crack cocaine. She was twenty-two, stiletto-thin, with eyes as old as tombs. She was living in two rooms in a welfare hotel with her children, who were two, three, and five years of age. Her story was the usual tangle of human woe: early pregnancy, dropping out of school, vanished men, smack and then crack, tricks with johns in parked cars to pay for dope. I asked her why she did drugs. She shrugged in an empty way and couldn't really answer beyond "makes me feel good." While we talked and she told her tale of squalor, the children ignored us. They were watching television.

Walking back to my office in the rain, I brooded about the woman, her zombielike children, and my own callous indifference. I'd heard so many versions of the same story that I almost never wrote them anymore; the sons of similar women, glimpsed a dozen years ago, are now in Dannemora or Soledad or Joliet; in a hundred cities, their daughters are moving into the same loveless rooms. As I walked, a series of homeless men approached me for change, most of them junkies. Others sat in doorways, staring at nothing. They were additional casualties of our time of plague, demoralized reminders that although this country holds only 2 percent of the world's population, it consumes 65 percent of the world's supply of hard drugs.

Why, for God's sake? Why do so many millions of Americans of 3
all ages, races, and classes choose to spend all or part of their lives
stupefied? I've talked to hundreds of addicts over the years; some
were my friends. But none could give sensible answers. They stutter
about the pain of the world, about despair or boredom, the urgent
need for magic or pleasure in a society empty of both. But then they
just shrug. Americans have the money to buy drugs; the supply is
plentiful. But almost nobody in power asks, *Why?* Least of all,
George Bush and his drug warriors.

William Bennett talks vaguely about the heritage of sixties permis- 4
siveness, the collapse of Traditional Values, and all that. But he and
Bush offer the traditional American excuse: It Is Somebody Else's
Fault. This posture set the stage for the self-righteous invasion of Pan-
ama, the bloodiest drug arrest in world history. Bush even accused
Manuel Noriega of "poisoning our children." But he never asked
why so many Americans demand the poison.

And then, on that rainy morning in New York, I saw another 5
one of those ragged men staring out at the rain from a doorway. I
suddenly remembered the inert postures of the children in that welfare hotel, and I thought: *television.*

Ah, no, I muttered to myself: too simple. Something as compli- 6
cated as drug addiction can't be blamed on television. Come on. . . .
but I remembered all those desperate places I'd visited as a reporter,
where there were no books and a TV set was always playing and the
older kids had gone off somewhere to shoot smack, except for the
kid who was at the mortuary in a coffin. I also remembered when I
was a boy in the forties and early fifties, and drugs were a minor side-
show, a kind of dark little rumor. And there was one major difference between that time and this: television.

We had unemployment then; illiteracy, poor living conditions, 7
racism, governmental stupidity, a gap between rich and poor. We
didn't have the all-consuming presence of television in our lives.
Now two generations of Americans have grown up with television
from their earliest moments of consciousness. Those same American
generations are afflicted by the pox of drug addiction.

Only thirty-five years ago, drug addiction was not a major prob- 8
lem in this country. There were drug addicts. We had some at the
end of the nineteenth century, hooked on the cocaine in patent medicines. During the placid fifties, Commissioner Harry Anslinger
pumped up the budget of the old Bureau of Narcotics with fantasies
of reefer madness. Heroin was sold and used in most major American cities, while the bebop generation of jazz musicians got jammed
up with horse.

But until the early sixties, narcotics were still marginal to American life; they weren't the $120-billion market they make up today. If anything, those years have an eerie innocence. In 1955 there were 31,700,000 TV sets in use in the country (the number is now past 184 million). But the majority of the audience had grown up without the dazzling new medium. They embraced it, were diverted by it, perhaps even loved it, but they weren't *formed* by it. That year, the New York police made a mere 1,234 felony drug arrests; in 1988 it was 43,901. They confiscated ninety-seven *ounces* of cocaine for the entire year; last year it was hundreds of pounds. During each year of the fifties in New York, there were only about a hundred narcotics-related deaths. But by the end of the sixties, when the first generation of children *formed* by television had come to maturity (and thus to the marketplace), the number of such deaths had risen to 1,200. The same phenomenon was true in every major American city.

In the last Nielsen survey of American viewers, the average family was watching television seven hours a day. This has never happened before in history. No people has even been entertained for seven hours a *day*. The Elizabethans didn't go to the theater seven hours a day. The pre-TV generation did not go to the movies seven hours a day. Common sense tells us that this all-pervasive diet of instant imagery, sustained now for forty years, must have changed us in profound ways.

Television, like drugs, dominates the lives of its addicts. And though some lonely Americans leave their sets on without watching them, using them as electronic companions, television usually absorbs its viewers the way drugs absorb their users. Viewers can't work or play while watching television; they can't read; they can't be out on the streets, falling in love with the wrong people, learning how to quarrel and compromise with other human beings. In short they are asocial. So are drug addicts.

One Michigan State University study in the early eighties offered a group of four- and five-year-olds the choice of giving up television or giving up their fathers. Fully one third said they would give up Daddy. Given a similar choice (between cocaine or heroin and father, mother, brother, sister, wife, husband, children, job), almost every stoned junkie would do the same.

There are other disturbing similarities. Television itself is a consciousness-altering instrument. With the touch of a button, it takes you out of the "real" world in which you reside and can place you at a basketball game, the back alleys of Miami, the streets of Bucharest, or the cartoony living rooms of Sitcom Land. Each move from

9

10

11

12

13

channel to channel alters moods, usually with music or a laugh track. On any given evening, you can laugh, be frightened, feel tension, thump with excitement. You can even tune in *MacNeil/Lehrer* and feel sober.

But none of these abrupt shifts in mood is *earned*. They are attained as easily as popping a pill. Getting news from television, for example, is simply not the same experience as reading it in a newspaper. Reading is *active*. The reader must decode little symbols called words, then create images or ideas and make them connect; at its most basic level, reading is an act of the imagination. But the television viewer doesn't go through that process. The words are spoken to him by Dan Rather or Tom Brokaw or Peter Jennings. There isn't much decoding to do when watching television, no time to think or ponder before the next set of images and spoken words appears to displace the present one. The reader, being active, works at his or her own pace; the viewer, being passive, proceeds at a pace determined by the show. Except at the highest levels, television never demands that its audience take part in an act of imagination. Reading always does.

In short, television works on the same imaginative and intellectual level as psychoactive drugs. If prolonged television viewing makes the young passive (dozens of studies indicate that it does), then moving to drugs has a certain coherence. Drugs provide an unearned high (in contrast to the earned rush that comes from a feat accomplished, a human breakthrough earned by sweat or thought or love).

And because the television addict and the drug addict are alienated from the hard and scary world, they also feel they make no difference in its complicated events. For the junkie, the world is reduced to him and the needle, pipe, or vial; the self is absolutely isolated, with no desire for choice. The television addict lives the same way. Many Americans who fail to vote in presidential elections must believe they have no more control over such a choice than they do over the casting of *L.A. Law.*

The drug plague also coincides with the unspoken assumption of most television shows: Life should be *easy*. The most complicated events are summarized on TV news in a minute or less. Cops confront murder, chase the criminals, and bring them to justice (usually violently) within an hour. In commercials, you drink the right beer and you get the girl. *Easy!* So why should real life be a grind? Why should any American have to spend years mastering a skill or a craft, or work eight hours a day at an unpleasant job, or endure the com-

14

15

16

17

promises and crises of a marriage? Nobody *works* on television (except cops, doctors, and lawyers). Love stories on television are about falling in love or breaking up; the long, steady growth of a marriage—its essential *dailiness*—is seldom explored, except as comedy. Life on television is almost always simple: good guys and bad, nice girls and whores, smart guys and dumb. And if life in the real world isn't that simple, well, hey, man, have some dope, man, be happy, feel good.

The doper always whines about how he *feels*; drugs are used to   18 enhance his feelings or obliterate them, and in this the doper is very American. No other people on earth spend so much time talking about their feelings; hundreds of thousands go to shrinks, they buy self-help books by the millions, they pour out intimate confessions to virtual strangers in bars or discos. Our political campaigns are about emotional issues now, stated in the simplicities of adolescence. Even alleged statesmen can start a sentence, "I feel that the Sandinistas should . . ." when they once might have said, "I *think*. . . ." I'm convinced that this exaltation of cheap emotions over logic and reason is one by-product of hundreds of thousands of hours of television.

Most Americans under the age of fifty have now spent their lives   19 absorbing television; that is, they've had the structures of drama pounded into them. Drama is always about conflict. So news shows, politics, and advertising are now all shaped by those structures. Nobody will pay attention to anything as complicated as the part played by Third World debt in the expanding production of cocaine; it's much easier to focus on Manuel Noriega, a character right out of *Miami Vice*, and believe that even in real life there's a Mister Big.

What is to be done? Television is certainly not going away, but   20 its addictive qualities can be controlled. It's a lot easier to "just say no" to television than to heroin or crack. As a beginning, parents must take immediate control of the sets, teaching children to watch specific television *programs*, not "television," to get out of the house and play with other kids. Elementary and high schools must begin teaching television as a subject, the way literature is taught, showing children how shows are made, how to distinguish between the true and the false, how to recognize cheap emotional manipulation. All Americans should spend more time reading. And thinking.

For years, the defenders of television have argued that the net-   21 works are only giving the people what they want. That might be true. But so is the Medellín cartel.

GETTING READY TO WRITE

■ *Step 1: Outlining an Argument*

One of the best ways to understand persuasive writing is to reduce the ideas to a simple list or outline. Most authors of persuasive essays use highly charged language and emotional appeals to influence their audience. Examining the major pieces of evidence from the essay separately, will allow you to analyze the relationship among its ideas objectively. Use the following format to list and organize the major steps of an argument.

Evidence (Reasons to Accept)

Responses to Opposing Viewpoints (if included)

Specific Action(s) Called for (if included)

In Step 2 on page 311 you will learn how to use this outlining format to evaluate an essay.

Here is a sample list for the persuasive essay included at the beginning of the chapter.

Evidence:

1. protect(s) from impact by holding you in place

2. protects vital organs

Responses to Opposing Viewpoints:

1. rather be thrown free—thrown at rate car is moving

2. fear being trapped inside—stunned—won't be able to escape

Specific Action:

1. *Buckle Up*

Exercise 14–8   Make a list or outline of Hamill's argument in "Crack and the Box" following the pattern presented on p. 309.

Step 2: Thinking Critically: Evaluating Persuasive Writing

Persuasive writing is meant to be convincing. As you read a convincing piece, it is easy to be swept along by the writer's line of reasoning. Although Hamill does not, some writers tug unfairly at your emotions, making it even more difficult not to "buy" the author's argument.

The best way to read persuasive writing is with a critical, questioning attitude. As you read, ask yourself questions such as: Why should I believe this? How do I know this is correct? Mark and annotate as you read. Place question marks next to ideas you want to question or consider further. Then, when you've finished reading, list and organize the argument into the form shown in Step 1. Now you are ready to evaluate the writer's evidence. Work through your list, item-by-item. For the first piece of evidence, ask the appropriate group of questions below.

Facts and Statistics

Are they relevant?

Are they up to date?

Do they logically connect with the issue in question?

Examples

Is the example relevant to the issue?

Does the example illustrate something that is typical or an exception?

Can you think of other examples that would confirm or disprove the writer's position?

Quotation from an Authority

Is the person an expert?

Would other experts agree?

What does the quotation contribute to the writer's ideas?

Personal Experience

Is the writer's personal experience relevant to the issue?

Is the writer's personal experience typical of most people's?

Can you think of other personal experiences that would confirm or dispute the writer's position?

Consider Hamill's first piece of supporting evidence linking drugs and television in paragraphs seven to nine. He presents facts to support his line of reasoning: When there was no television, there were no drugs. Those Americans who grew up with television are victims of drug addiction. Hamill establishes that these two developments—increased television viewing and drug addiction—occurred at the same time. The question that a critical reader must ask is whether this is a logical connection. Because the two events occurred at the same time does not prove that one *caused* the other. Hamill knows this; therefore, he provides additional reasons to support and develop the connection, such as explaining that television is a consciousness-altering "instrument" and that television alienates viewers from the real world. These additional reasons strengthen his stance and accentuate the article's argument about drug addiction and television viewing.

Exercise 14–9   Evaluate the remainder of the evidence Hamill provides. Write a paragraph explaining why you accept or reject each piece of evidence.

Step 3: Reacting to and Discussing Ideas

Get ready to write about the reading by discussing the following questions.

1. Hamill states that, unlike television, reading is active. It requires the reader "to take part in an act of the imagination." Do you agree?
2. Do you agree that television viewing alienates viewers from the real world?
3. Does television give a realistic view of life? Why or why not?
4. What factors, other than television, could account for the dramatic increase in drug use in America?
5. Does Hamill recognize and respond to the viewpoint a disagreeing audience might have? Why do you think he chose to respond or not respond?
6. Discuss the types of evidence Hamill offers in support of his thesis.

WRITING ABOUT THE READING

■ *Assignment 1*

Write a persuasive essay on the issue of whether a television watching skills course should be taught in elementary and high schools.

Assignment 2

Write a persuasive essay on the issue of whether parents should control their children's television viewing.

WRITING ABOUT YOUR IDEAS

■ *Assignment 1*

Is television addictive? Take a position on this issue and write a persuasive essay explaining your position.

Assignment 2

Should Americans read and think more, as Hamill suggests? Write a persuasive essay explaining your position.

Journal Writing Suggestions
1. Write an entry about possible solutions to the problems of drug abuse.
2. Write an entry describing how writing a persuasive essay differs from writing an expository essay.

REVISION CHECKLIST

1. Is your essay appropriate for your audience? Does it give them the background information they need? Will it interest them?
2. Will your essay accomplish your purpose?
3. Have you narrowed your topic so that you can cover your subject thoroughly in your essay?
4. Is your main point clearly expressed in a thesis statement in the introductory paragraph? Does your introductory paragraph capture the reader's interest and lead into the body of the essay?
5. Does each paragraph of your essay have a topic sentence that supports your essay's main point?
6. Is each paragraph's topic sentence supported by relevant and sufficient detail?
7. Are your paragraphs arranged in a logical sequence and connected by transitions?

8. Is the tone of your essay appropriate for your purpose and audience?
9. Does your conclusion reemphasize your thesis statement and draw the essay to a close?
10. Does your title identify the topic and interest the reader?

For PERSUASIVE Essays

1. Have you analyzed the position of your audience on the issue about which you are writing?
2. Have you researched your topic to obtain adequate and convincing evidence?
3. Does your thesis statement identify the issue and state your position toward it?
4. Does your thesis statement foreshadow your supporting points?
5. Have you provided convincing evidence?

PROOFREADING CHECKLIST

1. Does each sentence end with appropriate punctuation (period, question mark, or exclamation point)?
2. Is all punctuation within each sentence correct (commas, colons, semicolons, apostrophes, dashes, and quotation marks)?
3. Is each word spelled correctly?
4. Have you used capital letters where needed?
5. Are numbers and abbreviations used correctly?
6. Are any words omitted?
7. If your paper is typed, have you corrected all typographical errors?
8. If your paper is handwritten, is your handwriting always legible?
9. Are your pages in the correct order and numbered?

Using Colons and Semicolons

When to Use Colons

Colons are most commonly used

1. after an independent clause to introduce a concluding explanation or a long or formal quotation.

   Fashion is fickle: what looks stylish one year looks dated the next.

2. after an independent clause to introduce a list or series that follows a complete sentence.

   The American poetry class surveyed a wide range of poets: Whitman, Dickinson, Ashberry, and Pound.

When to Use Semicolons

Semicolons are most commonly used

1. between two independent clauses not connected by a coordinating conjunction (*and, but, for, nor, or, so, yet*)

   Each state has equal representation in the Senate; representation in the House of Representatives is based on population.

2. to separate items in a list when the items in the list themselves contain commas

   The library bulletin board has a display of "Pioneers in Thought," which includes Freud, the creator of psychoanalysis; Marx, the famous communist writer; Copernicus, the father of modern astronomy; and Watson and Crick, the alleged discoverers of DNA.

Rate Your Ability to Use Colons and Semicolons Correctly

Place colons and semicolons where needed in the following sentences.

1. Anthropologists believe human life began in the Middle East skeletons that have been found provide evidence for this.

2. The natural sciences include botany, the study of plants chemistry, the study of elements that compose matter and biology, the study of all living things.

3. The courses I am taking cover a wide range of subjects linguistics, racquetball, calculus, anatomy, and political science.

4. Introductory courses tend to be broad in scope they do give a good overview of the subject matter.

5. The poet, John Milton, tells how Eve must have felt when she was created "That day I remember, when from sleep / I first awaked, and found myself reposed / under a shade on flowers, much wond'ring where / and what I was, whence thither brought, and how."

6. Trigonometry incorporates many other math skills geometry, algebra and logic.

7. I enjoy a variety of sports tennis, which is my favorite golf, because it is relaxing basketball, because it is a team sport and racquetball, because it is a good workout.

8. When a skull is dug up by a gravedigger, Hamlet begins what is now a famous meditation on mortality "Alas, poor Yorick!—I knew him, Horatio . . ."

9. Spanish is important to learn because many Americans speak it exclusively it is also useful to understand another culture.

10. My botany text has a section about coniferous trees pines, firs, cedars, and spruces.

Score _____

Check your answers using the Answer Key on page 537. If you scored below 80 percent, you need additional review and practice recognizing when to use colons and semicolons. Refer to Section E.3 of Reviewing the Basics in Part 5.

SUMMARY

■   1. A persuasive essay presents reasons and arguments for accepting a belief or position or for taking a specific action.

2. To plan a persuasive essay
   • identify your topic and what position you will take.
   • analyze your audience, then decide if your audience is agreeing, neutral, or disagreeing.

3. Conduct necessary research to obtain adequate and convincing evidence to support your position.

4. Your thesis statement should identify the issue, state your position toward it, and if possible, foreshadow your supporting points.

5. Three common placements for the thesis statement are (1) at the beginning, (2) after responding to objections, and (3) at the end.

6. Use convincing evidence: facts and statistics, quotations, examples, and personal experience.

7. Organize your evidence using a logical method of development.

15 Writing Essay Exams and Competency Tests

In this chapter you will learn to

1. Plan and write essay exams.
2. Take competency tests.

This chapter will discuss how to prepare for, take, and write essay exams and competency or placement essay exams. Many instructors give essay exams because they reveal students' ability to think about the test material, whereas multiple choice and true/false tests only require that you *recognize* correct answers. Writing an essay exam involves the same steps as other kinds of writing: generating, planning, organizing, and writing ideas. But because exams are usually timed, there is little opportunity for revising or proofreading.

PREPARING FOR ESSAY EXAMS

■ The best way to prepare for an essay exam involves a thorough study and review of assigned textbook and lecture material. Simply rereading this material is seldom enough. Instead, work actively with it, identifying what is important, organizing and relating ideas and concepts, and expressing ideas in your own words. If you have been applying the "getting ready to write" techniques suggested throughout this book to your textbooks, you'll have a headstart. Reviewing these techniques will enable you to identify key points and express the author's ideas in your own words.

TABLE 15-1	Getting Ready to Write Strategies	
Strategy		**Chapter and Page Reference**
underlining		Ch. 3, p. 48;
immediate review		Ch. 3, p. 48;
recognizing supporting details		Ch. 4, p. 71
annotation		Ch. 12, p. 257
marking actions, descriptions, and statements		Ch. 7, p. 135
idea mapping		Ch. 5, p. 95; Ch. 6, p. 115; Ch. 8, p. 161; Ch. 9, p. 181; Ch. 10, p. 201
outlining		Ch. 11, p. 229; Ch. 14, p. 00
summarizing		Ch. 13, p. 284

In addition to reviewing your textbooks, you will want to review the following:

class notes (underline and annotate these, too)

in-class handouts (underline and mark)

assignments and papers (note key topics)

previous exams and quizzes (look for patterns of error and emphasized topics)

additional assigned readings (summarize these)

Using these materials as well as your textbook, make a study sheet listing key definitions, dates, facts, principles, or events that you must commit to memory. An excerpt from a study sheet for a psychology unit on consciousness is shown below. It illustrates how information can be concisely organized for easy review.

Study Sheet Excerpt

<u>Sleeping and Dreaming</u>

Stages 1. quiet sleep - 4 stages   move back
        2. REM sleep   & forth in
                                     these stages
                                     frequently

Purpose- not completely understood
     - part of circadian rhythm
     - rest and bodily repair
     - brain - check it's circuits

Dreams - storylike sequences of images
     and events
     - may be meaningless brain activity
     - but how a person recalls and
     organizes them is revealing
lucid dreaming- control own dreams

Disorders 1. insomnia - can't sleep
     2. hyper somnia - two much sleep

Predicting Exam Questions

Once you have assembled and reviewed all of your course materials, a good way to prepare for an essay exam is to predict questions that might be asked on the test. Essay exam questions are based on broad, general topics or themes that are important to the course. To predict these questions, then, you must identify the "big ideas"—important issues or concepts your instructor has emphasized. To identify these:

1. **Reread your course syllabus or objectives.** These are often distributed on the first day of class, and the major headings or objectives refer to the important issues. For example, a sociology course objective may read, "Students will understand the concept of socialization and the role of the family, peer, and reference groups." This objective identifies the key topic and suggests what you need to learn about it.

2. **Study your textbook's table of contents and the organization of individual chapters to be covered on the exam.** Identify important topics that run through several chapters. For example, in a business marketing textbook, you may discover that chapters on the impact of technology, federal regulations, and consumer protection legislation all relate to the market environment.

3. **Study your notes.** Identify lecture topics and group them into larger subjects or themes. For example, in a psychology course, individual lectures on retardation, creativity, and IQ can be grouped together into mental abilities.

4. **Evaluate previous exams to see what key ideas were emphasized.** For example, in a history course you may find questions on the historical significance of events appearing on each exam.

5. **Listen carefully when your instructor announces, discusses, or reviews for the exam.** He or she is likely to suggest or reveal important topics. Make detailed notes and study them later. For example, a biology instructor may say, "Be sure to review the structure of plants, as well as their reproduction, development, and growth cycles." This remark indicates that these topics will probably be on the exam.

As you'll see from Table 15-2 on p. 326, the way that essay exam questions are worded often suggests a method of development: narration, process, definition, classification, description, comparison and contrast, or cause and effect. Be sure to write the questions you predict in complete sentences, using one of the key words shown in Table 15-2. For example, the following question, "Trace the events that resulted in the dissolution of the Soviet Union" implies a chronological order of development. The question "Discuss similarities in the poetic works of Frost and Sandburg" suggests a comparison and contrast method of development.

Exercise 15–1   Predict and write an essay question for each of the following.

1. A mass communications textbook chapter titled "Newspapers" with the following headings:

   The Colonial Press

   Press of the New Republic

   The People's Publishers: Pulitzer, Hearst, and Scripps

   Twentieth Century Trends

   The Black Press

   New Latino and Native American Media

   Current Popular Journalists

   The Future of Journalism

2. "Understanding Society and Culture Through Eating," p. 280.
3. "The Uses of Advertising," p. 158.

Controlling Test Anxiety

Do you get nervous and anxious just before taking an exam? If so, you're like many other students. It's perfectly normal to feel some anxiety. It sharpens your attention and keeps you alert. Too much anxiety, however, can interfere with performance.

Use the following suggestions to reduce your level of anxiety about exams.

1. Become familiar with the building and room where the exam will be given. Take a seat in the room when it is empty and get used to your surroundings.

2. Visualize yourself taking the test. Visualize yourself working through the exam calmly and successfully.

3. Don't get to the exam room too early. You'll have too much time to get nervous. You'll see other nervous students, too, and their anxiety is sometimes contagious.

Preparation of Rough Draft Answers

Once you have predicted possible exam questions, the next step is to write rough draft answers. Generate ideas by locating information in your textbook and class notes that relate to the question. Organize the information, using the method of development suggested in the question, and write a rough draft answer. This draft will be helpful in several ways:

- Writing the draft will force you to think about and analyze ideas. This is a better way to review than just rereading your notes and underlining your textbook.
- The draft will give you practice expressing important ideas in your own words.
- Writing will increase your ability to retain the information.
- You will save time on the exam because you will already have thought about the ideas and how to organize and express them.

To be sure that you can recall important ideas at the time of the exam, you can take one more step: reduce your draft to a brief outline or list of key topics and details.

4. **Sit in the front of the room.** If you can make eye contact with the instructor, the situation will feel more personal and you'll feel more in control.

5. **Compose yourself before the test begins.** Take several deep breaths, close you eyes, and visualize yourself calmly working through the test.

6. **Take a minute to relax.** If you feel yourself getting nervous during the exam, close your eyes and stretch your legs and arms.

7. **Send yourself only** *positive* **messages.** Either before or during the exam, don't think such things as, "I'm not going to do well" or "what if I fail?" Negative thoughts just create more anxiety. Instead, send messages such as, "I know the material" or, "I have studied for this so I'll do well."

You probably won't be able to predict all of your essay exam questions. Some may take a different focus or require a different method of development than you predicted. However, this does *not* mean you have wasted your time. Whatever form a question may take, you will be well prepared to answer it if you've already thought about and organized your ideas on the topic.

TAKING ESSAY EXAMS

■ Here are a few general tips on taking essay exams. Many of these suggestions are useful for other types of exams as well.

1. **Arrive a few minutes early.** This will give you time to get organized and collect your thoughts.

2. **Sit in the front of the room.** You'll be able to hear directions and read changes or corrections written on the chalkboard. Also, you won't be easily distracted by other students in the exam room.

3. **Read the directions carefully.** They may, for example, tell you to answer only two out of four questions.

4. **If given a choice of questions, take time to make a careful choice.** Otherwise, you may realize midway through the exam that you've picked a question you're not really prepared to answer.

5. **Plan your time.** For example, if you have to answer two essay questions in a 50-minute class session, give yourself 20 to 25 minutes for each one. There is always a strong tendency to spend the most time on the first question, but you should guard against this tendency. Keep track of time so that enough time remains to finish both questions. Allow a few minutes at the end of an in-class exam to check and proofread your answer. Allow more time for a final exam.

6. **Know how many points each question is worth.** If that information is not written on the exam, ask the instructor. Use the information to budget your time and to decide how much to write for each question. Suppose you are taking an exam that has three essays with the following values:

Question 1: 20 points

Question 2: 30 points

Question 3: 50 points

Since Question 3 is worth the most points (half the total) you should spend approximately half of your time on it. Roughly divide the remaining time equally on Questions 1 and 2. Point distribution can suggest how many ideas to include in your answer. For a 20-point question, your instructor probably expects four or five main points. (4 $\times$ 5 = 20) and most instructors don't work with fractions of points. If you can think of additional ideas to include and time permits, include them, since point distribution is only an indicator, not a rule.

7. **Answer the easiest question first.** It may take you less time than you budgeted, and consequently, you can spend additional time on harder questions. Also, you'll get off to a positive and confident start.

Exercise 15–2   For each of the following sets of exam question values, decide how you would budget your time.

1. *Exam 1* (50 minute class)

Question 1   20 points   Time: _____

Question 2   20 points   Time: _____

Question 3   60 points   Time: _____

2. *Exam 2* (75 minute class)

Question 1   15 points   Time: _____

Question 2   30 points   Time: _____

Question 3   20 points   Time: _____

Question 4   35 points   Time: _____

3. *Exam 3* (two hour final exam)

Question 1   10 points   Time: _____

Question 2   30 points   Time: _____

Question 3   20 points   Time: _____

Question 4   40 points   Time: _____

Analyzing Exam Questions

Exam questions often follow a recognizable format that tells you not only *what* to write about, but also *how* to organize it. Here is a sample exam question.

Trace the history of advertising in the United States.

This question identifies the topic—the history of advertising. It also limits or narrows the topic to U.S. advertising. Now, notice the word "trace." This verb suggests the method of development to use in writing the essay. *Trace* means to track something through time. Therefore this word conveys time order for the method of development. Your answer should begin with the earliest example of advertising you know about and end with the present. Here is another example:

Justify the United Nations' decision to authorize military action against Iraq.

This question focuses on military action against Iraq, but limits the topic to the United Nations' decision to authorize it. The verb "justify" means to explain *why* something is correct or reasonable. *Justify*, then, suggests a cause and effect organization, and your answer should illustrate what caused the UN to make the decision.

Table 15-2 lists verbs commonly used in essay questions, gives an example of their use, and indicates the method of organization each suggests.

TABLE 15-2   **Verbs Commonly Used in Essay Questions**

Verb	Example	Information to Include and Method of Development
Trace	Trace changes in water pollution control methods over the past 20 years.	Describe the development or progress of a particular trend, event, or process in chronological order.
Describe	Describe the two types of chromosomal abnormalities that can cause Down's Syndrome.	Tell how something looks or happened, including *how, who, where, why.*
List	List the different types of family structures and marriage relationships.	List or discuss one-by-one. Use most-to-least or least-to-most organization.
Illustrate	Illustrate from your experience how religion shapes values.	Explain, using examples that demonstrate or clarify a point or idea.
Define	Define an institution and list three primary characteristics.	Give an accurate meaning of the term with enough detail to demonstrate you understand it.
Discuss	Discuss the antigen-antibody response in the immune system.	Consider important characteristics and main points.
Compare	Compare the poetry of Langston Hughes with one of his contemporaries.	Show how items are similar as well as different; include details or examples.
Contrast	Contrast Marx and Weber's theories of social stratification.	Show how the items are different; include details or examples.
Explain	Explain the functions of peptide and steroid hormones.	Give facts and details that make the idea or concept clear and understandable.
Evaluate	Explain the accomplishments of the civil rights movement over the past fifty years.	React to the topic in a logical way. Discuss the merits, strengths, weaknesses, advantages, or limitations of the topic.

Summarize	Summarize Parson's theory of social evolution.	Cover the major points in brief form; use a sentence and paragraph form.
Justify	Justify the use of racial quotas in police department hiring policies.	Give reasons that support an action, event, or policy.

Words other than verbs can also provide clues about how to organize essay answers. In a question that begins "Explain three common types of . . ." the key word is "types." The word *types* suggests classification. A question that directs you to explain the effects, implies a cause and effect organization.

Answering Two-Part Questions

Some essay questions have two verbs that ask you to do two different things. Here is an example:

> Describe the characteristics of psychotic behavior and explain how it can be treated.

This question asks you to *describe* characteristics and *explain* treatment methods. If you get a question like this, it is especially important to plan your time carefully. It is easy to get so involved in writing the first part that you don't leave enough time for the second.

Other two-part questions have only one verb, but they still require two separate discussions. Here is an example:

> Explain the effects of U.S. trade agreements on Canada and Mexico.

You would have to first discuss the effects on Canada, and then those on Mexico.

To make sure you respond to such questions accurately, underline and mark all of the exam questions as you read them. Underline the topic and any limitations, then draw a box around the verb(s) that suggest which method of development you should use. Number two-part questions clearly:

> Explain the effects of U.S. trade
>
> agreements on Canada and Mexico.

Exercise 15–3   For each of the following essay questions, underline the topic(s) and box the verb(s) that suggests the method of development (narration, description, process, definition, example, classification, comparison and contrast, or cause and effect). In the space provided, indicate the method(s) you would use to answer each question.

1. Define and illustrate the three approaches to collective behavior.

Method of Development: _____

2. Explain the function of memory cells in the human immune system and indicate how they differ from plasma cells.

Method of Development: _____

3. Discuss the advantages and disadvantages of the three basic market survey methods.

Method of Development: _____

4. Explain the three major types of shopping centers.

Method of Development: _____

5. Explain the stages involved in the process of establishing prices.

Method of Development: _____

6. Evaluate the statement, "Darwin unified the field of biology."

Method of Development: _____

7. Distinguish between cults and sects and give three examples of each.

Method of Development: _____

8. Define homeostasis and relate it to temperature regulation in cold-blooded animals.

Method of Development: _____

9. Describe the primary types of sensory receptors.

Method of Development: _____

10. Trace the increasing prominence for gender discrimination issues over the last three decades.

Method of Development: _____

Considering Audience and Purpose

The essay exam answer has a special audience and purpose. The audience consists of your instructor, and you know that he or she is knowledgeable about the topic of the essay. Your purpose in writing an essay answer is to demonstrate that *you* are knowledgeable about the topic. Consequently, your answer should explain the topic thoroughly and completely. It is best to write as if your audience were *not* knowledgeable about the topic.

Planning Your Answer

Because you are working within a time limit, you won't have time to revise your answer. Consequently, it is even more important than usual to plan your essay carefully before you begin.

After you have read and marked the question, jot down ideas you'll include in your essay on the back of the exam, or on a separate sheet of paper that you won't turn in. If the question is one that you predicted, jot down the outline of your draft essay, making adjustments and additions to fit the actual question. Arrange your ideas to follow the method of development suggested in the question. Number them to indicate the order in which you'll present them in your essay. Keep in mind, too, the point value of the essay, and be sure to include sufficient ideas and explanations.

Here is an example of what a student wrote in response to the following question.

Identify the stages of sleep and describe four sleep disorders.

<u>Stages</u>
1 wakefulness
2 quiet sleep
3 REM sleep (active)

<u>Disorders</u>
4 hypersomnia
1 insomnia
2 sleepwalking
3 night terrors

As you write, other ideas may occur to you; add them to your list so they won't slip your mind.

Exercise 15–4   Write a list of ideas to use in answering one of the following questions. Then number them to reflect how you plan to organize the essay.

1. The U.S. national debt has become an increasingly serious problem. One economist has suggested that each American take a 10 percent pay cut for one year. He presented statistics that demonstrated how this would drastically reduce the debt. Explain and justify your personal response to this proposal.

2. Describe the effects of the computerization of business and society on our daily lives.

WRITING YOUR ANSWER

■   Because you will have little time to make changes, it is important to write in complete sentences, supplying sufficient detail and following a logical organization. (Your instructor will not be put off by minor changes, additions, and corrections.)

Organize your essay answer as you would the other types of essays you've learned to write: Begin with a thesis statement, then explain and support it.

Writing Your Thesis Statement

Thesis statements in essay-answer tests should be simple and straightforward. In fact, you often can simply rephrase the essay question. Here are a few examples:

Essay Question	*Thesis Statement*
1. Describe the psychological factors that may affect the consumer buying decision process.	There are five psychological factors that may affect the consumer buying decision process.
2. Identify and give an example of the principal forms of price discrimination.	Retailers use numerous forms of price discrimination.
3. Coastal areas have more moderate temperatures than inland areas at the same latitude. Explain this phenomenon.	The high specific heat of water accounts for variations between coastal and inland areas at the same latitude.

At times you may decide to add more information, as in the following examples.

Essay Question	*Thesis Statement*
1. Describe the strategies individuals use to reinterpret a stressful event.	Individuals cope with stressful events by using reappraisal, social comparison, avoidance, or humor to reinterpret them.
2. Explain the differences between primary and secondary groups.	Primary groups differ from secondary groups in their membership, purpose, level of interaction, and level of intimacy.

In the above examples, the essay question provided a structure to which the writer added more information.

Make your thesis statement as concise and specific as possible. It should announce to your instructor that you know the answer and how you will organize it.

Exercise 15–5   Write a thesis statement for three of the following essay questions.

1. How does advertising differ from publicity?

Thesis Statement: _____

2. Explain the common types of magazines and identify the intended audience of each.

Thesis Statement: _____

3. Describe the rise of the women's movement over the past several decades.

Thesis Statement: _____

4. Discuss the major ways in which a group ensures that its members conform to its cultural rules.

Thesis Statement: _____

5. Discuss several ways to test the effectiveness of an advertising campaign.

Thesis Statement: _____

Presenting Supporting Details

Write a separate paragraph for each major supporting detail. Begin each one with a topic sentence that introduces each new point. Suppose your thesis statement is:

```
      There are five social factors that may af-
fect the consumer buying decision process.
```

Your topic sentences might read as follows:

```
Paragraph 1  First, role and family influence
             is a factor that influences con-
             sumer decisions . . .

Paragraph 2  Reference groups is a second so-
             cial factor . . .

Paragraph 3  Social class also affects the con-
             sumer's purchase decisions . . .

Paragraph 4  Finally, cultures and subcultures
             affect buying decisions . . .
```

The remainder of each paragraph should include supporting details about each factor.

Developing Your Answer with Supporting Details

Each paragraph should provide relevant and sufficient explanation of the topic sentence. For the above sample question on psychological factors, explain or define each factor and discuss how it affects the buying decision. Here is an example of how one student developed the first two paragraphs of this essay. Notice that he added a general explanation following the thesis statement.

```
      There are five social factors that may af-
fect the consumer buying decision process. So-
cial factors are those forces that other people
exert on a buyer. First, role and family influ-
ence affect who buys what. Everyone holds a po-
sition within a group. How you are expected to
act in that position is your role. Your role,
especially within your family, determines which
types of purchases you are in charge of. For
```

example, women are responsible for food and household supplies, while men buy home repair and auto supplies.

Reference groups is a second social factor influencing buying decisions. A reference group refers to the group a person connects himself or herself with. The person accepts the attitudes and behaviors of the reference group and thus tries to be like other members. As a result, a person buys the same things as others in the reference group. For example, teenagers in a particular high school class may all purchase one expensive brand of sneakers.

Social class also affects consumer purchase decisions. Social class is a group of people who have similar social rank, which is determined by such things as money, education, and possessions. People in the same social class have common attitudes and value the same things. Because they value the same things, they purchase similar items. For example, upper middle class business men and women buy luxury cars, like BMW's.

Finally, cultures and subcultures influence buying decisions. Culture means everything in our surroundings made by human beings and includes values and behavior. We tend to do things the way everyone else in our culture does. Because we imitate others, we buy the same things. For example, because many women in American culture work full-time, many of them buy convenience foods. Subcultures are subdivisions within a culture--they are often created on the basis of age, geography, or ethnic background. There are even more similarities in subcultures, so the buying influence is even stronger. Thus, since consumer buying decisions are determined by numerous social forces, retailers and advertisers find predicting consumer purchases challenging and complex.

Proofreading Your Answer

Be sure to leave enough time to proofread your answer. Check for errors in spelling, punctuation, and grammar. If time permits, make minor revisions, as well. If you think of an important fact to add, do so. Pay attention to sentences that do not make sense and make your changes as neatly as possible.

If You Run Out of Time . . .

If you run out of time before you have finished answering the last question, don't panic. Take the last minute or two to make a list or outline of the remaining points you planned to cover. Some instructors will give you partial credit for this outline.

COMPETENCY TESTS AND EXIT EXAMS

■ Some colleges require students to pass competency tests in skill areas such as reading, writing, and mathematics. These tests assess skills required in more advanced college courses, so think of them as readiness tests. Competency tests are designed so that you will not be placed into courses that are too difficult or for which you are inadequately prepared. Try your best, but don't be upset if you don't score at the required level. It is best to be certain you've got the skills you need before tackling more difficult courses. This section focuses on writing competency tests, but many suggestions apply to tests in other skill areas.

Finding Out About the Test

To feel confident and prepared for the test, find out as much about it as possible ahead of time. You'll want to know:

- What kinds of questions are included? (Do you write an essay or correct errors in paragraphs, for example?)
- How many questions are there?
- Is there a time limit, and if so, what is it?
- What skills does the test measure?
- How is the test scored? (Do some skills count more than others?)
- If it is an essay, are you expected to revise it? recopy it?

Your instructor may be able to answer many of these questions. Also, talk with other students who have taken the test. They may be able to offer useful tips and advice.

Preparing for Competency Tests

If you are taking the test right after you have finished a writing course, you will be well-prepared. Only a few last minute things remain.

If your test requires that you write an essay, use the following suggestions:

1. Study your error log (see Ch. 5, pages 88–90). If you haven't kept one, review papers your instructor has marked to identify and write a list of your most common errors. As you revise and proofread your competency test answers, check for each of these errors.

2. Construct a mental revision checklist before you go into the exam. Use revision checklists in this book as a guide. If time permits, jot it down on scrap paper during the exam; use it to revise your essay.

3. Reread sections of your learning journal in which you have written about skills you are learning and how well they work. If you have discovered that branching usually works well for generating ideas, for example, then use it during the test.

4. If your test is timed, plan how to divide your time. Estimate how much you will need for each step in the writing process. To find out, gauge your time on a practice test (see below). Wear a watch to the exam, and check periodically to see that you're on schedule.

5. Take a practice test. Ask a classmate to make up a topic or question for you to write about. It should be the same type of question as those that will be on the test. Give yourself the time limit that will be used on the test. Then ask your classmate to evaluate your essay. (see Writing Success Tip 5, Peer Review, p. 80.)

If your test requires you to edit or correct errors in another writer's sentences or paragraphs, follow the suggestions below:

1. Again, review your error log or graded papers. The errors you make when you write are likely to be those you'll have difficulty spotting on the test.

2. If time permits, read each sentence or paragraph several times, looking for different types of errors each time. For example, read it once looking for spelling errors, another time to evaluate sentence structure, and so forth.

3. Practice with a friend. Write sample test items for each other. Pay attention to the kinds of errors you are missing; you're likely to miss them on the test as well.

4. If you are taking a state exam, practice manuals or review books may be available. Check with your college bookstore. Take the sample

tests and work through the practice exercises, as well. Note your pattern of errors and get additional help with trouble spots if needed (see Writing Success Tip 4, College Services for Writing, p. 58.)

Taking Competency Tests

It is natural to become nervous before taking a test. The Writing Success Tip on pages 322–323 has suggestions about controlling test anxiety. Here are a few other tips for taking competency tests that can help you feel calm and confident:

1. If you are given a choice of topics to write about, choose the one you know the most about. One of the most common mistakes students make on competency tests is failing to support their ideas with specific detail. If you are familiar with a topic, you'll be able to supply details more easily.

2. If none of the topics seem familiar, spend a minute or two generating ideas on each topic before choosing one. You'll quickly see which will be the best choice.

3. Be sure to follow the writing process, step-by-step, as you've learned throughout this book.

4. If time permits, revise your essay, using your mental revision checklist and proofread, checking for common errors.

THINKING BEFORE READING

■   This reading was taken from a college textbook, *Human Anatomy and Physiology*, by Elaine Marieb. It represents the type of textbook material you might review for an essay exam.

1. Preview the reading using the steps listed in Chapter 3, p. 43.
2. Activate your thinking by completing the following questions.
   a. Is your mood different on dark dreary days than it is on bright sunny days?
   b. Have you ever worked night schedules or do you know someone who has? If so, what effects did you observe?
   c. Does the change from Standard to Daylight Savings Time affect you? How? Why?
   d. Do you know people who are "sun worshipers"—people who enjoy spending time in the sun? Why do they enjoy it, knowing the risk of skin cancer?

READING

SUNLIGHT AND THE CLOCK WITHIN

Elaine Marieb

It has been known for a long time that many body rhythms move in step with one another. Body temperature, pulse, and the sleep-wake cycles seem to follow the same "beat" over approximate 24-hour cycles, while other processes follow a different "drummer." What can throw these rhythms out of wack? Illness, drugs, jet travel, and changing to the night shift are all candidates. So is sunlight. [1]

Light exerts its internal biochemical effects through the eye. Light hitting the retina generates nerve impulses along the optic nerve, tract, and radiation to the visual cortex (where "seeing" occurs) and via the retinohypothalamic tracts to the superchiasmatic nucleus (SCN), the so-called biological clock of the hypothalamus. The SCN regulates multiple-drive rhythms, including the rhythmic melatonin output of the pineal gland and the output of various anterior pituitary hormones. Generally speaking, release of melatonin is inhibited by light and enhanced during darkness, and historically, the pineal gland has been called the "third eye." [2]

Light produces melatonin-mediated effects on reproductive, eating, and sleeping patterns of other animals, but until very recently, humans were believed to have evolved free of such effects. Thanks to the research of many scientists, however, we now know that people are influenced by three major variables of light: its intensity, its spectrum (color mixture), and its timing (day/night and seasonal changes). [3]

A number of human processes are known to be influenced by light: [4]

1. *Behavior and Mood.* Many people have seasonal mood rhythms, particularly those of us who live far from the equator, where the day/night cycle changes dramatically during the course of a year. We seem to feel better during the summer and become cranky and depressed in the long, gray days of winter. Is this just our imagination? Apparently not. Researchers have found a relatively rare emotional disorder called seasonal affective disorder, or SAD, in which these mood swings are grossly exaggerated. As the days grow shorter [5] each fall, people with SAD become irritable, anxious, sleepy, and socially withdrawn. Their appetite becomes insatiable; they crave carbohydrates and gain weight. Phototherapy, the use of very bright lights for 6 hours daily, reversed these symptoms in nearly 90% of patients studied in two to four days (considerably faster than any antidepressant drug could do it). When patients stopped receiving therapy or were given melatonin, their symptoms returned as quickly as they had lifted, indicating that melatonin may be the key to seasonal mood changes.

Symptoms of SAD are virtually identical to those of individuals   6
with *carbohydrate-craving obesity (CCO)* and *premenstrual syndrome (PMS)*, except that CCO sufferers are affected daily and PMS sufferers are affected monthly (2 weeks prior to menses onset). Photoperiodism appears to be the basis of these cyclic behavioral disorders as well, and phototherapy relieves PMS symptoms in some women.

2. *Night work schedules and jet lag.* People who work at night   7
(the graveyard shift) exhibit reversed melatonin secretion patterns, with no hormone released during the night (when they are exposed to light) and high levels secreted during daytime sleeping hours. Waking such people and exposing them to bright light causes their melatonin levels to drop. The same sort of melatonin inversion (but much more precipitous) occurs in those who fly from coast to coast.

3. *Immunity.* Ultraviolet light activates white blood cells called   8
suppressor T cells, which partially block the immune response. UV therapy has been found to stop rejection of tissue transplants from unrelated donors in animals. This technique offers the hope that diabetics who have become immune to their own pancreas islet tissue may be treated with pancreas transplants in the future.

People have worshipped sunlight since the earliest times. Scientists are just now beginning to understand the reasons for this, and   9
as they do, they are increasingly distressed about windowless offices, restricted and artificial illumination of work areas, and the growing numbers of institutionalized elderly who rarely feel the sun's warm rays. Artificial lights do not provide the full spectrum of sunlight: Incandescent bulbs used in homes provide primarily the red wavelengths, and fluorescent bulbs of institutions provide yellow-green; neither provides the invisible UV or infrared wavelengths that are also components of sunlight. Animals exposed for prolonged periods to artificial lighting exhibit reproductive abnormalities and an enhanced susceptibility to cancer. Could it be that some of us are unknowingly expressing the same effects?

from *Human Anatomy and Physiology*

GETTING READY TO WRITE

■ *Step 1—Underlining and Reviewing*

Reread and underline the reading, as if you were preparing for an exam that includes this material. Use any other "getting ready to write" strategy that will help you organize and recall the material. (Refer to Table 15–1, page 319, for a list of strategies.)

Step 2—Thinking Critically: Predicting Exam Questions

Predict at least one essay exam question that could be based on this reading.

Step 3—Reacting to and Discussing Ideas

Compare your essay question prediction with those of other students. Discuss ways you might respond to their questions as well as your own.

WRITING ABOUT THE READING

■

Answer the following essay question without quoting directly from the reading.
     Explain the effects of sunlight on humans, both biologically and psychologically.

WRITING ABOUT YOUR IDEAS

■ *Assignment 1*

Assume you are taking an exit exam for your writing course. Select one of the following assignments and approach it as you would a competency exam.

Assignment 2

Write an essay describing how seasonal and/or time changes affect you.

Assignment 3

Write an essay explaining factors that affect your mood.

Assignment 4

Write an essay describing how it feels when your biological clock is out of whack.

Journal Writing Suggestions

1. Write an entry describing whether sunlight affects you.
2. Write an entry describing your experiences with essay or exit exams.

REVISION CHECKLIST—ESSAY EXAMS

1. Is your essay written for an audience unfamiliar with the topic?
2. Does your essay demonstrate your purpose—that you are knowledgeable about the topic?
3. Is your thesis statement concise and straightforward?
4. Is each main point developed in a separate paragraph?
5. Does each paragraph provide relevant and sufficient detail?
6. Have you made minor revisions and have you proofread the essay?

REVISION CHECKLIST—COMPETENCY TESTS

1. Is your essay appropriate for your audience? Does it give them the background information they need? Will it interest them?
2. Will your essay accomplish your purpose?
3. Have you narrowed your topic so that you can cover your subject thoroughly in your essay?
4. Is your main point clearly expressed in a thesis statement in the introductory paragraph? Does your introductory paragraph capture the reader's interest and lead into the body of the essay?
5. Does each paragraph of your essay have a topic sentence that supports your essay's main point?
6. Is each paragraph's topic sentence supported by relevant and sufficient detail?
7. Are your paragraphs arranged in a logical sequence and connected by transitions?
8. Is the tone of your essay appropriate for your purpose and audience?
9. Does your conclusion reemphasize your thesis statement and draw the essay to a close?
10. Does your title identify the topic and interest the reader?
11. Have you proofread your paper and corrected any errors in grammar, mechanics, and spelling?

When to Use Capital Letters

Capital letters are commonly used to

    1. mark the beginning of a sentence.
    2. identify names of specific people, places, organizations, companies, products, titles, days, months, weeks, religions, and holidays.
    3. mark the beginning of a direct quotation.

Rate Your Ability to Use Capitalization Correctly

In each of the following sentences, capitalize wherever necessary by crossing out the letter and replacing it with a capital. If any words are incorrectly capitalized, change them to lower case letters.

  1. because I spent last sunday in pittsburgh, I missed my favorite television show—*60 minutes.*
  2. This summer I plan to visit the Baltic states—estonia, latvia, lithuania—former Republics of the soviet union.
  3. this may, professor gilbert will give us our final exam.
  4. Last week I rented my favorite movie from the video rental store on elmwood avenue.
  5. One of shakespeare's most famous plays is *hamlet.*
  6. I live next door to joe's mobile gas station.
  7. my brother will eat only rice krispies for breakfast.
  8. Jean Griffith is a senator who lives in washington county.
  9. I love to vacation in california because the pacific ocean is so beautiful.
10. My neighbors, mr and mrs wilson, have a checking account at the lincoln bank.

Score _____

Check your answers using the Answer Key on page 537. If you scored below 80 percent, you need additional review and practice recognizing when to use capital letters. Refer to Section F.1 of Reviewing the Basics in Part 5.

SUMMARY

■   1. Preparing for an essay exam involves identifying important ideas, organizing and relating ideas and concepts, and expressing them in your own words. Useful written strategies include underlining, immediate review, annotation, idea mapping, outlining, and summarizing.

2. Study sheets are useful in order to organize material concisely for review.

3. Predict possible exam questions by identifying important issues or concepts that your instructor has emphasized.

4. Practice answering the questions you predicted by writing rough draft answers.

5. When taking essay exams, read directions carefully, plan your time, and notice the point value of each question.

6. Analyze each question by identifying the topic, its limitations, and the method of development suggested.

7. Plan your answer by jotting down a brief outline.

8. Be sure your thesis statement is clear and direct.

9. Include sufficient supporting detail. Write a separate paragraph for each major detail.

10. To prepare for competency tests and exit exams:
   • find out about the test (content, time, scoring)
   • discover common errors you make using your error log
   • create a mental revision checklist
   • take a practice test

11. When taking competency tests and exit exams:
   • choose a familiar topic
   • follow the writing process, step-by-step

IV

Additional Readings

NARRATIVE

■

"I WILL DO ANYTHING WITHIN MY POWER TO KEEP 'BOARDER BABY' "

Jane Doe (*Jane Doe insisted on anonymity for fear of reprisals in efforts to adopt her boarder baby.*)

As work on a corporate project wound down, I made the call. I was ready to take home a "boarder baby."   1

Boarder babies are primarily victims of the crack epidemic, born of mothers who test positive for cocaine and cannot take care of them. They are taken by private agencies operating under the supervision of the city's Department of Social Services and given to foster parents temporarily, until they can be placed with relatives.   2

Unless people open their homes to them the babies languish in institutions, unloved, untouched, apathetic, cast off.   3

I had requested a boy. Having raised daughters of my own, I wanted the experience of a son. Next to "race" on my application I wrote "no preference," which meant he would most likely be black.   4

My only other request was that he be healthy, as crack babies go. I didn't have the courage my first time out to deal with the effects of extreme damage.   5

Two days later he was delivered to my apartment by a young man who had been commandeered as a messenger for the trip from Brooklyn to Manhattan by an overworked social worker friend. He put the infant in my arms and laid his worldly possessions down next to us: two small bottles of formula, one gray cotton sweater, one nightgown, three Pampers and the bright and pretty comforter he was wrapped in, made lovingly by some volunteer from some charity group.   6

In addition, there was a paper with his name, his mother's name, the hospital he was born in, date of birth and the information that he was on a three-hour feeding schedule. Then the messenger left. I don't remember if I signed a receipt. I think I did.   7

There we sat, this little being and I. Despite the oft-voiced concerns of my loved ones and friends, I felt perfectly capable of giving him up when the time came, knowing I had saved him from living death. Not without some pain and loss, of course, but I can always take another child and do it again.   8

Besides, deep down I believed some loving grandmother would   9 come looking for him, eager to return him to the welcoming arms of his family.

Well, my son has celebrated his first birthday. He's a real hunk 10 with "thunder thighs" and a smile and a squeal that sets my heart afire. His early, uncontrollable muscular tremors are gone and he is filled with the boundless excitement of discovery that all children feel when they are loved. I have gone back to the gym to be able to keep up with him.

No grandma has come to fetch him. No aunts, no uncles, no 11 cousins. No mother. No one has even come to see him.

But I was recently warned that his mother had entered a drug 12 rehab and wanted her baby back. I was told to bring him to the agency for a visit with her, and to be prepared for her taking him on weekends until she was well enough to keep him for good.

We showed up for the visit with him sweet-smelling, smiling and 13 full of trust, and me a teary, anxious mess.

She never showed up. Neither did her social worker. 14

We made another appointment for two weeks later. Again, she 15 didn't show. Neither did her social worker.

The pain of these episodes is indescribable. To be a mother, to 16 have that ferocious instinct of protectiveness and to be rendered impotent is truly hell. Rather than surrender to my helplessness I spent days on the telephone seeking the best advice I could find on my rights. Here is what I learned: I was as helpless as I felt.

The sanctity of the family rules supreme. Before the agency can 17 go to court and move to have the mother's rights terminated, they first have to exhaust every effort the law requires. Until he was with me for a year I had no rights whatsoever. I was a paid baby-sitter for New York City, bonding or no bonding.

I understand that these laws were created for another time, an- 18 other world, when mothers with emotional or financial problems deserved every opportunity to get their beloved children back, when grandmothers did come to fetch their precious babies if the mothers couldn't get it together.

But that was another time, before crack. The grandmothers are 19 getting all used up, and statistics on getting clean and staying that way are hardly encouraging.

I have engaged a lawyer and am seeking to terminate the 20 mother's rights. I will do anything within my power and possibly beyond to insure him a life where he will be valued and appreciated for the pure love and joy that he is.

New York Times, December 22, 1990

REACTING TO AND DISCUSSING IDEAS

■   1. If the natural mother of the child wants the child back after he has been cared for by "Jane Doe" for a year, do you think he should be returned to her? If so, are there certain conditions she should be required to meet?

2. What rights do you feel Jane Doe has after keeping the child for a year?

3. What does Jane Doe mean that she is willing to do anything within her power *and possibly beyond it* to ensure the child a life where he will be valued?

WRITING ABOUT THE READING

■   The narrative ends with two unresolved issues: a. Will the natural mother request to have the child returned to her? b. If so, will Jane Doe be successful in preventing her from doing so? Predict the answer to these questions and write a narrative paragraph describing what happens next. Be imaginative and create events and/or dialogue. Write this paragraph from the point of view of either Jane Doe or the natural mother.

WRITING ABOUT YOUR IDEAS

■   1. Write a process paragraph describing how you would explain to a child that he or she is adopted.

2. This assignment also encourages you to use your imagination. Suppose your mother, friend, or close relative did the same as Jane Doe, requested and received a boarder crack baby. Write a narrative paragraph describing what you would do and say when you learned of her decision.

NARRATION/ DESCRIPTION

■
THE WAVES OF WINTER

Lesley Choyce

Picture this. It's the third day of February in Nova Scotia. Along the Atlantic coast, arctic ghosts swirl up into the frigid air from the sea. The water, a tropical minus two degrees Celsius, is steaming up into the minus 18-degree atmosphere. A light north wind has recently arrived from Hudson Bay and stirs the morning sea wraiths into a vertical dance, then chases them off to sea.

I arrive at the Lawrencetown Headland in my old Pinto stationwagon. Looking out to sea I find near-perfect, six-foot-high waves breaking beyond the tip of the land. The short drive to this sacred spot has not allowed my engine to warm up enough to provide any semblance of heat. In fact, the engine had only groaned when I first urged it to turn over. It was sound asleep, hibernating. Winter wanted us all to freeze up into absolute zero mobility. But man is restless. He wants to get on with business, school, work. Some of us, however, just want to go surfing.

I put on my surfing gear in the house: socks, long underwear, hand-knitted gloves made of Alpaca hair from Peru. Then I climb into my drysuit. A surfing drysuit is just a big rubber bag shaped like a human body. You wear clothes underneath, a three-piece suit if you like. It's supposed to keep you dry but mine leaks a little so I have to wear old plastic bags over my gloves and socks as I slide my feet and hands into the drysuit. Next I pop my head through the neck seal. The fit has to be snug, so the feeling is that of a relatively mild Halifax nightclub bouncer trying to choke you to death.

Then it's outside into the frozen wasteland to find my board, buried by last night's snow storm. I find it's frozen into a minor glacier that has formed beneath the snow overnight, so I go back into the house to get a hammer. I have to literally mine my surfboard out of the ice.

By the time I get to the beach, my once warm body is already cold. But the waves are beautiful. The sun is out. The water is blue, clean, cracking cold hard tubes of Atlantic Ocean with immaculate precision beyond the stony shoreline.

I carry my board down the embankment, wading through drifted   6
snow as high as my chest. Along the shoreline there is no snow, but
each black and grey boulder is frozen over with a formidable head-
gear of ice. Slippery going: I have to half crawl, half walk over the
frozen rocks. I remind myself that even salt-water freezes if it isn't
stirred around and if the temperature has dropped below minus 20
degrees overnight.

At last my rubber feet find the open ocean. My board is still   7
heavy with ice cakes and I soak it in the sea until they drift off. Now
I'm wading through the shallows, walking over kelp and barnacle-
laden rocks. The sun is in my face as I hop up onto my board and begin to knee-paddle to sea. It almost feels warm. The water is so clear
I see everything on the bottom: fish, swaying kelp, rockweed, sea urchins, mussels, barnacles sharp as razor blades. I am at home here,
happy, in love with being alive.

Past the tip of the headland I arrive at where the hungry waves   8
are peaking and peeling off in two directions. From here I'll find my
spot, paddle hard down the face of a bulging heave of sea, then go
right or left, east or west, into the sunrise or off toward Halifax. Instead I sit for a minute, watch my breath turn to white ice as I
breathe out. Ten feet away a blubbery harbor seal pops up and
checks me out as a candidate for breakfast or mating. I'm never sure
which. He has the head of a giant dog with foot-long whiskers. He's
well insulated with fat, and the part of him under water that I can't
see probably weighs about 800 pounds. As usual, he's just curious.
His eyes are deep and dark with the mysteries of the sea and you can
tell he's never sold insurance.

He points his head to the sky, then slips back beneath the sur-   9
face. I see my wave on the horizon, shift further west to be at the precise point of the peak. Three deep strokes and I'm off, dropping
down the face of a pristine, blue North Atlantic wave. I dig in my
back foot hard and turn the board so that I'm sliding parallel to the
wave. I'm moving east at the speed of light straight into the burning
heart of the early morning sun. I tuck down because I see the wave is
about to break over my head. And then, for a brief but eternal instant, I'm inside the tube. The wave is leaping out over my head, my
feet are still firmly planted on the board and I'm surrounded on five
sides by water. I'm ecstatically inside the ocean and for the moment
completely dry. The sun itself is perfectly positioned in the doorway
of the only way out. I can hear the blood pounding in my ears over
the top of the roar of the winter sea collapsing all around. The trick

now is to find the hidden key to the front door and burst out into oxygen and blue sky.

But the warden sneaks up from behind, pulls me two critical inches further back into the tunnel and, with indifferent violence, the wave sucks me into its throat, gobbles me up, drags me to the top of the wave, then slams me to the bottom where I'm brutally thrashed around. It's like being a mouse and getting thrown into somebody's washing machine during a heavy rinse cycle. Only it's much cooler. Seconds under water in the winter stretch out into hours. When you pay your dues for hedonistic winter pleasures, the interest rates are extremely high. 10

I tell myself as usual to relax. The wave has always lost its appetite for me before, and vomited me back up into the world of air-breathing creatures. But first I'm punched around a few times until the oxygen is long gone from my lungs and I begin to see colors. Fortunately my arms are working of their own accord to send me to the surface. 11

I'm bouncing over rocks but they're all around and soft with sea-weed. It doesn't hurt, but I feel a bit like a silver ball in an old pin-ball machine. My lungs are ordering my chest to breathe, but my brain relays the news that seawater will not suffice for air. Then finally I feel the wave give up its grip and I'm out of the turbulent whitewater. I stick my head up into the air and breathe. My heart is pounding and my lungs are working overtime. I start to swim, my surfboard in tow, out of the way of the next incoming wave. I swim hard and sneak over the top of the feathering wall just as the ice-cream headache sets in. 12

An ice-cream headache is what happens after your head has been exposed to very cold water for more than three seconds. I wear a wetsuit hood over my head, but it's not quite enough to keep out the demons of cold. Once your brain is assaulted with below-zero water, it starts getting real angry at your skull and starts wanting out. The pain doesn't last long, maybe 30 seconds. But think about the worst migraine you could ever have, served up with a cherrybomb. That's what an ice-cream headache feels like. Fortunately, it goes away quite quickly and somehow you immediately forget that it happened. So you paddle back out to sea and hope to do it all over again. Maybe this time you'll make it through the tube. 13

Globe and Mail, March 7, 1987

REACTING TO AND DISCUSSING IDEAS

■   1. Identify Choyce's thesis statement.
2. What technique does Choyce use to conclude his essay?
3. Which paragraphs use a process method of development?
4. Is surfing dangerous? If so, why is it a popular sport?
5. Is an element of risk or danger necessary for a sport to be fun?

WRITING ABOUT THE READING

■   1. Write a paragraph explaining why Choyce enjoys winter surfing.
2. Write a paragraph describing Choyce's attitude toward the ocean.

WRITING ABOUT YOUR IDEAS

■   1. Choyce describes the ocean as "I am at home here, happy, in love with being alive." Write a paragraph describing a place or experience that makes you happy to be alive.
2. Write an essay describing a sport or activity you enjoy. Explain what makes it enjoyable.

PROCESS

■

SYMBOLS OF MANKIND

Don Lago

Many thousands of years ago, a man quietly resting on a log reached down and picked up a stick and with it began scratching upon the sand at his feet. He moved the stick slowly back and forth and up and down, carefully guiding it through curves and straight lines. He gazed upon what he had made, and a gentle satisfaction lighted his face.

Other people noticed this man drawing on the sand. They gazed upon the figures he had made, and though they at once recognized the shapes of familiar things such as fish or birds or humans, they took a bit longer to realize what the man had meant to say by arranging these familiar shapes in this particular way. Understanding what he had done, they nodded or smiled in recognition.

This small band of humans didn't realize what they were beginning. The images these people left in the sand would soon be swept away by the wind, but their new idea would slowly grow until it had remade the human species. These people had discovered writing.

Writing, early people would learn, could contain much more information than human memory could and contain it more accurately. It could carry thoughts much farther than mere sounds could—farther in distance and in time. Profound thoughts born in a single mind could spread and endure.

The first written messages were simply pictures relating familiar objects in some meaningful way—pictographs. Yet there were no images for much that was important in human life. What, for instance, was the image for sorrow or bravery? So from pictographs humans developed ideograms to represent more abstract ideas. An eye flowing with tears could represent sorrow, and a man with the head of a lion might be bravery.

The next leap occurred when the figures became independent of things or ideas and came to stand for spoken sounds. Written figures were free to lose all resemblance to actual objects. Some societies developed syllabic systems of writing in which several hundred signs correspond to several hundred spoken sounds. Others discovered the much simpler alphabetic system, in which a handful of signs represented the basic sounds the human voice can make.

At first, ideas flowed only slightly faster when written than they had through speech. But as technologies evolved, humans embodied their thoughts in new ways: through the printing press, in Morse code, in electromagnetic waves bouncing through the atmosphere and in the binary language of computers.   7

Today, when the Earth is covered with a swarming interchange of ideas, we are even trying to send our thoughts beyond our planet to other minds in the Universe. Our first efforts at sending our thoughts beyond Earth have taken a very ancient form: pictographs. The first message, on plaques aboard Pioneer spacecraft launched in 1972 and 1973, featured a simple line drawing of two humans, one male and one female, the male holding up his hand in greeting. Behind them was an outline of the Pioneer spacecraft, from which the size of the humans could be judged. The plaque also included the "address" of the two human figures: a picture of the solar system, with a spacecraft emerging from the third planet. Most scientists believe that when other civilizations attempt to communicate with us they too will use pictures.   8

All the accomplishments since humans first scribbled in the sand have led us back to where we began. Written language only works when two individuals know what the symbols mean. We can only return to the simplest form of symbol available and work from there. In interstellar communication, we are at the same stage our ancestors were when they used sticks to trace a few simple images in the sand.   9

We still hold their sticks in our hands and draw pictures with them. But the stick is no longer made of wood; over the ages that piece of wood has been transformed into a massive radio telescope. And we no longer scratch on sand; now we write our thoughts onto the emptiness of space itself.   10

Science Digest, March 1981

REACTING TO AND DISCUSSING IDEAS

■   1. What is the author's thesis?

2. By sending messages beyond our own universe, the senders have assumed that there is someone in other universes to receive the messages. Do you agree with this assumption?

3. Do we still communicate using forms of pictograms and ideograms?

4. The plaques aboard the Pioneer spacecraft featured a drawing of a man and a woman. Why was only the man holding up his hand in greeting?

5. If other civilizations attempt to communicate with us, why will they use pictures?

WRITING ABOUT THE READING

■   The author emphasizes that for communication to occur, two or more people must understand the same symbols. Think of a situation in which miscommunication or misunderstanding occurred. Write a process paragraph describing how it occurred or how you corrected it.

WRITING ABOUT YOUR IDEAS

■   1. Lago discusses writing as a means of preserving ideas. Write a paragraph describing the uses of writing that you have discovered.

2. Computers are one of the newest innovations in the transmission of ideas. Write an essay describing one or more effects computers have had on our society.

3. Suppose we received a communication from a civilization outside our universe. Write a paragraph describing what information that communication might contain.

DESCRIPTIVE

THE LIGHT STUFF

Douglas Colligan

Probably not since Christopher Columbus worried about skidding   1
off the edge of the earth have humans had to face such an awesome unknown as surviving, let alone living, in space. An almost total vacuum, an environment where temperatures of objects can routinely glide from 250 degrees Fahrenheit below zero to 250 degrees
above, a world where gravity is practically nonexistent, space has
hardly seemed inviting. Yet little by little scientists have learned, first,
how to get air-breathing, gravity-bred earthlings out to space and
back without killing them and, later on, how to get them to settle in
and actually enjoy outer space.

Getting a human back alive is largely a matter of packaging: 2
wrapping an astronaut in a cocoon of simulated earth atmosphere.
That problem was solved on the Mercury space flights and later refined with the Gemini and Apollo missions. Much trickier is how to
cope with all the weird challenges posed by the absence of gravity. If,
as some visionaries project, humans are to live and work in space,
making peace with zero gravity is vital.

As a result, over the years of space flight, including the Skylab   3
missions in 1973 and 1974 and culminating with the space shuttle,
there has evolved a whole zero-g technology. Earthbound engineers
and designers have begun to give present and future astronauts the
components of a world custom-built for weightlessness.

Much of the attention, naturally, is on outfitting the body for   4
weightlessness. Living in space, not just commuting through it on the
way to the moon, has some strange effects on the human form, as
NASA found out during the Skylab mission, when three crews of astronauts lived in zero-g for one, two, and three months. Joe Kosmo,
NASA engineer and space-suit expert, recalls one curious discovery:
"During flights the men had trouble getting into their space suits."
They complained they were too tight. No one knew what to make of
the complaint. Suits were custom-tailored, and each was meticulously
checked before the launch. Once the astronauts got back to earth the
mystery cleared up. The astronauts were taller than when they left
earth, sometimes by as much as two inches.

In-flight growth, NASA calls it. In weightlessness the spinal column becomes loose and stretches. With no gravity to compress the soft disks between the spinal bones, bodies expand and grow, at least temporarily. To compensate for this, suits now issued to space-shuttle astronauts are designed to grow with their wearers. Both the legs and sleeves of the suits have laced-in inserts to let out the suit a little when needed.

Zero-g bodies change shape as well as length. The body's fluids tend to migrate away from the lower half to the torso and head. As a result astronauts find they have skinnier feet and narrower waists and slightly larger chests and shoulders. Because of this, the standard-issue uniform for shuttle occupants has a jacket with elasticized pleats built in to expand with the body.

Of course, this fluid drift is reversed, with a vengeance, once the weightless person returns to earth's gravity. The sudden drop of fluid to the lower part of the body is so violent that anyone not prepared for it would black out. For that reason, astronauts have been routinely wearing what are called antigravity pants when they dress for reentry. Very simply, the pants are a pair of inflatable leggings that can be pumped to apply pressure to the lower body and minimize the fluid shock. The danger of blackout is very real, as Dr. Joseph Kerwin of the first Skylab crew found out. He had only partially inflated his suit before reentry and almost fainted. "Surprised the tar out of me," he later admitted.

Putting food into the weightless body has always been a special challenge for NASA. For a while no one was sure if a human could eat normally in zero-g. There were those who worried that when John Glenn made the first American around-the-world space flight he wouldn't be able to swallow his food in weightlessness and would choke to death. Once Glenn returned to earth, his stomach full, his throat clear, extraterrestrial meal planning began in earnest. Space meals have progressed from such items as gelatin-coated coconut cubes and peanut cubes to complete heat-and-serve meals on board Skylab and the space shuttle.

Space meals are not prepared so much as assembled. All the food is precooked and is either canned, dehydrated, or packed in aluminum-backed plastic envelopes called flex pouches. Because it's impossible to pour water in zero gravity (it congeals into silvery balls that drift around in a spacecraft), dehydrated food is revived by squirting water through a needle into the sealed plastic pouches. Each pouch has a flexible plastic top that lets the cook knead the water into the dried food. Liquids are drunk through a straw with a clamp attached to keep the straw pinched shut when not in use. All are in containers shaped to fit neatly into a compartmentalized and magnetized food tray, where they are anchored in place by Velcro tape.

Weightlessness affects not only how the food is packaged, but also what kind of food is inside. Even without gravity, it is possible to eat some foods off an open plate with a fork or spoon. Meals with sauces or gravies work especially well because they tend to stick to the plate and not float away. The Skylab astronauts, who tested out many space meals, found some were disasters. In one report to earth, the first crew crossed chili off their eating schedule. Every time they opened a container of it, there was an explosion of food: "Great gobbets of chili go flying all over; it's bad news."

Other adaptations to weightless eating include items like liquid salt and pepper. Ordinary crystals and granules are practically impossible to get out of shakers, and when something does come out, it tends not to hit the food but drift away in midair. Eating utensils are also made smaller because, in a gravity-free dining area, food sticks to the bottom as well as the top of the utensil. To keep an astronaut from spooning up more than he can chew, NASA provides utensils about three-fourths the size of what we use here on earth.

Even taste is affected by zero-g. "Body fluids migrate to your upper body, and you end up with engorged tissue around the nasal passages and ear," explains Gerald Carr, who was commander of the third and longest (84 days) Skylab mission. "You carry with you a constant state of nasal and head congestion in a weightless environment. It feels pretty much like you have a cold all the time." As with any head cold, the senses of taste and smell are numbed. To counter this some of the Skylab crews brought up spices and Tabasco sauce to jazz up the food, and shuttle crews will find barbecue and hot sauces in their meal packets.

And, of course, there is the matter of personal hygiene in zero-g, a great source of wonderment to earthlings. Using the toilet is much more of an adventure than here on earth. The toilet in the space shuttle has a footrest, handholds, and a seat belt to hold the user in position. The lack of gravity is solved by a suction fan. Fans are also used in water drains when astronauts wash. Getting clean is complicated by the fact that water is hard to contain in space. Using Skylab's shower, basically a collapsible cloth cylinder, was a time-consuming chore. To wash up, bathers squirted their bodies with a water gun. That turned out to be a messy design. For every astronaut scrubbing up, another would have to stand by with a vacuum cleaner to suck the escaping water globules out of the air. Designer Larry

Bell, who has been working on the plans for a space village for NASA at the University of Houston's School of Architecture, says a better design would be what he calls a "human car wash" or "human dishwasher" approach, in which the bather goes inside a sealed box, is sprayed with water, and is later completely air-dried.

Sleeping in space, on the other hand, is a relatively simple affair. 14 At bedtime the astronaut steps into a bag anchored vertically or horizontally to a firm surface, zips the bag up from toe to chest, and, after connecting a waist strap around the bag, tucks both arms under the strap to keep them from flailing around during sleep. Without gravity, sleepers can rest anywhere. Mattresses and pillows are unnecessary, since there's no reason for a body to sink into them; a padded board suffices. In the shuttle the sleeping area has what looks like a two-level bunk bed. One person sleeps on the top, a second on the bottom, and a third underneath the bottom bunk facing the floor. Only in zero gravity could you fit three persons this way into a two-person bed.

But even sleeping can have odd complications. Anyone sleeping 15 in weightlessness is in danger of suffering from the clouds of carbon dioxide-laden air exhaled during the night. On Skylab a fan kept a steady floor-to-ceiling current of air flowing by the sleepers' mouths. One astronaut, Charles Conrad, got so annoyed by this breeze constantly blowing up his nose that he once turned his sleeping bag upside down and tried to rest that way. (It would have worked except for the fact that the air then blew into his sleeping bag, billowing it out.)

With little resistance to struggle against, the human body tends to 16 lose muscle tone in weightlessness. Exercise regimens are usually prescribed for the longer space flights. Skylab astronauts kept in shape by riding a stationary bicycle exerciser and walking on an ingenious treadmill. It was nothing more than a large sheet of Teflon with some elastic bungee cords. To exercise, an astronaut would anchor himself to a spot on the floor with the cords and walk on the slippery Teflon in his socks. There will be no room for a bicycle exerciser on the shuttle, but it will be carrying a Teflon treadmill.

One problem weightless astronauts can encounter when exercis- 17 ing is that, without fans blowing directly on them, the air heated by their bodies tends to hover nearby. And perspiration doesn't dry but sticks to their skin in ever-thickening layers. The Skylab crews discovered this the hard way and rigged up a fan by the bicycle to help evaporate the sweat. That, however, blew the perspiration off their bodies in sheets, which then had to be vacuumed out of the air.

There is hardly a part of day-to-day space living that doesn't re- 18
quire some zero-g forethought. Standing still is impossible, for example. Astronauts in the shuttle attach suction-cup soles to their shoes
to keep them anchored. Without some means of fixing people in
place, Newton's third law of motion—for every action there is an
equal and opposite reaction—can conjure bizarre results from even
simple actions. When trying to unscrew a bolt, astronaut William
Pogue neglected to anchor himself; when he turned the screwdriver,
he suddenly found his body corkscrewing through the air. Without
some sort of brace, even a motion like bending over can send someone into a somersault. As a way of eliminating these problems,
NASA has packed aboard the shuttle handholds with suction cups
for use almost anywhere.

And because no one can truly sit down in the earthbound sense, 19
furniture has to be redesigned to suit the zero-g stoop, a quasi-fetal
slouch the human body naturally adopts when there is no gravity.
The space crews on Skylab complained that many of the tables and
control panels were too low and too hard to use. To remain seated
at a 90-degree angle, weightless people must tense their stomach muscles constantly. Skylab astronauts finally removed a chair from one
console because it was practically impossible to use. In deference to
this, the shuttle has removable working and eating tables that are
about a foot higher than an earth table, and their metal surfaces accommodate magnetic paperweights and magnetic food trays.

How well this kind of technology helps people adjust to a world 20
where notions like up, down, heavy, and light take on new meaning
is difficult to say. What is known is that astronauts do become totally acclimated to zero gravity. In *A House in Space*, a description
of the Skylab experience, author Henry Cooper, Jr., tells the story of
astronaut Jack Lousma shaving one morning after his return to
earth. Letting go of a can of shaving cream while it was poised in
midair, Lousma was genuinely surprised when it fell straight to the
floor.

Fellow Skylab veteran Gerald Carr chuckled when he heard the 21
story. "Yeah, I had the same problem," he recalled. "It's surprisingly
natural to become what I call a three-dimensional person, one who
can move in all three dimensions. It quickly gets to the point where
it is no bother." Carr may be screening out memories of hour-long
shower preparations and 3-D flotsam drifting through the cabin, but
it's clear that with the proper equipment, zero-g living can be enjoyed rather than just survived.

Technology Illustrated, February/March 1982

REACTING TO AND DISCUSSING IDEAS

■
1. Do you think lengthy exposure to near zero gravity could be harmful?
2. Does weightlessness create added stress for the astronauts?
3. What type of person would be well-suited to become an astronaut?
4. Would you enjoy outer space travel?

WRITING ABOUT THE READING

■ Write a paragraph supporting the following topic sentence. "Colligan uses vivid and descriptive detail to help his readers understand the effects of weightlessness."

WRITING ABOUT YOUR IDEAS

■
1. Jack Lousma (paragraph 20) quickly got used to weightlessness and, upon return to earth, had to get used to gravity again. The example of the can of shaving cream illustrates his adaptability. Write a paragraph describing a situation in which you had to adapt to new surroundings.

2. The reading describes the physical changes that occur during outer space travel. Write an essay describing what emotional or psychological changes an astronaut might experience.

DEFINITION

WHAT IS STRESS?

Douglas A. Bernstein, *et al.*

Stress is the process of adjusting to or dealing with circumstances   1
that disrupt, or threaten to disrupt a person's physical or psychological functioning. Here are two examples.

Marlene has spent ten hours of a sweltering August day on a   2
crowded bus from Cleveland, Ohio, to Muncie, Indiana. The air conditioner is not working, and she discovers that the person next to her has apparently not had a bath since the beginning of the decade. By the time she reaches Muncie, Marlene is hot, dizzy, depressed, tired, and irritable.

Jack is waiting in a room full of other college seniors to interview   3
for a job with a large accounting firm. His grades are not outstanding, but he hopes to get by on his personality. He feels that his parents and his fiancée expect him to land a high-prestige, high-paying position. He is very nervous. His mouth is dry, his stomach feels tight, his heart is pounding, and perspiration has begun to soak through his new suit.

These sketches illustrate that stress involves a relationship be-   4
tween people and their environments—more specifically, between stressors and stress reactions. **Stressors** are events and situations (such as bus rides or interviews) to which people must react. **Stress reactions** are the physical, psychological, and behavioral responses (such as nausea, nervousness, and fatigue) people display in the face of stressors. *Mediating factors*, such as the circumstances in which stressors occur and each person's characteristics, make people more or less sensitive to stressors and to stress responses. Thus, stress is

Figure 13.1   The Process of Stress

Stressors	Stress mediators	Stress reactions
Change Frustration Conflict Pressure Boredom Trauma	Predictability Control Cognitive interpretation Social support Coping skills	Physical Psychological Behavioral

not a specific event but a process (see Figure 13.1). We consider stressors and stress responses first and then examine some of the factors that influence the relationship between them.

STRESSORS

Many stressors involve physical demands such as invading viruses, extreme temperatures, or strenuous work. For humans, however, many of the most significant stressors are psychological. The person who must give a speech to impress a potential employer is facing stressors that can be just as demanding as a day of hard physical labor. Many, perhaps most, human stressors include both physical and psychological components. Athletes, for example, are challenged by the demands of physical exertion, as well as by the pressure of competition. In this section, we focus on the psychological stressors that, combined with the physical demands of life, contribute most significantly to the stress process.

MAJOR PSYCHOLOGICAL STRESSORS

Even very pleasant events can be stressors. For example, the increased salary and status associated with a promotion may be desirable, but the upgrade also requires finding ways of handling new responsibilities and increased pressures. Similarly, it is not uncommon for people to feel exhausted after the travel and intense fun-seeking of a vacation and somewhat depressed by the "real world" when the excitement of a wedding is over. Still, the events and situations most likely to be associated with stress are unpleasant ones—those involving frustration, pressure, boredom, trauma, conflict, or change.

Frustrating situations contain some obstacle that stands between a person and his or her goals. Waiting in a long line at the bank or being unable to find a phone to make an important call are simple examples of frustrating situations. More substantial illustrations include being unable to earn a decent living because of adverse economic conditions or job discrimination or failing in repeated attempts to find a love relationship.

Pressure situations require a person to do too much in too short a time. If you are trying to fix Thanksgiving dinner for twenty people on a day's notice, or if you are struggling to finish the last two questions on an essay test in ten minutes, you are under pressure. Many air-traffic controllers, physicians, nurses, and police officers face constant or long-lasting pressure. They must make many difficult decisions, sometimes involving life and death, under heavy time pressure.

People under such pressure day after day sometimes begin to perform poorly and develop physical illness, alcoholism, anxiety, and many of the other stress-related problems.

Boredom, or underestimulation, is the opposite of pressure, but it, too, can be a stressor, especially if it continues for a long time. The agony of solitary confinement in prison or the tedium of a remote military post are probably the most extreme examples.

Trauma is a shocking physical or emotional experience. Catastrophes such as rape, military combat, fire, tornadoes, or torture are only a few examples. More common disasters, such as a divorce or the sudden death of someone close, can be equally devastating.

Conflict is almost always stressful. The most obvious examples are disputes in which friends, family members, or coworkers fight with, insult, or otherwise get nasty with each other. If you can recall the last time you experienced one of these interpersonal conflicts (even if you were just a spectator), you can probably also remember the discomfort you felt. Internal conflicts can be equally, if not more, distressing than those with other people. Imagine, for example, the stress that might result when a woman stays with a man she does not love only because she fears he will commit suicide if she leaves.

Change can also be a major stressor. Divorce, illness in the family, unemployment, and moving to a new city are just a few examples of changes that create social, psychological, financial, and physical demands to which people must adapt and adjust. . . .

MEASURING STRESSORS

Attention to change was the keystone in a pioneering effort to find a standard way of measuring the stress in a person's life. Working from the assumption that *all* change, positive or negative, is stressful, Thomas Holmes and Richard Rahe developed in 1967 the Social Readjustment Rating Scale (SRRS). They asked a large number of people to rate a list of change-related stressors in terms of *life change units* (LCUs), the amount of change and demand for adjustment the stressor introduces into a person's life. Getting married, the point against which raters were told to compare all other stressors, was rated as slightly more stressful than losing one's job. Table 13.1 shows the forty-three items on the SRRS and their LCU ratings.

You can use the SRRS to measure the stressors in your own life by adding the LCUs associated with each item you have experienced within the past year. If your score strikes you as being high, don't be surprised. College students routinely face numerous stressors having to do with everything from course work to social life.

TABLE 13-1	**The Social Readjustment Rating Scale (SRRS)**

Each event in the SRRS has a life change unit (LCU) value associated with it. People with higher total LCUs may experience more stress-related problems, but stress mediators, such as social support and coping skills, also shape the effect of stressors.

Rank	Event	LCU Value
1	Death of spouse	100
2	Divorce	73
3	Marital separation	65
4	Jail term	63
5	Death of close family member	63
6	Personal injury or illness	53
7	Marriage	50
8	Fired at work	47
9	Marital reconciliation	45
10	Retirement	45
11	Change in health of family member	44
12	Pregnancy	40
13	Sex difficulties	39
14	Gain of new family member	39
15	Business readjustment	39
16	Change in financial state	38
17	Death of close friend	37
18	Change to different line of work	36
19	Change in number of arguments with spouse	35
20	Mortgage over $10,000	31
21	Foreclosure of mortgage or loan	30
22	Change in responsibilities at work	29
23	Son or daughter leaving home	29
24	Trouble with in-laws	29
25	Outstanding personal achievement	28
26	Wife begins or stops work	26
27	Begin or end school	26
28	Change in living conditions	25
29	Revision of personal habits	24
30	Trouble with boss	23
31	Change in work hours or conditions	20
32	Change in residence	20
33	Change in schools	20
34	Change in recreation	19
35	Change in church activities	19
36	Change in social activities	18
37	Mortgage or loan less than $10,000	17
38	Change in sleeping habits	16

(continued on next page)

TABLE 13-1	**The Social Readjustment Rating Scale (SRRS)**	
39	Change in number of family get-togethers	15
40	Change in eating habits	15
41	Vacation	13
42	Christmas	12
43	Minor violations of the law	11

from *Psychology*

REACTING TO AND DISCUSSING IDEAS

■   1. If this material were to be tested on an essay exam in a psychology class, what would you predict the question to be?

2. Why do different people react to stress differently?

3. Stress is usually thought of as caused by unpleasant events. Do you agree with the authors that pleasant events also can cause stress?

WRITING ABOUT THE READING

■   Compute your SRRS score using the table included in the reading. Then analyze your stressors. Write an essay explaining your major sources of stress.

WRITING ABOUT YOUR IDEAS

■   1. Think of a particularly stressful event or situation. Write a paragraph describing the event or situation.

2. College students face numerous stressors. Write an essay agreeing or disagreeing with this statement.

Example 365

EXAGEMPLE

■

| TODDLER TERRORISM |

Gerri Hirshey

Baby crime. You've seen it. You've probably been a victim. [1]
Baby crime is on the rise, all but unchecked by the current crop
of enthusiastic new parents. It's hard to blame the Infant Offender.
Yet when he strikes, his power is awesome. Take Teddy, a.k.a. Ninja
Tot, a wee terrorist in OshKosh B'Gosh and perpetrator[1] of a grisly
summer's day crime spree. It took place a few years ago at a baby
shower, the first in a monsoon of showers and birthings now blessing
my 30-and-counting friends. NT was with us because his parents had
declared themselves morally opposed to "adult occasions." A half
hour into the proceedings, it was clear that his mother—a witty,
savvy career woman, and the only experienced parent among us—
had turned into a simp, rendered stupid with mother love. "Oooh,
Teddy," she chirped, as NT upended a glass of wine. He howled for
the fuzzy bunnies and *Goodnight Moons* intended for the unborn.
He screeched, he whined, he climbed us and he slimed us. Mother
beamed. We bore it until he did the unspeakable and hijacked one
woman's purse, tore open the makeup case, and held a dozen women
at bay with an unsheathed mascara wand. He cackled, lurched toward a pale yellow armchair. Down came the mascara wand. The
purse owner dove and caught him by the wrist. She retrieved her
makeup and hissed to Mother:

"Don't you ever tell him NO?" [2]

At the time, I chalked Ninja Tot and his goony mom up as an ab- [3]
erration,[2] but the intervening years have yielded a growing tribe of
fine young savages. Wild things. Spoiled things, loved beyond measure and indulged to alarming excess. The resultant baby tyranny has
a swelling legion of silent victims, in public spaces and in private
homes. Baby tyranny's not cute. And it sure ain't pretty.

I have seen a two-year-old order his father out of an easy chair— [4]
successfully. I have had a three-year-old hand back a bagel I spread
with cream cheese and snort, "I want *Montrachet*."[3] At her parents'

1. person who commits a crime
2. abnormal situation
3. goat cheese

request, I have held dinner for six adults two and a half hours while a toddler was being "settled down" for the night. Oh, it wasn't that she was staying in a strange bed. They went through this *every* night. Had eaten cold suppers with the 11 o'clock news for the past three years. Yes, their wise 65-year-old pediatrician had counseled, "Let her cry," but that's so . . . '50s. So barbaric.

Standing over a withered chicken, I waved a wooden spoon and howled at the other hungry adults: "Who is this kid, the MESSIAH?"   5

Maybe. Boomer offspring are doubtless the most *awaited* children in the history of our species. Having babies at ages unprecedented in biological annals, we dare to dote in ways unimagined by millennia of loving parents. News magazines, TV features, even comic strips have chronicled the mania for boutique parenting—the teach-them-logarithms-in-the-womb school, the upscale kiddie health clubs. What the media hasn't addressed is the behavioral fallout of this delayed parenthood.   6

Maybe we've had too much time to think about it. After at least a decade of saying no to conception, new parents seem unable to use the N word on their offspring.   7

"It's so . . . negative," one new dad explains.   8

So are No Parking/Smoking/Dumping/Spitting signs. Negative, but necessary. If "No!" were such a traumatic concept, babes in arms wouldn't take to it so merrily themselves. *No* has always been   9

Example **367**

one of baby's first and favorite locutions, but never has it seemed so exclusively the property of the under-six set.

"I'm just too *tired* to fight it out," one 37-year-old new mom told me. 10

Understandable. Two-career or single-parent family life can make the most together folks lose their grip. But it just won't do to drop the ball in this ancient skirmish and let Junior run amok with it. Raising sweet, well-behaved children in the '90s is no day at the beach, but it is possible. I know a brace of swell tykes. They say please and thank you, they share, they get cranky, but THEY GET OVER IT. All of them have learned that use of the N word is a two-way street. 11

Admittedly, the archetype of the Infant Offender has been an amusing cultural constant, from Dickens' Infant Phenomenon in *Nicholas Nickleby* up through the Little Rascals and Dennis the Menace. Baby crime has been boffo at the box office. *She's Having a Baby. Baby Boom. Three Dorks and a Baby.* And the baby-as-wise-ass-savant flick, *Look Who's Talking*, soon to be a sitcom. On-screen, baby crime is cute as a bug. But in real life, the docket sheet grows. 12

Which brings us to a compendium of common Baby Crimes. Honk if you've been there. 13

Restaurant hell: Here they come, knapsack full o'baby, heads full of Attitude: We are the world, we are the PARENTS. Let Junior eat rice cake. And if he wants to, let him lob it into the next booth. Do not fetter the wee one, but let him roam the aisles like a free-range pullet, drooling on pant legs and grabbing tablecloths. Titter as he makes a beeline for the couple currently spending $8 an hour to leave their own little criminals with a sitter. 14

Recently, I dined with a fractious infant and his parents at a Chinese restaurant that discreetly reserves a back room for the little ones. The walls are stippled with the greasy skidmarks of airborne egg rolls. I asked the maitre d' about his savvy segregation and he said that such measures had only been necessary for the last half-decade—that of the boomer ninjas. He said the waiters had a Chinese name for the room and volunteered a translation: "Cage for baby pork." 15

Baby grandstanding: When I was growing up in *Leave It to Beaver*-Land, there was a crime more heinous than all: Showing Off for company. It was unspeakable. 16

These days, some children are *encouraged* to do this, like the young Sun King (not his real name). In a roomful of visitors, the Sun King has license to play earsplitting drums, records, videos. Try and 17 eat dinner and he starts the floor show—he's a LITTLE TEAPOT. Put down that fork, he's Tubby the Tuba now. HEY, YOU'RE NOT WATCHING . . . HEY. Mom and Dad giggle and beam. There is no uninterrupted conversation involving anything but THE CHILD—unless the Sun King is in bed, unconscious.

Such an imbalance of power is avoidable even in New York   18
City's cramped apartments. Kids can and should join the party—they just needn't run it.

My Sony/myself: Baby narcissism[4] is not new or unnatural to our   19
civilization. Examination of self in bathtub/mirror/wading pool is a longstanding learning tool. Not so for the super-long-playing game of See the Baby on the Family Sony. The impact of such intense coverage was apparent when I asked a three-year-old possessed of a state-of-the-art video library—Muppets, Disney, Raffi in concert—which was his favorite. He walked me to the cabinet bulging with cassettes bearing titles like "Nathan in Bathtub," "Nathan's First Haircut." Already, he'd starred in more miniseries than Ricardo Montalban.

I can't deny for a minute the joy of replaying baby's first upright   20
boogie, her first raspberry Frozfruit. But EDIT, for godsakes, and give some thought to airplay. Junior shouldn't watch himself more than Heidi or Big Bird.

Baby wars: Baby-to-baby crime is also ancient and natural, but   21
the latest methods for dealing with sandbox scuffles are not. There are few things more terrifying than a face-off of righteous and aggrieved begetters with conflicting parenting styles. It goes like this:

Young Dante is whacking petite Amber with the business end of   22
his Ghostbusters Proton Pack. Dante's mom is laissez-faire. Amber's is a commited interventionist; thus she yells at Dante's mom by speaking oh-so-adult-like to him, a clever bit of displaced aggression.

"DAN-TAYYY. I don't think our Amber is rilly enjoying what   23
you are doing, which is rilly unacceptable, don't you think, DAN-TAYYY. . . ."

Dante's mom: "Amber, you can tell Dante yourself just EX-   24
ACTLY HOW YOU FEEL, can't you, honey? Mommy's taught you how to express your feelings, HASN'T SHE?"

Whoa. Mommy's about to express *her* feelings. Neutral adults   25
yap feverishly to change the subject, fast. Do we miss Davey Johnson? Can the Simpsons really put a half Nielsen on Cosby this sea-

4. self-love

Example **369**

son? Never mind, it's the end of civility. Soon, the air is rent with the *zizzzz, zizzzz* of snowsuits being zipped in anger.

You've probably noticed that all these baby crimes are really born of the sins of adults. Men and women who love too much. Of course, there is no malice at the heart of baby crime, only love. And a hefty dollop of guilt, given the maddening strains of '90s family life. But baby love, untempered, does breed baby tyranny. [26]

Learning to say no doesn't have to be painful. Just for fun, why not consider it part of the nostalgia boom in progress—the nutty zeitgeist[5] that's brought back Donna Reed re-runs and nouvelle diners serving meatloaf and Tang. Why not try this one: "GO TO YOUR ROOM, YOUNG MAN." Call it retro discipline. The crazy kitsch of caring. Ward Cleaver was a stuffed shirt, but he was never baby-whipped. [27]

Nostalgia for those straitlaced times has reached the newest generation in some wacky ways. I've heard more than one liberated mom rue the current under-six craze for Barbie, who, at 31, is selling better than ever. Why has this busty relic made such a huge comeback? It's not ALL marketing. [28]

Little girls wanna have fun but they do crave some *structure*. Listen to a five-year-old's Barbie play and it has more special provisions that a SALT treaty: "No Kens on shopping trips," Leg warmers only with pants." As my seven-year-old friend Nina, a.k.a. Bananahead, once admonished me when I attempted to freewheel, "Me and my friend Victoria have lots of *rules*. We just have to." [29]

Play by them or perish. Anarchy isn't an altogether comfy state, even for the wee ninja. After all, Barbie has been saying no to Ken for 31 years now. She knows that you need the N word to keep the *dynamic*. [30]

What I'm pleading for here is a bilateral balance of power, at the very least. Nobody can tell any other body how to raise their kids. But as a hitherto silent victim of many baby crimes, I will undertake to counsel others similarly oppressed. The next time you see a baby crime in progress, say it loud, be firm and be proud: [31]

"NO." [32]

And if you must: [33]

"Pretty please? With Gummi Bears on top? [34]

---

5. trend

New York Woman, September 1990

REACTING TO AND DISCUSSING IDEAS

■   1. Discuss the author's use of humor in the essay. What parts were particularly effective?

2. Did the examples of baby crime "ring true"? That is, have you seen or experienced them yourself?

3. Why do parents allow "toddler terrorism"?

4. What should you do (or have you done) if you are the victim of "a baby crime"?

WRITING ABOUT THE READING

■   Although the essay is intended to be humorous, a serious message exists behind the humor. Write a paragraph explaining the author's serious message about childrearing.

WRITING ABOUT YOUR IDEAS

■   1. Write a paragraph describing a "baby crime" that you have observed. Try to invent your own "crime," if possible, and give your "criminal" a descriptive fictitious name, too.

2. Write an expository essay explaining your philsosophy of child rearing.

CLASSIFICATION

■

| TYPES OF CONSUMER |
| BUYING BEHAVIOR |

William M. Pride and O. C. Ferrell

Consumers usually want to create and maintain a collection of products that satisfy their needs and wants in both the present and future. To achieve this objective, consumers make many purchasing decisions. For example, people must make several decisions daily regarding food, clothing, shelter, medical care, education, recreation, or transportation. As they make these decisions, they engage in different decision-making behaviors. The amount of effort, both mental and physical, that buyers expend in decision making varies considerably from situation to situation. Consumer decisions can thus be classified into one of three broad categories: routine response behavior, limited decision making, and extensive decision making.[1]

A consumer practices **routine response behavior** when buying frequently purchased, low-cost items that need very little search and decision effort. When buying such items, a consumer may prefer a particular brand, but he or she is familiar with several brands in the product class and views more than one as being acceptable. The products that are bought through routine response behavior are purchased almost automatically. Most buyers, for example, do not spend much time or mental effort selecting a soft drink or a snack food. If the nearest soft-drink machine does not offer Sprite, they will quite likely choose a 7-Up or Slice instead.

Buyers engage in **limited decision making** when they buy products occasionally and when they need to obtain information about an unfamiliar brand in a familiar product category. This type of decision making requires a moderate amount of time for information gathering and deliberation. For example, if Procter & Gamble introduces an improved Tide laundry detergent, buyers will seek additional information about the new product, perhaps by asking a friend who has used the product or watching a commercial, before they make a trial purchase.

1. John A. Howard and Jagdish N. Sheth, *The Theory of Buyer Behavior* (New York: Wiley, 1969), pp. 27–28.

The most complex decision-making behavior, **extensive decision making,** comes into play when a purchase involves unfamiliar, expensive, or infrequently bought products—for instance, cars, homes, or an education in a college or university. The buyer uses many criteria to evaluate alternative brands or choices and spends much time seeking information and deciding on the purchase.   4

By contrast, **impulse buying** involves no conscious planning but rather a powerful, persistent urge to buy something immediately. For some individuals, impulse buying may be the dominant buying behavior. Impulse buying, however, often provokes emotional conflicts. For example, a man may want to have the new golf bag he just saw right away and so purchases it on the spot, but he also feels guilty because he knows his budget is limited that month.   5

The purchase of a particular product does not always elicit the same type of decision-making behavior. In some instances, we engage in extensive decision making the first time we buy a certain kind of product but find that limited decision making suffices when we buy the product again. If a routinely purchased, formerly satisfying brand no longer pleases us, we may use limited or extensive decision processes to switch to a new brand. For example, if we notice that the gasoline brand we normally buy is making our automobile's engine knock, we may seek out a higher octane brand through limited or extensive decision making.   6

from *Marketing*

REACTING TO AND DISCUSSING IDEAS

■   1. For each category of buying decisions, give some examples of purchases you have made that fit within that category.

2. Do you agree with the writer's classification of types of buying decisions? Are there other types? Would you classify your decisions differently?

3. Which type of buying decision do you make most frequently?

4. If this material were to be tested on an essay exam in a business course, what would you predict the question to be?

5. What type of decision making did you use in selecting the college you now attend?

WRITING ABOUT THE READING

■ Write a classification paragraph describing the types of consumer buying behavior. Include an example of each, chosen from your own experience as a consumer.

WRITING ABOUT YOUR IDEAS

■ 1. Write a classification paragraph in which you describe the types of products or services that require extensive decision making.

2. Write an essay explaining why you are or are not an impulse shopper.

COMPARISON
AND
CONTRAST

■
THE PACE OF LIFE

Robert V. Levine

When I was teaching in Brazil some years ago, I noticed that   1
students there were more casual than those in the United
States about arriving late for class. I was puzzled by their tardiness,
since their classroom work revealed them to be serious students who
were intent on learning the subject. I soon found, however, that they
were likely to be late not only in arriving for class but also in leaving
it afterward. Whatever the reason for the students' lateness, they
were not trying to minimize their time in the classroom.

In my classes in the United States I do not need to wear a watch   2
to know when the session is over. My students gather their books at
two minutes before the hour and show signs of severe anxiety if I do
not dismiss them on time. At the end of a class in Brazil, on the
other hand, some students would slowly drift out, others would stay
for a while to ask questions, and some would stay and chat for a
very long time. Having just spent two hours lecturing on statistics in
broken Portuguese, I could not attribute their lingering to my superb
teaching style. Apparently, staying late was just as routine as arriving
late. As I observed my students over the course of a year, I came to
realize that this casual approach to punctuality was a sign of some
fundamental differences between Anglo-American and Brazilian attitudes toward the pace of life.

My experience in Brazil inspired an ongoing research program   3
whose aim is to devise ways of measuring the tempo of a culture and
to assess peoples' attitudes toward time. Every traveler has observed
that the pace of life varies in different parts of the world, and even
from place to place within a single country, but it is not obvious
how to quantify these differences. We could question individuals
about their concern with time and about the course of their days, but
this method yields subjective descriptions that do not allow for systematic comparisons between groups. Without a suitable basis for
comparison, it becomes difficult to gauge the meaning of "fast" or
"slow."

In the past few years my colleagues and I have attempted to develop reliable, standardized measures of the pace of life. Our measurement techniques are based on simple observations that require no equipment more elaborate than a stopwatch. Much of the field work has been done by students in the course of their travels on summer vacation or during breaks between semesters. . . . 4

In general, our results confirmed the widespread impression that the Northeastern United States is fastpaced, whereas the West Coast is a little more relaxed. . . . Boston, Buffalo and New York are the fastest overall; a big surprise was that New York does not lead the list. (Manhattan residents might be excused a couple of steps, however, in order to watch the local events; during an interval of an hour and a half, our observer on one New York street corner reported an improvised concert, an attempted purse-snatching and a capsized mugger.) 5

The slowest pace is on the West Coast, and the slowest city overall is Los Angeles. The residents of that city scored 24th out of 36 in walking speed, next to last in speech rate and far behind everyone else in the speed of the bank tellers. The Los Angelenos' only concession to the clock was to wear one: the city was 13th highest in the proportion of the population wearing a watch. 6

PACE AND CONSEQUENCES

These temporal measures serve not only to inform us of differences between peoples, but they may also be used to examine relations between the pace of life and other traits of a population. One trait that has long been suspected of being associated with the pace of life is psychological and physical health. Of particular note is the reported association between a fast-paced life and a high incidence of heart disease. . . . 7

The precise mechanism linking time-urgent behavior to heart disease is not known. Nevertheless, some recent statistics from the Department of Health and Human Services hint at one possibility: the incidence of cigarette smoking follows the same regional pattern as that of ischemic heart disease and the pace of life. That is, the rates for cigarette smoking and ischemic heart disease are highest where the pace of life is fastest: the Northeastern United States. The Northeast is followed by the Midwest, the South and then the West on all three variables. 8

Cigarette smoking has been identified as the single most important preventable cause of heart disease. It is also well documented 9 that cigarette smoking is often related to psychological stress. These correlations suggest, but do not confirm, the possibility that a causal relation exists between these variables. One possibility is that stressful, time-pressured environments lead to unhealthy behaviors such as cigarette smoking and poor eating habits, which in turn increase the risk of heart disease. Our model of the fast-paced "type-A city" may provide a basis for examining this hypothesis. . . .

Although we have come to view the choice between rushing and leisurely activity as a trade-off between accomplishment and peace of mind, we should note that time pressure is not always stressful; it may also be challenging and energizing. The optimal pressure seems to depend on the characteristics of the task and the personality of the individual. Similarly, what we have characterized as a type-A environment will affect different people in different ways. What may be most important is fitting people to their environment. Although a type-A setting may be stressful to a type-B individual, a type-A person may experience more distress in a type-B environment. Given that heart disease remains the single largest cause of death in the United States, the search for a healthy person-environment fit takes on great importance.

American Scientist, September/October 1990

REACTING TO AND DISCUSSING IDEAS

■ 1. Discuss differences in the pace of life that you have observed.

2. Why do you think different geographical areas have different paces of life?

3. Are the author's findings on differences in pace of life in various cities and areas consistent with what you've imagined or with what you know about those areas?

4. Discuss the method the author used to reach his conclusions.

WRITING ABOUT THE READING

■ Write a paragraph describing how the author organized the comparison and contrast sections of the essay.

WRITING ABOUT YOUR IDEAS

■   1. Write a paragraph explaining how you react to time pressures.

2. Write an essay explaining how you would measure the pace of life in your community and to what areas you would compare it.

3. Write a comparison and contrast essay explaining similarities and/or differences between your community and another you've lived in or visited.

CAUSE AND EFFECT

WIVES OFTEN TAKE A BEATING
WHEN THE TEAM LOSES

Mike Capuzzo

After Penn State lost its home opener to Texas in September, a grim-faced Joe Paterno, at 63 a paragon of wholesome American sportsmanship, ended his post-game news conference with a forced smile. 1

"I'm going to go home," he said, "and beat my wife." 2

Coach Joe was joking. 3

Charles Barkley was just joking, too, after the Philadelphia 76ers almost lost to the New Jersey Nets in November. "This is a game that if you lose," said the 253-pound 76ers star, "you go home and beat your wife and kids." 4

It's just an expression, locker room talk, part of sports culture. 5

Part of the scene at Madison Square Garden, where for years New York Rangers hockey fans heckled a particular opponent: "Beat your wife! Beat your wife!" 6

And at Boston Garden, where Celtics fans hung a banner at the dawn of the Larry Bird era, declaring that they liked to beat rival teams almost as much as they like to "beat our wives." 7

And at Veterans Stadium, where Philadelphia Eagles fans have voiced many variations on the theme over the years: "If the Eagles lose this one, I'm gonna beat my wife" or "I told my wife she better stay at her mother's tonight." 8

The fans are just kidding, right? 9

"No," said Roberta Hacker, director of Women in Transition, a Philadelphia battered women's group. "Some of them mean it." 10

Rallying to protest Barkley's widely reported comment, battered women's advocates say they are alarmed by a correlation they're starting to see between the aggressions unleashed by sports viewing—especially of pro football and basketball—and violence against women. 11

Although perceptions of this link are so new that few studies have been done, "I think it's incredibly significant, the tie between 12 sports and battering," said Anne Menard, director of the Connecticut Coalition Against Domestic Violence.

Professional sports viewing is a primary setting for domestic violence, Ms. Hacker said. "Often whether a woman gets beat or not depends on whether her husband's team wins or loses." 13

Ms. Hacker says she has noticed that the style of battering is influenced by the sport. "The women say they are tackled, like in football, or her arms are twisted, and he sits on top of her punching her repeatedly in the face, like a hockey fight." 14

Ms. Menard and other experts on domestic violence don't claim that playing or watching sports causes battering, but that sports viewing—with its frequent setting of family, betting and beer—provides one more trigger. 15

"It's an interesting question for a sociologist," said Irene Basil of the Women's Program at Lutheran Settlement House in Philadelphia. "Is it that watching that kind of violence triggers aggression or creates an illusion that it's OK to behave in that fashion? I don't know. But certainly the kind of aggressions that are displayed in the sports arena can be translated into domestic life and brought home, and clearly they are." 16

Consider: 17

• Of the approximately 300 men who annually seek counseling at the Family Services Agency in Philadelphia to stop battering their wives, about 25 percent of the cases involve sports-related violence, said Paul Bukovic, director of Project Rap. 18

"I've been in the business 14 years now," adds Ms. Basil, "and so many times on a Monday morning women will call the hot line and say, 'Yesterday he was watching a football game; his brother was there; they were drinking beer; they had a $50 bet on the game and my husband lost. He was really (angry) and he started to hit one of the kids. I told him to stop, and he beat me.' 19

"Or, 'He was watching the football game, and the kids were making too much noise playing in the living room, or they wanted to play Nintendo and he got violent.' . . . 20

"Or if the wife isn't behaving properly, if she runs out of potato chips, his buddies are there, and he goes after her." 21

• Super Bowl Sunday is the most violent day of the year for women, when the caseload at battered women's shelters soars, according to separate studies in the late 1980s by women's groups in Marin County, Calif., Denver and Los Angeles. 22

Sue Ostroff, director of the National Clearinghouse for the Defense of Battered Women, keeps a file on sports figures arrested on 23 suspicion of battering—more than 20 have made police blotters and headlines in the past two years. Among them:

Former Buffalo Bills star O. J. Simpson was placed on two years' probation last year after pleading no contest to charges that he beat his wife during a New Year's Day argument. Los Angeles Dodgers slugger Darryl Strawberry was arrested after allegations that he threatened his wife with a gun in January; although he was not charged, he underwent treatment for alcohol abuse. Boston Red Sox pitcher Wes Gardner was arrested on charges he assaulted his wife in a Baltimore hotel room in August 1989, but she dropped the charges when he agreed to attend domestic violence counseling. 24

"I think we have a bizarre heroism attached to professional and college athletes," Ms. Basil said, "and we give them essentially the right to be unaccountable, and that feeling travels down to the fans." 25

"The pro sports leagues make a huge deal about drugs," said Sue Schecter, author of "Women and Male Violence." "But battering is also criminal activity. . . . What are the policies of leagues and teams when sports stars keep beating their wives? What happens to them when they talk about it? What public stand do we take against this?" 26

A woman who works as a medical technician and lives near Cherry Hill, N.J., felt furious and betrayed when she heard Charles Barkley's "joke." 27

"I thought: 'How dare you! How dare you be so insensitive!' " 28

She was battered by her ex-husband, who was 6-feet-4, repeatedly after 76ers games in the late '70s. She is still in counseling over it. 29

"He'd say: 'You're not sorry they lost. You're not sharing my interests!' Once he pulled a gun on me after a Sixers loss." 30

She shudders when she sees football coaches scream at her young son to "have that killer instinct, to destroy and control and dominate. . . . I think we just need to look at what we're saying to our male children when we encourage them to get into sports." 31

The *Buffalo News*, December 10, 1990

REACTING TO AND DISCUSSING IDEAS

■ 1. Do you agree or disagree with the author's position that wife abuse is related to professional sports?

2. Do you think sports are violent? If so, does the article suggest that violence occuring during sporting events causes some violence against women?

3. In the last paragraph of the reading, the author quotes a woman who shudders at what coaches say to her young son. Why does the woman feel this way? In other words, what is she afraid of?

4. The author states that 20 professional sports figures (players) have been involved in wife abuse over the past two years. Should the fact that players themselves are abusing their wives be used as evidence that viewing sports causes wife abuse?

5. Wife abuse, according to the reading, occurs after men view professional sporting events. The assumption made here is that since the occurrences follow each other in time, one causes the other. Could there be other explanations for abuse other than the sports game itself? Does the article suggest other causes?

WRITING ABOUT THE READING

■ Write a paragraph explaining (giving reasons) whether you feel the author has provided sufficient evidence for you to agree with her claim that sports viewing is a cause of wife abuse. If you feel there is insufficient evidence, explain what types of evidence are needed or why the evidence provided is insufficient.

WRITING ABOUT YOUR IDEAS

■ 1. The reading attempts to establish a relationship between professional sports and wife abuse. Write a paragraph that answers the question: What other effects do professional sports have on people's lives or on your life?

2. The reading discusses one possible cause of wife abuse, although sociologists agree there are many other causes. Write a paragraph that discusses other reasons why you think men abuse their wives.

3. The reading presents a negative view of professional sports by discussing the problems it creates. Write an essay explaining (giving reasons) why professional sports are beneficial.

EXPOSITORY

■
FATHERS, SONS, AND SPORTS

Scott Russell Sanders

The lore of sports may be all that some fathers have to pass   1
down to their sons in place of lore about hunting animals, planting seeds, killing enemies, or placating[1] the gods. Instead of telling
him how to shoot a buffalo, the father whispers in the son's ear how
to shoot a lay-up. Instead of consulting the stars or the entrails of
birds, father and son consult the smudged newspapers to see how
their chosen spirits are faring. They fiddle with the dials of radios,
hoping to catch the oracular murmur of a distant game. The father
recounts heroic deeds, not from the field of battle but from the field
of play. The seasons about which he speaks lead not to harvests but
to championships. No longer intimate with the wilderness, no longer
familiar even with the tamed land of farms, we create artificial land-
scapes bounded by lines of paint or lime. Within those boundaries,
as within the frame of a chessboard or painting, life achieves a memorable, seductive clarity. The lore[2] of sports is a step down from that
of nature, perhaps even a tragic step, but it is lore nonetheless, with
its own demigods and demons, magic and myths.

The sporting legends I carry from my father are private rather   2
than public. I am haunted by scenes that no journalist recorded, no
camera filmed. Father is playing a solo round of golf, for example,
early one morning in April. The fairways glisten with dew. Crows
rasp and fluster in the pines that border the course. Father lofts a
shot toward a par-three hole, and the white ball arcs over the pond,
over the sand trap, over the shaggy apron of grass, onto the green,
where it bounces, settles down, then rolls toward the flag, rolls unerr-
ingly, inevitably, until it falls with a scarcely audible click into the
hole. The only eyes within sight besides his own are the crows'. For
once, the ball has obeyed him perfectly, harmonizing wind and gravity and the revolution of the spheres; one shot has gone where all are
meant to go, and there is nobody else to watch. He stands on the
tee, gazing at the distant hole, knowing what he has done and that
he will never do it again.

1. quiet the anger of
2. traditional knowledge

Here is another story I live by: The man who will become my fa- 3
ther is twenty-two, a catcher for a bush-league baseball team in Ten-
nessee. He will never make it to the majors, but on weekends he
earns a few dollars for squatting behind the plate and nailing runners
foolish enough to try stealing second base. From all those bus rides,
all those red-dirt diamonds, the event he will describe for his son
with deepest emotion is an exhibition game. Father's team of whites,
most of them fresh from two-mule farms, is playing a touring black
team, a rare event for that day and place. To make it even rarer, and
the sides fairer, the managers agree to mix the teams. And so my father, son of a Mississippi cotton farmer, bruised with racial notions
that will take a lifetime to heal, crouches behind the plate and for
nine innings catches fastballs and curves; change-ups and screwballs
from a whirling muttering wizard of the Negro Baseball League, one
Leroy Robert Paige, known to the world as Satchel. Afterward,
Satchel Paige tells the farm boy, "You catch a good game," and the
farm boy answers, "You've got the stuff, mister." And for the rest of
my father's life, this man's pitching serves as a measure of mastery.

I am conscious of my father's example whenever I teach a game 4
to my son. Demonstrating a stroke in tennis or golf, I amplify my gestures, like a ham actor playing to the balcony. My pleasure in the
part is increased by the knowledge that others, and especially my father, have played it before me. What I know about hitting a curve or
shooting a hook shot or throwing a left jab, I know less by words
than by feel. When I take Jesse's hand and curl his fingers over the
baseball's red stitches, explaining how to make it deviously spin, I
feel my father's hands slip over mine like gloves. Move like so, like
so. I feel the same ghostly guidance when I hammer nails or fix a fau-
cet or pluck a banjo. Working on the house or garden or car, I find
myself wearing more than my father's hands, find myself clad entirely in his skin.

As Jesse nears thirteen, his estimate of my knowledge and my 5
powers declines rapidly. If I were a potter, say, or a carpenter, my
skill would outreach his for decades to come. But where speed and
stamina are the essence, a father in his forties will be overtaken by a
son in his teens. Training for soccer, Jesse carries a stopwatch as he
jogs around the park. I am not training for anything, only knocking
rust from joints and beguiling my heart, but I run along with him,
puffing to keep up. I know that his times will keep going down,
while I will never run faster than I do now. This is as it should be,
for his turn has come. Slow as I am, and doomed to be slower, I relish his company.

I mean to live the present year before rushing off to any future   6
ones. I mean to keep playing games with my son, so long as flesh
will permit, as my father played games with me well past his own
physical prime. Now that sports have begun to give me lessons in
mortality, I realize they have also been giving me, all the while, lessons in immortality. These games, these contests, these grunting conversations of body to body, father to son, are not substitutes for
some other way of being alive. They are the sweet and sweaty thing
itself.

from *Secrets of the Universe*

REACTING TO AND DISCUSSING IDEAS

■   1. What is the author's main point? Explain the connection among
fathers, sons, and sports.
    2. Have you observed or experienced the relationship the author
describes among fathers, sons, and sports?
    3. If sports link fathers and sons, what activities or experiences
link mothers and daughters?
    4. Have you experienced knowing how to do something by feel
rather than by words?

WRITING ABOUT THE READING

■   Write a paragraph explaining what you think Sanders meant when he
said, "Now that sports have begun to give me lessons in mortality, I
realize they have also been giving me, all the while, lessons in
immortality."

WRITING ABOUT YOUR IDEAS

■   1. Write a paragraph describing an experience in which you have
felt as if you were wearing your father's or mother's hands.
    2. Write an essay describing an experience you shared with your
mother or father that provided a bond or permanent link between you.

EXPOSITORY

■
HOMELESS

Anna Quindlen

Her name was Ann, and we met in the Port Authority Bus Termi-   1
nal several Januarys ago. I was doing a story on homeless people. She said I was wasting my time talking to her; she was just passing through, although she'd been passing through for more than two
weeks. To prove to me that this was true, she rummaged through a
tote bag and a manila envelope and finally unfolded a sheet of typing
paper and brought out her photographs.

They were not pictures of family, or friends, or even a dog or   2
cat, its eyes brown-red in the flashbulb's light. They were pictures of
a house. It was like a thousand houses in a hundred towns, not sub-
urb, not city, but somewhere in between, with aluminum siding and
a chain-link fence, a narrow driveway running up to a one-car garage and a patch of backyard. The house was yellow. I looked on the
back for a date or a name, but neither was there. There was no need
for discussion. I knew what she was trying to tell me, for it was
something I had often felt. She was not adrift, alone, anonymous, although her bags and her raincoat with the grime shadowing its
creases had made me believe she was. She had a house, or at least
once upon a time had had one. Inside were curtains, a couch, a
stove, potholders. You are where you live. She was somebody.

I've never been very good at looking at the big picture, taking the   3
global view, and I've always been a person with an overactive sense
of place, the legacy of an Irish grandfather. So it is natural that the
thing that seems most wrong with the world to me right now is that
there are so many people with no homes. I'm not simply talking
about shelter from the elements, or three square meals a day or a
mailing address to which the welfare people can send the check—although I know that all these are important for survival. I'm talking
about a home, about precisely those kinds of feelings that have
wound up in cross-stitch and French knots on samplers over the
years.

Home is where the heart is. There's no place like it. I love my   4
home with a ferocity totally out of proportion to its appearance or location. I love dumb things about: the hot-water heater, the plastic

rack you drain dishes in, the roof over my head, which occasionally leaks. And yet it is precisely those dumb things that make it what it is—a place of certainty, stability, predictability, privacy, for me and for my family. It is where I live. What more can you say about a place than that? That is everything.

Yet it is something that we have been edging away from gradu-   5
ally during my lifetime and the lifetimes of my parents and grandparents. There was a time when where you lived often was where you worked and where you grew the food you ate and even where you were buried. When that era passed, where you lived at least was where your parents had lived and where you would live with your children when you became enfeebled. Then, suddenly where you lived was where you lived for three years, until you could move on to something else and something else again.

And so we have come to something else again, to children who   6
do not understand what it means to go to their rooms because they have never had a room, to men and women whose fantasy is a wall they can paint a color of their own choosing, to old people reduced to sitting on molded plastic chairs, their skin blue-white in the lights of a bus station, who pull pictures of houses out of their bags. Homes have stopped being homes. Now they are real estate.

People find it curious that those without homes would rather   7
sleep sitting up on benches or huddled in doorways than go to shelters. Certainly some prefer to do so because they are emotionally ill, because they have been locked in before and they are damned if they will be locked in again. Others are afraid of the violence and trouble they may find there. But some seem to want something that is not available in shelters, and they will not compromise, not for a cot, or oatmeal, or a shower with special soap that kills the bugs. "One room," a woman with a baby who was sleeping on her sister's floor, once told me, "painted blue." That was the crux of it; not size or location, but pride of ownership. Painted blue.

This is a difficult problem, and some wise and compassionate peo-   8
ple are working hard at it. But in the main I think we work around it, just as we walk around it when it is lying on the sidewalk or sitting in the bus terminal—the problem, that is. It has been customary to take people's pain and lessen our own participation in it by turning it into an issue, not a collection of human beings. We turn an adjective into a noun: the poor, not poor people; the homeless, not Ann or the man who lives in the box or the woman who sleeps on the subway grate.

Sometimes I think we would be better off if we forgot about the broad strokes and concentrated on the details. Here is a woman without a bureau. There is a man with no mirror, no wall to hang it on. They are not the homeless. They are people who have no homes. No drawer that holds the spoons. No window to look out upon the world. My God. That is everything. 9

from *Living Out Loud*

REACTING TO AND DISCUSSING IDEAS

■ 1. Does the meaning of home change when you move or is it a constant regardless of its location?

2. The author says we call poor people "the poor" as a means of distancing ourselves from their problems. What other problems have become impersonal issues rather than human beings in need of help?

3. What effects might frequent changes of homes produce?

4. Does Quindlen use descriptive details effectively? Underline several examples.

5. Analyze Quindlen's introductory paragraphs. What hook does she use?

6. What is the purpose of the essay?

WRITING ABOUT THE READING

■ 1. Write a paragraph explaining what home means to you. (Hints: security? comfort? base of operations?)

2. Write an essay explaining the statement "You are where you live."

WRITING ABOUT YOUR IDEAS

■ 1. Write an essay in which you offer and defend an action(s) that should be taken to assist homeless people or to prevent the problem.

2. Write a paragraph identifying and describing another social issue or problem that we "walk around" rather than address.

EXPOSITORY

OZETTE: A MAKAH VILLAGE IN 1491

Maria Parker-Pascua

When I was a girl, I often wondered about my ancestors. I lived then, as now, in the village of Neah Bay on the Olympic Peninsula in the northwest corner of Washington State, where the sea and the forest surround us. I knew that in times past the most powerful men in our Makah tribe were whalers. My great-grandfather Wilson Parker was a whaler, as were his father and grandfather. Stories of the rituals that had empowered them filled my childhood. 1

But growing up in the 1960s, I never saw a harpoon, or a lance, or a buoy made of the skin of a hair seal. The last whale hunt took place in 1913, and the hunters' gear was packed away. 2

And then, as if in answer to a prayer, the past returned. In early January 1970, Pacific storm surf began to expose wondrous things at the abandoned village of Ozette, 30 miles away. Those artifacts had been buried when a mudslide covered a cluster of cedar longhouses about A.D. 1500. A decade-long excavation by Washington State University archaeologists, in cooperation with the tribe, recovered har- 3

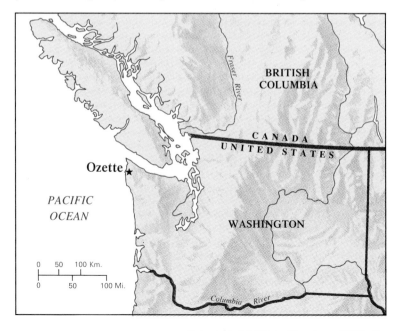

poons, lances, implements of daily life, and precious ceremonial objects that I could see and sometimes even touch.

Then later, as an employee of our local Makah Cultural and Research Center, I was asked to collect the songs and stories of our elders so that these and the Makah language itself might not vanish. The words poured over me, giving further substance to the past. 4

We first knew ourselves as Qwidicca-atx (Kwee-DITCH-chuh-aht): "people who live on the cape by the rocks and seagulls." The name Makah, "generous with food," is what we were called by neighboring Klallam Indians, one of whom served as translator when we signed a treaty with the U.S. government in 1855. Federal agents found Makah easier to pronounce, and we now use it when speaking English. But we know who we are. 5

British and Spanish explorers made brief contact with us at the end of the 18th century, but we had little dealings with whites until the mid-1800s. Soon after, two-thirds of the tribe was dead from smallpox, measles, and other diseases brought by the traders we had welcomed. Our bodies lined the beaches, and they buried us in trenches. 6

Today about a thousand Makah live at Neah Bay. The people began to leave Ozette and other villages in 1896 when the U.S. government said our children must attend school in Neah Bay, where federal agents had set up office. 7

But in 1491 Ozette, with its long beach on the Pacific, was the most important Makah sea-mammal-hunting village. No site was better for launching the spring hunts. It had then been occupied—and defended against competing tribes—"since the first Daylight." Let us go back to that time, before the sails of "people who live in houses on the water" came over the horizon. 8

I want the sea. That is my country.
—OZETTE CHIEF TSE-, KAW-WOOTL AT THE 1855 TREATY NEGOTIATIONS

Like the hearts of the Makah, the doors of Ozette's longhouses in 1491 face the sea. The sounds are the wash of the surf, the sea gulls' chorus, a sea lion's bark, the sighing of hemlock, spruce, and cedar, and the voices of a thousand people. 9

The women are wearing soft skirts woven from shredded cedar bark. When they laugh, they toss back long tooth shell earrings. The men too have pierced ears and noses but save their jewelry for special occasions. There is no word for shoes, nor is there any footgear. Both men and women bear tattoos on legs and forearms. 10

Behind Ozette's longhouses towers the rain forest, lush with ferns 11 and mosses, that gives the wood from which nearly all Makah possessions are made. Especially in winter, "the time for wind," the ocean and forest seem to talk to each other—the song of the waves answered by the song of the boughs.

The woods and the water are mystically linked. Because a cedar   12
can become a canoe, Makah can harvest the sea. Because an elk's antlers can be carved to hold a harpoon blade of sharpened mussel shell, gray whales can be captured. Because the cry of the wolf so echoes the cry of the killer whale, the Makah understand that this is the same animal, using one body for land and another for sea.

Even in the sky the Makah see the ocean; they call the Big Dip   13
per the Skate. Every type of wave and current, every rock and navigational landmark, has been given a name. There are a dozen words to describe the varying tides. In deep fog the hunters navigate by reading the sea's currents, swells, and sounds, as if tracking a living creature.

The whale always gives our people something. The whale always helps someone who needs him.
—JOHN THOMAS (NITINAHT), 1913–1990

Of the sea's creatures, the gray whale is the most important. Its   14
gifts are meat and oil for food, sinew for binding harpoons, giant bones that can be shaped into war clubs. But it has given the tribe something greater—it has shaped Makah society.

The first Makah men bold enough to pursue the gray whale be   15
came chiefs and created a hereditary rulership. Only a chief or his sons can harpoon a whale, and these sons must marry the daughters of whalers. Their marriage must be a deep spiritual kinship marked by preparatory fasting and prayer, or the whales will not come.

At Ozette there are as many as six chiefs, ranked according to   16
wealth. Beneath them and allied to them are the commoner families. It is the quality of his allies' skills—sealing, fishing, canoe carving, basketry, a woman's closely guarded recipe for berry cakes—that helps bring a chief wealth.

The chief in turn offers protection, and commoners gain status ac   17
cording to his status. Whales caught by the chief and seals and fish caught by commoners are shared among a chief's allied families. Highly skilled commoners, if they feel unappreciated, can shift their allegiance to another chief. But however great their talents, commoners can never rise into the elite. In Makah society, you are who you are the day you are born.

I have come to see how your house is. Is it prepared for large crowds?
—SONG OF THE WHALE, SUNG BY WILSON PARKER, 1855–1926

Everyone has something to do, and it is a disgrace for anybody to sleep late. Older relatives, as much as parents, teach Ozette's children the Makah ways. Boys are given miniature canoes and harpoons; girls receive tiny baskets and cradles—not just as toys but for training too. 18

A boy may start out carving play canoes and paddles. If he shows aptitude, he'll begin carving the one-man fishing canoes, then the sealing canoes. Then, as a man, he will be prepared to shape 36-foot whaling canoes and larger war canoes from a single red cedar log. 19

In summer women and girls walk the beach at low tide gathering clams, mussels, periwinkles, limpets, barnacles, and sea urchins. They also walk the woods and bogs picking salmonberries, huckleberries, salal berries, and cranberries. 20

During the winter women weave baskets, clothing, canoe mats, pouches for fishing equipment, and diapers—mostly out of the cedar bark they gather with orange-stained hands in late spring. 21

Normally there is more than abundant food, but famine sometimes strikes. One Makah story recalls a hard winter when it was impossible to fish, there was no game to be found, and the food-storage baskets became empty. One man went up on the mountain to pray. Hearing a noise, he looked up: 22

> *There was the Thunderbird, so huge it darkened the sky. He made the thunder sound with the beat of his wings. His eyes were flashing lightning. Then he flew straight down. Just as he was about to hit the water, he swooped back up carrying a whale in his talons. He flew toward the village. He flew close to the beach, and there he dropped the whale. Then he flew away. The man who saw all this said to the people, "We're saved, we're saved."*
> —MAKAH TRIBAL STORY

The Thunderbird is a supernatural being, a giant man who changes into his bird nature to hunt. He has appeared in visions and dreams and has taught people many things. 23

By both the creatures of the physical world and the creatures of the supernatural, the Makah are shown how to take care of what they have been given, how to take care of one another, how to respect the One who has given them these things. 24

> *Women prayed, "Make me better, let me live, let me be healthy." They prayed to the One up in the Sky.*
> —KATIE HUNTER, 1886–1985

The medicines of Ozette are gathered from the forest. A tea of thimbleberry leaves strengthens the blood. The bark of a salmon- 25 berry bush numbs a toothache. Head lice are doused with powdered hemlock mixed with seal oil, and a poultice of chewed hemlock stops bleeding. The sea contributes too. The heads of lingcod, their bodies eaten by sharks and seals, wash up on the beach in the winter. They are boiled into a delicious broth that is soothing for colds.

For illness beyond common remedies, a doctor is called. No one   26
can choose to be a doctor. The Creator of Daylight chooses, male and female alike. This election crosses class boundaries and, like the Wolf Society,[1] balances the life of the village. A doctor may be assisted by members of a secret healing society who have received powerful songs of prayer in visions. The ceremony proceeds for hours.

Of course, in time death comes to all: 27

The people believed that when you die, your spirit leaves your body. Sometimes they believed that some of your people come to meet you. They are waiting there to take you with them. People were not afraid to die. Long before, they used to talk about how they were going to be wrapped in a certain blanket or shawl.
—HELEN PETERSON, MAKAH ELDER

More valuable than a family's material possessions are its songs.   28
Most songs are received in visions or dreams. Their verses are brief, woven in and out of a chanting melody as a box drum keeps beat.

Songs are a privilege and must be cared for, honored, and prop-   29
erly sung and danced. Their origin and history must be learned, repeated, and passed down to each generation.

A song can be sung only by its owners, though others may be   30
asked to learn a song to help perform it. If the owner of a song dies before passing it down at a potlatch,[2] the song dies also, unless permission was given for someone to carry it on.

There are songs of joy, of war, and of love: 31

No matter how hard I try to forget you, you always come back to my mind, and when you hear me singing you may know I am weeping for you.
—RECORDED BY YOUNG DOCTOR, 1851–1934

When a chief hosts a potlatch, families are invited to dance their   32
songs and to display the ceremonial dress and masks they usually keep hidden. Important occasions call for a potlatch—a wedding, a daughter's coming of age, the end of a year of mourning.

But the primary purpose is to validate a Makah chief's ownership   33
of his family songs, his ceremonial names, the crests that decorate his

1. a secret society based on invitation and initiation
2. *Potlatch* means "to give." A potlatch is a ceremonial feast.

robes and possessions. To repay his guests for witnessing and validating his claims, the host will give away virtually everything he owns.

Messengers fan out in canoes to invite families from the other Makah villages and from neighboring villages where other languages are spoken. Several interpreters are needed. 34

How much a chief is able to give away will affect his standing. His guests will be fed the best food, given the finest blankets and the most handsome boxes. The chief knows that his gifts will be reciprocated with interest at future potlatches. 35

The families are called by rank to perform their songs. This is their great gift to the host, to which they add presents for his family and fellow guests. 36

If a family is in mourning and therefore unable to sing and dance, it will ask another family if it can "ride in their canoe." In this way the mourning family can be spiritually present in the other family's song. Then, finally, the host's family performs its songs. 37

The Makah elders alive in 1991 remember potlatches that went for two weeks without a song being repeated. Today a potlatch lasts but a night. We have no way of knowing how many songs were lost in the epidemics, how many were lost through the persistent efforts of missionaries and federal Indian agents to suppress our language and culture. 38

I am a Christian; I am not sorry the missionaries came. But I wish they had known how to let their news change peoples' lives from the inside, without imposing their culture over our ways. 39

We have lost so much. But when we needed it most, the 15th century came back to us. We have the artifacts of our ancestors. And, more important, we still have songs that are carried in the hearts of the people. 40

National Geographic, October 1991

REACTING TO AND DISCUSSING IDEAS

■ 1. Why does the author include quotes by her ancestors? What effect do they achieve?

2. What is the function(s) of Makah songs?

3. Describe the Makah culture's relationship with nature.

4. Discuss what it would be like to live in a society in which "you are who you are the day you are born," without any opportunity for change or advancement.

5. Discuss the ways in which the Makah culture is similar to and different from your culture.

WRITING ABOUT THE READING

■   Write a paragraph describing the author's attitude toward or the effects of U.S. government intervenion in the Makah culture.

WRITING ABOUT YOUR IDEAS

■   1. Pascua values the artifacts of her ancestors. Write a paragraph describing an object you value or explaining why you value it.

2. The Makah pass songs from generation to generation. Families also have ceremonial names, crests, robes, and possessions. Write an essay describing a tradition or object that is passed from generation to generation in your family.

EXPOSITORY

JUDY BACA'S ART FOR PEACE

Anne Estrada

Now known as a muralist,[1] activist, and spokesperson for the Hispanic community, as well as a professor at the University of California in Irvine, Judy Baca could not speak English when she entered public school in East Los Angeles in the '50s. But she could paint, and so began the power of her art to communicate what sometimes can't be said in words.

Baca recalls her role in the beginning of the Chicano Mural Movement when she was searching for a way to express her own experience as a Hispanic American artist. Greatly influenced by the Mexican muralists, Baca discovered a means of community empowerment.[2]

Her first mural projects began when she was working for the city of Los Angeles teaching art classes. During her lunch breaks, she spent time in the parks getting to know some of the kids who hung out there. As she observed the graffiti, the tattoos, and the decorated cars, she recognized a visual language used by these teenagers to express who they are and how they feel about their lives. Painting walls became a vehicle of communication as she brought them together to negotiate treaties in order to make it possible for the kids to cross rival gang territory, and reach the mural site safely. This work led to the project she is best known for, the "Great Wall of Los Angeles," which she began in 1976.

Located in the San Fernando Valley, the "Great Wall" is a half mile long and depicts scenes from the history of California. The muralists were young people from various ethnic communities in Los Angeles, some of whom were recruited when the court offered the choice of mural painting over reform school. The project proved to be an extraordinary educational experience for all those involved. In 1976 Baca founded her own non-profit organization, Social and Public Art Resource Center (SPARC), as a means of supporting community art projects.

Where has Judy Baca found the will to overcome obstacles and

1. artist who paints large pictures, often on walls
2. gaining power and self-control

accomplish her goals? She believes that her greatest source of strength comes from her early years, when she learned the meaning of human pride and dignity. She was raised by her grandmother because her single mother had to work long hours to support her family. "I was surrounded by extraordinary women," she remembers. Through her grandmother, Baca learned how to approach life in a philosophical manner. Baca remembers an experience she had with her grandmother. At the store, her grandmother realized that she had been given incorrect change and asked Judy to tell the cashier that he had made a mistake. Apparently, he had been trying to cheat them because they couldn't speak English well, and he became angry and threw the coins down. Although Baca couldn't understand why the man acted this way, she noticed a tattoo across his wrist that was given to prisoners in Nazi concentration camps. Her grandmother said, "You shouldn't be angry with him because people have hurt him. Every time you see that tattoo, you must remember what happened to those people." These early lessons nurtured the genuine compassion that Baca now calls upon when she works with those who might otherwise be written off as hopeless. She is able to work with them in a way that is not condescending, but empowering. She also has the insight needed to find compassion for the oppressor, as well as the oppressed. "When people are treated badly, they treat other people badly," she says.

Baca has now moved from interracial to international relations with her current project, "World Wall: A Vision of a Future Without Fear." The "World Wall," when completed, will consist of seven portable panels with artwork on both sides, each measuring 10 by 30

6

feet, assembled into an octagon 80 to 100 feet in diameter. The images depict the material and spiritual transformations that must occur before world peace can be achieved. Baca traveled to Finland and the Soviet Union, where artists in those countries created their own murals to add to the series. Among the themes that emerge are the elimination of racism and sexism, the creation of positive interdependence between countries, and the need for people of all backgrounds to work together for world harmony. The "World Wall" now consists of six works, and is expected to grow as Baca travels over the next few years. The completed panels were on view in Los Angeles at Plaza de la Raza on April 6 and 7 and will travel to the Smithsonian Institute in Washington, D.C. in July.

Judy Baca claims that adversity[3] breeds a certain kind of strength. Nourished by this strength, her artistic vision has reached out to inspire those around her.   7

3. misfortune, trouble

Hispanic, May 1991

REACTING TO AND DISCUSSING IDEAS

1. What effects on peace do you think Baca's murals will have or have had?

2. Do you agree that teenagers have a visual language?

3. Discuss the themes depicted on the world murals. Are these necessary for world peace? What other themes would you add?

4. Baca's murals seem directed toward specific goals, such as world peace. Do or should all pieces of art have goals?

WRITING ABOUT THE READING

Write a paragraph explaining why you agree or disagree with the Los Angeles court when it offered teenagers the choice of mural painting over reform school.

WRITING ABOUT YOUR IDEAS

1. Baca's greatest source of strength was her grandmother. Write a paragraph explaining how a person you know has been a source of strength.

2. Judy Baca claims that adversity breeds a certain kind of strength. Write an essay explaining why this statement is true or not true in your life.

PERSUASIVE

■

THE CAPTIVE PANTHER

Michael W. Fox

Some experiences can be so painfully intense that they are soon forgotten. Amnesia protects the psyche.[1] Then again, in anticipation of vicarious suffering, we may simply tune out certain experiences altogether. Other times, perhaps for good reason, the psyche is not so protected. It is as if the soul—the observing, feeling self—is actually burned by certain experiences. The imprint is branded so indelibly that we can go back and review every detail so completely that the experience is actually relived. I had just such an experience with a panther in a zoo many years ago.

The first time that I ever really *saw* an animal in a cage was in a small zoo at the Jardin des Plantes, a natural history museum in Paris. I entered a large, ornate Victorian rotunda that housed a few animals in small wrought-iron cages. I now recall seeing only one animal there. At first it appeared not to see me even though I stood beside its cage for a long time.

Time did end that day as a part of me separated and was incorporated as part of the creature in the cage.

In retrospect, I was probably mesmerized by what at first appeared to be a shiny black serpent in constant motion. It's liquid form brushed across the front of the cage. After insinuating itself around some artificial rocks and a body-polished tree stump toward the back of the enclosure, it ricocheted off a ceramic-tiled wall to again caress the front of the cage. Form and motion were so unified and the pattern of movement within the confines of the cage so repetitive that at first encounter the creature was barely recognizable as a panther, or black leopard. Her movements were executed with such precision—even to the point of always touching the tree trunk with her left hip and the same ceramic tile with her right front paw—that she was more like a perpetual motion machine than a sentient being.

And then I saw the blood—a streak of blood down her left thigh, draining from an open sore that would never heal until the cat was freed from the hypnotic lines she traced and was so inexorably bound to execute. Each scraping turn around the tree trunk kept the

1. mind

sore open, like a broken heart bleeding for the loss of all that was wild and free.

I wondered if she felt any pain. Her yellow-green eyes were like cold glass, with neither fire nor luster. Perhaps this was a slow ritual form of suicide, gradually grinding and rubbing and shredding the body to pieces to free the wild spirit within. I saw the glint of white bone—or was it tendon—through the cat's thigh muscles winking as she turned and paced before me. And there was no pad left on the right front paw that struck the tile wall polished ocher with the patina of dried blood and serum. Yet still the crippled creature continued her measured minuet.[2]

The panther body, denied freedom of expression and fulfillment of purpose, had become a prison for the creature spirit within. Following and anticipating every movement she made, I began to breathe in rhythm with the cat. I felt part of myself entering her cage while the rotunda started to revolve faster and faster around that part of my consciousness that remained in my body outside of the cage. Then when I entered the prison of her body the other visitors strolling around the rotunda became ephemeral[3] shadow-beings, as if they were part of a dream and the only thing that was real was the measured universe of the tortured panther.

Confined in such limited space, how else could this boundless spirit of the jungle respond? Her rhythmic, trancelike actions were more than thwarted attempts to escape. Was her compulsive animation designed simply to help her cope with the emptiness of existing in body without any purpose for the spirit, a kind of living death? . . .

The cage may be the last refuge for many endangered species, but such "protective custody" is a sad reflection indeed of how far we have desecrated[4] nature's creation. Zoos have been as slow to address the psychological needs of the animals they keep as they have to question their own purpose. But times are changing; more and more people have begun to feel and see the world through the eyes of the animals. The cage bars are disappearing as we begin to empathize and come to realize that the fate of the animal kingdom is inextricably linked with the fate of humanity. The black panther in the cage is a mirror reflecting our own condition. And we are not helpless to do something about both.

But when we reach into the cage with our hearts, we may feel

2. dance
3. short-lived
4. treat as if not sacred

very differently about keeping animals in zoos or ever visiting a zoo again. . . .

Do zoos educate the public adequately to political action and compassionate concern for the plight of wildlife and nature? Are they not too tame, sanitized, and beautiful? They are becoming facsimiles of how animals once were in the wild. Some zoo safari parks are run for profit and secondarily for entertainment. And zoos are also an illusion, a false assurance to the public that lions and cheetahs and tigers and elephants are plentiful and lead free and easy lives. Some amusement parks even have safari zoos purely for public entertainment. This is surely an unethical exploitation of wildlife.

Even the best of zoos cannot justify their existence if they do not sufficiently inform and even shock the public into compassionate concern and political action. I know of no zoo that exhibits crippled but otherwise healthy animals that have been maimed by trappers and hunters.

Regarding the claim that the best zoos are helping save species from extinction by breeding them in captivity, it may be best to let them become extinct if there is no place for them in the wild. Life in captivity can never fulfill any species or individual, because the animal *is* its natural environment, and no species lives in isolation from others. Certainly the better zoos have seminatural environments—miniswamps, artificial rivers, climatrons, and mixed-species exhibits. But to what end? For exhibition. They are not conserving nature by creating high-tech facsimiles thereof. And even if such artificial environments enhance the overall welfare and reproductivity of endangered species, where are their offspring to go? To other zoo collections. . . .

I believe that even the best zoos and aquaria in the world are not doing an adequate job of nature conservation. They have taken more species from the wild than they have ever put back, and until this situation is dramatically reversed, zoos cannot make any claim to effective nature conservation. Breeding endangered species in captivity is animal preservation, not conservation, and animals preserved forever in a cage or synthetic habitat are at best unreal.

As for zoos' often high-blown research into exotic animal diseases, nutrition, and reproduction, all of this would be unnecessary if we had just left wildlife alone and respected their rights and protected their habitats. . . .

Are zoos a necessary evil? Wildlife's last refuge? Sometimes I think so. Sometimes I think not. I respect the many people who are dedicated to good zoo management, research, species preservation, and veterinary medicine. But all this dedication may be seriously misplaced if we lose sight of the fact that the problems of zoo animals and the crisis of wildlife's threatened annihilation are primarily manmade.

17 Building better zoos at the expense of efforts to conserve nature is wrong. We should need no zoos and we are misguided if we do not work toward this end, however far into the future it might be. Zoos are not so much a necessary evil as they are a tragic mirror of an evil for which we may yet atone.

18 As it is estimated that at the current rate of habitat destruction, some 500,000 to 2 million plant and animal (including insect) species will be extinct by the year 2000, obviously captive breeding in zoos is not the answer. Habitat protection is the only solution, and all nations and peoples must be prepared to make the necessary adjustments and sacrifices if the health and vitality of the Earth is to be preserved.

19 One of the best exhibits in any zoo that I have ever visited was a large mirror behind bars. The caption read: *Homo sapiens*, a dangerous, predatorial tool and weapon-making primate. Status: endangered by its own doing.

20 There can be no communion with our animal kin when they are held captive, no matter what the justifications may be for their "protective custody." The zoo is a trick mirror that can delude us into believing that we love and respect animals and are helping to preserve them. And like the animal circus, the zoo can have a pernicious influence on children's attitudes toward wild creatures. We cannot recognize or celebrate the sanctity and dignity of nonhuman life under such conditions. There can be no communion: only amusement, curiosity, amazement, and perhaps sympathy. The deprivation of these creatures and the loss of wildness and wilderness are ours also. When we fail collectively to feel these things, and in the process come to accept and patronize the zoo as some cultural norm, we lose something of our own humanity—that intuitive wisdom and a sense of reverence for all life that are the hallmarks of a truly civilized society.

from *Inhumane Society: The American Way of Exploiting Animals*

REACTING TO AND DISCUSSING IDEAS

1. What is Fox's thesis?

2. Analyze the audience for whom the essay is written. Does Fox perceive his audience as agreeing, disagreeing, or neutral?

3. What is the most and least convincing evidence Fox offers?

4. Why did Fox begin the essay with the description of the panther?

5. What is the difference between animal preservation and animal conservation?

6. Do you agree that the zoo is "a trick mirror," which deludes us into believing that we love and respect animals?

WRITING ABOUT THE READING

Write a persuasive essay to your state or local officials either a) urging the closing of a nearby zoo, b) urging a more humane zoo be built, or c) urging expansion of the existing zoo.

WRITING ABOUT YOUR IDEAS

1. Write a paragraph describing an animal you have observed. Reflect your attitude toward the animal through your description.

2. Write a persuasive essay arguing for or against using animals in a circus.

3. Write an essay for or against humans wearing coats made of animal fur.

EXPOSITORY

■
ALTRUISM AND HELPING BEHAVIOR

Douglas A. Bernstein, et al.

On a winter day several years ago, an airliner crashed into the [1] ice-filled Potomac River in Washington, D.C. Many of the survivors were thrown, injured or unconscious, into the water and were in danger of drowning or freezing to death. A bystander named Lenny Skutnik dove into the river and helped several people to shore before exhaustion and the frigid temperatures nearly killed him. Skutnik acted as he did, not for money or any other material benefit, but simply to help other human beings.

Skutnik's actions provide a dramatic example of a common situa- [2] tion: people helping one another by doing everything from picking up dropped packages to donating kidneys. **Helping behavior** is defined as any act that is intended to benefit another person. Closely related to it is **altruism**, an unselfish concern with another's welfare (Batson, 1987). In the following sections we examine some of the reasons for altruism and helping and some of the conditions in which people are most likely to help others.

WHY DO PEOPLE HELP?

The tendency to help others begins early, and it follows a predictable [3] pattern. Around age six, children begin to help others as a form of self-punishment (Kenrick, 1989). They try to "make-up" for a bad deed by doing a good deed. As they grow older, children use helping behavior to gain social approval, and their efforts at helping become more elaborate (Zahn-Waxler et al., 1982). Often they follow examples set by people around them; their helping behaviors are shaped by the norms established in their families and other reference groups. Further, children are praised and given other rewards for helpfulness, but scolded for selfishness. Eventually children come to believe that being helpful is good and that they are good when they are helpful. By the late teens, people often help others even when no one is watching and no one will know that they did so (Cialdini, 1981).

There are two major theories of why people help even when they [4] cannot expect others to reward them for doing so. According to the **negative state relief model,** helping aids in eliminating negative moods and unpleasant feelings (Cialdini et al., 1987). Indeed, there is evidence that people in a bad mood are often most likely to help others (Carlson & Miller, 1987), and people usually report feeling much better after having helped someone (Millar et al., 1988). It appears that people learn to reward themselves after acts of good will by saying to themselves something like "I'm a good person for having done that." According to the negative state relief model, then, people help for essentially selfish reasons: to eliminate their own unpleasant emotional state or to make themselves feel good.

Of course, people do not have to be feeling bad in order to help others, and several studies suggest that truly unselfish forms of altruism also exist (Batson et al., 1989; Schroeder et al., 1988). The second major theory of helping, the **empathy-altruism model**, holds that unselfish helping can occur as a result of empathy with another person (Batson, 1987). Simply seeing another person's suffering or need can create **empathy**, which involves understanding or experiencing that person's emotional state (Eisenberg & Strayer, 1987). People are much more likely to help when they empathize with the other person (Eisenberg & Miller, 1987). Experiments have shown that people will help others even when their own personal distress is prolonged or increased. Thus, it appears that although people sometimes help others in order to reduce their own unpleasant emotional state, empathizing with another person can lead to unselfish helping.

WHEN ARE PEOPLE MOST LIKELY TO HELP?

Deeply rooted and well learned as they are, human altruism and helping behaviors are neither automatic nor invariable. This fact was dramatically demonstrated in New York City in 1964, when a woman named Kitty Genovese was repeatedly attacked and ultimately killed by a man with a knife, in full view and hearing of dozens of her neighbors. The tragic episode took more than thirty minutes to unfold, but no one physically intervened, and no one called the police until it was too late.

Public dismay and disbelief followed. Psychologists thought it unlikely that everyone in the neighborhood was callous and wondered whether something about the situation that night had deterred people from helping. Numerous studies of helping behavior followed; many of them led to important insights about the characteristics of situations that promote or inhibit helping. Among the most important characteristics of the situation are the clarity of the need for help, the attractiveness of the person in need, the familiarity of the situation, and the number of people available to help.

Is the Need Recognized? The clarity of someone's need for help 8
has a major impact on whether others provide help (Clark & Word,
1974). In one study, undergraduate students waiting alone in a campus building observed what appeared to be an accident involving a
window washer. The man screamed as he and his ladder fell to the
ground; then he began to clutch his ankle and groan in pain. All of
the students looked out of the window to see what had happened,
but only 29 percent of them did anything to help. Other students experienced the same situation, with one important difference: the man
said he was hurt and needed help. In this case, more than 80 percent
of the subjects came to his aid (Yakimovich & Saltz, 1971). Apparently, this one additional cue eliminated any ambiguity in the situation and led the vast majority of people to offer their help. In a similar experiment, 100 percent of the observers responded to a direct
request for help (Clark & Word, 1972).

The Attractiveness of the Person in Need People are much more 9
likely to provide help to those they find attractive or likable than to
others. In one study people with a large birthmark were less likely to
receive help than those without such a mark (Piliavin, Piliavin & Rodin, 1975). Similarly, stranded motorists are more likely to receive
help if they are dressed neatly than if their clothes are dirty and their
hair is messy (Graf & Riddell, 1972; Morgan, 1973). Males are also
more likely to help female rather than male motorists with car trouble (West, Whitney & Schnedler, 1975), and they are more likely to
assist physically attractive than unattractive females (West & Brown,
1975).

Familiarity with the Surroundings The probability that people 10
will offer help also increases if they are in a familiar situation. This
relationship was demonstrated in an experiment that set up an apparent emergency in a New York City subway station (where most of
the observers were commuters who had come to the station many
times) and in New York's LaGuardia Airport (where many of the
travelers had never been before). A man with a bandaged leg and
crutches hobbled along until he came upon a person sitting alone.
Then he tripped, fell to the ground, and grasped his knee as if in
pain (Latané & Darley, 1970). More than twice as many people
helped in the subway station than in the airport. Further, habitual
subway users were much more likely to help than those who used
the subway infrequently.

The Presence of Others The tendency to help is strongly influ- 11
enced by the number of other people present. Somewhat surprisingly,
however, the presence of others *inhibits* helping behavior (Miller &

McFarland, 1987). This phenomenon was true in the Genovese case, and it has been demonstrated time and time again in everyday life— when a group of people watches but does nothing to stop a rape or a mugging—as well as in controlled experiments (Latané & Darley, 1968).

One explanation for this inhibiting effect is that each person   12
thinks that someone else will help the victim. The tendency to deny any personal responsbility for responding when others are present is known as **diffusion of responsibility** (Mynatt & Sherman, 1975).

The degree to which the presence of other people will inhibit   13
helping may depend on who those other people are. When they are strangers, perhaps poor communication inhibits helping. People have difficulty speaking to strangers, particularly in an emergency, and without speaking, it is difficult to know what the others intend to do. According to this logic, if people are with friends rather than strangers, they should be less embarrassed, more willing to discuss the problem, and thus more likely to help.

In one experiment designed to test this idea, a female experi-   14
menter led the subject to a room where he or she was to wait either alone, with a friend, with a stranger, or with a stranger who was a confederate of the experimenter (Latané & Rodin, 1969). The experimenter then stepped behind a curtain into an office. For nearly five minutes, she could be heard doing normal chores—opening and closing the drawers of her desk, shuffling papers, and so on. Then she could be heard climbing up on a chair. Soon there was a loud crash, and she screamed, "Oh, my God. . . . My foot, I . . . I can't move it. Oh, my ankle. . . . I can't get this . . . thing off me." Then the subject heard her groan and cry.

Would the subject go behind the curtain to help? Once again,   15
people were most likely to help if they were alone. When one other person was present, subjects were more likely both to communicate with one another and to offer help if they were friends than if they were strangers. When the stranger was the experimenter's confederate (who had been instructed not to help the woman in distress), virtually no subject offered to help. Other studies have confirmed that bystanders' tendency to help increases when they are coworkers, members of the same club, or know each other in some other way (Rutkowski, Gruder & Romer, 1983).

Conclusions   Whether helping and altruism are displayed de-   16
pends on an interaction between the people involved and the situation. Understanding the complexities underlying helping and altruism is of practical as well as theoretical importance. Indeed, the tendency

to interpret emergency situations as emergencies and to take responsibility for doing something about them appear to be strengthened by an understanding of the social psychology of helping. For example, when confronted with a contrived emergency under circumstances unlikely to promote helping, students who had recently learned about diffusion of responsibility offered help nearly twice as often as those who had not received that information (Beaman et al., 1978). There is also a lesson here for the victims of mishaps. Especially if a number of people are present, it is important not only to ask for help but to tell a specific onlooker to take some specific action (e.g., "You, in the yellow shirt, please call an ambulance!").

from *Psychology*

REACTING TO AND DISCUSSING IDEAS

■   1. Identify the method(s) of organization used in this reading.

2. Summarize the two major theories concerning why people help one another. Which seems more plausible to you?

3. How would you feel upon learning that you had been one part of the experiments described in the reading?

4. Why do people take risks to help others?

5. The authors cite numerous situations intended to demonstrate conditions in which people are willing to help others. Can you think of explanations, other than the one given by the author, for the behavior described?

WRITING ABOUT THE READING

■ Write an essay explaining why no one helped Kitty Genovese when she was attacked and killed.

WRITING ABOUT YOUR IDEAS

■   1. The author describes numerous experiments that were done to evaluate conditions under which people help others. Design an experiment that you could conduct to test one or more conditions for helping behavior. Write a paragraph describing your experiment.

2. Write an essay describing a situation in which you helped someone. Analyze your motivation and the conditions at the time.

V

. . . .

Reviewing the Basics

Most of us have an intuitive knowledge of how to communicate in our language. When we talk or write, we put our thoughts into words, and, by and large, we make ourselves understood. But no one has an intuitive knowledge of the specific terms and rules of grammar, the complex system that describes how language is put together. Grammar must be learned, almost as if it is a foreign language.

Why is it important to study grammar, to understand grammatical terms like *verb, participle, gerund,* and concepts like *predication* and *subordination?* There are several good reasons. Knowing grammar will allow you to

- **recognize an error in your writing and correct it.** Your papers will read more smoothly and communicate more effectively when error-free.
- **understand the comments of your teachers and peers.** People who read and critique your writing may point out a "fragment" or a "dangling modifier." You will be able to revise and correct the problems.
- **write with more impact.** Grammatically correct sentences are signs of clear thinking. Your readers will get your message without distraction or confusion.

As you will see in this section "Reviewing the Basics," the different areas of grammatical study are highly interconnected. The sections on parts of speech, sentences, punctuation, and mechanics and spelling fit together into a logical whole. To recognize and correct a run-on sentence, for example, you need to know both sentence structure *and* punctuation. To avoid errors in capitalization, you need to know parts of speech *and* mechanics. In other words, grammar can neither be studied piecemeal, nor can it be studied superficially. If grammar is to do you any good, your knowledge of it must be thorough. As you review the following "Basics," be alert to the interconnections that make language study so interesting.

Grammatical terms and rules demand your serious attention. Mastering them will pay handsome dividends: error-free papers, clear thinking, and effective writing.

A Understanding the Parts of Speech

A.1 Nouns

A.2 Pronouns

A.3 Verbs

A.4 Adjectives

A.5 Adverbs

A.6 Conjunctions

A.7 Prepositions

A.8 Interjections

The eight parts of speech are **nouns, pronouns, verbs, adjectives, adverbs, conjunctions, prepositions,** and **interjections.** Each word in a sentence functions as one of these parts of speech. Being able to identify the parts of speech in sentences allows you to analyze and improve your writing and to understand grammatical principles discussed later in this book.

It is important to keep in mind that *how* a word functions in a sentence determines *what* part of speech it is. Thus, the same word can be a noun, verb, or an adjective, depending on how it is used.

noun
↓
He needed some blue <u>wallpaper</u>.

verb
↓
He will <u>wallpaper</u> the hall.

adjective
↓
He went to a <u>wallpaper</u> store.

A.1 NOUNS

■ A **noun** names a person, place, thing, or idea.

People	*woman, winner, John Smith*
Places	*mall, hill, Indiana*
Things	*lamp, ship, air*
Ideas	*goodness, perfection, harmony*

The form of a noun can change depending on **gender** (male, female, neuter), **number** (singular, plural), and **case** (subjective, possessive).

Noun changing with gender	waiter, waitress
Noun changing with number	book, books
Noun changing with case	cat (subjective), cat's (possessive)

    noun   noun   noun

Our cat will not eat from the other cat's dish.

Nouns are classified as **proper, common, collective, abstract,** and **concrete.**

1. **Proper nouns** name specific people, places, or things and are always capitalized: *John F. Kennedy, East Lansing, IBM Selectric.* Days of the week and months are considered proper nouns and are capitalized.

   proper noun   proper noun   proper noun

In September Allen will attend Loyola University.

2. **Common nouns** name one or more of a general class or type of people, place, thing, or idea and are not capitalized: *presidents, city, typewriter.*

   common noun   common noun   common noun

Next fall the students will enter college.

3. **Collective nouns** name a whole group or collection of people, places, and things: *committee, team, jury.* They are singular in form.

   collective noun   collective noun

The flock of mallards flew over the herd of bison.

4. **Abstract nouns** name ideas, qualities, beliefs, and conditions: *honesty, goodness, poverty.*

                    abstract nouns

Their marriage was based upon love, honor, and trust.

5. **Concrete nouns** name tangible things that can be tasted, seen, touched, smelled, or heard: *sandwich, radio, pen.*

     concrete noun   concrete noun

The frozen pizza was stuck in the freezer.

A.2 PRONOUNS

■ A **pronoun** is a word that substitutes for a noun or refers to a noun. A pronoun is generally used in place of a noun that has already been mentioned, called the **antecedent.** The antecedent is the noun or group of words acting as a noun to which a pronoun refers. A pronoun identifies the antecedent without re-naming it by agreeing with the antecedent in person, number, and gender (see discussion of these terms below.)

> After the campers discovered the cave, they mapped it for the next group, who were arriving next week. [The pronoun *they* refers to its antecedent *campers;* the pronoun *it* refers to its antecedent *cave;* the pronoun *who* refers to its antecedent *group.*]

The eight kinds of pronouns are **personal, possessive, demonstrative, reflexive, intensive, interrogative, relative,** and **indefinite.**

1. **Personal pronoun** take the place of nouns that name people or things. Personal pronouns change form depending on whether they are used in the sentence as subjects, objects, or to show possession. (Pronouns can take three forms known as the **subjective case, possessive case,** and **objective case.** See p. 485.)

	SUBJECTIVE	*POSSESSIVE*	*OBJECTIVE*
Singular			
1st person	I	my, mine	me
2nd person	you	your, yours	you
3rd person	he	his	him
	she	her, hers	her
	it	its	it
Plural			
1st person	we	our, ours	us
2nd person	you	your, yours	you
3rd person	they	their, theirs	them

Which personal pronoun you use depends on the **person, gender,** and **number** of the antecedent, and on the **case** of the pronoun (how the pronoun functions within the specific sentence or clause).

Person is the grammatical term used to distinguished among the speaker (first person), the person or thing spoken to (second person), and the person or thing spoken about (third person).

> Magda, the twins are visiting. I wrote to you about them. [The first person singular pronoun I agrees with the first person singular antecedent, the

pro

speaker of the sentence; the second person singular pronoun you agrees with its second person singular antecedent, Magda; the third person plural pronoun them agrees with its third person plural antecedent, twins.]

Gender is a term that classifies nouns and pronouns into masculine (*congressman, he*), feminine (*congresswoman, she*), and neuter (*rock, it*) categories.

When the reporter asked about the proposed bill, the congresswoman told him that she would support it. [The masculine pronoun him agrees with its masculine antecedent, reporter; the feminine pronoun she agrees with its feminine antecedent, congresswoman; and the neuter pronoun it agrees with its neuter antecedent, bill.]

Number is a term that classifies nouns and pronouns into singular (one) and plural (more than one).

The scarf was beautiful. It was handmade. [The singular pronoun it agrees with the singular antecedent, scarf.]

Homes were lost. They can be rebuilt. [The plural pronoun they agrees with the plural antecedent, homes.]

The authors were looking for a picture of the rare watercress darter. They wanted it for a new book on fish. [The plural pronoun they agrees with its plural antecedent, authors; the singular pronoun it agrees with its singular antecedent, picture.]

Case is the form of the personal pronoun that indicates whether the pronoun is being used as a **subject** (the person, place, thing, or idea that is acting or being described), an **object** (the person, place, thing, or idea that is being affected by the action), or to indicate **possession**. (See p. 437 for more on subjects and see p. 441 for more on objects. See p. 485 for more on case.)

pronoun
as subject
↓
John changed. He learned to cook.

pronoun
as object
↓
John changed. The cooking lessons changed him.

pronoun showing
possession
↓
John changed. His cooking lessons helped bring about the change.

2. **Possessive pronouns** are personal pronouns that show ownership.

	SINGULAR	*PLURAL*
1st person	my, mine	our, ours
2nd person	your, yours	your, yours
3rd person	his	
	her, hers	their, theirs
	its	

Leslie wrote the newspaper about <u>her</u> opinions. The editorial in support of the four-day work week is <u>hers</u>.

3. **Demonstrative pronouns** refer to particular people or objects. The demonstrative pronouns are *this* and *that* (to refer to singular nouns) and *these* and *those* (to refer to plural nouns).

<u>This</u> biography is more thorough than <u>that</u>.

The red shuttle buses stop here. <u>These</u> go to the airport every hour.

4. **Reflexive pronouns** indicate that the subject performs actions to, for, or upon itself. Reflexive pronouns end in *-self* or *-selves*.

	SINGULAR	*PLURAL*
1st person	myself	ourselves
2nd person	yourself	yourselves
3rd person	himself	
	herself	themselves
	itself	

We painted <u>ourselves</u> into a corner.

5. An **intensive pronoun** emphasizes the word that comes before it in a sentence. Like reflexive pronouns, intensive pronouns end in *-self* or *-selves*.

The filmmaker <u>herself</u> could not explain the ending.

Note: A reflexive or intensive pronoun should not be used as a subject of a sentence. An antecedent for the reflexive pronoun must appear within the same sentence.

INCORRECT: <u>Myself</u> create colorful sculpture.

CORRECT: I <u>myself</u> create colorful sculpture.

6. **Interrogative pronouns** are used to ask questions: *who, whom, whoever, whomever, what, which, whose.* How the pronoun is used in the sentence or clause determines the form of the interrogative pronouns,

pro

who and *whom.* When the pronoun functions as a subject of a sentence or clause, use *who.* When the pronoun functions as an object of a sentence or clause, use *whom.* (See pp. 437 and 441 for more on subjects and objects.)

What happened?

What street runs parallel to Crosby Street?

Who wrote Ragtime? [Who is the subject of the sentence.]

Whom should I notify? [Whom is the object of the sentence.]

7. **Relative pronouns** relate groups of words to nouns or other pronouns, and often introduce adjective clauses (see p. 452) or noun clauses (see p. 452). The relative pronouns are *who, whom, whoever, whomever,* and *whose* (referring to people) and *that, what, whatever,* and *which* (referring to things).

In 1836 Charles Dickens met John Forster, who became his friend and biographer.

The smoke alarm, which often goes off accidentally, is no longer taken seriously.

We read some articles that were written by former astronauts.

Like the personal pronouns *I, he, she, we,* and *they,* the relative pronouns *who* and *whoever* change form depending on how they function in a sentence or clause. *Who* and *whoever* are used for subjects; *whom* and *whomever* are used for objects. (See p. 483.)

subject
of clause
↓
Anna is certain [who is invited].

object of
clause
↓
Anna stated [whom she invited].

8. **Indefinite pronouns** are pronouns without specific antecedents. Indefinite pronouns refer to people, places, or things in general. When used as the subject of a sentence, indefinite pronouns, some of which are singular and some plural, must agree in number with the verb. (See p. 478.)

Someone has been rearranging my papers.

Many knew the woman, but few could say they knew her well.

Here are some frequently used indefinite pronouns:

SINGULAR		PLURAL
another	everything	all
any	neither	both
anybody	nobody	few
anyone	none	many
anything	no one	more
each	nothing	most
either	one	much
enough	somebody	plenty
everybody	someone	several
everyone	something	some

Exercise 1   In each of the following sentences (a) circle each noun and (b) underline each pronoun.

EXAMPLE: (Mark) parked his (car) in the (lot) that is reserved for (commuters) like himself.

1. Toronto is an exciting city to visit because it has so many distinctive neighborhoods.

2. Hannah finds roller coasters thrilling to ride, but they frighten me.

3. Whoever dropped these papers should pick them up before someone steps on them.

4. Although no one expected her to do so, the boss delivered the flowers herself.

5. Hilary's mother passed the cookies and urged us to have another.

6. Ray's garden has many flowers, but those pictured in the catalogue are larger and more colorful.

7. Some of the record albums that we donated to the United Way auction were from Pete's Elvis collection.

8. I could not think of an answer to what the child asked.

9. After the couple had read the menu, they handed it to the waiter and asked him to bring them the appetizer that came with a pickled mango relish.

10. Many gorillas are difficult to raise in captivity, but Seattle's Woodland Park Zoo has succeeded by carefully recreating the animal's natural habitat.

A.3 VERBS

■ Verbs express action or state of being. A grammatically complete sentence has at least one verb in it.

There are three kinds of verbs: **action verbs, linking verbs,** and **helping verbs** (also known as **auxiliary verbs**).

1. **Action verbs** express physical and mental activities.

Mr. Royce <u>dashed</u> for the bus.

The incinerator <u>burns</u> garbage at high temperatures.

I <u>think</u> that seat is taken.

Action verbs are either **transitive** or **intransitive.** The action of a **transitive verb** is directed toward someone or something, called the **direct object** of the verb. Direct objects receive the action of the verb. Transitive verbs require direct objects to complete the meaning of the sentence.

subject (noun)	transitive verb	object (noun)
Sam	<u>made</u>	clocks.

An **intransitive verb** does not need a direct object (a receiver of the action of the verb) to complete the meaning of the sentence.

       intransitive
        verb
         ↓
The traffic <u>stopped.</u>

2. A **linking verb** expresses a state of being or a condition. A linking verb connects a noun or pronoun to words that describe that noun or pronoun. Common linking verbs are forms of the verb *to be (is, are, was, were, be, being, been), become, feel, grow, look, remain, seem, smell, sound, stay,* and *taste.*

Their child <u>grew</u> tall.

The boat <u>smells</u> fishy.

Mr. Davenport <u>is</u> our accountant.

3. A **helping verb** (**auxiliary**) helps another verb, called the **main verb,** to convey when the action occurred (through verb tense) and to form questions. One or more helping verbs and the main verb together form a **verb phrase.** Here are some common helping verbs:

am, are, be, been, is, was, were

have, has, had

do, does, did

shall, should

may, might

can, could

will, would

must

helping   main
verb   verb

The cat <u>will</u> <u>nap</u> on that window sill for hours.

Forms of the Verb

A verb changes form according to how it is used. It changes to agree in **person** and **number** with its subject and to express **mood** (whether the action is thought of as fact, command, wish, or speculation) and **tense** (when the action occurred). (See p. 475 for a discussion of subject-verb agreement.)

Mood

A verb changes according to how the writer regards the action, process, occurrence, condition, or assertion being expressed. The English language has three moods: **indicative, imperative,** and **subjunctive.**

A writer uses the **indicative mood** for ordinary statements of fact and questions:

This flashlight <u>is</u> broken.

<u>Have</u> you <u>checked</u> the batteries?

My eyes <u>are</u> getting accustomed to the dark.

The **imperative mood** is used to plead and make suggestions and commands.

<u>Stop</u> shouting!

<u>Stay</u> here with me.

<u>Come</u> to New York for a visit.

The **subjunctive mood** is used for wishes, recommendations, speculations, hypotheses, certain expressions of command, and ideas contrary to fact. *Were* and *be* are the most common subjunctive forms.

> I recommend that the house be sold.
>
> If I were him, I would take the high road.
>
> Presumably, the Army would know if UFOs were landing.

Principal Parts of Verbs

Verb tense relates the time of an action to a point of reference, usually the time of writing (or speaking). To express tense, verbs in English have four basic forms or **principal parts:** the **infinitive,** the **present participle,** the **past tense,** and the **past participle.** (See p. 468 for more on verb tenses.)

The **infinitive** is the main form of the verb as it appears in the dictionary (*jump, predict, create*). When infinitives are used in sentences, the word *to* usually, but not always appears before the verb.

> infinitive
> ↓
> Michael Jordan knows how to jump.

> infinitive
> ↓
> The coach made us sprint. [Here, the to of the infinitive is implied before the word sprint, not stated.]

The **present participle** combines the infinitive and the ending *-ing,* and uses a form of the verb *be* as a helping verb. (When the infinitive ends in *-e,* as in *type* or *shove,* the final *-e* is dropped before the *-ing* is added.)

> form of verb   present
> be   participle
> ↓   ↓
> The meteorologist is predicting a sunny day.

The **past tense** and **past participle** are generally formed by adding *-ed* or *-d* to the infinitive. The past participle is used with a form of the verb *have* as a helping verb. In the lists below, the helping verbs in parentheses indicate that, in a sentence, a form of the verb *be* accompanies the present participle, and a form of the verb *have* accompanies the past participle.

Principal Parts of Some Regular Verbs

INFINITIVE	PRESENT PARTICIPLE	PAST	PAST PARTICIPLE
plant	(is) planting	planted	(has) planted
wash	(is) washing	washed	(has) washed
type	(is) typing	typed	(has) typed

past tense

PAST TENSE: The man and woman walked to the flower show.

form of
verb have   past participle

PAST PARTICIPLE: The major has offered to speak to our class.

Verbs are classified as either **regular verbs** or **irregular verbs** depending on how their past tense and past participles are formed. Regular verbs add *-d* or *-ed* to the infinitive. Irregular verbs follow no set pattern for their formation. Instead, they are formed in a variety of ways. Consult the list below and your dictionary for the principal parts of irregular verbs.

Principal Parts of Some Irregular Verbs

INFINITIVE	PRESENT PARTICIPLE	PAST	PAST PARTICIPLE
be	(is) being	was	(has) been
become	(is) becoming	became	(has) become
begin	(is) beginning	began	(has) begun
bite	(is) biting	bit	(has) bitten
blow	(is) blowing	blew	(has) blown
burst	(is) bursting	burst	(has) burst
catch	(is) catching	caught	(has) caught
choose	(is) choosing	chose	(has) chosen
come	(is) coming	came	(has) come
dive	(is) diving	dived, dove	(has) dived
do	(is) doing	did	(has) done

vb

INFINITIVE	PRESENT PARTICIPLE	PAST	PAST PARTICIPLE
draw	(is) drawing	drew	(has) drawn
drive	(is) driving	drove	(has) driven
eat	(is) eating	ate	(has) eaten
fall	(is) falling	fell	(has) fallen
find	(is) finding	found	(has) found
fling	(is) flinging	flung	(has) flung
fly	(is) flying	flew	(has) flown
get	(is) getting	got	(has) gotten
give	(is) giving	gave	(has) given
go	(is) going	went	(has) gone
grow	(is) growing	grew	(has) grown
have	(is) having	had	(has) had
know	(is) knowing	knew	(has) known
lay	(is) laying	laid	(has) laid
lead	(is) leading	led	(has) led
leave	(is) leaving	left	(has) left
lie	(is) lying	lay	(has) lain
lose	(is) losing	lost	(has) lost
ride	(is) riding	rode	(has) ridden
ring	(is) ringing	rang	(has) rung
rise	(is) rising	rose	(has) risen
say	(is) saying	said	(has) said
set	(is) setting	set	(has) set
sit	(is) sitting	sat	(has) sat
speak	(is) speaking	spoke	(has) spoken
swear	(is) swearing	swore	(has) sworn
swim	(is) swimming	swam	(has) swum
tear	(is) tearing	tore	(has) torn
tell	(is) telling	told	(has) told
throw	(is) throwing	threw	(has) thrown
wear	(is) wearing	wore	(has) worn
write	(is) writing	wrote	(has) written

Simple, Perfect, and Progressive Verb Tenses

Tenses are the forms of a verb that express time. They convey whether an action, process, or occurrence takes place in the present, past, or future. There are three **simple tenses: present** (*I arrive*), **past** (*I arrived*), and **future** (*I will arrive*); and three **perfect tenses—present perfect**, (*I have arrived*), **past perfect** (*I had arrived*), and **future perfect** (*I will have arrived*). Perfect tenses indicate completed action.

In addition to the simple and perfect tenses, there are three **progressive tenses** (or **aspects**), formed by adding the helping verb *be* to the present participle: **present progressive** (*I am arriving*), the **past progressive** (*I was arriving*), and the **future progressive** (*I will be arriving*). The progressive tenses indicate continuing action. (See p. 468 for more on verb tenses.)

The chart below shows the first person singular forms of two verbs in each tense.

	PRESENT	*PAST*	*FUTURE*
		Simple	
REGULAR	I talk	I talked	I shall (will) talk
IRREGULAR	I go	I went	I shall (will) go
		Perfect	
REGULAR	I have talked	I had talked	I shall (will) have talked
IRREGULAR	I have gone	I had gone	I shall (will) have gone
		Progressive	
REGULAR	I am talking	I was talking	I shall (will) be talking
IRREGULAR	I am going	I was going	I shall (will) be going

Voice

Transitive verbs (verbs that take objects) may be in either the **active voice** or the **passive voice**. (See pp. 472–474.) When a verb is used in an **active voice** sentence, the subject does the action described by the verb. In other words, the subject names the actor. Active voice sentences emphasize the person or thing performing the action and tend to be lively and straightforward.

Active voice: Dr. Hillel <u>delivered</u> the report on global warming.

When a verb is used in a **passive voice** sentence, the subject is not the person or thing that acts. Instead, the subject names the object or receiver of the action. In the passive voice, the appropriate form of the helping verb *be* exists, plus the past participle of the main verb. Passive voice sentences emphasize the person, place, or thing being acted upon. Repeated use of passive voice sentences can be dull and wordy.

Passive voice: The report on global warming <u>was delivered</u> by Dr. Hillel.

Exercise 2   Revise the following sentences changing each verb from the present tense to the tense indicated on the line following the sentence.

> EXAMPLE: I <u>know</u> the right answer.
>
> PAST TENSE: I <u>knew</u> the right answer.

vb

1. The desk clerk answers the phone.

    future: _____

2. The giraffe walks across the field.

    present perfect: _____

3. I run ten miles.

    past perfect: _____

4. The movie stars Goldie Hawn.

    future: _____

5. The artist paints ocean scenes.

    past perfect: _____

6. My cousin mows the lawn each week.

    future perfect: _____

7. The subway train stops six times.

    past perfect: _____

8. The Ontario Science Center changes its exhibits frequently.

    past: _____

9. The president answers questions from the press.

    future perfect: _____

10. The professor lays his notes on the table.

    past: _____

Verbals and Finite Verbs

A **verbal** (also known as a **non-finite verb**) is a word derived from a verb, but used as a noun, adjective, or adverb. For example, *swimming* is a word used as a noun or adjective that is derived from the verb *to swim*. The adjectives *frozen* and *forbidden* are derived from the verbs *to freeze* and *to forbid*. The three kinds of verbals are **gerunds, participles,** and **infinitives.** (See p. 467 for descriptions of each specific type of verbals.)

A verbal cannot function by itself as the verb of a sentence. It cannot make an assertion about an action or process without the addition of a helping verb. You can recognize a verbal because it does not change form when a third person subject changes from singular to plural.

third person
singular subject   verbal

The **boy** is sledding.

third person
plural subject   verbal

The **boys** are sledding.

Similarly, a verbal does not change form to show past, present, and future tenses.

verbal

The boy sledding (was/is/will be) cold.

In contrast, a **finite verb** functions by itself as the verb in a sentence. A finite verb can make an assertion about actions or processes without the addition of a helping verb. Finite verbs do change form when the third person subject changes from singular to plural.

third person
singular subject   finite verb

The **boy** sleds.

third person
plural subject   finite verb

The **boys** sled.

Unlike a verbal, a finite verb does change form to show past, present, and future tenses.

finite
verb

He (sledded/sleds/will sled.)

The distinction between finite verbs and verbals is important when you are studying how to correct and avoid **sentence fragments** (See p. 457).

A.4 ADJECTIVES

■ **Adjectives** modify nouns and pronouns. They describe, identify, qualify, or limit the meaning of nouns and pronouns, thus making the meaning of those nouns and pronouns more specific. Adjectives answer the questions *which? what kind? how many? whose?* about the words they modify.

adj

WHICH? The twisted, torn umbrella was of no use to its owner.

WHAT KIND? The spotted owl has caused controversy in the Northwest.

HOW MANY? There were eighty seats in the club, and one hundred people in line outside to see the show.

WHOSE? The class visited William Faulkner's house in Oxford, Mississippi.

In form, adjectives can be **positive** (implying no comparison), **comparative** (comparing two items), or **superlative** (comparing three or more items). (See p. 488 for more on the forms of adjectives.)

positive adjective
↓
The scissors are sharp.

comparative adjective
↓
Your scissors are sharper than mine.

superlative adjective
↓
These are the sharpest scissors I have ever used.

There are two general categories of adjectives. **Descriptive adjectives** name a quality of the person, place, thing, or idea being described (*mysterious* man, *green* pond, *healthy* complexion). **Limiting adjectives** narrow the scope of the person, place, or thing being described (*my* hat, *this* tool, *second* try).

Descriptive Adjectives

1. **Regular** (or **attributive**) **adjectives** appear next to (usually before) the word they modify. Several adjectives can modify the same word.

adjectives   adjectives
↓   ↘   ↙   ↘
The enthusiastic new barber gave three lopsided haircuts.

adjective   adjectives
↓   ↙   ↓ ↘
The antique dealer sold an immense, ornate, porcelain vase.

2. **Predicate adjectives** follow linking verbs and modify the subject of the sentence or clause. (A clause is a group of related words containing both a subject and a predicate. See p. 436.)

subject　　　predicate adjective

The meeting was long. [The adjective long describes the subject.]

Limiting Adjectives

3. The one **definite article**, *the*, and the two **indefinite articles**, *a* and *an*, are classified as adjectives. Singular nouns that name something countable (**a** carrot, **a** train) take an indefinite article. *A* and *an* are used when it is *not* important to specify a particular, individualized noun or when the object named is *not* known to the reader ("A radish adds color to **a** salad"). The definite article, *the*, is used when specifying one or more of a particular, individualized noun is important or when the object named is known to the reader ("**The** radishes from **the** garden are on **the** table").

indefinite　　　definite
article　　　　article

A squirrel visited the feeder.

4. The **possessive adjectives** are *my, your, his, her, its, our,* and *their*. They modify nouns and pronouns and indicate possession or ownership.

Your friend borrowed my jacket for his wife because she left her sweater in their car.

5. The **demonstrative adjectives** are *this* and *that* (for singular nouns and pronouns) and *these* and *those* (for plural nouns and pronouns). They act to call attention to or point out the nouns they modify. *This* and *these* modify nouns close to the writer, and *that* and *those* modify nouns more distant from the writer.

Eat these sandwiches, not those sardines.

This freshman course is a prerequisite for those advanced courses.

6. **Cardinal adjectives** are words used in counting: *one, two, twenty,* etc. They tell the reader precisely "How many?"

I read four biographies of Jack Kerouac and seven articles.

7. **Ordinal adjectives** note position in a series.

The first biography I read was too sketchy, while the second one was too detailed.

adj

adj

8. **Indefinite adjectives** provide more general information about quantities and amounts than do cardinal or ordinal adjectives. Indefinite adjectives give the reader general or approximate information about "How much?" or "How many?" Some common indefinite adjectives are *another, any, enough, few, less, little, many, more, much, several,* and *some.*

> <u>Several</u> people asked me if I had <u>enough</u> blankets, if I needed the thermostat turned up a <u>few</u> degrees, or if I wanted <u>some</u> hot soup.

9. The **interrogative adjectives** are *what, which,* and *whose.* Interrogative adjectives modify nouns and pronouns that are having something asked about them.

> <u>Which</u> radio stations do you like? <u>Whose</u> music do you prefer?

10. **Proper adjectives** are proper nouns used as adjectives or altered to function as adjectives. Proper adjectives are capitalized.

> <u>New York</u> cabbies are known for their friendliness.

> Please give me the <u>Beatles</u> record.

> The parrot spoke <u>French</u> expressions.

11. **Nouns used as adjectives** usually precede the word they modify. In form they are nouns, but in function they are adjectives, serving to define or limit another person, place, thing, or idea.

> The <u>terrace</u> chairs were more expensive than the <u>porch</u> swing.

> I threw away the <u>hamburger</u> bun.

Exercise 3   Revise each of the following sentences by adding at least three adjectives.

> EXAMPLE: The cat slept on the pillow.

> REVISED: The <u>old,</u> <u>yellow</u> cat slept on the <u>expensive</u> pillow.

1. The band performed four numbers after the intermission.
2. The boat departed from the dock.
3. The quiz was easy, but the exam was difficult.
4. The mystery had an ending I enjoyed.
5. As the concert ended, the crowd left the theater.
6. The museum was filled with sculptures and paintings.
7. The tigers paced around their cages.
8. Our hostess served chicken, rice, and asparagus before the dessert.
9. The guitar rested on the table.
10. Laura's behavior is as unusual as her clothing.

A.5 ADVERBS

■ **Adverbs** modify a verb, an adjective, another adverb, or an entire sentence or clause (a group of related words containing a subject and a predicate). Like adjectives, adverbs describe, qualify, or limit the meaning of the words they modify. Many adverbs end in *-ly* (*lazily, happily*), but there are words generally used as adverbs that do not end in *-ly* (*fast, here, much, well, rather, everywhere, never, so*), and words that end in *-ly* that are not adverbs (*lively, unfriendly, lonely*). Like all parts of speech, an adverb may be best identified by examining its function within the sentence.

adv

> ADVERB MODIFYING A VERB: I <u>quickly</u> skimmed the book.
>
> ADVERB MODIFYING AN ADJECTIVE: <u>Very</u> cold water came from the shower.
>
> ADVERB MODIFYING ANOTHER ADVERB: He was injured <u>quite</u> seriously.
>
> ADVERB MODIFYING A SENTENCE: <u>Apparently</u>, the job was bungled.

Adverbs answer the questions *how? when? where? how often?* or *to what extent?* about the words they modify.

> HOW? Cheryl moved <u>awkwardly</u> because of her stiff neck.
>
> WHEN? I arrived <u>yesterday</u>.
>
> WHERE? They searched <u>everywhere</u>.
>
> HOW OFTEN? He telephoned <u>repeatedly</u>.
>
> TO WHAT EXTENT? Simon was <u>rather</u> slow to answer his doorbell.

Some adverbs, called **conjunctive adverbs** (or **adverbial conjunctions**), have a different function. Conjunctive adverbs are words like *however, therefore*, and *besides*. They connect the ideas of one sentence or clause to those of a previous sentence or clause. These adverbs show the logical relation between two sentences or main clauses. They can appear anywhere in a sentence. (See p. 464 for how to punctuate sentences containing conjunctive adverbs.)

> conjunctive adverb
> ↓
> James did not want to go to the library on Saturday; <u>however</u>, he knew he needed to write his paper.

> conjunctive adverb
> ↓
> The telephone book was an old one. <u>Furthermore</u>, many of its pages were missing.

The sporting goods store was crowded because of the sale. Leila

conjunctive adverb
↓

decided, <u>nonetheless</u>, to look for new sneakers.

Some common conjunctive adverbs are listed below. The list includes several phrases that function as conjunctive adverbs.

accordingly	further	moreover	similarly
also	furthermore	namely	still
anyway	hence	nevertheless	then
as a result	however	next	thereafter
at the same time	incidentally	nonetheless	therefore
besides	indeed	now	thus
certainly	instead	on the contrary	undoubtedly
consequently	likewise	on the other hand	
finally	meanwhile	otherwise	

Like adjectives, adverbs have three forms: **positive** (modifies a verb, adjective, adverb, sentence, or clause, but does not suggest any comparison), **comparative** (compares two actions or conditions), and **superlative** (compares three or more actions or conditions). (See also p. 489.)

positive adverb   positive adverb
↓   ↓

Andy rose <u>early</u> and crept downstairs <u>quietly</u>.

comparative adverb   comparative adverb
↓   ↓

Jim rose <u>earlier</u> than Andy and crept downstairs <u>more quietly</u>.

superlative adverb
↓

Bill rose <u>earliest</u> of anyone in the house and crept downstairs

superlative adverb
↓

<u>most quietly</u>.

In general, to make the comparative form of an adverb, place either the word *more* or the word *less* before the adverb. To make the superlative form of an adverb, place the word *most* or *least* before the adverb.

A few common adverbs, however, have irregular comparative and superlative adverb forms:

POSITIVE	COMPARATIVE	SUPERLATIVE
well	better	best
badly	worse	worst
much	more	most
far (in distance)	farther	farthest
far (in time, degree)	further	furthest

Exercise 4   Write a sentence using each of the following comparative or superlative adverbs.

> EXAMPLE: better
>   This beach looks <u>better</u> than it did before the clean-up.

1. worst
2. heavier
3. earlier
4. more maturely
5. least quickly
6. more
7. fewer
8. farthest
9. most warmly
10. less smoothly

conj

A.6 CONJUNCTIONS

Conjunctions connect words, phrases, and clauses. There are three kinds of conjunctions: **coordinating, correlative,** and **subordinating. Coordinating** and **correlative conjunctions** connect words, phrases, or clauses of equal grammatical rank. (A **phrase** is a group of related words lacking a subject, a predicate, or both. A **clause** is a group of words containing a subject and a predicate. See p. 436.)

The **coordinating conjunctions** are *and, but, or, nor, for, so,* and *yet.* These words must connect words or word groups of the same kind. In other words, two nouns may be connected by *and.* A noun and clause cannot be. *For* and *so* can only connect main clauses.

coordinating conjunction
connecting nouns
↓

We studied the novels of Toni Morrison <u>and</u> Alice Walker.

coordinating conjunction
connecting verbs
↓

The copilot successfully flew <u>and</u> landed the disabled plane,

coordinating conjunction
connecting main clauses
↓

<u>but</u> he did not want to be considered a hero.

coordinating conjunction connecting
main clauses
↓

The carpentry course sounded interesting, <u>so</u> Meg enrolled.

Correlative conjunctions are pairs of words that link and relate parts of a sentence. Some common correlative conjunctions are *both . . . and, either . . . or, neither . . . nor, not only . . . but also*, and *whether . . . or*. Correlative conjunctions are always used in pairs.

correlative conjunctions
↙　　　　　　↘

<u>Either</u> the electricity was off, <u>or</u> the bulb had burned out.

Some common **subordinating conjunctions** are *although, because, if, since, until, when, where, while*. They connect subordinate, or dependent, elements of the sentence to the main sentence. (See p. 450 for a further discussion of subordinating conjunctions.)

subordinating conjunction
↓

<u>Although</u> the movie got bad reviews, it drew big crowds.

subordinating conjunction
↓

<u>Because</u> she was a reliable correspondent, she received a lot of mail.

A.7 PREPOSITIONS

■　A **preposition** links and relates its **object** (a noun or a pronoun) to the rest of the sentence. Prepositions often show relationships of time and space.

preposition　object of prep.
↓　　　　　↓

I walked <u>around</u> the **block**.

preposition   object of prep.

She called <u>during</u> our **vacation.**

object of   object of
preposition   prep.   preposition   prep.

Dillon searched <u>for</u> his **gloves** <u>in</u> the **closet.**

Multiple-word prepositions are called **phrasal prepositions** (or **compound prepositions**).

phrasal preposition   object of prep.

<u>According to</u> our **records**, you have enough credits to graduate.

phrasal preposition   object of prep.

We decided to make the trip <u>in spite of</u> the **snowstorm.**

Often the object of the preposition will have modifiers itself.

preposition   modifiers   object of prep.

We set up our tent <u>beneath</u> the <u>tall pine</u> **trees.**

prep.   modifier   obj. of prep.   prep.   modifier   obj. of prep.

Not a sound came <u>from</u> the <u>child's</u> **room** <u>except</u> a <u>gentle</u> **snoring.**

Usually the preposition comes before its object, a noun or a pronoun. In interrogative sentences, however, the preposition sometimes follows its object.

object of preposition   preposition

What did your supervisor ask you <u>about</u>? [<u>What</u> is the object of the preposition <u>about</u>.]

Together the preposition, the object of the preposition, and the object's modifiers form a **prepositional phrase**. A prepositional phrase may have more than one object (**a compound object**).

prepositional phrase   prepositional phrase

The water <u>from the open hydrant</u> flowed <u>into the street.</u>

prepositional phrase with compound object

The laundromat was <u>between campus and home.</u>

prepositional phrase with compound object

The scientist conducted her experiment <u>throughout the afternoon and early evening.</u>

prep

There may be many prepositional phrases in a sentence.

> The noisy kennel was underneath the beauty parlor, despite the complaints of customers.

> Alongside the weedy railroad tracks, an old hotel stood with faded grandeur near the abandoned brick station on the edge of town.

The prepositional phrase as a unit acts as one part of speech, frequently as an adjective or adverb. (As such it can be part of the complete subject or complete predicate of a sentence. See pp. 437–438.) If the prepositional phrase modifies a noun or pronoun, it functions as an adjective. If it modifies a verb, adjective, or adverb, it functions as an adverb.

> The **auditorium** inside the new building has a special **sound system** for the hearing impaired. [These prepositional phrases function as adjectives; they modify the nouns auditorium and sound system.]

> The doctor **looked** cheerfully at the patient and **handed** the lab results across the desk. [These prepositional phrases function as adverbs; they modify the verbs looked and handed.]

prep

Here are some words commonly used as prepositions.

along	beyond	off	to
among	by	on	toward
around	despite	onto	under
at	down	out	underneath
before	during	outside	until
behind	except	over	up
below	for	past	upon
beneath	from	since	with
beside	in	through	within
besides	near	till	without
between			

Here are some common compound prepositions.

according to	in addition to	on account of
aside from	in front of	out of
as of	in place of	prior to
as well as	in regard to	with regard to
because of	in spite of	with respect to
by means of	instead of	

A.8 INTERJECTIONS

■ **Interjections** are words that express emotion or surprise. They are followed by an exclamation point, comma, or period, depending on whether they stand alone or serve as a part or a whole of a sentence. Interjections are used in speech more than in writing.

<u>Oh</u>!

<u>Wow</u>! What a hat!

<u>So</u>, was that lost letter ever found?

<u>Well</u>, I'd better be going.

Exercise 5   Expand each of the following sentences by adding a prepositional phrase where indicated.

EXAMPLE: The car _____ was severely damaged.

The car <u>in the ditch</u> was severely damaged.

1. The diamond ring _____ sparkled.

2. Stories _____ filled the newspaper.

3. The maple tree _____ was cut down.

4. Termites had damaged the building _____.

5. The chairs _____ dried off quickly after the rainstorm.

6. The history professor lectured _____.

7. Lunch was served _____.

8. The chest _____ was not empty.

9. The bookstore was located _____.

10. The dictionary _____ is tattered and torn from frequent use.

int

B   Understanding the Parts of Sentences

B.1 Subjects

B.2 Predicates

B.3 Complements

B.4 Basic Sentence Patterns

B.5 Expanding the Sentence with Adjectives and Adverbs

B.6 Expanding the Sentence with Phrases

B.7 Expanding the Sentence with Clauses

B.8 Basic Sentence Classifications

sub

A sentence is a group of words that expresses a complete thought about something or someone. A sentence must contain a **subject** and a **predicate**.

SUBJECT	*PREDICATE*
Children	grow.
Larry	laughed.
Fish	swim.
Wheels	turn.
Time	will tell.

Depending on their purpose and punctuation, sentences are either **declarative, interrogative, exclamatory,** or **imperative.**

A **declarative sentence** makes a statement. It ends with a period.

subject   predicate

The snow fell steadily.

An **interrogative sentence** asks a question. It ends with a question mark (?).

subject   predicate

Who called?

An **exclamatory sentence** conveys strong emotion. It ends with an exclamation point (!).

subject   predicate

Your picture is in the paper!

An **imperative sentence** makes a request or gives an order. It ends with either a period or an exclamation point, depending on how mild or strong the command or request is.

subject   predicate

We need a fire extinguisher!

predicate

Please close that window. [The subject of this sentence is understood to be you. Please [you] close that window.]

B.1 SUBJECTS

■ The subject of a sentence tells you who or what the sentence is about. It tells you who or what performs the action expressed in the predicate. The subject is often a **noun**, a word that names a person, place, thing, or idea.

Michael Jackson released a new video.

My sister drives a used van.

The rose bushes must be watered.

Honesty is the best policy.

The subject of a sentence can also be a **pronoun**, a word that refers to or substitutes for a noun (for example, *I, you, he, she, it, they, we*).

They saw the movie three times.

I will attend the rally.

Although the ink spilled, it did not go on my shirt.

The subject of a sentence can also be a group of words.

Lying on a beach is my idea of a good time.

Simple vs. Complete Subjects

The **simple subject** is the noun or pronoun that names what the sentence is about. It does not include any **modifiers**—that is, words that describe, identify, qualify, or limit the meaning of the noun or pronoun.

sub

simple subject
↓

The bright red concert <u>poster</u> caught everyone's eye.

simple subject
↓

High speed <u>computers</u> have revolutionized the banking industry.

When the subject of a sentence is a proper noun (a name of a particular person, place, or thing), the entire name is considered the simple subject.

simple subject
↓

<u>Martin Luther King, Jr.</u> was a great leader.

The simple subject of an imperative sentence is *you*. In imperative sentences the word *you* as a subject is often understood, not explicitly stated.

simple subject
↓

[<u>You</u>] Remember to bring the cooler.

The **complete subject** is the simple subject plus its modifiers.

complete subject
↓

<u>The sleek, black limousine</u> waited outside the church.

complete subject
↓

<u>Fondly remembered as a gifted songwriter, fiddle player, and story teller, Quintin Lotus Dickey</u> lived in a cabin in Paoli, Indiana.

sub

Compound Subjects

Some sentences contain two or more subjects, joined together with a coordinating conjunction (specifically *and, but, or, nor*). When there are a series of subjects, commas appear after each subject except the last. The subjects that are linked together form a **compound subject**.

compound subject
↓   ↓

Neither <u>Maria</u> nor <u>I</u> completed the marathon.

compound subject
↙   ↓   ↘

The <u>microwave oven</u>, the <u>dishwasher</u>, and the <u>refrigerator</u> were not usable during the blackout.

B.2 PREDICATES

■ The **predicate** indicates what the subject does, what happened to the subject, or what is said about the subject. The predicate must include a verb. A **verb** is a word or group of words that expresses action or state of being (for example, *run, invent, build, know, be*). The verb is the essential part of the predicate.

> Joy <u>swam</u> sixty laps.
>
> The thunderstorm <u>replenished</u> the reservoir.

Sometimes the verb consists of only one word ("The athlete *runs*"). Often, however, the main verb is accompanied by a **helping verb** (also known as an **auxiliary verb**): "The athlete *has* run," or "He *is* running." In the sentences below, the main verb is in boldface and the helping verb is underlined.

> By the end of the week, I <u>will have</u> **worked** twenty-five hours.
>
> The play <u>had</u> **begun.**
>
> The professor <u>did</u> **return** the journal assignments.

Helping verbs help the main verb indicate **tense, voice, number,** and **mood.** (See pp. 423, 423, 412, and 419 for definitions of these terms.) Helping verbs may also indicate necessity, possibility, or permission.

> You <u>must</u> **leave** now.
>
> You <u>might</u> **leave** now.
>
> You <u>may</u> **leave** now.

Simple vs. Complete Predicates

The **simple predicate** is the verb in a sentence or clause (a group of words containing a subject and a predicate), including helping verbs. It does not include words that modify the verb, complements (words that complete the meaning of the verb), or the words *not* or *never*. The simple predicate contains the verb or the helping verb and the verb together (known as the **verb phrase**).

simple predicate
↓

The proctor hastily <u>collected</u> the blue books.

simple predicate
↓

The master of ceremonies <u>had introduced</u> the next performer.

pred

The **complete predicate** consists of the simple predicate, its modifiers, and any complements (words that complete the meaning of the verb). In general, the complete predicate includes everything in the sentence or independent clause except the complete subject (the subject and its modifiers).

Subject   complete predicate

Bill decided to change the name of his band to something less potentially confusing and alienating.

complete subject   complete predicate

The brown bats that flew out of the barn each night helped us keep the mosquito population under control.

Compound Predicates

Some sentences have two or more predicates joined together with a coordinating conjunction. The predicates that are linked together form a **compound predicate**.

compound predicate

Mark started his car and drove it home.

compound predicate

The supermarket store owner will survey his customers and order the specialized foods they desire.

Linking Verbs

A linking verb does not express action, but links the subject to other words in the sentence that rename or describe the subject. Some linking verbs are *be, become, seem, feel, look, appear, taste, smell,* and *sound.* (See p. 418.)

Sharon was polite to the reference librarian. [The linking verb was (a form of the verb be) links Sharon with the word polite that describes her.]

By the end of March, the days become balmy. [The linking verb become links days with the word balmy that describes them.]

Be and *become* are the most common linking verbs, but other verbs can function as linking verbs.

Yvonne seems happy lately.

The music sounds better from the back of the room.

This cheese tastes moldy.

Copyright © 1993 by Houghton Mifflin Company.

pred

Exercise 6   Underline the simple subject(s) and circle the simple predicate(s) in each of the following sentences.

EXAMPLE: Pam Master (photographed) a hummingbird.

1. Sue's chemistry lab group completed the experiment.
2. The American family takes many forms these days.
3. Lynn and Bruce seem relieved to have completed their psychology exam.
4. The geraniums and pansies had been weeded and watered regularly.
5. The leather couch with the snakeskin pillows looked out of place in the small, yellow, flowered living room.
6. The whales dove and swam around our boat.
7. Sherman, with his sister beside him, hurried home.
8. The students were glad when the semester was over.
9. Thirty-nine men signed the U.S. Constitution and forwarded it to the Congress of the Confederation.
10. The local news anchorwoman visited our communication class and spoke about jobs in the media.

B.3 COMPLEMENTS

■ A **complement** is a word (or words) that completes the meaning of a transitive verb in a sentence or clause. The action of a transitive verb is directed toward someone or something, creating a complement. Complements are part of the complete predicate. They follow the verb, and, like subjects and predicates, can be simple or compound.

There are five kinds of complements: **direct objects, indirect objects, objective complements, predicate nominatives** (also known as **predicate nouns**), and **predicate adjectives**. The last two, predicate nominatives and predicate adjectives, are known as the **subjective complements**.

comp

Direct Objects

A **direct object** is a noun or pronoun that receives the action of a transitive verb in the active voice (see p. 472). A direct object answers the question *what?* or *whom?*

transitive verb   direct object
↓   ↓
The pharmacist helped us. [The pharmacist helped whom?]

transitive verb   compound direct object
↓   ↓   ↓
Jillian borrowed a bicycle and a visor. [Jillian borrowed what?]

Indirect Objects

An **indirect object** is a noun or pronoun that receives the action of the verb indirectly. Indirect objects name the person or thing *to whom* or *for whom* something is done.

transitive verb   indirect object   direct object
↘   ↓   ↙
The oil delivery man gave me the bill. [He gave the bill to whom?]

transitive verb   compound indirect object   compound direct object
↓   ↙   ↓   ↙   ↘
Eric bought his wife and son some sandwiches and milk. [He bought food for whom?]

Objective Complements

An **objective complement** is a noun or adjective that follows the direct object and modifies or renames that direct object. Objective complements appear with verbs like *name, find, think, elect, appoint, choose,* and *consider.*

direct object   noun as objective complement
↘   ↓
We appointed Dean our representative. [Representative renames the direct object Dean.]

direct object   adjective as objective complement
↓   ↓
The judge found the defendant innocent of the charges. [Innocent modifies the direct object defendant.]

Predicate Nominatives

A **predicate nominative** (also known as a **predicate noun**) is a noun or pronoun that follows a linking verb and restates, renames, or identifies the subject of the sentence. Because it restates the subject, it is known as a **subjective complement.**

subject   predicate nominative
↓   ↓
Murasaki Shikibu was an early Japanese novelist. [Novelist identifies the subject **Murasaki Shikibu**.]

subject   compound predicate nominative

The **party** will be either a <u>luncheon</u> or a <u>dinner</u>. [Luncheon or dinner identifies the subject **party**.]

Predicate Adjectives

A **predicate adjective** follows a linking verb and modifies the subject of a sentence. Because it modifies the subject, it is known as a subjective complement.

subject   linking verb   predicate adjectives

The Cadillac was <u>pink</u> and <u>white</u>.

subject   linking verb   predicate adjective

The candidate sounded <u>confident</u>.

B.4 BASIC SENTENCE PATTERNS

■ Having reviewed parts of speech and subjects, predicates, and complements, we can now look at the five basic sentence patterns in English. The order of elements within a sentence may change, as when the sentence is a question. Some elements of the sentence may be understood (not explicitly stated) as in an imperative sentence when the subject is omitted. A sentence might become long and intricate through the addition of descriptive words, qualifying phrases, or additional clauses. Nonetheless, five basic patterns stand at the heart of how we build sentences.

Pattern 1

Subject + Predicate

Intransitive verb

I   shivered.

Cynthia   swam.

Pattern 2

Subject + Predicate   **+ Direct Object**

Transitive verb

Anthony   bought   a sofa.

We   wanted   freedom.

sent pat

Pattern 3

Subject + Predicate		+ Subject Complement
	Linking verb	*[Noun or Adjective]*
The woman	was	a welder.
Our course	is	interesting.

Pattern 4

Subject + Predicate		+ Indirect Object	+ Direct Object
	Transitive verb		
My friend	loaned	me	a typewriter.
The company	sent	employees	a questionnaire.

Pattern 5

Subject + Predicate		+ Direct Object	+ Objective Complement
	Transitive verb		*[Noun or Adjective]*
I	consider	her singing	exceptional.
Lampwick	called	Jiminy Cricket	a beetle.

Exercise 7   Complete each sentence with a word or words that will function as the type of complement indicated.

EXAMPLE: George Washington was _____.

George Washington was ____our first president____.
　　　　　　　　　　　　　　　　predicate nominative

1. The school bus struck the _____.
　　　　　　　　　　　　　　　　　　　　　direct object

2. Samantha gave _____ a rawhide bone to chew.
　　　　　　　　　　　indirect object

3. Jonas considers Elvis Presley _____.
　　　　　　　　　　　　　　　　　　　objective complement

4. The test will be either _____.
　　　　　　　　　　　　　　　predicate nominative

5. The jockey checked to make sure his helmet was _____
before beginning the race.　　　　　　　　　　predicate adjective

sent
pat

6. Michael helped _____ fold the laundry.
   indirect object

7. Lucinda finds the novel _____.
   objective complement

8. The kindergarten teacher gave each of his students a _____.
   direct object

9. Learning to drive a car for the first time was _____.
   predicate adjective

10. Picasso is a famous _____.
    predicate nominative

B.5 EXPANDING THE SENTENCE WITH ADJECTIVES AND ADVERBS

■ A sentence may consist of just a subject and a verb.

Linda studied.

Rumors circulated.

Most sentences, however, contain additional information about the subject and the verb. Information is commonly added in three ways:

- by using adjectives and adverbs
- by using phrases (groups of words that do not contain both a subject and a predicate)
- by using clauses (groups of words that do contain both a subject and a predicate).

Using Adjectives and Adverbs to Expand Your Sentences

Adjectives are words that modify or describe nouns and pronouns. (See p. 426.) Adjectives answer questions about nouns and pronouns such as *which one? what kind? how many?* Adjectives allow you to add detail and meaning to your sentences.

WITHOUT ADJECTIVES: Dogs barked at cats.

WITH ADJECTIVES: Our three, large, brown dogs barked at the neighbor's two terrified, tiny, spotted cats.

Adverbs also add information to a sentence. Adverbs are words that modify or describe a verb, an adjective, or another adverb (See p. 429).

**adj
adv**

Adverbs usually explain where, when, how, or to what extent an action occurred.

WITHOUT ADVERBS: I will clean.

The audience applauded.

WITH ADVERBS: I will clean <u>everywhere</u> <u>very</u> <u>thoroughly</u> <u>tomorrow</u>.

The audience applauded <u>loudly</u> and <u>enthusiastically</u>.

Note: Sometimes nouns and verbals (see p. 425.) are used as adjectives and thus can expand and add information to our sentence.

noun used as adjective
↓

People are rediscovering the <u>milk</u> bottle.

verbal (present participle)   verbal (past participle)
used as adjective   used as adjective
↓   ↓

Mrs. Simon had a <u>swimming</u> pool with a <u>broken</u> drain.

B.6 EXPANDING THE SENTENCE WITH PHRASES

■ A **phrase** is a group of related words that lacks a subject, predicate, or both. A phrase by itself cannot stand alone as a sentence, but must be attached to a complete sentence. Phrases can appear at various positions in a sentence, either at the beginning, middle, or end. They add information to a sentence.

WITHOUT PHRASES: I noticed the stain.

Sal researched the topic.

Felix arose.

WITH PHRASES: <u>Upon entering the room</u>, I noticed the stain <u>on the expensive carpet</u>.

<u>At the local aquarium</u>, Sal researched the topic <u>of shark attacks</u>.

<u>An amateur astronomer</u>, Felix arose <u>in the middle of the night</u> to observe the lunar eclipse, but, <u>after waiting ten minutes</u> <u>in the cold</u>, gave up.

There are eight kinds of phrases: **Noun, verb, prepositional,** three kinds of **verbal phrases** (**participial, gerund,** and **infinitive**), **appositive,** and **absolute.**

A noun plus its modifiers is a **noun phrase** (*red shoes, quiet house*). A main verb plus its helping verbs (auxiliaries) is a **verb phrase** (*had been exploring, is sleeping*).

A **prepositional phrase** consists of a preposition (for example, *in, above, with, at, behind*), an object of a preposition (a noun or pronoun), and any modifiers of the object. (See p. 434 for a list of common prepositions.) A prepositional phrase functions like an adjective (modifying a noun or pronoun) or an adverb (modifying a verb, adjective, or adverb). A prepositional phrase generally adds information about time, place, direction, manner, or degree.

Prepositional phrases used as adjectives

The woman with the briefcase is giving a presentation on meditation techniques.

Both of the telephones behind the partition were ringing.

Prepositional phrases used as adverbs

The fire drill occurred in the morning.

I was curious about the new coffee shop.

My niece came over from Australia.

With horror, the crowd watched the rhinoceros's tether stretch to the breaking point.

A prepositional phrase can function as part of the complete subject or as part of the complete predicate, but should not be confused with the simple subject or simple predicate.

complete subject
simple subject   prepositional phrase

The red leather-bound **volumes** on the dusty shelf were filled with obscure facts.

complete predicate
simple predicate   prepositional phrase

Pat **ducked** quickly behind the potted fern.

Verbal Phrases (Participial Phrases, Gerund Phrases, Infinitive Phrases)

A **verbal phrase** is composed of a **verbal** (a form of a verb that functions as a noun, adjective, or adverb), a complement (a word or words that complete the meaning of the verb), and any modifiers of the complement. Each verbal phrase contains one of the three types of verbals: **participles, gerunds,** and **infinitives.**

Participles and Participial Phrases

A **participle** is a form of a verb that functions like an adjective and therefore modifies nouns and pronouns.

> <u>Irritated</u>, Martha circled the <u>confusing</u> traffic rotary once again.

> My paper was about recent changes in the <u>trucking</u> industry.

Helping verbs may be attached to the participle. The participle and the helping verb function together to modify a noun or pronoun.

> <u>Having been caught</u>, the groundhog circled his cage.

There are two kinds of participles: present and past. Present and past participles are two of the four principal parts of verbs (See p. 420). The present participle is formed by adding *-ing* to the infinitive form of a verb. The past participle of regular verbs is formed by adding either *-d* or *-ed* to the infinitive form of the verb. (For past participles of irregular verbs, consult the list on p. 421.)

A **participial phrase** is composed of a participle (either present or past), its modifiers, and any complements (words that complete the meaning of a verb). Like the participles discussed above, the participial phrase functions as an adjective to modify a noun or pronoun.

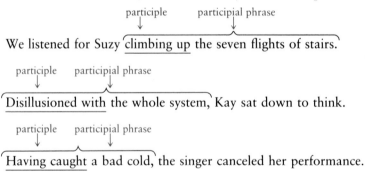

Gerunds and Gerund Phrases

A **gerund** is a verb form that functions as a noun. Gerunds always end in *-ing*.

Note: Present participles also end in *-ing*, but function as adjectives, not as nouns.

> <u>Shoveling</u> is good exercise.

> Rex enjoyed <u>gardening</u>.

> <u>Recycling</u> has become a national priority.

A **gerund phrase** contains a gerund, its modifiers, and complements. Like gerunds, these phrases function as nouns and thus may be a sentence's subject, direct or indirect object, object of a preposition, predicate nominative, or appositive.

> The knitting of the sweater took longer than Alice anticipated. [Gerund phrase functions as a subject.]
>
> The director considered making another monster movie. [Gerund phrase functions as a direct object.]
>
> He gave running three miles credit for his helath. [Gerund phrase functions as an indirect object.]
>
> Prior to learning Greek, Omar spoke only English. [Gerund phrase functions as an object of the preposition.]
>
> One fountain is showering the passersby with water. [Gerund phrase functions as a predicate nominative.]
>
> Wayne's trick, memorizing license plates, has come in handy. [Gerund phrase functions as an appositive.]

Infinitives and Infinitive Phrases

An **infinitive** is a verb's first principal part (see p. 420). In a sentence the infinitive is usually preceded by the word *to*, although sometimes *to* is understood, not explicitly stated. An infinitive may function as a noun, an adjective, or an adverb.

> To travel is to see history come alive.
>
> Ricardo is the runner to watch.
>
> I could not get to sleep.
>
> I saw her flinch. [The word to before flinch is understood, not stated.]

Note: Since *to* is a common preposition, prepositional phrases may also start with the word *to*. In an infinitive the word *to* will be followed by a verb; in a prepositional phrase, *to* will be followed by a noun or pronoun.

An **infinitive phrase** contains an infinitive, its modifiers, and its complements. An infinitive phrase can function as a noun, adjective, or adverb. As with infinitives, sometimes the *to* is understood, not explicitly stated.

To love one's enemy is a noble goal.

The season to plant bulbs is fall.

The chess club met to practice for the state championship.

I must go select a tuxedo. [The to before select is understood.]

Frank and Mary Beth help us learn the dance. [The to before learn is understood, not stated.]

Appositive Phrases

An **appositive phrase** explains, restates, or adds new information about a noun. If the appositive phrase is necessary to the meaning of the sentence, no commas are needed to set if off from the rest of the sentence. If the appositive phrase provides nonessential information, it needs to be set off with commas.

Francis, my neighbor, lent me a wrench.

Claude Monet completed the painting Water Lilies around 1903.

Absolute Phrases

An **absolute phrase** consists of a noun or pronoun, a participle, and any modifiers of the noun or pronoun. An absolute phrase often modifies an entire sentence. It does not modify any particular word within the sentence, but instead adds related information about its own subject. Unlike participial phrases, absolute phrases always contain a subject. They can appear in a variety of places within the sentence, but must be set off from the rest of the sentence with a comma or commas.

The winter being over, the geese returned. [Absolute phrase adds information about its subject, winter.]

The bulletin board, its cork surface cluttered with month-old posters and messages, was ignored by students in the hall. [Absolute phrase adds information about its subject, surface.]

There may be more than one absolute phrase in a sentence.

The modern research lab was impressive, its staff working with quiet efficiency and its massive banks of computer equipment humming.

Exercise 8 Expand each of the following sentences by adding adjectives, adverbs and/or phrases (prepositional, verbal, appositive, or absolute).

> EXAMPLE: I bought a pair of jeans.
> EXPANDED: At the Galleria Mall, I finally bought a new pair of stone-washed jeans with pleated pockets.

1. Edmund visited Montreal.
2. I was alarmed.
3. Katrina cooked dinner.
4. The class began.
5. Rudy threw a book.
6. My alarm rang.
7. The car struck the truck.
8. I answered the telephone.
9. I will study tonight.
10. The sky became cloudy.

B.7 EXPANDING THE SENTENCE WITH CLAUSES

■ A **clause** is a group of words that contains a subject and a predicate. A clause is either **independent** (also called **main**) or **subordinate** (also called **dependent**).

An **independent clause** can stand alone as a grammatically complete and correct sentence.

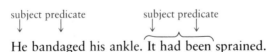

He bandaged his ankle. It had been sprained.

The rooster crowed. I awoke.

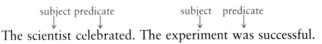

The scientist celebrated. The experiment was successful.

A **subordinate clause** has a subject and a predicate, but cannot stand alone as a grammatically complete and correct sentence. It does not express a complete thought. Most subordinate clauses begin with either a **subordinating conjunction** or a **relative pronoun.** (See the lists on p. 453). These words are part of the subordinate clause and serve to connect it to an independent clause.

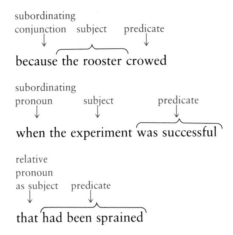

subordinating
conjunction   subject   predicate

because the rooster crowed

subordinating
pronoun   subject   predicate

when the experiment was successful

relative
pronoun
as subject   predicate

that had been sprained

These clauses do not express complete thoughts, therefore, they cannot stand alone as sentences. When joined to independent clauses, however, subordinate clauses function as adjectives, adverbs, and nouns. Depending on how they are used in a sentence, these clauses are known as **adjective clauses, adverb clauses,** and **noun clauses.**

Adjective Clause

subordinate clause as adjective

He bandaged his ankle that had been sprained.

Adverb Clause

subordinate clause as adverb

Because the rooster crowed, I awoke.

[Also correct: I woke up because the rooster crowed.]

Noun Clause

subordinate clause as noun (direct object)

The scientist celebrated when the experiment was successful.

As mentioned above, subordinate clauses are most often connected to independent clauses with two kinds of words: **subordinating conjunctions** and **relative pronouns.** These words establish a relationship between the material in the subordinate clause and the material in the independent clause.

Some of the most common subordinating conjunctions are

after	if	supposing that
although	inasmuch as	than
as	in case that	though
as if	in order that	unless
as far as	insofar as	until
as soon as	in that	when
as though	now that	whenever
because	once	where
before	provided that	wherever
even if	rather than	whether
even though	since	while
how	so that	

The relative pronouns are

which	what
that	who (whose, whom)
whatever	whoever (whomever)

Note: Relative pronouns are generally the subject or object in their clauses. Two relative pronouns, *who* and *whom*, change form depending on whether the relative pronoun functions as the subject or object of the phrase (see p. 483).

Sometimes the relative pronoun or subordinating conjunction is implied or understood rather than stated, or the subordinate clause contains an implied predicate. When a subordinate clause is missing an element that can clearly be supplied from the context of the sentence, it is called an **elliptical clause**.

understood predicate
in subordinate clause
↓

The circus is more entertaining than the television [is].

understood subordinating conjunction
in subordinate clause
↓

Canadian history is among the subjects [that] the book discusses.

B.8 BASIC SENTENCE CLASSIFICATIONS

■ Depending on their structure, sentences are classified into four basic categories: **simple, compound, complex,** and **compound-complex.**

Simple Sentences

A **simple sentence** has one independent (main) clause and no subordinate (dependent) clauses. A simple sentence contains at least one subject and one predicate. It may have a compound subject, a compound predicate, and many various kinds of phrases, but it has only one clause.

subject   predicate

Sap rises.

In the spring the sap rises in the maple trees of the Northeast and is collected and boiled to make thick, delicious maple syrup.

Compound Sentences

A **compound sentence** has at least two independent (main) clauses and no subordinate (dependent) clauses. The clauses are usually joined with a comma and a coordinating conjunction (*and, but, nor, or, for, so,* or *yet*). Sometimes the two independent clauses are joined with a semicolon and no coordinating conjunction or with a semicolon and a conjunctive adverb like *nonetheless* or *still,* followed by a comma.

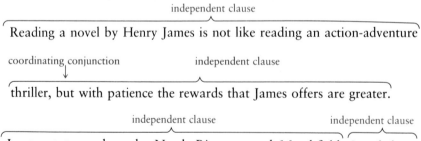

independent clause

Reading a novel by Henry James is not like reading an action-adventure

coordinating conjunction   independent clause

thriller, but with patience the rewards that James offers are greater.

independent clause   independent clause

I set out to explore the North River around Marshfield; I ended up stranded on a dune at high tide.

Complex Sentences

A **complex sentence** has one independent clause and one or more subordinate (dependent) clauses. The clauses are joined by subordinating conjunctions or relative pronouns.

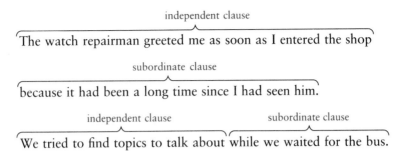

independent clause

The watch repairman greeted me as soon as I entered the shop

subordinate clause

because it had been a long time since I had seen him.

independent clause   subordinate clause

We tried to find topics to talk about while we waited for the bus.

Compound-complex Sentences

A **compound-complex sentence** contains two or more independent clauses and one or more subordinate clauses.

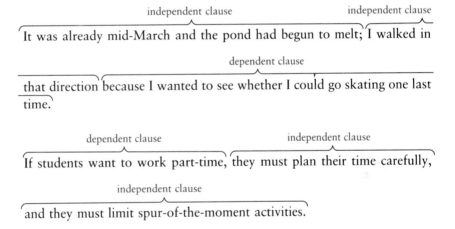

independent clause   independent clause

It was already mid-March and the pond had begun to melt; I walked in

dependent clause

that direction because I wanted to see whether I could go skating one last time.

dependent clause   independent clause

If students want to work part-time, they must plan their time carefully,

independent clause

and they must limit spur-of-the-moment activities.

Exercise 9   Combine the following pairs of sentences into a single sentence by forming independent and/or subordinate clauses.

EXAMPLE: a. The weather vane crashed to the ground.
            b. A strong, gusty wind was blowing.

COMBINED: Because a strong, gusty wind was blowing, the weather vane crashed to the ground.

  1. a. Doug gift-wrapped the box of candy.
      b. Doug bought the candy for his wife for Valentine's Day.

sent
class

2. a. Mark experienced a lot of stress about job interviews.
    b. Mark learned relaxation techniques to reduce stress.
3. a. Tuesday was the last class before our spring break.
    b. The students talked about their vacation plans.
4. a. Angry students lined up outside the Registrar's Office.
    b. A computer error had cancelled their registration.
5. a. Diana was daydreaming during the lecture.
    b. Diana missed an important announcement.
6. a. Leon works sixty hours per week in his brother's landscaping business.
    b. Leon has little time to spend with his two children.
7. a. Jeff refused to even look at the dessert menu.
    b. Jeff's friend, Sam, ordered two desserts.
8. a. Harry cleaned the garage.
    b. At the same time, Rita washed and waxed the car.
9. a. We may have hot dogs and chili for dinner.
    b. We may order pizza from Dominick's.
10. a. The political candidate said she believed in lowering state taxes.
    b. Her voting record on lower state taxes was poor.

C Avoiding Sentence Errors

C.1 SENTENCE FRAGMENTS

■ A complete sentence contains at least one subject and one verb and expresses a complete thought. It begins with a capital letter and ends with a period. A **fragment** is an incomplete sentence because it lacks either a subject, verb, or both, or is a subordinate (dependent) clause unattached to a complete sentence and, therefore, does not express a complete thought. Avoid fragments in your writing; instead, use complete sentences.

FRAGMENT: Walked across campus this afternoon. [This group of words lacks a subject.]

COMPLETE SENTENCE: Pete walked across campus this afternoon.

FRAGMENT: The car next to the fence. [This group of words lacks a verb.]

COMPLETE SENTENCE: The car next to the fence was muddy.

FRAGMENT: Alert and ready. [This group of words lacks a subject and a verb.]

COMPLETE SENTENCE: Sam appeared alert and ready for his morning interview.

FRAGMENT: While I was waiting in line. [In this group of words the thought is incomplete.]

COMPLETE SENTENCE: While I was waiting in line, I studied the faces of people walking by.

How to Spot Fragments

To find sentence fragments in your writing, use the following questions to evaluate each group of words you have written.

1. **Does the group of words have a verb?** Be sure that the verb is a finite verb (see p. 425) and not a verbal or part of a verbal phrase (see p. 425). In the following examples, the verbal phrases (underlined) are fragments. The finite verbs (in bold) are part of complete sentences.

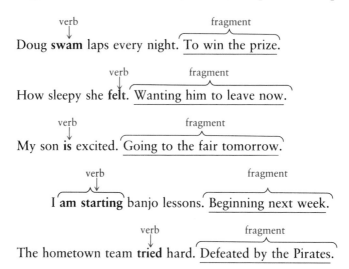

Each of the underlined phrases needs to be either (1) rewritten as a complete sentence or (2) combined with a complete sentence.

REWRITTEN: Doug swam laps every night. He practiced to win the prize.

REWRITTEN: How sleepy she felt. She wanted him to leave now.

COMBINED: My son is excited because he is going to the fair tomorrow.

COMBINED: Beginning next week, I am starting banjo lessons.

COMBINED: The hometown team tried hard, but they were defeated by the Pirates.

To distinguish between a finite verb (the main verb of the sentence) and a verbal phrase, keep in mind the following rule: A finite verb can change tense to show differences in time—past, present, and future. A verbal phrase cannot demonstrate these shifts in time. In the sentence *I have a lot of homework*, the verb *have* could change to *had* or *will have.* In the sentence *Mary enjoyed riding a horse,* the verbal phrase *riding a horse* cannot be changed to show differences in time.

2. **Does your group of words have a subject?** After you have found the verb, look for the subject. The subject is a noun or pronoun that performs the action of the sentence. To find the subject, ask *who* or *what* performs the action of the verb.

> subject   verb
>
> The corner bookstore opens at noon. [*What* opens? The bookstore opens.]

frag

Notice, however, what happens when you ask *who?* or *what?* about the following fragments.

> Will study math with a tutor. [*Who* will study? The question cannot be answered; no subject exists.]
>
> And walked away quickly. [*Who* walked away? Again, the question cannot be answered because there is no subject.]

Every sentence must have a subject. Even if one sentence has a clear subject, the sentence that follows it must also have a subject, or else it is a fragment.

> sentence   fragment
>
> Peter slammed the door. And stormed out into the hall.

You know from the first sentence that it was Peter who stormed out, but the second group of words is nonetheless a fragment because it lacks a subject. Combining it with the first sentence would solve the problem.

> COMBINED: Peter slammed the door and stormed out into the hall.

Imperative sentences (sentences that make a command or suggestion) have a subject that is understood, not explicitly stated. They are not fragments.

> Follow me. [The subject *you* is understood. **You** *follow me.*]

3. **Does the group of words begin with a subordinating conjunction (*after, because, as, that, however, although, since,* etc.)?** A subordinating conjunction used at the beginning of a group of words can create a fragment, unless that group of words (a subordinate clause) is attached

to an independent (main) clause. (See list of subordinating conjunctions on p. 453.)

subordinating
conjunction
↓
FRAGMENT: While I was waiting for the express train.

COMPLETE SENTENCE: I was waiting for the express train.

or

independent clause
COMPLETE SENTENCE: While I was waiting for the train, I saw Robert DeNiro.

subordinating
conjunction
↓
FRAGMENT: Although the politician campaigned feverishly.

COMPLETE SENTENCE: The politician campaigned feverishly.

or

COMPLETE SENTENCE: Although the politician campaigned feverishly,

independent clause
the public supported her opponent.

4. Does the group of words begin with a relative pronoun (*who, whoever, whom, whomever, that, what, which*)? Unless the group of words forms a question, exists as an independent clause, or is attached to an independent clause, it is a fragment.

relative
pronoun
↓
FRAGMENT: Who lost these keys.

COMPLETE SENTENCE: Who lost these keys?

or

COMPLETE SENTENCE: I am looking for the person who lost these keys.

relative
pronoun
↓
FRAGMENT: Which we discussed after class.

COMPLETE SENTENCE: This assignment is the one which we discussed after class.

A group of words beginning *how, what, when, where,* and *why* should also be carefully checked. If the clause beginning with one of these words neither asks a question nor is attached to an independent clause, then the clause is a fragment.

FRAGMENT: Where there is smoke.

COMPLETE SENTENCE: Where is there smoke?

or

COMPLETE SENTENCE: Where there is smoke, there is usually fire.

frag

How to Revise Fragments

1. Combine the fragment with a complete sentence or independent clause (see p. 451). Fragments below are underlined.

FRAGMENT: While my toddler was bathing. She began to eat the soap.

REVISED: While my toddler was bathing, she began to eat the soap.
[A comma here combines the subordinate clause with the independent clause.]

FRAGMENT: Students who missed five classes. They are ineligible for the final exam.

REVISED: Students who missed five classes are ineligible for the final exam.

FRAGMENT: Marge sketched portraits all morning. And read art history all afternoon.

REVISED: Marge sketched portraits all morning and read art history all afternoon.

2. Remove the subordinating conjunction or relative pronoun from a group of words that could stand alone as a separate sentence.

FRAGMENT: I did not finish the book. Because its tedious style bored me.

REVISED: I did not finish the book. Its tedious style bored me.

3. Add the missing verb or subject.

FRAGMENT: The baby knocked over her glass of milk. Spilled all over the table.

REVISED: The baby knocked over her glass. The milk spilled all over the table.

FRAGMENT: The Winter Olympics were held in France. <u>The speed skaters at the starting line.</u>

REVISED: The Winter Olympics were held in France. The speed skaters

verb added
↓

<u>approached</u> the starting line.

Exercise 10   Revise each sentence fragment into a complete sentence, either by combining it with a complete sentence, removing the subordinating conjunction or relative pronoun, or adding the missing subject or verb.

EXAMPLE: The forestry department received many letters about their logging plan. Which they sorted and counted.

REVISED: The forestry department received many letters about their logging plan, which they sorted and counted.

1. Maria slipped on an icy step. Hurrying to get home.
2. Wishing the class would end.
3. Students who are older with families.
4. Anthony knew the locks had been changed. But didn't tell anyone.
5. A strange old uncle, always telling weird stories about his childhood in Denmark.
6. The top drawer of my desk.
7. Farmworkers who live in poverty.
8. Even though we painted the room.
9. Because she took an accounting class on Tuesday night.
10. Mark forgot what time it was. Until the doorbell rang.

C.2 RUN-ON SENTENCES AND COMMA SPLICES

■ Independent clauses contain both a subject and a predicate. When joined in one sentence, independent clauses must be separated from each other by either proper punctuation or by a coordinating conjunction. When you do not properly indicate the break between independent clauses, your writing will contain errors called **run-on sentences** and **comma splices**.

A **run-on sentence** (or fused sentence) contains two independent clauses that are not separated by the correct punctuation or by a coordinating conjunction (*and, but, or, nor, for, so, yet*).

A **comma splice** (or comma fault) contains two independent clauses joined with only a comma (and no coordinating conjunction). A comma by itself cannot join two independent clauses.

Examine the following four ways comma splices and run-on sentences may be corrected (four ways, in other words, that related independent clauses may correctly be separated from each other):

1. **Place a period between the two clauses, making two complete sentences.**

   RUN-ON SENTENCE: The clouds had darkened the boats were still out.

   COMMA SPLICE: The clouds had darkened, the boats were still out.

   CORRECT: The clouds had darkened. The boats were still out.

2. **Place a semicolon between the two clauses.**

   CORRECT: The clouds had darkened; the boats were still out.

3. **Use a comma and a coordinating conjunction to join the clauses and show the relationship between them.**

   CORRECT: The clouds had darkened, but the boats were still out.

4. **Make one clause a dependent clause, and insert by adding a subordinating conjunction, and join it to the independent clause.**

   CORRECT: Although the clouds had darkened, the boats were still out.

How to Spot Run-ons and Comma Splices

1. **You can often spot run-ons by reading them aloud. Listen for a pause or a change in your voice when you move from the first clause to the second.** Read the following run-ons and see if you can hear where the two clauses should be separated.

   RUN-ON: We watched the football game then we ordered pizza.

   CORRECT: We watched the football game. Then we ordered pizza.

or

   CORRECT: After we watched the football game, we ordered pizza.

   RUN-ON: My car sounds terrible I hope the transmission does not need to be replaced.

   CORRECT: My car sounds terrible; I hope the transmission does not need to be replaced.

2. You can spot a comma splice by looking carefully at your usage and placement of commas. If there are independent clauses before and after a comma with no coordinating conjunction in between, then chances are you have spotted a comma splice.

COMMA SPLICE: Television is an important influence in America, most people spend at least ten to twenty hours a week watching it.

CORRECT: Television is an important influence in America; most people spend at least ten to twenty hours a week watching it.

How to Correct Run-ons and Comma Splices

There are four ways to correct a run-on sentence or a comma splice.

1. Create two separate sentences. End the first complete thought with a period. Begin the next with a capital letter.

RUN-ON: We went for a walk in the woods we saw the leaves turning red and orange.

CORRECT: We went for a walk in the woods. We saw the leaves turning red and orange.

2. Use a semicolon. A semicolon can be used to join two complete thoughts. Use a semicolon when two thoughts are closely related and you want to emphasize that relationship. The word immediately following the semicolon does not begin with a capital letter unless it is a proper noun.

RUN-ON: It is unlikely that school taxes will increase this year citizens have expressed their opposition.

CORRECT: It is unlikely that school taxes will increase this year; citizens have expressed their opposition.

Note: A clause containing a conjunctive adverb (for example, *finally, however, meanwhile, otherwise, therefore*) must be separated from another independent clause with a period or semicolon. The conjunctive adverb is set off in most cases with a comma or commas.

COMMA SPLICE: The road crew was repairing pot holes, therefore traffic was snarled.

CORRECT: The road crew was repairing pot holes; therefore, traffic was snarled.

3. **Insert a comma and a coordinating conjunction** (*and, or, but, for, nor, so, yet*).

RUN-ON: Americans are changing their eating habits they still eat too much red meat.

CORRECT: Americans are changing their eating habits, but they still eat too much red meat.

4. **Subordinate one clause to another.** This effective method allows you to show the relationship between ideas, especially when the idea expressed in one of the clauses is more important than the idea expressed in the other clause. By adding a subordinating conjunction (*after, although, because, until*), you can create a subordinate (dependent) clause that can then be linked to an independent clause.

A subordinating conjunction explains the relationship between the subordinate (dependent) clause and the independent clause (a complete thought) to which it is joined.

subordinate clause independent clause

Before I left the house, I shut off all the lights.

The word before indicates the time sequence in which the two actions were performed. In addition to time, subordinate conjunctions can indicate place, cause, condition, manner, result, comparison, or contrast.

MEANING	SUBORDINATING CONJUNCTION	EXAMPLE
place	where, wherever	I will go wherever you go.
time	after, before, when, until, during, once, while	After I left work, I went to the mall.
cause or effect	because, since, so that, that, as	I missed the bus because I overslept.
condition or circumstance	if, unless, as long as, in case, whenever, once, provided that	If I get an A on the paper, I'll be happy.
contrast	although, even though, even if, whereas, while	Even though I lost my job, I have to make my car payment.
manner	as, as if, as though	Marge acted as if she were angry.

The subordinate clause can be placed *before* or *after* the independent clause. If it is placed before the independent clause, put a comma at the end of the subordinate clause. No comma is needed when the independent clause comes first.

COMMA SPLICE: I studied psychology, I was thinking about some of Freud's findings.

REVISED: When I studied psychology, I was thinking about some of Freud's findings.

REVISED: I was thinking about some of Freud's findings when I studied psychology.

You may add a dependent clause to a sentence that has more than one independent clause.

RUN-ON: We toured the hospital we met with its chief administrator she invited us to lunch.

REVISED: After we toured the hospital, we met with its chief administrator, and she invited us to lunch.

Exercise 11   Identify run-ons and comma splices in the sentences below. Revise or rewrite to eliminate these errors.

EXAMPLE: The cashier at the convenience store had worked in the neighborhood for many years he knew everyone. [A run-on sentence.]

REVISED: The cashier at the convenience store had worked in the neighborhood for many years. He knew everyone.

1. My sister's newborn baby is learning to smile and reach for objects, I enjoy taking care of him.

2. Although her favorite pastime is skiing, Suzanne goes skiing only once or twice a year when she visits her parents at the cabin they own in the mountains.

3. My friends agree that the laundromat is a great place to meet people, everyone has to do laundry, and there is always someone there.

4. Jerry's new sweater shrunk the first time he washed it he returned it to the store.

5. When I broke my leg I knew the doctor who treated me in the emergency room, he is one of my sister's professors in medical school, and she talks about how brilliant he is all the time.

6. Joselyn loves her new answering machine because she doesn't have to worry about missing important phone calls.

7. When Steve moved out of the dorm, he bought a lot of new furniture, he bought a couch, a kitchen table and chairs, a bed, an armchair, and a dresser.

8. Because he was behind on his car payments, Jose sold his collection of baseball cards.

9. Our team lost the game, the quarterback was throwing terribly, and the receivers kept dropping the ball.

10. It was so hot yesterday that everyone had all their car windows rolled down, offices had the air conditioning running on high.

C.3 FORMS OF THE VERB (THE PRINCIPAL PARTS OF THE VERB)

■   The four basic forms of a verb are the **infinitive** (for example, *jump*), the **present participle** (is *jumping*), the **past** (*jumped*), and the **past participle** (has *jumped*). These forms are called the principal parts of the verb (see p. 420). By using these forms alone or with helping verbs, you can communicate a verb's **tense**. Tense indicates when an action or sequence of actions occurred, relative to the time of writing. It is important to use the correct forms of verbs when you write, and to avoid unnecessary shifts in verb tense that may confuse your reader.

vf

There are two kinds of verbs: regular and irregular. Regular verbs all construct their past and past participles by adding *-ed* or *-d* to the infinitive: *wash* in the infinitive becomes *washed* in the past and past participle forms. Irregular verbs do not follow this pattern for the formation of their past tense and past participle. For example, the past tense of *drive* is *drove*, not *drived*. (See p. 421 for a list of the principal parts of some common irregular verbs.)

If you are unsure of whether a verb is regular or not, check your dictionary. Following the pronunciation of the verb in the infinitive form, your dictionary lists forms of irregular verbs. For example, after the irregular verb *drive*, the dictionary says, "*drove, driven, driving, drives.*" If the dictionary lists no verb forms after the infinitive, you can assume that the verb is a regular one that forms its past tense and past participle forms by adding *-ed* or *-d*.

Writing all the forms of a verb for all the tenses is called conjugating a verb. A conjugation shows the verb forms for singular and plural subjects and for the first, second, and third person pronouns.

C.4 VERB TENSES

■ The three most common tenses are present, past, and future.

TENSE	*TIME*	*EXAMPLE*
present	at time of writing	You <u>work</u>.
past	has already occurred	You <u>worked</u>.
future	will occur in future	You <u>will work</u>.

In addition, each of these three tenses has **perfect tense** forms (**present perfect, past perfect,** and **future perfect**) that indicate completed action, and **progressive tense** forms (**present progressive, past progressive,** and **future progressive**) that indicate continuing action.

PRESENT PERFECT: They have recognized their rights.

PAST PERFECT: They had recognized their rights.

FUTURE PERFECT: They will have recognized their rights.

PRESENT PROGRESSIVE: She has been considering the job offer.

PAST PROGRESSIVE: She had been considering the job offer.

FUTURE PROGRESSIVE: She will have been considering the job offer.

Writing all the forms of a verb for all the tenses is called conjugating a verb. A conjugation shows the verb forms for singular and plural subjects and for the first, second, and third person pronouns.

Conjugation of the Regular Verb Walk

	SINGULAR	*PLURAL*
Present Tense	I walk	we walk
	you walk	you walk
	he/she/it walks	they walk
Past Tense	I walked	we walked
	you walked	you walked
	he/she/it walked	they walked
Future Tense	I will (shall) walk	we will (shall) walk
	you will walk	you will walk
	he/she/it will walk	they will walk
Present Perfect Tense	I have walked	we have walked
	you have walked	you have walked
	he/she/it has walked	they have walked

	SINGULAR	*PLURAL*
Past Perfect Tense	I had walked	we had walked
	you had walked	you had walked
	he/she/it has walked	they had walked
Future Perfect Tense	I will (shall) have walked	we will (shall) have walked
	you will have walked	you will have walked
	he/she/it will have walked	they will have walked
Present Progressive Tense	I am walking	we are walking
	you are walking	you are walking
	he/she/it is walking	they are walking
Past Progressive Tense	I was walking	we were walking
	you were walking	you were walking
	he/she/it was walking	they were walking
Future Progressive Tense	I will be walking	we will be walking
	you will be walking	you will be walking
	he/she/it will be walking	they will be walking
Present Perfect Progressive Tense	I have been walking	we have been walking
	you have been walking	you have been walking
	he/she/it has been walking	they have been walking
Past Perfect Progressive Tense	I had been walking	we had been walking
	you had been walking	you had been walking
	he/she/it had been walking	they had been walking
Future Perfect Progressive Tense	I will have been walking	we will have been walking
	you will have been walking	you will have been walking
	he/she/it will have been walking	they will have been walking

vt

Emphatic Forms, Modals, and Use of the Infinitive

The **emphatic forms** of a verb (formed by using the present or past tense of the verb *do* with the infinitive) add emphasis to the present and past tenses.

> PRESENT EMPHATIC: Malcolm <u>does</u> have the same birthday as his father.
>
> PAST EMPHATIC: Judy <u>did</u> complete her residency program while caring for her newborn daughter.

Modals are helping verbs used with main verbs to add emphasis and nuances of meaning. The most common modals are *can, could, do, did, may, might, must, shall, will,* and *would.*

> <u>Could</u> we have another ticket?
>
> <u>May</u> we have a front row seat?

The **infinitive** (*to* plus the present tense of a verb) describes an action occurring at the same time as the action of the main verb.

> I asked <u>to go</u> along for the ride.
>
> She hoped <u>to avoid</u> a scene.

Common Mistakes with Verb Tense

There are a few common mistakes often made with verb tenses. Try to avoid:

1. omitting *-d* or *-ed* or *-s* or *-es* endings
   INCORRECT: I walk a mile yesterday.

   CORRECT: I walk<u>ed</u> a mile yesterday.

2. misusing irregular verbs
   INCORRECT: I will lay down for a nap.
   CORRECT: I will <u>lie</u> down for a nap.

3. omitting helping verbs
   INCORRECT: I go to class tomorrow.
   CORRECT: I <u>will</u> go to class tomorrow.

4. using dialect (casual, everyday language) forms of *be, have,* and *do.*
   INCORRECT: The train be gone.
   CORRECT: The train <u>has</u> gone.

A brief review of the correct present and past tense of these common irregular verbs follows.

Have

PRESENT	PAST
I have	I had
You have	You had
He, she, it has	They had

Be

PRESENT	PAST
I am	I was
You are	You were
He, she, it is	They were

Do

PRESENT	PAST
I do	I did
You do	You did
He, she, it does	They did

Also try to avoid

1. failing to make your subject and verb agree (see p. 475)
2. inconsistent or shifting tenses (see p. 495). In general, when you write, keep your verbs in the same tense, unless you need to show a sequence of events in time. If you need to shift from one time period to another, follow these rules.

   a. If two actions occurred at different times in the past, but close in time, use the past tense. Otherwise use the past perfect for the earlier and the past for the later event.

earlier occurrence:
past perfect

later occurrence:
past tense

Dickens had become famous in America before he visited there.

   b. If two actions occur in the present but one began in the past, use the present perfect tense for the earlier action and the present tense for the later one.

earlier occurrence:
present perfect

later occurrence:
present

Because Debbi has been editing the ASPCA newsletter, she knows many veterinarians.

c. Similarly, if two actions occur in the future, use the future perfect tense for the action that will take place earlier and the future tense for the action that will occur later.

earlier occurrence: later occurrence:
future perfect   future
↓   ↓
After the campaign we will have been running, we will know how to organize local support.

Exercise 12   Identify and correct sentences that contain an error in verb form or verb tense. Some sentences are correct.

EXAMPLE: Pat builded a porch on the summer house.

CORRECT: Pat built a porch on the summer house.

1. This summer, my brother take me to Las Vegas.
2. The lecture hall is so big that the professor seems to be just a tiny dot at the front of it.
3. Jonathan is suppose to meet Kathy at the library, and if he doesn't hurry, he would be late.
4. Barb has a fifty dollar phone bill last month.
5. After the concert, Madelaine remember she had a paper due the next day.
6. I park my car somewhere in this parking lot, and now, although I looked everywhere, I cannot find it.
7. The instructor had showed a film about the life of Martin Luther King.
8. Soon it will be January, and New Year Resolutions will began to appear.
9. Moths destroyed my wool jacket, even though I keep it all summer in a tightly sealed box.
10. Brad takes his daughter to the circus, but she was afraid of the clowns.

**act
pass**

C.5 ACTIVE AND PASSIVE VOICE

■ When a verb is in the active voice, the subject performs the action of the verb. The direct object receives the action. The active voice expresses points in a lively, vivid, energetic way.

subject   verb   direct object
↓   ↓   ↓
ACTIVE VOICE: Sam dropped his calculator.

When a verb is in the passive voice, the subject receives the action of the verb. The passive voice tends to express points in an evasive, dull way.

$$\text{subject} \quad \text{verb} \quad \text{object of preposition}$$

PASSIVE VOICE: The calculator was dropped by Sam.

Notice that the form of the verb changed as the above sentence was changed from active to passive voice. The verb changed from the past to the past participle. Here are a few more examples.

ACTIVE: I did not take down the Halloween decorations until Christmas.

PASSIVE: The Halloween decorations were not taken down until Christmas.

ACTIVE: The supermarket gave samples of prepared foods.

PASSIVE: Samples of prepared food were given by the supermarket.

Both active and passive sentence arrangements *are* grammatically correct. However, active voice is usually more effective because it is simpler and more direct. As a general rule, use the active rather than the passive voice unless

1. It is unknown who performs the action of the verb.

    PASSIVE: The handle of the dagger had been wiped clean of fingerprints.

2. The object of the action is more important than who performs the action.

    PASSIVE: The poem "The Chicago Defender Sends a Man to Little Rock" by Gwendolyn Brooks was discussed in class. [Here, exactly who discussed the poem is less important than the title of the poem.]

**act
pass**

Exercise 13   Revise each of the following sentences by changing them from passive voice into active voice.

EXAMPLE: The china dolls were handled carefully by Julia and her friends.

REVISED: Julia and her friends carefully handled the china dolls.

1. The speech to the Hispanic Students Association was given by Rosa.

2. The plane was brought in for a safe landing by the pilot.
3. The submarine sandwich was purchased by Ricardo for lunch.
4. Lou got a feeling of assurance from the exam grade.
5. Our campus will be visited by Jay Leno.
6. Carlos was praised by Professor Black for the excellent paper he wrote on the history of the bayonet.
7. Joshua's pant leg was clawed by my cat.
8. Michelle was stopped by a police officer for going through a red light.
9. Peaches are bought by pie makers and fruit canners.
10. My grandfather's extensive coin collection was given to me when I turned twenty-five.

C.6 SUBJUNCTIVE MOOD

■ Verbs change forms to express mood, as well as as to express tense and voice. The mood of the verb conveys the writer's attitude toward the expressed thought. There are three moods in the English language: the **indicative mood** (used to make ordinary statements of fact and to ask questions); the **imperative mood** (used to give commands or make suggestions); and the **subjunctive mood** (used to express something that is not true or that you doubt will ever be true, and to make wishes, recommendations, speculations, and hypotheses).

INDICATIVE: Laurel lies in the sun every afternoon.

IMPERATIVE: Lie down and rest!

SUBJUNCTIVE: It is urgent that she lie down and rest.

The **subjunctive** mood requires some special attention because it uses unusual verb forms. Verbs can be in the subjunctive mood in both the present and the past tense.

PRESENT SUBJUNCTIVE: If the whole story be told, Jacob is luckier than he knows.

PAST SUBJUNCTIVE: If the whole story were told, Jacob would have been luckier than he knew.

The verb *be* is the one most commonly used in the subjunctive mood. The following chart presents present and past forms of this irregular verb. The word *if* appears in parentheses to remind you that the subjunctive is used to propose wishful or doubting thoughts.

present

(if) I be	(if) we be
(if) you be	(if) you be
(if) he be	(if) they be

past

(if) I were	(if) we were
(if) you were	(if) you were
(if) he were	(if) they were

Here are several rules for using the subjunctive correctly:

1. With the verb *be*, use *be* for the present subjunctive no matter what the subject.

Mr. Kenefick requires that his students be drilled daily in safety procedures.

2. With the verb *be*, use *were* for the past subjunctive no matter what the subject.

If Andrew were older than five, we would be angry that he had broken the clock.

3. With verbs other than *be*, form the present subjunctive by using the infinitive form, no matter what the subject.

I ask that my son wash his hands before dinner.

4. With verbs other than *be*, form the past subjunctive by using *had* as a helping verb with the past participle of the main verb.

If I had known her, I would have said hello.

If the cadets had seen the President, they would have saluted.

5. To express something you know is contrary to fact, use the subjunctive mood in clauses that begin with *if, as if, that*, and *as though*.

If I were you, I would take my umbrella.

We wished that lunch hour were not over.

sv agree

C.7 SUBJECT-VERB AGREEMENT

■ A subject and its verb must agree (be consistent) in number.

Agreement Rules

1. A **singular subject** (one person, place, thing, or idea) must be used with a singular form of the verb.

SINGULAR SUBJECT	VERB
I	dance
you	dance
he she it	dances
Sally	dances
a boy	dances

2. A **plural subject** (more than one person, place, thing, or idea) must be used with a plural form of the verb.

PLURAL SUBJECT	VERB
we	dance
you	dance
they	dance
Sally and James	dance
boys	dance

Note: In general, an *-s* or *-es* ending makes a noun plural (*boy* becomes *boys*), while the same ending makes a verb in the present tense singular (*A boy dances* becomes *Boys dance*).

Common Errors

In the example sentences below, the subjects are underlined and the verbs are in boldface.

1. **Third person plural.** It is incorrect in Standard English to omit the *-s* or *-es* in a singular verb, when used with he, she, or it, or when used with a noun that could be replaced with he, she, or it.

INCORRECT: She **dance** like a professional.

CORRECT: She **dances** like a professional.

INCORRECT: Professor Simmons **pace** while he lectures.

CORRECT: Professor Simmons **paces** while he lectures.

2. **Compound Subjects (two or more subjects).** A compound subject containing the word *and* requires a plural verb, even though one or both of the subjects are singular.

INCORRECT: Anita and Mark **plays** cards.

CORRECT: <u>Anita and Mark</u> **play** cards.

When both of the subjects refer to the same person or thing, however, use a singular verb.

INCORRECT: <u>Research and Development</u> **are** a fast-growing division of my company.

CORRECT: <u>Research and Development</u> **is** a fast-growing division of my company.

When your compound subject contains the conjunctions *or, nor, either . . . or, neither . . . nor, not . . . but, not only . . . but also,* your verb should agree with the subject nearest to it.

<u>Neither book nor the magazine articles</u> on Edith Wharton **were** helpful to my research.

3. **Verbs Before Subjects.** When a verb comes before a subject, as in sentences beginning with *here* and *there*, it is easy to make an agreement error. *Here* and *there* are never subjects of a sentence and do not determine how you choose the correct form of the verb. Instead, locate the subject and, depending on its number, choose a singular or plural verb.

singular singular
verb   subject
↓   ↓
There **is** a <u>bone</u> in my soup.

plural   plural
verb   subject
↓   ↓
There **are** two <u>bones</u> in my soup.

4. **Words Between Subject and Verb.** Words, phrases, and clauses coming between the subject and verb do not change the fact that the subject must agree with the verb. To check that the form is correct, mentally cancel everything in between the subject and the verb. Make sure your verb agrees in number with the subject of the sentence, not an intervening word.

singular subject   singular verb
↓   ↓
A <u>list</u> of degree requirements **is** printed in the college catalog.

plural subject   plural verb
↓   ↓
<u>Expenses</u> surrounding the sale of the house **were** unexpectedly low.

sv agree

singular subject
↓

The l̲a̲m̲p̲, together with some plates, glasses, and china tea cups,

singular verb
↓

was b̲roken during the move.

5. **Indefinite Pronouns as Subjects.** Indefinite pronouns (words like *everyone, neither, anybody, nobody, one, something*, and *each*) are words that do not refer to a specific person or thing. Many indefinite pronouns take a singular verb.

E̲v̲e̲r̲y̲o̲n̲e̲ **likes** my father.

N̲e̲i̲t̲h̲e̲r̲ apple **smells** rotten.

Some indefinite pronouns, such as *both, many, others, several*, and *few*, always take a plural verb. Some indefinite pronouns, such as *all, any, none, part, half*, and *some*, may take either a singular or plural verb. Treat the indefinite pronoun as singular if it refers to something that cannot be counted and as plural if it refers to more than one of something that can be counted.

S̲o̲m̲e̲ of the ice **is** still on the road.

S̲o̲m̲e̲ of the ice cubes **are** still in the tray.

H̲a̲l̲f̲ of the spaghetti **tastes** overcooked.

H̲a̲l̲f̲ of the spaghetti dishes **taste** too spicy.

6. **Collective nouns.** A collective noun is a word that refers to a group of people or things (*audience, class, flock, jury, team, family*). When the noun refers to the group as one unit, use a singular verb.

The h̲e̲r̲d̲ **stampedes** towards us.

When the noun is used to mean the group members as separate individuals, use a plural verb.

The h̲e̲r̲d̲ **scatter** in all directions.

7. **Nouns with Plural Forms but Singular Meaning.** Some words appear plural (that is, they end in *-s* or *-es*), but they often have a singular meaning. *Measles, hysterics, news*, and *mathematics* are examples. Use a singular verb with them.

M̲a̲t̲h̲e̲m̲a̲t̲i̲c̲s̲ **is** a required course.

Note: Other nouns look plural, have singular meanings, but take a plural verb: *braces, glasses, trousers, slacks, jeans, jodhpurs*, and

sv agree

pajamas. Even though, when used in the singular, they refer to a single thing (to one pair of jeans, for example), these words take a plural verb.

His pajamas **were covered** with pictures of tumbling dice.

8. Relative Pronouns in Adjective Clauses. The relative pronouns *who, which,* and *that* sometimes function as the subject of an adjective clause (see p. 452). When the relative pronoun refers to a singular noun, use a singular verb. When the pronoun refers to a plural noun, use a plural verb.

Anita is a person who never **forgets** faces. [Who refers to "person," which is singular, so who here takes a singular verb: **forgets**.

Exercise 14 Circle the verb that correctly completes each sentence.

EXAMPLE: Dr. Martin is a professor who never (remember, (remembers)) to take attendance.

1. Molly and Michael (sit, sits) next to each other in human anatomy class.
2. Peanut butter and jelly (is, are) my favorite sandwich.
3. Physics (is, are) an interesting course.
4. The class (deserve, deserves) a day off for working so hard.
5. Students (is, are) not suspected of committing yesterday's theft.
6. The eight person committee (make, makes) all the important decisions for the club.
7. There (are, is) two reasons why I dropped the course.
8. The lawns in this neighborhood (look, looks) like golf courses.
9. Professor Harris should listen closely to the students who (is, are) in her class.
10. Neither of the biscuits (is, are) made with buttermilk.

C.8 PRONOUN-ANTECEDENT AGREEMENT

■ A pronoun must agree with the word it refers to or replaces (its antecedent) in person (first, second, or third) and in number (singular or plural), and gender (masculine, feminine, or neuter). This rule applies to all pronouns: personal, indefinite, relative, reflexive, or intensive. (See pp. 413–417.)

Ronald attended the party, but I did not have a chance to talk with **him**. [Ronald, a third person, masculine, singular noun, is the antecedent of him, a third person, masculine, singular pronoun.]

pa agree

We had planned to call **our** sister, but **her** line was busy. [We is the antecedent of our; sister is the antecedent of her.]

I took my rolls of film to the developer and asked him to print them on glossy stock. [I is the antecedent of my; developer is the antecedent of him; rolls is the antecedent of them.]

Rules to Follow

1. Use a singular pronoun to refer to or replace a singular noun. (A singular noun names one person, place, or thing.)

Juanita washed her car.

2. Use a plural pronoun to refer to or replace a plural noun. (A plural noun names more than one person, place, or thing.)

The shirts are hung on their hangers.

3. (a) Many indefinite pronouns are singular in meaning. Use singular pronouns to refer to these indefinite pronouns:

anybody	everybody	nobody	someone
anyone	everyone	one	something
anything	everything	nothing	
each	much	other	
either	neither	somebody	

singular | singular
antecedent | pronoun

Someone left her handbag under this table.

singular antecedent   singular pronouns

Everyone in the office must do his or her own photocopying.

Note: To avoid the awkwardness of *his or her*, consider rephrasing your sentence with a plural antecedent and plural pronoun.

plural antecedent   plural pronoun

Office workers must do their own photocopying.

3. (b) Some indefinite pronouns, such as *both, few, several, others*, and *many* are plural in meaning. To refer to one of them, use a plural pronoun.

Both of the journalists said that, as far as they could tell, no violations of the cease-fire had occurred.

3. (c) **Some indefinite pronouns, such as *all, most, some,* or *any,* can be singular or plural, depending on how they are used. If the indefinite pronoun refers to something that cannot be counted, use a singular pronoun to refer to it. If the indefinite pronoun refers to something that can be counted, use a plural pronoun to refer to it.**

Most voters feel they can make a difference.

Most air on airplanes is recycled repeatedly, so it becomes stale.

4. **Antecedents joined by *and* require a plural pronoun, unless both nouns refer to the same person, place, or thing.**

<pre>
      plural antecedent   plural pronoun
     ⌒‿‿‿‿‿‿‿⌒   ↓
My girlfriend and I planned our wedding.
</pre>

<pre>
          singular antecedent   singular pronoun
     ⌒‿‿‿‿‿‿‿‿‿‿‿⌒   ↓
My neighbor and best friend Joy started her book bindery at the local
warehouse.
</pre>

5. **When antecedents are joined by *or, nor, either/or, neither/nor, not/but,* or *not only/but also,* the pronoun agrees in number with the nearer antecedent. To apply this rule can result in changes in your sentence's meaning, however. Reword if necessary to convey the point you intend.**

Neither his brothers nor Sam have made his plane reservations. [This
sentence suggests that Sam will be traveling alone.]

Neither Sam nor his brothers have made their plane reservations. [This
sentence suggests that Sam will be traveling with his brothers.]

Note: Two or more singular antecedents joined by *or* or *nor* require a
singular pronoun.

Neither Larry nor Richard replaced his broken CD player.

Margaret or Anita will bring her saxophone.

6. **Collective nouns are words that refer to a specific group (*army, class, family*). When the group acts as a unit, use a singular pronoun to refer to it. When each member of the group acts individually, use a plural pronoun to refer to them.**

The band marched its most intricate formation.

The band found their seats in the bleachers, but could not see the game
because the sun was in their eyes.

**pa
agree**

Exercise 15   Revise sentences that contain agreement errors. Some sentences do not contain errors.

> EXAMPLE: Either of the payment plans has their advantages and disadvantages.

> REVISED: Either of the payment plans has <u>its</u> advantages and disadvantages.

1. The legislature reached their decision about the bill.
2. Neither the oak trees nor the maple tree in our yard has dropped their leaves yet.
3. Each gas station in town has raised their prices in the past week.
4. Jane and Lena want to take Professor Shrub's Shakespeare class because she was told it is a terrific class.
5. No one handed in his or her assignment late.
6. Professional athletes must devote their lives to their sport.
7. The jury decided to have lunch at restaurants of their own choice.
8. Either the neighbors or their guest, Sam Mallery, raised their voice so that we could hear it across the street.
9. Tom and Steven went to the store to pick up the baseball gloves he needed for Sunday's game.
10. When senior citizens go to the movie theater he can get a senior citizen discount.

C.9 PRONOUN REFERENCE

■ A pronoun refers to or replaces a noun or nouns previously mentioned, called the pronoun's antecedent. As you write, you must always make sure that a reader knows to which noun or nouns a pronoun refers. The antecedent of each pronoun must be clear.

> UNCLEAR: Lois accompanied Pam because <u>she</u> did not know the route. [Who did not know the route? The antecedent of <u>she</u> is unclear.]

> CORRECT: Lois did not know the route, so she walked with Pam.

pr

How to Use Pronouns Correctly

1. A pronoun may refer to two or more nouns in a compound antecedent.

<u>Mark and Dennis</u> combined <u>their</u> efforts to fix the leaky faucet.

2. **Avoid using a pronoun that could refer to more than one possible antecedent.**

UNCLEAR: Rick told Garry that he was right.

CORRECT: Rick told Garry, "You are right."

3. **Avoid using vague pronouns like *they* and *it* that often have no clear antecedent.**

INCORRECT: It says in the paper that K-Mart is expanding the Williamsville store.

CORRECT: The article in the paper says that K-Mart is expanding the Williamsville store.

INCORRECT: They told me that we were required to wear surgeons' masks to view the newborns.

CORRECT: The obstetrics nurse told me that we were required to wear surgeons' masks to view the newborns.

INCORRECT: On the bulletin board it says that there is a fire drill today.

CORRECT: The notice on the bulletin board says that there is a fire drill today.

4. **Avoid unnecessary or repetitious pronouns.**

INCORRECT: My sister she said that she lost her diamond ring.

CORRECT: My sister said that she lost her diamond ring.

5. **Be sure to use the relative pronouns *who*, *whom*, *which*, and *that* with the appropriate antecedent.**

Who and *whom* refer to persons or named animals. As relative pronouns, *who* and *whom* introduce subordinate clauses. Use *who* or *whoever* when the relative pronoun is functioning as the subject of a subordinate clause. Use *whom* or *whomever* when the relative pronoun is functioning as the object in a main clause. (See p. 487.)

Mary Anne became the team member who scored the most points this year.

Dublin, who is a golden retriever, barked at everyone.

That refers to animals, things, and anonymous people. *That* introduces an **essential clause,** an adjective clause that is necessary to identify a noun or pronoun.

The ring that my sister gave me has three opals.

The majority of the teen-agers that were surveyed did not listen to the classical music station.

pr

Which refers to both animals and things. *Which* introduces a **nonessential clause**, an adjective clause that is not necessary to identify a noun or pronoun. Nonessential clauses are set off from the rest of the sentence with commas.

Highway 33, which has ten hairpin turns, is difficult to drive.

6. **Use *one* if you are not referring specifically to the reader.** Use the second person pronoun *you* only to refer to the reader. In academic writing, avoid using *you*.

INCORRECT: Last year, you had to watch the news every night to keep up with world events.

CORRECT: Last year, one had to watch the news every night to keep up with world events.

7. **Place the pronoun close to its antecedent so the relationship is clear.**

INCORRECT: Margaux found a shell on the beach that her sister wanted.

CORRECT: On the beach Margaux found a shell that her sister wanted.

Exercise 16   Revise each of the sentences to correct problems in pronoun reference.

EXAMPLE: It says in the college catalog that one math course is required for a degree in Liberal Arts.

REVISED: The college catalog states that one math course is required for a degree in Liberal Arts.

1. Anthony is the man that called about mice in his apartment.
2. It shows in the dictionary that the word "run" has 110 meanings.
3. The doctor she noticed a mole that needed to be removed.
4. In the Middle Ages in England, you had to pay a tax to the church, called a tithe.
5. On soap operas they make life seem much more complicated than it really is.
6. Margaret chose a dress in a store that was expensive.
7. Although the sun was not shining yesterday, it was quite warm.
8. When Larry set the plate on the table it broke.
9. Dr. Harris is a well-known scholar which is an expert on Middle Eastern politics.

pr

10. In Mark Twain's *Huckleberry Finn*, he spends a lot of time describing the Mississippi River.

C.10 PRONOUN CASE

■ A pronoun's form, or **case**, changes depending on its grammatical function in a sentence. Pronouns may be in the **nominative case**, the **objective case**, or the **possessive case**.

Here is a chart showing the cases of pronouns:

PERSONAL PRONOUNS

Singular	*Nominative*	*Objective*	*Possessive*
First person	I	me	my, mine
Second person	you	you	your, yours
Third person	he, she, it	him, her, it	his, her, hers, its

Plural	*Nominative*	*Objective*	*Possessive*
First person	we	us	our, ours
Second person	you	you	your, yours
Third person	they	them	their, theirs

RELATIVE OR INTERROGATIVE PRONOUNS

Number	*Nominative*	*Objective*	*Possessive*
Singular	who	whom	whose
Plural	who	whom	whose

Pronouns in the Nominative Case

Use the nominative case (also known as the subjective case) when the pronoun functions as a subject of the sentence (see p. 414) or as a predicate nominative (see p. 443). A predicate nominative is a noun or pronoun that follows a linking verb and identifies or re-names the subject of the sentence.

subject

She has won recognition as a landscape architect.

predicate nominative

Cathie volunteers at the local hospital. A great volunteer is she.

pc

Note: The nominative case is also used when the pronoun functions as an appositive to a subject or predicate nominative (see p. 442).

Pronouns in the Objective Case

Use the objective case when a pronoun functions as a direct object or an indirect object. (See pp. 441–442.)

direct object

George helped her with the assignment.

indirect object

George gave her a book.

Note: The objective case is also used when the pronoun functions as an objective complement, the object of a preposition, the subject of an infinitive clause, an appositive to a direct or indirect object, or an appositive to an object of a preposition.

When a sentence has a compound subject or compound objects of a preposition, the correct pronoun case may be difficult to determine. To determine how the pronoun functions, and hence whether to use the nominative or objective case, mentally recast the sentence without the conjunction and other noun or pronoun in the compound construction. Determine how the pronoun functions by itself, then decide which case is correct.

subjective case

Mary Jo and they brought the beverages. [Think, "They brought the beverages." They is the subject of the sentence, so the subjective case is correct.]

objective case

Behind you and me, the drapery rustled. [Think, "Behind me . . ." Me is the object of the preposition behind, so the objective case is correct.]

Pronouns in the Possessive Case

Possessive pronouns indicate to whom or to what something belongs. They are not used with apostrophes. Some possessive pronouns (*mine, yours, his, hers, its, ours,* and *theirs*) function just as nouns do.

subject

Hers is the hat with the long green feather.

direct object
↓
I liked <u>hers</u> the best.

Other possessive pronouns (*my, your, his, her, its, our,* and *their*), sometimes known as **pronominal adjectives**, are used to modify nouns and gerunds.

<u>Our</u> high school reunion surprised everyone by <u>its</u> size.

<u>Your</u> attending that reunion will depend on <u>your</u> travel schedule.

Who and *Whom* as Interrogative Pronouns

Interrogative pronouns introduce questions. When *who, whoever, whom, whomever,* and *whose* introduce questions, they are interrogative pronouns. As such, their form or **case** changes depending on how the pronoun is used in its sentence or clause. How an interrogative pronoun is used in its own clause determines its case. Use *who* and *whoever* (the nominative case) when the interrogative pronoun functions as a subject or predicate nominative. Use *whom* and *whomever* (the objective case) when the interrogative pronoun functions as an object of a verb or an object of a preposition.

Nominative Case

pronoun as subject
↓
<u>Who</u> is there?

Objective Case

pronoun as
object of preposition
↓
To <u>whom</u> did you give the letter?

Who and *Whom* as Relative Pronouns

When *who, whoever, whom,* and *whomever* introduce subordinate clauses, they are relative pronouns. How a relative pronoun is used in its own clause determines its case. Use *who* or *whoever* when a relative pronoun functions as the subject of the subordinate clause. Use *whom* or *whomever* when a relative pronoun functions as the object within the subordinate clause.

Nominative Case

The lecturer, <u>who</u> is a journalist from New York, speaks with great insight and wit. [<u>Who</u> is the subject of the clause in which it appears.]

pc

Objective Case

The journalist, <u>whom</u> I know from college days, came to give a lecture. [<u>Whom</u> is the direct object of the clause in which it appears.]

C.11 CORRECT ADJECTIVE AND ADVERB USE

■ Adjectives and adverbs modify, describe, explain, qualify, or restrict words to which they relate. (See pp. 426 and 429.) **Adjectives** modify nouns and pronouns; adverbs modify verbs, adjectives, and other adverbs; and adverbs can also modify phrases, clauses, or whole sentences.

	MODIFY	*EXAMPLE*
ADJECTIVES:	nouns	*red* car
	pronouns	*nearly* everyone
ADVERBS:	verbs	*quickly* finish
	adjectives	*only* four reasons
	adverbs	*very* angrily

Positive and Comparative Adjectives and Adverbs

Positive adjectives and positive adverbs modify but do not involve any comparison: *green, bright, lively.* Comparative adjectives and comparative adverbs compare two persons, things, actions, or ideas.

COMPARATIVE ADJECTIVE: Michael is <u>taller</u> than Bob.

COMPARATIVE ADVERB: Sam reacted <u>more</u> calmly than Bob.

Here is how to form comparative adjectives and adverbs.

1. **If the word has one syllable, add -*er*.**

   fast ⟶ faster
   slow ⟶ slower

2. **For words of two or more syllables, place the word *more* in front of the word.**

reasonable	more reasonable
interesting	more interesting
important	more important

3. **For two-syllable adjectives ending in -*y*, change the -*y* to -*i* and add -*er*.**

drowsy   drowsier

lazy   lazier

Superlative Adjectives and Adverbs

Superlative adjectives and adverbs compare more than two persons, things, actions, or ideas.

SUPERLATIVE ADJECTIVE: Michael is the <u>tallest</u> member of the team.

SUPERLATIVE ADJECTIVE: Mark was selected as the team's <u>most valuable</u> player.

Here is how to form superlative adjectives and adverbs.

1. **Add -*est* to one-syllable adjectives and adverbs.**

slow   slowest

fast   fastest

2. **For words of two or more syllables, place the word *most* in front of the word.**

reasonable   most reasonable

interesting   most interesting

3. **For two syllable adjectives ending in -*y*, change the -*y* to -*i* and add -*est*.**

drowsy   drowsiest

lazy   laziest

Irregular Adjectives and Adverbs

A quick review follows the comparative and superlative forms of some troublesome irregular adjective and adverbs. (See also p. 431.)

POSITIVE	*COMPARATIVE*	*SUPERLATIVE*
little	less, littler	least, littlest
good	better	best
bad	worse	worst
many } some } much }	more	most

**adj
adv**

Common Mistakes to Avoid

1. **Adjectives can modify only nouns and pronouns.** Do not use them to modify verbs, other adjectives, or adverbs.

> INCORRECT: Peter and Mary take each other serious.
>
> CORRECT: Peter and Mary take each other seriously.

2. **Writers often use the words *good* and *bad* (adjectives) when they should use *well* and *badly* (adverbs).**

> INCORRECT: Juan did good on the exam.
>
> CORRECT: Juan did well on the exam.

3. **Writers often use the words *real* and *sure* (adjectives) when they should use *really* and *surely*.**

> INCORRECT: Jan scored real well on the exam.
>
> CORRECT: Jan scored really well on the exam.
>
> INCORRECT: I sure was surprised to win the lottery.
>
> CORRECT: I surely was surprised to win the lottery.

4. **Writers should avoid double negatives, or two negatives in the same clause.** The negatives cancel each other out in the reader's mind and cause confusion.

> INCORRECT: The steak cannot scarcely be more rare.
>
> CORRECT: The steak can scarcely be more rare.

5. **When using the comparative and superlative forms of adverbs, do not create an incomplete comparison.**

> INCORRECT: The heater works more efficiently. [It works more efficiently than what?]
>
> CORRECT: The heater works more efficiently than it did before the repairman came.

6. **Certain adjectives and adverbs cannot be used in the comparative form because they name a quality that has no degrees.** It is incorrect to write, for example, *more square, most perfect* (adjectives) or *more equally* or *most straight* (adverbs). See lists below for additional examples.

adj
adv

ADJECTIVES

complete	equal	impossible	parallel	unanimous
dead	eternal	infinite	pregnant	universal
empty	everlasting	invisible	square	vertical
endless	favorite	matchless	supreme	whole

ADVERBS

endlessly	infinitely	uniquely
equally	invisibly	universally
eternally	perpendicularly	
impossibly	straight	

Exercise 17   Revise each of the following sentences so that all adjectives and adverbs are used correctly.

EXAMPLE: I was <u>real</u> surprised that I won the raffle.

REVISED: I was <u>really</u> surprised that I won the raffle.

1. The bigger book of the five assigned in the World Literature class is *Anna Karenina*.
2. Even though the quarterback played bad, the team still won.
3. Of all the students in the French class, Marguerite has the better accent.
4. When Peter and Jose practice the trumpet together, Peter plays worst.
5. Jennifer completed the tennis match quick.
6. The car runs more smoothly.
7. Our doorbell rings worst than any of the other doorbells in the apartment building.
8. Bruno has the most high grade in the class.
9. Mr. Santelo spoke more eloquently of all the panel members.
10. The used television worked good, considering we paid $25 for it.

D Writing Effective Sentences

D.1 Misplaced and Dangling
      Modifiers

D.2 Shifts in Person, Number, and
      Tense

D.3 Coordination

D.4 Subordination

D.5 Parallelism

D.6 Sentence Variety

D.7 Redundancy and Wordiness

D.8 Diction

D.1 MISPLACED AND DANGLING MODIFIERS

■ Misplaced modifiers are words or phrases that do not describe or explain the words the way the writer intended them to. Instead, modifiers make a sentence unclear and confusing.

MISPLACED: Max bought a chair at the used furniture shop <u>that was large and dark</u>. [Was the chair large and dark or <u>the furniture shop</u>?]

MISPLACED: The instructor announced that the term paper was due on April 25 <u>at the beginning</u> of class. [Are the papers due at the beginning of class on the 25th, or did the instructor make the announcement at the beginning of class?]

You can easily avoid misplaced modifiers if you place the modifier immediately before or after the word it modifies. Notice how the above sentences have been revised by following this rule.

CORRECT: Max bought <u>a large, dark</u> chair at the used furniture shop.

CORRECT: At the beginning of class, the instructor announced that the term paper was due on April 25.

Dangling Modifiers

Dangling modifiers are words or phrases that do not clearly describe or explain any part of the sentence. Dangling modifiers create confusion, if not unintentional humor. To avoid dangling modifiers, make sure each of your modifying phrases or clauses has a clear antecedent.

DANGLING: Rounding the curve, a fire hydrant was hit by the speeding car. [The opening modifier suggests that the hydrant rounded the curve.]

CORRECT: Rounding the curve, the speeding car hit the fire hydrant.

DANGLING: Uncertain of what courses to take next semester, the academic advisor listed five options. [The opening modifier suggests that the advisor was uncertain of what courses to take.]

CORRECT: Uncertain of what courses to take next semester, the student spoke to an academic advisor, who listed five options.

DANGLING: Flood damage was visible crossing the river. [This sentence makes it sound as though flood damage was crossing the river. A reader might also ask, "To whom was the damage visible? Who was crossing the river?"]

CORRECT: Flood damage was visible as we crossed the river.

There are two common ways to revise dangling modifiers.

1. Add a word or words so that the modifier describes the word or words it is actually intended to describe. Place the new material just after the modifier, and rearrange other parts of the sentence as necessary.

DANGLING: While watching television, the cake burned. [The opening modifier implies that the cake is watching television.]

CORRECT: While watching television, Sarah burned the cake.

2. Change the dangling modifier to a subordinate clause. (See p. 451.) You may need to change the verb in the modifier.

DANGLING: While watching television, the cake burned.

CORRECT: While Pat was watching television, the cake burned.

Exercise 18   Revise each of the following sentences to correct misplaced or dangling modifiers.

EXAMPLE: Walking across campus, a flock of Canadian geese was seen.

REVISED: While I walked across campus, I saw a flock of Canadian geese.

1. Running up the stairs, the tray of food fell.
2. The fax machine was out of order at the store.
3. Being almost asleep, it was difficult to concentrate.

shift

4. The professor returned to campus after a summer vacation on Thursday.
5. Hoping to earn enough money for an out of town weekend, several extra jobs were taken.
6. On Halloween the restaurant served hamburgers to the kids wrapped in orange and black paper.
7. After skiing all day, a cup of hot cider was served.
8. Marcia received a letter from her mother with a check enclosed.
9. Studying my horoscope, the answer to my dilemma became clear.
10. The car is an antique that needs repainting.

D.2 SHIFTS IN PERSON, NUMBER, AND TENSE

■ The parts of a sentence should be consistent. Shifts within a sentence in person, number, or tense make sentences confusing and difficult to read.

Shifts in Person

Person is a term used to distinguish between the speaker or writer (known as *first person*), the person spoken to (the *second person*) and the person spoken about (*third person*). Using a consistent person means using the same person throughout the sentence. The first person pronoun refers to *I* or *we*. The second person pronoun refers to *you*. The third person pronoun refers to *he, she, it,* or *they.*

FIRST: I will write the essay.

SECOND: You will write the essay.

THIRD: He will write the essay.

The pronoun must agree in person with the noun it refers to (its antecedent).

SHIFT: If a student studies effectively, you will get good grades.

Here the writer shifts from a third person noun, *student*, to a second person pronoun, *you.*

CORRECT: If a student studies effectively, he or she will learn a lot.

CORRECT: If you study effectively, you will learn a lot.

Note: Revision of person may require a change in verb tense as well, as in the second revision.

Shifts in Number

Number means the distinction between singular and plural. A pronoun must agree in number with its antecedent. A singular pronoun must be used to refer to a singular noun, and, likewise, a plural pronoun must refer to a plural noun (see p. 480).

Nouns within a sentence must also agree in number.

SHIFT: All the houses have a screened-in porch.

CORRECT: All the houses have screened-in porches.

SHIFT: A plumber repairs water lines, but he will not replace drenched floorboard.

CORRECT: A plumber repairs water lines, but he will not replace drenched floorboards.

Shifts in Tense

The same verb tense should be used throughout the sentence unless meaning requires a shift.

third person   first person
present   future
↓   ↓

REQUIRED SHIFT: After my cousin arrives, we will go to the movies.

Unnecessary shifts

INCORRECT: After Marguerite joined the food co-op, she seems healthier.

CORRECT: After Marguerite joined the food co-op, she seemed healthier.

INCORRECT: Pamela watched the moon rise, and then she goes for a midnight swim.

CORRECT: Pamela watched the moon rise, and then she went for a midnight swim.

Exercise 19   Revise each of the following sentences. Correct errors in shift of person, number, or tense.

EXAMPLE: The decoy carver carefully sands before he painted the wooden duck.

REVISED: The decoy carver carefully sanded before he painted the wooden duck.

1. If a person shops carefully, you can save a lot of money.
2. If an older man has chest pains, they should go to the doctor.

shift

3. When everyday stresses begin to overpower students, one should learn some relaxation techniques.

4. In the beginning of the film, the main character was a young boy; by the end he is a wealthy businessman and is seated by a pool.

5. After he began college, Ralph joins a study group.

6. Many people think your opinions don't count and never contact their congressional leaders.

7. I enjoy swimming; you can clear your mind, and you feel great afterwards.

8. Only one of the mothers of the kindergarten students have a job.

9. In the morning, Mark exercised by jogging, and in the afternoon, he will study calculus.

10. All of my friends have an active imagination.

D.3 COORDINATION

■ **Coordination** is a way that, you, as a writer can give related ideas equal emphasis within a single sentence. Your readers will better understand the flow of your thought if you connect coordinate ideas.

How to Combine Ideas of Equal Importance

There are three ways to combine ideas of equal importance.
Method 1: Join the two independent clauses using a comma and a coordinating conjunction.

I passed the ball, <u>but</u> Sam failed to catch it.

The coordinating conjunction that connects the two clauses provides information about the relationship of the two ideas. Here is a list of coordinating conjunctions, along with their meanings.

COORDINATING CONJUNCTION	MEANING	EXAMPLE
and	addition; one idea added to another	I went shopping, *and* I spent too much money.
but, yet	the two ideas are different, opposite, or to be contrasted	I wanted to grill fish, *but* Peter was a vegetarian

or	alternatives or choices	Tonight I might go to the movies, *or* I might work out.
nor	not either	Julie was not in class, *nor* was she in the snack bar.
for	one idea is the cause of another	We went for a walk, *for* it was a beautiful evening.
so	as a result	I was early for the appointment, *so* I decided to doze for a few minutes.

CO

Method 2: Join the clauses using a semicolon.

> We decided to see the new Spike Lee film; it was playing at three local theaters.

Use this method when the relationship between the two ideas is clear and requires no explanation. Usually, the two clauses must be very closely related. If you join two clauses but fail to use a conjunction along with the comma, you will produce a comma splice. When two clauses are joined without using either punctuation or a coordinating conjunction, it is called a run-on sentence. (See p. 462.)

Method 3: Join the clauses using a semicolon and a conjunctive adverb followed by a comma. A conjunctive adverb can also be used at the beginning of a sentence to link the sentence with an earlier sentence. Here is a list of common conjunctive adverbs and their meanings.

CONJUNCTIVE ADVERB	MEANING	EXAMPLE
therefore, consequently, thus, hence	as a result—one idea is the effect of another	I am planning to become a nurse; *consequently*, I'm volunteering at local hospitals.

CO

however, nevertheless, nonetheless, conversely	but—suggests differences or contrast	We had planned to go bowling; *however,* we went to hear music instead.
furthermore, moreover, also	in addition—a continuation of the same idea	To save money I am packing my lunch; *also,* I am walking to school instead of taking the bus.
similarly, likewise	comparison	I left class as soon as I finished the exam. *Likewise,* other students also left.
then, subsequently, next	follows one another in time	I walked home; *then,* I massaged my aching feet.

Exercise 20   Complete each of the following sentences by adding a coordinating conjunction or a conjunctive adverb and the appropriate punctuation.

> EXAMPLE: We found an old sofa in the barn; <u>therefore,</u> we took it to the upholsterer.

1. Ahmad unplugged his phone _____ he missed an important call from his sister.
2. Jack loves chocolate _____ I made a double chocolate layer cake for his birthday.
3. Olivia hates television _____ she loves to go to see live theatre.
4. The band played until midnight _____ we danced to every song.
5. Bob's Hardware Store was bought by Value Home Centers _____ the name was not changed.
6. I forgot yesterday was Mother's Day _____ I called my mother to apologize.
7. We do not have enough money for a take-out Chinese dinner _____ I will make fried chicken.
8. My favorite TV shows are on tonight _____ I won't get much homework done.

9. Several defensive ends were injured _____ several defensive backs were injured.

10. The newspaper article on global warming contained some useful information _____ it was not detailed enough about the effects on wheat production.

D.4 SUBORDINATION

■ Subordination is a way of showing that one idea is not as important as another. When two clauses are related, but one is less important, the less important one can be expressed as a subordinate clause. Subordinate clauses do contain a subject and a verb, but they do not express a complete thought. They are always added to a complete sentence or independent clause. If a subordinate clause is used alone, it is a fragment and must be corrected. (See p. 457.)

sub

How to Combine Ideas of Unequal Importance

Method 1: Use a subordinating conjunction. When a less important idea is combined with one of greater importance, it is helpful to show how the ideas relate to one another. The subordinate (less important) idea often begins with a word or phrase that explains its relationship to the more important idea. Words such as *after, although, before, unless, while, when*, and *because* are examples. These words are called *subordinating conjunctions*. (See p. 453 for an extensive list.)

Here are a few examples of sentences that use a subordinate conjunction to combine a subordinating clause with an independent clause.

subordinate clause   independent clause

After I finished cleaning my fish tank, I worked on my paper.

subordinate clause   independent clause

Unless I win the lottery, I will not be able to buy a new car.

A subordinate conjunction suggests the relationship between the two clauses.

Method 2: Use a relative pronoun. A special type of subordinate clause begins with a relative pronoun:

who (whose, whom)   that   what

whoever (whomever)   which   whatever

A subordinate clause can begin with one of these words. Often, this type of subordinate clause is placed within the independent clause.

The professor <u>who won the award</u> is on leave this semester.

The courses <u>that I am taking this semester</u> are challenging.

The waiter, <u>whose name I forgot</u>, was cheerful.

Commas are used to set off subordinate clauses that supply non-essential information. Commas are not used when the subordinate clause provides essential information.

Exercise 21

sub

Combine each of the following pairs of sentences into a single sentence. Use a subordinating conjunction or a relative pronoun to combine the sentences.

EXAMPLE: The melons that were bred to taste like bananas were easy to grow.
The groundhog ate the melons that were bred to taste like bananas.

COMBINED: The melons that were bred to taste like bananas were easy to grow, but they were eaten by the groundhog.

1. The mishap occurred at the interstate exit.
   The mishap injured no one.
2. The muffler on Lucinda's car fell off.
   Lucinda was driving to school.
3. Tony asked Lydia to marry him next month.
   Tony is working only part-time and is still in school.
4. The landfill will decrease property values.
   The landfill was unsuccessfully opposed by our citizens' group.
5. It is never necessary to order double cheese on D'Angelo's pizzas.
   D'Angelo's Pizza uses a lot of cheese on their pizzas.
6. The professor spoke slowly.
   The professor noticed students were having trouble taking notes.
7. The red dress fit perfectly.
   My husband bought the red dress.
8. I slept soundly.
   The alarm clock rang.
9. Paulette asked her roommates to be quiet.
   Paulette was studying for a psychology midterm exam.
10. The bride and groom kissed.
    The minister pronounced the couple man and wife.

D.5 PARALLELISM

■ Parallelism means that words, phrases, or clauses in a series should have similar grammatical form. When elements within a sentence are not balanced, they exhibit faulty parallelism.

What Should Be Parallel?

1. **Words or phrases in series.** When two or more nouns, verbs, or adjectives appear together in a sentence, they should be parallel (similar) in grammatical form. Verbs should be written in the same tense.

INCORRECT: The dentist told my sister to stop eating so much candy and that she should floss her teeth.

CORRECT: The dentist told my sister to stop eating so much candy and to floss her teeth.

INCORRECT: My history professor gives pop quizzes and assigned homework for each class.

CORRECT: My history professor gives pop quizzes and assigns homework for each class.

2. **Clauses within sentences.** The clauses within a sentence should be parallel.

INCORRECT: Barry wanted to go to the concert, but Julia wants to stay home and watch a video.

CORRECT: Barry wanted to go to the concert, but Julia wanted to stay home and watch a video.

3. **Items being compared.** When elements of a sentence are compared or contrasted, use the same grammatical form for each.

INCORRECT: Mark wanted a vacation rather than to save money to buy a house.

CORRECT: Mark wanted to take a vacation rather than to save money to buy a house.

Exercise 22 Revise each of the following sentences to achieve parallelism.

EXAMPLE: I saved money by not buying magazines and did not go out to dinner.

REVISED: I saved money by not buying magazines and by not going out to dinner.

1. Abdul decided either to paint the shelves or clean them.
2. Cynthia has had a desire to and was interested in riding horses since she was young.
3. Jose wanted his own car rather than to take the bus every day.
4. Most people exercise to shape up, to lose weight, and so they feel better.
5. The doctor explained that a good diet, exercising, and to get enough sleep are important in avoiding stress.
6. Because Darin was late leaving work and having noticed that the traffic was congested, he called his wife to tell her he was going to be late getting home.
7. Cherie would rather have a dog than being a mother.
8. The class was dull because the textbook is terrible, long, boring lectures, and classmates who wouldn't participate in discussions.
9. Estaphano wanted both the leather jacket he saw in S & P's window and to buy the acid-washed jeans he saw at The Gap.
10. Not only did the snowstorm make driving impossible, but also to even go outside was dangerous because it was so cold.

---

var

D.6 SENTENCE VARIETY

■ Good writers use a variety of sentence structures to avoid wordiness and monotony and to show the relationships between thoughts. To achieve good **sentence variety**, do not use all simple sentences or all coordinate sentences and do not begin or end all sentences in the same way. Instead, vary the length, amount of detail, and structure of your sentences. Here are a few suggestions for improving sentence variety.

1. **Use sentences of varying lengths.**
2. **Avoid stringing simple sentences together with coordinating conjunctions.** Instead use introductory participial phrases (see p. 448).

SIMPLE: There was a long line at the deli, <u>so</u> Chris decided to leave.

VARIED: <u>Seeing the long line at the deli</u>, Chris decided to leave.

3. **Begin some sentences with a prepositional phrase.** A preposition shows relationships between things (*during, over, toward, before, across, within, inside, over, above*). Many suggest direction or location.

<u>During the concert</u>, the fire alarm rang.

<u>Inside the theater</u>, it was damp and cold.

4. Begin some sentences with an *-ing* verb or phrase.

<u>Barking</u> and <u>jumping</u>, the dogs greeted their master.

<u>Still laughing</u>, two girls left the movie.

5. Begin some sentences with an *-ed* verb or phrase.

<u>Tired</u> and <u>exhausted</u>, the mountain climbers fell asleep quickly.

6. Begin some sentences with adverbs, frequently known as *-ly* words.

<u>Angrily</u>, the student left the room.

<u>Patiently</u>, the math instructor explained the assignment again.

7. Begin some sentences with *to* (infinitives and infinitive phrases).

<u>To</u> get breakfast ready on time, I got up at 7 a.m.

8. Begin with a subordinating conjunction.

<u>Because</u> I ate shellfish, I developed hives.

9. Begin with a conjunctive adverb.

<u>Consequently</u>, we decided on steak for dinner.

var

Exercise 23 Combine each pair of simple sentences into one sentence using the technique suggested in parentheses.

EXAMPLE: The child whined and cried. The angry child refused to come out from under the table. (use *-ing* verb)

COMBINED: Whining and crying, the angry child refused to come out from under the table.

1. The truck delivered the merchandise into the storefront.
   It double parked for an hour.
   (use an introductory participial phrase, *-ing*)
2. Susan and Rhonda studied in the library.
   They studied after class.
   (use prepositional phrase)
3. Kim spends a great deal of time exercising.
   Kim is worried about her weight.
   (use *-ed* verb)

4. I am planning to travel to Baltimore.
   I am going in the spring.
   (use prepositional phrase)
5. The student requested a retest.
   He spoke in a loud voice.
   (use adverb, *-ly*)
6. Sharon has been reading child-care books.
   Sharon is excited about her pregnancy.
   (use *-ed* verb)
7. Pat cleaned all the upholstery in the living and dining room.
   Pat worked hard and feverishly.
   (use *-ing* verb)
8. Doug wanted to surprise his wife.
   Doug rented a store sign that announced his wife had turned thirty years old.
   (use *to*)
9. The professor explained the causes of inflation.
   The professor gave several examples.
   (use *-ing* verb)
10. The waiter likes to impress his customers.
    The waiter uses a French accent.
    (use *to*)

D.7 REDUNDANCY AND WORDINESS

■ Redundancy results when a writer has said the same thing twice. Wordiness results when a writer uses more words than necessary to convey a meaning. Both redundancy and wordiness detract from clear, effective sentences by distracting and confusing the reader.

Eliminating Redundancy

A common mistake is to repeat the same idea in slightly different words.

The <u>remaining</u> chocolate chip cookie is the <u>only one left</u>, so I saved it for you.

Here *remaining* and *only one left* mean the same thing, so only one is needed.

The vase was <u>oval in shape</u>.

Oval is a shape, so *in shape* becomes redundant. To revise a redundant sentence, eliminate one of the redundant elements.

Eliminating Wordiness

1. Eliminate wordiness by cutting out words that do not add to the meaning of your sentence.

WORDY: In the final analysis, choosing the field of accounting as my major resulted in my realizing that college is tough, hard work.

REVISED: Choosing accounting as my major made me realize that college is hard work.

WORDY: The type of imitative behavior that I notice among teenagers is a very important, helpful aspect of their learning to function in groups.

REVISED: The imitative behavior of teenagers helps them learn to function in groups.

Watch out in particular for empty words and phrases.

PHRASE	SUBSTITUTE
until such time as	until
due to the fact that	because
at this point in time	now

2. Express your ideas simply and directly, using as few words as possible. Often by rearranging your wording, you can eliminate two or three words.

the fleas that my dog has—my dog's fleas
workers with jobs that are low in pay—workers with low-paying jobs

3. Use strong active verbs that convey movement and express additional meaning.

WORDY: I was in charge of two other employees and needed to watch over their work and performance.

REVISED: I supervised two employees, monitored their performance, and checked their work.

4. Avoid sentences that begin with "There is . . ." and "There are . . ." These empty phrases add no meaning to the sentence and give no energy or life to the writing.

WORDY: There are many children that suffer from malnutrition.

REVISED: Many children suffer from malnutrition.

Exercise 24   Revise each of the following sentences to eliminate redundancy and wordiness.

> EXAMPLE: I will not know my exam grade on the sociology test until the papers are returned in class next week by the professor.

> REVISED: I will not know my sociology exam grade until the papers are returned in class next week.

1. I have observed that most parents see their children misbehave, and the parents don't do anything to correct their misbehavior.

2. Dominic planned to revisit again his native Italy.

3. Though the players made some improvement since the last game they played, they are still lacking in defensive strategies until such time as they improve.

4. Linda knew she needed to revise and change her essay before handing it in.

5. Because they are lab partners, Natalie and Dave have agreed to cooperate and work together.

6. There are numerous theories that can explain the reasons how the planets were created.

7. Geoff, who is soft-spoken, sometimes speaks so quietly that people are unable to hear him.

8. The exam that I took in sociology had several essay questions that were difficult.

9. For the reason that my work schedule seems to be changing all the time, at the present time I cannot say what I'll do next weekend or make any plans.

10. In the event that my sister should decide to visit my parents who live in Baltimore, it will be necessary for me to leave campus by means of bus.

D.8 DICTION

dic

■ Diction means the use and choice of words. Words that you choose should be appropriate for your audience and express your meaning clearly. Note the following suggestions for improving your diction.

1. **Avoid slang expressions.** Slang refers to the informal, unique expressions created and used by groups of people who want to identify themselves as a group. Slang is an appropriate and useful way to communicate in some conversational and social situations and in some forms of creative writing. However, it is not appropriate for academic or career writing.

SLANG: My sister seems permanently <u>out to lunch</u>.

REVISED: My sister seems out of touch with the world.

SLANG: We <u>pigged out</u> at the ice-cream shop.

REVISED: We consumed enormous quantities of ice cream at the ice-cream shop.

2. **Avoid colloquial language**. Colloquial language refers to casual, everyday, spoken language. It should be avoided in formal situations. Words that fall into this category are labeled *informal* or *colloquial* in your dictionary.

COLLOQUIAL: I almost <u>flunked</u> <u>bio</u> last <u>sem</u>.

REVISED: I almost failed biology last semester.

COLLOQUIAL: What <u>are you all</u> doing later?

REVISED: What are your plans for this evening?

3. **Avoid non-standard language**. Non-standard language is words and grammatical forms that are used in conversation, but are neither correct nor acceptable standard written English.

INCORRECT	*REVISED*
hisself	himself
knowed	known
hadn't ought	should not
she want	she wants
he go	he goes

4. **Avoid trite expressions**. Trite expression are old, worn-out words and phrases that have become stale and do not convey meaning as effectively as possible. These expressions are sometimes called clichés.

TRITE EXPRESSIONS
needle in a haystack

hard as a rock

face the music

sadder but wiser

white as snow

gentle as a lamb

as old as the hills

pretty as a picture

dic

Exercise 25   Revise each of the following sentences by using correct diction.

I was <u>wacked out</u> after graduation weekend.

I was <u>exhausted</u> after graduation weekend.

1. Keith's father is strong as an ox and can rip a phone book in half with his bare hands.

2. Martina could of graduated this year, but she decided to go after a second major in marketing.

3. Bo's boss gave him the ax because he was slacking off on the job.

4. That there checkout line appears to be the shortest.

5. The class went crazy when the professor cancelled class on Friday.

6. Martha buzzed her assistant to let her know she was taking off for lunch.

7. Harold wore an awesome new tie for his interview with Mattel.

8. The professor put Arthur's question on ice for a few minutes while he finished summarizing the events that led up to the American Revolution.

9. He want tuna for lunch and steak for dinner.

10. When Trina realized she had forgotten to pay her rent, she decided to face the music and speak to her landlord.

---

dic

E Using Punctuation Correctly

E.1 COMMAS

■ The comma is used to separate parts of a sentence from one another. If you omit a comma when it is needed or add an unnecessary comma, a clear and direct sentence can become confusing.

When to Use Commas

Use a comma in the following situations:

1. **Before a coordinating conjunction that joins two independent clauses.** (See p. 496.)

Terry had planned to leave work early, but he was delayed.

2. **To separate a dependent clause from an independent clause when the dependent clause comes first in the sentence.** (See p. 465.)

After I left the library, I went to the computer lab.

3. **To separate introductory words and phrases from the remainder of the sentences.** These introductory words modify a word or words in the remainder of the sentence.

Unfortunately, I forgot my umbrella.

To pass the baton, I will need to locate my teammate.

Exuberant over their victory, the football team carried the quarterback on their shoulders.

com

> **4. To separate information that is added to a sentence but does not change its basic meaning.**

My cousin, <u>Janet Sanchez</u>, is majoring in engineering.

To decide whether a comma is needed, read the sentence without the added information. If the meaning changes, then commas are *not* needed.

> Mail carriers who have been bitten by dogs are afraid of them. [If the clause <u>who have been bitten by dogs</u> is deleted, the meaning of the sentence is changed. It reads as if all mail carriers are afraid of dogs. Consequently, no commas are needed.]

> My sister, who is a mail carrier, is afraid of dogs. [In this sentence, deletion of the fact that the sister is a mail carrier does not change the basic meaning of the sentence, so commas are needed.]

> **5. To separate three or more items in a series, a comma is *not* used *after* the last item.**

I plan to take math, psychology, and writing next semester.

> **6. To separate two or more adjectives not linked by a conjunction that modify the same noun or pronoun.**

The <u>thirsty, hungry</u> children returned from a day at the beach.

Note: When the adjective closer to the noun is closely related to the noun's meaning, they are *not* separated by commas.

> I threw a ragged wool skirt away.

Here *ragged* modifies *wool skirt*, not skirt.

To discover if a comma is needed between two adjectives, use the following test. Insert the word *and* between the two adjectives. Also try reversing the order of the two adjectives. If the phrase makes sense that way, then a comma is needed. If it does not make sense, do not use a comma.

> The <u>tired, angry</u> child fell asleep.

In this sentence *and* could be inserted between *tired* and *angry*. Also, *tired* and *angry* could be reversed; consequently, a comma is needed.

> Sarah is an <u>excellent psychology</u> student.

The word *and* cannot be inserted between the two adjectives, nor does it make sense to reverse the two words. No comma is needed.

7. **To separate parenthetical expressions from the clause they modify. Parenthetical expressions are added pieces of information that are not essential to the meaning of the sentence.**

Most students, I imagine, can get jobs on campus.

8. **To separate transitions from the clause they modify.**

Next, I will rake leaves.

9. **To separate a quotation from the words that introduce or explain it.**

Barbara explained, "Shopping is a form of relaxation for me."

10. **To separate dates, place names, and long numbers. Commas follow the year and the state name (see first two examples.)**

October 10, 1961, is my birthday.

Dayton, Ohio, was the first stop on the tour.

1,777,716 people took part in the study.

11. **To separate phrases expressing contrast.**

Sam's good nature, not his wealth, explains his popularity.

Exercise 26   Revise each of the following sentences by adding commas where needed.

EXAMPLE: Because Sam felt pressured by school and job responsibilities he reduced his work hours.

REVISED: Because Sam felt pressured by school and job responsibilities, he reduced his work hours.

1. The woman who lives next door in the blue house with the wide front porch loves her dog but does not allow him into her garden.

2. "Yes" Mr. Murray answered "The car has air conditioning, cruise control and power windows."

3. Julio was born on March 25 1966 a date which his mother we suppose remembers well.

4. After T.J. decided to major in economics he dropped his art class.

5. The doctor and the many nurses agreed that the heart transplant was a success although the patient felt worse than he had expected.

6. Marlena asked "Why doesn't the softball team have uniforms yet?"

com

7. Luckily Cheryl was able to locate the hubcap which had fallen off of her car at Main Street and Oakview Road the busiest intersection in the city.

8. Well it certainly seems as if we will have a hot summer this year doesn't it?

9. Our big beautiful leafy oak tree and our neighbor's maple tree were blown over in a windstorm last fall.

10. Charlene for example has a double major in English literature and political science but she still has time to take some interesting electives as well.

E.2 UNNECESSARY COMMAS

■   It is as important to know where *not* to place commas as it is to know where to place them. Note the following rules for places where it is incorrect to place commas.

1. Do not place a comma between subject and verb, between verb (or verbal) and complement, or between an adjective and the word it modifies. (A comma can, however, set off a word or phrase that occurs between a subject and verb: *The saguaro, a kind of cactus, is becoming rare.*)

INCORRECT: The stunning, imaginative, and intriguing, work of art became the hit of the show.

CORRECT: The stunning, imaginative, and intriguing work of art became the hit of the show.

2. Do not place a comma between two or more compound verbs, subjects, or complements.

INCORRECT: Sue called, and asked me to come by her office. [To correct, remove the comma.]

3. Do not place a comma before a coordinating conjunction joining two subordinate clauses. (See p. 496.)

INCORRECT: The city planner examined blueprints that the park designer had submitted, and the budget officer had approved. [To correct, remove the comma.]

4. Do not place a comma after coordinating conjunctions that begin sentences.

INCORRECT: And, the rest is history. [To correct, remove the comma.]

5. **Do not place commas around restrictive clauses, phrases, or appositives.** Restrictive clauses, phrases, and appositives are essential to the identification of the noun they modify. (See pp. 450 and 452.)

INCORRECT: The <u>girl, who</u> grew up down the <u>block, became</u> my lifelong friend. [To correct, remove the commas.]

6. **Do not place a comma before a subordinating conjunction when an adverbial clause follows an independent clause.** (See p. 466.)

INCORRECT: You may buy the golden <u>necklace, when</u> the store opens tomorrow. [To correct, remove the comma.]

7. **Do not place a comma before the word *than* when you are writing a comparison, after the words *like* and *such as*, nor before *such as* when it introduces a restrictive phrase.**

INCORRECT: Some snails, <u>such as,</u> the Oahu Tree Snail and the Banded Tree Snail, have colorful shells.

CORRECT: Some <u>snails, such as</u> the Oahu Tree Snail and the Banded Tree <u>Snail, have</u> colorful shells.

8. **No commas are used next to periods, question marks, exclamation marks, and dashes, or before opening parentheses.**

INCORRECT: "When will you come <u>back?,</u>" Dillon's son asked him. [To correct, remove the comma.]

INCORRECT: The bachelor <u>button, (also</u> known as the cornflower) grows well in ordinary garden soil. [To correct, remove the comma.]

9. **Do not place a comma between adjectives that are not coordinate.** Place a comma between coordinate adjectives only. Coordinate adjectives modify a noun independently and cannot be replaced with the word *and*.

INCORRECT: The light, yellow, <u>rose, blossom</u> was a pleasant birthday surprise. [To correct, remove comma.]

E.3 COLONS AND SEMICOLONS

■ Colons and semicolons also separate elements within a sentence.

When to Use a Colon

The colon is usually used to introduce a sentence element. It often signals that the preceding statement is to be explained or elaborated upon. Use a colon in the following situations.

C
S

1. **To introduce items in a series after a complete sentence.**

   I am wearing three popular colors: magenta, black, and white.

The colon should always follow a complete thought. It should not be used in the middle of a clause.

INCORRECT: My favorite colors are: red, pink, and green.

CORRECT: My favorite colors are red, pink, and green.

2. **With statements introduced by "the following" or "as follows."**

   The directions are as follows: take Main Street to Oak Avenue and then turn left.

3. **When an independent clause comes before a quotation, you may use a colon to introduce the quotation.**

   My brother made his point quite clear: "Never borrow my car without asking me first!"

4. **To introduce an explanation.**

   Mathematics is enjoyable: it requires a high degree of accuracy and peak concentration.

5. **To separate titles and subtitles of books.**

   Biology: A Study of Life

When to Use a Semicolon

Use a semicolon to:

1. **Separate two closely related independent clauses not connected by a coordinating conjunction.** (See p. 463.)

   Sam had a 99 average in math; he earned an "A" in the course.

2. **Separate two complete thoughts joined by a conjunctive adverb.** (See p. 464.)

   Margaret earned an "A" on her term paper; consequently, she was exempt from the final exam.

3. **Separate independent clauses if they are very long or if they contain numerous commas.**

   By late afternoon, having tried on every pair of black checked pants in the mall, Marsha was tired and cranky; but she still had not found what she needed to complete her new outfit.

4. **Separate items in a series if the items are lengthy or contain commas.**

The soap opera characters include Marianne Loundsberry, the wife; Ellen and Sarah, her children; Barry, her ex-husband; and Louise, Marianne's best friend.

5. **Revise a comma splice or run-on sentence (See pp. 463–466.)**

Exercise 27   Revise each sentence by placing colons and semicolons where necessary. Delete any incorrect punctuation.

> EXAMPLE: The textbook for my sociology course is titled Societies Read-
> ings and Case Studies.
>
> REVISED: The textbook for my sociology course is titled Societies: Read-
> ings and Case Studies.

1. Nick decided to go to the mall after dinner, he needed to purchase a suit to wear to his sister's wedding.

2. Marguerite has an allergy to chalk dust therefore, she always sits in the back of the classroom.

3. Sid invited three friends over for pizza, Neal, his neighbor Pam, a friend from childhood and Charlene, a woman he met in his sociology class.

4. The bookstore was sold out of textbooks for Professor Kenyatta's course, although she had ordered plenty thus I have to wait until the bookstore orders more.

5. Enrico had read every chapter in the textbook and attended every class, but he still did poorly on the exam he failed to organize the material and to review it.

6. Josephine bowls every Wednesday with members of her husband's family Sally, his sister June, his aunt Trish, his cousin Eric and Tina, his sister-in-law.

7. My aquarium has a large variety of fish angelfish, black mollies, goldfish, and many exotic tropical fish.

8. After his apartment building burned down, Troy moved in with his brother he quickly moved out again because his brother is so temperamental.

9. Joining the military is Jeff's goal his girlfriend hopes he will change his mind.

10. Marty dropped his wallet in the cafeteria consequently, I found him there crawling around on the floor looking for it.

C
S

E.4 DASHES, PARENTHESES, HYPHENS, APOSTROPHES, QUOTATION MARKS

■ Dashes (—)

The dash is used to separate non-essential elements from the main part of the sentence. It creates a stronger separation, or interruption, than when commas or parentheses are used. The dash is used to emphasize an idea, to create a dramatic effect, or to indicate a sudden change in thought.

My sister—the friendliest person I know—will visit me this weekend.

My brother's most striking quality is his ability to make money—or so I thought until I heard of his bankruptcy.

When typing or word processing, use two hyphens (--) to indicate a dash. No space appears between the dash and the words it separates.

Parentheses (   )

Parentheses are used in pairs to separate extra or non-essential information from the rest of the sentence. Parentheses often contain material that amplifies, clarifies, or acts as an aside to the main point. Parentheses, unlike dashes, de-emphasize information.

Some large breeds of dogs (Golden Retrievers and Newfoundlands) are susceptible to hip deformities.

The prize was dinner for two (maximum value $50.00) at a restaurant of your choice.

Hyphens (-)

Hyphens have two primary uses:

1. to split a word when dividing it between two lines of writing or typing. (See p. 523.)
2. to join two or more words that function as a single unit when describing a noun.

   single-parent families
   school-age children
   state-of-the-art sound system

punc

Apostrophes (')

Use apostrophes in the following ways:

1. to show ownership or possession.

When the person, place, or thing doing the possessing is a singular noun, add *'s* to the end of it, regardless of what its final letter is.

> Sam's CD player
> Aretha's best friend
> John Keats's poetry

With plural nouns that end in *-s,* add only an apostrophe to the end of the word.

> the twins' bedroom
> teachers' salaries
> postal workers' hours

With plural nouns that do not end in *-s,* add *'s.*

> children's books
> men's slacks

Do not use an apostrophe with possessive adjectives (see p. 427).

> INCORRECT: It's frame is damaged.
>
> CORRECT: Its frame is damaged.
>
> INCORRECT: You're wallet is on the floor.
>
> CORRECT: Your wallet is on the floor.
>
> INCORRECT: They're parents arrived yesterday.
>
> CORRECT: Their parents arrived yesterday.

2. to indicate omission of one or more letters in a word or number.
Contractions are used in informal writing, but not in formal situations.

it's [it is]	you're [you are]	'57 Ford [1957 Ford]
doesn't [does not]	hasn't [has not]	class of '89
		[class of 1989]

Quotation Marks (" ")

Quotation marks separate direct quotations from the sentence that contains them. Here are some rules to follow in using quotation marks.

punc

1. **Quotation marks are always used in pairs.** Even if the quotation completes the sentence, two quotation marks are needed. Note that a comma or period goes at the end of the quotation, inside the quotation marks.

Marge exclaimed, "I never expected Peter to give me a watch for Christmas."

2. **Use double quotations to enclose the quotation.** Use single quotation marks for a quotation within a quotation.

My literature professor said, "Byron's line 'She walks in beauty like the night' is one of his most sensual."

Note: When quoting long prose passages of more than four lines, no quotation marks are used. Instead, separate the quote by indenting each line.

The opening lines of the *Declaration of Independence* establish the purpose of the document:

When in the Course of human events it becomes necessary for one

people to dissolve the political bonds which have connected them

with another, and to assume among the powers of the earth, the

separate and equal station to which the Laws of Nature and of

Nature's God entitle them, a decent respect to the opinions of

mankind requires that they should declare the causes which impel

them to the separation.

3. **Use quotations to indicate titles of songs, short stories, poems, articles, and essays.** (Books, movies, and the names of television series are underlined.)

"Rappaccini's Daughter"
"The Road Not Taken"
60 Minutes

punc

Exercise 28   Add dashes, apostrophes, parentheses, and quotations where necessary.

EXAMPLE: As I came in the door, Maria shouted Watch out for the slippery floor!

REVISED: As I came in the door, Maria shouted, "Watch out for the slippery floor!"

1. Her dog picked up its bone chewed and ragged and brought it into Johns house.

2. Although I forgot my shopping list, I remembered the items I needed shrimp, cocktail sauce, beer, cheese, and crackers for the dinner I was having.

3. Its very hot out, Moira said even though it didn't seem warm to anyone else.

4. Jonah asked me if I wanted to come to the party he called it a party but I knew I was the only guest.

5. Apples a fruit eaten by millions of children can be dangerous if they are sprayed with pesticides; Dr. Martin Lenns article, The Fruit of the Tree, discusses the dangers of pesticides on apples.

6. Barry handed out the employees bonus five hundred dollars apiece in cash!

7. Students who park in the lots by the gym lots 25, 26, and 27 must purchase special parking permits.

8. Muhammad Ali claimed, I will float like a butterfly, but sting like a bee.

9. When Todd reminded me that the football game began at 4 p.m., I said I hope the Jets win!

10. Tina is a redhead this week, and many people have not recognized her at first glance.

punc

F Managing Mechanics and Spelling

F.1 Capitalization

F.2 Abbreviations

F.3 Hyphenation and
     Word Division

F.4 Numbers

F.5 Suggestions for Improving
     Spelling

F.6 Six Useful Spelling Rules

F.1 CAPITALIZATION

■ In general, capital letters are used to mark the beginning of a sentence or the beginning of a quotation and to identify specific or unique nouns (proper nouns). The list below provides guidelines on what to capitalize.

WHAT TO CAPITALIZE	*EXAMPLE*
1. the first word in every sentence	Prewriting is useful.
2. the first word in a direct quotation	Sarah commented, "That exam was difficult!"
3. the names of people and animals, including the pronoun "I"	Madonna Michael Jackson Spot Fido
4. names of specific places, cities, states, nations, geographic areas or regions	New Orleans the Southwest Lake Erie
5. government and public offices, departments, buildings	Williamsville Library House of Representatives
6. names of social, political, business, sporting, cultural organizations	Boy Scouts Buffalo Bills

7. days of the month, week, and holidays — Halloween / August

8. the first word following a colon, the first and last word of a title, and all other words except short articles, prepositions, and conjunctions. — "Once More to the Lake" / *Biology: The World of Life*

9. races, nationalities, languages — Afro-American / Italian, English

10. religions, religious figures, sacred books — Hindu, Hinduism, God, Allah, the Bible

11. names of products — Tide, Buick

12. titles when they come before a name — Professor Rodriquez / Senator Hatch

13. historic events — World War I

14. specific course titles — History 201 / Introduction to Psychology

Exercise 29   Capitalize words as necessary in the following sentences.

EXAMPLE: The fans will be disappointed if the buffalo bills do not play in the super bowl.

REVISED: The fans will be disappointed if the Buffalo Bills do not play in the Super Bowl.

1. Jorge, a democrat, took political science 101 and was unhappy with the political ideals professed by the doctor Martinez.

2. When my family visited europe we saw the eiffel tower in paris and the tower of london in england, and we swam in the english channel.

3. the reporter asked at the press conference, "mr. president, what kinds of changes do you plan to make in the state department?"

4. Our host served us spam and kraft cheddar cheese.

5. Next thursday is thanksgiving, a holiday first celebrated by the pilgrims.

6. One of melinda's ancestors signed the constitution.

7. Trent was born in texas but was raised in the appalachian mountains.

abbr

8. Joanna and Mark were married by bishop tunis, the same priest who had baptized Mark.

9. The silvertone theater is on southeast street, near the football stadium, about a mile from maroon's department store.

10. We watched the new york jets last night on *monday night football*.

F.2 ABBREVIATIONS

■ Abbreviations are shortened forms of a word or phrase used to represent the complete form. The following is a list of the most common acceptable abbreviations.

WHAT TO ABBREVIATE	*EXAMPLE*
1. titles before and after a person's name	Mr. Ling Samuel Rosen, M.D.
2. names of familiar organizations, corporations, countries (no periods are used if the name consists of three or more words)	CIA, IBM, USA
3. time references preceded or followed by a number	a.m., p.m., B.C.
4. Latin references when used in footnotes, references, or in parentheses	i.e. (that is) et al. (and others)
5. Parts of the names of companies	Marcus Bros. Moving and Storage, Fred/Alan, Inc., The Boston Co.

Here is a list of common mistakes:

	Example	
WHAT NOT TO ABBREVIATE	*INCORRECT*	*CORRECT*
1. units of measurement	thirty in.	thirty inches
2. geographical names when used in sentences	N.Y., N.O.	New York New Orleans
3. parts of written works	Ch. 3	Chapter 3
4. names of days, months, holidays	Tues.	Tuesday
5. names of subject areas	psych.	psychology

Exercise 30   Revise the following sentences to correct the inappropriate use of abbreviations. If a sentence contains no error, mark **C** next to its number.

> EXAMPLE: My bio. professor cancelled class for Tues. but rescheduled for Thu. p.m.
>
> REVISED: My biology professor cancelled class for Tuesday but rescheduled for Thursday afternoon.

hyph

1. Susan's grandfather worked for the FBI before he became a prof. of history at the local U.
2. Myron Thomas, Ph.D., is giving a lecture on Mon. about art from 30 B.C.
3. Dr. Sufed told the young mother that her baby weighed 8 lbs.
4. When we were working out at the YMCA one day in Aug., we met a foreign student who speaks four languages, i.e. Ger., Eng., Fr. and Sp.
5. Rev. Hult read to the congregation from *Genesis* while the Sunday school class reviewed Ch. 4 of their book.
6. When our communications class drew numbers to determine the order in which we would give our speeches, I got no. 25 and Ron got no. 2; when he complained to the T.A. said she was sorry, but there was nothing she could do.
7. Terri used to work for the Pacific Gas and Fuel Co. when she lived in CA.
8. Renee's housemates planned a trip to NYC over spring break.
9. Tom never began his shopping until two wks. before Xmas.
10. Although the book on L.A. was long, Felicia finished reading it by 3 p.m. on the day she began it.

F.3 HYPHENATION AND WORD DIVISION

■ On occasion a writer must divide and hyphenate a word between the end of one line and the beginning of the next. Here are some guidelines to follow in dividing words.

1. **Divide words only when absolutely necessary.** Frequent word divisions make a paper difficult to read.
2. **Divide words between syllables.** Consult a dictionary if you are unsure of how to break a word into syllables.

di-vi-sion

pro-tect

num

3. **Do not divide one-syllable words.**

4. **Do not divide a word so that a single letter is left at the end of a line.**

> INCORRECT: a-typical [Dividing the word between *a* and *typ* leaves a single letter at the end of a line.]
>
> CORRECT: atyp-ical

5. **Do not divide a word so that less than three letters begin the new line.**

> INCORRECT: caus-al [Dividing this word results in a new line starting with a syllable of less than three letters.]

6. **Divide compound words only between the words.**

some-thing

any-one

7. **Divide words that are already hyphenated only at the hyphen.**

ex-policeman

Exercise 31

Place diagonal slash mark—solidus or virgule—(/) to indicate where each word should be divided. Mark N in the margin if the word should not be divided.

Connect
Con/nect

1. stepsister
2. soloist
3. cross-indexed
4. crops
5. purchased
6. roughly
7. subject
8. dependent
9. replanted
10. electorate

F.4 NUMBERS

■ Numbers can be written as numerals (600) or words (six hundred). Here are some guidelines for when to use numerals and when to use words.

WHEN TO USE NUMERALS	EXAMPLE
1. numbers that use more than two words	375 students
2. days and years	August 10, 1993
3. decimals, percentages, fractions	59% 56.7
4. times	9:27 a.m.
5. pages, volumes, acts, lines, chapters	Chapter 12 Volume 4
6. addresses	122 Peach Street
7. exact amounts of money	$5.60
8. scores and statistics	23 to 6 1 out of every 5

WHEN TO USE WORDS	EXAMPLE
1. numbers that begin sentences	Twenty students attended the lecture.
2. numbers of one or two words	sixty students

num

Exercise 32

Revise the following sentences to correct misuse of numbers. If a sentence is correct, mark "C" in the margin.

EXAMPLE: The lecture hall can seat 200 students.

REVISED: The lecture hall can seat two hundred students.

1. 158 children sang in the choral concert.
2. Mary will miss a French class because she has a dental appointment at 3 p.m. on October 10.
3. Lee was surprised to learn it was 11 forty-five already.
4. The used car lot contained 50 2-door cars and 20 4-door cars.
5. Our professor stated that 20% of adults cannot read.
6. Thomasita received a $15,000 inheritance from her grandmother.
7. Allan's team won the game, 9 to 4.
8. We were surprised to learn that Pat's social security number is 111-22-3333.
9. On page A-3 of the newspaper there was a 4-column story about the latest outbreak of fleas in our area.

10. Tomorrow in my Shakespeare class we are going to focus on Act III of *Hamlet*, after we complete the daily 3-question, 6-point quiz on the reading assignment.

F.5 SUGGESTIONS FOR IMPROVING SPELLING

■ Correct spelling is important to a well-written paragraph. Note the following advice to help you submit papers without misspellings.

1. Do not worry about spelling as you write your first draft. Checking a word in a dictionary at this point will interrupt your flow of ideas. If you do not know how a word is spelled, spell it the way it sounds. Circle or underline the word so you remember to check it later.

2. Keep a list of words you commonly misspell. This list can be part of your error log (see Chapter 5) or of your writing journal (see Writing Success Tip 2).

3. Every time you catch an error or find a misspelled word on a paper returned by your instructor, add it to your list.

4. Study your list. Ask a friend to quiz you on the list. Eliminate words from the list after you have passed several quizzes on them.

5. Develop a spelling awareness. You'll find that your spelling will improve just by being aware that spelling is important. When you encounter a new word, notice how it is spelled and practice writing it.

6. Pronounce words you are having difficulty spelling. Pronounce each syllable distinctly.

7. Review basic spelling rules. Your college library or learning lab may have manuals, workbooks, or computer programs that review basic rules and provide guided practice.

8. Be sure to have a dictionary readily available when you write. (See Writing Success Tip 8)

9. Read your final draft through once, checking only for spelling errors. Look at each word carefully and check the spelling of those words of which you are uncertain.

F.6 SIX USEFUL SPELLING RULES

■ The following six rules focus on common spelling trouble spots.
Troublespot 1: Is it *ei* or *ie*?

sp

Rule: Use *i* before *e*, except after *c* or when the syllable is pronounced "ay" as in the word weigh.

> EXAMPLE: *I* before *e*: believe, niece
>   except after *c*: receive, conceive
>   or when pronounced "ay": neighbor, sleigh

Exceptions to this rule include the following words:

either	neither
foreign	forfeit
height	leisure
weird	seize

Exercise 33   Complete each word by supplying "ie" or "ei."

> EXAMPLE: bel--ve
>
> COMPLETED: believe

1. sc--nce
2. th--r
3. effic--nt
4. exper--nce
5. conc--ve
6. w--rd
7. n--ghbor
8. th--f
9. ach--ve
10. ch--f

Troublespot 2: When adding an ending to a word, do you keep or drop the final *e*?

Rules: 1. Keep the final *e* when adding an ending that begins with a consonant.

> hope—hopeful   aware—awareness
> live—lively   force—forceful

        2. Drop the final *e* when adding an ending that begins with a vowel.

> hope—hoping   file—filing
> note—notable   write—writing

sp

(Vowels are a, e, i, o, u, and sometimes y; all other letters are consonants)
Exceptions: To avoid confusion or mispronunciation, the following words are exceptions.

argument	truly
awful	noticeable
manageable	changeable
judgment	courageous
outrageous	

Exercise 34

Combine the following words and endings.

EXAMPLE: Captive + ity

COMBINED: Captivity

1. love + less
2. argue + able
3. advise + ment
4. time + ly
5. complete + ness
6. arrive + ing
7. courage + ous
8. care + ful
9. argue + ment
10. surprise + ed

Troublespot 3: When adding an ending do you keep or drop the final *y*?

Rules: 1. Keep the *y* if the letter before the *y* is a vowel.

delay—delaying   buy—buying

2. Change the *y* to *i* if the letter before the *y* is a consonant.

defy—defiance   marry—married

Exercise 35

Combine the following words and endings.

EXAMPLE: captive + ity
COMBINED: captivity

EXAMPLE: angry + ly
COMBINED: angrily

1. buy + ing
2. messy + ness
3. copy + ed
4. way + s
5. happy + est
6. comply + ing
7. study + ous
8. ready + ness
9. worry + ed
10. bury + al

Troublespot 4: When adding an ending to a one-syllable word, when do you double the final consonant?

Rules: 1. In one-syllable words, double the final consonant when a single vowel comes before it.

drop—dropped   shop—shopped

pit—pitted

2. In one syllable words, *don't* double the final consonant when two vowels come before it.

repair—repairable

real—realize

Exercise 36   Add *-ed* or *-ing* to each of the following words.

EXAMPLE: fit

COMBINED: fitted

1. turn
2. slap
3. hop
4. laugh
5. fail
6. lift
7. ban
8. steal
9. map
10. bark

Troublespot 5: When adding an ending to a word with more than one syllable, when do you double the final consonant?

Rules: 1. In multi-syllable words, double the final consonant when a single vowel comes before it *and* the stress falls on the last syllable. Vowels are a, e, i, o, u, and sometimes y. All other letters are consonants.

begin—beginning

repel—repelling

2. In multi-syllable words, do *not* double the final consonant when two vowels or a vowel and another consonant come before it *or* when the stress is *not* on the last syllable.

despair—despairing

conceal—concealing

benefit—benefited

sp

Exercise 37   Add *-ed* or *-ing* to each of the following words.

EXAMPLE: reveal

COMBINED: revealing

1. ponder
2. question
3. repel
4. deduct
5. unlock
6. recommend
7. construct
8. travel
9. refer
10. cover

Troublespot 6: To form a plural, do you add *s* or *-es*?

Rules: 1. For most nouns, add *-s*.

cat—cats

house—houses

2. Add *-es* instead of *-s* for words that end in *-o*.

hero—heroes

echo—echoes

(Exceptions: zoos, radios, ratios, and other words ending with two vowels.)

        3. Add -*es* instead of -*s* for words ending in *ch, sh, ss, x,* or *z.*
            church—churches
            dish—dishes
            fox—foxes

Exercise 38   Add -*s* or -*es* to each of the following words.

        EXAMPLE: zero

        COMBINED: zeros

    1. hobo
    2. try
    3. hush
    4. glass
    5. fez
    6. money
    7. boss
    8. quarry
    9. church
  10. box

sp

G Error Correction Exercises

Revise each of the following paragraphs. Look for errors in sentence structure, grammar, punctuation, mechanics, and spelling. Rewrite these paragraphs with corrections.

Paragraph 1

err
corr

Jazz is a type of music, originating in New orleans in the early Twenties, and contained a mixture of Afro-American and European musical elements. There are a wide variety of types of jazz including: the blues, swing, bop and modern. Jazz includes both hard and soft music and it doesn't get to radical. Unlike rock music, rock it does not goes to extremes. Rock bands play so loud you can't understand half of the words. As a result, jazz is more relacking and enjoyable.

Paragraph 2

every one thinks vacations are great fun but that isnt allways so. Some people are too hyper to relax when their on vaccation. My sister Sally is like that. She has to be on the move at alltimes. She can never slow down and take it easy. She goes from activitiy to activity at a wild pace. When Sally does have a spare moment between activities, she spends her freetime thinking about work problems and her family and their problems and what she should do about them when she gets back. Consequently, when Sally gets back from a vacation she is exhausted and more tense and upset then when she left home.

Paragraph 3

Soap operas are usually serious eposodes of different people in the world of today. There about fictuous people whom are supposed to look real. But each character has their unique prblems, crazzy relationships and nonrealistical quirks and habits.In real live, it would never happen.The actors are aways getting themself into wiered and unusall situation that are so of the wall that they could never be real. Its just to unreal to have 20 looney people all good frinds.

Paragraph 4

Here are two forms of music, we have rock music and we have country music. First, these two sound differen. Rock music is very loud and with a high base sound, sometimes you can't even understand the words that the singer is singing. On the other hand, country music is a bit softer with a mellow but up beat sound. Although country music sometimes sounds boring, at least you can understand the lyrics when listening to it. Country singers usually have a country western accent also unlike rock singers.

err corr.

Essay 1

What A Good Friend Is

I have this friend Margaret who is really not too intelligent. It took awhile before I could accept her limitations. But, I had to get to know Margaret and her feelings. We are like two hands that wash each other.

I help her, she helps me. when I need her to babysit for me while I'm at work it's done. If she needs a ride to the dentist she's got it. All I need is to be given time to do them. We help each other and that is why we are friends.

Good friends; Friends that do for one another. To tell the friend the truth about something that is asked of them. And for the other to respect your views as you would theirs. A friend is there to listen if you have a problem and to suggest something to help solve the problem but, yet not telling you just what to do. Or just to be the shoulder to cry on. Good friends go places and do things together. Good Friends are always there when you need them.

err corr

Essay 2

Putting Labels on People

People tend to label someone as stupid if they are slower and takes more time in figuring out an assignment or just trying to understand directions. My friend Georgette is a good example. People make fun of her. When a person has to deal with this type of ridicule by her fellow students or friend she start to feel insecure in speaking up. She start to think she is slower mentally, she gets extremely paranoid when asked to give answer in class. She feels any answer out of her mouth will be wrong. Her self-image shoots down drastically, like a bottom less pit. that She will avoyd in answering all answers even when she's almost positive she's right. It's the possibility of being wrong that will keep her from speaking. Then when some one else gives the answer she seess she was right, she would become extremely anoid at herself for not answering the question. As a result, she start to run away from all challenges, even the slightest challenge will frighten her away. Do from the teasing of her friends, Georgette will lock herself away from trying to understand and her famous words when facing to a challenge will be I can't do it!

Therefore, when a person makes a mistake, you should think of what you say before you say it and be sure it's not going to hurt the person. You comments may help destroy that person self confidence.

err corr

Skill Refresher
Score Chart

Skill Refresher	Score (%)	Where to Get Help in Part Five: Reviewing the Basics
Sentence Fragments *(page 52)*	_____	C.1 *(page 457)*
Run-on Sentences *(page 74)*	_____	C.2 *(page 462)*
Subject-Verb Agreement *(page 98)*	_____	C.7 *(page 475)*
Pronoun-Antecedent Agreement *(page 120)*	_____	C.8 *(page 479)*
Pronoun Reference *(page 139)*	_____	C.9 *(page 482)*
Dangling Modifiers *(page 166)*	_____	D.1 *(page 492)*
Misplaced Modifiers *(page 186)*	_____	D.1 *(page 492)*
Coordinate Sentences *(page 206)*	_____	D.3 *(page 496)*
Subordinate Clauses *(page 232)*	_____	D.4 *(page 499)*
Parallelism *(page 263)*	_____	D.5 *(page 501)*
When to Use Commas *(page 289)*	_____	E.1, E.2 *(pages 509, 512)*
Using Colons and Semicolons *(page 315)*	_____	E.3 *(page 513)*
When to Use Capital Letters *(page 341)*	_____	F.1 *(page 520)*

Skill Refresher Answer Key

. . . .

SKILL REFRESHER—CHAPTER 3

■ Sentence Fragments (page 54)

Answers may vary.

1. Correct
2. Correct
3. Because we're good friends, I remembered her birthday.
   I remembered her birthday because we're good friends.
4. After I left the classroom, I realized I forgot my book.
   I realized I forgot my book after I left the classroom.
5. Before the professor moved on to the next topic, Jason asked a question about centrifugal force.
   Jason asked a question about centrifugal force before the professor moved on to the next topic.
6. The phone rang, and the answering machine answered.
   The phone rang; the answering machine answered.
7. I was hoping I would do well on the test.
   I studied fervently, hoping I would do well on the test.
8. Martha scheduled a conference with her art history professor to discuss the topic for her final paper.
9. I got a "B" on the quiz because I reread my notes.
   Because I reread my notes, I got a "B" on the quiz.
10. Marcus was interested in the course that focused on the rise of communism.
    Marcus was interested in the course because it focused on the rise of communism.

SKILL REFRESHER—CHAPTER 4

■ Run-On Sentences (page 75)

Answers may vary.

1. The Civil War ended in 1865; the period of Reconstruction followed.
   The Civil War ended in 1865, and the period of Reconstruction followed.
2. Although light and sound both emit waves, they do so in different ways.
3. Correct
4. Archaeologists study the physical remains of cultures; anthropologists study the cultures themselves.
   Archaeologists study the physical remains of cultures, while anthropologists study the cultures themselves.
5. The body's nervous system carries electrical and chemical messages. These messages tell parts of the body how to react and what to do.
   The body's nervous system carries electrical and chemical messages that tell parts of the body how to react and what to do.
6. Neil Armstrong was the first human to walk on the moon. This event occurred in 1969.
   Neil Armstrong was the first human to walk on the moon; this event occurred in 1969.
7. Robert Frost is a well-known American poet; his most famous poem is "The Road Not Taken."
   Robert Frost is a well-known American poet. His most famous poem is "The Road Not Taken."
8. Algebra and geometry are areas of study of mathematics; calculus and trigonometry are other branches.
9. Correct
10. Since it is easy to become distracted by other thoughts and responsibilities while studying, it helps to make a list of these distractors.
    It is easy to become distracted by other thoughts and responsibilities while studying. It helps to make a list of these distractors.

SKILL REFRESHER—CHAPTER 5

■ Subject-Verb Agreement (page 99)

1. wants
2. are
3. agrees
4. swim
5. knows
6. are
7. are
8. Candy
9. Sabrina
10. were

SKILL REFRESHER—CHAPTER 6

■ Pronoun-Antecedent Agreement (page 121)

1. our
2. his
3. his or her
4. it
5. his or her
6. their
7. he or she
8. his or her
9. their
10. he or she

SKILL REFRESHER—CHAPTER 7

■ Pronoun Reference (page 139)

Answers may vary.

1. Marissa told Kristin, "My car wouldn't start."
2. In the trunk, Brian found a book that his mother owned.
   Brian found a book in his mother's trunk.
3. Naomi put the cake on the table, and Roberta moved it to the
   counter after she noticed the cake was still hot.

4. The professor asked the student to loan him a book.
   The professor asked the student, "Could I borrow that book?"
5. Our waiter, who was named Burt, described the restaurant's specials.
6. Aaron's sister was injured in a car accident, but she would heal.
7. Correct
8. Another car, which was swerving crazily, hit mine.
   The car that was swerving crazily hit mine.
9. In hockey games, the players frequently injure each other in fights.
10. The hunting lodge had lots of deer and moose antlers hanging on its walls, and Ryan said he had killed some of the deer.
    The hunting lodge had lots of deer and moose antlers hanging on its walls, and Ryan said he had killed some of these animals.

SKILL REFRESHER—CHAPTER 8

■ Dangling Modifiers (page 166)

Answers may vary.

1. While standing on the ladder, Harvey patched the roof with tar paper.
2. Since I was nervous, the test seemed more difficult than it was.
   The test seemed more difficult than it was because I was nervous.
3. I was waiting to drop a class at the Record's Office; the line seemed to go on forever.
   Everyone was waiting to drop a class at the Record's Office; thus, the line seemed to go on forever.
4. Correct
5. The elevator was, of course, out of order while I was moving the couch.
   We discovered, while moving the couch, that the elevator was, of course, out of order.
6. While we were watching the evening news, the power went out.
   The power went out while Marge was watching the evening news.

7. After I decided to mow the lawn, it began to rain.
8. Since I was very tired, the long wait was unbearable.
   The long wait was unbearable because I was very tired.
9. While I was skiing downhill, the wind picked up.
   Skiing downhill, we noticed that the wind picked up.
10. The phone company hired me at the age of eighteen.

SKILL REFRESHER—CHAPTER 9

■ Misplaced Modifiers (page 186)

Answers may vary.

1. Marietta studiously previewed the test before she began answering the questions.
2. The book that Mark had returned late was checked out by another student.
3. Correct
4. The shocking article about the large donations political candidates receive from interest groups caused Lily to reconsider how she viewed candidates and their campaign promises.
   The article about the large donations political candidates receive shocked Lily, causing her to reconsider how she viewed candidates and their campaign promises.
5. Bryant cashed the student loan check that he desperately needed.
6. The angry crowd booed the referee when he finally arrived.
   Angry with the delay, the crowd booed the referee when he finally arrived.
7. Correct
8. The poetry of Emily Dickinson, a young, unhappy, and lovelorn woman, reveals a particular kind of misery and pain.
   The poetry of the young, unhappy, and love-lorn Emily Dickinson reveals a particular kind of misery and pain.
9. The governors of all the states met to discuss homelessness, a national problem.
10. Because health care workers are concerned about the risk of being exposed to the virus, they refuse treatment to many AIDS patients.

SKILL REFRESHER—CHAPTER 10

■ Coordinate Sentences (page 206)

Answers will vary.

1. A field study observes subjects in their natural settings; therefore, only a small number of subjects can be studied at one time.
2. The Grand Canyon is an incredible sight; it was formed less than ten million years ago.
3. Alaska and Siberia used to be connected twenty-five thousand years ago; consequently, many anthropologists believe that Native Americans migrated to North and South America from Asia.
4. Neon, argon, and helium are called inert gases, and they are never found in chemical compounds.
5. The professor returned the tests, but he did not comment on them.
6. Ponce de Leon was successful because he was the first European to "discover" Florida; however, he did not succeed in finding the fountain of youth he was searching for.
7. The lecture focused on the cardio-pulmonary system; therefore, the students needed to draw diagrams in their notes.
8. Rudy had never read *Hamlet*, nor had Rufus ever read *Hamlet*.
9. Presidents Lincoln and Kennedy did not survive assassination attempts, but President Ford escaped two assassination attempts.
10. Marguerite might write her paper about *Moll Flanders*, or she might write her paper about its author, Daniel Defoe.

SKILL REFRESHER—CHAPTER 11

■ Subordinate Clauses (page 232)

Answers will vary.

1. Although mushrooms are a type of fungus, some types are safe to eat.
2. When grape juice is fermented, it becomes wine.
3. It is important for children to be immunized since children who are not immunized are vulnerable to many dangerous diseases.
4. After a poem is read carefully, it should be analyzed.

5. Although the Vikings were probably the first Europeans to set foot in North America, Columbus "discovered" America much later.
6. While I was giving a speech in my communications class, Carl Sagan was giving a speech on campus.
7. When I started my assignment for French class, I was relieved that it was very easy.
8. Although infants may seem unaware and oblivious to their surroundings, they are able to recognize their mother's voice and smell from birth.
9. Because Neo-Freudians disagreed with Freud's focus on biological instincts and sexual drive, they formed new theories.
10. Although the hypothalamus is a tiny part of the brain, it has many very important functions, including the regulation of hormones, body temperature, and hunger.

SKILL REFRESHER—CHAPTER 12

■ Parallelism (page 263)

Answers may vary.

1. Melinda's professor drew an organizational chart of the human nervous system on the board, passed out a handout of it, and lectured about the way the nervous system is divided into subcategories.
2. Correct
3. Ski jumping, speed skating, and hang gliding are sports that require consideration and manipulation of velocity and wind resistance.
4. Professor Bargo's poetry class read famous poets, analyzed their poetry, and researched their lives.
   Professor Bargo's poetry class reads famous poets, analyzes their poetry and researches their lives.
5. Clams, oysters, and mussels are examples of mollusks.
   The clam, the oyster, and the mussel are examples of mollusks.
6. Correct
7. The United Nations was formed in 1945 to renounce war, uphold personal freedoms, and bring about worldwide peace and well-being.
8. In the 1980's Sandra Day O'Connor was appointed the first

female Supreme Court Justice, Geraldine Ferraro became the first female presidential candidate, and the Equal Rights Amendment was defeated.

9. The Eighteenth Amendment to the Constitution implemented Prohibition, but the Twenty-First Amendment, ratified fourteen years later, repealed it.

10. Correct

SKILL REFRESHER—CHAPTER 13

■ When to Use Commas (page 289)

1. Although I was late, my sister was still waiting for me at the restaurant.
2. Tom invited Marie, Ted, Leah, and Pete.
3. Following the movie, we had a late lunch.
4. I bumped into a beautiful woman, Lisa's mother, on my way into the grocery store.
5. The phone rang, but I was outside.
6. My niece began to yell, "I'm Tarzan, king of the jungle."
7. Bill, a friend from school, sent me a postcard from Florida.
8. When I entered the room, everyone was watching television.
9. I heard her call, "Wait for me."
10. Although I have visited Vancouver, I have never been to Vancouver Island.

SKILL REFRESHER—CHAPTER 14

■ Using Colons and Semicolons (page 315)

1. Anthropologists believe human life began in the Middle East; skeletons that have been found provide evidence for this.
2. The natural sciences include botany, the study of plants; chemistry, the study of elements that compose matter; and biology, the study of all living things.
3. The courses I am taking cover a wide range of subjects: linguistics, racquetball, calculus, anatomy, and political science.
4. Introductory courses tend to be broad in scope; they do give a good overview of the subject matter.
5. The poet, John Milton, tells how Eve must have felt when she was created: "That day I remember, when from sleep / I first

awaked, and found myself reposed / under a shade on flowers, much wond'ring where / and what I was, whence thither brought, and how."

6. Trigonometry incorporates many other math skills: geometry, algebra, and logic.
7. I enjoy a variety of sports: tennis, which is my favorite; golf, because it is relaxing; basketball, because it is a team sport; and racquetball, because it is a good workout.
8. When a skull is dug up by a gravedigger, Hamlet begins what is now a famous meditation on mortality: "Alas, poor Yorick, I remember him well."
9. Spanish is important to learn because many Americans speak it exclusively; it is also useful to understand another culture.
10. My botany text has a section about coniferous trees: pines, firs, cedars, and spruces.

SKILL REFRESHER—CHAPTER 15

■ **When to Use Capital Letters (page 341)**

1. Because I spent last Sunday in Pittsburgh, I missed my favorite television show—*60 Minutes*.
2. This summer I plan to visit the Baltic states—Estonia, Latvia, Lithuania—former Republics of the Soviet Union.
3. This May, Professor Gilbert will give us our final exam.
4. Last week I rented my favorite movie from the video rental store on Elmwood Avenue.
5. One of Shakespeare's most famous plays is *Hamlet*.
6. I live next door to Joe's Mobile gas station.
7. My brother will only eat Rice Krispies for breakfast.
8. Jean Griffith is a senator who lives in Washington County.
9. I love to vacation in California because the Pacific Ocean is so beautiful.
10. My neighbors, Mr. and Mrs. Wilson, have a checking account at the Lincoln Bank.

Text and Art Credits

Chapter 3

FRED MOODY   From "Divorce: Sometimes a Bad Notion." *Seattle Weekly,* Nov. 22, 1989. Used with permission.

Chapter 4

BILL GIFFORD   From *Rolling Stone,* 8/22/91. By Straight Arrow Publishers, Inc. 1992. All Rights Reserved. Reprinted by permission.

Chapter 5

E. B. WHITE   Reprinted courtesy of Cornell University Library, Department of Rare Books.

PHOTO OF FIRST FLAG ON MOON   Used with permission of NASA.

Chapter 6

L. RUST HILLS   From "How to Eat an Ice-Cream Cone," *How to Do Things Right: The Revelations of a Fussy Man* (New York: Doubleday, 1972). Reprinted by permission of the author.

GORDON PARKS   From *Voices in the Mirror* by Gordon Parks. Copyright © 1990 by Gordon Parks. Used by permission of Doubleday, a division of Bantam Doubleday Dell Publishing Group, Inc.

PHOTO OF ELLA WATSON   From *Voices in the Mirror* by Gordon Parks. Copyright © 1990 by Gordon Parks. Used by permission of Doubleday, a division of Bantam Doubleday Dell Publishing Group, Inc.

Chapter 7

PHOTO OF COACH   Carl Skalak/Sports Illustrated.

Chapter 8

WILLIAM PRIDE AND O. C. FERRELL   From *Marketing,* Seventh Edition. Copyright © 1991 by Houghton Mifflin Company. Used with Permission.

DAIRY AD   America's Dairy Farmers, National Dairy Board.

Chapter 9
JOE SCHWARTZ AND THOMAS MILLER   From "The Earth's Best Friends," *American Demographics*, Feb. 1991, pp. 26–35. Excerpt used with permission. © *American Demographics*, February 1991.

Chapter 10
DEBORAH PROTHEROW-STITH   From *Deadly Consequences: How Violence is Destroying Our Teenage Population* by Deborah Protherow-Stith and Michaele Weissman. Reprinted by permission of Harper-Collins Publishers Inc.

Chapter 11
MICHELE MANGES   "The Dead End Kids," The Wall Street Journal February 2, 1990. Reprinted by permission of The Wall Street Journal, © 1990 by Dow Jones & Company, Inc. All rights reserved worldwide.

Chapter 12
BARBARA LAZEAR ASCHER   "Hers: A Brother's Death," *New York Times Magazine*, November 19, 1989. Copyright © 1989 by The New York Times Company. Reprinted by permission.

Chapter 13
PETER FARB AND GEORGE ARMELAGOS   From *Consuming Passions: The Anthropology of Eating* by Peter Farb and George Armelagos. Copyright © 1980 by the Estate of Peter Farb and Houghton Mifflin. Reprinted by permission of Houghton Mifflin Company and Brandt & Brandt Literary Agents, Inc. All rights reserved.

Chapter 14
PETE HAMILL   Copyright © by Deidre Enterprises, Inc. Originally published in *Esquire* Magazine. Reprinted by permission of Pete Hamill.

Chapter 15
ELAINE MARIEB   from *Human Anatomy and Physiology*, Second Edition, by Elaine Marieb (Redwood City, CA: Benjamin/Cummings Publishing Company, 1992), p. 570. Reprinted with permission.

Additional Readings
"JANE DOE"   "Why Should I Give My Baby Back," *New York Times*, Op-ED December 22, 1990. Copyright © 1990 by The New York Times Company. Reprinted by permission.

LESLEY CHOYCE   "The Waves of Winter." First appeared in the *Globe and Mail*, March 7, 1987. Reprinted by permission of the author.

DOUGLAS COLLIGAN   "The Light Stuff." First appeared in *Technology Illustrated*, Feb–Mar, 1982; pp. 44–52. Reprinted by permission of the author.

DOUGLAS BERNSTEIN, ET AL.   "What is Stress" from, *Psychology*, Second Edition. Houghton Mifflin, 1991. Copyright © 1991 by Houghton Mifflin Company. Used with permission.

"WHAT IS STRESS" TABLE 13-1   Reprinted with permission of Journal of Psychosomatic Research, Vol. 29, pp. 213–218, Thomas H. Holmes and Richard H. Rahe, "The Social Adjustment Rating Scale," Copyright 1967, Pergamon Press, plc.

GERRI HIRSHEY   "Toddler Terrorism," New York Woman, Sept, 1990. Reprinted by permission of Sterling Lord Literistic, Inc. Copyright 1991 by Gerri Hirshey.

CARTOON   Illustration by Elwood Smith.

WILLIAM PRIDE AND O. C. FERRELL   From *Marketing*, Seventh Edition. Copyright © 1991 by Houghton Mifflin Company. Used with permission.

ROBERT LEVINE   From "The Pace of Life," *American Scientist* 78, (Sept.–Oct. 1990). Reprinted with permission.

MIKE CAPUZZO   "Wives Often Take a Beating When the Team Loses." Reprinted with permission from *The* *Philadelphia Inquirer*.

SCOTT RUSSELL SANDERS   From *Secrets of the Universe* by Scott Russell Sanders. Copyright © 1991 by Scott Russell Sanders. Reprinted by permission of Beacon Press, Boston.

ANNA QUINDLEN   From *Living Out Loud* by Anna Quindlen. Copyright © 1987 by Anna Quindlen. Reprinted by permission of Random House, Inc.

MARIA PARKER-PASCUA   From "Ozette: A Makah Village in 1491." *National Geographic*, Oct. 1991, pp. 38–53. Reprinted by permission of the author.

ANNE ESTRADA   "Judy Baca's Art for Peace," *Hispanic*, May 1991, pp. 16–18. reprinted with permission from HISPANIC Magazine.

PHOTO   World Wall © Social and Public Art Resource Center.

MICHAEL FOX   From *Inhuman Society: The American Way of Exploiting Animals* by Michael Fox. © 1990 St. Martin's Press, Inc., New York, NY. Reprinted with permission of St. Martin's Press and Lecture Literary Management, Inc.

DOUGLAS BERNSTEIN, ET AL.   "Altruism and Helping Behavior" from *Psychology*, Second Edition. Houghton Mifflin, 1991. Copyright © 1991 by Houghton Mifflin Company. Used with permission.

Index

Instructor's Resource Manual

to Accompany

THE WRITER'S EXPRESS

Instructor's Resource Manual

to Accompany

THE WRITER'S EXPRESS

Kathleen T. McWhorter

Niagara County Community College

Sponsoring Editor: Mary Jo Southern
Developmental Editor: Martha Bustin
Project Editor: Robin Hogan
Production Coordinator: Karen Rappaport
Senior Manufacturing Coordinator: Priscilla Bailey
Marketing Manager: George Kane

Printed in the U.S.A.

ISBN: 0-395-59896-6

123456789-DH-96 95 94 93 92

Contents

Chapter 3   Critical Thinking Skills   21

Chapter 4   Suggestions for Approaching the Readings   25

Chapter 5   Practical Suggestions for Teaching Writing   32

Chapter 6   Notes on Individual Chapters   39

Chapter 7 Using *Expressways*, the Computer Software Ancillary   48

Expressways Software Table of Contents   48
Overview   49
Benefits   58
Suggested Uses   58

Chapter 8 Overhead Transparency Masters   60

Figure Number	*Transparency Title*
2.1	The Writing Process
3.1	Previewing Steps
3.2	Sample Journal Entry for Chapter 3
4.1	Common Methods of Arranging Details
4.2	Using Specific Words
5.1	Revision: Examining Your Ideas
5.2	Draft 1
5.3	Draft 2
5.4	Draft 3
6.1	Parks's Day in Washington
8.1a	Sample Map: The Uses of Advertising
8.1b	Sample Map: The Uses of Advertising (continued)
10.1a	Exercise 10.8: Causes of Poor Community-Police Relationships
10.1b	Exercise 10.8 (continued): Community Policing
11.1	Similarities Between Paragraphs and Essays
11.2	Sample Essay Map
12.1a	Revision Checklist
12.1b	Revision Checklist (continued)
12.2	Proofreading Checklist
12.3a	Useful Transitions
12.3b	Useful Transitions (continued)
12.4	Exercise 12.13
13.1	Sample Student Summary

Preface

The primary purpose of this manual is to enable you, the instructor, to use *The Writer's Express* efficiently. Included here are a variety of resources designed to supplement the main text and to save you time.

Within this manual you will find ideas for using the text's features and classroom exercises for developing the writing and critical thinking abilities of your students. You will find brief discussions of ways to use the book's readings and information on thematic and rhetorical groupings that can be found within the reading program. There are, in addition, chapters on techniques for writing teachers, supplemental classroom activities for each chapter, an overview of *Expressways* (the software that accompanies *The Writer's Express*), and thirty-three overhead or copy masters of material that can be used in class. The final chapter of this manual provides a complete answer key for the grammar exercises that appear in the handbook section of the main text and for objective exercises in Parts One through Three.

I have developed the material in this Instructor's Resource Manual, like that in *The Writer's Express,* from my own experiences as teacher of writing. I encourage you to use and modify what you find here to suit your teaching style and the specific needs of your students. It is my hope that this manual will stimulate creative use of the text, not dictate a single way to use it, and that it will enhance your teaching experience and the success you achieve in the classroom.

Kathleen T. McWhorter

Instructor's Resource Manual

to Accompany

THE WRITER'S EXPRESS

CHAPTER 1
Overview of the Text

PURPOSE OF THE TEXT

The Writer's Express is a developmental composition text focusing on paragraph and essay writing skills. Its overall purpose is to teach basic writing students the fundamentals of paragraph and essay writing through structured, sequential instruction and practice. The text approaches writing as a process while providing encouragement, support, and practical applications throughout. The text links writing and reading, using readings as springboards to writing.

ORGANIZATION OF THE TEXT

The text is organized into five parts. It opens with an introductory chapter intended to establish the importance of good writing and to place writing within the context of the college experience. The chapter discusses elements of effective writing and offers students encouragement and advice for getting started. Because it is important for students to begin writing as early in the course as possible, numerous assessment exercises are included in the chapter. The chapter concludes with a "How to Use This Book" section, which explains the organization of Chapters 3 through 15 and the purpose of each section.

Part One focuses on paragraph writing strategies. Chapter 2 emphasizes the writing process and leads the student through each step. Chapter 3 presents an overview of paragraph structure and offers strategies for writing effective topic sentences. The focus of Chapter 4 is developing and arranging details. The use of relevant and sufficient detail and the use of specific words are emphasized. Chapter 5 discusses the revision process and describes strategies for examining ideas and editing for errors.

1

Part Two presents methods of developing paragraphs. Chapters cover narration and process; description; example, classification, and example; comparison and contrast; and cause and effect. Each chapter describes the rhetorical mode, explains its use, and offers specific strategies for organizing and developing a paragraph.

Part Three is concerned with essay writing techniques. Chapter 11 defines the essay and deals with planning strategies, including selecting and narrowing a topic and generating ideas. Chapter 12 describes techniques for drafting and revising the essay. Chapter 13 discusses planning and drafting expository essays, and Chapter 14 is concerned with persuasive essays. Strategies for writing essay exams and competency tests are addressed in Chapter 15.

Part Four contains fifteen additional readings. Questions for discussion and writing assignments are included for each. Part Five, "Reviewing the Basics," contains a brief handbook, which reviews principles of grammar, sentence structure, mechanics, and spelling.

ORGANIZATION OF CHAPTERS

Beginning with Chapter 3, each chapter follows a consistent organization and includes the following sections.

Writing Strategies

This section presents, explains, and demonstrates a key aspect of the writing process. Each skill is introduced, usually within the context of an everyday example, and its use and importance are discussed. Strategies and techniques are then presented. Students begin writing very early within this section, applying strategies as they are introduced. Sample student writing is included to demonstrate how skills are used. This section comprises the bulk of each chapter. The remaining, briefer sections build toward end-of-chapter writing assignments, emphasizing connections between reading and writing.

Thinking Before Reading

The purpose of this section is to introduce students to the reading that follows. Students preview the reading and discover what of their background knowledge and experience relates to the reading.

Previewing

Students are directed to skim through a reading before reading it. Previewing acquaints students with the content and organization of the reading while improving their comprehension and retention.

Questions to Activate Background Knowledge

Students are asked several questions that enable them to discover what they already know about the topic and to relate the topic to their experience. Verbal learning research has demonstrated that activating background knowledge improves comprehension, increases students' confidence in approaching new reading material, and builds or sustains interest.

Reading

The reading serves two primary functions. First, it serves as a springboard for writing. This function is discussed in more detail in a later section of this chapter. Second, the reading serves as a model, providing the students with the opportunity to see how other writers work with the techniques presented in the chapter. Each reading was carefully chosen to exemplify good writing in general, and, in particular, the writing strategies discussed in the chapter in which the reading is found. For example, the reading found in Chapter 6, "Narration and Process," is a narrative essay illustrating aspects of narrative style.

Getting Ready to Write

This section provides three steps that prepare students to write. The first demonstrates methods for reviewing and organizing the reading's literal content. For example, students learn techniques for underlining, outlining, and annotating.

The second step presents strategies that enable students to react to, interpret, and evaluate ideas expressed in the reading. The third step offers questions for discussion and reaction.

Writing About the Reading

This section contains one or more writing assignments about ideas expressed in the reading. The assignments are designed to encourage students to apply the writing strategies presented in the chapter.

Writing About Your Ideas

This section contains several writing assignments that encourage students to express their own ideas on topics related to the reading. This section also contains journal writing suggestions.

Revision Checklist

A Revision Checklist is included at the end of each chapter, beginning with Chapter 5. It provides a review of writing strategies learned in the chapter as well as a cumulative review of strategies learned in previous chapters.

Writing Success Tips

Each chapter includes a boxed insert that offers practical advice on topics related to writing. They are intended to address student concerns, suggest new strategies, and overcome common writing problems.

Skill Refresher

Each chapter offers a review of a topic related to sentence structure, grammar, or punctuation. The review begins with a brief refresher, followed by a 10-item self-assessment quiz. Students are directed to record their score on the Skill Refresher Score Chart. Students who score below 80 percent on the quiz are directed to pages in Part Five that present a more detailed explanation of the topic.

Summary

Chapters conclude with a brief summary that reviews key points of the chapter.

PEDAGOGICAL FEATURES OF THE TEXT

This text is distinct from numerous other developmental paragraph-to-essay texts currently on the market. Unique features include:

Supportive introductory chapter. Because many students are anxious about taking a writing course, the text opens with a positive, unthreatening introductory chapter, which offers students encouragement and support. It offers practical tips for getting started while focusing the student's attention on the importance and characteristics of good writing.

Assessment exercises. Chapter 1 contains six assignments that will enable the student and instructor to assess the student's writing experiences, attitudes, and approaches. These assignments encourage writing early in the course and emphasize its importance as a vehicle of communication between instructor and student.

Overview of the writing process. Chapter 2 introduces the student to a five-step writing process: generating ideas, organizing ideas, writing a first draft, revising and rewriting, and proofreading. This chapter establishes a process used throughout the book and focuses on writing as a process.

Use of practical, everyday situations to illustrate writing strategies. Students are shown that they are already familiar with the rhetorical modes by describing everyday situations that involve the same organization of ideas. Comparison-contrast, for instance, is introduced with the example of shopping for a used car and having to compare and contrast a Nissan and a Chevrolet. Because comparison shopping has been done by most students, they are able to more easily grasp the comparison-contrast concept.

Student writing samples. Each chapter contains one or more pieces of student writing used as an example or model of a particular writing strategy. The samples are motivational and enable students to establish realistic expectations of their own writing.

Incremental instruction. The writing strategies section approaches each skill incrementally. Students learn and apply skills in succession, building upon previously mastered skills. This progression occurs throughout the text, within each chapter as well as from chapter to chapter.

Realistic writing exercises. Students are given numerous and frequent practice exercises, usually within the context of a writing assignment. Routine drill exercises are minimal. Instead, students develop and revise paragraphs as they apply new writing strategies. The focus is on writing and revision, rather than error recognition.

Numerous visual and graphic aids. Many developmental students are visual learners; that is, they respond positively to and learn more easily through a visual medium. The text offers numerous tables, charts, diagrams, and checklists to accommodate this learning characteristic.

Idea mapping. The text uses idea maps (visual representations of the organization of a paragraph or essay) to demonstrate organization of ideas and to teach revision. This feature also accommodates students' visual learning style.

Chapter readings. The readings have wide appeal and interest. They touch on important topics within the students' realm of experience, such as environmental conservation, community policing, and family issues.

Additional readings. Fifteen additional readings comprise Part Four. The readings, identified by rhetorical mode, can be used as a substitute for or supplement to chapter readings. Chapter 4 of this Manual suggests ways these readings may be combined with chapter readings for a themed approach to the text.

READING AS A SPRINGBOARD TO WRITING

Beginning with Chapter 3, each chapter contains a reading on an interesting topic within the students' realm of experience. The reading serves as a springboard, or source of ideas, for student writing. Many developmental students have difficulty finding a topic to write about. Some lack confidence in expressing their own ideas. Because some students feel their ideas are not important or worthwhile, they are reluctant to write about them. Many students fail to recognize the wealth of their personal experience and do not readily draw on it when writing. The readings are intended to activate students' thinking, engage them in dialogue, build their confidence in their own ideas, and enable them to generate new ideas. In effect, the readings provide a source of ideas and lead the student toward self-expression.

Each reading is followed by two sets of writing assignments: Writing About the Reading and Writing About Your Ideas. The Writing About the Reading assignments direct the student to respond or react to ideas presented in the reading or to evaluate an aspect of the reading. These assignments ease the students into writing by asking them to write responses to specific topics. The Writing About Your Ideas assignments encourage students to relate reading topics to their own experience.

The Writing About the Reading assignments also introduce the student to one aspect of academic writing: responding to the ideas of others presented in written form. While many students may not be ready for a formal introduction to academic writing, it is important that they be exposed to the concept early in any college writing course.

In addition to serving as a springboard for writing, the readings also serve as models for writing. This feature of the readings is discussed in more detail in Chapter 2 of this Manual.

CORRELATIONS TO STATEWIDE WRITING COMPETENCY TESTS

Several states require college students to pass writing competency tests. Chapter 15 of the text offers students specific suggestions for preparing for and taking competency tests. Tables 1.1 and 1.2 list the writing skills evaluated by two representative states and indicate where in the text each skill is covered.

Table 1.1 **Texas Academic Skills Program (TASP)**

Writing-Skill Description	*Pages*
Recognize purpose and audience	
Purpose	5, 78, 270–272, 329
Audience	78, 269–270, 271–272, 275–276, 294–296, 329
Recognize unity, focus, and development in writing	
Shifts in point of view	494–495
Developing a main idea	32–41, 106–107, 110–111, 124–126, 143, 151, 153–154, 173–174, 192–193
Revising for unity and focus	77–87, 119, 138, 165, 185, 205, 247–252, 262, 287–288, 313–314, 340
Recognize effective organization in writing	
Methods of paragraph and essay organization	61–65, 107–108, 111, 131–132, 146, 152, 156, 174–177, 193, 223–225, 271–272, 299, 302
Transitional words or phrases	66–67, 108–109, 131–132, 157, 177–178, 196, 244–245, 277–278
Reorganizing sentences for cohesion	61–65, 84–86, 107–108, 131–132, 146, 152, 156, 174–177, 193–195, 223–225, 243, 248–252, 271–272, 302
Recognize effective sentences	
Identifying sentence fragments and run-on sentences	52–53, 74–75, 457–462, 462–466
Standard subject-verb agreement	98–99, 475–479

Placement of modifiers	166–167, 186–187, 492–493
Parallel structure	263–264, 501
Use of negatives in sentence formation	490
Word choice	506–507

Recognize edited American-English usage

Use of verb forms and pronouns	413–417, 419–420, 420–422, 452–453, 460–461, 467–472, 474–475, 483–484, 487–488, 499–500
Use of adverbs, adjectives, comparatives, superlatives	426–428, 429–431, 445–446, 487–498, 503
Plural and possessive forms of nouns	412, 517
Punctuation	289–290, 315–316, 464, 465–466, 509–518

THE WRITING SAMPLE

The following characteristics may be considered in scoring the writing samples.

Characteristic	*Pages*
Appropriateness	
Use of language	65–66, 86, 129–130, 506–507
Audience and purpose	5, 78, 269–272, 275–276, 294–296, 329
Unity and focus	
Main idea	32–41, 106–107, 110–111, 124–126, 143, 151, 153–154, 173–174, 192–193
Point of view	4–5, 78, 269–270, 294–296, 329, 494–495

Development

Amount, depth, and specificity of detail	55–65, 79–83, 268–272

Organization

Clarity and logical sequence of ideas	61–65, 107–108, 111, 131–132, 146, 152, 156, 174–177, 193, 223–225, 271–272, 299, 302

Sentence structure

Effective sentences	436–437, 443–444, 453–455, 492–507

Usage

Word choice	65–66, 129–130, 136, 259, 506–507

Mechanical conventions

Spelling	125, 526–531
Capitalization	341, 520–521
Punctuation	289–290, 315–316, 464, 465, 466, 509–518

Table 1.2 **Florida College-Level Academic Skills Test (CLAST)**

Writing-Skill Description	*Pages*
Identifying subjects for expository writing	38–40, 104–105, 110, 215
Determine the purpose for writing	5, 78, 270–272, 329
Meet requirements of time, purpose, and audience	4–6, 78, 269–270, 271–272, 275–276, 294–296, 329
Thesis statements	
Develop generalized v. concrete evidence	55–57, 60–61
Organizing main ideas	61–65, 107–108, 111, 131–132, 146, 152, 156, 174–177, 193, 223–225, 271–272, 299, 302
Unified prose	61–65, 107–108, 111, 131–132, 146, 152, 156, 174–177, 193, 223–225, 271–272, 299, 302
Transitional devices	66–67, 108–109, 131–132, 157, 177–178, 196, 244–245, 277–278
Demonstrate effective word choice	
Denotative v. connotative meanings	136–137
Slang, jargon, clichés	506–507
Word choice	506–507
Employ conventional sentence structure	
Placing modifiers	166–167, 186–187, 492–493
Coordinate and subordinate sentence elements	206–207, 232–233, 451–452, 465–466, 496–498, 499–500

CHAPTER 2
Instructional Features: Teaching Suggestions

After the first two introductory chapters, each chapter in *The Writer's Express* follows a consistent format. This format, which divides chapters into ten sections, was devised to emphasize the sequence of skills that lead from reading to writing. The nature and purpose of each of the ten sections were briefly described in Chapter 1 of this Manual, in the Organization of Chapters section. This chapter offers suggestions for approaching each of the ten elements.

WRITING STRATEGIES

The Writing Strategies form the longest and most important segment of each chapter. It is here that students learn techniques and skills for writing effective paragraphs and essays. Therefore, a significant portion of class time should be devoted to this section. Chapter 6 of this Manual offers specific suggestions for approaching each chapter's strategies; Chapter 8 contains useful overhead transparencies to be used in conjunction with specific strategies. The computer software *Expressways*, described in Chapter 7 of this Manual, provides supplementary instruction on particular writing strategies.

THINKING BEFORE READING

This section, intended to activate students' thinking, background knowledge, and experience, contains directions to preview the assignment, followed by thought-provoking questions related to the reading.

13

Previewing

Previewing is a popular technique with students. It is a technique they can use easily and with which they can experience immediate success. When introducing previewing (covered in Chapter 3 of the text), it is helpful to emphasize its benefits. Previewing makes reading easier, acquaints the reader with the content and organization of the material to be read, improves comprehension and retention, and may also have a slight facilitory effect on reading rate. Material is easier to read because the reader knows what to expect and can follow the writer's progression of thought more easily.

The first time students preview a reading should be in class. Then, once students are comfortable with the technique, previewing may be done during class or outside of class, depending on how the questions that follow are used. Transparency Master 3.1 lists steps in the preview process. Project this list (especially the first time students are using the technique) to guide students through the process.

Previewing is a useful technique for most types of reading material, especially textbooks. Encourage students to experiment with previewing in their other college courses. An evaluation of the benefits of previewing is a possible journal writing topic.

Questions

The questions that follow previewing and precede the reading may be used in several ways. They can serve as a basis for class or small-groups discussion. The questions may be used as additional writing assignments, or students may be directed to freewrite about one or more of the questions. If the questions are to be discussed in class, students should preview the reading prior to the discussion. Class discussion is advantageous because it builds interest and motivates students to do the reading.

Both previewing and the questions that follow guide the student toward formulating a purpose for reading. Knowledge of the readings' content and organization, along with connection with the students' experiences, will enable the students to decide what they intend to learn from the reading, that is, what information they need.

READINGS

The reading is best given as an outside assignment. Because some students may read very slowly and all read at differing rates, it may be difficult to have students complete the reading during class time without some students awkwardly waiting for others to finish.

The readings present numerous and diverse opportunities to analyze a writer's technique. To accompany the reading, various assignments can be created that further emphasize or reinforce the writing strategies taught in the chapter. For example, for

Chapter 7, "Description," students could be asked to underline particularly strong examples of the use of descriptive language. Additional class activities for each chapter are included in Chapter 6 of this Manual. Analysis of the reading in class is also useful in reinforcing writing strategies previously taught. For example, the author's use and placement of topic sentences could be analyzed and evaluated, or the arrangement of details might be studied.

If students need additional exposure to a particular mode, or if a reading is not well suited to their needs or interests, you may choose from fifteen additional readings included in Part Four of the text. The additional readings are arranged by mode and include writing assignments.

GETTING READY TO WRITE STRATEGIES

This section contains three steps designed to facilitate students' movement from reading to writing.

Step 1: Review of Literal Content

Before students can analyze, discuss, or write about a reading, they must grasp its literal content and organization. Each chapter presents a different strategy for reviewing literal content, as shown in Table 2.1.

This table also appears as Transparency Master 15.1. Reviewing this list of strategies with students may be helpful in encouraging students to use them.

Not all strategies are effective for every type of reading material. Encourage students to regard these strategies as choices or options. The strategy they choose should depend on the nature of the material and the students' purposes in reading.

Students will find each of these skills useful in reading and reviewing college textbooks, particularly when preparing for exams. As a class activity, students may discuss their success with a particular technique in other academic disciplines, identifying disciplines in which the technique is especially useful. Students may conclude, for example, that outlining is helpful in biology or that underlining topic sentences is effective in introductory social science courses.

Step 2: Thinking Critically

Critical reaction to and evaluation of text are necessary skills, but ones that few students possess. Each chapter presents a different critical reading strategy intended to enable students to interpret and evaluate the reading. The skills included are listed in Table 2.2.

Table 2.1 **Review of the Literal Content Strategies**

Strategy	Chapter	Page
Immediate review; underlining topic sentences	3	48–49
Recognizing types of supporting details	4	71
Drawing idea maps	5	95
Using idea mapping (sequence maps)	6	116
Marking revealing actions, descriptions, and statements	7	136
Using idea mapping to review and organize ideas (charts)	8	161–162
Using the three-column list for review (comparison-contrast)	9	181
Reviewing and organizing ideas	10	201–202
Outlining	11	229
Annotation	12	257–258
Summarizing	13	284
Outlining an argument	14	309–310
Underlining and reviewing	15	339

Table 2.2 **Critical Thinking Strategies**

Strategy	Chapter	Page
Discovering the author's purpose	3	49–50
Making inferences	4	72
Understanding symbols	5	95
Point of view	6	117
Understanding connotative language	7	136–137
Applying and transferring information	8	163
Distinguishing fact from opinion	9	182–183
Evaluating cause-and-effect relationships	10	203
Examining assumptions	11	229–230
Figurative language	12	259
Analyzing source and authority	13	284–285
Evaluating persuasive writing	14	311–312
Predicting exam questions	15	339

Refer to Chapter 3 of this Manual for a more detailed discussion of critical thinking skills.

Step 3: Reacting to and Discussing Ideas

Like all students, developmental students are able to write more easily about a topic after they have discussed it. The questions included in this section provide a means for students to move from spoken to written expression, while generating interest, exposing students to each other's ideas, and building self-confidence.

Students enjoy discussing the reading; for many it is the "reward" for completing the reading. Discussion may be conducted with the whole class, or small groups of three to four students may be formed. For additional suggestions on collaborative learning, refer to Chapter 5 of this Manual. It may be necessary to announce a time limit for discussion, unless you plan to devote the entire class session. Sometimes, it may also be necessary to focus the discussion, leading students back to topics that will be most useful in generating ideas about which to write.

The discussion questions may be used as additional writing assignments, either following discussion or replacing it.

WRITING ABOUT THE READING

This section includes a formal writing assignment and suggested journal writing topics. Each writing assignment directs the student to respond to ideas presented in the reading. This assignment moves students toward academic writing, giving them some experience in responding to the ideas of others.

Depending in part on the skill level of the students, this assignment may be given to complete outside of class, or the instructor may help students get started during class. To help students begin the assignment, divide the class into small groups and direct each group to generate ideas about the assignment using such techniques as brainstorming.

Because some students may have difficulty with the assignment, it may be useful to provide parameters within which students can work. At first, you might provide the students with a topic sentence or suggest three possible topic sentences at the time you make the assignment. Later, as students become more skilled, reduce the cues provided. For more on cue reduction, see Chapter 5. Uses for journal writing assignments are also discussed in that chapter.

WRITING ABOUT YOUR IDEAS

The assignments are offered as sources for additional writing assignments. They may be used before, after, or in place of the Writing About the Reading assignment. Alternatively, they may be used as topics for collaborative learning activities or further class discussion.

REVISION CHECKLISTS

The Revision Checklists begin in Chapter 5, once students have been acquainted with the basics of paragraph development and given strategies for revising. The checklists are cumulative, building on previously learned skills and adding new strategies, and their primary purpose is to guide students in the revision process. Encourage students to use the checklists each time they revise an assignment. The checklists are also useful for peer review of papers.

SKILL REFRESHERS

The Skill Refreshers may be completed during class or assigned as homework. If done in class, they work well at the beginning of class; they direct the students' attention to a specific task and open the class with a focused activity. Skills covered in the refreshers are listed in Table 2.3.

Answers for the refreshers are included in the Answer Key in the text. Encourage students to correct their errors, and be sure they understand *why* wrong answers are incorrect. If students score below 80 percent on the refresher, they are directed to a specific section of Part Five, "Reviewing the Basics," that provides a more comprehensive review of the skill. Instructors may assign the appropriate section of Part Five and ask students to complete and submit the exercise that follows the section. Alternately, students may work in groups or pairs to complete the exercise.

As a class or in groups, students may be directed to write their own skill refresher quizzes, then to exchange and complete each other's quizzes. When questions over correct answers occur, first refer students to the appropriate section of Part Five, "Reviewing the Basics." If the question is unresolved, it may be used as a class example or the instructor may provide an explanation.

Table 2.3 **Skill Refresher Topics**

Topic	Chapter	Page
Sentence fragments	3	52–54
Run-on sentences	4	74–76
Subject-verb agreement	5	98–99
Pronoun-antecedent agreement	6	120–121
Pronoun reference	7	139–140
Dangling modifiers	8	166–167
Misplaced modifiers	9	186–187
Coordinate sentences	10	206–207
Subordinate sentences	11	232–233
Parallelism	12	263–264
When to use commas	13	289–290
Using colons and semicolons	14	315–316
When to use capital letters	15	341

WRITING SUCCESS TIPS

Placed as a boxed insert within each chapter, the Writing Success Tips offer practical advice while providing a brief diversion from the regular text. Success tips are listed in Table 2.4.

The success tips may be used as a writing stimulus, either in student journals or as a writing assignment. Students may be asked to evaluate the tips or describe situations in which they used one or more of the tips.

Students enjoy writing their own success tips. As a collaborative learning activity, students may be asked to contribute additional tips on the same topic or generate tips on a topic not covered within the text. Groups may "publish" their tips, or the instructor may compile tips from each group and distribute a packet to all class members. Students should be encouraged to share their tip sheets with friends not enrolled in the course.

SUMMARY

Encourage students to read the summary before beginning a chapter and once again after completing it.

Table 2.4 **Writing Success Tips**

Topic	Chapter	Page
Keeping a journal, part one	1	11–12
Keeping a journal, part two	2	16–17
Organizing a place and time to write	3	34–35
College services for writing	4	58–59
Peer review	5	80–81
Should you use a word processor?	6	104–105
Spelling tips	7	125
Dictionaries and other reference works for writers	8	144–145
Building your concentration	9	170–171
How to summarize	10	190–191
Using a computer to organize and write papers	11	212–213
An overview of library resources and services	12	236–237
Taking notes when researching a topic	13	268–269
Writing for college courses	14	294–295
Controlling test anxiety	15	322–323

CHAPTER 3
Critical Thinking Skills

A unique feature of *The Writer's Express* is its emphasis on critical thinking. This emphasis predominates in sections relating to the chapter reading. The Getting Ready to Write section of each chapter presents a specific critical reading strategy, and the questions for reaction and discussion promote interpretation and evaluation. The Writing About the Reading assignment in each chapter requires the students to react critically to the chapter reading. The Journal Writing Suggestions and the Writing About Your Ideas assignments encourage reaction to, synthesis of, and application of ideas.

THE IMPORTANCE OF CRITICAL THINKING SKILLS

Because critical thinking is important to writing and reading, it is a vital and necessary skill in nearly all college courses. To organize and present ideas effectively in written form, a writer must think critically about them, evaluating the relevance of an idea and noting connections and relationships among ideas. Critical thinking is also necessary to grasp and evaluate another writer's ideas. After understanding a writer's literal meaning, the reader must be able to evaluate content, judging its worth, appropriateness, and relevance.

Despite its extreme importance, critical thinking is seldom taught. Many educators expect their students to think critically, yet few are prepared to explain the process. Critical thinking, like many other skills, has component parts, or subskills. Twelve important subskills are presented in the text. (For a list of these subskills, refer to Table 2.2, Critical Thinking Strategies, on p. 16 of this Manual.) Both chapter readings and additional readings serve as vehicles for the presentation of additional skills, as appropriate.

INTRODUCING STUDENTS TO
CRITICAL EVALUATION OF TEXT

Many developmental students view reading as an additive process of recognizing or pronouncing individual words to arrive at an understanding of what the writer is saying. Their focus is essentially literal. They regard reading as a visual process of seeing what is on the page rather than a mental process of understanding, interpreting, and evaluating the writer's meaning, intent, and process.

To simply encourage students to think critically is seldom sufficient. Students are unaware of the process and do not know how to begin. Instead, specific activities are often needed to demonstrate the process. Several useful activities are:

1. Use a seemingly simplistic piece of writing to demonstrate the types of critical thinking skills involved in all reading. For instance, the following text is seemingly straightforward:

    Sam ate dinner at Burger Heaven. The french fries were soggy.

    A reader automatically makes numerous assumptions and inferences about this text:

    a. Burger Heaven is a restaurant.
    b. Sam ate in the evening.
    c. Sam bought the french fries at Burger Heaven.
    d. Sam ordered more than french fries.
    e. Sam didn't like the french fries.
    f. Sam didn't expect the french fries to be soggy.
    g. The french fries are not always soggy.

    Use several examples, each of increasing complexity, to guide students in grasping the concept of critical thinking. Once they are able to recognize the kinds of inferences they already make, they are ready to move to unfamiliar text and toward more complex critical analysis.

2. Use a familiar nursery rhyme to demonstrate critical thinking.* For example, distribute copies of or ask students to reconstruct the Little Jack Horner rhyme. Then ask the students questions such as:

   a. Was Jack little or is "Little" part of his name?

   b. How little is little?

   c. Was Jack "good," or did he perceive himself as "good"? What does "good" mean?

   d. At what time of year did this event occur? Was it Christmas, or was he eating a previously frozen Christmas pie in February?

   e. What kind of pie was he eating? (When students respond with "plum," ask them how they know it was entirely plum and not, for example, plum and cherry or an apple pie with one plum in it. This question can lead to a discussion of hasty generalizations.)

   Work through several other rhymes in a similar way. Students will enjoy asking each other questions and, at the same time, will gain experience in critical thinking.

3. Present the students with two differing accounts or viewpoints of a single event. If possible, locate two articles from different sources describing a recent national or local news event. Select articles with fairly obvious differences or opposing viewpoints. Ask students to compare and contrast the articles by evaluating the content, the evidence supplied, the authors' purpose, the authors' objectivity or bias, and each article's effectiveness.

PRINCIPLES OF CRITICAL THINKING

While introducing students to the concept of critical thinking, try to incorporate some of the following principles into the discussions.

1. Most writers are reliable and trustworthy, but some are not. (Discuss sensational press.)

2. Everything that appears in print is not true. (Discuss opinions, value judgments.)

3. Some writers may include misleading information, either intentionally or unintentionally.

---

* Based on an exercise suggested by Anita Harnadek in *Critical Reading Improvement* (New York: McGraw-Hill, 1963).

4. Writers may express bias, but readers must recognize it.

5. Persuasive writing may contain both logical and emotional appeals.

Each of these principles will seem abstract to students unless demonstrated with concrete examples. Once students grasp these principles, suggest that they search for examples and describe them in their journal.

ADDITIONAL TEACHING STRATEGIES

The chapter readings and the additional readings are both excellent source material for teaching critical thinking. Here are a few suggestions on how to use the readings in addition to how they are used within the text.

1. *Apply skills cumulatively.* Each chapter of the text presents a different critical thinking strategy. However, while introducing a new skill, previously taught skills should be reinforced. For example, Chapter 3 teaches students how to discover the author's purpose. When working with the new skill in Chapter 4, also be sure to ask students to evaluate the author's purpose. As students progress through the book, then, they should build a repertoire of skills useful in evaluating text.

2. *Suggest critical thinking journal topics.* Encourage students to write journal entries describing or demonstrating their application of critical thinking skills. For instance, students may critically evaluate a political campaign speech, television coverage of an event, or a radio talk show host's objectivity or bias.

3. *Use advertising to demonstrate skills.* Advertising is clear and obvious material on which to practice many critical thinking skills. Bring to class several magazine ads and ask students questions such as: What is it designed to sell? (What is the author's purpose?) What evidence is given? How does it try to convince us? What is the writer's point of view? Advertisements also can serve as the basis for additional writing assignments.

4. *Encourage students to read with a pen or pencil in hand.* Direct students to underline revealing sections of the text and make marginal notes that reflect their critical thinking. Refer to the Getting Ready to Write strategies "Marking Revealing Actions, Descriptions, and Statements" (in Chapter 7) and "Annotations" (in Chapter 12).

CHAPTER 4
Suggestions for Approaching the Readings

Beyond the uses ascribed within the text, the readings may serve as the basis for further instruction on specific features of writing or the basis for thematic organization of a course.

READINGS AS MODELS

Each chapter's readings were chosen as models of the writing strategy or strategies taught in the chapter. The chapters do *not* include an apparatus for a detailed analysis of specific features of writing illustrated in the readings. Often, exegesis is best accomplished through discussion and reaction, with frequent references to the reading. (Paragraphs in each reading are numbered to facilitate reference and discussion.) To prepare students for discussion and analysis of the reading, however, specific assignments are helpful. For example, for Chapter 7, "Description," instructors may ask students to prepare to discuss and analyze the reading by underlining effective descriptive details and highlighting particularly strong examples of descriptive language. Or, for "The Uses of Advertising," the classification reading for Chapter 8, students could prepare for discussion by identifying the subgroups and underlining details describing each subgroup.

Although each reading was chosen as a model of the writing strategy taught in the chapter in which the reading was placed, only readings that exemplify all primary features of effective writing were chosen. Each reading is not only a model of a particular skill, then, but of all other skills taught throughout the text. For example, although "The Uses of Advertising" is a model of classification, it is also a model of effective use of topic sentences, use of relevant and sufficient detail, and so forth. Thus, students can be given numerous and varied assignments in preparation for analyzing a reading. Students might be asked to underline topic sentences or to note the arrangement of details in each paragraph. For essays, students might be asked to identify the thesis statement and draw an idea map of the remainder of the essay.

For each rhetorical mode represented by chapter readings, another reading is included in Part Four, "Additional Readings." Readings representing the same rhetorical mode may be paired for comparison and further analysis. For easy reference, comparable readings are listed in Table 4.1.

Table 4.1 **Rhetorical Table of Contents**

Narration

Gordon Parks, "The Charwoman" (Chapter 6, p. 112)
Barbara Lazear Ascher, "A Brother's Death" (Chapter 12, p. 255)
Jane Doe, "I Will Do Anything within My Power to Keep 'Boarder Baby'" (Additional Readings, p. 344)
Lesley Choyce, "The Waves of Winter" (Additional Readings, p. 347)

Process

Don Lago, "Symbols of Mankind" (Additional Readings, p. 351)

Description

Gail Y. Miyasaki, "Obāchan" (Chapter 7, p. 133)
Douglas Colligan, "The Light Stuff" (Additional Readings, p. 354)

Classification

William Pride and O. C. Ferrell, "The Uses of Advertising" (Chapter 8, p. 158)
William M. Pride and O. C. Ferrell, "Types of Consumer Buying Behavior" (Additional Readings, p. 371)

Definition

Douglas A. Bernstein, *et al.,* "What Is Stress?" (Additional Readings, p. 360)

Example

Gerri Hirshey, "Toddler Terrorism" (Additional Readings, p. 365)

Comparison and contrast

Joe Schwartz and Thomas Miller, "The Environment: What We Say Versus What We Do" (Chapter 9, p. 179)

Robert V. Levine, "The Pace of Life" (Additional Readings, p. 374)

Cause and effect

Deborah Prothrow-Stith, M.D., "Community Policing" (Chapter 10, p. 198)
Mike Capuzzo, "Wives Often Take a Beating When the Team Loses" (Additional Readings, p. 378)

Expository

Bill Gifford, "The Greening of the Golden Arches" (Chapter 4, p. 68)
E. B. White, "Moon-Walk" (Chapter 5, p. 92)
Michele Manges, "The Dead-End Kids" (Chapter 11, p. 226)
Peter Farb and George Armelagos, "Understanding Society Through Eating" (Chapter 13, p. 280)
Elaine Marieb, "Sunlight and the Clock Within" (Chapter 15, p. 337)
Scott Russell Sanders, "Fathers, Sons, and Sports" (Additional Readings, p. 382)
Anna Quindlen, "Homeless" (Additional Readings, p. 385)
Maria Parker-Pascua, "Ozette: A Makeh Village in 1491" (Additional Readings, p. 388)
Anna Estrada, "Judy Baca's Art for Peace" (Additional Readings, p. 395)
Douglas A. Bernstein, *et al.,* "Altruism and Helping Behavior" (Additional Readings, p. 403)

Persuasive

Fred Moody, "Divorce: Sometimes a Bad Notion" (Chapter 3, p. 44)
Pete Hamill, "Crack and the Box" (Chapter 14, p. 304)
Michael W. Fox, "The Captive Panther" (Additional Readings, p. 398)

Students may be assigned the additional reading for the same mode as the chapter on which they are working. After both readings have been completed, class discussion could focus on similarities and differences in the writer's approach, organization, audience, purpose, use of topic sentences, type of supporting detail, and diction.

USING A THEMATIC APPROACH

Readings may be approached thematically. In fact, some instructors may prefer to rearrange chapter sequence as well, thereby organizing the course thematically. Table 4.2 lists readings by thematic group.

Table 4.2 **Thematic Table of Contents**

Pete Hamill, "Crack and the Box" (Chapter 14, p. 304)
Douglas A. Bernstein, *et al.*, "What Is Stress?" (Additional Readings, p. 360)
Robert V. Levine, "The Pace of Life" (Additional Readings, p. 374)
Mike Capuzzo, "Wives Often Take a Beating When the Team Loses" (Additional Readings, p. 378)
Anna Quindlen, "Homeless" (Additional Readings, p. 385)
Douglas A. Bernstein, *et al.*, "Altruism and Helping Behavior" (Additional Readings, p. 403)

Science and humanity

E. B. White, "Moon-Walk" (Chapter 5, p. 92)
Elaine Marieb, "Sunlight and the Clock Within" (Chapter 15, p. 337)
Douglas Colligan, "The Light Stuff" (Additional Readings, p. 354)

Sports and sports-related issues

Lesley Choyce, "The Waves of Winter" (Additional Readings, p. 347)
Mike Capuzzo, "Wives Often Take a Beating When the Team Loses" (Additional Readings, p. 378)
Scott Russell Sanders, "Fathers, Sons, and Sports" (Additional Readings, p. 382)

Class discussions and writing assignments could focus on the thematic unit. Sample thematic-unit writing assignments are shown in Table 4.3. Due to their complexity, assignments are essay, rather than paragraph, length.

Table 4.3 **Sample Thematic Writing Assignments**

Theme	*Assignment*
Family issues	Write an essay explaining why the family seems important to one or more of the authors in this thematic group.
Art	Write an essay comparing the goals of Judy Baca with those of Gordon Parks.
Business	Describe the type(s) of advertising that would help McDonald's make consumers aware of and respond positively to the corporation's "greening."

Communication	Write a brief essay describing a situation in which you were able to communicate more effectively using a visual medium (drawing, diagram, or photo) rather than a verbal medium (writing, speaking), or vice versa.
The environment and nature	Each of the readings in this group identifies environmental problems and offers or describes solutions. Write an essay explaining whether you think we are being "tough" enough in mandating environmental change. Support your position with references to the readings.
Social issues	Select one social issue and write an essay offering alternative solutions to the problem identified in the readings.
Science	Write an essay describing how scientific writing differs from other types of expository writing. Support your ideas with examples from the readings.
Sports and sports-related issues	Compare the view of sports presented in "Fathers, Sons, and Sports" with that presented in "The Waves of Winter."

STUDENTS WITH READING DIFFICULTIES

Although the readings were selected to be of a reading level appropriate for most developmental students, there may be some students who have difficulty understanding them. You can identify students with reading difficulty by their inability to respond or react to the reading. Most often you will notice partial or incomplete comprehension, rather than a complete lack of comprehension. If these students are not concurrently enrolled in a reading course, they should be referred to the campus learning lab or academic skills center for assistance.

Figure 4.1 lists suggestions that may help students with difficult readings and is prepared in the form of a student handout. Instructors may wish to distribute copies to the entire class. If a student continues to experience difficulty with the readings, suggest a team or "buddy" approach in which the student reviews the reading with another student.

Figure 4.1 **Tips for Reading Difficult Material**

1. *Analyze the time and place in which you are reading.* If you have been reading or studying for several hours, mental fatigue may be the source of the problem. If you are reading in a place with numerous distractions or interruptions, lack of concentration may contribute to comprehension loss.

2. *Rephrase each paragraph in your own words.* You might approach extremely complicated material sentence by sentence, expressing each in your own words.

3. *Read aloud sentences or sections that are particularly difficult.* The auditory feedback signals that oral reading provides often aid comprehension.

4. *Look up unfamiliar words.* Keep a dictionary handy and refer to it as needed.

5. *Write a brief outline of the major points of the reading.* An outline will help you see the overall organization and progression of ideas of the material.

6. *Do not hesitate to reread difficult or complicated sections.* In fact, sometimes several rereadings are appropriate and necessary.

7. *Underline key ideas.* After you have read several paragraphs, think about what you have read and underline what is important. Underlining forces you to sort out what is important, which facilitates overall comprehension and recall.

8. *Slow down your reading rate if you feel you are beginning to lose comprehension.* On occasion, simply reading more slowly will provide the needed boost in comprehension.

9. *Summarize.* Test your recall by summarizing each section after you have read it.

CHAPTER 5
Practical Suggestions for Teaching Writing

This chapter offers a range of suggestions for how to teach writing effectively. Instructors may find some suggestions more helpful than others, depending on the nature of their students, specific course objectives, and teaching style.

COLLABORATIVE LEARNING

Recent research indicates that students can learn effectively from one another, especially in structured situations designed to facilitate the exchange of ideas. Collaborative learning, then, has become an important vehicle in the writing classroom. The following features of the text are particularly well-suited for small-group activities.

1. *Thinking Before Reading*. The questions that appear in this section may be used as topics for small-group discussions.

2. *Getting Ready to Write*. Each of the three activities contained in this section can be worked on by teams of two to three students. A team approach to Step 1, Review of the Literal Content of the Reading, will be particularly helpful if some or many of the students in the class find the readings difficult. Collectively, students can discover what is important and be sure they have grasped key ideas. Steps 2 and 3, Critical Thinking and the Questions for Reaction and Discussion, are also adaptable to group activity. Critical thinking skills are demanding and challenging for students and are often more easily explained by one student to another. (Student exchanges like, "Don't you see . . . ?" "You mean that . . . ?" and "OK, I've got it," are particularly likely when the topic is critical evaluation and interpretation.) The discussion questions can be discussed in small groups, which can prepare a summary

response to one or more questions and have a designated spokesperson present the response to the class.

3. *Writing Assignments.* One or more of the writing assignments could be begun in small groups or student teams. The generation and organization of idea stages work particularly well in groups or teams: students not only generate their own ideas, but they also benefit by observing the thought processes of others. Assignments, once written, can be reviewed by groups as well. (See Peer Review, below.)

4. *Writing Success Tips.* Small groups can be formed to discuss and evaluate the tips and to add additional advice or suggestions.

5. *Skill Refreshers.* Students may work together to complete skill refreshers, discussing how to respond to each item.

6. *Part Five: Reviewing the Basics.* Students may work through exercises in this section in teams of two or three students.

Here are a few suggestions for dividing the class into collaborative learning groups.

1. Decide, or experiment until you are able to decide, whether you will keep students in the same group for the semester or will rearrange them. There are advantages and disadvantages to either plan; the tasks the groups will perform are a determining factor, as is the student composition of particular classes.

2. Specify the size of each group and divide the class according to specific criteria (alphabetically, seating in the classroom, etc.).

3. To function effectively, groups need structure and direction. Specify the task they are to perform in as much detail as possible. If you are not using an activity directly from the text, printed directions may be helpful.

4. Decide how leadership in the group will function. The instructor may appoint a leader, or the group may appoint its own leader or rotate leadership. Determine who will report back to the class, if reporting is part of the activity.

5. The instructor may sit in on groups or work with groups not functioning as effectively as expected.

PEER REVIEW

Writing Success Tip 5, included in Chapter 5, introduces students to the process of peer review. Peer review is an excellent means for students to learn from one another, exchange ideas, share and solve problems, and observe one another's thinking. Peer review can be a step in the revision process, before a student submits a paper to the instructor, or it can be an end in itself.

Many instructors would like to assign more writing to students, but find it impossible to do so given the reading and correction time each assignment requires. Peer review is a practical way for students to receive feedback on their writing without adding to the instructor's load. Peer review can also be done in conjunction with *Expressways,* the computer software that accompanies the text (see Chapter 7 of this Manual).

JOURNAL WRITING

Beginning with Chapter 3, each chapter presents suggested topics for journal writing. Many students will need encouragement and support before they begin to keep a journal. At the beginning of the semester, read students' journals frequently. Most instructors agree that it is not necessary to read every entry; sampling is sufficient. Error correction is unnecessary and, in fact, is generally avoided because it may inhibit students from responding freely and openly. Try to make several positive comments, because they will build the student's confidence in the journal-writing process. Comments in which you respond to the ideas expressed are particularly useful.

CONFERENCING

Conferencing, although time-consuming, is rewarding for both the student and the instructor. If possible, try to meet with each student for 10 to 15 minutes every three or four weeks. Conferences provide students with the opportunity to build rapport with the instructor, a difficult task for students who feel uncomfortable in or unfamiliar with an academic environment. Conferences enable students to see the personable side of the instructor, and they provide a balance or counterpoint to the authority-figure image most students hold. Because the instructor is the audience for many papers students will write, it is important that students feel knowledgeable about and comfortable with the instructor. Conferences enable the instructor to relate to students, discuss individual problems, check assigned work, make specific recommendations, and assign additional work in areas of weakness.

Here are a few specific suggestions for conducting effective conferences.

1. Make sure students view conferences as a requirement. Some instructors refuse to grade or return papers until conferencing requirements have been met. Others incorporate conferencing into their grading system.

2. Scheduling a specific time (such as Tuesday at 3:15 P.M.) for each student is more effective than telling students to see you anytime during a time block (Monday or Wednesday between 2 and 4 P.M., for example). Be sure each student writes down the conference time. Some instructors distribute colored slips of paper for this purpose.

3. It is usually best to discuss only one paper per conference.

4. Be sure to begin your conference positively, praising the student for an area of strength.

5. Review the student's writing, pointing out several key problem areas. Don't try to cover too many weaknesses in one conference; the student will feel overwhelmed.

6. Discuss content and organization first, thereby placing emphasis on the expression of ideas. Later, you may call the student's attention to grammatical errors and assign, or refer him or her to, appropriate sections of Part Five, "Reviewing the Basics." Some instructors prefer to identify the line in which an error has occurred and ask the student to locate and correct it, thus simulating the revision and error-correction process.

7. Instructors may use conference time to be sure students have been keeping up with chapter assignments in Part Five, "Reviewing the Basics," or with journal assignments.

8. Encourage students to contribute to the agenda of the conference; they may have specific questions or concerns to discuss.

9. Conclude the conference with two or three specific suggestions or areas on which the students should focus.

Most instructors immediately recognize the benefits of conferencing, but have difficulty finding enough time to conduct them. Here are some timesavers.

1. Conduct some conferences while the other students are completing an in-class writing assignment. Place two seats in the corridor outside the classroom, and conduct conferences there to avoid breaking the concentration of the other students.

2. You will need to spend less time reading, correcting, and commenting on papers if they are discussed during conferences. Often, a fairly quick reading prior to the conference is sufficient. If necessary, you can also make a few brief reminder notes.

3. By having students complete sections of the text at home or in collaborative learning groups that meet outside of class, you may be able to cancel classes occasionally and conduct conferences throughout the day.

4. By using peer review in place of instructor grading on some assignments, you may be able to allocate more time for conferencing.

CREATING A SENSE OF COMMUNITY

Students need to feel that they are part of a community, that they belong to a group that shares goals, problems, and concerns. Classmates at a nonresidential college often make little effort or have little time to get to know one another. Some are busy working long hours, caring for children, and maintaining a household. Others feel comfortable within their residential community of old friends and do not recognize the value of building new communities.

An "ice-breaking" activity during the first week of classes often helps students develop a positive, trusting rapport among themselves. Two activities are suggested below; many others are available through campus library resources. Each activity enables the students to get to know each other while providing the instructor with information about each one.

Activity 1

Announce to the class that, instead of calling roll, you will use a different strategy to discover who is present. Tell the class that you would like each person to learn the name of one other person and discover some interesting or unique fact about the person (something more interesting than what town the person lives in or what he or she is majoring in). Leave the room for ten minutes and on returning ask the students to tell you who they met and to share the facts they learned.

Activity 2

On the first day of class, distribute to students a brief questionnaire asking for demographic and biographical data (name, address, other courses they are taking, etc.). Using the questionnaires, write a set of questions on index cards, each question on a separate card (for example, Who lives in Sanborn? Who is taking karate?). During the second class, randomly distribute one card to each student, directing him or her to find the answer to the question by talking individually to the other class members.

BUILDING A WRITING VOCABULARY

Students know more words than they use in their writing. There are thousands of words students recognize or understand through reading or listening that they do not use in writing (or speaking). Many students think they should improve their writing vocabulary by locating and learning new words—often a laborious task and one to which few students are truly committed. A more manageable approach is for students to transfer words from their reading and listening vocabularies to their writing vocabulary.

Encourage students to keep a file of useful words that they feel would make their writing more precise, exact, or descriptive. The file may be kept on index cards, with the word on the front and a synonym or brief definition on the back. The source of the words may be varied: instructors' lectures, reading assignments, other students, recreational reading, and so forth. Students should review the file frequently. Eventually, these words will be transferred to their writing.

CUE REDUCTION

Cue reduction is a teaching strategy involving successive reduction of cues or assistance to students as they perform a task. In the beginning, when a task is new and unfamiliar, students require numerous cues. As the task becomes more familiar and as the students become more skilled, fewer prompts are necessary. For example, when students begin writing descriptive paragraphs, help them form a dominant impression of a topic through class activities before giving a writing assignment on the topic. You might even assist students in drafting possible topic sentences. Later, offer successively less assistance until the student is able to write a descriptive paragraph by himself or herself.

ERROR LOG

Chapter 5 of the text encourages students to keep an error log in which they record types of errors. Students often need encouragement to keep up with and refer to this log. Once they begin using it, however, they quickly become convinced of its value. Once the log has been introduced, the instructor may occasionally spot-check error logs to emphasize their importance and assist students who may not be developing them correctly.

COMMENTING ON STUDENT PAPERS

An instructor's comments are extremely valuable to students. Instructors may find the following suggestions useful.

1. Make positive, as well as negative, comments. Do not assume students know what they have done well. Positive comments build students' self-confidence as writers.

2. Announce in advance the criteria on which the paper will be evaluated and limit criticisms to those criteria. This strategy will make evaluation easier (and faster) and, more importantly, will not overwhelm or discourage students.

3. Suggest to the student *how* to revise the paper. For instance, students may recognize that the organization of a paragraph is weak, but may not know what to do to strengthen it.

4. When students submit revised papers, ask them to resubmit the original versions. With both versions at hand, the instructor can more easily discover and evaluate the writer's revision strategies.

5. When a weakness is identified and the student is unable to remedy it, make referrals for additional study and practice. For grammatical and mechanical errors, refer students to a specific section of Part Five, "Reviewing the Basics." For problems in generating, organizing, and expressing ideas, assign specific units in *Expressways,* the computer software that accompanies the text.

6. Sections in Part Five, "Reviewing the Basics," are coded for easy reference. Refer to the inside back cover of the text for a summary chart of the coding system. If you mark errors and indicate the codes in the margins, students will be able to refer to the sections that explain their errors.

CHAPTER 6
Notes on Individual Chapters

This chapter offers suggestions, tips, and additional class activities for each chapter in *The Writer's Express*.

CHAPTER 1   AN INTRODUCTION TO WRITING

This chapter is intended to get students started with their writing course in a positive, nonthreatening, supportive manner while building expectations about what effective writing involves. It concludes with a How to Use This Book section, which explains the organization of subsequent chapters.

The six assessment exercises contained in this chapter are primarily intended to get students writing as soon as possible and to provide both students and instructor with information on the students' writing experiences, views, and approaches. These exercises are best ungraded. Because students have not as yet learned any new skills, it seems inappropriate to grade them on prior learning.

Because many students will want to know "how they did," instructors might provide students with feedback in conferences or by indicating *both* strengths and one or two primary areas of weakness on which to concentrate first.

After students have read Success Tip 1, Keeping a Writing Journal, Part One, instructors should announce their expectations or requirements, if any, of journal writing. Give students specific guidelines: indicate how often they should write and when they are to submit their writings.

Class Activities

1. To introduce this chapter, you might ask students to brainstorm lists of everyday, academic, and career situations in which writing is necessary. Brainstorming this list will build an awareness of the importance of writing and its role within academic and occupational or career environments.

2. Ask the class or small groups of students to generate two lists: Characteristics of Good Writing and Characteristics of Poor Writing. You might distribute several samples of good and poor writing for students to examine. The poor samples should not be filled with grammatical or mechanical errors (papers of this sort will focus students' attention on such errors). Instead, they should be examples of problems in the expression and organization of ideas.

CHAPTER 2   THE WRITING PROCESS: AN OVERVIEW

Chapter 2 introduces students to each step of the writing process and offers four specific techniques for generating ideas: freewriting, brainstorming, branching, and questioning. The chapter also foreshadows topics to follow in later chapters, while reassuring students that they will learn more about each step as they progress through the text. Emphasize to students that the purpose of the chapter is to *introduce* the writing process. After reading the chapter, students should be *aware* of the process, but by no means should have mastered it.

Class Activities

1. There are two concepts about the writing process that students should understand: (1) the process is learned gradually and (2) writing skills can always be improved. To assist students in grasping these concepts, draw an analogy to other skill learning. Ask students to think of a skill at which they feel accomplished (sports, arts, crafts, etc.). Discuss how long they have been performing the skill, how they learned it, and whether or not there is room for further improvement.

2. Students should be aware early in the course that not all techniques are equally effective and that they must choose ones that work best. The four methods of generating ideas are a good case in point. Ask students to state their preliminary preference for techniques by listing them in priority order. Then divide the class into four groups, based on their first preference. Direct each group to:

   a. Compare their rankings of the other techniques.

b. Discuss why everyone in the group preferred the technique they did. Urge students to consider how they learn (auditorily, visually, or spatially) and how they approach tasks (systematically or creatively, in an organized way or unstructured one).

Students are likely to recognize that their preference is related to their learning style and their task orientation. For example, students who prefer branching are likely to be visual, systematic learners, while students who prefer freewriting tend to be more creative, unstructured learners.

CHAPTER 3 WRITING TOPIC SENTENCES

This chapter defines a paragraph and focuses on choosing manageable topics and writing effective topic sentences.

Class Activities

1. To help students grasp the importance of topic sentences, show several examples of paragraphs in which the topic sentence has been deleted and, as a result, the text is difficult to understand.

2. Present students with several paragraphs in which the topic sentence has been deleted, and ask students, individually or in groups, to draft a topic sentence that fits the paragraph. Alternatively the instructor can supply three possible topic sentences and ask students to select the most appropriate one, indicating why the others are less appropriate.

CHAPTER 4 DEVELOPING AND ARRANGING DETAILS

This chapter focuses on the development and arrangement of details to support the topic sentence. Students tend to have difficulty including specific details; many tend to write in generalities and lack the sense of how vivid and specific language contributes to a paragraph's development.

Class Activities

1. To demonstrate the importance of vivid and specific detail, show two versions of a student sample, the first of which lacks vivid and specific detail and the second of which has been revised to include it.

2. To build student skill in arranging details, present student groups with paragraphs for which each sentence is typed on an index card or individual strip of paper. Scramble the order of the cards or strips, and direct students to unscramble them to produce a coherent paragraph.

CHAPTER 5   STRATEGIES FOR REVISING

Revising is one of the more difficult steps in the writing process to teach. Many students are satisfied with their first draft; others are willing to rethink their work, but don't know how to begin. The revision process is effectively taught through demonstration, both in groups and individually. Using an overhead projector, show a piece of student writing and ask students for suggestions on how to begin revising the paper. Refer them to the Revision Checklist used in the chapter; work through one or more revisions on the overhead screen.

It is important to get students accustomed to using the revision checklist introduced in this chapter because it is used in each subsequent chapter throughout the remainder of the text.

Some students may need assistance in studying the revision process, which is demonstrated in the reading "Moon-Walk." Class discussion and evaluation of the three drafts would be helpful.

Class Activities

1. After students have completed the first draft of a writing assignment, divide the class into pairs. Direct students to exchange papers, evaluate each other's draft using the Revision Checklist, and make specific suggestions for revision.

2. Divide the class into groups and present each group with a piece of student writing. Ask them to use the Revision Checklist to evaluate the writing and make suggestions for revision.

3. Either as a whole or in groups, ask students to apply the Revision Checklist to the final draft of "Moon-Walk."

CHAPTER 6   NARRATION AND PROCESS

Narration and process seem to be the easiest methods of development for students to grasp. Most students have some experience in writing in the mode and especially enjoy writing narratives. In many writing situations, students have difficulty including detail adequate to support their main point. In writing narratives, the opposite seems to be true: students have a wealth of detail, but have difficulty shaping a topic sentence that makes a point about the events they are describing or story they are telling.

Class Activities

1. Think of a recent local or national event or incident; a controversial event is ideal. Ask each student to write a narrative paragraph explaining the event. Students will, in all likelihood, express differing views of the event. Direct students to systematically exchange papers until they have read everyone's paragraph. Explain to students that this activity demonstrates that it is possible to have a variety of viewpoints on a single event. (The instructor might list topic sentences on the chalkboard or use an overhead projector.)

2. Conduct a demonstration of a process in front of the class (or ask a student to do so). Demonstrations might include assembling an object or assembling ingredients for a cake (then passing out samples of a baked one). Try to choose an odd, exotic, or humorous demonstration to make the activity fun. After the demonstration, ask students to write a paragraph describing the process. Students can compare paragraphs, noting discrepancies, missing information, etc.

CHAPTER 7   DESCRIPTION

Students enjoy descriptive writing, but often experience difficulty in expressing a dominant impression and in arranging details in a logical sequence. The following activities are designed to assist students in these areas.

Class Activities

1. Bring to class several photographs that reveal a strong, clear impression. Discuss each photo.

2. Present students with descriptive paragraphs for which the topic sentence has been deleted. Ask students to supply topic sentences that produce dominant impressions that the details support. (This activity may be conducted with the entire class, in pairs, or in small groups.)

3. Bring an unusual object to class and ask the students to write a paragraph describing it. Compare dominant impressions and methods of arranging details.

CHAPTER 8
EXAMPLE, CLASSIFICATION, AND DEFINITION

Example, classification, and definition are alternative methods of explaining. You might introduce the chapter by listing numerous topics on the chalkboard and discussing how each might best be explained (possible topics include toothpaste, love, living room furniture, rude behavior, junk food).

Class Activities

1. To introduce the classification mode, bring a collection of 15 to 20 objects from around your household to class, arrange them on a table in random order, and ask students to discuss how they might be classified. Alternatively, you could select 15 to 20 different periodicals from the library and ask students to classify them.

2. To help students grasp the elements of a definition, give them practice in class (as a whole or in groups) composing oral definitions of terms. Students especially enjoy defining slang terms.

CHAPTER 9   COMPARISON AND CONTRAST

The comparison-contrast mode is one of the most commonly used in academic writing. You might introduce the chapter by giving students examples of academic assignments that require comparison-contrast analysis (include specific term paper topics and essay exam questions from other campus courses).

Class Activity

Bring two photographs, two advertisements, or two objects to class. Introduce the two-column list by asking students (individually or in groups) to identify characteristics of each. Then ask students to match up their lists, identifying items that describe the same feature or characteristic.

CHAPTER 10   CAUSE AND EFFECT

Cause and effect is often a complicated thought process and one students have difficulty writing about. Students often need help in distinguishing cause and effect. You might present numerous case situations and ask students to generate both causes and effects.

Class Activities

1. Use a recent international, national, local, or campus incident or hypothetical situation to analyze causes and effects. Students could be asked to speculate about causes of the incident and to project both immediate and long-range effects. You could then work with students to determine how the effects could be organized.
2. Discuss causes and possible effects of a proposed piece of legislation or campus policy.

CHAPTER 11   PLANNING YOUR ESSAY

This chapter begins by emphasizing similarities between paragraphs and essays, then discusses the organization of an essay. Choosing and narrowing a topic are discussed briefly in Chapter 3, "Writing Topic Sentences," and discussed in more detail here. Students may need additional examples and practice with topic narrowing. This activity lends itself well to small-group work.

Class Activity

Present students with a brief essay for which the thesis statement has been deleted. Direct students (individually or in groups) to draft a thesis statement that the details seem to support.

CHAPTER 12   DRAFTING AND REVISING YOUR ESSAY

This chapter focuses on the development and revision of the essay. Tone is sometimes a difficult concept for students to grasp. Activities 1 and 2 are very useful in developing the concept of tone.

Class Activities

1. Bring to class several pieces of writing with different tones. Good sources include magazine ads, literature, newspapers, manuals, and textbooks. First ask students to identify the tone of each piece, then closely analyze how the tone was established.

2. Ask students to review several of the chapter readings or additional readings they have completed and to identify the tone of each.

3. Present students with an essay lacking an introduction and another lacking a conclusion. Discuss the effect of the deletion—for example, what information the reader lacks—then ask students to draft possible introductions and conclusions.

CHAPTER 13   WRITING EXPOSITORY ESSAYS

Emphasize that this chapter is an important one since most academic writing is expository. Instructors will find that expository-essay writing flows easily for their students because of the various methods of paragraph development previously covered. Many students lack experience in using and documenting sources correctly. Many college libraries or learning labs offer workshops, videotapes, or individualized assistance in research and documentation procedures. If students lack such skills, refer them to one or more of these sources.

Class Activities

1. Assign an expository essay on how to research and take notes on a topic.
2. Assign an expository essay on plagiarism and its consequences at college.

CHAPTER 14   WRITING PERSUASIVE ESSAYS

Persuasive essays are difficult for students because they require careful and reasoned selection and presentation of evidence in support of a specific position on an issue. As the chapter emphasizes, analysis of audience is a critical aspect in persuasive writing.

Class Activities

1. Students often need assistance in developing the line of reasoning, or argument, used in persuasive essays. It often helps to begin with a simplified example in which the thought process is more transparent. Magazine advertisements work well in this capacity. They are familiar sources of persuasion that can provoke discussion, particularly since some ads do not offer relevant or convincing evidence.

2. Split the class into two groups. Assign a familiar topic. Direct one group to consider their audience as in agreement with them; direct the other group to consider their audience as being in disagreement. Ask both groups to discuss evidence they would include and how they would organize it, and to report their strategies. Discuss with the students similarities and differences in the groups' approaches.

CHAPTER 15
WRITING FOR ESSAY EXAMS AND COMPETENCY TESTS

This chapter offers strategies and techniques for approaching essay exams and competency tests, which students are likely to encounter early in their college career.

Class Activities

1. Ask students to predict several essay exam questions for another course they are taking this semester.

2. Select one of the chapter readings or additional readings that students have already read and that could fit in the context of an academic course. Divide students into groups and ask them to predict an essay question based on the reading.

3. Conduct a simulation of a competency exam. Use peer review to provide student feedback on the papers.

CHAPTER 7
Using *Expressways,*
The Computer Software Ancillary

Expressways is an interactive tutorial software program designed to accompany *The Writer's Express*. It mirrors the text's organization and pedagogy, reinforces the instruction given in the text, and provides the student with extra writing practice.

A demonstration disk is available from your Houghton Mifflin Company sales representative or regional Houghton Mifflin office. The complete program is available to instructors who adopt the text. The software is available in both IBM or Macintosh versions. When requesting software, please be sure to specify which version you need.

EXPRESSWAYS SOFTWARE TABLE OF CONTENTS

The program consists of eighteen modules, covering the following topics:

1. Getting Started (Prewriting Techniques)

The Paragraph

2. The Topic and Writing Effective Topic Sentences
3. Generating Ideas for Writing
4. Rewriting and Revising Strategies

Paragraph Modes

5. Narration
6. Process
7. Description

OVERVIEW

Expressways is designed to teach the writing process in conjunction with *The Writer's Express*. The software focuses on the five-step writing process on which the text is built. Using a clear, consistent format, each module immediately engages the student in the writing process. Students receive a brief introduction of the writing strategy or rhetorical mode under discussion and an example, and then they begin to select a topic and generate ideas. They are guided through each stage of the writing process by on-screen prompts. They are given many opportunities for practice and review and frequent summaries to reinforce important points. Boxes, diagrams, and flow charts throughout the program help make the structure of paragraphs and essays easy to visualize. A short, relevant reading near the end of each module provides more opportunities for writing within the software. Following are some sample screens from the module on writing process paragraphs. Actual screens may vary in appearance.

Expressways Sample

Guidelines for Writing Effective Process Paragraphs

1. The steps in a process should be presented in the order in which they occur. In a "how-it-works" paragraph, the steps should be presented in a logical, easy-to-follow fashion.

2. Be sure to include only essential, necessary steps. Avoid comments, opinion, or unnecessary information. They may confuse your reader.

3. Assume, unless you know otherwise, that your reader is unfamiliar with your topic. Be sure to define unfamiliar terms and identify clearly any technical or specialized tools, procedures, or objects.

4. Use a consistent point of view. Use either the first person "I" or the second person "you" throughout. Don't switch between them.

(Menu)

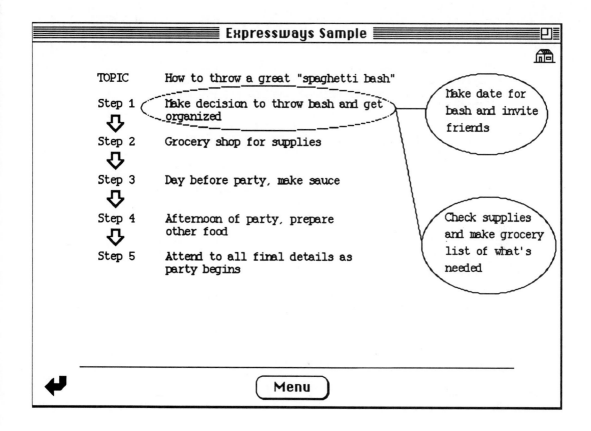

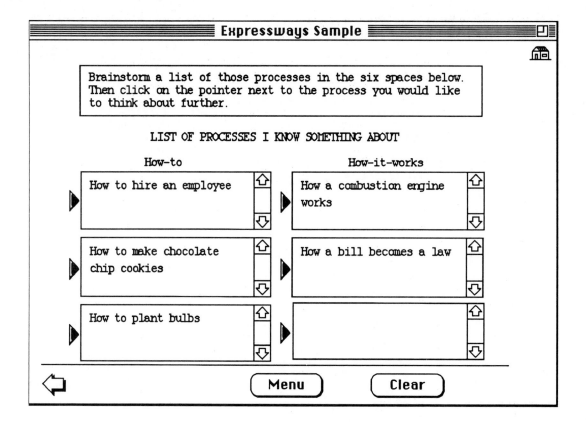

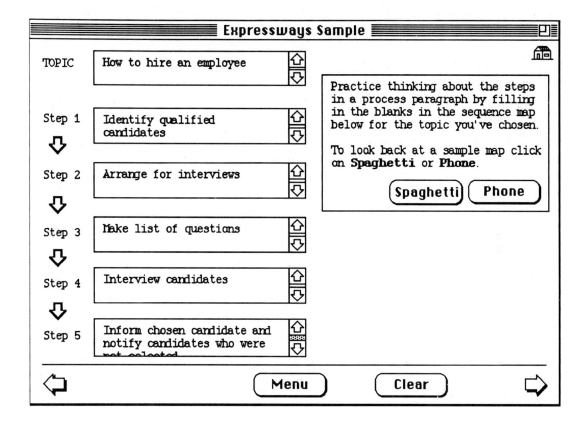

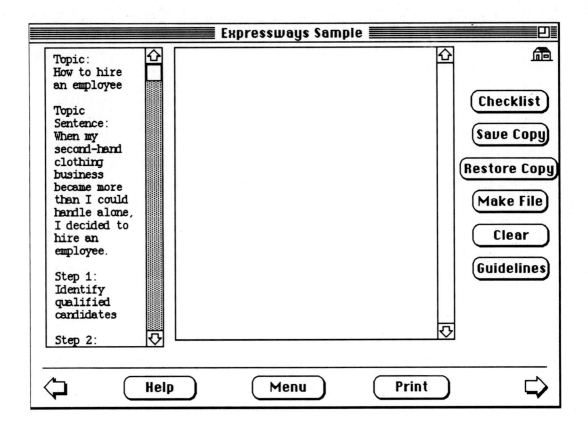

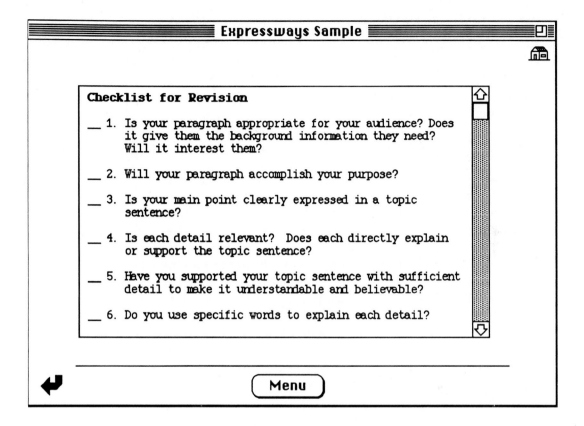

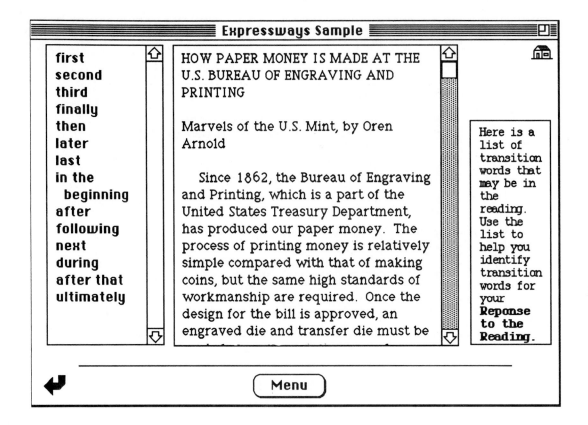

Expressways Sample

| |
| |
first
second
third
finally
then
later
last
in the
  beginning
after
following
next
during
after that
ultimately

HOW PAPER MONEY IS MADE AT THE U.S. BUREAU OF ENGRAVING AND PRINTING

Marvels of the U.S. Mint, by Oren Arnold

Since 1862, the Bureau of Engraving and Printing, which is a part of the United States Treasury Department, has produced our paper money. The process of printing money is relatively simple compared with that of making coins, but the same high standards of workmanship are required. Once the design for the bill is approved, an engraved die and transfer die must be

Here is a list of transition words that may be in the reading. Use the list to help you identify transition words for your **Reponse to the Reading.**

Menu

========================= **Expressways Sample** =========================

SUMMARY

A process paragraph describes how something is done or how
something works.   To write effective process paragraphs

- write about a topic that is familiar.

- be sure your topic sentence identifies the process or
  procedure you are writing about.

- be sure your topic sentence explains why your topic is
  useful or important.

- arrange your details in the order in which they occur, or in
  a logical, easy-to-follow sequence.

- use transitions to connect your details.

[**Menu**]

BENEFITS

Computer instruction offers many instructional advantages that make it particularly appealing to developmental students.

- The computer is a "silent," nonthreatening partner. Students can make mistakes, repeat segments, or reread frequently without embarrassment.
- The computer encourages participation and interaction, allowing students to become both mentally and physically involved with instruction.
- The computer is a visual instructional mode and accommodates the visual learning style.

SUGGESTED USES

Each module corresponds to and complements a chapter or section of *The Writer's Express*. The software modules can enhance or supplement classroom writing instruction in a variety of ways. Any part of the student's work in *Expressways* can be printed out at any time.

1. *Instructional preview.* Students can be assigned software units as instructional previews of textbook chapters. Explain to students that the unit introduces skills and strategies that will be emphasized in the text and in class activities and assignments. Used in this way, the software generates interest and enthusiasm for the skill while providing a condensed, brief overview and closely guided step-by-step application. This preview approach may be particularly appropriate for students with reading problems who may experience difficulty reading portions of the text. Once these students gain some knowledge about the skill at hand through interacting with the software, they may be able to comprehend the text more completely.

2. *Prewriting activity.* The software can be assigned to students *after* the corresponding text instructional material has been assigned and discussed in class, but before the reading and text writing assignments are assigned. Because the software features shorter and simpler readings than are used in the text, the software can thus function as an intermediary step; it can provide instructional review and additional practice before culminating (and evaluative) text writing assignments are given. Students may view the software as a helpful step "before the test"—that is, as an opportunity to practice before a formal evaluation.

This approach would be appropriate for particularly weak classes or individual students who need additional skill instruction, practice, and reinforcement before they fully grasp skills and concepts.

3. *Instructional review.* The software can be assigned after students have completed all corresponding text material. Used in this way, the software provides closure and final reinforcement, functioning in much the same way as a chapter summary does.

    This use allows students to apply what they have learned from text exercises as well as instructor-evaluated writing assignments.

4. *Selective remedial use.* The software can be assigned selectively to students who, through in-text exercises or writing assignments, demonstrate the need for additional instruction and guided practice. Or it can be assigned to students who are absent when skills are presented or who during conferencing with instructors request additional work.

5. *Precondition for submission of revisions.* Particular software units can be used as required assignments for students who demonstrate weaknesses on graded writing assignments. Students can be asked to complete a specific software module before submitting a revision of the graded paper.

CHAPTER 8
Overhead Transparency Masters

THE WRITING PROCESS

1. **Generating
    ideas**
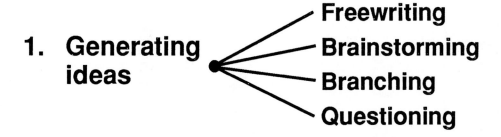
Freewriting

Brainstorming

Branching

Questioning

2. **Organizing your ideas**

3. **Writing a first draft**

4. **Revising and rewriting**

5. **Proofreading**

PREVIEWING STEPS

1. Read and think about the title.

2. Check the author.

3. Read the first paragraph.

4. Read all dark print headings.

5. Read the first sentence under each heading.

6. Read the first sentence of each paragraph.

7. Read the last paragraph.

SAMPLE JOURNAL ENTRY FOR CHAPTER 3

A major cause of divorce in this country is stress. People are so busy and do so much that their marriages suffer. Because people are so busy, they don't make time for their spouse, and many marriages end up in divorce. My Uncle Mark and Aunt Pat are good examples. They both work two jobs and never saw each other. When they did see each other, they'd argue. Also, many people don't consider family to be important and so they don't spend time at home or with their extended family where the emphasis is on marriage and family.

COMMON METHODS OF ARRANGING DETAILS

1. Time sequence

2. Spatial

3. Advantages/disadvantages

4. Most/least

USING SPECIFIC WORDS

1. Use specific, active verbs.

2. Give exact names.

3. Use adjectives before nouns to convey details.

4. Use words that appeal to the senses.

REVISION: EXAMINING YOUR IDEAS

1. Is your paragraph suited to your audience and purpose?

2. Have you provided relevant and sufficient detail?

3. Is your paragraph logically organized?

4. Is your language vivid and specific?

DRAFT 1

Planning trip to moon similar to planning trip to beach
  – **decide what to take & leave behind**
    (thermos? horse? pickels?)
  – **fateful decisions — success or failure**
    – **something gets in way**
    – **something is needed**

Moon list — planned long and hard
  – **vacuum cleaner?**
  – **sent pole and flag**
    – **traditional among explorers to plant flag**

Men who landed on moon in class by themselves
  – **should have been equipped accordingly**
  – **new breed; seen whole earth**
  – **flag — fumbling with past**

Moon plant last chapter in book of nationalism
  – **should have been omitted**

Moon holds key to madness — universal

Moon controls tides

Moon guards lovers everywhere

Pity we couldn't have planted white handkerchief
  – **symbol of common cold — affects us all, like the
    moon**

DRAFT 2

Moon is great place for men
- **Aldrich and Armstrong danced from sheer exuberance; sight to see**

Moon is poor place for flags
- **flag cannot float in breeze**
- **flag out of place**
- **moon belongs to none and all**
- **should have planted white handkerchief, symbol of common cold**
  - **colds, like the moon, affect us all**
- **flag is traditional for explorers**
  - **astronauts followed custom**
- **moon holds key to madness**
- **controls tides**
- **guards lovers**

Should have planted white handkerchief
- **symbol of common cold**
- **like the moon, cold affects us all**

DRAFT 3

Moon is a great place for men
- one-sixth gravity is fun
- Armstrong and Aldrich's dance was moment of triumph, sight to see

Moon is poor place for flags
- flag looked stiff in breeze that didn't blow
- lesson here somewhere
- it is traditional for explorers to plant flags, but our men were universal men
    - should be equipped accordingly
- moon belongs to none and all of us
- still holds key to madness
- controls tides
- guards lovers

Should have planted device acceptable to all
- white handkerchief — common-cold symbol
- colds, like the moon, affect us all

PARKS'S DAY IN WASHINGTON

Parks recalls past experience with racism.

Stryker sends Parks out to learn about city.

Parks experiences racism in Washington.

Parks is reminded of childhood.

Parks becomes angry.

Parks storms into Stryker's office.

Stryker offers Parks advice: get at the source of bigotry.

Parks mulls over Stryker's advice.

Parks talks to a black charwoman and takes pictures of her.

Parks goes home to supper.

SAMPLE MAP: THE USES OF ADVERTISING

ADVERTISING TYPE	CHARACTERISTIC	EXAMPLE
Institutional	Promotes organizational images, ideas, or political issues	To create and develop a socially responsible image, Seagram's advertising promotes the idea that drinking and driving don't mix
Product	Promotes goods and services; used by businesses, government, and private nonprofit organizations to promote uses, features, images, and benefits of their products	Johnson & Johnson used advertising for disposable lenses to tout their benefits; ads include a toll-free phone number to get more information
Pioneer	Informs people about a product, what it is, what it does, how it can be used, where it can be purchased	National Dairy Board sponsors ads to promote the nutritional value of dairy products
Competitive	Points at a brand's uses, features, advantages that benefit customers and that may not be available in competing brands	Volvo promotes the safety and crash-worthiness of its autos

SAMPLE MAP: THE USES OF ADVERTISING

ADVERTISING TYPE	CHARACTERISTIC	EXAMPLE
Comparative	Two or more specified brands are compared on the basis of one or more product attributes	Sorrell Ridge's fruit preserves ad said their preserves were made only from fruit and fruit juice, but Smucker's contained corn syrup and refined sugar
Defensive	Offsets or lessens effects of a competitor's ads	Pizza Hut emphasized its pizza is from scratch, but McDonald's uses frozen dough
Reminder	Lets consumers know an established brand is still around and has certain uses, characteristics, and benefits	Proctor & Gamble reminds consumers that Crest is still best for preventing cavities
Reinforcement	Assures current users that they have made the right choice; tells them how to get the most satisfaction from the product	AT&T tells customers that its services are "the right choice"

CAUSES OF POOR COMMUNITY-POLICE RELATIONSHIPS

COMMUNITY

Blames police for instigating violence and failing to stop violence

Thinks if police really cared, they would restore order

African-Americans resent the way their males are demeaned by the police

POLICE

Do not recognize the positive aspects of the community

Have trouble seeing that poor people of color are more victimized by violence and crime than other citizens

Focus on the hostile attitude with which their presence is often greeted and feel betrayed by the people for whom they are risking their lives

COMMUNITY POLICING

POSITIVE EFFECTS

Reduction in the number of arrests

Sets free the intelligence of the police

Police and community work together to solve problems; heal the rift between them

WHY PRESENT SYSTEM IS INEFFECTIVE

Police are removed from the street and are anonymous in their cars

Police react to each criminal act as if it were a unique occurrence, but they should approach the problem more holistically

Situations in which crimes occur need to be changed to prevent crimes

SIMILARITIES BETWEEN PARAGRAPHS AND ESSAYS

PARAGRAPH	DESCRIPTION	ESSAY
Topic	The one thing the writing is about	Subject
Topic sentence	Statement of the one key point of the writing	Thesis statement
Supporting details	Explanation of the one key point	Supporting paragraphs or body
Transitional words	Connections among ideas	Transitional words or sentences
Last sentence	Statement that connects all ideas to key point	Conclusion

SAMPLE ESSAY MAP

Paragraph	Contents
1	**Introductory ideas** **Thesis statement**
2	**Topic sentence** **– detail** **– detail** **– detail**
3	**Topic sentence** **– detail** **– detail** **– detail**
4	**Topic sentence** **– detail** **– detail** **– detail**
5	**Conclusion**

REVISION CHECKLIST

1. Is your essay appropriate for your audience? Does it give them the background information they need? Will it interest them?

2. Will your essay accomplish your purpose?

3. Have you narrowed your topic so that you can cover your subject thoroughly in your essay?

4. Is your main point clearly expressed in a thesis statement in the introductory paragraph? Does your introductory paragraph capture the reader's interest and lead in to the body of the essay?

5. Does each paragraph of your essay have a topic sentence that supports your essay's main point?

REVISION CHECKLIST (cont.)

6. Is each paragraph's topic sentence supported by relevant and sufficient detail?

7. Are your paragraphs arranged in a logical sequence and connected by transitions?

8. Is the tone of your essay appropriate for your purpose and audience?

9. Does your conclusion reemphasize your thesis statement and draw the essay to a close?

10. Does your title identify the topic and interest the reader?

11. Have you proofread your paper and corrected any errors in grammar, mechanics, and spelling?

PROOFREADING CHECKLIST

1. Does each sentence end with appropriate punctuation (period, question mark, or exclamation point)?

2. Is all punctuation within each sentence correct (commas, colons, semicolons, apostrophes, dashes, and quotation marks)?

3. Is each word spelled correctly?

4. Have you used capital letters where needed?

5. Are numbers and abbreviations used correctly?

6. Are any words omitted?

7. If your paper is typed, have you corrected all typographical errors?

8. If your paper is handwritten, is your handwriting always legible?

9. Are your pages in the correct order and numbered?

USEFUL TRANSITIONS

METHOD OF DEVELOPMENT	TRANSITIONAL WORDS
Most-least	Most important, above all, especially, particularly important
Advantages/disadvantages	One, another, first, second, etc.
Spatial	Above, below, behind, beside, next to, inside, outside, to the west (north, etc.), beneath, near, nearby
Time sequence	First, next, now, before, during, after, eventually, finally, at last, later, meanwhile, soon, then, suddenly, currently, afterward, after a while, as soon as, until

USEFUL TRANSITIONS (cont.)

METHOD OF DEVELOPMENT	TRANSITIONAL WORDS
Process/narration	First, second, then, later, in the beginning, when, after, following, next, during, again, after that, at last, finally
Description	See Spatial and Most-least
Example	For example, for instance, to illustrate
Classification	One, another, second, third
Definition	Means, can be defined as, refers to, is
Comparison	Likewise, similarly, in the same way, too, also
Contrast	However, on the contrary, unlike, on the other hand, although, even though, but, in contrast, yet
Cause-effect	Because, consequently, since, as a result, for this reason, therefore, thus

EXERCISE 12.13

PARAGRAPH	FIGURATIVE LANGUAGE
2	"disease dismissed courage and defiantly claimed their friends"
4	"The sun beat down on us alone"
6	"we, in the cast, sat as still as stones"
6	"Still as stone we rode"
7	"He kept flying into windows"
7	"he flew south"
9	"The horizon is filling up with parents"
10	"numbers don't touch our hearts"
17	"began a journey into paralysis"
19	"grief . . . yawning like the gaping mouth in Munch's painting"
19	"grieving is like walking"
20	"death tugs at our own shirttails"
21	"Grief doesn't read schedules"
25	"Grief will fool you with its disguises"
26	"Grief is like the wind"
26	"he heard the final click of a door as it closed on possibility"
28	"he was just beginning to look out at the world and make maps"

SAMPLE STUDENT SUMMARY

For humans, eating is a very important part of culture. In all societies, eating is the most important way in which relationships are begun and maintained. Food is so emotionally important that it is often linked with occurrences that are not about eating, like the Boston Tea Party.

Eating is linked to sex roles. People are given different responsibilities for getting and preparing different foods based on their sex. The order in which people eat is also often determined by sex. Culture is communicated to children through meals with the family; customs are taught and reinforced while eating.

The food that is eaten is determined by one's social, religious, and ethnic membership. Different groups have different prohibitions and requirements. Because so much emphasis is placed on eating, food is an important factor in holding a society together. Food also is often believed to have magical effects and has symbolic meanings in various religions.

SAMPLE STUDENT OUTLINE OF ARGUMENT

Crack and the Box

Position: Television causes drug addiction

Evidence

1. When television wasn't as important in our lives, drug addiction wasn't a problem.

2. Generations that have grown up with television have problems with drug addiction.

3. Today's children are addicted to television in the same way they become addicted to drugs.

4. Television works on the same imaginative and intellectual level as psychoactive drugs by supplying abrupt unearned shifts in moods.

5. Television and drugs alienate addicts from the world.

6. Television shows assume life should be easy and simple and when it is not, people turn to drugs.

SAMPLE STUDENT OUTLINE OF ARGUMENT (cont.)

Responses to Opposing Viewpoints

1. Television is only giving people what they want — so are the drug cartels

Specific Action

1. Parents must take control of the television set.

2. Parents must teach children to watch specific shows, not just television in general.

3. Schools should teach television the way literature is taught, showing students how to distinguish between the true and false.

4. Americans should spend more time reading and thinking.

REVIEW OF THE LITERAL CONTENT STRATEGIES

STRATEGY	CHAPTER	PAGE
Immediate review; underlining topic sentences	3	48-49
Recognizing types of supporting details	4	71
Drawing idea maps	5	95
Using idea mapping (sequence maps)	6	116
Marking revealing actions, descriptions, and statements	7	136
Using idea mapping to review and organize ideas (charts)	8	161-162
Using the three-column list for review (comparison-contrast)	9	181
Reviewing and organizing ideas	10	201-202
Outlining	11	229
Annotation	12	257-258
Summarizing	13	284
Outlining an argument	14	309-310
Underlining and reviewing	15	339

TABLE 15.2. VERBS COMMONLY USED IN ESSAY QUESTIONS

VERB	EXAMPLE	INFORMATION TO INCLUDE AND METHOD OF DEVELOPMENT
Trace	Trace changes in water pollution control methods over the past twenty years.	Describe the development or progress of a particular trend, event, or process in chronological order.
Describe	Describe the two types of chromosomal abnormalities that can cause Down's syndrome.	Tell how something looks or happened, including the answers to how, who, where, why.
List	List the different types of family structures and marriage relationships.	List or discuss one by one. Use most-to-least or least-to-most organization.
Illustrate	Illustrate with examples from your experience how religion shapes value.	Explain with examples that demonstrate or clarify a point or idea.

TABLE 15.2. VERBS COMMONLY USED IN ESSAY QUESTIONS (cont.)

VERB	EXAMPLE	INFORMATION TO INCLUDE AND METHOD OF DEVELOPMENT
Define	Define an institution and list three primary characteristics.	Give an accurate meaning of the term with enough detail to show that you really understand it.
Discuss	Discuss the antigen-antibody response in the immune system.	Consider important characteristics and main points.
Compare	Compare the poetry of Langston Hughes with the poetry of one of his contemporaries.	Show how items are similar as well as different; include details or examples.
Contrast	Contrast the social-stratification theories of Marx and Weber.	Show how the items are different; include details or examples.

TABLE 15.2. VERBS COMMONLY USED IN ESSAY QUESTIONS (cont.)

VERB	EXAMPLE	INFORMATION TO INCLUDE AND METHOD OF DEVELOPMENT
Explain	Explain the functions of peptide and steroid hormones.	State facts and details that make the idea or concept clear and understandable.
Evaluate	Explain the accomplishments of the civil rights movement over the past fifty years.	React to the topic in a logical way. Discuss the merits, strengths, weaknesses, advantages, or limitations of the topic.
Summarize	Summarize Parson's theory of social evolution.	Cover the major points in brief; use a sentence-and-paragraph form.
Justify	Justify the use of racial quotas in police department hiring policies.	Give reasons that support an action, event, or policy.

SUNLIGHT AND THE CLOCK WITHIN
ELAINE MARIEB

It has been known for a long time that many <u>body rhythms move in step with one another</u>. Body temperature, pulse, and the sleep-wake cycles seem to follow the same "beat" over approximate 24-hour cycles, while other processes follow a different "drummer." What can throw these rhythms out of whack? Illness, drugs, jet travel, and changing to the night shift are all candidates. So is sunlight.

   <u>Light exerts its internal biochemical effects through the eye.</u> Light hitting the retina generates nerve impulses along the optic nerve, tract, and radiation to the visual cortex (where "seeing" occurs) and via the retinohypothalamic tracts to the suprachiasmatic nucleus (SCN), the so-called biological clock of the hypothalamus. The SCN regulates multiple-drive rhythms including the rhythmic melatonin output of the pineal gland and the output of various anterior pituitary hormones. <u>Melatonin secretion is inhibited by light and enhanced during darkness</u>, and historically the pineal gland has been called the "third eye."

   Light produces melatonin-mediated effects on reproductive, eating, and sleeping patterns of other animals, but until very recently, humans were believed to have evolved free of such effects. Thanks to the research of many scientists, however, we now know that <u>people are influenced by three major variables of light</u>: its <u>intensity</u>, its <u>spectrum</u> (color mixture), and its <u>timing</u> (day/night and seasonal changes).

Source: From *Human Anatomy and Physiology*, Second Edition, by Elaine Marieb (Redwood City, CA: Benjamin/Cummings Publishing Company, 1992), p. 570. Reprinted by permission.

SUNLIGHT AND THE CLOCK WITHIN (cont.)

A number of <u>human processes</u> are known to be influenced by light:

1. *Behavior and mood*. Many people have <u>seasonal mood rhythms</u>, particularly those of us who live far from the equator, where the day/night cycle changes dramatically during the course of the year. We seem to <u>feel better during the summer</u> and become <u>cranky</u> and <u>depressed</u> in the short, gray days of <u>winter</u>. Is this just our imagination? Apparently not. Researchers have found a relatively <u>common emotional disorder</u> called <u>seasonal affective disorder</u>, or <u>SAD</u>, in which these mood swings are grossly exaggerated. As the days grow shorter each fall, people with SAD become irritable, anxious, sleepy, and socially withdrawn. Their appetite becomes insatiable; they crave carbohydrates and gain weight. <u>Phototherapy</u>, the use of very bright <u>lights for 2 hours daily, reversed these symptoms</u> in nearly 90% of patients studied in two to four days (considerably faster than any antidepressant drug could do it). When patients stopped receiving therapy or were given melatonin, their symptoms returned as quickly as they had lifted, indicating that melatonin may be the key to seasonal mood changes.

<u>Symptoms of SAD</u> are virtually <u>identical</u> to those of individuals with *<u>carbohydrate-craving obesity</u> (CCO)* and *<u>premenstrual syndrome</u> (PMS)*, except that CCO sufferers are affected daily and PMS sufferers are affected monthly (2 weeks prior to menses onset). <u>Photoperiodism</u> appears to be the <u>basis</u> of these <u>cyclic behavioral disorders</u> as well, and phototherapy relieves PMS symptoms in some women.

Source: From *Human Anatomy and Physiology*, Second Edition, by Elaine Marieb (Redwood City, CA: Benjamin/Cummings Publishing Company, 1992), p. 570. Reprinted by permission.

SUNLIGHT AND THE CLOCK WITHIN (cont.)

2. *Night work schedules and jetlag.* People who work at night (the graveyard shift) exhibit reversed melatonin secretion patterns, with no hormone released during the night (when they are exposed to light) and high levels secreted during daytime sleeping hours. Waking such people and exposing them to bright light causes their melatonin levels to drop. The same sort of melatonin inversion (but much more precipitous) occurs in those who fly from coast to coast.

3. *Immunity.* Ultraviolet light activates white blood cells called suppressor T cells, which partially block the immune response. UV therapy has been found to stop rejection of tissue transplants from unrelated donors in animals. This technique offers the hope that diabetics who have become immune to their own pancreas islet tissue may be treated with pancreas transplants in the future.

People have worshipped the sunlight since the earliest times. Scientists are just now beginning to understand the reasons for this, and as they do, they are increasingly distressed about windowless offices, restricted and artificial illumination of work areas, and the growing number of institutionalized elderly who rarely feel the sun's warm rays. Artificial lights do not provide the full spectrum of sunlight: Incandescent bulbs used in homes provide primarily the red wavelengths and fluorescent bulbs of institutions provide yellow-green. Animals exposed for prolonged periods to artificial lighting exhibit reproductive abnormalities and an enhanced susceptibility to cancer. Could it be that some of us are unknowingly expressing the same effects?

Source: From *Human Anatomy and Physiology,* Second Edition, by Elaine Marieb (Redwood City, CA: Benjamin/Cummings Publishing Company, 1992), p. 570. Reprinted by permission.

SAMPLE ESSAY ANSWER

Sunlight can disturb body rhythms through a biochemical reaction that occurs through the eye. Light inhibits the release of melatonin, a chemical released by the pineal gland. The light's intensity, color mixture, and timing all affect its release. Mood, work schedules, behavior, and immunity are all affected by light. People's mood may change with the season; some suffer from SAD (seasonal affective disorder), which produces serious behavior changes. People who work night shifts have reversed patterns of melatonin secretions; similar symptoms are associated with jet lag. Ultraviolet light can partially block the immune response and is useful in preventing rejection of tissue transplants. Artificial light is not an adequate substitute for sunlight, and prolonged exposure has caused abnormalities in animals.

CHAPTER 9
Answer Key for In-text Exercises

Part I: Paragraph Writing Strategies

CHAPTER 3

Exercise 3–1

Following are sample answers; students' answers will vary.

1. Disease, poverty, environmental preservation
2. Personal loans, part-time jobs, grants, scholarships
3. Used cars may be damaged from involvement in accidents.
   Used cars may have high mileage.
4. Only positive aspects of products are described.
   Advertisers lead us to believe "everyone" buys the product.
5. Television offers soap operas.
   Television offers coverage of sporting events.
   Television offers situation comedies.
6. Accountants must learn to keep financial records.
   Attorneys must learn state and national laws.
7. Commercials use several different techniques to persuade consumers to buy their products.
8. Newspapers provide readers with a variety of information.

Exercise 3–2

Topic	View
1. Sunday morning	Time for reading and relaxing
2. My part-time job at department store	Is providing valuable sales experience
3. Publicly funded FM radio stations	Need your financial support
4. *Time*	Presents thorough coverage of world events
5. Danny Everett	Gets my day off to a bright and humorous start

Exercise 3–3

Following are sample answers: students' answers will vary.

1. Liquor advertisements are often appealing to teenagers.
2. Most fast-food restaurants are not concerned with their customers' health and nutrition.
3. Monday morning is a time to get organized for the week.
4. Violence on television may promote physical aggressiveness among young children.
5. College professors make sincere efforts to understand their students' needs.

Exercise 3–4

1. G
2. S
3. G
4. G
5. S

Exercise 3–5

1. A
2. G

3. S
4. E
5. A
6. G
7. S
8. E
9. E
10. G

Exercise 3–6

Following are sample answers; students' answers will vary.

1. Hunger in less-developed African countries is increasing dramatically.
2. Freud was the founder of a school of psychotherapy in which patients talk about their problems and past lives.
3. There are several easy ways to conserve energy in the home.
4. Congress is responsible for enacting laws.
5. Chemical pollution poses a threat to Lake Erie.

CHAPTER 4

Exercise 4–1

1. c
2. a, c
3. a, c
4. b, c

Exercise 4–9

Following are sample answers; students' answers will vary.

1. Specific verbs: Paragraphs 1 (flipping), 2 (searching), 3 (deep-six), 4 (check out), and 7 (blast)
2. Exact names: Paragraphs 1, 4, 6, 7, and 8
3. Adjectives: Paragraphs 3 (corrugated), 4 (strange), 5 (nerdy), and 7 (pearly white)
4. Words that appeal to the senses: Paragraphs 2 (Niagara of waste), 6 (a little chewy), and 9 (thorns out of our paw)

Exercise 4–10

1. EDF's relationship was bad news for the plastics industry because EDF and McDonald's were working together to reduce the amount of plastic waste in the environment.
2. In 1967 EDF did not show concern for economic needs, instead concentrating on lawsuits as the means to an end. Today its environmentalists try to satisfy economic and environmental concerns.
3. Cows cause a lot of negative environmental effects; these effects could be lessened if McDonald's did not sell meat.
4. Changes were made behind the counter to avoid inconveniencing customers and because most of the trash is generated behind the counter.
5. The changes environmental groups are able to make will encourage other people to donate to their cause.

CHAPTER 5

Exercise 5–2

Irrelevant details are as follows:

1. Being a union leader is a difficult but important job.
2. Sometimes strikes don't work and people are out of work for long periods of time.
3. A lot of times this is on the news.

Exercise 5–7

Paragraph 1: Narrow the topic; include additional detail

Paragraph 2: Eliminate generalities; include specific detail; develop the paragraph around the incident of the writer's being run over

Paragraph 3: Create a stronger topic sentence; include more specific detail; improve the paragraph's organization; eliminate sentence fragments

Exercise 5–8

See Transparency Masters 5.2, 5.3, and 5.4 in Chapter 8 of this Manual.

Part II: Methods of Developing Paragraphs

CHAPTER 6

Exercise 6–6

1. Making pizza at home can save time and money; it involves five steps.
2. Because lecture material is often included on exams, taking notes is an essential skill that requires good listening and writing skills.
3. Through a smell-identification process, bloodhounds can locate criminals before they can harm others or commit other crimes.
4. My dentist showed me how to use dental floss, an important habit that helps prevent gum disease.
5. In case of an emergency, here's how to change a flat tire.

Exercise 6–10

See Transparency Master 6.1 in Chapter 8 of this Manual.

CHAPTER 7

Exercise 7–1

Following are sample answers; students' answers will vary.

1. A thunderstorm reminds us of the power of nature.
   Thunderstorms frighten my dog.
   Thunderstorms can be dangerous to human life.

2. Many professional athletes are community-oriented and make worthwhile contributions to their community.
   Professional athletes serve as role models to impressionable teenagers.
   Professional athletes are egotistical, over-paid actors.

3. Brownies are the perfect comfort food.
   Brownies, although delicious, are high in calories and fat.
   Brownies are quick and easy to make.

4. _____ was a frightening thriller.
   _____ was not worth the admission price.
   _____ was so exciting I've seen it four times.

5. I couldn't make it through the day without my wristwatch.
   My wristwatch reminds me that valuable time is passing.
   My wristwatch is primarily a piece of jewelry.

Exercise 7–3

1. b, d
2. b, d
3. b, c
4. b, d
5. d

Exercise 7–5

2. The rubbery, greasy, and overly spiced chicken served with floury, runny potatoes and hockey puck-like biscuits, was inedible.

3. The nervous bride wearing an ice pink lace white gown frantically glanced around the reception hall in search of her new husband.

4. The crumbling, worn yellow brick sidewalk with grass shooting between its blocks led to the garden.

5. A German shepherd named Molly, with brown-marked ears and muzzle, barked ferociously and growled continuously as we walked past her yard.

CHAPTER 8

Exercise 8–3

Following are sample answers; students' answers will vary.

1. Location, price, size, type of building, number of bedrooms
2. Destination, duration, type of activities involved
3. Alone or with others; reason, activities to remedy
4. Age, gender, type of crime
5. Type of vehicle, destination, purpose

Exercise 8–4

1. Ways of classifying: ratings, length, country of origin, by producer, by language
   Subgroups for ratings: X, R, PG, G
2. Ways of classifying: popularity, type of alphabet, difficulty
   Subgroups for popularity: most widely spoken, less widely spoken, least widely spoken
3. Ways of classifying: price, location, facilities
   Subgroups for price: less than $40, $40–$80, more than $80
4. Ways of classifying: sources, effects, geographical area
   Subgroups for sources: landfills, automobile exhaust, industrial waste
5. Ways of classifying: price, size, purpose, memory capacity
   Subgroups for price: less than $1000, $1000–$3000, more than $3000

Exercise 8–6

Following are sample answers; students' answers will vary.

1. A brat is a child who misbehaves by calling attention to him or herself and disturbs others.
2. Holiday spirit is a feeling of joy or excitement related to an upcoming special day.
3. Sex appeal is a sense of physical attraction and personal charm usually between members of the opposite sex.

4. Loneliness is a feeling of separation or isolation that occurs when a person is apart physically or emotionally from others.

5. Autumn is a season that comes between summer and winter during which changes occur in nature to anticipate the arrival of winter.

Exercise 8–9

See Transparency Masters 8.1a and b in Chapter 8 of this Manual.

CHAPTER 9

Exercise 9–3

Following are sample answers; students' answers will vary.

1. a. Type of film (comedy, horror, etc.)
    b. Photography
    c. Music
    d. Actors and actresses
    e. Dialogue

2. a. Artists who perform
    b. Type of person who listens
    c. Age of person who listens
    d. Where it is played
    e. Musical instruments

3. a. Age
    b. Salary
    c. Physical requirements
    d. Celebrity status
    e. Training

Exercise 9–8

Point of Comparison	What We Say	What We Do
Quality of environment	Must improve	Can do little to help
Recycle newspapers	Should recycle	52% recycle
Products from irresponsible companies	Avoid	Only 7% avoid
Driving	Reduce	76% drive as usual

Exercise 9–9

1. Opinion: Saving the environment is a high priority for Americans.
   Evidence: Study conducted by the Roper Organization.

2. Opinion: Americans blame businesses for environmental problems.
   Evidence: Six of ten Americans blame businesses for not developing better products.

3. Opinion: Americans blame themselves for environmental problems.
   Evidence: Fifty-three percent of Americans admit they are not willing to pay extra for safer products.

4. Opinion: Recycling is a rapidly growing behavior.
   Evidence: Statistics on growth of recycling bottles and cans and newspapers.

5. Opinion: Only a minority of Americans have adopted a more environmentally responsible lifestyle.
   Evidence: Only 7 percent of consumers avoid restaurants that use foam containers.

CHAPTER 10

Exercise 10–1

1. Cause
2. Effect
3. Cause
4. Cause
5. Effect

Exercise 10–6

1. Because
2. Therefore
3. Consequently
4. Because

Exercise 10–8

See Transparency Masters 10.1a and b in Chapter 8 of this Manual.

Part III: Strategies for Writing Essays

CHAPTER 11

Exercise 11–1

1. Mobile home ownership.
2. Paragraph 1, sentences 1 and 2.
3. Paragraph 1, sentence 3.
4. Local zoning laws, loan rates, government agency financing.
5. The writer concludes the essay restating the thesis statement.

Exercise 11–6 (sample answers)

1. Jogging benefits one's cardiovascular system.
2. Counseling can help unemployed workers regain their sense of self-worth.
3. Getting involved in campus activities is an excellent way to make new friends.
4. Building a weekly time schedule will help balance the demands of work and school.
5. Commuting to college is time-consuming and expensive.

Exercise 11–8

1. Comparison-contrast
2. Most-to-least, classification
3. Cause and effect
4. Most-to-least, process
5. Cause and effect
6. Most-to-least, classification

CHAPTER 12

Exercise 12–1

Following are sample answers; students' answers will vary.

1. Outlawing abortion denies a woman's right to make decisions about her own body.
2. Television sitcoms are an insult to human intelligence.
3. Romance or mystery novels are mindless diversions that waste our valuable time.
4. Political campaigning gives voters the opportunity to evaluate the candidates' platforms and suitability for public office.
5. My writing class is teaching me the basics I will need for both academic and career writing tasks.

Exercise 12–3

Tone	*Potential Audience*
1. Serious, engaging	Farmers
2. Outrage	Potential mugging victim
3. Sentimental	Friend of family member
4. Sympathetic	General interest audience

Exercise 12–5

1. Startling fact
2. Question
3. Story or anecdote
4. Quotation
5. Startling fact

Exercise 12–13

See Transparency Master 12.4 in Chapter 8 of this Manual.

CHAPTER 13

Exercise 13–2

1. Narrative, description
2. Example, cause and effect
3. Most-to-least, cause and effect, classification
4. Example, cause and effect, classification
5. Example, cause and effect, comparison-contrast

Exercise 13–4

1. When I was in high school, I did not take education seriously, but now I recognize its value.
2. Sam is very attractive to women.
3. Because Marco is relaxed and easy-going, people try to take advantage of him.
4. Ronald Reagan was a popular president and, at every opportunity, his staff reminded us of his popularity.
5. Emily Dickinson is a sensitive and creative poet; some of her poems carry a strong emotional impact.

Exercise 13–6

See Transparency Master 13.1 in Chapter 8 of this Manual.

CHAPTER 14

Exercise 14–3

1. Recycling garbage can significantly improve our environment by reducing landfills and reducing pollution.
2. Lengthening the school year will place a financial drain on school districts and dampen both teachers' and students' enthusiasm toward school.
3. Television sitcoms offer a relaxing escape from one's daily routine.
4. Volunteer work can function as an eye-opening learning experience for college students.
5. The use of steroids by athletes should be banned in all countries.

Exercise 14–5

1. Personal experience, quotations, examples
2. Statistics, quotations
3. Examples, statistics
4. Statistics, quotations
5. Statistics, quotations

Exercise 14–8

See Transparency Masters 14.1a and b in Chapter 8 of this Manual.

CHAPTER 15

Exercise 15–1

Following are sample answers; students' answers will vary.

1. Trace the history of the development of newspapers from colonial to modern times.
2. Explain the various functions of food within our society.
or Defend the statement: "All animals feed, but humans alone eat."
3. Discuss the various types of advertising; include an example of each.
or Identify and compare three forms of advertising.

Exercise 15–2

Following are sample answers; students' answers will vary.

1. 10 minutes, 10 minutes, 30 minutes
2. 10 minutes, 20 minutes, 15 minutes, 30 minutes
3. 10 minutes, 35 minutes, 25 minutes, 50 minutes

Exercise 15–3

1. Topic: collective behavior
   Verbs: define and illustrate
   Methods: definition, example, description
2. Topic: memory cells
   Verbs: explain and indicate
   Methods: comparison-contrast, description, process
3. Topic: market survey methods
   Verb: discuss
   Methods: description, comparison-contrast, example
4. Topic: shopping centers
   Verb: explain
   Methods: description, comparison-contrast, example, definition
5. Topic: establishing prices
   Verb: explain
   Methods: process, description, example, definition
6. Topic: unification of biology by Darwin
   Verb: evaluate
   Methods: description, example

7. Topics: cults and sects
   Verbs: distinguish and give (examples)
   Methods: comparison-contrast, example, description, definition

8. Topics: homeostasis, temperature regulation
   Verbs: define, relate
   Methods: definition, process, example

9. Topic: sensory receptors
   Verb: describe
   Methods: description, classification, definition, example

10. Topic: gender discrimination issues
    Verb: trace
    Methods: time sequence, description, example, process, cause and effect

Exercise 15–5

1. Advertising differs from publicity in three primary ways.

2. There are four common types of magazines; each is intended for a different, but specific audience.

3. There have been three significant events contributing to the women's movement over the past several decades.

4. There are three major ways a group ensures that its members conform to its cultural rules.

5. The effectiveness of an advertising campaign can be evaluated in three ways.

Step 2, page 339

Explain the effects of sunlight, both biologically and psychologically.

Part V: Reviewing the Basics

A. UNDERSTANDING THE PARTS OF SPEECH

Exercise 1

	Nouns	*Pronouns*
1.	Toronto, city, neighborhoods	It
2.	Hannah, roller coasters	They, me
3.	Papers	Whoever, these, them, someone, them
4.	Boss, flowers	No one, her, herself
5.	Hilary's mother, cookies	Us, another
6.	Ray's garden, flowers, catalogue	Those
7.	Albums, United Way auction, Elvis collection	Some, we
8.	Answer, child	I, what
9.	Couple, menu, waiter, appetizer, mango relish	They, it, him, them, that
10.	Gorillas, captivity, Seattle's Woodland Park Zoo, habitat	Many

Exercise 2

1. will answer
2. has walked
3. had ran
4. will star
5. had painted
6. will have mowed
7. had stopped
8. changed
9. will have answered
10. laid

Exercise 3

Following are sample answers; students' answers will vary.

1. The rock band performed four fast numbers after the brief intermission.
2. The enormous, multicolored boat departed from the littered dock.
3. The short math quiz was easy, but the sociology midterm exam was difficult.
4. The new murder mystery had a surprising ending I enjoyed.
5. As the lengthy concert ended, the exhausted crowd left the hot, humid theater.
6. The historic museum was filled with Greek sculpture and Italian paintings.
7. The restless tigers paced around their tiny, confining cages.
8. Our young hostess served baked chicken, brown rice, and fresh asparagus before the chocolate dessert.
9. The electric guitar rested on the old wooden table.
10. Laura's courteous behavior is as unusual as her neat, stylish clothing.

Exercise 4

Following are sample answers; students' answers will vary.

1. This is the worst storm we have had in thirty years.
2. Uncle Mark is heavier than I expected him to be.
3. Each morning we rose earlier than the last one.
4. Joe acts more maturely than his cousin.
5. Fire Company C responded to the fire least quickly of all companies on duty.
6. More interesting food was served at dinner than at breakfast.
7. Fewer than ten students submitted their papers on time.
8. Of all my family attending the reunion, my grandfather lives the farthest away.
9. Of all the party guests, the hostess greeted us most warmly.
10. The last performance went less smoothly than the first.

Exercise 5

Following are sample answers; students' answers will vary.

1. The diamond ring on the starlet's finger sparkled.
   The diamond ring in the jewelry store window sparkled.

2. Stories about the protest filled the newspaper.
   Stories of horror filled the newspaper.

3. The maple tree beside the church was cut down.
   The maple tree next to the house was cut down.

4. Termites had damaged the building on its north side.
   Termites had damaged the building beyond repair.

5. The chairs on the lawn dried off quickly after the rainstorm.
   The chairs behind the table dried off quickly after the rainstorm.

6. The history professor lectured about constitutional amendments.
   The history professor lectured for two hours.

7. Lunch was served on the patio.
   Lunch was served before noon.

8. The chest in the attic was not empty.
   The chest with the antique handle was not empty.

9. The bookstore was located across from the library.
   The bookstore was located on the corner.

10. The dictionary in the hallway is tattered and torn from frequent use.
    The dictionary with the red cover is tattered and torn from frequent use.

B. UNDERSTANDING THE PARTS OF A SENTENCE

Exercise 6

	Simple Subject(s)	*Simple Predicate(s)*
1.	Group	Completed
2.	Family	Takes
3.	Lynn, Bruce	Seem
4.	Geraniums, pansies	Had been weeded, watered
5.	Couch	Looked
6.	Whales	Dove, swam
7.	Sherman	Hurried

Simple Subject(s)	Simple Predicate(s)
8. Students	Were
9. Men	Signed, forwarded
10. Anchorwoman	Visited, spoke

Exercise 7

Following are sample answers; students' answers will vary.

1. Sign
2. Barney
3. Heroic
4. Objective or essay
5. Secure
6. Paul
7. Exciting and humorous
8. Valentine card
9. Challenging
10. Painter

Exercise 8

Following are sample answers; students' answers will vary.

1. Edmund, my uncle's only son, visited Montreal for the summer.
2. I was suddenly alarmed by the intensity of the baby's crying.
3. Exhausted, Katrina cooked a quick dinner after a busy day at work.
4. The psychology class, held in Norton Hall, began ten minutes late.
5. Angry that his offer for a used car was not accepted, Rudy threw a book across the room.
6. My alarm, ringing loudly across the room, forced me to get out of bed.
7. Speeding out of control, the compact car struck the gasoline truck parked alongside the road.

8. Anticipating news about my recent job interview, I answered the telephone anxiously.

9. To pass my history exam I will study for four hours tonight.

10. As dusk approached, the late summer sky became cloudy.

Exercise 9

1. Doug gift-wrapped the box of candy that he bought for his wife for Valentine's Day.

2. Because Mark experienced a lot of stress about job interviews, he learned relaxation techniques to reduce stress.

3. Since Tuesday was the last class before our spring break, the students talked about their vacation plans.

4. Angry students lined up outside the Registrar's office; a computer error had canceled their registrations.

5. Because Diana was daydreaming during the lecture, she missed an important announcement.

6. Leon has little time to spend with his two children because he works sixty hours per week in his brother's landscaping business.

7. Although Jeff's friend, Sam, ordered two desserts, Jeff refused to even look at the dessert menu.

8. While Harry cleaned the garage, Rita washed and waxed the car.

9. We may have hot dogs and chili for dinner, or we may order pizza from Dominick's.

10. The political candidate said she believed in lowering state taxes, but her voting record on lowering taxes was poor.

C. AVOIDING SENTENCE ERRORS

Exercise 10

Following are sample answers; students' answers will vary.

1. Hurrying to get home, Maria slipped on an icy step.

2. We wished the class would end.

3. Older students with families are usually very serious about college.

4. Anthony knew the locks had been changed, but he didn't tell anyone.

5. Mike was a strange old uncle, always telling weird stories about his childhood in Denmark.

6. The top drawer of my desk is cluttered.

7. Farmworkers who live in poverty may lack proper medical care.

8. Even though we painted the room, it looked no better.

9. Because she took an accounting class on Tuesday night, Mary was often late for work on Wednesday morning.

10. Until the doorbell rang, Mark forgot what time it was.

Exercise 11

Following are sample answers; students' answers will vary.

1. Because my sister's newborn baby is learning to smile and reach for objects, I enjoy taking care of him.

2. Correct

3. My friends agree that the laundromat is a great place to meet people. Everyone has to do laundry, and there is always someone there.

4. Jerry's new sweater shrunk the first time he washed it, so he returned it to the store.

5. When I broke my leg, I knew the doctor who treated me in the emergency room. He is one of my sister's professors in medical school, and she talks about how brilliant he is all the time.

6. Correct

7. When Steve moved out of the dorm, he bought a lot of new furniture. He bought a couch, a kitchen table and chairs, a bed, an armchair, and a dresser.

8. Correct

9. Our team lost the game; the quarterback was throwing terribly, and the receivers kept dropping the ball.

10. It was so hot yesterday that everyone had all their car windows rolled down; offices had the air conditioning running on high.

Exercise 12

1. This summer, my brother took me to Las Vegas.

2. Correct

3. Jonathan is supposed to meet Kathy at the library, and if he doesn't hurry, he will be late.

4. Barb had a fifty-dollar phone bill last month.

5. After the concert, Madelaine remembered she had a paper due the next day.

6. I parked my car somewhere in this parking lot, and now, although I have looked everywhere, I cannot find it.

7. The instructor had shown a film about the life of Martin Luther King.

8. Soon it will be January, and New Year Resolutions will begin to appear.

9. Moths destroyed my wool jacket, even though I kept it all summer in a tightly sealed box.

10. Brad took his daughter to the circus, but she was afraid of the clowns.

Exercise 13

1. Rosa gave a speech to the Hispanic Students Association.

2. The pilot brought the plane in for a safe landing.

3. Richardo purchased the submarine sandwich for lunch.

4. The exam grade gave Lou a feeling of assurance.

5. Jay Leno will be visiting our campus.

6. Professor Black praised Carlos for the excellent paper he wrote on the history of the bayonet.

7. My cat clawed Joshua's pant leg.

8. A police officer stopped Michelle for going through a red light.

9. Pie makers and fruit canners buy peaches.

10. I was given my grandfather's extensive coin collection when I turned twenty-five.

Exercise 14

1. Sit

2. Is

3. Is

4. Deserves

5. Are

6. Makes
7. Are
8. Look
9. Are
10. Is

Exercise 15

1. The legislature reached its decision about the bill.
2. Neither the oak tree nor the maple trees have dropped their leaves yet.
3. Each gas station in town has raised its prices in the past week.
4. Jane and Lena want to take Professor Shrub's Shakespeare class because they were told it is a terrific class.
5. Correct
6. Correct
7. Correct
8. Either the neighbors or their guest, Sam Mallery, raised their voices so that we could hear them across the street.
9. Tom and Steven went to the store to pick up the baseball gloves they needed for Sunday's game.
10. When senior citizens go to the movie theater they can get a senior citizen discount.

Exercise 16

1. Anthony is the man who called about mice in his apartment.
2. The dictionary shows that the word "run" has 110 meanings.
3. The doctor noticed a mole that needed to be removed.
4. In the Middle Ages in England, one had to pay a tax to the church, called a tithe.
5. Soap operas make life seem much more complicated than it really is.
6. Margaret chose an expensive dress in a store.
7. Although the sun was not shining yesterday, the weather was quite warm.
8. The plate broke when Larry set it on the table.
9. Dr. Harris, who is an expert on Middle Eastern politics, is a well-known scholar.

10. In *Huckleberry Finn,* Mark Twain spends a lot of time describing the Mississippi River.

Exercise 17

1. The biggest book of the five assigned in the world literature class is *Anna Karenina.*
2. Even though the quarterback played badly, the team still won.
3. Of all the students in the French class, Marguerite has the best accent.
4. When Peter and José practice trumpet together, Peter plays worse than José.
5. Jennifer completed the tennis match quickly.
6. The car runs more smoothly than before the tune-up.
7. Our doorbell rings worse than any of the other doorbells in the apartment building.
8. Bruno has the highest grade in the class.
9. Mr. Santelo spoke most eloquently of all the panel members.
10. The used television worked well, considering we paid $25 for it.

D. WRITING EFFECTIVE SENTENCES

Exercise 18

Following are sample answers; students' answers will vary.

1. While I was running up the stairs, the tray of food fell.
2. The fax machine at the store was out of order.
3. Because I was almost asleep, it was difficult to concentrate.
4. The professor returned to campus on Thursday after a summer vacation.
5. Hoping to earn enough money for an out-of-town weekend, I took several extra jobs.
6. On Halloween the restaurant served hamburgers wrapped in orange and black paper to the kids.
7. After we skied all day, our hostess served us cups of hot cider.
8. Marcia received a letter with a check enclosed from her mother.
9. After I studied history, the answer to my dilemma became clear.
10. The car that needs repainting is an antique.

Exercise 19

1. If you shop carefully, you can save a lot of money.
2. If an older man has chest pains, he should go to the doctor.
3. When everyday stresses begin to overpower students, they should learn some relaxation techniques.
4. In the beginning of the film, the main character was a young boy; by the end he was a wealthy businessman, seated by a pool.
5. After he began college, Ralph joined a study group.
6. Many people think their opinions don't count and never contact their congressional leaders.
7. I enjoy swimming; it clears my mind, and I feel great afterwards.
8. Only one of the mothers of the kindergarten students has a job.
9. In the morning, Mark exercised by jogging, and in the afternoon, he studied calculus.
10. All of my friends have active imaginations.

Exercise 20

1. Ahmad unplugged his phone; consequently he missed an important call from his sister.
2. Jack loves chocolate; therefore, I made a double-chocolate-layer cake for his birthday.
3. Olivia hates television, but she loves to go to see live theater.
4. The band played until midnight, and we danced to every song.
5. Bob's Hardware Store was bought by Value Home Centers; however, the name was not changed.
6. I forgot yesterday was Mother's Day, so I called my mother to apologize.
7. We do not have enough money for a take-out Chinese dinner; therefore, I will make fried chicken.
8. My favorite TV shows are on tonight, so I won't get much homework done.
9. Several defensive ends were injured; subsequently, several defensive backs were injured.
10. The newspaper article on global warming contained some useful information; however, it was not detailed enough about the effects on wheat production.

Exercise 21

1. The mishap that occurred at the interstate exit injured no one.
2. The muffler on the car that Lucinda was driving to school fell off.
3. Tony, who is working only part-time and is still in school, asked Lydia to marry him next month.
4. The landfill that will decrease property values was unsuccessfully opposed by our citizens group.
5. It is never necessary to order double cheese on D'Angelo's pizzas since D'Angelo's uses a lot of cheese on their pizzas.
6. The professor spoke slowly because he noticed some students were having trouble taking notes.
7. Because the red dress fit perfectly, my husband bought it.
8. I slept soundly until the alarm clock rang.
9. Because Paulette was studying for a psychology midterm exam, she asked her roommates to be quiet.
10. After the bride and groom kissed, the minister pronounced the couple man and wife.

Exercise 22

1. Abdul decided either to paint the shelves or to clean them.
2. Cynthia has had a desire to and has been interested in riding horses since she was young.
3. José wants to own a car rather than to take the bus every day.
4. Most people exercise to shape up, to lose weight, and to feel better.
5. The doctor explained that a good diet, exercise, and enough sleep are important in avoiding stress.
6. Because Darin was late leaving work and he noticed that the traffic was congested, he called his wife to tell her he was going to be late getting home.
7. Cherie would rather have a dog than a child.
8. The class is dull because the textbook is terrible, the lectures are long and boring, and classmates will not participate in discussions.
9. Estaphano wanted both the leather jacket he saw in S & P's window and the acid-washed jeans he saw at the Gap.

10. Not only did the snowstorm make driving impossible, but it also made going outside dangerous because it was so cold.

Exercise 23

1. Double-parking for an hour, the truck delivered the merchandise into the storefront.
2. After class, Susan and Rhonda studied in the library.
3. Worried about her weight, Kim spends a great deal of time exercising.
4. In the spring, I am planning to travel to Baltimore.
5. Loudly, the student requested a retest.
6. Excited about her pregnancy, Sharon has been reading child-care books.
7. Working hard and feverishly, Pat cleaned all the upholstery in the living and dining rooms.
8. To surprise his wife, Doug rented a stork sign that announced his wife had turned thirty years old.
9. Giving several examples, the professor explained the causes of inflation.
10. To impress his customers, the waiter uses a French accent.

Exercise 24

1. Most parents see their children misbehave, but they do nothing to correct it.
2. Dominic planned to revisit his native Italy.
3. Though the players have made some improvement since their last game, they still lack defensive strategies.
4. Linda knew she needed to revise her essay before handing it in.
5. Because they are lab partners, Natalie and Dave have agreed to cooperate.
6. Numerous theories can explain how the planets were created.
7. Geoff sometimes speak so quietly that people are unable to hear him.
8. My sociology exam had several difficult essay questions.
9. Because my work schedule fluctuates, I cannot make any plans for next weekend.
10. If my sister decides to visit my parents in Baltimore, then I must go by bus.

Exercise 25

1. Keith's father has enormous strength; he has particularly powerful arms and hands.
2. Martina could have graduated this year, but she decided to pursue a second major in marketing.
3. Bo's boss fired him because he was not performing as well as expected.
4. The checkout line nearest the exit appears to be the shortest.
5. The class was ecstatic when the professor canceled class on Friday.
6. Martha phoned her assistant to let her know she was leaving for lunch.
7. Harold wore a striking new tie for his interview with Mattel.
8. The professor delayed answering Arthur's question for a few minutes while he finished summarizing the events that led up to the American Revolution.
9. He wants tuna for lunch and steak for dinner.
10. When Trina realized she had forgotten to pay her rent, she decided to accept the consequences and speak to her landlord.

E. USING PUNCTUATION CORRECTLY

Exercise 26

1. The woman who lives next door in the blue house with the wide front porch loves her dog, but doesn't allow him into her garden.
2. "Yes," Mr. Murray answered, "the car has air conditioning, cruise control, and power windows."
3. Julio was born on March 25, 1966, a date that his mother, we suppose, remembers well.
4. After T.J. decided to major in economics, he dropped his art class.
5. Correct
6. Marlena asked, "Why doesn't the softball team have uniforms yet?"
7. Luckily, Cheryl was able to locate the hubcap that had fallen off her car at Main Street and Oakview Road, the busiest intersection in the city.
8. Well, it certainly seems as if we will have a hot summer this year, doesn't it?

9. Our big, beautiful, leafy oak tree and our neighbor's maple tree were blown over in a windstorm last fall.

10. Charlene, for example, has a double major in English literature and political science, but she still has time to take some interesting electives, as well.

Exercise 27

1. Nick decided to go to the mall after dinner; he needed to purchase a suit to wear to his sister's wedding.

2. Marguerite has an allergy to chalkdust; therefore, she always sits in the back of the classroom.

3. Sid invited three friends over for pizza: Neal, his neighbor; Pam, a friend from childhood; and Charlene, a woman he met in his sociology class.

4. The bookstore was sold out of textbooks for Professor Kenyatta's course, although she had ordered plenty; thus, I have to wait until the bookstore orders more.

5. Enrico had read every chapter in the textbook and attended every class, but he still did poorly on the exam; he failed to organize the material and to review it.

6. Josephine bowls every Wednesday with members of her husband's family: Sally; his sister June; his aunt Trish; his cousin Eric; and Tina, his sister-in-law.

7. My aquarium has a large variety of fish: angelfish, black mollies, goldfish, and many exotic tropical fish.

8. After his apartment building burned down, Troy moved in with his brother; he quickly moved out again because his brother is so temperamental.

9. Joining the military is Jeff's goal; his girlfriend hopes he will change his mind.

10. Marty dropped his wallet in the cafeteria; consequently, I found him there crawling around on the floor looking for it.

Exercise 28

1. Her dog picked up its bone—chewed and ragged—and brought it into John's house.

2. Although I forgot my shopping list, I remembered the items I needed (shrimp, cocktail sauce, beer, cheese, and crackers) for the dinner I was having.

3. "It's very hot out," Moira said—even though it didn't seem warm to anyone else.

4. Jonah asked me if I wanted to come to the party—he called it a party—but I knew I was the only guest.

5. Apples (a fruit eaten by millions of children) can be dangerous if they are sprayed with pesticides; Dr. Martin Lenns' article, "The Fruit of the Tree," discusses the danger of pesticides on apples.

6. Barry handed out the employees' bonuses—five hundred dollars apiece in cash!

7. Students who park in the lots by the gym (lots 25, 26, and 27) must purchase special parking permits.

8. Muhammed Ali claimed, "I will float like a butterfly, but sting like a bee."

9. When Todd reminded me that the football game began at 4 p.m., I said, "I hope the Jets win!"

10. Correct

F. MANAGING MECHANICS AND SPELLING

Exercise 29

1. Jorge, a Democrat, took Political Science 101 and was unhappy with the political ideals professed by Dr. Martinez.

2. When my family visited Europe we saw the Eiffel Power in Paris and the Tower of London in England, and we swam in the English Channel.

3. The reporter asked at the press conference "Mr. President, what kinds of changes do you plan to make in the State Department?"

4. Our host served us Spam and Kraft cheddar cheese.

5. Next Thursday is Thanksgiving, a holiday first celebrated by the Pilgrims.

6. One of Melinda's ancestors signed the Constitution.

7. Trent was born in Texas but was raised in the Appalachian Mountains.

8. Joanna and Mark were married by Bishop Tunis, the same priest who had baptized Mark.

9. The Silverstone Theater is on Southeast Street, near the football stadium, about a mile from Maroon's Department Store.

10. We watched the New York Jets last night on "Monday Night Football."

Exercise 30

1. Susan's grandfather worked for the FBI before he became a professor of history at the local university.

2. Myron Thomas, Ph.D., is giving a lecture on Monday about art from 30 B.C.

3. Dr. Sufed told the young mother that her baby weighed eight pounds.

4. When we were working out at the YMCA one day in August, we met a foreign student who speaks four languages: German, English, French, and Spanish.

5. Rev. Hult read to the congregation from Genesis while the Sunday school students reviewed Chapter 4 of their book.

6. When our communications class drew numbers to determine the order in which we would give our speeches, I got number 25 and Ron got number 2; when he complained, the technical assistant said she was sorry, but there was nothing she could do.

7. Terri used to work for the Pacific Gas and Fuel Company when she lived in California.

8. Renee's housemates planned a trip to New York City over spring break.

9. Tom never began his shopping until two weeks before Christmas.

10. Although the book on Los Angeles was long, Felicia finished reading it by 3 p.m. on the day she began it.

Exercise 31

1. step\sister
2. so\lo\ist
3. cross\-indexed
4. N
5. pur\chased
6. N
7. sub\ject
8. de\pend\ent
9. re\planted
10. elec\tor\ate

Exercise 32

1. One hundred fifty-eight children sang in the choral concert.
2. Correct
3. Lee was surprised to learn it was 11:45 already.
4. The used car lot contained fifty 2-door cars and thirty 4-door cars.
5. Correct
6. Correct
7. Correct
8. Correct
9. On page A-3 of the newspaper there was a four-column story about the latest outbreak of fleas in our area.
10. Tomorrow in my Shakespeare class we are going to focus on Act III of *Hamlet,* after we complete the daily three-question, six-point quiz on the reading assignment.

Exercise 33

1. Science
2. Their
3. Efficient
4. Experience
5. Conceive
6. Weird
7. Neighbor
8. Thief
9. Achieve
10. Chief

Exercise 34

1. Loveless
2. Arguable
3. Advisement

4. Timely
5. Completeness
6. Arriving
7. Courageous
8. Careful
9. Argument
10. Surprised

Exercise 35

1. Buying
2. Messiness
3. Copied
4. Ways
5. Happiest
6. Complying
7. Studious
8. Readiness
9. Worried
10. Burial

Exercise 36

1. Turned, turning
2. Slapped, slapping
3. Hopped, hopping
4. Laughed, laughing
5. Failed, failing
6. Lifted, lifting
7. Banned, banning
8. Stole, stealing
9. Mapped, mapping
10. Barked, barking

Exercise 37

1. Pondered, pondering
2. Questioned, questioning
3. Repelled, repelling
4. Deducted, deducting
5. Unlocked, unlocking
6. Recommended, recommending
7. Constructed, constructing
8. Traveled, traveling
9. Referred, referring
10. Covered, covering

Exercise 38

1. Hoboes
2. Tries
3. Shushes
4. Glasses
5. Fezes
6. Denies
7. Bosses
8. Quarries
9. Churches
10. Boxes

SECTION G: ERROR CORRECTION EXERCISES

Paragraph 1

Jazz is a type of music, originating in New Orleans in the early Twenties and containing a mixture of Afro-American and European musical elements. There is a wide variety of jazz including the blues, swing, bop, and modern. Jazz includes both hard and soft music, and it does not get too radical. Unlike rock music, jazz does not go to extremes. Rock bands play so loud you can't understand half of the words. As a result, jazz is more relaxing and enjoyable.

Paragraph 2

Everyone thinks vacations are great fun, but that isn't always so. Some people are too nervous to relax when they are on vacation. My sister Sally is like that. She has to be on the move at all times. Never able to slow down and take it easy, she goes from activity to activity at a wild pace. When Sally does have a spare moment between activities, she spends her free time thinking about work problems, her family and their problems, and what she should do about the problems when she gets back. Consequently, when Sally gets back from a vacation, she is exhausted and more tense and upset than when she left home.

Paragraph 3

Soap operas are usually serious episodes of different people in the world of today. They are about fictitious people who are supposed to look real. Each character has his or her unique problems, crazy relationships, and nonrealistic quirks and habits. In real life, these events would never happen. The actors are always getting themselves into weird and unusual situations that are so bizarre that they could never be real. It's just too unreal to have twenty insane people who are all good friends.

Paragraph 4

Two forms of music are rock and country. Each sounds different. Rock music is very loud and has a high bass sound; sometimes you cannot even understand the words that the singer is singing. On the other hand, country music is a bit softer with a mellow but upbeat sound. Although country music is sometimes boring, at least you can understand the lyrics. Also, unlike rock singers, country singers usually have a country-western accent.

Essay 1

What A Good Friend Is

I have a friend Margaret who is not very intelligent. It took awhile before I could accept her limitations; first I had to get to know her and her feelings. We are like two hands that wash each other. I help her; she helps me. When I need her to babysit for me while I'm at work, it's done. If she needs a ride to the dentist, she's got it. All I need is to be given time to do so. We help each other and that is why we are friends.

Good friends are friends that do things for one another. Friendship involves telling the truth about something when it is asked. It is also a respect for one another's views. A friend is there to listen if you have a problem and to suggest something to help solve the problem; however, a friend should not just tell you just what to do. A friend is more than a shoulder to cry on. Good friends go places and do things together. Good friends are always there when you need them.

Essay 2

Putting Labels on People

People tend to label someone as stupid if he or she is slow, takes more time figuring out an assignment, or has difficulty understanding directions. My friend Georgette is a good example of someone who is labeled as stupid. People make fun of her. When she has to deal with ridicule by her fellow students or friends, she starts to feel insecure in speaking up. She starts to think she is slower mentally; she gets extremely paranoid when asked to give an answer in class. She feels any answer out of her mouth will be wrong. Her self-image is drastically reduced, like a bottomless pit. She will avoid answering questions even when she's almost positive that she's right. The possibility of being wrong keeps her from speaking. Then when someone else gives the correct answer that she would have given, she becomes extremely annoyed with herself for not answering the question. As a result, she starts to avoid the challenges; even the slightest challenge will frighten her away. Because her friends tease her, Georgette locks herself away from trying to understand. Her famous words when facing a challenge is, "I can't do it!"

Therefore, when a person makes a mistake, you should think of what you say before you say it and be sure it's not going to hurt the person. Your comments may help destroy that person's self-confidence.